"This book gives insights in the increasing importance of innovation for economic and social development and offers interesting lessons for scholars and policy makers in low and middle income countries around the world".

Bengt Åke Bertil Lundvall,
Professor Emeritus in Economics at Department of Business and Management at Aalborg University

"At a time when most academics in the field of economics are padding their biographies with marginal contributions, Lakhwinder Singh stands out as a rare professor who has demonstrated through his publications the prime role with insightful scientific findings that will serve society good. I found his work on innovation systems and knowledge spill-over illuminating and with strong focus on development in such critical areas as the agrarian crisis and sustainable development. Indeed, Lakhwinder Singh deserves a distinction as a Professor as he has trained so many development economists who shall carry the brilliant torch that he lit to serve society in the many decades to come. Indeed, the chapter contributions eminent scholars and researchers in a volume edited by his students rightfully hold him in high esteem, which is indeed a fitting tribute to such a passionate researcher and enthusiastic mentor".

Rajah Rasiah,
Distinguished Professor of Economics, University of Malaya

Innovation Systems, Economic Development and Public Policy

This book looks at the policy challenges confronting India and other developing countries in creating a robust, sustainable and industrialized economy. It investigates different facets of the nature, structure, growth and impact of innovation in industries, education and within institutions to foster greater productivity and growth.

The volume examines systems adopted to boost innovation and diffusion of technology in different economies while also mapping their success and failures. It offers suggestions for the future for long-term growth, sustainability and inclusiveness amidst dynamic, fast-changing technological frontiers using examples and case studies from India, Sri Lanka and Malaysia, among others. The chapters in the book, written to honour the academic work of Professor Lakhwinder Singh in the field of development economics and innovation economics, highlight the importance of adopting and adapting new technologies and development models to local contexts and small industries.

An important contribution to research on innovation economics, this interdisciplinary book will be of interest to students, researchers, practitioners and policy-makers working in industrial economics, international economics, political economy, innovation economics, institutional economics, industrial organization and international trade.

Swati Mehta is Assistant Professor at Punjab School of Economics, Guru Nanak Dev University, Amritsar. She is Associate Editor of the *African Journal of Science, Technology, Innovation and Development* at Routledge, Taylor & Francis Group. She is a member of the Board of Management at the International Joseph A. Schumpeter Society (ISS) (2022–24). With a PhD from the Department of Economics, Punjabi University, Patiala, she was a Visiting Researcher at the Institute of Economic Research, Seoul National University, Seoul, South Korea, with the award of the International Scholar Exchange Fellowship (ISEF) of Korea/Chey Foundation for Advanced Study during March–August 2019. Her area of research includes Economics of Innovation, Innovation Systems Approach, Global Value Chains,

Development Economics and Manufacturing Industries in developing countries. She is a member of 'The Global Network of Economics of Learning, Innovation and Competence Building Systems' (Globelics). She is a founding member of earlier career Innovation Researchers, CRIS, https://www.cris-is.org. She has published articles in journals like *Asian Journal of Technology Innovation*, *Seoul Journal of Economics*, *International Journal of Technology Management and Sustainable Development*, *Economic and Political Weekly* and *Innovation and Development*. She is a referee to journals of repute including *Economic Modelling*, *Millennial Asia*, *Innovation and Development*, *Asian Journal of Technology Innovation* and *African Journal of Science, Technology, Innovation and Development*.

Baldev Singh Shergill is Assistant Professor in the Department of Economics, Punjabi University South Campus, Talwandi Sabo, Punjab. He did his PhD in Economics at Punjabi University, Patiala. Prior to his current position, he taught at the University of Delhi. He has published widely in journals of repute like *Economic and Political Weekly*, *Journal of Development Policy and Practice*, and the *International Journal of Economics and Development*, amongst others. He is a referee to many journals including *Millenial Asia and Man & Development*.

Innovation Systems, Economic Development and Public Policy

Sustainable Options from Emerging Economies

Essays in Honour of Lakhwinder Singh

Edited by Swati Mehta and Baldev Singh Shergill

Routledge
Taylor & Francis Group
LONDON AND NEW YORK

First published 2023
by Routledge
4 Park Square, Milton Park, Abingdon, Oxon OX14 4RN

and by Routledge
605 Third Avenue, New York, NY 10158

Routledge is an imprint of the Taylor & Francis Group, an informa business

British Library Cataloguing-in-Publication Data
A catalogue record for this book is available from the British Library

ISBN: 978-1-032-26605-3 (hbk)
ISBN: 978-1-032-43537-4 (pbk)
ISBN: 978-1-003-35390-4 (ebk)

DOI: 10.4324/9781003353904

Typeset in Sabon
by Apex CoVantage, LLC

Thinking Minds which infuse Thinking Ability in Others

Contents

Figures

Tables

Contributors

Anand, Anurag is currently working with CTIER-Pune as a research TDB. He holds a doctorate degree in Economics from the Centre for Development Studies (CDS) - Trivandrum, Kerala. He also obtained his M.Phil. degree in Economics from the Central University of Gujarat in 2013. His research interest includes economics of innovation, exports and technology performance of foreign MNCs in Indian high-tech industries. He has been a visiting PhD scholar at the Department of International Economics & Management, Copenhagen Business School, Denmark. He was associated with the National Cheng Kung University (Department of Business Administration), Taiwan as a visiting research scholar under the Ministry of Education, Government of Taiwan.

Anand, Manish is a policy researcher working as Senior Fellow at The Energy and Resources Institute (TERI), New Delhi. He is a multidisciplinary research professional with basic training in agricultural sciences and advanced training in interdisciplinary fields of science policy, innovation studies and developmental studies. In his professional career of over 16 years grounded in interdisciplinary research, project coordination and management, outreach and capacity building, he has worked in diverse areas of agriculture, energy and environment and emerging technology policy, essentially focusing on the governance of science, technology and innovation to address sustainable development challenges from a global as well as local perspective. Currently, his research and policy analysis work focuses on generating evidence, strategies and methodologies based on systems thinking approaches towards sustainable food and land use systems including sustainable agricultural practices, natural resource use, rural livelihoods, human health and nutrition and climate change. Besides publishing in peer-reviewed international journals he has also contributed to writing policy briefs, newspaper articles and blog posts.

Angathevar, Baskaran is Associate Professor, Department of Development Studies, Faculty of Business and Economics; Head, UM North-South Research Centre, Universiti Malaya, Malaysia; Senior Research Associate of SARChI (Innovation & Development), Tshwane University of Technology, Pretoria, South Africa. Email: baskaran@um.edu.myis

Ashta, Arvind is Professor of Finance at the Burgundy School of Business, Université Bourgogne Franche-Comté in Dijon, France and is a member of its research center CEREN, EA 7477. He is a member of research associations (RRI, CERMi, PRME Anti-poverty Working Group, among others) and has been associated with the European Microfinance Platform. He has over seventy publications in international journals. He has edited "Advanced Technologies for Microfinance", co-edited "MIS in Microfinance" and "Slow Management" and authored "Microfinance: Battling a Wicked Problem" and "A Realistic Theory of Social Entrepreneurship: A Life Cycle Analysis of Micro-Finance". He is a member of a club of micro-investors.

Chandran, VGR is Associate Professor, Department of Development Studies, Faculty of Economics and Administration, University of Malaya, Kuala Lampur.

Das, Keshab is Professor, Gujarat Institute of Development Research, Ahmedabad. Gujarat. He holds M.Phil. (Applied Economics) and Ph.D. (Economics) degrees from the Jawaharlal Nehru University, New Delhi (through the Centre for Development Studies, Trivandrum). He is a recipient of the VKRV Rao Prize in Social Sciences (Economics) for the year 2004 (www.isec.ac.in/vkrvraoprize.htm). He has been a visiting research fellow/faculty at the following: Tshwane University of Technology, Pretoria, South Africa; University of Insubria, Varese, Italy (twice); International Institute of Social Studies (ISS), The Hague, Netherlands; University of Manchester, Manchester, UK; Institute of Developing Economies (IDE), Chiba, Japan; CNRS-REGARDS, Bordeaux, France (twice); Maison des Sciences de lHomme (MSH), Paris, France; Institute of Development Studies (IDS), University of Sussex, Brighton, UK; NKC Centre for Development Studies, Bhubaneswar, India; Punjabi University, Patiala, India and Institute for Studies in Industrial Development (ISID), New Delhi, India. He has been empanelled as an Indian Council of Cultural Relations (ICCR) Chair Professor in Economics (2015–16). He is the Executive Editor of the *Odisha Economic Journal* and President of the Orissa Economic Association (2022–23). With ten books (authored/co-authored/edited/co-edited) and over a hundred articles, his research and policy engagements concern issues in local and regional development; industrialization strategies; informal sector; MSMEs, industrial clusters and globalization; innovation; labor; infrastructure; and politics of development.

Johnson, K.N. Daniel is Professor at Department of Economics and Business, Colorado College, Colorado Springs USA. He earned his PhD from

Yale University, USA and masters from London School of Economics, and taught at Harvard University and Wellesley College. He was invited for TEDx Talks at Yale University in October 2016. He received an Honorable Mention from the United States Patent Office Cancer Moonshot Challenge, October 2016; was a Fulbright Specialist in Innovation and Entrepreneurship, Myanmar, 2016; Faculty Fellow, Teaching Integrity in Economics Research, Alfred P. Sloan Foundation and Haverford College, 2016–17 and Fulbright Specialist Roster, 2015–2020. His website is at http://faculty1.coloradocollege.edu/~djohnson/. His research papers are available at http://papers.ssrn.com/sol3/cf_dev/AbsByAuth.cfm?per_id=57030

Kathuria, Vinish is Professor, SJM School of Management, Indian Institute of Management, Bombay, Mumbai. He was Adjunct Professor at Jiangsu University, PR China (2014). UNESCO Ph.D. Thesis Award 2000–01: Ph.D. thesis among 8 theses selected by the Scientific Steering Committee of the UNESCO for their 'Management of Social Transformation (MOST)' program for the year 2000–01. Fulbright Senior Researcher at the Department of Economics, University of Colorado at Boulder, Colorado, US from October 2, 2006 to July 29, 2007. Visiting Scientist Position at The Beijer Institute, The International Institute for Ecological Economics, Stockholm, Sweden from June 2001 to August 2001. Post-doctoral fellowship at the Environmental Economics Unit (EEU) of Department of Economics and Commercial Law of University of Göteborg at Göteborg, Sweden, April 2000 to September 2000 and from February 2001 to June 2001. Ph.D. Internship at the United Nations University/Institute for New Technologies (UNU/INTECH) at Maastricht, The Netherlands, August – December 1996. Visiting Chair Professor (Contemporary India) at the International Business division, University of Sydney, Sydney (Australia) from September 3, 2017 to December 1, 2017. Visiting Professor at the Department of Economics, University of Toronto, Mississauga (Canada) from June 3 to July 31, 2017. UGC-DSA Visiting Fellow at Department of Business Management, University of Calcutta, Calcutta from March 22 to March 27, 2013. Visiting Senior Fellow at the School of Environment and Development, University of Manchester, Manchester (UK) from October 1, 2010 to September 30, 2011 and from January 11 to January 18, 2010. Visiting Fellow at School of Business, University of New South Wales, Sydney (Australia) from October 18 to 29, 2012. Research Scholar (Hon.) at Department of International Development (QEH), University of Oxford, Oxford (UK) (July 2009 onwards). Website www.som.iitb.ac.in/?p=989

Kedia, Shailly is a policy researcher who is a Senior Fellow and Associate Director with The Energy and Resources Institute (TERI), New Delhi. With over 17 years of experience, she has worked in interdisciplinary projects on sustainable development and climate action. She has a doctoral degree from the School of International Studies, Jawaharlal Nehru University.

Kumar, Manish is at Department of Economics, School of Liberal Arts and Social Sciences, SRM University AP, Andhra Pradesh. He was Research Scholar, Department of Humanities and Social Sciences at Indian Institute of Technology Bombay, Mumbai.

Lanzona, Leonardo Jr., A. is Professor of Economics at the Ateneo de Manila University. He has a PhD in Economics from University of the Philippines and did postdoctoral studies at Yale University Economic Growth Center. He has published books and journal articles internationally and specializes in demographic, labor and economic development.

Mor, Surender is Professor of Economics in B. P. S. Women University, Sonipat, India. He is one of the Founder Members in the Global Partnership for Poverty and Entrepreneurship (GPPE) initiated by University of Notre Dame, Indiana, U.S.A. He has published 85 papers, edited eight books and reviewed three books, as well as having more than 25 years of teaching experience. His book 'Sino-US Trade War: A New Challenge to Globalisation' has been reviewed by Prof. Kenneth S. Friedman, Regis University, U.S.A. Prof. Mor supervised six PhD and fifteen MPhil and was a reviewer in many journals from SGAE, Emerald, Inderscience, etc. His areas of interest include Microfinance, Entrepreneurship, and Environmental Economics.

Muchie, Mammo is DST-NRF SARChI Chair in Innovation Studies. He did his postgraduate MPhil and DPhil in Science, Technology, and Innovation for Development (STI&D) from the University of Sussex, UK. He is currently a DST-NRF research chair in Innovation Studies at the Faculty of Management Sciences, Tshwane University of Technology. He is editor of African Journal of Science, Technology, Innovation and Development. Website: https://sarchi.org

Panda, Bhagirathi currently works as a Professor of Economics at North Eastern Hill University, Shillong and as the Honorary Director of ICSSR-NERC, Ministry of Education, Government of India, Shillong. Earlier, he was also the Dean of the School of Economics, Management and Information Sciences and Head of the Department of Economics, North Eastern Hill University, Shillong. During 2008–09, Prof. Panda was also on the faculty of IIM, Shillong. Prof. Panda is an Asia fellow of Asian Scholarship Foundation, Bangkok and in this capacity worked as a Visiting Fellow in Thammasart University, Thailand and Asian Institute of Technology, Bangkok during the year 2003. He has more than 30 years of teaching and research experience in different universities and colleges of the country and abroad and has also published more than 50 research articles in different national and international journals. He has guided 11 Ph.D. Scholars. Prof. Panda was a member of a number of expert committees formed by Ministry Rural Development, Government of India and currently is also the editor of the UGC CARE Listed Journal 'Man and Development' published by ICSSR-NERC, Shillong.

Pandey, Rita is Senior Fellow, National Institute of Public Finance and Policy. PhD from IIT Kanpur; she was Post-Doctoral Fellow at Yale University, Connecticut, USA.

Daniel K.N. Johnson and Tianyi (Lincy) Qin is Paraprofessional of the Economics and Business Department at Colorado College for the 2020–21 academic year and supports department administrative tasks and student learning/research needs. Her hometown is Shanghai, China, a global center for finance and innovation. Influenced by a wealth of international perspectives that she grew up with, she came to the United States to enrich her understanding of a different culture and economic system. She has a BA in Mathematical Economics from Colorado College (2020) and plans on pursuing graduate studies. At CC, she builds and shares stimulating economics knowledge through tutoring and research activities. Her research interests lie in how heterogeneous higher education characteristics introduce differing labor market matching and outcomes. Recently she began to explore the use of computational tools for more efficient research efforts and aspires to further study advanced deep learning methods. For leisure, she enjoys listening to and performing classical music and turning unique recipes into reality.

Rajesh GK is a development practitioner with 25 years of experience in public administration and agricultural technology management under Government of Kerala, India. He holds an M.Phil in Applied Economics from Jawaharlal Nehru University (Centre for Development Studies) and PhD from Gandhigram Rural University. He founded CRIS-IS.ORG, the global network of innovation scholars and co-founded the UK-based Association for South-South Cooperation in Innovation Systems Transformation (ASSIST), and is member of several international organizations such as AFRICALICS and GLOBELICS.

Ramanayake, Sanika Sulochani is Senior Lecturer, Department of Social Statistics, University of Kelaniya, Sri Lanka. She holds PhD from Department of Economics, Seoul National University, Seoul. Earlier, she was a Post-Doctoral researcher at International Development Research Centre (IDRC), Canada, affiliated to the Indira Gandhi Institute of Development Research (IGIDR), Mumbai (from 2016 to 2018), and a Post-Doctoral researcher at Seoul National University and Inha University, which was funded by the Social Science Korea (SSK) program in South Korea (from 2013 to 2016).

Selvarajan, Sonia Kumari is Senior Lecturer, Department of Development Studies, Faculty of Business and Economics, Universiti Malaya. Email: soniakumari@um.edu.my

Singh, Nidhi is Senior Policy Fellow, Department of Science of Technology, Government of India.

Singh, Nirvikar is Distinguished Professor of Economics at the University of California, Santa Cruz. He is currently Co-Director of the Center for Analytical Finance at UCSC, of which he was the founding director. He has served as a member of the Advisory Group to the Finance Minister of India on G-20 matters, Consultant to the Chief Economic Advisor, Ministry of Finance, Government of India, and a member of the Expert Group on post-Covid-19 economic recovery formed by the Chief Minister of Punjab state in India. At UCSC, he has previously served as Director of the Santa Cruz Center for International Economics, Co-Director of the Center for Global, International and Regional Studies, and Special Advisor to the Chancellor. In the 1990s, he organized one of the first major US conferences on Indian economic reform. He received his PhD from the University of California, Berkeley, and his BSc and MSc from the London School of Economics, where he was awarded the Allyn Young Prize, Gonner Prize and Ely Devons Prize.

Professor Singh's current research topics include entrepreneurship, information technology and development, electronic commerce, business strategy, political economy, federalism, economic growth, the Indian economy and Sikh and Punjabi studies. He has authored over 100 research papers and co-authored or co-edited six books: *Joint Ventures, International Investment and Technology Transfer; The Political Economy of Federalism in India*; and *Waiting to Connect: India IT Revolution Bypasses the Domestic Industry; Handbook of the Economics of the Pacific Rim; Economic Transformation of a Developing Economy: The Experience of Punjab, India;* and *The Other One Percent: Indians in America.* He has also served as an advisor for several start-ups and knowledge services firms in Silicon Valley and in India.

Singh, Sukhpal is Professor and former Chairperson of the Centre for Management in Agriculture at the Indian Institute of Management (IIM), Ahmedabad. He has been the former Director General of the Centre for Research in Rural and Industrial Development (CRRID), Chandigarh and the Former Professor and Head of the Agricultural Economic Research Unit (AERU) at the Institute of Economic Growth (IEG), New Delhi. He has been conferred the title of the Fellow of the Indian Society of Agricultural Economics for his contributions to the discipline and the Society in 2018. A PhD from the Institute for Social and Economic Change (ISEC), Bangalore, Prof. Singh was a visiting fellow at the Institute of

Development Studies (IDS), Sussex, UK and the Copenhagen Business School. He was an ASIA fellow of the Asian Scholarship Foundation, Bangkok at Chulalongkorn University, Bangkok, and an ESRC-ICSSR Exchange Scholar at the University of Manchester, UK. He is the Founding Editor of *Millennial Asia: An International Journal of Asian Studies*, published by Sage Publications. He has been a member of numerous high-level committees at the national and the state levels in India. He has authored/co-authored/edited 14 books and published widely in top-ranked reputed international and national journals and national dailies. He has delivered many invited and memorial lectures. Professor Singh specializes in issues of value chain analysis and management, vertical co-ordination in agribusiness, small producer organizations and agribusiness marketing and regulation. His research interests lie in small producer and worker livelihoods and collectivization of such stakeholders in the context of agribusiness value chains and deregulation of agricultural markets in India and the developing world. He is on the boards of many academic and non-profit organizations. Website: www.iima.ac.in

Trivedi, Pushpa is Senior Professor, Shiv Nadar University, Chennai. She was Professor of Economics, Department of Humanities and Social Sciences, Indian Institute of Technology, Bombay, Mumbai. She was Head, Department of Humanities and Social Sciences, IIT- Bombay. She was Visiting Faculty, Centre for Development Economics (CDE), Delhi School of Economics, New Delhi. Her areas of research include open economy macroeconomics, international finance, productivity measurements and the Indian economy.

Foreword

I feel honored to write a foreword for this book, published to honor Dr. Lakhwinder Singh on the occasion of his retirement from the university. Until today, he has devoted his academic life to teaching and research, based in Punjabi University, India.

It is wonderful to have a collection of essays in honor of him and all related to his research topics, such as innovation systems and sustainable and inclusive development. I think this collection of essays from diverse authors is not easy, but reflects the wide network Dr. Singh has built over his engagement with *Millennial Asia* (a journal) and Indialics (academic association in partnership with Globelics).

As a longtime friend and colleague, I have found him always a person of gentleness, a passion for research, and amusing interactions. I am sure that this formal retirement will not stop him from continuing his academic endeavor and journey. Also, his academic and professional leadership will continue to impact his school, students and colleagues, and this book would be a starting place for that. The book is nicely divided into four parts on industrial linkages, national innovation systems, sub-national systems and sustainability, which are all timely and relevant topics. These chapters would help us to find out a way out of the pandemic crisis from innovation and capability building perspectives, which are badly needed now.

Finally, I appreciate the efforts and contribution by two former students of Dr. Singh – Swati Mehta and Baldev Singh Shergill – for their remarkable job of having this book out finally.

Keun Lee, Distinguished Professor,
Seoul National University, January 2022

Preface

Innovation Economics delves on 'ideas' at the core. Ideas have the innate ability to grow in varied phases and places unboundedly. The ability to generate ideas and transform them into innovations has been a continuous process that is difficult to decipher. New technological advancements open new pathways of opportunities with undoubtedly many challenges. Economists for centuries have tried to capture the realities and complexities of socio-economic behavior at different macro and micro levels. The past economic thinking and schools of thoughts have been transformed by the dynamics of realities. Classical economists stood against the mercantilist in the 18th century, while Keynes challenged Classical thinking during the Great Depression of the 1930s. Neoclassical thinkers saw greener pastures with greater internationalization and globalization that also showed contrary outcomes in some countries. Schumpeterian 'creative destruction' found innovation as the ultimate source of growth that helped in the progress of a distinct branch of theoretical frameworks revolving around opening the 'black box' of innovation. The notion of 'equilibriums' are being challenged by 'evolutionary' economists, putting skepticism to the strength of capturing the dynamics of real interlinked actors in the world's economies with fast-changing technological frontiers through primarily algebraic modeling. The pioneering contributions of Nelson and Winter in the epoch-making book "The Evolutionary Theory of Economic Change" in 1982 has shown the way for greater understanding, thinking and deliberations to capture the economic complexities of the ever-evolving world. This contribution has challenged the earlier theoretical frameworks by placing the power of 'ideas', 'technological changes' and 'innovations' in the center stage of long-run growth and sustainability. Given the nature of the *intangible* source of growth, it is challenging, but stimulating and inspiring for researchers to quantify and examine the complex structures and process of generating innovations. Henceforth, the research in the field has increased manifold in the past five decades, and the focus remains on understanding the process of generating innovation, the measurement of innovation and building the overall innovative capability and capacity of different entities across sectors and regions. The field largely attracted the attention of scholars across disciplines ranging from science to the social sciences, with focus on technological generation and its relationship with socio-economic, political, historical and legal aspects of generating, absorbing and disseminating innovations. The policy prescribers and practitioners have concentrated their efforts in understanding 'innovation' for survival, growth, inclusiveness, sustainability and catching-up of different entities.

In the early 1980s, Christopher Freeman of SPRU, Sussex University, Brighton, England and Bengt Åke Lundvall from Aalborg, Denmark introduced a framework known as the 'National Innovation Systems' (NIS) approach after Fredrich List (1891). In their approach, they emphasized that interlinkages of various actors, organizations and institutions for 'learning' and 'technological' capability building are the core of the NIS. Hence, economic strategies are influenced by and influence the nature of different organizations and institutions, at different levels of analysis. Successively, many offshoots of the approach also emerged. The growing internationalization calls for deeper understanding of 'sectoral innovation systems' and technological innovation systems. The growth of industrial agglomerates, manufacturing clusters and industrial districts lead to the notion of 'regional innovation systems'.

Dynamic technological paradigms, the changing international world economic order and altering world production structures are raising different issues and posing new problems. What strategies should be adopted by the frontrunners to remain hegemonic, and how can followers 'catch up' with frontrunners? These remain the core concerns for different firms, industries and countries. How can the evolution of systems of innovation be synchronized with long-term inclusive growth and environmental sustainability? These are some concerns that hold prominence in current times and thus constitute the broad scope of this book.

Specifically, the distinct paradigm of the 'systems of innovation' (SI) approach acknowledges uniqueness, diversity and evolutionary perspective. Therefore, whatever is valid for one firm/industry or country under certain circumstances, historical backgrounds, current challenges and opportunities may not be applicable to others. This diversity and uniqueness demand systematic understandings of different structures and growth patterns concerning divergent entities, which this book aims to fulfill.

In context of these discussions, the present book aspires to be an important contribution to the growing field of 'Economics of Innovation', 'Systems of Innovation' and broader field of 'Evolutionary Economics' and 'Development Economics'. The book aims to present different facets of looking into the nature, structure, growth and impact of innovation on different entities. The broader aim is to present a way forward for the future approaches for long-term growth, sustainability and inclusiveness amidst dynamic and fast-changing technological frontiers.

This book is going to be of interest to young researchers, early-career researchers, scholars, practitioners and policy-makers working in related areas of research. This book is a tribute to all the thinkers who aspire for 'alternatives' to the orthodoxy and respect 'individual thinking' and divergent viewpoints. These are the traits infused in us by our teacher and mentor, Professor Lakhwinder Singh, for whom this book is planned. The 'idea' for this book came about a week before his superannuation on 31st December 2020 from the Department of Economics, Punjabi University, Patiala, where he served for more than two and a half decades. We both are fortunate to have done our PhD research under the guidance of the open-minded and hardworking Professor Singh, who not only taught us the 'skills' of becoming an 'economist', but also a humane human being.

We cordially thank the authors who contributed chapters for this volume. Thanks are also due to the reviewers for their constructive comments that helped immensely in improving the quality of the book. The team at Routledge, India, especially Shoma Choudhary and Shloka Chauhan, provided effective support for this project.

The chapters in the volume are contributed by both young and senior scholars who present a mix of experience and futuristic approach towards the pressing issues of our times and the contribution to the larger scope of 'innovation studies'.

Swati Mehta
and
Baldev Singh Shergill
December 2021
India

Abbreviations

ACC	Automatic Cruise Control
AEP	Act East Policy
AFNU	Animal Feed and Nutrition Unit
AIC	Akaike Information Criterion
AKIS	Agriculture Knowledge Information System
BIC	Bayesian Information Criterion
BIPP	Biotechnology Industry Partnership Programme
BIRAC	Biotechnology Industry Research Assistance Council
BIRAP	Biotechnology Industry Research Assistance Programme
BMC	Bulk Milk Chillers
BMPC	Baani Milk Producer Company
BVHT	Bivoltine-Hybrid Technology
CCC	Commerce, Culture and Connectivity
CCP	Central Committee of Communist Party of China
CCSAMMN	Climate Change and Sustainable Agriculture: Monitoring, Modeling and Networking
CESCRA	Centre for Environment Science and Climate Resilient Agriculture
CFD	Computational fluid dynamics
CHED	Commission on Higher Education
CMIE	Centre for Monitoring Indian Economy
COE	Community-Own Enterprises
CSC	Common Service Centres
CSIR	Council for Scientific and Industrial Research
CSO	Civil Society Organisations
CSP	Concentrated Solar Power Systems
DAI	Digital Adoption Index
DIPP	Department of Industrial Policy and Promotion
DNA	Deoxyribonucleic Acid
DOAFW	Department of Agriculture and Farmers Welfare
DSIR	Department of Scientific and Industrial Research
DST	Department of Science and Technology

DTC	Diamond Trading Company
EMI	Electronic Money Issuers
ERP	Extramural Research Projects
FAA	Federal Aviation Administration
GII	Global Innovation Index
GJEPCI	Gems and Jewellery Export Promotion Council of India
GMM	Generalized Method of Moments
GPN	Global Production Networks
GVC	Global Value Chains
HHI	Herfindahl Hirschman index
IAe	Indonesian Aerospace
ICT	Information and Communications Technology
IIS	Innovation Index Score
IOM	Industry of manufacture
IPR	Intellectual Property Rights
IPTN	Industri Pesawat Terbang Nusantara
IREDA	Indian Renewable Energy Development Agency Limited
ISIC	International Standard Industrial Classification
ISTS	Interstate Transmission System
ITA	Information Technology Agreement
ITES	IT-Enabled Services
JICA	Japan International Cooperation Agency
LEP	Look East Policy
MIS	Management Information System
MMF	Manmade Fibre
MNC	Multinational Companies
MOAFW	Ministry of Agriculture and Farmers Welfare
MOST	Ministry of Science and Technology
MPP	Milk Pooling Point
MRG	Member Relations Group
MVI	Motor Vehicle Industry
NAC	National Advisory Committee
NAPCC	National Action Plan on Climate Change
NBM	National Bamboo Mission
NCVET	National Council for Vocational Education and Training
NDLM	National Digital Literacy Mission
NEP	National Education Policy
NER	North Eastern Region
NGO	Non-Governmental Organisations
NIC	National Industrial Classification
NICRA	National Innovation for Climate Resilient Agriculture
NIE	Newly Industrialized Economies
NIS	National Innovation System

NMITLI	The New Millennium Indian Technology Leadership Initiative
NMSA	National Mission for Sustainable Agriculture
NMSKCC	National Mission on Strategic Knowledge for Climate Change
NSDC	National Skill Development Corporation
NSI	National Systems of Innovation
NSTMIS	Department of National Science and Technology Management Information System
NVEQF	National Vocational Education Qualification Framework
OECD	Organisation for Economic Cooperation and Development
PCT	Patent Cooperation Treaty
PETS-QSDS	Public Education Expenditure Tracking and Quantitative Service Delivery Study
PIM	Perpetual Inventory Method
PMP	Progressive Manufacturing Programme
PRISM	People's Right to Information and Development Implementing Society of Mizoram
PTID	PT Industri Dirgantara
QIC	Quinn information criterion
R&D	Research and Development
RAAKS	Rapid Appraisal of Agricultural Knowledge Systems
RAD	Rainfed Area Development
RCDF	Rajasthan Co-operative Dairy Federation
RNA	Ribonucleic Acid
RPSSGP	Rooftop PV and Small Solar Power Generation Programme
RRR	Retreat, Reimagine and Reclaim
S&T	Science and Technology
SBIRI	The Small Business Innovation Research Initiative
SDA	Surat Diamond Association
SDPC	Surat Diamond Polishing Cluster
SHG	Self-Help Group
SHM	Soil Health Management
SIS	Sericulture Innovation System
SLUSI	Soil and Land Use Survey of India
SMAF	Sub-Mission on Agroforestry
SMEs	Small and Medium Enterprises
SMSA	State Mission for Sustainable Agriculture
SOE	State owned enterprises
SOU	Sector of Use
SPRU	Science Policy Research Unit
SSTC	State Science and Technology Commission
STIP	Science, Technology, and Innovation Policy

TIPO	Taiwan Intellectual Property Office
TIS	Technological Innovation System
TKC	Tiruppur Knitwear Cluster
TT	Technology Transfer
UIL	University-Industry Linkages
UIR	University-Industry Relations
UMB	Urea Molasses Blocks
UP	University of the Philippines system
VAR	Vector Autoregression Model
VCG	Village Contact Group
WIOD	World Input–Output database
WIPO	World Intellectual Property Organisation
WTO	World Trade Organization

Chapter 1

Innovation, Institutions and Organizations

Growth and Sustainability

Swati Mehta and Baldev Singh Shergill

1. Introduction

Innovation has been changing human lives. The journey from conceiving an 'idea' to its final acceptability as 'innovation' is a long process that takes time, energy and resources. It took years until the middle of the twentieth century before scholars explicitly recognized the importance and strength of intangible factors generating 'knowledge' for increasing productivity, economic growth and economic development. Innovations increase human welfare in a responsible way (Von Schomberg, 2011). Similarly, innovation generates new jobs opportunities to be strategically adopted (Edquist et al., 2001). Opening the 'black box' of innovation processes become necessary for policy perspectives, mainly for firms/industries and countries to grow and sustain themselves in the complex technology world. The journey from 'Schumpeter Mark-I' to 'Schumpeter Mark-II' increases the scope of understanding the process of innovation from individual to the firm (Fagerberg, 2005). Schumpeter focused upon understanding 'industrial dynamics' in long-term economic change with 'technological competition'. The firms can either innovate to gain the 'first mover advantage' or become the 'imitator' to learn and later innovate to compete, catch up or leapfrog (Lee, 2019). Nelson and Winter extended the Schumpeterian perspective of 'capitalism as the engine of growth' (Fagerberg, 2005) in their monumental book published in 1982, *An Evolutionary Theory of Economic Change*. Conceptually based on biology with non-equilibrium notions, Nelson and Winter accommodate diverse socio-economic environments, heterogeneous actors and uncertainty through simulations with varying key values of the parameters that impact innovation. This clearly shows that "innovation does not originate in isolation" (Saviotti, 1997). Rather, a multitude of actors, organizations, institutions and their complex interactions create a 'system' that leads to innovation. These underlying inter-connecting process of generating innovation leading to economic growth were identified by Christopher Freeman in the 1974 book *The Economics of Industrial Innovation*. Initially influenced by the ideas of Karl Marx, Freeman has had a great influence on

DOI: 10.4324/9781003353904-1

natural scientist J.D. Bernal, that led him to frame his thoughts around the power of science for social scientists. He conceptually adopted the framework from List's 1841 work *The National System of Political Economy* with its English edition published in 1904, and the concept of the 'National System of Innovation' along with Bengt Åke Lundvall. Although they were united in thought, the concept was published first by Freeman in his book on *Technology Policy and Economic Performance in Japan*, published in 1987. But Freeman (1995) wrote that the Lundvall used the expression 'National System of Innovation' for the first time in the book edited by Dosi et al. (1988) (Edquist, 1997).

2. Organizations, Institutions and Inter-Linkages

The 'system' approach connotes the importance of various components, broadly classified as organisations and institutions and the inter-linkages among these that work in a complex manner for the actors, like individuals, firms, industries and countries. Organizations play an important role in the process of innovation as it reflects the intrinsic dynamic historical growth. (Refer to Chapter 5 for this diagrammatic notion.) Edquist (1997) explains these concepts very clearly in the chapter on the System of Innovation in an edited volume by Fagerberg et al. The basic idea of Edquist's 'System of Innovation' approach is to find the commonalities in the offshoots: like the sectoral innovation system (Malerba and Orsenigo, 1997), regional innovation system (Saxenian, 1994), technological innovation system (Carlsson and Stankiewicz, 1995).

Organizations, as explained by Edquist (1997), are the:

> formal structures that are consciously created and have an explicit purpose . . . they are the players or actors. Some of the important organizations in SI are firms, universities, venture capital organizations and public agencies responsible for innovation policy, competition policy or drug regulation.

Similarly, Edquist (1997) also explains institutions as:

> sets of common habits, norms, routines, established practices, rules or laws that regulate the relations and interactions between individuals, groups, and organizations . . .. Examples include . . . patent laws, as well as rules and norms influencing the relations between universities and firms.

Edquist (1997) focuses upon drawing generalities as a way towards theorizing. But a lot of ambiguity engulfs the Innovation System approach due to distinct views about the scope of the concept. The foundational concept of 'National Innovation Systems' finds it difficult to draw boundaries for what comes under 'national' when the opening of the national economies has been happening on an even greater scale (Lundvall, 1992). However, when the delimitation of the regional boundaries happens, then it becomes difficult to explain that one region is ahead of the other due to an internationalization of 'technological systems', and 'sectoral systems' also have overlaps that need further empirical analysis and case studies. Therefore, as the 'framework' is in its infancy, it is undoubtedly a much broader, flexible and more open approach that "intended to capture process of innovation, their determinants, and some of their consequences (eg. productivity growth and employment) in a useful way" (Edquist, 1997).

The aim of this book is to focus upon different dimensions of the Innovation System approach to contribute to the existing literature.

3. Overview of the Chapters

In total, there are 17 chapters, including an introduction titled '*Innovation, Organization and Institutions: Growth and Sustainability*'. The rest of the chapters are divided into four sections, the overview of which is as follows:

3.1. Inter-Industrial Inter-Linkages and Evolving Economies

In this section there are four chapters. The chapters dealing with macro aspects of innovation approach are included in the section. With an evolutionary approach dealing largely with the ever-changing aspects of inter-linkages within different actors of the economy, the sub-sections try to present these concerns in different arrangements.

Daniel K.N. Johnson and Tianyi (Lincy) Qin (Chapter 2) revisited their 1990s research (Johnson and Evenson, 1997; Johnson, 2002; Evenson and Johnson, 1997; Johnson and Van Wagoner, 2021) concerning the invention input–output tables, to link those to traditional product/service input–output tables in a Granger-causal fashion. They constructed invention input–output tables using patent data (for a given nation and time period). The chapter explores whether the invention Granger-causes product/service linkages or vice versa, using a vector autoregressive (VAR) format for industry and services sector for India and the United States. The results depict that at the national level, innovation Granger-causes production and not vice versa, except where it Granger-causes more innovation instead. The authors here call for a cautious approach for policy prescription for divergent sectors across divergent countries and times.

The role of technology and technology transfer (TT) is predominant in understanding the innovation capability of recipient countries. The literature is also replete with studies that have argued a) the kind of technology transferred may be inappropriate to the recipient country's factor conditions, and b) foreign firms are the carrier of these technology forming enclaves, thereby creating a bigger wedge in the economy. Despite all these concerns, the countries continue to depend on technology transferred in order to not reinvent the wheel. One of the aims of the technology transfer, apart from bringing productivity improvement, is spurring local innovation activities. Technology transfer has different facets. These are a) from one application domain to another – for example, several of the civil applications have their origin in military use; b) from one country to another – which has three different aspects: from one developed country to another developed country (North-North transfer), from one developed county to a developing country, termed as North-South transfer, and lastly, from one developing country to another, called South-South technology transfer; and c) from labs/universities to market. These facets are mostly mutually exclusive with little overlap. In this context, the chapter by ***Vinish Kathuria*** (Chapter 3) talks about the role of technology transfer in satisfying the country's needs and requirements – be it transferred from one application domain to another, or from one country to another, or from labs to market. The discussion is mainly oriented towards developing countries, which are often in dire need of technology. The chapter ends with some suggestions on what needs to be done to maximize the recipient country's benefits from the transferred technology.

For understanding the nature of 'absorptive capability and capacity' in different entities, ***Leonardo A. Lanzona, Jr*** (Chapter 4) aims to explore the relationship between higher education sectors in selected Asian countries. Education plays a huge role in developing human capital and innovation. These in turn contribute to economic development – as society is more skilled and has more technology at hand, productivity improves and translates to economic outputs. The chapter provides an empirical analysis for analyzing the impact of foreign participation on the supply of education quality, particularly teachers and investments in education. The cross-country analysis on the degree of liberalization in the education sector was done in Vietnam, Indonesia, Thailand, Bolivia and Guatemala. The study argues that the higher education sector in these countries could collaborate with the industrial sector to assimilate the transferred foreign technology and make the adaptations necessary for foreign technology to fit within the local technical, economic and social context. Some alliances between industry and leading research universities were also capable of leading to a deeper assimilation and diffusion of foreign technology through reverse engineering and R&D to make modifications to the transferred foreign technology.

To highlight the complexity and uncertainty of capturing innovation quantitatively, ***Mehta and Shergill*** (Chapter 5) discuss the various input and output indicators that can be used for this purpose. Knowledge is widely acclaimed as the de facto source of growth. The endogenous growth theories regard investment in research and development as the main source of growth and achieving competitiveness. But the evolutionary theories regarded that the accumulation of technology is not a simple linear process where the output is generated with the subsequent quantum of inputs. During the early 1980s, the term 'national innovation system' was coined, and since then scholars have worked on understanding the mechanism of generations, accumulation and diffusion of technology that could be converted to productivity and lead to competitiveness. With these issues at hand, the chapter attempts to analyze the national system of innovation of India and China. Both theoretical and empirical analyses are done for the purpose. The study is based on secondary data sources.

3.2. Innovation Systems and Developing Economies

Change is the law of nature. Economic history is full of numerous cases wherein some laggard entities catch up with the frontrunners while others fell apart. But the important concern is how transformation occurs within the successful entities, which become the role models for imitation and aspirations for the laggards. In this context, five different chapters address the peculiar issues concerning developing countries.

Sanika Sulochani Ramanayake (Chapter 6) explores the nature of National Innovation Systems (NIS) and Technology Innovation System (TIS) that transformed the Asian tigers, namely South Korea, Taiwan, Hong Kong and Singapore, over the years. The broader aim of the chapter is to understand the NIS and TIS of developed Asian tigers and compare it with the developing countries of South Asia: namely, Sri Lanka, to draw broad policy implications. East Asian tigers like South Korea, Taiwan, Hong Kong and Singapore were known as high-income countries with rapid economic catch-up within a short time period. At the same time, these tigers were famous for structural changes with new technological innovations (mostly Korea and Taiwan) through the national innovation system. In other words, they were able to do a quick structural transformation from labour-intensive industries to high technological manufacturing industries, which most developing countries are unable to do. These changes led to fast and sustained economic growth. Therefore, the chapter discusses how Asian tigers used NIS and TIS for sustaining growth. Furthermore, this chapter researches the role of NIS and TIS in the context of Sri Lanka. The findings suggest that strong national innovation systems can overcome the low- to middle-income trap and sustain economic growth in the long run.

The chapter by ***Mammo Muchi and Rajesh GK*** (Chapter 7) concerns the state of agricultural system of social innovation (ASI) in developing countries with the aim of examining the rich literature to question the theoretical foundations for ASI.

Apart from these chapters based upon country-level analysis, the other two chapters in the section are industry-specific. ***Manish Kumar and Pushpa***

Trivedi (Chapter 8) examine the determinants of productivity of the Indian electronics industry for the period 2004–05 to 2016–17. The electronics industry is a very important short-cycle industry. The electronics industry has played a prominent role in the development and economic transformation of many East Asian countries, like Japan, South Korea, Taiwan, Singapore and now many other developing countries like Vietnam, Chile, the Philippines, Malaysia, etc. The authors estimate the productivity of the electronics industry employing control function approach and compare coefficients using semi-parametric Levinsohn-Petrin and Wooldridge methods. Following a two-stage approach, fixed effects model of determinants of productivity shows that firm size, profitability and oligopolistic market structure positively affect productivity, while the impact of the firm's age is not conclusive. The import of inputs plays a significant role in explaining firm-level productivity performance along with R&D, despite a small number of firms involved in it. The role of exports is neither significant nor positive in explaining productivity performance. Their results conform to broader characteristics of Indian manufacturing of better productivity performance of old, large and low-profit firms. The authors propose an active government role in resource (re)allocation and industry-specific policy to foster innovation and entrepreneurship to reduce import dependency in the long run.

Anurag Anand (Chapter 9) examines another important industry, the Indian motor vehicle industry. He examines the role and importance of multinational corporations in the Indian motor vehicle manufacturing sector with the aim of exploring the relationship of MNC's affiliation and its export performance.

3.3. Institutions, Organizations and Inter-linkages in Sub-National Innovation Systems

Development of sub-sectors and different regions are important for the holistic development of innovation systems of the nation's concerns. The four chapters in this section deal with different aspects of innovation like digitalization, production networks and inter-linkages between various institutions and organisations.

Nirvikar Singh (Chapter 10) aims to focus upon the role of digitalization on innovation systems from the institutional approach. 'Digital India' commonly refers to an initiative of the Government of India, which includes three areas: digital infrastructure as a utility for all citizens, governance and services on demand, and digital empowerment of citizens. This chapter discusses the components of a possible successful innovation system for digital technology-based growth. A digital technology innovation system extends beyond highly-skilled software engineers to include maintenance, repair and technical support for the hardware and software of digital infrastructure and applications. Basic education in a digitally-driven economy includes facility in using a variety of software applications. The interlinkage and feedback loops between different components of the digital economy are analyzed. The chapter also considers the impact of digitization on specific sectors such as education, health, agriculture and financial services, as well as retailing (e-commerce) and government. Government policies that will support Digital India as an innovation system are discussed, including tax incentives, investment policies, spectrum allocation, competition policy, and education policy.

The relationship between structural transformation and regional innovation systems is the objective that ***Bhagirathi Panda*** (Chapter 11) aims to explore while considering the case of the North Eastern region of India. Rich in natural resources, the North Eastern region showed minimal structural transformation from primitive economic activities to advanced value-generation activities, which the author examined into by focusing on institutional factors and the role of important stakeholders.

Studying the linkage of the local firms in the global production networks has assumed more importance in the last few decades. Increasing globalization and opening of the economies has different implications in different sectors across regions spanning countries. Assuming this important aspect, ***Keshab Das*** (Chapter 12) focus on micro, small and medium enterprises (MSMEs) belonging to the Tiruppur knitwear Cluster in South India and the Surat diamond polishing cluster in western India, mainly from the perspective of labour engaged and their working conditions amidst the role of various actors and institutions.

Surender Mor and Arvind Ashta (Chapter 13) aim to explore the importance of Reverse Innovation for the development of the microfinance sector in South Asia with the larger objective of understanding the nature of technology diffusion. The innovations in new products and services that are carried out mostly in capital-intensive countries and trickle down to developing countries for consumption by adapting them as per the market requirement are termed 'Glocalisation'. 'Reverse innovation' refers to those innovations that are rendered to a product in a developing country before launching it to a developed country. One particular type refers to innovations overtly designed and invented in developing markets and later introduced into developed countries' markets. Others are first innovated in developed countries then further improved in developing countries and then taken back to developed countries. They propose calling the first 'indigenous reverse innovations' and the others 'exogenous reverse innovations'. The authors illustrate these concepts with two examples from the microfinance world: banking correspondent models and mobile payments, and show that the banking correspondent seems to be an indigenous reverse innovation, while mobile payments may be an exogenous reverse innovation.

3.4. Innovation, Growth and Sustainability

Institutional innovation plays a very important role in building innovation systems. Agriculture and allied activities contribute significantly in many developing countries, notably in India as it is the largest employment-generating sector. But there are numerous problems that engulf the sector, mainly related to the paucity of resources. Co-operatives at various levels remain an important part of the larger agricultural and allied activities that also face much failure due to numerous bottlenecks in the system. However, a novel form of farmer organizations, Producers Organizations, has started emerging in India after being introduced in Sri Lanka. To compare and examine the two forms of production and cooperation, ***Sukhpal Singh*** (Chapter 14) examines the case of NDDBs Milk Producer companies in India to understand the performance, viability and sustainability of these entities. India had thousands of co-operatives at various levels but most of them have been failures due to political capture and interference, elite capture and mismanagement or to the very lack of 'fertile grounds' in most parts of India, with the exception of Gujarat and Maharashtra. Therefore, in the search for a better form of farmer organization of small producers, the Producer Company (PC) was born as a legal provision in the early 2000s. Since many of the PCs have faced both governance and management challenges over the years across regions which have led to these problems, Singh examines this issue with the help of case studies of NDDB's Milk Producers' Companies (MPCs) in terms of governance and management innovations designed by the promoting entity – National Dairy Services (NDS) of National Dairy Development Board (NDDB) – and adopted by the individual PCs, which has led to their better performance over the years.

Nidhi Singh (Chapter 15) attempts to ascertain the number of system failure issues of the innovative actors of Molecular Diagnostics (MDs) in India. As such, the objective of her chapter is to evaluate the issues and challenges experienced in the performance of system building activities by the Science Base, Translational Base and Industrial Base for the development of an emerging MD innovation system in India. By examining these challenges, she was able to identify the underlying system weakness and underperforming component of the MD's innovation structure. The existence of various structural weaknesses and rigidities reveals that there are number of important system failures that challenge the efficient and well-functioning technological innovations in India's MD sector.

VGR Chandran, Angathevar Baskaran, & Sonia Kumari Selvarajan (Chapter 16) explore the solar industry ecosystem in Malaysia by focusing on identifying the roles of different stakeholders in the development of renewable energy sources for sustainable growth.

Manish Anand, Rita Pandey and Shailly Kedia (Chapter 17) explored the innovation framework of India with the scope of integrating the issues of poverty, inclusivity and environment by taking two cases: the agriculture sector and renewable energy sector.

The volume contains chapters that cater to divergent dimensions of the broader scope of innovation systems. The evolutionary perspective underlying the dynamisms in different sectors across regions hits the boundaries of orthodoxy. The dynamics of the real world where the entities from the Global South are trying to find a place has important policy implications. The innovation system with the defined geographical boundaries has accumulated knowledge that is reflected in its development over the years (Chapters 5 and 6); the sectoral growth with the geographical boundaries had an altogether different momentum (Chapters 2, 7, 8, 9, 14 and 15). The regional divergence of growth and development are an important dimension that depicts the factors determining the knowledge flows (Chapters 2 and 11). However, the core remains confined to the factors determining innovation, focusing upon the mix of internal and external knowledge (Chapter 3). The internal factors include education (Chapter 4), finance (chapter 13), digitalization (Chapter 10), labour (Chapter 12) and sustainability (Chapters 16 and 17).

References

Carlsson, B. and Stankiewicz, R. (1995) On the Nature, Function and Composition of Technological Systems, in B. Carlsson (ed.) *Technological Systems and Economic Performance: The Case of Factory Automation*. Dordrecht: Kluwer.

Dosi, G., Freeman, C., Nelson, R., Silverberg, G. and Soete, L. (eds.) (1988) *Technical Change and Economic Theory*. London and New York: Pinter.

Edquist, C. (1997) Systems of Innovation Approaches: The Emergence and Characteristics, in E. Charles (ed.) *Systems of Innovation: Technologies, Institutions and Organisations*. London and Washington, DC: Pinter.

Edquist, C., Hommen, L. and McKelvey, M. (2001) *Innovation and Employment: Process Versus Product Innovation*. Cheltenham, UK: Edward Elgar Publishing.

Evenson, R. E. and Johnson, D. K. N. (1997) Introduction: Invention Input–Output Analysis. *Economic Systems Research* 9(2), 149–160.

Fagerberg, J. (2005) Innovation: A Guide to the Literature, in J. Fagerberg, D. C. Mowery and R. R. Nelson (eds) *The Oxford Handbook of Innovation*. Oxford: Oxford University Press.

Freeman, C. (1995) The National System of Innovation in Historical Perspective. *Cambridge Journal of Economics* 19(1), 5–24.

Johnson, D. K. N. (2002) The OECD Technology Concordance (OTC): Patents by Industry of Manufacture and Sector of Use. Organization for Economic Cooperation and Development, Science Technology and Industry Working Paper 2002/05. Available at: https://www.oecdilibrary.org/docserver/521138670407.pdf?expires=1665067937&id=id&accname=guest&checksum=3E7BD8F58DCC567FF47A0449EACB215

Johnson, D. K. N. and Evenson, R. E. (1997) Innovation and Invention in Canada. *Economic Systems Research* 9(2), 177–192.

Lee, K. (2019) *The Art of Economic Catch-up: Barriers, Detours and Leapfrogging in Innovation Systems*. Cambridge: Cambridge University Press.
Lundvall, B-Å. (ed) (1992) *National Innovation Systems: Towards a Theory of Innovation and Interactive Learning*. London: Pinter.
Johnson, D. K. N. and Van Wagoner, P. (2021) The Chicken or the Egg: Causality Between Trade and Innovation. *Journal of Industry, Competition and Trade: From Theory to Policy* 21(4), 527–541.
Malerba, F. and Orsenigo, L. (1997) Technological Regimes and Sectoral Pattern of Innovative Activities. *Industrial and Corporate Change* 6, 83–117.
Saviotti, P. P. (1997) Innovation Systems and Evolutionary Theories, in E. Charles (ed.) *Systems of Innovation: Technologies, Institutions and Organisations*. London and Washington, DC: Pinter.
Saxenian, A. (1994) *Regional Advantage. Culture and Competition in Silicon Valley and Route 128*. Cambridge, MA: Harvard University Press.
Von Schomberg, R. (2011) Towards Responsible Research and Innovation in the Information and Communication Technologies and Security Technologies Fields (November 13). Available at: https://ssrn.com/abstract=2436399

I

Inter-Industrial Inter-Linkages and Evolving Economies

Chapter 2

But What Came Before That?

Granger-Causality, Innovation and Input–Output Coefficients

Daniel K.N. Johnson and Tianyi (Lincy) Qin

1. Introduction

In a book such as this, celebrating the career and contributions of Lakhwinder Singh, it seemed appropriate to revisit a topic that interested us both when we first met almost 30 years ago. At that time, our mutual friend and mentor, Bob Evenson, was considering how input–output tables could be built to reflect not only flows of goods and services but the industrial distribution of innovation as well. This chapter is an attempt to draw those together, to link sectoral input–output flows across both typical economic activity and patents.

Our motivating question is simple: do more innovative sectors grow faster/slower economically, or is the causality reversed, such that growing/stagnant sectors become more/less innovative? Naturally, one or both directions are possible, as more vibrant economic sectors might become more creative to deal with change and economic competition, or more vibrant growth might leave less room for viable innovative activity as the easier frontiers are made more expensive by growth. Indeed, Evenson might very well agree with that latter claim of potential technological exhaustion. In the other causal direction, innovation might engender growth by opening up new market opportunities or it could plausibly hinder economic activity by drawing resources away from profits by competitive research efforts. In short, this is a causality whose sign and direction might vary by empirical context rather than by theory, so we intend to rely on data across time, across nations, and across economic sectors to reflect on patterns. To keep this chapter in line with our personal historical connection with Lakhwinder Singh, we will be analyzing the patterns for India and the United States over the years 1995–2011.

We propose no theoretical underpinning for this macro- (or technically, meso-) economic study, instead relying on industry-level VAR analysis. In doing so, we propose limited exogenous variables, allowing for level effects and inertial effects, but otherwise asking the data to directly inform our findings. There is clear evidence that trade between nations helps to foster innovation and technological progress (Beckerman, 1962; Kaldor, 1970; Balassa, 1989; Liu and Wang, 2003; MacGarvie, 2005, 2006; Vogel and Wagner,

DOI: 10.4324/9781003353904-3

2010; Castellani and Pieri, 2010), and that knowledge spillovers are associated with trade (Madsen, 2007), so it seems natural to assume that subnational trade would exhibit some of the same impacts. Further, knowledge spillovers contribute to innovation and economic growth within all sectors (Baier et al., 2006; Johnson and Evenson, 1997); their ability to have an impact across physical distance is well-documented (Jaffe, 1989; Acs et al., 1994; Jaffe et al., 2000; Funke and Niebuhr, 2005; Johnson and Lybecker, 2012), and learning through economic activity is clearly present (Beckerman, 1962; Kaldor, 1970; Balassa, 1989; Vogel and Wagner, 2010, Castellani and Pieri, 2010). However, empirical studies are inconclusive on the direction of causality or even on how to model the causality (Giles and Williams, 2000; Van Beveren and Vandenbussche, 2010; Johnson and van Wagoner, 2021).

At the national level, international trade correlates with innovation and learning (Edwards, 1997; Chand and Sen, 2002; Derakhshan and Sakunasingha, 2008), with more interconnected nations/industries benefiting more (Mankiw et al., 1992; Grossman and Helpman, 1991; Barro et al., 1995).

2. Model

We propose a VAR analysis of commercial activities and innovation in an input–output format, where each input–output cell's annual change is potentially a function of its previous level, of the relative size of its specific industry of manufacture (IOM, or row) and sector of use (SOU, or column), and of its historical counterpart in the other variable. Our goal is to discern whether innovation Granger-causes economic activity (ceteris paribus) or vice versa. So, we propose the following panel vector autoregression model, with fixed effects by sector:

$$\begin{bmatrix} \Delta g_{i,j,t} \\ \Delta p_{i,j,t} \end{bmatrix} = \begin{bmatrix} \beta_{gg} & \beta_{gp} \\ \beta_{pg} & \beta_{pp} \end{bmatrix} \begin{bmatrix} \Delta g_{i,j,t\text{-}1} \\ \Delta p_{i,j,t\text{-}1} \end{bmatrix} + \begin{bmatrix} \gamma_{gg} & \gamma_{gp} \\ \gamma_{pg} & \gamma_{pp} \end{bmatrix} \begin{bmatrix} \sum_{t=1}^{m} \sum_{\substack{k=0 \\ k<>j}}^{n} g_{i,k,t} + \sum_{t=1}^{m} \sum_{\substack{k=0 \\ k<>i}}^{n} g_{k,j,t} \\ \sum_{t=1}^{m} \sum_{\substack{k=0 \\ k<>j}}^{n} p_{i,k,t} + \sum_{t=1}^{m} \sum_{\substack{k=0 \\ k<>i}}^{n} p_{k,j,t} + \end{bmatrix}$$

$$+ \begin{bmatrix} u_{i,j,g} \\ u_{i,j,p} \end{bmatrix} + \begin{bmatrix} e_{i,j,t,g} \\ e_{i,j,t,p} \end{bmatrix}$$

Where:

$\Delta g_{i,j,t}$ is the change in goods/services from IOM i to SOU j from time t–1 to time t,

$\Delta p_{i,j,t}$ is the change in patents from IOM i to SOU j from time t–1 to time t,

$\sum_{t=1}^{m} \sum_{\substack{k=0 \\ k<>j}}^{m} g_{i,k,t} + \sum_{t=1}^{m} \sum_{\substack{k=0 \\ k<>i}}^{m} g_{k,j,t}$ represents the sum of goods and services flows from IOM i to all j SOUs except j and from all n IOMs except i to SOU j, both for all m time periods,

$\sum_{t=1}^{m}\sum_{\substack{k=0 \\ k<>j}}^{m} p_{i,k,t} + \sum_{t=1}^{m}\sum_{\substack{k=0 \\ k<>i}}^{m} p_{k,j,t}$ represents the sum of patents flows from IOM i to all n SOUs except j and from all n IOMs except i to SOU j, both for all m time periods,

$u_{i,j,g}$ is the panel-fixed effects specific to goods/services in IOM i and SOU j,
$u_{i,j,p}$ is the panel-fixed effects specific to patents in IOM i and SOU j,
and $\begin{bmatrix} e_{i,j,t,g} \\ e_{i,j,t,p} \end{bmatrix}$ is a vector of random errors.

The model parameters in matrices $\begin{bmatrix} \beta_{gg}\,\beta_{gp} \\ \beta_{pg}\,\beta_{pp} \end{bmatrix}$ and $\begin{bmatrix} \gamma_{gg}\,\gamma_{gp} \\ \gamma_{pg}\,\gamma_{pp} \end{bmatrix}$ are estimated using the generalized method of moments (GMM) via the PVAR process in Stata (Abrigo and Love, 2016).

3. Data

Traditional goods/services input–output data (in current prices, millions of US$) were obtained from the World Input–Output Database (WIOD), Release 2013, which covers the years from 1995 to 2011 for 40 countries in total (Timmer et al., 2015). WIOD is so far the only publicly available database that includes both our countries of interest in this study, India and the United States. We limit our focus to the intersectoral economic activities within a country so that we can spotlight the relationship between goods and services flows and patents flows for that country, but future work might consider using trading flows as a robustness check. These tables are in a square-matrix format with 35 IOMs (rows) and 35 SOUs (columns), which allow us to explore the inter-linkages across industries for the overall economy.

Unfortunately, innovation is inevitably more difficult to quantify. We elected to use Patent Cooperation Treaty (PCT) data to consider only patented innovations, and only those valuable enough to warrant international protection (and presumably therefore are large enough to transform inter-industrial linkages). This results in potential bias by sector if there is non-uniformity based on trade secrets or informal economic activity that might reduce reliance on PCT. Further, since patent documents do not carry IOM or SOU identifiers, we assigned probable IOMs and SOUs to each patent using the 1980 Canadian Standard Industrial Classification (SIC) version E to compare to goods/services sector definitions that are based on the two-digit International Standard Industrial Classification (ISIC) Revision 3 (Kortum and Putnam, 1997; Timmer et al., 2015). We then applied the crosswalk known as the OECD Technology Concordance to bridge definitions from the Canadian SIC-E to the ISIC-based definitions (Johnson, 2002). The resulting panel dataset details goods and services input–output and PCT patent publications by nation, by year, and by IOM-SOU pair. This introduces ambiguity due to the choice of crosswalks, but permitted us to aggregate patent counts to the precise sectors available for WIOD comparisons. PCT patent data therefore consist of 12,590 patent publications for India and 981,798 patent publications for the United States for the years from 1995 to 2011 (WIPO, 2020).

As a standard practice to prepare data for VAR analysis, we performed the Harris-Tzavalis unit-root test, which works well for data with a large panel size and a relatively small time dimension. The null hypothesis of unit roots was not rejected, so we tested the two variables for cointegration and rejected the Kao test null hypothesis, thus accepting the alternative hypothesis that both panels are cointegrated. Based on these results, we created the first difference of the panel series (Δg and Δp, as shown in our earlier model) for stationarity purposes and used this model for further analysis.

In choosing the optimal lag order for VAR model selection, we determined that the first-order panel VAR, or VAR(1), was appropriate for all sectors based on the Akaike information criterion (AIC), the Bayesian information criterion (BIC), and the Quinn information criterion (QIC). We also computed Hansen's J statistic and found that any over-identifying restrictions remained valid.

Notice that the exogenous variables are fixed in value over time to avoid stationarity or cointegration complications with the endogenous variables. Instead, they are included to reflect size/scale effects for each sector.

4. Results

We present the panel vector autoregression results as comparisons of India and the United States, first for the overall economy (in Table 2.1), then for selected large sectors (in Tables 2.2 and 2.3). In all cases, we report robust standard errors for coefficients as they affect the annual change in goods/services flows ($\Delta g_{i,j,t}$) and the change in patent flows ($\Delta p_{i,j,t}$).

In the top panel of Table 2.1, we present a comparison of the coefficients affecting cell values of the traditional goods/services input–output tables. Notice that the results show interesting statistical significance in very different ways across the two nations: in India, innovation appears to Granger-cause goods/services growth, while in the U.S. there is (statistically insignificant) evidence that innovation leads to fewer goods/services flows in that same input–output cell. Furthermore, large economic sectors in India (as measured by historical goods/services stocks) appear to grow more slowly, while large economic sectors grow more quickly in the United States (whether measured by historically large goods/services stocks or patent stocks). In short, India's input–output table values seem to be responding more promptly to innovative change, which is then lessened in sectors that are difficult to change due to large economic weight; in contrast, American input–output table values seem to be set more by historical norms than by recent change, and those norms suggest that large sectors change more quickly than small ones do.

In the bottom panel of Table 2.1, we investigate the factors affecting innovation input–output table cell values. There is less statistical significance evident here, and where it exists, it again highlights a difference between India and the United States. In India, a sector with more historical patents

Table 2.1 Panel VAR results for the overall economies of India and the U.S., 1995 to 2011

Variable	*Coefficient*	*t-stat*	*Coefficient*	*t-stat*
	India		**United States**	
	ΔGoods/Services flow ($\Delta g_{i,j,t}$)			
Lagged ΔGoods/Services flow	−0.030	−0.17	0.028	0.31
Lagged ΔPatents flow	670.568	2.96**	−3.993	−1.56
Sector goods/services total stock	−0.059	−3.89***	0.042	2.36*
Sector patents total stock	1.120	0.07	4.546	2.58*
	ΔPatents flow ($\Delta p_{i,j,t}$)			
Lagged ΔGoods/Services flow	0.001	0.68	0.001	0.74
Lagged ΔPatents flow	−0.174	−0.84	0.727	7.90***
Sector goods/services total stock	0.001	−0.06	0.001	−1.54
Sector patents total stock	−0.033	−2.17*	−0.017	−0.21

sees less patent activity in that same sector (perhaps evidence of technological exhaustion). This is frustrating, as it suggests that perhaps Indian innovation, at least at the internationally competitive PCT level, is stymied by competition in sectors that already have experienced a strong history of innovation. In contrast, the United States sees innovation Granger-causing more innovation in the same input–output cell, suggesting technological optimism where invention leads to follow-up breakthroughs at the knowledge frontier. These polar opposite responses suggest that policy advice in the two nations should not follow similar pathways at all.

Given these differences, we were eager to understand whether specific sectors drove these results. Therefore, we estimated the same model at the sectoral level for all 35 sectors, estimating separately for both IOMs and SOUs. In fact, there is a great degree of diversity among sectors. In India, only 8 of 35 IOMs mirror the aggregate result of innovation Granger-causing goods/services flows, just fewer than half of the 35 IOMs reflect the aggregate result of larger goods/services sectors growing more slowly, and only slightly more than half of all IOMs show a history of innovation slowing future innovation. Those results are quite similar if we group evidence by SOU, and most importantly, there is great diversity between sectors. In the United States, it is even more rare for an IOM (or SOU) to follow the aggregate economy-wide patterns of innovation Granger-causing more innovation or of historical size leading to more annual growth. Rather than present all 70 sets of results (which are available from the authors), we present 5 of the largest sectors here for comparison across IOM and SOU, and between nations.

Table 2.2 presents results for India's primary sector (agriculture/hunting/forestry/fishing), petroleum/nuclear fuels, chemicals, machinery, and

Table 2.2 India panel VAR results for five large sectors from 1995 to 2011

	IOM		*SOU*	
Variable	*Coeff.*	*t–stat.*	*Coeff.*	*t–stat.*
Agriculture, Hunting, Forestry and Fishing				
	ΔGoods/Services flow ($\Delta g_{i,j,t}$)			
Lagged ΔGoods/Services flow	−0.157	−1.17	−0.331	−2.10*
Lagged ΔPatents flow	−1314.412	−0.65	44.985	2.31*
Sector goods/services total stock	−0.066	−4.14***	−0.121	−6.45***
Sector patents total stock	−1969.932	−1.85	5.227	1.57
	ΔPatents flow ($\Delta p_{i,j,t}$)			
Lagged ΔGoods/Services flow	0.000	−1.37	0.000	0.57
Lagged ΔPatents flow	−0.765	−2.35*	−1.615	−3.27**
Sector goods/services total stock	0.001	−0.10	0.001	0.10
Sector patents total stock	−0.062	−0.73	−0.099	−2.40*
Coke, Refined Petroleum and Nuclear Fuel				
	ΔGoods/Services flow ($\Delta g_{i,j,t}$)			
Lagged ΔGoods/Services flow	−0.198	−0.83	−0.353	−1.16
Lagged ΔPatents flow	−210.724	−8.93***	558.698	0.73
Sector goods/services total stock	−0.022	−1.52	−0.039	−0.71
Sector patents total stock	21.449	1.99*	−121.562	−1.00
	ΔPatents flow ($\Delta p_{i,j,t}$)			
Lagged ΔGoods/Services flow	0.001	0.01	0.001	−0.72
Lagged ΔPatents flow	0.216	1.79	−0.209	−1.49
Sector goods/services total stock	0.001	−0.74	0.001	−0.54
Sector patents total stock	0.012	0.50	−0.021	−0.68
Chemicals and Chemical Products				
	ΔGoods/Services flow ($\Delta g_{i,j,t}$)			
Lagged ΔGoods/Services flow	−0.082	−1.00	−0.171	−3.87***
Lagged ΔPatents flow	57.124	9.53***	58.001	13.81***
Sector goods/services total stock	−0.034	−2.26*	−0.064	−2.63**
Sector patents total stock	0.403	0.38	2.046	1.28
	ΔPatents flow ($\Delta p_{i,j,t}$)			
Lagged ΔGoods/Services flow	−0.002	−0.50	−0.002	−0.53
Lagged ΔPatents flow	−0.194	−0.97	−0.302	−1.89
Sector goods/services total stock	0.001	−1.89 0.27	0.001	−0.44
Sector patents total stock	0.005		0.014	0.45

Table 2.2 (Continued)

	IOM		SOU	
Variable	*Coeff.*	*t–stat.*	*Coeff.*	*t–stat.*
Machinery				
	ΔGoods/Services flow ($\Delta g_{i,j,t}$)			
Lagged ΔGoods/Services flow	−0.235	−1.81	−0.161	−1.15
Lagged ΔPatents flow	−25.057	−2.01*	31.197	1.40
Sector goods/services total stock	−0.075	−3.56***	−0.089	−4.57***
Sector patents total stock	−1.292	−1.01	1.124	0.62
	ΔPatents flow ($\Delta p_{i,j,t}$)			
Lagged ΔGoods/Services flow	0.003	2.01*	0.000	1.65
Lagged ΔPatents flow	−0.046	−0.57	−0.131	−1.30
Sector goods/services total stock	0.001	2.40*	0.001	1.22
Sector patents total stock	−0.101	−5.03***	−0.073	−4.92***
Electrical and Optical Equipment				
	ΔGoods/Services flow ($\Delta g_{i,j,t}$)			
Lagged ΔGoods/Services flow	−0.747	−7.86***	−0.039	−0.25
Lagged ΔPatents flow	−96.548	−18.42***	−167.976	−19.95***
Sector goods/services total stock	−0.071	−2.94**	−0.037	−3.00**
Sector patents total stock	0.104	0.08	−1.797	−1.22
	ΔPatents flow ($\Delta p_{i,j,t}$)			
Lagged ΔGoods/Services flow	0.007	2.71**	0.002	1.27
Lagged ΔPatents flow	1.037	7.92***	1.314	9.19***
Sector goods/services total stock	0.001	1.70	0.001	0.24
Sector patents total stock	−0.095	−4.84***	−0.032	−1.82

electronic/optical equipment, while Table 2.3 parallels that content for the United States. Our objective here is to display diverse but important sectors, and to showcase the ways in which they differ between nations. Notice here that in results for single industries, the interpretations of sector-wide stocks of previous goods/services or patents take on a slightly different meaning; within a given sector, the reason for variation here is the omission of the history of the cell itself, because the historical stock is composed of the historical sum of all cells in the row and column other than the cell itself. Thus, a negative coefficient signifies that the remainder of the input–output row/column detracts from growth of the highest cell values; in other words, it signifies an evenly distributed row/column of values. In contrast, a positive

Table 2.3 United States panel VAR results for five large sectors from 1995 to 2011

	IOM		SOU	
Variable	*Coeff.*	*t–stat.*	*Coeff.*	*t–stat.*
Agriculture, Hunting, Forestry and Fishing				
	ΔGoods/Services flow ($\Delta g_{i,j,t}$)			
Lagged ΔGoods/Services flow	−0.087	−0.50	−0.140	−0.80
Lagged ΔPatents flow	−3220.293	−1.21	−120.660	−4.83***
Sector goods/services total stock	−0.121	−1.30	−0.058	−0.86
Sector patents total stock	−116.203	−0.19	1.147	0.26
	ΔPatents flow ($\Delta p_{i,j,t}$)			
Lagged ΔGoods/Services flow	0.001	1.67	0.001	0.24
Lagged ΔPatents flow	0.258	1.90	0.125	1.42
Sector goods/services total stock	0.001	2.02*	0.001	0.75
Sector patents total stock	−0.119	−3.18**	0.019	0.74
Coke, Refined Petroleum and Nuclear Fuel				
	ΔGoods/Services flow ($\Delta g_{i,j,t}$)			
Lagged ΔGoods/Services flow	−0.319	−4.89***	−0.271	−2.33*
Lagged ΔPatents flow	18.545	2.30*	−523.556	−1.06
Sector goods/services total stock	−0.006	−0.27	−0.111	−0.66
Sector patents total stock	−2.515	−0.31	−122.433	−0.40
	ΔPatents flow ($\Delta p_{i,j,t}$)			
Lagged ΔGoods/Services flow	0.001	−1.09	0.001	0.29
Lagged ΔPatents flow	0.272	1.32	−0.355	−3.85***
Sector goods/services total stock	0.001	−0.28	0.001	−0.05
Sector patents total stock	−0.127	−1.25	−0.037	−0.51
Chemicals and Chemical Products				
	ΔGoods/Services flow ($\Delta g_{i,j,t}$)			
Lagged ΔGoods/Services flow	−0.183	−0.58	0.162	2.00*
Lagged ΔPatents flow	3.621	0.35	8.574	2.18*
Sector goods/services total stock	0.389	1.53	0.001	−0.02
Sector patents total stock	−24.349	−1.87	−1.724	−0.66
	ΔPatents flow ($\Delta p_{i,j,t}$)			
Lagged ΔGoods/Services flow	−0.019	−1.24	0.001	0.39
Lagged ΔPatents flow	0.352	0.83	0.134	1.50
Sector goods/services total stock	0.016	2.61**	0.001	0.23
Sector patents total stock	−1.029	−2.54*	0.021	0.60

Table 2.3 (Continued)

	IOM		*SOU*	
Variable	*Coeff.*	*t–stat.*	*Coeff.*	*t–stat.*
Machinery				
	ΔGoods/Services flow ($\Delta g_{i,j,t}$)			
Lagged ΔGoods/Services flow	0.405	2.30*	0.027	0.27
Lagged ΔPatents flow	−3.829	−2.24*	−13.208	−2.64**
Sector goods/services total stock	0.097	0.76	−0.147	−1.27
Sector patents total stock	1.987	3.10**	5.401	4.02***
	ΔPatents flow ($\Delta p_{i,j,t}$)			
Lagged ΔGoods/Services flow	−0.004	−0.46	0.001	0.04
Lagged ΔPatents flow	0.033	0.22	0.428	2.98**
Sector goods/services total stock	−0.013	−2.40*	−0.001	−0.85
Sector patents total stock	0.182	2.35*	0.048	0.49
Electrical and Optical Equipment				
	ΔGoods/Services flow ($\Delta g_{i,j,t}$)			
Lagged ΔGoods/Services flow	0.566	4.95***	0.351	4.84***
Lagged ΔPatents flow	−4.947	−10.22***	0.178	0.20
Sector goods/services total stock	−0.094	−1.82	0.091	2.78**
Sector patents total stock	−1.664	−2.34*	1.631	2.63**
	ΔPatents flow ($\Delta p_{i,j,t}$)			
Lagged ΔGoods/Services flow	0.013	1.02	0.015	1.53
Lagged ΔPatents flow	0.763	8.13***	0.396	1.80
Sector goods/services total stock	−0.002	−0.39	0.002	1.82
Sector patents total stock	−0.042	−0.41	−0.264	−3.45**

coefficient signifies oscillation or spikes and valleys in the row/column where high (or low) values elsewhere in the row/column lead to even higher (or lower) values in this input–output cell.

By this logic, the primary sectors show a flat distribution of cell values in India (Table 2.2), and no statistical evidence of any pattern at all in the United States (Table 2.3). There is evidence of bi-directional Granger-causality in India's primary sector as an SOU, because sectors which contribute to agriculture are cyclical in both goods/services and innovation (with lagged flows dampening current flows in both goods and patents) and goods/services flows are strongly encouraged by innovation.

In contrast, within the fuel sector innovation Granger-causes reductions in Indian fuel IOM goods/services flows (presumably because those

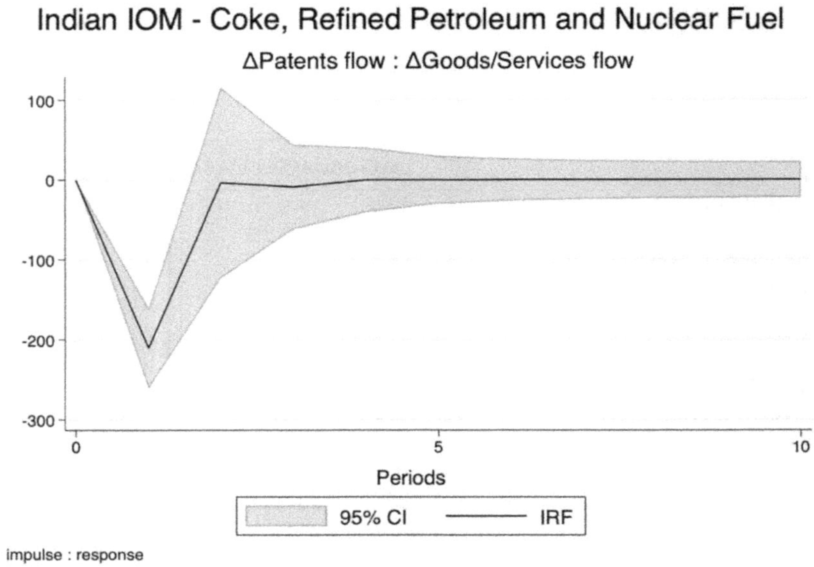

Figure 2.1 Indian Industries of Manufacture: Coke, Refined Petroleum and Fuel

innovations are energy-saving). As a result, the impulse response function for innovation's effect on goods/services flows in India is fairly dramatic but relatively short-lived, as seen in Figure 2.1. The same does not appear true in the American fuel sector.

In the American table, goods/services oscillate annually (perhaps due to fuel costs), innovation oscillates annually, and innovation Granger-causes increases in fuel IOM goods/services (perhaps due to technologies that push the frontier of exploration, like fracking techniques and equipment).

Innovation strongly Granger-causes increased sales in the Indian chemical industry as defined by both IOM and SOU, which is displayed in the impulse response function in Figure 2.2. That effect is weakly emulated in the American chemical industry, at least by SOU.

The Indian machinery sector is dominated by even distributions of input–output coefficients with little evidence of Granger-causality. In contrast, the American machinery sector is characterized by strong Granger-causality from innovation that reduces goods/services flows to and of machinery (by IOM and SOU).

Finally, in the electronics/optics sector, India shows strong Granger-causality by innovation that sharply reduces goods/services flows. That effect is also shown in the US, albeit more gradually, and is presumably due

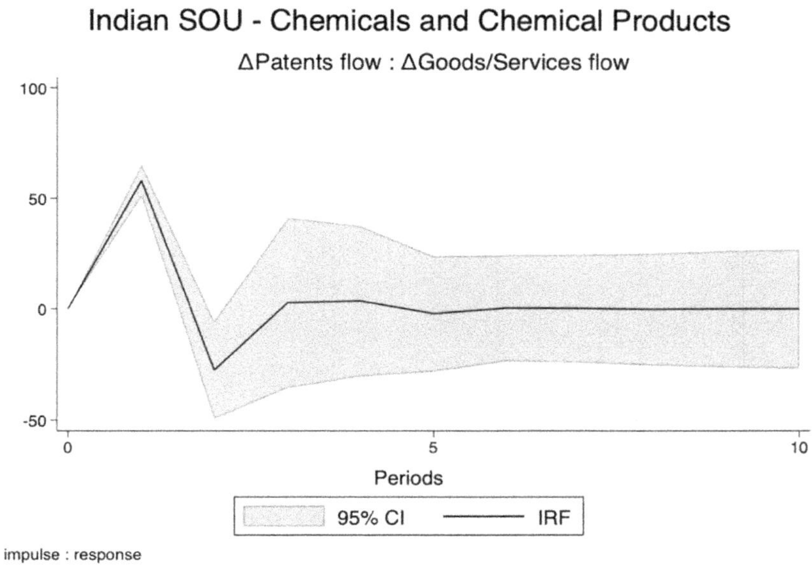

Figure 2.2 Indian Sectors of Use: Chemicals and Chemical Products

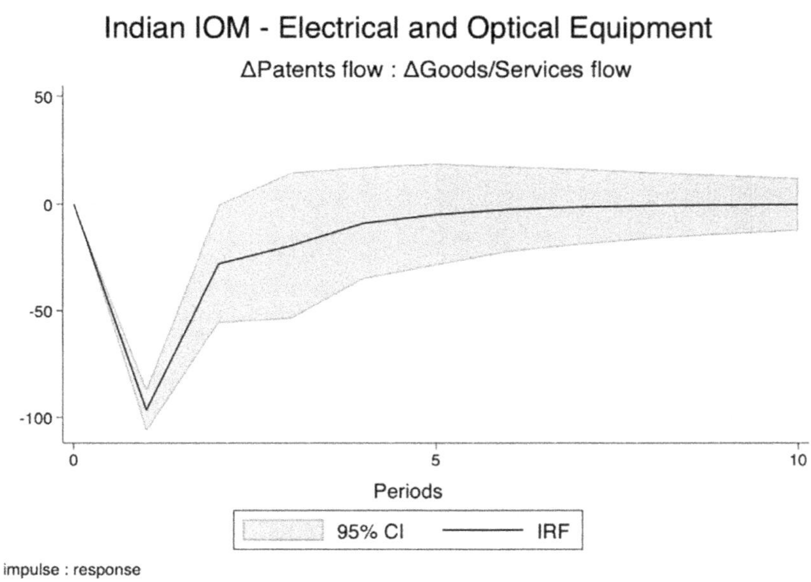

Figure 2.3 Indian Industries of Manufacture: Electrical and Optical Equipment

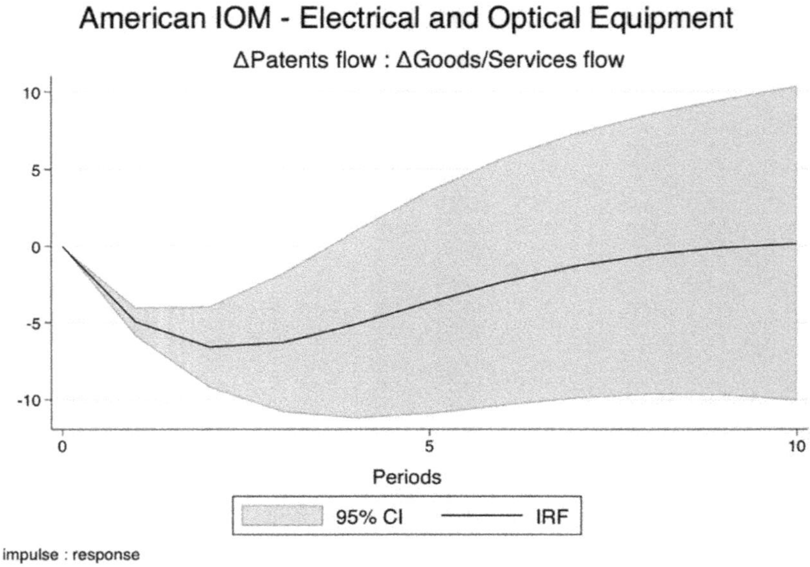

Figure 2.4 American Industries of Manufacture: Electrical and Optical Equipment

to cost reductions by induced innovation. Those two impulse response functions are displayed in Figures 2.3 and 2.4 for comparison.

Interestingly, Granger-causality from production that increases innovation to complete an unstable an unstable or oscillating equilibrium. That is, a small perturbation in production leading to more innovation would lead to smaller goods/services flows and a subsequent reduction in innovation.

5. Conclusions

We realize that it is unsatisfying to offer a conclusion that exhorts further study on the topic. However, what we have offered in this chapter is only a preliminary exploration of the idea that the coefficients of traditional input–output tables might be considered as potential partners with the coefficients of innovation input–output tables. In fact, innovation coefficients might be Granger-causing, or Granger-caused by, goods/services coefficients. We have indeed found evidence in both directions.

At the national level across 35 sectors, Indian innovation appears to stimulate (or technically, to Granger-cause) goods/flows in the same input–output cells, while American innovation appears to Granger-cause further innovation and perhaps even dampen goods/services flows there. That poses an interesting insight: that perhaps Indian innovation is more practical, more implementable, more readily applied to market sales, while American innovation is more theoretical and more prone to engender follow-on innovation than production. This narrative is consistent with the American race for continual change (perhaps regardless of the cost or the end goal), and the Indian goal of increased income per capita.

However, the coefficients at the national level mask a frankly puzzling array of diversity at the industry level. Here we see innovation slowing goods/services (Indian fuel IOM) or speeding up goods/services (Indian chemicals both IOM and SOU); we see evidence of production speeding up innovation (Indian electrical/optics both IOM and SOU); we even have some limited evidence of production acting to deter innovation (although it is rare). The spectrum of possible Granger-causalities is not contained to India but is mirrored in the United States, albeit by different sectors. In short, there are presumably narratives to tell and case studies to relate that will flesh out the sectoral differences. As a result, simple conclusions are dangerous and would mislead policy-makers. Instead, our conclusion must be nuanced and thoughtful: at the national level, innovation Granger-causes production and not vice versa, except where it Granger-causes more innovation instead, but a plurality of causal linkages is possible within specific sectors.

References

Abrigo, M. R. M., & Love, I. (2016). "Estimation of panel vector autoregression in Stata". *The Stata Journal*, 16(3): 778–804.

Acs, Z. J., Audretsch, D. B., & Feldman, M. P. (1994). "R & D spillovers and recipient firm size". *The Review of Economics and Statistics*, 76(2): 336–340.

Baier, S. L., Dwyer, G. P., & Tamura, R. (2006). "How important are capital and total factor productivity for economic growth?" *Economic Inquiry*, 44(1): 23–49. doi:10.1093/ei/cbj003

Balassa, B. (1989). "Outward orientation", in *Handbook of Development Economics*, Hollis Chenery & T.N. Srinivasan (eds.), edition 1, volume 2, chapter 31, pp. 1645–1689. New York: Elsevier.

Barro, R. J., Mankiw, N. G., & Sala-i-Martin, X. (1995). "Capital mobility in neoclassical models of growth", *NBER Working Paper* 4206.

Beckerman, W. (1962). "Projecting Europe's growth". *The Economic Journal*, 72(288): 912–925.

Castellani, D., & Pieri, F. (2010). "Foreign investments and productivity". *Quaderni del Dipartimento di Economia, Finanza e Statistica* 83.

Chand, S., & Sen, K. (2002). "Trade liberalization and productivity growth: Evidence from Indian manufacturing". *Review of Development Economics*, 6(1): 120–132.

Derakhshan, F., & Sakunasingha, B. (2008). "Importing technology: A theoretical paradigm". *Business Renaissance Quarterly*, 3(4).

Edwards, S. (1997). "Trade policy, growth, and income distribution". *American Economic Review*, 87(2): 205–210.

Evenson, R. E., & Johnson, D. K. N. (1997). "Introduction: Invention input–output analysis". *Economic Systems Research*, 9(2): 149–160.

Funke, M., & Niebuhr, A. (2005). "Regional geographic research and development spillovers and economic growth: Evidence from West Germany". *Regional Studies*, 39(1): 143–153.

Giles, J. A., & Williams, C. L. (2000). "Export-led growth: A survey of the empirical literature and some non-causality results". *Journal of International Trade & Economic Development*, 9(4): 445–470.

Grossman, G. M., & Helpman, E. (1991). "Trade, knowledge spillovers, and growth". *European Economic Review*, 35(2): 517–526.

Jaffe, A. B. (1989). "Real effects of academic research". *American Economic Review*, 79(5): 957–970.

Jaffe, A. B., Trajtenberg, M., & Fogarty, M. S. (2000). "Knowledge spillovers and patent citations: Evidence from a survey of inventors". *American Economic Review*, 90(2): 215–218.

Johnson, D. K. N. (2002). "The OECD Technology Concordance (OTC): Patents by industry of Manufacture and Sector of Use". Organization for Economic Cooperation and Development, *Science Technology and Industry Working Paper* 2002–5.

Johnson, D. K. N., & Evenson, R. E. (1997). "Innovation and invention in Canada". *Economic Systems Research*, 9(2): 177–192.

Johnson, D. K. N., & Lybecker, K. M. (2012). "Does distance matter less now? The changing role of geography in biotechnology innovation". *Review of Industrial Organization*, 40(1): 21–35.

Johnson, D. K. N., & van Wagoner, H. (2021). "The chicken or the egg: Granger-causality between trade and innovation". *Journal of Industry, Competition and Trade*, 21(4).

Kaldor, N. (1970). "The case for regional policies". *Scottish Journal of Political Economy*, 17(3): 337–348.

Kortum, S., & Putnam, J. (1997). "Assigning patents to industries: Tests of the Yale Technology concordance". *Economic Systems Research*, 9(2): 161–176.

Liu, X., & Wang, C. (2003). "Does foreign direct investment facilitate technological progress? Evidence from Chinese industries". *Research Policy*, 32(6): 945–953.

MacGarvie, M. (2005). "The determinants of international knowledge diffusion as measured by patent citations". *Economics Letters*, 87(1): 121–126.

MacGarvie, M. (2006). "Do firms learn from international trade?" *Review of Economics and Statistics*, 88(1): 46–60.

Madsen, J. B. (2007). "Technology spillover through trade and TFP convergence: 135 years of evidence for the OECD countries". *Journal of International Economics*, 72(2): 464–480.

Mankiw, N. G., Romer, D., & Weil, D. N. (1992). "A Contribution to the Empirics of Economic Growth". *Quarterly Journal of Economics*, 107(2): 407–437.

Timmer, M. P., Dietzenbacher, E., Los, B., Stehrer, R., & de Vries, G. J. (2015). "An illustrated user guide to the world input – output database: The case of global automotive production". *Review of International Economics*, 23: 575–605.

Van Beveren, I., & Vandenbussche, H. (2010). "Product and process innovation and firms' decision to export". *Journal of Economic Policy Reform*, 13(1): 3–24.

Vogel, A., & Wagner, J. (2010). "Higher productivity in importing German manufacturing firms: Self-selection, learning from importing, or both?" *Review of World Economics*, 145(4): 641–665.

World Intellectual Property Organization (WIPO). (2020). "IP Statistics Data Center". https://www3.wipo.int/ipstats/editSearchForm.htm?tab=pct

Chapter 3

Technology Transfer to Developing Countries

Facets and Challenges

Vinish Kathuria

1. Introduction

The role of technology and international technology transfer (TT) in the growth and welfare of economies is well-established (UNCTAD, 2014; Hoppe, 2005).[1] The literature is also replete with studies that have argued a) the kind of technology transferred being inappropriate to the recipient country's factor conditions (Mytelka, 1978, Stewart, 1978); b) foreign firms that are the carrier of these technology forming enclaves (Kathuria, 2002a; Eriksson, 2013a), thereby creating a bigger wedge in the economy; and c) technology transfer not resulting in catch-up with the leader, as is often presumed (Steenhuis et al., 2007; Eriksson, 2013a).[2] Despite all these concerns, the developing countries continue to depend on technology transferred to not have to reinvent the wheel.

Importantly, in the S-shaped curve of technology diffusion, where technology acquisition through transfer is often the first step for developing countries, it allows the late starters to catch up or even leapfrog (Steenhuis et al., 2007). Besides, one of the aims of the TT, apart from bringing productivity improvement, is spurring local innovation activities. It has also been pointed out that owing to their small size and resource constraints, small and medium enterprises (SMEs) in these countries cannot carry out research and development (R&D) activities to generate their own technologies; consequently, they depend on TT as a strategic means to meet globalization challenges (Mayer and Blass, 2002).

Technology transfer has different facets. These are: a) from one application domain to another – for example, several of the civil applications have their origin in military use; b) from one country to another – which has three different aspects: from one developed country to another developed country (North-North transfer), from a developed county to a developing country (North-South transfer), and lastly, from one developing country to another (South-South transfer); and c) from labs/universities to market or university to industry TT.[3] These facets are mostly mutually exclusive, with little overlap. Sufficient literature and evidence exist looking into the issues

DOI: 10.4324/9781003353904-4

encountered in each of these facets of technology transfer (see, for example, the works of Mansfield, 1975; Godkin, 1988; Eriksson, 2000; Steenhuis et al., 2007; Eriksson, 2013a, 2013b; Majidpour, 2017). Evidence also exists about successful as well as failed TT in each of these facets.

This chapter talks about the role of TT and issues encountered when it is transferred from one country to another (mainly developed to developing/industrializing), and also from labs to market. The discussion is oriented toward developing countries, which are often in dire need of technology. This is because it is the developed countries that are acknowledged as the generator of new technology. For developing countries, technological progress is inextricably linked to their ability to access, adapt and diffuse technological knowledge having its origin abroad (UNCTAD, 2014). The chapter ends with some suggestions on what needs to be done to maximize the recipient country's benefits from the transferred technology.

2. Technology Transfer – Key Terms and Views

Before we look into different facets of technology transfer, we need to know the difference between technology diffusion and TT. The former means the passive spreading of technological knowledge related to innovation around technology (Hameri, 1996). In contrast, TT is an active and intentional process through licensing, foreign investment, or outright buying to disseminate or acquire knowledge, experience and related products. Since diffusion is passive, the process does not involve money transfer, whereas TT involves payment. Another difference between the two is diffusion concerns the knowledge itself, whereas transfer involves both the replication of knowledge and the physical products linked to the innovation. Despite being different concepts, the boundaries between the two concepts are mostly blurred (Radosevic, 1999).

There are two distinct views of technology: the neoclassical view perceiving technology as information, whereas the alternate view perceives technology as knowledge. The neoclassical or the growth models developed by Solow (1957), which perceive technology as information, imply that it is easily available to producer and consumer. This makes it easily reproducible and transferable. The alternate view (Mowery and Rosenberg, 1989; Pavitt, 1991) argues that technology is knowledge, which is primarily tacit and cumulative within individual firms. This implies that reproducing and transferring it is not easy. Radosevic (1999) illustrates these differences based on 8 attributes as given in Table 3.1. Notably, both these aspects of technology co-exist in any economy or within the same firm. The firms rely on both these sources and types with varying mixes.

As is clear from the table, if technology is perceived as information, then problems of technology transfer are reduced to an issue of incentives only (Radosevic, 1999). On the other hand, the firm-specific nature of technology

Table 3.1 Technology as information or knowledge – attributes

Sno	*Attributes*	*Technology as Information*	*Technology as firm-specific knowledge*
1	Unit of analysis	Technique	Capability
2	Characteristic of Technology	Flexible/Substitutable/ Generic/Reversible/ Adaptable	Local/cumulative/Path dependent
3	Dominant View	Static	Dynamic
4	Access	Easy, No problem	Limited (Difficult)
5	Concept	Transaction	Investment
6	Focus	Price	Spillovers, Externalities – dynamic
7	Transfer Mode	Arm's length as a norm	Various forms of technology transfer (JV, FDI)
8	Transfer Costs	Negligible to small	High

Source: Adapted from Radosevic (1999)

renders it difficult and costly to transfer the technology. Given that technology is an embodied knowledge, for a matured manufacturing process, its successful transfer would require new investments in learning (Grant and Gregory, 1997). If technology is embodied, it results in huge transaction/ transfer costs. An earlier study by Teece (1977) finds that the transfer costs averaged 19% of the total costs of the project (with a range of 2 to 56 percent for 26 projects).

As discussed earlier, TT has different facets involving transfer from one application domain to another, from one country to another, or from labs/ universities to market. These facets are mostly mutually exclusive with little overlap. A recent study by UNCTAD (2014) argues that irrespective of the facet, TT is often linked to the movement of physical persons or more specifically to the movement of a specific set of capabilities.

2.1. TT – One Application Domain to Another

Several of the civil applications have their origin in military use. For example, use of vision enhancement in road vehicles, the use of the World Wide Web (WWW) or the modern computers, or the use of transistors have a history of first use in the military and then successfully transferred to civil applications (Mowery and Rosenberg, 1982; Markusen and Yudken, 1992). Several of the applications developed for motor vehicles are based on the principles first applied in aviation (Harris and Harris, 2004). For example, autopilot mode in the aircraft resulted in automatic cruise control (ACC) in cars. Similarly, the technology of lightweight materials was accepted in Formula 1 after it was proven successful in the aeronautical industry. Computational fluid dynamics (CFD) was a limited resource available to few

Table 3.2 Parallel technological concepts – from one domain to another

	Technology	*Domain 1*	*Domain 2*	*Source*
1		Aircraft	Car	Harris and Harris (2004)
	Automatic Control	Auto Pilot, Flight management system (FMS)	Adaptive Cruise control, Automatic Lane keeping	
	Navigation	Moving map displays, FMS	Route Guidance system, Route Finders	
	Vision Enhancement	Night vision goggles, Forward-looking infrared	Vision Enhancement system	
	Collision Avoidance	Traffic Alert and Collision Avoidance System (TCAS), Ground Proximity Warning Systems (GPWS)	Collision Avoidance System	
2		Aviation	Civil	
	Material and Coating technologies	Jet Engine	Gas Turbines	Majidpour (2017)
3	Pistons, Hydraulics, advanced engine parts	Defense cluster (military engine)	Traditional clusters such as power generation, transportation	Eriksson (2000); Solvell *et al.* (1993)
		Aviation/Automobile	Health/Defense/ Spaceí™.	
4	Laser Beam	For metal cutting and welding	Diverse domains as holography, micro and power electronics, space science, medical science, directed military weapons	Ahmed *et al.* (2021)

Source: Own compilation from different sources

aeronautical companies. However, its advantages of cost reduction of prototype testing and quicker product development time found its users in F1, for which making the fastest car in the quickest possible time is sine quo non. Similarly, material and coating technologies in gas turbines first occurred in aircraft jet engines (Majidpour, 2012). Table 3.2 compiles some of these domain transfer examples.

2.2. TT – From One Country to Another

The international TT occurs through different channels, and these channels encompass the varying role of the donor and recipients moderated and mediated through the magnitude of TT. Key among them is a) trade, especially in capital goods, b) explicit trade in technology measured by the global payment of fees and royalties, c) technology transferred through foreign direct investment (FDI), and d) channels like the movement of people, scientific literature, etc.

Radosevic (1999), however, goes one step further and argues that even development assistance can also involve TT.[4] He characterizes TT based on three key dimensions: a) is it embodied or disembodied? b) What is the transfer mode? – market mediated or through the network; and c) What is the role of the seller? – active, passive or enabler. Table 3.3 reproduces the characterization. From the table, one can see that with so many dimensions, especially when technology is disembodied, the seller is a passive or mere enabler, and technology involves a network partner, the transfer may not yield the desired result of the building of capabilities and may fall flat more than realizing the benefits as envisaged.

Regarding relevance of different channels of TT over a period of time, the data shows that capital goods trade, which formed nearly 23 percent of total trade in 1975, increased to nearly 30 percent by 1996 and after that to 33 percent by 2019.[5] However, the real explosion has happened in market-mediated international TT, measured by royalty payment, which has gone from US$ 0.5 bn in 1970 to nearly US $100 bn in 2003 and then to over US $440 bn in 2019 (a CAGR of 14.7 since 1970). Figure 3.1 shows the trend in royalty payments over the period.

The increased relevance of royalty payments also points to the increased importance of high-technology (high-tech) industries such as pharmaceuticals or electronics or aviation. In the following sub-section, we see how TT in such sectors brings about industrialization and technological change, resulting in economic growth.

2.3. From Developed Countries to Developing Countries (North-South Transfer)

High-tech industries are frequently targeted to further regional development policy (Eriksson, 2013a). This is because they are the most probable sources of innovation, successful entrepreneurs, new firms, and new industries (Maleci, 1997), besides their spillover effects (Eriksson, 2000). In terms of product characteristics, industries can be divided into a) mass-produced or bulk commodities such as steel, or b) complex product systems, which are largely customized goods (Miller et al., 1995), thus having a distinctive role in innovation. The latter include aerospace, flight simulation, nuclear power plants and heavy electrical equipment.

Miller et al. (1995) stresses three key characteristics of the complex system. First, they are made of many interconnected but customized elements, which are hierarchical; second, they exhibit dynamic non-linear properties when a small perturbation in part results in large changes elsewhere; and last, they have a high degree of user involvement in the innovation process. Several of the high-tech industries form or are complex systems.

Table 3.3 Types with dimensions of technology transfer – role of supplier/buyer

Transfer Mechanism	*Embodiment Type*			*Transfer Mode*			*Role of seller/partner*		
	Capital	*Embodied*	*Disembodied*	*Market (explicit)*	*Network (intermediate)*	*Hierarchies (implicit)*	*Active*	*Enabling*	*Passive*
FDI	X	X	X			X	X		
JV	X	X	X			X	X		
Licensing			X	X					X
Goods Import		X		X					X
Co-operative alliances		X			X		X		X
Subcontracting		X			X		X	X	X
Export		X		X					X
Transfer by people		X			X			X	
Development Assistance	X	X		X	X		X		

Notes: Co-operative alliances include production sharing agreements, management & marketing contracts, service agreements, R&D consortia and other co-operative alliances, franchising, technical services contracts.
Source: Adapted from Radosevic (1999)

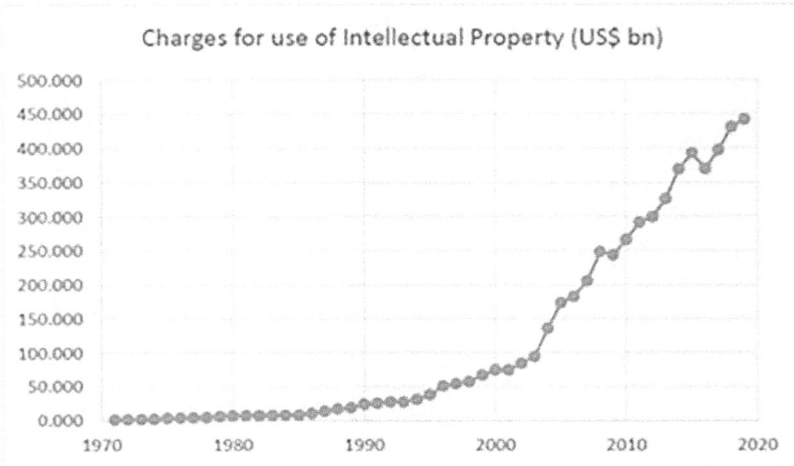

Figure 3.1 Trend of World Charges for the Use of Intellectual Property (US$ bn)
Data Source: World Bank

UNCTAD (1995) has characterized industries into four tiers based on their technological sophistication: tier 1 are labor-intensive light industries and include clothing, footwear, sports goods; tier 2 are scale-intensive heavy and chemical industries such as steel, fertilizers etc.; tier 3 are assembly-based industries, where both scale and scope economics exist and product differentiation is the rule; and in tier 4, we have R&D or innovation-intensive Schumpeterian industries, where R&D and close customer interactions are the keys. Aircraft, pharmaceuticals, turbines, etc. fall into this.

Importantly, it is the developed countries that control and dominate these tier 4 or high-tech industries. Given the importance of these industries, any effort by developing countries to nurture them and to ever pose a serious challenge to the developed countries would first require importing the technology. Paradoxically, the catch-up and technological leadership in these industries in the future may also be tough as the aim is at moving target due to the "red-queen effect," where the leader would invest in next-generation technology to be ahead of the pack. Thus, by the time technology is imported and assimilated, the leader moves on (Freeman, 1988: p. 73). This implies that investment and TT in such industries is highly risky, and capabilities to absorb them should exist before embarking on the technology transfer process (Kathuria and Oh, 2018). This is very much exemplified in the case of aircraft industries in Indonesia and Romania, where transfer did not yield a leadership position, whereas in Brazil and to some extent in China, the transfer could help them to carve out a niche due to already existing capabilities (see Steenhuis *et al.*, 2007; Eriksson, 2013b for details about these two countries).

An important aspect of catch-up is leapfrogging. Information and communication technology (ICT) is one example where developing countries could catch up and leapfrog without investing in outdated technology (James, 2009; Kathuria and Oh, 2018). Interestingly, in high-tech industries for leapfrogging, the traditional S-curve becomes more of a sequential S-curve. Over time, the technological complexity increases, and a new S-curve emerges. This is illustrated in Figure 3.2 for two such high-tech industries: aircraft and locomotives.

The technology catch-up through TT in a high-tech industry can be considered to consist of four phases (Eriksson, 2013a; Steenhuis et al., 2007). In phase 1, technology is transferred for licensed production. This implies phase 1 uses existing production and management technologies to produce goods already in the market. Phase 2 is the technology integration phase, where current technologies are used to design and produce a new product. This could be done indigenously or jointly. In phase 3, the technology development phase is to develop existing technologies further and invest in new technologies. The last phase is to support the first three phases and is termed "large-scale basic research." This is to defend technological superiority if attained.

We take an example from one country for one such key industry to see what challenges this country has faced while benefitting/learning from the technology transferred. Did the TT facilitate catch-up? The industry chosen

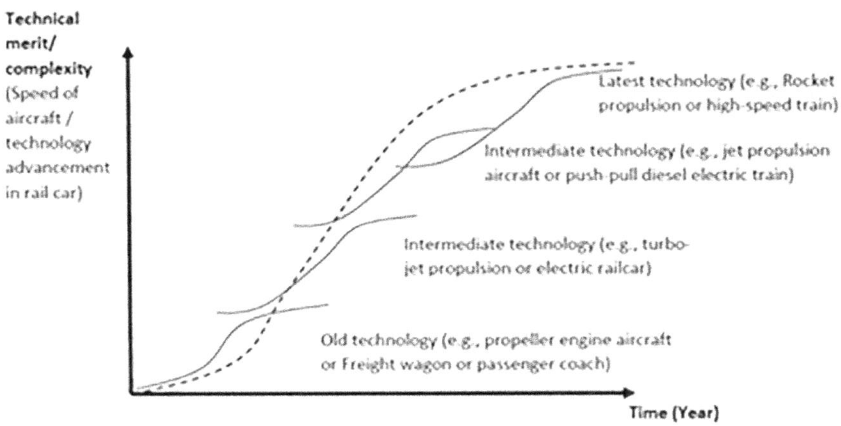

Figure 3.2 Sequential S-shaped Technological Process for Dynamic Industries

Source: Adapted from Steenhuis *et al.* (2007), Putranto *et al.* (2003)

is the aviation industry (also termed commercial aircraft industry), and the country is Indonesia.

3. Aircraft Industry

Given the widespread linkages of the aircraft industry with software, electronics, mechanical, materials and paints, several countries (Indonesia, China, Brazil, Taiwan and Romania) in the past have tried to develop the industry. Some have become successful, and others have to cease the activity and have become the component supplier.

This tier 4 industry is characterized by complex and high-value-added products made in relatively small quantities by few players (Eriksson, 2000). The development period is long and the technological requirement is high, which necessitates high R&D investment. According to Eriksson (2013a), there is no other industry requiring such interdependence and cross-fertilization of advanced technology. The extremely demanding required level of functional performance, reliability, safety and efficiency at a system level makes aircraft technology very complex, where different components have to withstand a temperature gradient of over 100 degrees within a few hours. Consequently, much of the investment in developing a new aircraft is spent on integrating from varied fields such as metallurgy, composite materials, electronics, hydraulics and petroleum. The catch-up becomes all the more difficult because of a lack of technical and technological competence, industrial infrastructure and above all, financial resources in several of the developing countries (Eriksson, 2013a).

Though the industry has widespread linkages, it has several other characteristics that result in catch-up difficulties. The sector requires: a) skilled labor for aircraft production and design; b) large tied-up investments due to long design lead-time, production lead-time[6] and cyclical demand; and c) reliance on the international market, as profitability requires selling a large number of quantities (Steenhuis *et al.*, 2007). An international selling in the absence of a domestic market makes catch-up even more difficult as it would necessitate approval from international aviation authorities for certification.

We take an example from the aviation sector for Indonesia. The country (as well as Romania and China), knowing the sector's benefit potential, emphasized building the local aviation sector from scratch. Incidentally, it failed to a great extent but provided enormous lessons to other countries.

3.1. Indonesia – IPTN/IAe/PTDI[7]

Indonesia, with over 17,500 islands spread over 3 time zones with limited or no road access to most islands, depends heavily on air transportation. To boost Indonesia's industrialization and to cater to these islands, the country embarked on a program to spur the local aircraft industry (Steenhuis *et al.*,

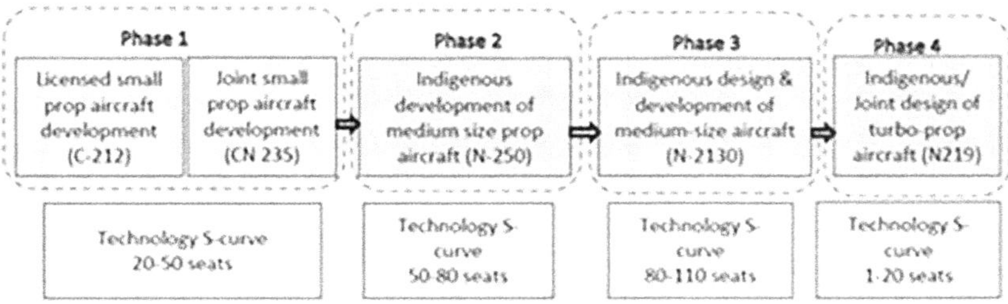

Figure 3.3 Technology Transferred and Phases in Indonesia's Quest for Dominance in Aircraft Technology

2007). A company named Peasawat Terbang Nurtanio (Nurtanio Aircraft Industry Ltd) was established in 1976. In 1985, its name was changed to Industri Pesawat Terbang Nusantara, or IPTN. In August 2000, the name was again changed to PT Industri Dirgantara (PTDI) to cater to the domestic market, and Indonesian Aerospace (Iae) as the global identity (Eriksson, 2013a).

The aviation program in Indonesia had all four phases (Figure 3.3) discussed earlier, starting with licensed production, followed by a joint venture and indigenous efforts in phases 3 and 4 with increased technological sophistication. Phase 1 started with the manufacturing of a 24-passenger turbo aircraft (C-212 Aviocar) with a license from CASA, Spain. A key feature of the aviation program was focus on the Progressive Manufacturing Programme (PMP)[8] to build local capabilities. The first Indonesian C-212 Aviocar was assembled using major components in 1976. Subsequently, over a period of time, PMP resulted in increased content from Indonesia, with IPTN able to manufacture it completely by 1987 (Eriksson, 2013a). As can be seen from Table 3.4 and Figure 3.3, the learning/catch-up in phase 1 was successful. IPTN could produce more than 100 C-212 with complete indigenization.

In the second phase, which started in 1979, IPTN went into a joint venture with CASA to produce a small propeller (CN235) aircraft. An important aspect of this JV and earlier licensing was that the parent company (CASA) continued to produce the same aircraft in its Spanish plant. From a learning and catch-up perspective, it is heartening to note that the first Spanish-built CN235 flew in November 1983, while the first Indonesian-built CN235 flew in December 1983 – a mere six-week delay (Steenhuis *et al.*, 2007). The program was moderately successful; by December 2002, IPTN could sell only 47 CN235, whereas CASA could sell over 250. Two key problems for IPTN not able to commercially sell as identified were: a) high cost;[9] b) not able to secure certification from the Federal Aviation Administration

Table 3.4 Indonesia's efforts in the aviation sector – a phase-wise summary

Phase	*Aircraft*	*Type*	*Licensed/JV/ Indigenous*	*Year Started*	*Number Mfrd*	*Status*	*Reason*
1	C-212	Small Prop (21–28 passengers)	Licensed from CASA Spain	1976	>100 (CASA sold over 460 in 42 countries)	Successful (By 1987, IPTN was able to mfr it completely)	In 2014, PTDI stopped producing the -400 series and moved production to the improved NC-212i model
2	CN235	Small Prop (44 passengers)	Jointly with CASA Spain	Oct. 1979	57 (up to 2011)	Moderately successful	Number far from breakeven; IAe not able to export any version based on pure commercial grounds and also due to certification issues
3	N250	Medium size prop (64–68-seater)	Indigenous development	June 1989	Two prototypes	Not successful	Development & production cost too high, No international certification, Financial constraint
4	N2130	Medium size (100–130-seater)	Indigenous design & development	1996	Project closed down in 1999	Not successful	Financial constraint; IMF insisted on no subsidy – had to stop
5	N219	Small Turbo prop (19-seater)	Indigenous design & development	2006	Two prototypes – MSN 001 in Nov. 2015 and MNS 002 in Sep. 2018	Still not successful	Certification received on 11 Feb 2020 (extended twice). IAe plans to go for commercialization in 2021
6	N245	Medium size turbo prop (50-seater)	Jointly with Turkish Aerospace	2016		Under development	

Source: Eriksson, 2013a; Steenhuis et al., 2007; www.flightglobal.com/aerospace/indonesia-certifies-n219-regional-turboprop/141763.article; https://en.wikipedia.org/wiki/Indonesian_Aerospace_N-245 accessed in June 2021

(FAA) – a sine quo non for selling to the US market. Interestingly, the FAA certification required a bilateral treaty between Indonesia and the USA.

In the third phase, IPTN decided to develop its first fully indigenized turboprop 50-seater aircraft, N250, with Western Assistance using modern technology such as fly-by-wire in 1989. This was subsequently redesigned in 1993 as a 64–68 seater with full authority digital engine control and other state-of-the-art technology, such as a Doppler turbulence weather radar and a collision-avoidance system (Eriksson, 2013a). The first aircraft was rolled out in Nov. 1994, a year later than planned, and had its maiden flight in August 1995. Learning from the experiences of CN235, IAe decided to open an assembly line in the US, which would have yielded multiple benefits, such as a large US market with easy FAA certification, access to foreign investors and reduced cost as most input suppliers were from the USA, among other things (Steenhuis et al., 2007). Failing to get FAA certification, IPTN moved to Europe and sought the help of European Aerospace consultants to get JAA certification. In 1997, IPTN signed a technical and marketing JV with a German group to assemble and market N250 in Germany. Post the 1997 East Asian crises, IMF blocked government support (financial and other privileges) to IPTN (Eriksson, 2013a). Subsequently, IPTN looked to China for support to bail it out of its financial troubles. Despite spending in excess of US $650 million on development, the third prototype of the N250 has not seen the light, and no production has taken place either in the USA or in Germany. Eventually, the project closed down.

Though the third phase was still on, IPTN entered its fourth phase in 1995 with the announcement of an 80–130-seat regional jet, the N2130, with a US $2 bn development program. The phase can be described as the implementation and R&D of future technology. Similar to N250, it was decided that N2130 would be developed with help from Western companies. A special company, PT Dua Satu Tiga Puluh (DSTP), was founded in 1996 to raise funds for N2130. By late 1996, three versions of N2130 were envisaged, with a 29.45m-long airframe serving as the baseline 100-seat design. This version was to be followed by an 80-seater, 22.20m-shrink version and a third version with 39.20m-stretch derivative, seating up to 130 passengers, in a single-class configuration. However, subsequent consultations with regional airlines revealed little support for either an 80-seater or a five-abreast cabin cross-section. In response, by 1997, IPTN had dropped the plan to develop a shortened, 80-seat version and opted for a larger-aircraft family with six-abreast seating for between 104 and 132 passengers.[10]

The initial timetable stated that the all-Indonesian-made aircraft would have its maiden flight on March 2004 and would be delivered to its first operator for the June 2006 Indonesia Air Show.[11] A wing part of a 1:7.89 scale half-span wind tunnel model was designed and built for IPTN in 1999/2000 by Vojnotehnièki Institut Ratka Resanoviæa (VTI), Beograd, Serbia. The project continued for some years, including wind tunnel testing and some work on the prototype. However, by 1998, the Indonesian aircraft industry faced serious economic and political uncertainty because of the region's financial crisis. In September 1999, DSTP was officially closed. The company handed over the preliminary design of N2130 to the Ministry of Industry and Trade, and the US$ 70 million spent on the design process was considered as "sunk-cost."

Apart from becoming a major international aircraft producer, IPTN intended to be a global supplier of aircraft components and parts. The company has been successful in this, as in 2012 it carried out subcontracting for Airbus 380 (various components), Airbus 320/321 (leading edge skin, pylons, and D-nose skin), Boeing B747–9 (steel retainers) and Boeing B767 (flaps) (Eriksson, 2013a). Besides, it has done subcontracting work for Fokker, General Dynamics/Lockheed and Mitsubishi. The main business for IPTN has been the continued production of airframe sections for the Spanish-built CN-235.

3.2. Learning

From this discussion, it is very much evident that with government support, an industry can be set up, but there is no guarantee that it will be successful. This is because several other enabling factors are needed. One key factor that has been highlighted elsewhere is nurturing advanced suppliers at the local and regional level. IPTN, however, neglected to nurture suppliers (Eriksson, 2013a). Material imports accounted for over 95 percent of the entire value of its inputs in 1994 (Sutanto, 1996 as referred in Eriksson, 2013a). On the contrary, local private technology firms were coerced to contribute financially to aircraft development activities (Fromhold-Eisebith and Eisebith, 2002). Once the government changed, these regional airlines withdrew this support. Moreover, regional dynamism is required for the growth and catch-up of such an industry, which the Bandung region lacks.

On the other hand, one key factor that emerges from the successful transfer of technology in the gas turbine industry in Iran's MAPNA is the physical proximity of its subsidiaries manufacturing equipment such as turbines, generators and boilers (Majidpour, 2017). The physical proximity facilitated knowledge and experience-sharing through face-to-face interaction.

Another key learning from the long-term failure of the IPTN case is the excessive focus of the company on technology without looking at marketing, business development and management (Eriksson, 2013a). This is because the company could not acquire an airworthiness certificate and did not secure enough orders to keep it financially afloat. A huge supporting infrastructure of suppliers, services firms and industry-university interaction together with financial resources are needed for the success of such an industry. If these enabling factors are missing, such firms can only become an industrial enclave with little connection to the rest of the economy.

3.3. TT – From Universities/Labs to Market

The TT from universities/labs to market assumes importance if we recognize that invention does not only take place in research labs/controlled experimental settings, termed "primary inventions" by Young, 1991 (Hoppe, 2005). The refinement and improvement of these technologies, now termed "secondary inventions," takes place in market/industry through learning-by-doing (Arrow, 1962), dynamic learning (Radosevic, 1999) or learning-to-learn (Connolly, 1997). Based on this, we can say there exist 3 kinds of inventive activities: the invention of new goods (mostly primary), quality improving nature and cost-reducing nature (mostly secondary).

An earlier study by Mansfield (1991) and Pavitt (1991) studying linkages between academic research and industrial innovation, concludes that 10 percent of the new products and processes commercialized during 1975–1985 by 76 randomly chosen top American firms would have been significantly delayed (gestation lag of seven years) if there was no academic research. An issue with university-to-market research is how to measure the output of the R&D project. The criteria vary, depending upon what is being measured and the phase of the innovation process. Macroeconomic models study the effect of R&D expenditure on productivity at firm, industry, national or international level, whereas business models calculate revenue from R&D investment, and scientometric or technometric models evaluate the results from an epistemological view by analyzing the bibliometric data (i.e., citations) and other achievements of the project (patents or prizes) (Hameri, 1996). The success of TT in scientific-industry R&D projects has to be broad-based and can be measured a number of ways (Phillmore, 1989), including: a) new product, processes and services produced; b) patents and licenses produced; c) scientific publications, doctoral theses and other academic output accomplished; d) congresses, workshops, seminars, briefings and other information dissemination activities carried out; e) spin-off companies, joint ventures and other business units founded; and f) mobility of people from industry to research and vice versa.

What kind of collaborators are interested in participating in R&D projects with a fundamental research center (say CSIR lab or university)? Freeman (1982) has outlined that of the six innovation strategies: offensive, defensive, imitative, dependent, traditional and opportunist. The firms with offensive strategies provide the best opportunities for collaboration with universities.

3.4. Conclusions and Policy Implications

Based on the case study and discussion, it can be summarized that there are three key concerns in technology transfer that have implications for innovation and growth for developing countries. The first concern is whether appropriate technology is being transferred. This requires need mapping. The issue is more glaring when technology is transferred from a setting with different factors prevailing than the one in the transferee location. These issues are more glaring from developed to developing countries TT, but as can be seen from China's Kpatawee rice project in Liberia, the issue can also emerge in South-to-South TT. Another dimension which reflects the relevance of this need mapping is support for TT. In the 1990s, several of the solar PV projects in India and Africa failed as they were donor-driven (Kathuria, 2002b), and once donors left, the project also died down. The same can be stated based on the aircraft industry in Indonesia, which mainly was state-supported. Once the external economic environment changed, the government was forced to stop funding through the IMF dictate and several initiatives died down.

The second issue is that once the technology is acquired, it has to be diffused. For diffusion, however, the acquisition is only one necessary condition; the sufficient condition is absorption, which requires capabilities in the form of domestic R&D, domestic research labs, local enabling environment in the form of industries to supply parts and components, besides two-way interaction from university to industry and vice versa. The failed Indonesian example is testimony to the importance of all of these.

Another issue related to diffusion and catch-up is identifying an appropriate technology S-curve (Steenhuis et al., 2007) for a particular industry. The identification is essential if a country has to catch up in that industry. The identification of the S-curve is based on two things: technological characteristics and market characteristics of the industry. The latter is important as it often drives the innovation process, resulting in technological change. In the commercial aircraft industry, the technological characteristics imply the type of engine technology – jet vs. propeller and market characteristics emanate from the different sizes of aircraft based on seats. The size (1-20 seats, 20-50 seats, 50-80 seats, and 80-110 seats) becomes important as each size caters to a different market segment with varying technological change and patterns of innovation (Steenhuis et al., 2007).

The fourth crucial dimension of TT Is that if technology has to serve people, then it has to be not only adapted to local conditions but also be affordable to them. Again, the Indonesian example highlights the relevance of cost. A high leasing cost of an aircraft (regardless of the reasons), whereas better and more reliable are available at the same or lower prices, is a testimony to the role of other factors apart from the only transfer of technology.

The Iranian example demonstrates the role of geographical proximity on the technological catch-up process, which facilitates knowledge flows, spillovers of knowledge and infrastructural benefits.

In conclusion, to remain competitive, a nation should continuously upgrade and innovate. Technology transfer and the related functions in the economy play a crucial role and are a significant source of innovations.

Accounting for the concerns mentioned, besides enhancing collaboration between fundamental research through universities or research labs and industry, can leverage a nation. However, for effective transfer of technology, absorptive capacity, a concept given by Cohen and Levinthal (1990), is required. The concept has two elements: the prior knowledge base and intensity of effort. Thus, for any technology transfer and absorption, prior indigenous capacity-building efforts and the extent of efforts made would be required (Kathuria, 2010).

The technology (for example, blueprints) can be transferred rather easily, but to benefit from this technology or to catch up, capabilities must be developed. If the human capital formation does not match up with the technology transfer, there will be a delay in catch-up (Keller, 1996). The role of technological capabilities, which are a function of the existing knowledge base and the extent of R&D effort, has been well-documented for other countries as well (see for example, Lee and Lim, 2001 for South Korea, Steenhuis *et al.*, 2007 Indonesia, Romania, Brazil and China).

Lastly, the aircraft technology transfer examples demonstrate that transferring or acquiring manufacturing skills does not necessarily translate into design skills (as is exemplified in the case of Indonesia). In contrast, the Brazilian (Embraer) example demonstrates that having design skills can result in manufacturing skills and thus can facilitate catch-up.

Notes

1 Nearly half a century ago, Mansfield (1975) pointed out that "One of the fundamental processes that influence the economic performance of nations and firms is technology transfer. Economists have long recognized that the transfer of technology is at the heart of the process of economic growth, and the progress of both developed and developing countries depends on the extent and efficiency of such transfer. In recent years, economists have also come to realize (or rediscover) the important effects of international technology transfer on the size and pattern of the world trade."

2 Putranto et al. (2003) has documented that it took nearly 20 years for the Indonesian rolling stock industry to catch up.

3 The relevance of the third facet is evident from the fact that most research offices and universities have opened up offices of technology transfer (Siegel et al., 2004).

4 An interesting example of such a technology transfer is supplying turbine-generator by Sumitomo Corporation to Sardar Sarovar Dam, India, as part of its loan/financing (Gelder et al., 2002: p. 87).

5 Data Source: World Bank.

6 It takes a minimum of 1-2 years to design a typical large commercial aircraft, and after that, once the design is frozen, it takes 5-6 years before it is ready for delivery (US International Trade Commission, 1993). The intermediate steps, such as procurement of parts, assembly, engine procurement, prototype, first flight and then certification are key steps that can easily prolong this period, as was amply demonstrated in Indonesia.

7 This and the next sub-section is based on Steenhuis et al. (2007) and Eriksson (2013a).

8 This is similar to India's Phased Manufacturing Programme implemented before 1991 and subsequently from 2015–16 onwards. For details about PMP programme of the government of India for Cellular Handsets and Medical X-ray machines, kindly refer to www.meity.gov.in/content/phased-manufacturing-programme.
9 A high cost is reflected from the fact that a local Indonesian airline declined to lease CN235 for the quoted price ($110,000 per month), stating that for such a high price, the company can lease a Boeing 737 (Steenhuis et al., 2007; Eriksson, 2013a).
10 www.globalsecurity.org/military/world/indonesia/n2130.htm accessed in June 2021.
11 Ibid.

References

Ahmed, S.A., M. Mohsin and S.M.Z. Ali (2021) Survey and technological analysis of laser and its defense applications, *Defence Technology*, 17: 583–592.

Arrow, K.J. (1962) The economic implications of learning by doing, *Review of Economic Studies*, 29: 155–173.

Cohen, W.M. and D.A. Levinthal (1990) Absorptive capacity: A new perspective in learning and innovation, *Administrative Science Quarterly*, 35(1): 128–152.

Connolly, M. (1997) Learning to learn: The role of imitation and trade in technological diffusion, Duke University, Working paper no. 97–25.

Eriksson, S. (2000) Technology spillovers from the aircraft industry: The case of Volvo Aero, *Technovation*, 20: 653–664.

Eriksson, S. (2013a) The aircraft industry as a tool for economic and industrial development – the case of Indonesia, in S. Ericksson (ed.) *Clusters and Economic Growth in Asia*, Cheltenham: Edward Elgar (Chapter 7: 141–164).

Eriksson, S. (2013b) Foreign knowledge transfer in the development of aircraft industry clusters – the case of Chengdu, China, in S. Ericksson (ed.) *Clusters and Economic Growth in Asia*, Cheltenham: Edward Elgar (Chapter 8: 165–181).

Freeman, C. (1982) *The Economics of Industrial Innovation* (2nd ed.), London: Frances Pinter.

Freeman, C. (1988) Technology gaps, international trade and the problems of smaller and less developed economies, in Christopher Freeman and Bengt-Ake Lundvall (eds.) *Small Countries Facing the Technological Revolution*, London: Pinter Publishers (67–84).

Fromhold-Eisebith, M. and G. Eisebith (2002) The Indonesian technology region of Bandung, *International Development Planning Review*, 24(1): 41–57.

Godkin, L. (1988) Problems and practicalities of technology transfer: A survey of the literature, *International Journal of Technology Management*, 3(5): 587–603.

Grant, E.B. and M.J. Gregory (1997) Tacit knowledge, the life cycle and international manufacturing transfer, *Technology Analysis & Strategic Management*, 9(2): 149–162.

Hameri, A-P. (1996) Technology transfer between basic research and industry, *Technovation*, 16(2): 51–57.

Harris, D. and F.J. Harris (2004) Evaluating the transfer of technology between application domains: A critical evaluation of the human component in the system, *Technology in Society*, 26: 551–565.

Hoppe, M. (2005) Technology transfer through trade, European Commission, Brussels. www.feem.it/Feem/Pub/Publications/WPapers/default.htm (accessed in February 2020).
James, J. (2009) From the relative to the absolute digital divide in developing countries, *Technological Forecasting and Social Change*, 76(8): 1124–1129.
Kathuria, V. (2002a) Liberalisation, FDI and productivity spillovers: An analysis of Indian manufacturing firms, *Oxford Economic Papers*, 54: 688–718.
Kathuria, V. (2002b) Technology transfer for GHG reduction: A framework with application to India, *Technological Forecasting and Social Change*, 69: 405–430.
Kathuria, V. (2010) Does the technology gap influence spillovers? – A post-liberalisation analysis of Indian Manufacturing Industries, *Oxford Development Studies*, 38(2): 145–170.
Kathuria, V. and K.Y. Oh (2018) ICTs access – testing for convergence across countries, *The Information Society*, 34(3): 166–182.
Keller, W. (1996) Absorptive capacity: On the creation and acquisition of technology in development, *Journal of Development Economics*, 49: 199–227.
Lee, K. and C. Lim (2001) Technological regimes, catching-up and leapfrogging: Findings from Korean industries, *Research Policy*, 30: 459–483.
Majidpour, M. (2012) Heavy duty gas turbines in Iran, India and China: Do national energy policies drive the industries, *Energy Policy*, 41: 723–732.
Majidpour, M. (2017) International technology transfer and the dynamics of complementarity: A new approach, *Technological Forecasting and Social Change*, 122: 196–206.
Maleci, E.J. (1997) *Technology & Economic Development: The Dynamics of Local, Regional and National Competitiveness* (2nd ed.), London: Longman.
Mansfield, E. (1975) East-West technology transfer issues and problems, international technology transfer: Forms, resource requirements and policies, *American Economic Review*, 65(2): 372–376.
Mansfield, E. (1991) Academic research and industrial innovation, *Research Policy*, 20: 1–12.
Markusen, A. and J. Yudken (1992) Building a new economic order, *Technology Review*, April, pp. 23–30.
Mayer, S. and W. Blass (2002) Technology transfer: An opportunity for small open economies, *Journal of Technology Transfer*, 27(3): 275–289.
Miller, R., M. Hobday, T. Thierry Leroux-Demers and X. Olleros (1995) Innovation in complex systems industries: The case of flight simulation, *Industrial and Corporate Change*, 4(2): 363–400.
Mowery, D.C. and N. Rosenberg (1982) Government policy and innovation in the commercial aircraft industry, 1925–75, in R.R. Nelson (ed.) *Government and Technical Change: A Cross-Industry Analysis*, New York: Pergamon Press.
Mytelka, L.K. (1978) Licensing and technology dependence in the Andean group, *World Development*, 6(4): 447–459.
Pavitt, K. (1991) What makes basic research economically useful?, *Research Policy*, 20: 109–119.
Phillmore, A.J. (1989) University research performance indicators in practice: The University Grants Committee's evaluation of British Universities, *Research Policy*, 18(5): 255–271.

Putranto, K., D. Stewart, G. Moore and R. Diatmoko (2003) Implementing a technology strategy in developing countries: The experience of the Indonesian rolling stock industry, *Technological Forecasting and Social Change*, 70(2): 163–176.

Radosevic, S. (1999) *International technology transfer and catch-up in economic development*, Cheltenham: Edward Elgar.

Siegel, D.S., D.A. Waldman, L.E. Atwater and A.N. Link (2004) Toward a model of the effective transfer of scientific knowledge from academics to practitioners: Quantitative evidence from the commercialization of university technologies, *Journal of Engineering and Technology Management*, 21: 115–142.

Solow, R.M. (1957) Technical change and aggregate production function, *The Review of Economics and Statistics*, 39(3): 312–320.

Solvell, Q., I. Zander and M. Porter (1993) *Advantage Sweden* (2nd ed.), Stockholm: Norstedts Juridik.

Steenhuis, H.-J., E.J. de Bruijn and H. Heerkens (2007) Technology transfer and catch-up: Lessons from the commercial aircraft industry, *International Journal of Technology Transfer and Commercialization*, 6(2/3/4): 250–278.

Stewart, F. (1978) *Technology and Underdevelopment*, London: Palgrave Macmillan.

Sutanto, A. (1996) *Penilaian Dempak Ekonomi PT: IPTN Terhadap Perekonomian Jawa Barat dan Nasional Dengan Menggunakan Metoda Input–Output* (unpublished thesis), Bandung: Department f Regional and City Planning, Institut Teknologi Bandung.

Teece, D.J. (1977) Technology transfer by multinational corporations: The resource cost of transferring technological know-how, *Economic Journal*, 87(346): 242–261.

UNCTAD (1995) *World Investment Report 1995: Transnational Corporations and Competitiveness*, New York: United Nations.

UNCTAD (2014) *Transfer of technology and knowledge sharing for development: Science, technology and innovation issues for developing countries, UNCTAD current studies on Science, Technology and Innovation – No. 8*, New York and Geneva: United Nations.

US International Trade Commission (1993) *Global Competitiveness of US Advanced-Technology Manufacturing Industries: Large Civil Aircraft*, Washington DC: US International Trade Commission.

Van Gelder, J.W., F.V.D. Walk, J.M. Dros and J. Worm (2002) The impacts and financing of large dams (p. 87). http://awsassets.panda.org/downloads/aidenvdamfinancereport.pdf.

Young, A. (1991) Learning-by-doing and the dynamic effects of international trade, *Quarterly Journal of Economics*, 106: 369–405.

Chapter 4

Educational Liberalization, Innovation, and Economic Growth

Leonardo A. Lanzona, Jr.

1. Introduction

Professors Lakhwinder Singh and (his mentor) Robert Evenson (1997) provided evidence of significant international technological spillover effects from developed countries to Asian countries. Lower-income countries can benefit from the innovations that originate from the developed countries, but the benefits can be attained only if these countries simultaneously interact with developed countries through trade and investing in education to generate domestic technological capabilities. This last point is the subject of this chapter.

Innovation is recognized as a necessary factor of industrialization and growth in developing countries but is costly, risky, and path-dependent, and even now ground-breaking innovation is highly concentrated in a few rich countries, linked with specific forms of university science and research capacity, and amongst a small number of firms (Zanello et al., 2015). Therefore, external sources of technology account for a large component of productivity growth in most developing countries. If foreign technologies were easy to diffuse and adopt, a country with meager technological capacity could follow a catch-up strategy to acquire and more rapidly deploy the most advanced technologies (Bell and Pavitt, 1993). Currently, this positive association between innovation and growth is one emerging consensus, ranging from the broad diffusion and impacts of mobile technologies to associated value-adding financial and health services (Aker and Mbiti, 2010).

This consensus is well-grounded in the theory of endogenous growth. As one of this theory's proponents, Romer (1989) highlighted the value of education in the economic growth of developing countries, underlining the importance of scientific skill as the means of introducing innovation. Unlike capital and labor, scientific skills are unbounded, and combined with innovation produce greater additional outputs as these are utilized. In effect, the sustainability of growth is dependent on how new technology may influence not just one sector but various sectors, either directly or indirectly through a series of backward and forward linkages.

DOI: 10.4324/9781003353904-5

For this to be done on a more efficient scale, the economy must then be a large-scale exporter. Only by exploiting scale economies would a country benefit in terms of additional output, greater employment, and lower costs. This will also mean that the firms should not only be content in servicing the local economy. Instead, their market should be the world, and knowledge of the existing technology used abroad is necessary to maximize production possibilities.

Cirera and Maloney (2017) show that optimal investment in innovation does not depend on economic conditions, but on disincentives and non-economic restrictions that prevent countries from having the capacity to take advantage of the current technology, which shows that there is no correlation between optimal innovation investment[1] and percentage of R&D over GDP. As shown in Figure 4.1, South Korea, which has a high percentage of the latter, has a greater divergence than the Philippines from what is considered optimal innovation investment.

In the case of the Philippines, this lack of capacity originates from the restriction of allowing more foreign participation. The Philippine Constitution partly restricts foreigner ownership of educational institutions to 40 percent and prohibits them entirely from teaching, except in exceptional cases. In other Asian countries, however, universities paid more attention to research in recent decades, prompted by government incentives (Hershberg et al., 2007). The higher education sector in these countries could collaborate with the industrial sector to assimilate the transferred foreign technology and make the adaptations necessary for foreign technology to fit within the local technical, economic, and social context. Some alliances between industry and leading research universities were also capable of

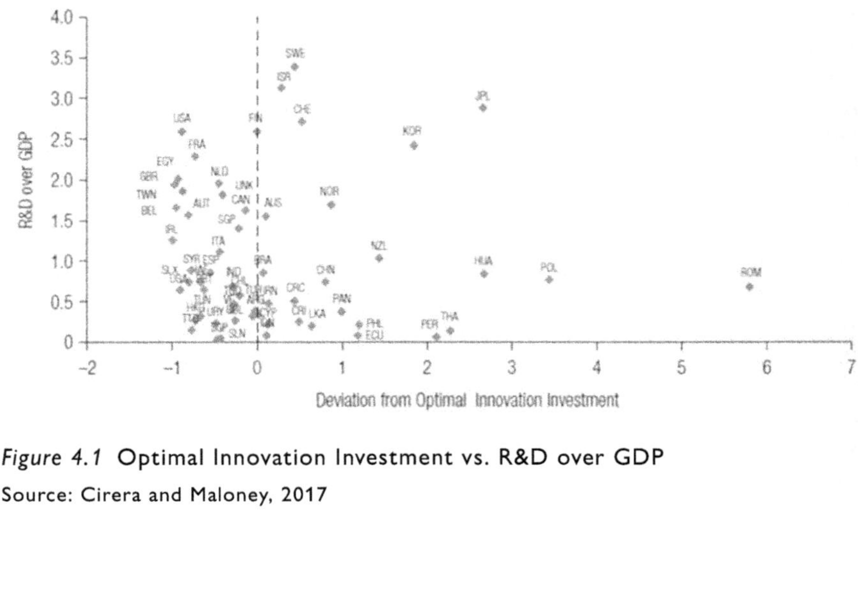

Figure 4.1 Optimal Innovation Investment vs. R&D over GDP

Source: Cirera and Maloney, 2017

leading to deeper assimilation and diffusion of foreign technology through reverse engineering and R&D to make modifications to the transferred foreign technology (Fu and Li, 2016).

By allowing more foreign participation in terms of investment and labor, the country is expected to experience the following. First, greater efficiency in the production of quality education, as less-qualified educators and lower-standard institutions will be weeded out by the competition process. Along with adequate regulation, the lower quality inputs from abroad will presumably not be allowed to enter the sector. Second, given equal access to these schools, graduates from this system will best be able to manage the changes in the labor market, since education quality and innovation can be expected to create greater employment opportunities. Empirical evidence suggests that innovation tends to create rather than destroy jobs (Vivarelli, 1995). In effect, the education sector becomes competitive in the way the chapter has defined it. Third, while supporting R&D investments and promoting emerging and high-tech sectors can be a means of fostering competitiveness, economic growth, and job creation, industrial policies, innovation policies, and education policies need carefully to take into account a series of complex interactions between a process innovation and product innovation, between mature sectors and new sectors, between job creation and job destruction, and between reputable processes and untrustworthy schools or training centers. These complex interrelationships, difficult to predict in advance, highlight the need for continuous monitoring of policy implementation.

This chapter aims to show the impact of foreign participation constraints on the educational and economic outcome using the Differential Diagnosis/Growth Diagnostics framework (Hausmann et al., 2008). Specifically, the goal is to determine if the limitations on foreign participation in the education sector are binding constraints to the development of educational institutions and eventually to the creation of human capital needed for growth. Many internal constraints are affecting the education sector. Addressing all these constraints may distract from eliminating the key restrictions. The chapter aims to assess whether foreign limitations are one of the most important constrictions, such that eliminating this will allow the countries to benefit from technological spillovers as predicted by Evenson and Singh (1997).

To conduct the diagnostics, a cross-country analysis based on the degree of liberalization in the education sector of Vietnam, Indonesia, Thailand, Bolivia, and Guatemala is conducted, comparing planned and ongoing education initiatives and reforms related to foreign participation.

These comparator countries were selected to apply the principles of differential diagnosis by controlling for common characteristics and to benchmark various socio-economic indicators. We analyzed the degree of liberalization by focusing on foreign ownership of educational institutions, labor mobility, and internationalization of higher education. These criteria are aligned with the definition of foreign participation set out at the beginning of the report.

2. Empirical Strategy: Growth Diagnostics

Growth diagnostics is a relatively new approach to reform. Unlike previous models, this is much more contingent on the economic environment. The country, we argue, needs to figure out one or two *most binding constraints* on its education sector and then focus on lifting them. Presented with a list of needed reforms, policy-makers have either tried to fix all of the problems at once or started with reforms that were not crucial to their country's growth potential. And often, reforms have gotten in each other's way, with reform in one area creating unanticipated distortions in another area. Since the 1970s, the Philippine education system has decidedly taken a nationalist position. In the absence of counterfactual evidence, we performed a cross-country analysis using the growth diagnostics approach developed by Hausmann et al. (2006). This approach operates around four tests for identifying binding constraints. Specifically, these tests indicate that a constraint is potentially binding if:

1 The shadow price of the constraint is high, resulting in greater access and lower relative cost of quality education.
2 Easing the constraint produces results in significant movements in the objectives, leading to improved quality of education or other benefits, particularly employment and on-the-job training.
3 Agents in the economy are attempting to overcome or bypass the constraint, highlighting more general and service-oriented education instead of emphasizing specialized skills which tend to be more expensive.
4 Agents less affected by the constraint are more likely to survive and thrive, and vice versa, causing certain schools or individuals to flourish in this restricted environment at the expense of other, more qualified institutions and persons.

Initially modeled strictly as an approach to identify and prioritize factors that are most binding to a country's growth, the growth diagnostics approach has evolved to become a more flexible framework that can be customized based on need. For instance, it may incorporate differential diagnosis to concretely link the tests to specific factors and objectives, such as foreign participation and education quality, rather than private investment or economic growth.

The first two tests are to be conducted using cross-country comparisons, while the last two tests are implications on specific effects in the local institutions. All these tests indicate key features of the countries involved and are presumed to have economic consequences.

To apply the principles of differential diagnosis, the Philippines can be benchmarked against other comparable countries or "comparators." Comparator countries play a central role in applying the principles of differential diagnosis by controlling for common characteristics (e.g., geography, demography, colonial history) among country peers as well as in benchmarking the progress on various socio-economic indicators.

Using World Bank statistics, several indicators to ensure consistency were selected based on their perceived importance in describing the Philippine economy from economic, demographic, and geographic perspectives. Based on these criteria, the following comparator countries were selected – Bolivia, Guatemala, Indonesia, and Vietnam – as illustrated in Table 4.1. Thailand was also included as an "aspirational" country in terms of development level. The final list of comparator countries and regional and income group averages will be used consistently throughout the analysis.

The main assumption of the Growth Diagnostic Tests is if the economic variables in comparator countries are comparable, then the differences in education outcomes and economic conditions associated with education can be traced to differences in education policies. This association cannot be made if we compare these countries with Singapore, Malaysia, or other groups of countries, since the differences in economic conditions can also explain the differences in educational outcomes.

Using the findings of a previous study (PriceWaterhouseCoopers, 2019), the degree of liberalization in the education sector of the comparator countries is seen to be quite diverse. Unlike the Philippines, Vietnam, Indonesia, and Thailand have aggressively pursued a policy of educational liberalism, especially at the basic level and the technical schools. Foreign ownership in these countries has been encouraged, and the teaching requirements for foreigners have been much simplified compared to the stringent requirements found in the Philippines. More importantly, education has been structured in a way that will make it relevant to the country's drive to learn the English language as the means to have access to improved technology for greater industrialization.

There is limited data on the condition of foreign ownership of educational institutions, teacher mobility, and internationalization of higher education in Bolivia and Guatemala. Based on research on the constitution of these countries, there is no foreign restriction specifically for the establishment of educational institutions. There have been numerous efforts for decades in the region to establish cooperative links between the institutions of different countries. However, they have not produced significant results in the integration of the higher education systems of Latin American countries. In this regard, Uribe (2007) wrote:

> It is surprising that in spite of repeated policy declarations of the countries of the region, the growing importance of the different inter-university

Table 4.1 Selected economic and demographic criteria, Philippines and comparator countries

Country	*GDP Per Capita, PPP (Constant 2011 International $)*	*Personal Remittances, Received (% Of GDP)*	*Employment In Agriculture (% Of Total Employment)*	*Population Ages 0–14 (% Of Total)*	*Informal Employment (% Of Total Non-Agricultural Employment)*	*Manufacturing, Value Added (% Of GDP)*	*Poverty Headcount Ratio At $3.10 A Day (2011 PPP, % Of Population)*	*Rural Population (% Of Total Population)*
Philippines	5778	11	33	34	70	21	11	55
Bolivia	5602	5	28	34	73	14	9	33
Guatemala	6853	11	34	39	68	19	10	50
Indonesia	8693	1	38	29	73	24	15	50
Thailand	13633	1	40	19	33	29	0	55
Vietnam	4621	7	46	24	68	15	9	69
Singapore	72862	N.A.	1	17	N.A.	20	N.A.	0
Malaysia	21798	0.5	14	28	N.A.	24	0	29
Lower middle-income countries	5095	5	45	32	N.A.	17	52	63
East Asia Pacific region countries, excluding high-income	9283	1	36	21	N.A.	30	N.A.	52

Source: World Bank

networks, the trans-continental initiatives of cooperation in education, and combined actions of regional inter-governmental organizations, no potent force of cohesion has appeared that lends vigor to the renewed Latin American interest in achieving an integration that transcends the exclusionary inequitable dynamics of the threatening mercantilization of Higher Education and of at times paternalistic policies and actions coming from European academic cooperation.

It can thus be assumed that Latin American countries, although open to foreign investment in the education sector, are not as aggressive as the Asian countries in developing and implementing complementary programs to make the sector more accessible to foreign players.

Across the comparator countries, the impact analyzed does not only pertain to foreign participation, but also to the initiatives to modernize the

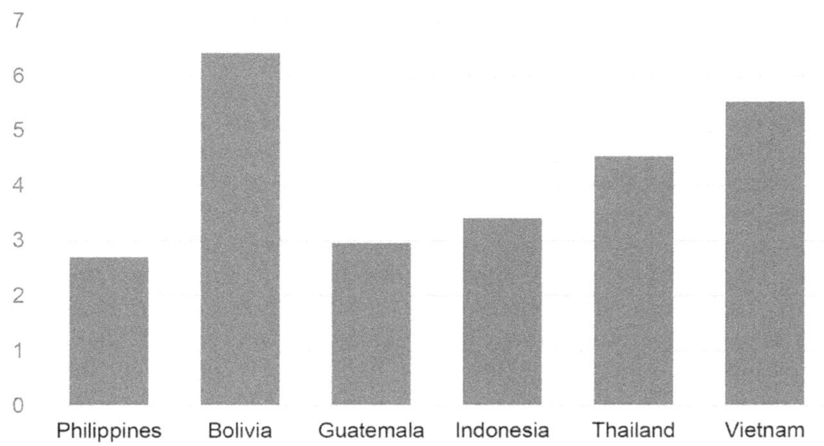

Figure 4.2 Percentage of Government Education Expenditures to GDP

Note: The reference year here is 2012.

Source: World Bank Data

sector. ***Increasing foreign participation, in other words, is difficult to isolate from the rest of the other education reforms and is merely one part of the modernization program of these countries.***

One way of examining the interaction of education reforms and foreign limitations is to look at the percentage of government education expenditures to GDP (see Figure 4.2). Note that the Philippines has the lowest percentage, and Bolivia has the highest percentage. One may assume that because of the larger proportion of education expenses, Bolivia[2] should have a better quality of education than the Philippines and the rest of the other counties given the premium that this country places on education.

However, unlike the other countries, Bolivia has the least exposure to internationalization. Clausen (2012) notes that the country has adopted the theory of dependency that argues that nation-states can and should craft an internally directed development policy by implementing import substitution policies. In short, the premise of this development strategy is to lessen the number of imports, favor an economic policy that nationalizes essential industries, and heighten the national economic production primarily for local consumption.

In the case of education, what this theory implied was the lack of efficiency in the sector. Following the 2005 presidential election, legislative initiatives targeted reforms to the existing 1994 Education Law and advocated a new "indigenous" model of education. In the end, reforms were to become piecemeal and the debate about a new education law continued throughout the remainder of the decade (with a new education law passed in 2010).

The original reforms included the language of colonization, anti-neoliberalism, imperialism, and indigeneity. The dependency-inspired leaders viewed social systems in the developing world as being under the sway of elites in developed nations, international institutions, and in the international education development field. This influence is seen as a form of cultural manipulation that creates a culture of education policy, teaching, and learning based on alienation, decolonizing, or anti-globalization.

This cross-country discussion on education policies indicates two main points. First, while the Philippines is more open to foreign participation than its Latin American counterparts, the other Asian countries seem to be more aggressive in reducing the foreign limitations. Second, these other Asian countries, except the Philippines, had a more aggressive education program as seen by the percentage of government education expenditures to GDP. The Latin American comparators also seem more aggressive than the Philippines in this sense, but as already noted these countries are less open to foreign influence.

Table 4.2 is based on the World Economic Forum Surveys and will serve as our starting point in comparing the quality of education and analyzing the impact of foreign participation in these countries. Except for enrollment rates, the values in the table are on a 1-to-7 scale with 7 as the highest possible value. These numbers are based on a "perception" survey of businessmen who are members of the World Economic Forum (WEF).

Four points are noteworthy from the table. First, figures on the South East Asian countries are not diversified and are starting at relatively the same level. It can be assumed from these figures that these countries are facing the same quality problems and at the same time, pushing for changes to catch up with the quality of the education system of more developed countries such as Singapore and Malaysia, which scored 5.8 and 5.2, respectively, placing 2nd and 14th out of 137 countries based on the 2017–2018 WEF Global Competitiveness Report.

Second, it is important to put these numbers in their proper perspective. The Philippines was the first among these Asian countries to establish an education system modeled after the West. With its colonial history, the first Asian universities were established there, even earlier than in the USA. However, because of years of neglect and the isolationist policy on education, data show that other countries have caught up to if not overtaken the Philippines.

Third, Latin American countries seem to be falling behind in terms of the quality of the education system and are not able to adapt to all the changes in the international market. External factors such as the attractiveness of the domestic markets to foreign investment may also impact this. As compared with Vietnam, Indonesia, and Thailand, although Latin American countries

Table 4.2 Selected education indicators based on the World Economic Forum Surveys

Country	*Quality of primary education*	*Higher education*					*Enrollment rates (gross %)*		
		Quality of the educational system	*Quality of manage-ment schools*	*Quality of math and science education*	*Local availability of specialized training services*	*Extent of staff training*	*Primary*	*Secondary*	*Tertiary*
Philippines	4.1	4.2	4.8	3.9	4.8	4.4	96.0	88.4	35.8
Bolivia	2.8	2.8	3.5	3.0	3.6	3.1	94.1	84.7	38.4
Guatemala	2.6	2.6	4.5	2.6	5.0	4.3	85.5	65.6	21.8
Vietnam	3.4	3.6	3.3	3.7	3.8	3.9	98.0	92.5	28.8
Indonesia	4.5	4.4	4.6	4.6	4.7	4.6	89.7	85.8	24.3
Thailand	3.5	3.7	4.1	3.8	4.1	4.2	90.8	129.0	48.9
Singapore	6.2	5.8	6.0	6.5	6.0	5.4	100	108.1	92.2
Malaysia	5.1	5.2	5.3	5.3	5.6	5.3	98.1	77.6	26.1

Note: The figures for Bolivia are based on the 2016–2017 report

Source: 2016–2017 and 2017–2018 World Competitiveness Reports, World Economic Forum

have some niche demands on language study, South East Asian countries are more attractive to foreign investors because of the economic growth, language and talent skills, and growth potential.

Finally, Thailand appears to have the most accessible education system, given its high enrollment rates at each level. The low tertiary enrollment rates of Indonesia and Vietnam indicate perhaps the need for more structural reforms that will make the level more accessible. The Philippines and Bolivia seem to be at the same level in terms of accessibility, but the quality of the former is observed to be higher.

It can be noted from this table that the Philippines seem to be ranked better than the other Asian comparator countries that had taken a more liberalized position. While this may be the case, this finding does not undermine the narrative concerning the importance of foreign participation. This simply strengthens our assertion that education reforms combined with liberalization, and the associated institutional changes, are simultaneously affecting the quality of education. The WEF rankings all seem to reflect these components together. Since these are all based on perceptions, their rankings were not computed based on actual tests or available data. These cannot distinguish the liberalization from institutional structures, including the regulatory ability.

The point is that these rankings do not reflect only the degree of liberalization. In effect, the impact of foreign participation cannot be isolated from these rankings. A more sophisticated system of rankings is the Global Innovation Index (GII) developed by Cornell University, the INSEAD Business School, and the World Intellectual Property Organization (WIPO). Consisting of several components, the index aims to find metrics and approaches that better capture the depth of innovation in society, going beyond such traditional measures of innovation as the number of research articles and the level of research and development (R&D) expenditure. One of the variables used is called market sophistication, which measures the availability of credit and the environment that supports investment, access to the international market, competition, and market scale. These components capture the market conditions for trade by measuring the average tariff rate weighted by import shares and the intensity of competition in local markets. To a large extent, this measures the degree of liberalization that the economy has allowed.

Table 4.3 shows the GII rankings for the selected countries in this study, as well as a few of the components used in deriving such comparisons. These include institutions that measure the political conditions found in the country, including their adherence to the rule of law, human capital, and research, which defines the degree of investment that the country makes in innovation, and knowledge and technology, which considers the country's exposure to the knowledge economy and social media. These, along with market sophistication, infrastructure, and creativity, determine the country's level of innovation.

Table 4.3 2018 Global Innovation Index Rankings with key components, selected countries

Country	*Global Innovation Index*	*Institutions*	*Human Capital and Research*				*Market Sophistication*	*Knowledge and Technology*
			Total	*Basic Education*	*Tertiary*	*Research*		
Philippines	73	93	86	105	54	68	100	49
Bolivia	117	125	82	56	N.A.	102	75	103
Guatemala	102	115	122	116	114	114	105	82
Indonesia	85	97	94	101	91	60	59	86
Thailand	44	65	57	92	55	39	28	40
Vietnam	45	78	66	18	84	81	33	35
Singapore	5	1	1	42	1	10	4	11
Malaysia	35	43	31	75	15	30	22	33

Source: Global Innovation Index 2018

The following points are important. First, the rankings in terms of market sophistication also match the rankings that have been made for education liberalization levels. As in the case of the Philippines, a country's policy on trade can be reflected in its education sector. The economic protectionism that is adopted by the Philippines and the South American countries seems to have influenced their nationalist position in education, while the openness policy of the other Asian countries is reflected in the education policy as well.

Second, Vietnam, Bolivia, and to some extent Indonesia seem to have placed more emphasis on Basic Education instead of Tertiary Education and Research in building up their human capital. For these countries, greater returns in basic education are evident as language forms a fundamental source of transaction costs. Poor command of English is viewed as a constraint to growth. Hence, for these countries, innovation is hinged on developing directly its Basic Education. In the case of Indonesia and Vietnam, foreign participation has targeted Basic Education. In contrast, the Philippines, given its command of English, indirectly raised its innovation ratings by improving its tertiary sector. To a large extent, its innovation is fundamentally linked to its Tertiary Education, as in the cases of Singapore and Malaysia.

Third, as exemplified by the case of Indonesia, greater openness to the global market does not automatically result in innovation. One needs to complement this with institutional reforms and human capital investments, along with improvements in the knowledge economy. In the case of the Philippines, the failure to liberalize creates a barrier to innovation.

Fourth, except for Bolivia and Indonesia, the value of market sophistication directly corresponds to the rankings of the countries in terms of overall global innovation. The former ranks second to last in market sophistication but is the last in the innovation index, while the latter ranks fifth in market sophistication but ranks third to last in overall innovation. This situation is caused by their poor political institutions and their limited exposure to the knowledge. Because of this, the Philippines have been ranked higher in innovation despite its poorer rankings in market sophistication.

The data presented here seems to indicate the impact of the interaction of the overall education reform and foreign participation. In the following section, we conduct several tests to determine if limitations in foreign participation are significant and binding. This does not mean that the other constraints are not binding as well. While foreign participation may not be sufficient for further growth, we intend to show that allowing greater liberalization is necessary for the country and can affect the other constraints as well.

3. Results of the Diagnostic Tests

The results of the Growth Diagnostic Tests are presented here. With the use of secondary data, the various hypotheses suggested by the methodology are examined.

3.1. Shadow Price

While it is challenging to identify and measure shadow prices as these are not observed directly, the growth diagnostics framework states that shadow prices are "often signaled by actual or implied market prices, or other symptoms of unmet demand" (Hausmann et al., 2008). Following this suggestion, the shadow price for this study is expressed as the cost of producing quality education, thus leading to lower completion rates and greater training costs. A high shadow price measured by high completion rates would indicate that supply or presence is scarce of foreign participation relative to demand.

High costs of producing quality education may be reflected in terms of negative impact completion rates as households are left to shoulder these costs, especially in countries where there is limited financial aid available. Likewise, private firms may not be willing to spend resources to train workers with unfinished or low-quality education. Completion rates thereby can serve as a proxy variable for the shadow price of quality. If completion rates are low, then the costs of quality education are high, and vice versa. In this study, completion rates of basic and higher education students, therefore, may be lower in countries with stricter regulations on foreign investment, which may contribute to improving access to quality education and decreasing its costs.

Figure 4.3 shows the completion rates for lower secondary and primary levels for the six comparators in the study. The data indicate that Guatemala, which has the lowest amount of resources devoted to education and is the least liberalized of these countries, also exhibits the lowest completion rates. Another important point is that if resources can be made available,

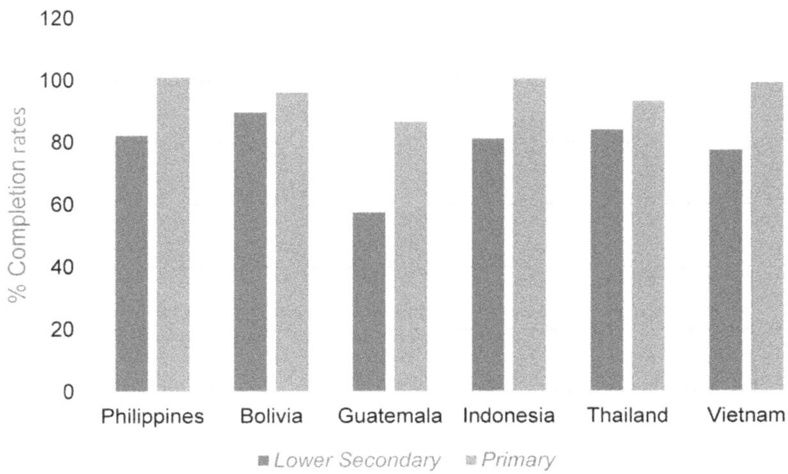

Figure 4.3 Completion Rates for Lower Secondary and Primary Levels

Note: The reference year for all countries is 2013, except for Thailand, which is set in 2015.

Source: World Bank Data

foreign participation is not necessary to decrease the cost of education, as shown in the cases of the Philippines and Bolivia. Guatemala, which has limited foreign exposure and relatively lower education resources, would seem to have the lowest completion rate.

Figure 4.4 features the tertiary enrollment rates for the comparator countries. Note that Thailand, which devoted fewer resources for education than Bolivia, recorded a higher enrollment rate than the latter. The difference can perhaps be attributed to the more liberalized structure of its system. Other Asian countries, like Vietnam and Indonesia, did register substantially low rates as the majority of their resources may have been devoted to secondary and primary education. The strong government support that the Philippines and Bolivia have committed traditionally to their tertiary education explains why tertiary enrollment rates are higher in these countries.

Recent studies that assessed tertiary education costs in Vietnam relative to the average monthly income of households highlighted the rapid increase in education fees. The World Bank (2014) reported that students from less wealthy backgrounds often drop out because they are unable to finance the tuition and non-tuition as well as opportunity costs associated with education and training. A survey conducted in 2013 further stressed the level of costs imposed by private colleges and questioned whether this translates to better education quality. Annual tuition ranged from US$ 473 to 3,500,

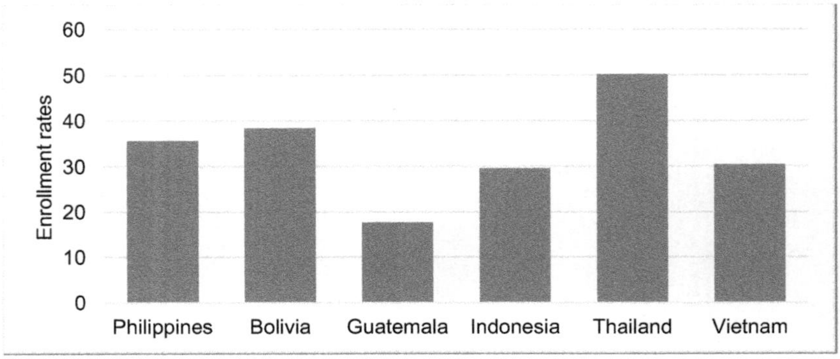

Figure 4.4 Enrollment Rates in Tertiary Education

Note: The reference year here is 2007, except for the Philippines, which is 2008.

Source: World Bank Data

which was at that time 15 times higher than the average fees that public schools charge.

However, higher fees do not necessarily ensure higher-quality education, as public colleges are still believed to outperform private ones. The current university ranking for Vietnam seems to be consistent with this observation, as 9 of the top 10 universities in the country are public institutions (UniRank, 2018). Nonetheless, the growth of private institutions, including those that are 100 percent foreign-owned, helped address the unmet demand for tertiary education. Despite the estimated 125 percent increase in the number of enrollees from 2010 to 2020, as of 2009, only 6.7 percent of people above 25 held tertiary degree attainment, a percentage that is one of the lowest in the region.

Given these statistics and trends, the hypothesis that quality implies higher costs does not hold as private institutions, generally private schools, do not have a good reputation in Vietnam. Since public universities remain the top performers in the sector, the cost of producing quality education would remain low with or without foreign participation unless public confidence in non-public institutions increases. Nevertheless, with the massive demand for higher education, as seen in Thailand, the presence of foreign universities can help expand access, especially with the government's move towards privatization of education. The impact of reducing foreign limitations is thus higher in tertiary education. In Vietnam, for instance, greater liberalization aims to increase the number of students in private institutions from 10% to 40% of all students enrolled.

Higher completion rates in basic education and thus lower costs of education can be achieved if government resources are used to maintain students

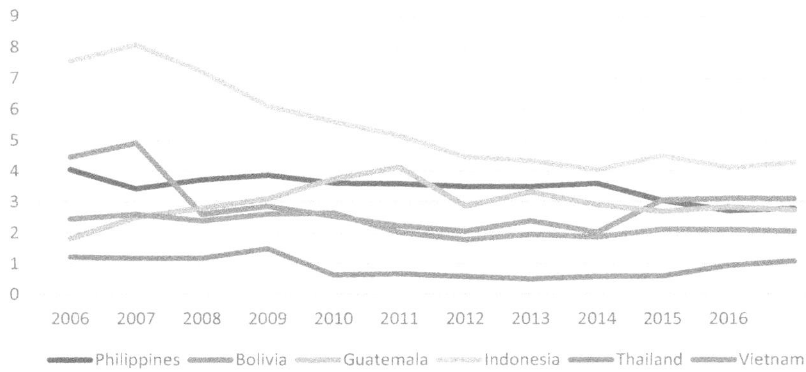

Figure 4.5 Unemployment Rates for Comparator Countries

Source: World Bank Data

in school. However, Thailand, which offers incentives to higher-level foreign institutions and possesses a more developed education structure, has a higher completion rate in tertiary education. Greater access to tertiary education can mean greater worker adaptability and assimilation to new technologies, thus leading to greater employment rates. Figure 4.5 features the unemployment rates in the comparator countries. Note that the lowest unemployment rates are found in Thailand.

In effect, Thai workers were able to obtain greater access to markets by having more access to higher-level education. Given new technologies, a modern strategy of developed countries is based on the concept of human capital (Asian Development Bank, 2012) and the knowledge economy: the competitiveness of the country today is determined not only by the presence of rich natural resources, but primarily by the human factor, by the ability to create and develop high technologies, to provide a new technological level of production, to adapt to the rapidly changing information environment, to be competitive in the labor market and, as a result, to have higher incomes.

3.2. Impulse-Repulse

Figure 4.6 shows the out-of-school rate for children of primary school age. It is expected that if the quality of schooling is poor and if households do not perceive the relevance of education, the probability of the children being out of school is greater (UNESCO, 2018). The figure indicates that those countries with limited foreign participation are also those that exhibit

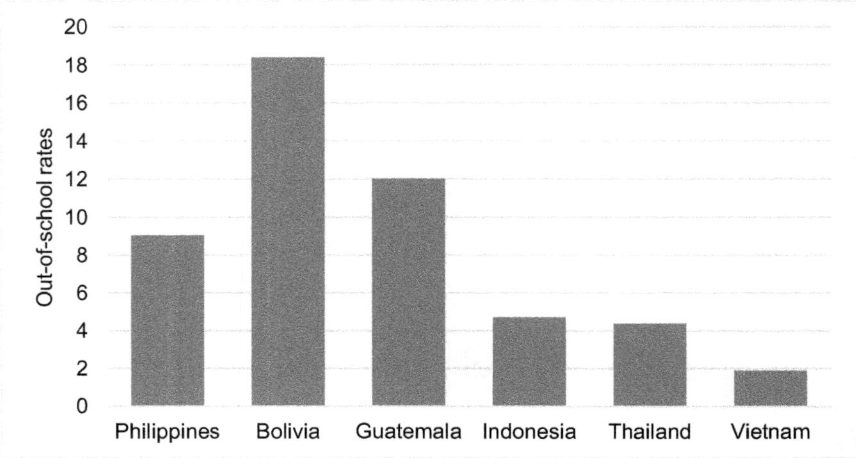

Figure 4.6 Out-of-school Rates for Children of Primary School Age

Note: The reference year is 2013, except for Thailand (2009) and Indonesia (2012).

Source: UNESCO data

higher rates of out-of-school primary school-age children. It needs to be noted that Bolivia and the Philippines are also countries that have higher completion rates and significant resources devoted to education. The main issue is fundamental: whether the education system introduces concepts that are innovative and practical to the households. Such qualities are factors that can keep children in school.

This seeming irrelevance in education in the Philippines can be fundamentally traced to other factors, especially the poor quality of teachers at the primary level. Figure 4.7 features the results of tests of the Public Education Expenditure Tracking and Quantitative Service Delivery Study (PETS-QSDS), which indicate that knowledge of subject matter among elementary and high school teachers is low in most subjects. Except for English at the elementary level, the average elementary or high school teacher could answer fewer than half of the questions on the subject content tests correctly. Since these tests are closely aligned with the curriculum, the results suggest that teachers face significant challenges in teaching a considerable portion of the current curriculum.

This lack of qualified teachers in turn can be traced to a lackluster tertiary education. Teachers in basic education are, after all, crucial in embedding the foundational skills in students. If basic education does not challenge its students and cannot meet the necessary standards in higher education, tertiary education will only produce mediocre teachers. A high-quality tertiary

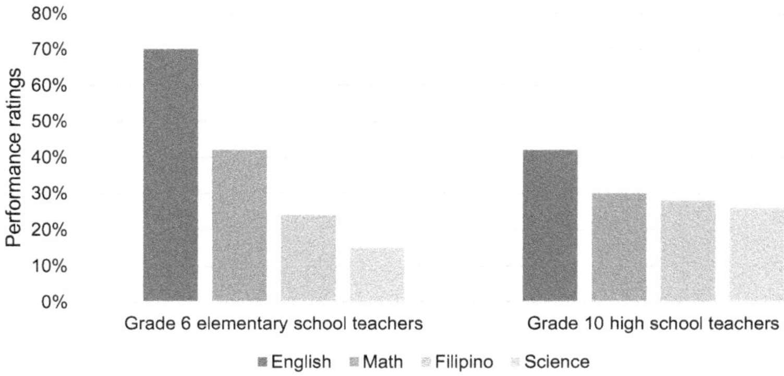

Figure 4.7 Basic Education Teachers' Performance in Content Knowledge Assessment

Source: World Bank Group (2016), Assessing Basic Education Service Delivery in the Philippines

level is fundamentally one that creates new knowledge. For this, two inputs are necessary: a significant number of investments in research and development (R&D) and the number of students going to other countries to learn better technologies.

Figure 4.8 features the total value of R&D investments of major ASEAN countries. Singapore and Malaysia are the leaders of innovation which in turn have incurred positive gains to their economies. Thailand and Indonesia come next, with the Philippines occupying a lower position. As a result, the education provided to the children in the country may not be innovative and relevant to the changing environment they work in. Note that the top four countries are also those countries that have expressed greater openness in allowing foreign participation in their education systems.

Within the South East Asian region, universities in Singapore and Malaysia dominate the Asia University Rankings in 2018, with four HEIs in these countries included in the top 100 (Times Higher Education, 2018). Universities in the less developed countries of Vietnam, Indonesia, and Thailand rank lower, as problems on the quality and institutional capability persist.

As we have noted, these countries have only recently liberalized their education reforms, a policy which they considered as one solution to the internal issues they face. Specifically, in Vietnam, the primary goal of internationalization is to expand English-language education in the country (World Education News + Review, 2017). Foreign universities are also expected to absorb the excess supply of students and decentralize the sector from public institutions.

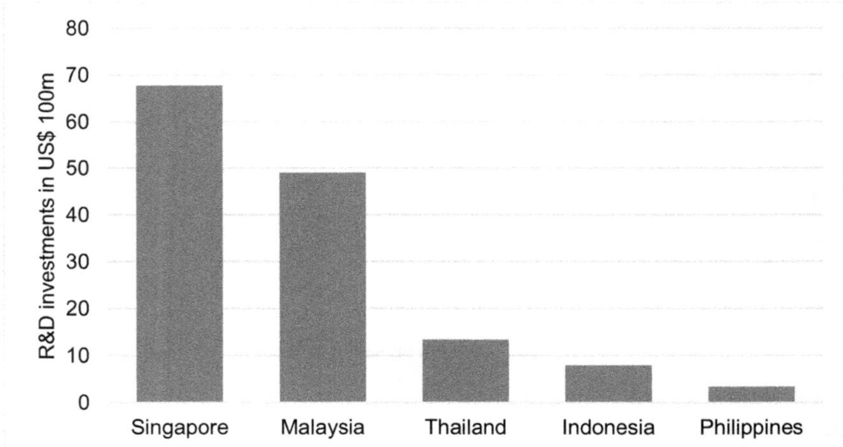

Figure 4.8 R&D Investments (in US$100m, PPP parity conversion)

Note: The reference year is 2009 for Thailand and Indonesia, 2012 for Singapore, 2011 for Malaysia, and 2007 for the Philippines.

Source: UNESCO Institute for Statistics

Part of the reason why R&D is low in the Philippines is the lack of researchers who are qualified to conduct valid R&D initiatives and projects. For the second input, the training of new researchers on new technologies will have to be conducted abroad if these are not available in the country.

Table 4.4 shows the number of students abroad for the Asian countries that are comparators in our study. Several points are important. First, the Philippines lags significantly behind these countries. The limited amount of quality research in turn contributes to the failure of the education to deliver what households may be expecting from their children's education. Vietnam, which we ranked highest in terms of liberalization, is also the country with the greatest number of students abroad, indicating the country's drive to innovate and maximize the available technology. Third, the issue of proximity and language seems important, as more students from Thailand, Indonesia, and Vietnam have chosen China as the country of destination. Allowing more foreign institutions and teachers in the country will be a more practical way of learning new ideas.

In the end, these students or researchers should end up as teachers. Except for the Philippines, where studying abroad is donor-driven, these countries have allocated a portion of their government budget for international scholarships. Thailand, for instance, recognizes that stronger foreign

Table 4.4 No. of students abroad in top 5 destination areas, 2012

Origin	*5 Top Destination and Number of Students Abroad*					*Total*
	1	*2*	*3*	*4*	*5*	
Thailand	China 16,675	US 7,386	UK 6,098	Australia 3,282	Japan 2,476	35,917
Indonesia	China 13,144	Australia 9,431	US 6,907	Malaysia 6,222	Japan 2,213	37,917
Vietnam	China 13,038	US 15,083	Australia 11,081	France 5,642	Japan 4,047	48,891
Philippines	US 3,094	Australia 2,374	UK 1,306	Japan 632	NZ 429	7,835

Source: UNESCO (2012)

participation is likely to improve the quality of Thai researchers, teachers, administrators, and students such that they can compete with the new players (The PIE News, 2017). This point of view is closely related to Thailand's aspiration to be the center of international education in South East Asia. The drastic increase in international schools and students in the country over the past two decades was brought about by an "enhanced awareness of the academic and career benefits graduation from an institution offering a curriculum that adheres to global KPIs and is taught in English can deliver" (Maxwell, 2015).

Educators and researchers, however, emphasize that the weak state of higher education in Vietnam, Indonesia, and Thailand cannot be completely addressed by increased foreign participation. The high cost of foreign education, whether through a branch campus or a joint venture with a local university, is a key factor that may discourage the majority from entering these universities. Only privileged individuals can take advantage of foreign program offerings unless huge amounts of scholarship packages are offered, collaborations between foreign and local academic workers are frequent, and learning from these collaborations is sustained and applied in local universities. Indeed, foreign participation should be accompanied by substantial reform and accessibility.

In any case, despite these issues of access, studies have indicated that the ASEAN countries have been able to attract more foreign direct investments because of their efforts to form human capital. In Thailand, for instance, the ability of the industry to identify, assimilate, transform, and apply valuable external knowledge, or its absorptive capacity, drew more direct foreign investments since this reduced their training costs (Tanna and Topaiboul, 2005). Figure 4.9 shows the FDI Inward Stock for the comparator countries. Note that except for the Philippines, FDI stock is higher in the Asian countries.

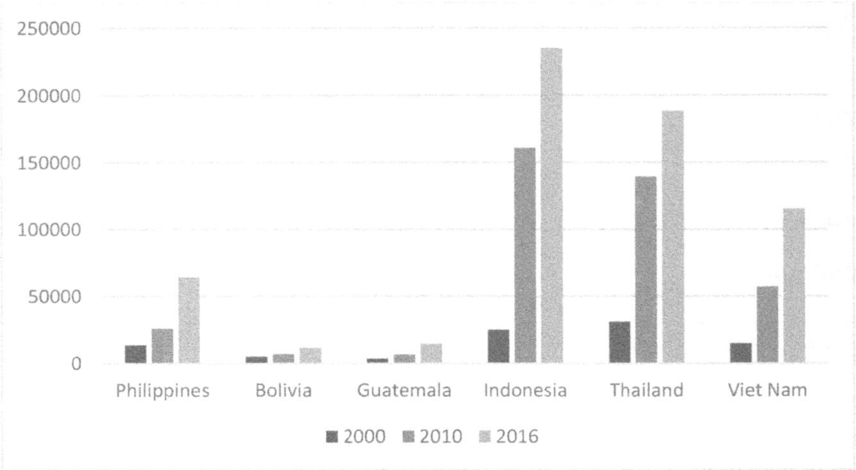

Figure 4.9 FDI Inward Stock for Comparator Countries (in US$100m)

Source: UNCTAD, World Investment Report 2017

3.3. Circumvention

Having noted that the poorer quality of education in the Philippines can be associated with its foreign restrictions, we now consider how this constraint may lead educational institutions and other industry actors to bypass or overcome the constraint. Because of limited funding, tertiary schools would, since the latter would entail higher costs. Basic or general education is less likely to produce employable graduates.

Limitations on foreign participation are assumed to limit opportunities in developing science, technology, engineering, and mathematics (STEM) disciplines in a country. Education in these fields of study is generally more expensive to fund due to specialized resources – faculty, equipment, and facilities – needed. Tuition fees in the business, education, vocational, liberal arts, and social sciences undergraduate and graduate programs are considerably lower on average. As developing economies implement reforms to advance STEM fields, funding for public and private schools to develop and maintain quality programs remains a constraint. Higher tuition fees charged by private institutions, in particular, may discourage students from pursuing STEM degrees.

Figure 4.10 presents the proportion of graduates in priority disciplines relative to the total graduates in a given year. Based on consultations with business groups, such as the Philippine Business for Education (PBED), the CHED has identified a set of disciplines that are in demand by the industry and service sectors. The government has then provided a set of incentives to

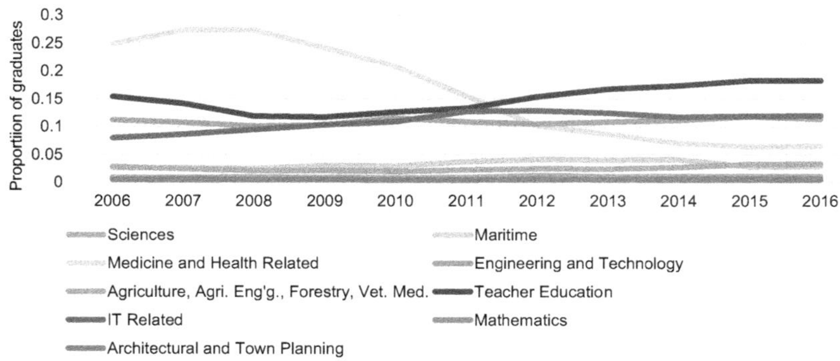

Figure 4.10 Proportion of Graduates in Selected Priority Disciplines

Source: Philippine Commission on Higher Education (CHED) Statistics

ensure that the share of graduates in these disciplines should increase over time. However, despite the high demand for these disciplines, the existing universities are not able to supply the needed graduates to fill these skills gaps. Most of the graduates are in areas that are not demanded in the market.

Note that these disciplines are primarily technical. Mathematics and the natural sciences degrees were less than 0.2 percent of the total HEI students. To begin with, only a handful of HEIs offer these fields, and more math and natural science graduates are produced by SUCs than by private HEIs.

Comparator countries in this study scored among the lowest in the region in WEF's 2017 ranking of the quality of math and science education. Indonesia, though ranked higher than Vietnam and Thailand, was a far third behind Singapore and Malaysia. The presence of foreign universities in the comparator countries is recognized to improve competence in STEM fields and to drive research capabilities.

In Vietnam, however, the presence of private institutions is more demand-driven, as these are encouraged to absorb excess demand of students regardless of the academic discipline. In recent years, the majority of students enrolled in business studies, education, information technology, and foreign languages, and almost none enrolled in hard sciences (SMEC, 2010). Except for education, the study of which is fully funded by the government, non-public institutions concentrate on the other areas that exceed the capacity of public institutions.

Similar trends are observed in Indonesia wherein social sciences and business remain popular fields among students. Though there are still no foreign-owned universities in Indonesia, the government has identified science, technology, engineering, mathematics, business, and management as priority subject areas for interested players. These areas, except for business and management, are not that developed in the country, as more specialized institutions are built around those with high demand, such as banking, finance and accountancy, and tourism.

In contrast with Vietnam and Indonesia, Thailand has distinct requirements for foreign universities that want to set a branch campus in the country. Recognizing the low scores of Thai students in math and science and the low science and technology budget, the government aims to attract top-tier foreign universities to bridge the gap and to produce highly-skilled employees. This initiative is in line with the country's goal to become the international education hub in the region and to progress into an innovation-driven economy.

Because of the failure to develop the priority disciplines, more students entered service-oriented positions as schooling became more accessible. Because of limited workers, the country has not been able to fully develop its manufacturing sector. With this, employment shares have been skewed toward services (see Table 4.5). While most of the workers are in the service sector, these are mostly in retail or entrepreneurial work.

This trend toward more employment in the services sector can be seen in the comparator countries. Figure 4.11 shows that the countries which have limited foreign participation have a significant proportion of their workers in the service sector relative to the Asian countries which are more open to foreign exposure.

One may argue that these trends are simply responses to market conditions. However, circumvention has been most apparent in the Philippines in maintaining its supply of nurses. The sudden increase in the number of graduates in nursing was a market response to the demand in the said profession; however, when the demand declined, the country's education system continued to produce nurses – therefore inducing a surplus.

However, when the manufacturing sector was experiencing a "revival," the education system was not able to sustain the demand for workers in

Table 4.5 Sectoral employment shares

ALL INDUSTRIES	*2006*	*2007*	*2008*	*2009*	*2010*	*2011*	*2012*	*2013*	*2014*	*2015*	*2016*
	1.00	*1.00*	*1.00*	*1.00*	*1.00*	*1.00*	*1.00*	*1.00*	*1.00*	*1.00*	*1.00*
AGRICULTURE	**0.34**	**0.35**	**0.36**	**0.35**	**0.33**	**0.33**	**0.33**	**0.31**	**0.31**	**0.29**	**0.26**
INDUSTRY	**0.16**	**0.16**	**0.15**	**0.15**	**0.15**	**0.15**	**0.16**	**0.16**	**0.16**	**0.17**	**0.18**
Mining and Quarrying	0.01	0.01	0.00	0.00	0.01	0.01	0.01	0.01	0.01	0.01	0.01
Manufacturing	0.10	0.09	0.09	0.08	0.09	0.08	0.08	0.08	0.09	0.08	0.09
Electricity, Gas and Water Supply	0.00	0.00	0.00	0.00	0.00	0.00	0.00	0.00	0.00	0.00	0.00
Construction	0.05	0.06	0.05	0.06	0.06	0.06	0.06	0.07	0.07	0.07	0.09
SERVICES	**0.49**	**0.49**	**0.50**	**0.50**	**0.52**	**0.52**	**0.51**	**0.53**	**0.53**	**0.54**	**0.56**

Source: Philippine Statistics Authority

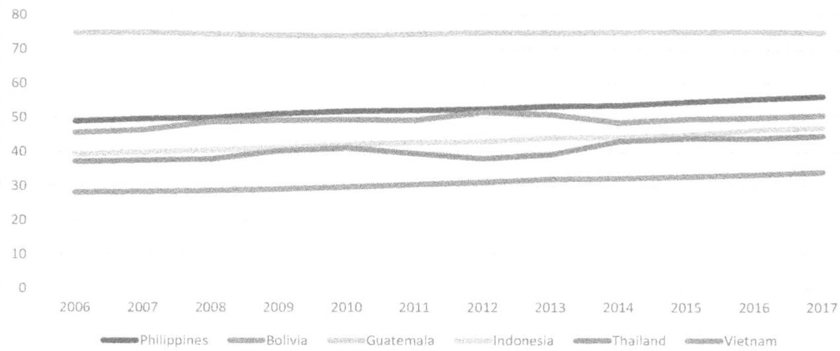

Figure 4.11 Proportion of Workers Employed in the Service Sector
Source: World Bank data

the sector due to the lack of relevant courses (e.g., TVET and engineering), institutional capacity, technical expertise, and capital.

Thus, the data does not simply reflect market conditions, but is more indicative of schools' inability to produce courses that will provide graduates to the priority sectors. Because of this inability, courses that need more resources or effort in executing are not provided by schools, despite the sectoral demand for the same.

3.4. *Camels and Hippos*

In the case of the Philippine education system, it would be interesting to analyze why most religious schools or institutions rank higher in quality assessment compared with state and local universities, which have a higher status in other countries. Religious institutions are treated as "camels and hippos" in this case, as perhaps they are benefiting from the exemptions on tax and limitations on foreign ownership.

Moreover, since the University of the Philippines (UP) system is allocated a majority of the budget for state and local universities and colleges, UP Diliman, which is the main campus, is the only public university thriving based on world rankings, while some continue to offer low-quality programs. Foreign participation, especially in terms of the entry of highly skilled foreign academic workers, may be a binding constraint in the education sector as it prevents the growth and development of low-quality HEIs and other current players.

Table 4.6 shows the percentage of graduates from both the private and public HEIs. Several points are important.

First, the public sector offers almost the same courses as the private sector, and in the process, competes with them. Theoretically, the public sector

Table 4.6 Percent distribution of higher education graduates by discipline group, program level: private and public HE, 2011/12

	Panel A: Private Higher Education Institutions						*Panel B: Public Higher Education Institutions*					
Discipline group	*Pre-bacc.*	*Baccal*	*Post-bacc.*	*Master's*	*Doctorate*	*Share of discipline*	*Pre-bacc.*	*Baccal.*	*Post-bacc.*	*Master's*	*Doctorate*	*Share of discipline*
Agriculture, Forestry, Fisheries	4.1	92	2	1.3	0.7	0.2	23.5	72.2	–	3.1	1.1	5
Architecture and Town Planning	2.4	97.5	–	–	–	0.4	16.7	73.9	3	6.1	0.3	0.5
Bus. Adm. and related	5.7	88	–	5.9	0.3	29.3	17.6	80	0.2	2	0.2	23.9
Education science and Teacher Training	0.7	73.8	1.4	21.5	2.6	9.1	1.4	82.8	4.7	9.8	1.4	19.1
Engineering and Tech	2.7	95.4	0.1	1.2	–	5.7	37.1	62.1	0.3	0.3	0.3	17.7
Fine and Applied Arts	0.4	98.7	–	0.9	–	0.5	31.9	50.4	0.1	17.4	0.1	0.7
Humanities	0.7	91.1	–	5.2	3	0.9	–	84.6	–	8.1	7.2	1.3
IT–Related Disciplines	20.5	78.9	–	0.5	–	12.4	32.2	67.4	–	0.3	0.2	13.3
Law and Jurisprudence	–	98.9	–	1.1	–	0.8	–	98.4	–	1.6	–	–
Maritime	21	76.9	2	–	–	5.7	27.8	72.2	–	–	–	1.2
Mass Communication and Documentation	0.2	96.9	–	2.9	–	1.1	0.6	95.3	0.4	2.6	0.7	0.9
Mathematics	–	78.3	–	21.1	0.6	0.02	1.2	91	–	7.3	0.5	0.8
Medical and Allied	4.9	91.5	–	3.6	–	23.1	16.5	79.9	–	3.6	–	5.2

Natural Science	–	93.4	1.2	4.8	0.6	0.5	–	91.1	1.3	6.2	1.3	1.3
Social and Behavioral Sciences	–	97.1	–	2.4	0.5	2.7	–	92.6	–	6.6	0.8	2.6
Others	6.7	88.7	–	4.1	0.5	7.8	38.6	58	1.3	1.4	0.7	6.5
Share by program level	7.3	8.7	0.1	5.3	0.4	100	20	74.3	1.2	3.8	0.6	100
Total number of graduates	21,865	260,034	535	15,788	1,246	299,468	44,748	165,867	2,570	8,528	1,389	223,102

Note: Row entries per field in each panel sum up to 100 except for rounding errors.
Source: Tan (2017)

is needed if the returns to the activity cannot be fully appropriated by the private firms, as in the case of public goods. In this case, the private sector is already operating in the market. Given the subsidies and grants that SUCs receive from the government, an undue advantage is given to them since these institutions do not compete directly with the private HEIs.

Second, the discipline that has the greatest number of graduates are business administration and related disciplines. This is offered by public and private institutions. Students in the public sector are attracted to these courses since there may be scholarships offered, freeing them from the cost of education.

Third, because of the annual budget given to these SUCs, they are not affected by competition from the private sector, especially from the emerging players with limited resources. For this reason, they flourish because of the policy environment found in the sector, with no clear incentive to improve quality since they are assured of their budgets no matter what happens. These public universities have then become the new "camels and hippos."

Across the comparator countries, public universities are associated with a higher quality of education than private universities. Public schools receive a greater number of applicants and therefore are harder to get into. On the other hand, private universities, especially in Vietnam and Indonesia, are expected to absorb non-passers and offer easier entrance examinations.

In the Philippines, however, the tertiary education system was founded by the private sector. The higher education system has evolved from what was an essentially private system to one with a fairly large public sector that now absorbs 50 percent of tertiary students. Until the late 1950s, there was only one state university, UP, which was established by the American colonial government in 1908. The Americans also established the Philippine Normal School in 1906 to train teachers for the new and fast-growing public schools.

The same period also saw the establishment of technical-vocational schools for training in clerical work, construction skills, and agriculture. Most of the original TVET schools decided to develop their programs into degree programs and got legislative approval to convert their schools into colleges.

From only 1 university until the late 1950s, the number of SUCs grew to the current 112. Once established, many SUCs followed the expansionary trend by establishing branches. These 112 SUCs now have 451 satellite campuses. UP itself increased its branches from 1 agricultural campus in 1950 to 8 campuses now. From its origins as the small Philippine College of Commerce, the Polytechnic University of the Philippines is now the country's largest SUC, with enrollment reaching 80,000 in its numerous branches. Figure 4.12 shows that the share of graduates in public HEIs have slowly taken the share of the private HEIs.

In 2012, the Commission on Higher Education (CHED) allocated PHP 26 billion to support SUCs, aligned with the country's commitment to

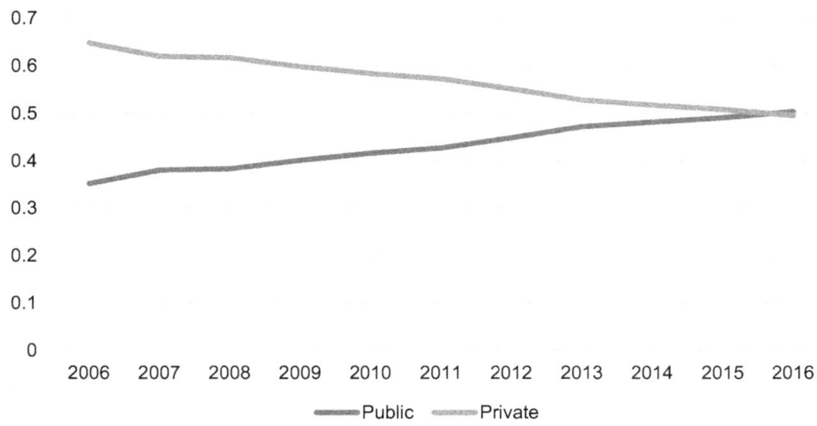

Figure 4.12 Share of Graduates from Public and Private HEIs

Source: Philippine Commission on Higher Education Statistics

promoting human capital development and improving the country's economic competitiveness. But how well have SUCs contributed to realizing that commitment? Manasan and Parel (2015) describe a dismal performance that puts to question the cost and the efficiency of SUC management relative to the quality of education they provide.

The study measures SUCs' performance using the results of 36 professional board exams (PBEs) as an indicator of the quality of instruction. Overall, the numbers reflect very low averages for SUCs. "The weighted passing rate of all SUCs combined in all the PBEs taken together is 4 to 9 percent lower than the national passing rate in 2004–2011," reveals the study. Only 9 out of the 36 PBEs had average passing rates above 60 percent, and only 3 had passing rates above 70 percent.

The SUCs' performance in PBEs dropped in 12 course programs, namely accountancy, aeronautical engineering, civil engineering, criminology, electrical engineering, electronics engineering, library science, mechanical engineering, medical technology, physical therapy, social work, and veterinary medicine. The authors add, "More worrisome is the preponderance of SUCs and private higher education institutions (PHEIs) with zero passing rates in many PBEs in 2004–2011."

In short, SUCs are not meeting the expectations that come with increased budget allocation for their institutions and are siphoning away resources that could have been spent for basic education as well as for health and housing. Instead of producing more worker productivity, SUCs are not producing qualified people in the courses they offer. Manasan and Parel surmise that the root of the problem comes down to the collective management issues of the CHED and the SUCs, particularly where duplication of programs distracts a big number of SUCs from carrying out their core mandates efficiently. Because of the advantage given to SUCs and the restrictions in foreign participation, foreign institutions may not be interested in entering the market.[3] In the process, apart from the subsidies given to SUCs, the ability of the private institutions to offer courses different from the ones offered by the public schools is hampered by foreign restrictions.

Some stakeholders who argue against foreign participation are also concerned that these foreign institutions may operate as diploma or degree mills. In the course of liberalizing the education sector, some comparator countries made sure to include strict policies and procedures to regulate foreign schools. However, the complex and lengthy approval process serves as a disadvantage for interested players who can meet or even exceed high quality standards that the governments impose. In the case of Vietnam and Indonesia, these foreign schools are required to have a local partner and still comply with the minimum curriculum requirements for higher education.

For the TVET subsector, the restriction on foreign equity is a binding constraint, but for the other levels, it may not be the heaviest limitation that greatly inhibits the sector from actualizing opportunities for improvement. A number of the Philippine universities have already started to internationalize. Foreign universities, if they wish to partner with the local universities, have generally been able to do so. In contrast, TVET schools can partner with foreign industries that can benefit from such a collaboration. The foreign limitations on investments can hinder these firms from managing the schools in a manner that suits them.

4. Synthesis and Policy Direction

Based on the current data, the actual impact of opening up the sector is minimal in these countries as of now. All three South East Asian nations implemented significant reforms on foreign participation very recently, and whether the perceived benefits are achieved is still unknown. Nevertheless, most legislators believe that an open education sector will improve the quality of teachers and the quality of graduates produced, enhancing the global competitiveness of the sector. Most also recognized that limiting foreign participation may be a disadvantage in a globalized world and a region working toward integration.

On the other hand, some local educators and experts in Vietnam, Indonesia, and Thailand emphasize that increased foreign participation will not significantly address serious problems on the quality of education in these countries unless institutional capacity, openness to local-foreign collaboration, teacher training, and funding are improved. Some also pointed out that even though reforms were introduced, several factors may still discourage interested foreign players and teachers from entering the sector. Increasingly bureaucratic permit and licensing processes and a highly politicized education sector are some of the hindrances to a successful sector liberalization.

Findings suggest that the poor quality of education in the Philippines is due to different reasons, where each cause is equally vital in the development of the sector. ASEAN countries that have recently liberalized the sector recognize that the weak state of higher education in their countries is not completely addressable by increasing foreign participation in the country. This is evident when observing the reforms made by Indonesia, Thailand, and Vietnam in their education sectors – aside from liberalizing the foreign restrictions, they have also made aggressive changes in providing universal education, infrastructure, and research, among others. That said, the limitations imposed by the Philippine government on foreign participation are, indeed, binding. However, in addition to the restrictions on foreign participation constraining the country from exploring options in making the education sector more competitive, there are many other problems encountered by educational institutions. This said, opening up the sector is not the only solution to improve the quality of education in the country – it may, however, serve as a catalyst for development.

More importantly, results from the diagnostic tests and sentiments from FGDs and KIIs seem to point out that the restrictions on the mobility of professionals may be more inhibiting, given how tedious it is for foreigners to apply for the numerous permits, all from different government agencies, to allow the practice of their professions in the country. The level of compensation is also seen as a challenge in attracting the best talents in teaching, as the salaries in the Philippines are meager compared to developed economies.

To make for a holistic improvement of the sector, an initiative toward the liberalization of the sector must be done in concurrence with an aggressive reform or improvement program which addresses all the gaps identified in this study. As Evenson and Singh (1997) indicate, "a public policy which encourages faster growth of international technological spillovers would be conducive to generate higher productivity growth in the developing countries" (p. 12).

Notes

1 These pertain to investments that allow the country to reach its production possibility frontier.
2 Bolivia was a recipient of a large amount of international aid to improve its schooling system. All of the funds were earmarked for education.
3 Additionally, part of the reason the private sector is weakening is because of the limited capacity to offer TVET and courses different from those offered in

public. The increasing dominance of the public schools may be due to the subsidies offered to them. At the same time, even if there had been subsidies, the private schools could have been more competitive had they been allowed to partner with better schools abroad and offer better courses than what the public schools can offer.

References

Aker, J. C., & Mbiti, I. M. (2010). Mobile phones and economic development in Africa. *The Journal of Economic Perspectives, 24*, 207–232.

Asian Development Bank. (2012). *Regional cooperation and cross-border collaboration in higher education in Asia (RPS124784)*. Retrieved from Asian Development Bank website

Bell, M., & Pavitt, K. (1993). Technological accumulation and industrial growth: Contrasts between developed and developing countries. *Industrial and Corporate Change*, 2, 157–210.

Cirera, X., & Maloney, W. F. (2017). *The innovation paradox: Developing-country capabilities and the unrealized promise of technological catch-up*. Washington, DC: The World Bank.

Clausen, R. L. (2012). *Education for all priorities in the education policies of Bolivia and Mexico*. Dissertation submitted to the Pennsylvania State University College of Education.

Evenson, R., & Singh, L. (1997). *Economic growth, international technological spillovers and public policy: Theory and empirical evidence from Asia* (Discussion Paper No. 777). New Haven, CT: Yale Economic Growth Center.

Fu, X., & Li, J. (2016). Collaboration with foreign universities for innovation: Evidence from Chinese manufacturing firms. *International Journal of Technology Management*, *70*, 193–217.

Hausmann, R., Klinger, B., & Wagner, R. (2008). *Doing growth diagnostics in practice: A 'mindbook* (CID working paper no. 177). Cambridge, MA: Center for International Development Harvard University.

Hausmann, R., Rodrik, D., & Velasco, A. (2006). Getting the diagnosis right. *Finance and Development*, *43*(1), 12–15.

Hershberg, E., Nabeshima, K., & Yusuf, S. (2007). Opening the ivory tower to business: University-industry linkages and the development of knowledge-intensive clusters in Asian cities. *World Development*, *35*(6), 931–940.

Manasan, R., & Parel, D. (2015). *Review and assessment of programs offered by State Universities and Colleges* (Research Paper Series No. 2015–02). Makati: PIDS.

Maxwell, D. (2015, January 19). Could Thailand become Southeast Asia's international education hub? *Asian Correspondent*. Retrieved from https://asiancorrespondent.com/2015/01/could-thailand-become-southeast-asias-international-education-hub/#Dro6Atmbyt6dQg7q.97

The PIE News. (2017, June 6). *Thailand to open up to foreign higher education institutions*. Retrieved from https://thepienews.com/news/thailand-open-up-to-foreign-institutions/

PriceWaterhouseCoopers (PWC). (2019). *Study on limitations of foreign participation in educational institutions and teaching in the Philippines*. Pasig City, Manila: Report Submitted to the National Economic Development Authority.

Romer, P. M. (1989). *Human capital and growth: Theory and evidence* (Research No w3173). New York: National Bureau of Economic.

SMEC International Pty. Ltd. (2010). Viet Nam: Preparing the Higher Education Sector Development Project (HESDP). *Asian Development Bank*. Retrieved from www.adb.org/projects/documents/preparing-higher-education-sector-development-project-hesdp-viet-nam-higher-education

Tan, E. (2017). Quality, inequality and recent education reform. *The Philippine Review of Economics*, *54*(2), 110–137.

Tanna, S., & Topaiboul, K. (2005). *Human capital, trade, FDI and economic growth in Thailand: What causes what?* DEGIT Conference Papers (No. c010-046).

Times Higher Education. (2018). *World University rankings*. Retrieved from www.timeshighereducation.com/world-university-rankings

UNCTAD. (2017). *World Investment Report 2017: Investment and the digital economy*. Geneva: United Nations Publications.

UNESCO. (2012). *Students from a given country studying abroad*. Retrieved from http://data.un.org/Data.aspx?d=UNESCO&f=series%3AED_FSOABS

UNESCO. (2018). *One in five children, adolescents and youth is out of school*. UNESCO fact sheet no. 48. Retrieved from https://uis.unesco.org/sites/default/files/documents/fs48-one-five-children-adolescents-youth-out-school-2018-en.pdf

UniRank. (2018). *Top Universities in Vietnam|2018 Vietnamese University ranking*. Retrieved from www.4icu.org/vn/

Uribe, R. J. (2007). *Integración, cooperación internacional, redes y asociaciones*. Unpublished Document.

Vivarelli, M. (1995). *The economics of technology and employment: Theory and empirical evidence*. Aldershot: Edward Elgar.

World Bank. (2014). *Skilling up Vietnam: Preparing the work force for a modern market economy*. Washington, DC: World Bank.

World Bank Group. (2016). *Assessing basic education service delivery in the Philippines: Public education expenditure tracking and quantitative service delivery study* (No. AUS6799, pp. 1–191). The World Bank.

World Education News + Review. (2017, November 8). *Education in Vietnam – current trends and qualifications*. Retrieved from https://wenr.wes.org/2017/11/education-in-vietnam

Zanello, G., Fu, X., Mohnen, P., & Ventresca, M. (2015). The creation and diffusion of innovation in developing countries: A systematic literature review. *Journal of Economic Surveys*, 884–912.

Chapter 5

Innovation System in Making

Comparing India and China

Swati Mehta and Baldev Singh Shergill

1. Introduction

Innovation has been regarded as the main ingredient of long-term growth, structural transformation and gainful employment (Edquist, 1997). Scholars since ages have been engaged in understanding 'innovation', and more importantly its 'process'. Since the late twentieth century, a new paradigm of understanding has emerged in the field of 'innovation studies' that has further broadened the scope of the studies. Broadly defined as the 'system of innovation' approach by, Christopher Freeman (1987), the framework has assumed a significant position in theoretical literature to understand the pattern of growth in different economies.

History is witness to numerous struggles resulting in different arrays of economic and political gains. Since World War II, the power has been vested in the West. But the last two decades have seen a change in the world economy. The two Asian countries, namely China[1] and India, are trying to catch up with the Western developed countries, which is posing a serious challenge to the hegemony of the West. This could also lead to an advent of a bipolar world. Regarding this trend, Nayyar (2013) acclaimed that 'The robust growth in Asia provides stimulus to the old engines of growth and such processes is although not large enough to shift the hegemonic balance, but it is undoubtedly a beginning of change'. However, Bosworth and Collins (2008) optimistically view the continued growth of China and India will dominate the world economy for several decades.

It is pertinent to note that over the last four decades, China and India have been growing at an average annual rate of 9.4 percent and 6.1 percent respectively, relative to the world's average of 2.8 percent. Figure 5.1 shows that China touched the peak of around 14 percent GDP growth three times during the last 40 years, in 1984 (15.1%), 1992 (14.2%) and 2007 (14.2%), while India touched its highest level of GDP growth in 1988 (9.6%), 1999 (8.8%) and 2010 (8.8%).

It was evident that the global economic crisis of 2008 also failed to deter the growth momentum of these two Asian countries. The annual GDP growth

DOI: 10.4324/9781003353904-6

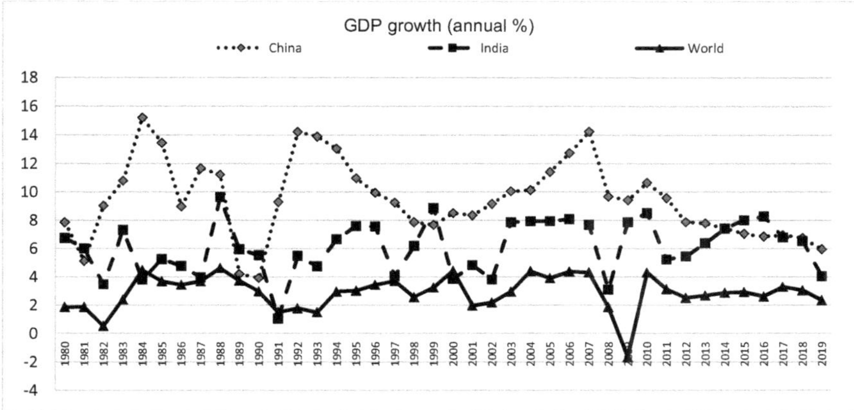

Figure 5.1 Annual Gross Domestic Growth (percentage)

Source: World Development Indicators

did dip to 9.6 percent in 2008 from 14.2 percent in 2007 for China; while for India, it was 3.1 percent and 7.6 percent, respectively. This resilience from the global recession is remarkable for these emerging Asian economies.

The GDP per capita of India and China (Figure 5.2) started with almost similar magnitude in the early 1990s, but the gap between the two giants started swelling. China's average GDP per capita for the years 2017–19 was 2.5 times that of India's.

Despite being a part of same continent, these two Asian economies have the highest population in the world and also have the highest economic growth rate over the years. But despite some similarities, India and China are two different countries with a multitude of differences and divergences. Both India and China initiated their growth journey with the planned model of development, albeit at different degrees, during the 1940s. Predominantly agrarian in nature, both India and China adopted liberalization policies almost during the same period[2]. But despite these similarities, there exist varied differences (Dahlman, 2009). The socio-political[3] demarcation leads these two giants to part ways on the path of success and development. The patterns of development and growth witnessed in both the countries are very different. The manner in which the policies are targeted, framed and executed is also varied and thus produced different results.

Under this background, it is imperative to understand the structure of 'innovation' in both these countries, using the 'system of innovation' approach. The chapter assumes the following structure. After building up the argument in the introduction and Part I, Section II presents the evolution

Figure 5.2 Gross Domestic Product per Capita in India and China

Source: World Development Indicators

of the National Innovation System followed by a review of the literature in Section III. In Section IV, we present the foundation and the growth of innovation in India and China. The analysis and comparison of growth and structure of the NIS in India and China is presented in Section V. Some policy recommendations, along with some broader means to develop the NIS, are contained in Section VI, followed by the conclusion.

2. National Innovation System: The Framework

Coined by Christopher Freeman in his 1987 book on Japan, the System of Innovation approach has 'innovation' in its core. The importance of 'innovation' has been recognized by growth theorists for ages. Innovation is regarded as an important source of growth in theories since the Classical economists (Mehta, 2013). The explicit importance of 'technical change' as an ingredient of growth can be found in the work of Solow (1956). These exogenous growth models consider 'knowledge' as 'manna from heaven'. But the real breakthrough in the literature of 'innovation studies' could be traced to the advent of endogenous growth models in the late 1980s with the publication of papers by Romer (1986), Lucas (1988), Grossman and Helpman (1991). These models assumed knowledge to possess certain characteristics unlike the tangible factors of production. Numerous scholars started taking up the issues like understanding the 'nature', 'processes', 'determinants' and 'consequences' of innovation.

Innovation is widely considered to be 'complex', 'dynamic' and 'non-linear' in nature. These theoretical underpinnings produced varied theoretical models dealing with the process of technology accumulation. Neoclassical models talked about the 'global' knowledge pool, which led to producing welfare enhancing consequences in the 'competitive' 'laissez-faire' market framework.

However, the other stream of literature, pioneered by Nelson and Winter (1982), considered 'innovation' as a complex process that could be accumulated through a multiplicity of variables under conducive accumulative environments. These evolutionary theories (Saviotti, 1997) considered the biological nature of non-optimality and non-equilibrium in the process of innovation. The concentration of Nelson and Winter's (1982) model is on a single industry consisting of heterogeneous firms producing homogenous products, which are searching for higher productivity routines than they were using in a particular period (Andersen, 1992), leading to a 'path-dependence' process (Saviotti, 1997).

But a new paradigm to the 'studies of innovation' is found with the introduction of the 'system of innovations' approach. Interdisciplinary in nature, this approach tries to capture the 'process of innovation' unanimously that is composed of various actors, institutions, organisations and the inter-relationship between them. To reflect upon the complexity, Edquist (1997) referred *'all important economic, social, political, organizational, institutional, and other factors that influence the development, diffusion, and use of innovation'* as a 'system'. This 'system' is a *'complex of elements or components which mutually condition and constrain one another'* (Fleck, 1992 quoted in Edquist, 1997) leading to innovation.

Figure 5.3 presents the complex process of technological accumulation that is evolutionary in character. The two components of the 'systems of

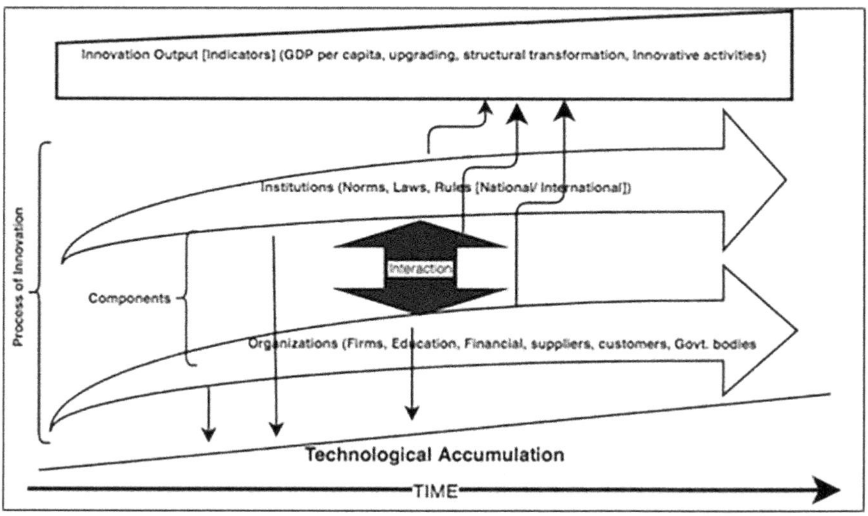

Figure 5.3 Systems of Innovation Approach: Diagrammatic Representation

Source: First Author

innovation' approach are Institutions and Organisations that are interrelated with each other in the process of innovation. Institutions are considered as the 'rules of the games', like habits, norms, routines, rules and laws, both at the national and at the international level. Organisations are 'formal structures that are consciously created and have an explicit purpose' (Edquist and Johnson, 1997). The firms, educational institutions, research institutions, venture capital organisations and government bodies and ministries are the important organisations. The close inter-linkages between the various actors or organisations and institutions compose a 'system' with the aim of achieving some innovation output. These innovation outputs can take the form of increasing productivity, increase in gross domestic product per capita, increase in high-tech exports, structural transformation towards high value-added activities/sectors, increase in employment along with adoption of advanced technologies, increase in scientific research and increase in patents.

It was initially started to reflect upon the nature of the 'system' that leads to 'innovation' at the 'national' level, trying to understand its various processes, determinants and consequences (Edquist, 1997). Then it turned to the different units of analysis like 'sectoral', 'regional' and 'technological' innovation systems. These advances mainly resulted from the increasing integration amongst nations.

3. Review of Literature

A rich literature exists that has analysed, examined, described and compare the various dimensions including economic, political and social policies of the two Asian giants, India and China. These comparisons have been done by various scholars for decades. But the basic issue that attracted the attention of the scholars was the comparison of the developmental path, the process taken up and more importantly the policies that have shaped the growth path of these economic giants that have grown at a phenomenal rate for the last two decades.

Development literature has tried to examine the source of this growth. During the 1980s and 1990s, the importance of innovation and technology for economic growth was well evident in the theoretical literature. However, two major approaches emerged with competing paradigms concerning the means, process and source of technological accumulation – neoclassical endogenous growth models and evolutionary approaches (Verspagen, 2005). The former approach (Romer, 1986) assumes technology as a 'public good' which could be accumulated through both indigenous investment in R&D and through technology spillover (Coe and Helpman, 1995; Lichtenberg and Potterie, 1998; Keller, 1998) between firms through various channels like trade, FDI and human capital apart from direct purchase of technology. These models (Grossman and Helpman, 1991) emphasised the efficiency of market models as the requisite policy framework for technology accumulation. Thus, more'openness' of the economies were emphasised as a development policy by neoclassical endogenous theoretical models.

Contrarily, the evolutionary models of economic growth also emerged during the same time (Nelson and Winter, 1982). These models assume heterogeneity of firms and accumulation of technology as a complex process. The evolutionary approach embraces micro-complication of the innovative process (Verspagen, 2005) that requires consistent and strategic policy initiatives from the government to lead the private sector prosper and excel.

However, the literature that has studied both these countries found that China has mostly performed well compared to India in terms of a number of quantitative indicators (Dahlman, 2009). It was found that the Chinese economy is almost three times that of India, and its per capita income is more than twice as high as India.

Some scholars compared the level of productivity in these two emerging countries. A very comprehensive study on the issue of comparing the growth and productivity of industries in India and China was done by Bosworth and Collins (2008). They found that growth of output and productivity of labour are constantly higher than that witnessed by the Indian industry for the period of 1978 to 2004. Trivedi (2010) also presented a review of literature on the issue and concluded that both production and productivity growth rate in India have been moderate compared to China. Precisely, Siddharthan and Nollen (2010) found that the Chinese software industry is also bigger in size than India's. Siddharthan and Narayanan (2010) also found empirically that the outward FDI as a percentage of GDP from China is doubled compared to India in 2005. Emphasising the importance of FDI for Indian technological accumulation, Beule (2010) found that due to irregular investment in R&D, India is not able to reap the benefit of foreign investment in R&D labs. Discussing the case for China, Beule found that Chinese used foreign investments to jumpstart domestic firms into technology activity. Therefore, the number of patents and inventions has grown exponentially in China compared to India. The overall literature shows that China is ahead of India in many quantitative economic indicators. However, the scholars have different opinions for the reasons that China has surged ahead of India.

Explaining the reason for the lagging of India, Dahlman (2009) observed that China has embraced globalisation more profoundly, whereas India remained more autarkic and circumspect. He further asserted that India opened up much later and much more slowly and is still not as globally integrated as China. On the other hand, Amsden (2001) reasoned the strategically consistent policy of China was to make the industry competitive. Some studies regarded that in China, the institutional innovations like development of the household responsibility system, township and village enterprise and special economic zones in coastal areas lead to rapid growth in the country over the last few years (Sachs and Woo, 1997). However, some (Zhang and Liu, 2009) also highlighted the various bottlenecks in the continuing growth in China, including unbalanced economic structure with a greater share of exports than internal consumption. The country faces a demographic divide, income disparity and massive environmental degradation.

Apart from the literature discussed earlier that considers some partial elements of the national innovation system of these countries, there are some who specifically examined the national innovation system in more detail. However, the literature is very scarce in the field, but it is certainly not non-existent. Ahmad (1978) presented a comparative analysis of India and China regarding their social, economic and political perspective that has varied impact upon the growth and structure of science and technology in both countries. Aiming for self-reliance, it was found that these countries followed different paths. From importing technology initially, these countries tried to develop technologies.

Xiwei and Xiangdong (2007) discussed the different stages of S&T reforms and policy frameworks in China that helped it to build a strong national innovation system. A very consistent study regarding the national innovation system of China was done by Schaaper (2009). He found that the Chinese state council regarded science and technology (S&T) as the key driving force for sustainable economic growth and structural transformation into an innovation-orientation nation. The study analysed the S&T system of China by examining the various indicators from 1996 to 2006. It was found that over the years, China has raised the ratio of R&D to GDP very rapidly as a targeted policy which has made it a global R&D player, ranking behind only the USA and Japan in purchasing power parity (PPP) terms. The study further found that the NIS of China is lacking in R&D intensity in high-technology industries, emphasis on applied research, lack of science-industry linkage and lack of resources for the higher education sector.

Thus, the brief review of literature shows that there is a need to specifically compare and understand the structure of the national innovation systems of India and China in order to understand the source of development of these two Asian giants and to decipher the patterns of growth. Thus, the aim of the present chapter is: (i) to compare the national innovation systems of India and China, and (ii) to examine the different paths undertaken by these countries in terms of policy framework, institutional build-ups and networking patterns to build up their national innovation system.

4. Innovation in India and China: Foundation and Growth

This section is about what governments in India and China have done to promote the national innovation system in their countries. It is evident that governments of all industrialised and a growing number of developing countries have adopted the policies that implicitly and explicitly affect the development of an indigenous innovation system (Conroy, 1984; Cimoli et al., 2009). In the present era of fast-moving technological frontiers and rapidly changing technologies, the policy-makers face moving targets for which dynamism is also required in framing policies with consistent framework for proper and timely implementation.

a *Historical foundations (Before 1950s):* Both India and China were basically agrarian and highly populated with a set of similar constraints. In China, widespread political turmoil during the Great Leap Forward (1958–9) and the Cultural Revolution (1966–76), increased the desire of administration units for self-sufficiency. In India, the culmination of dominion from the British Empire in 1947 aroused the quest for 'self-sufficiency'. Before the 1950s, China's economy remained firmly Stalinist in key features like commitment to administration planning, absence of a market for labour or capital, collective farms, bias towards large scale and relative isolation from the international economy (Nolan, 2004). India, under the first Prime Minister, Pt. Jawaharlal Nehru, adopted Fabian Socialism, central planning with State control.

b *State and Self-Sufficiency (1950s to 1980s):* Following the establishment of the People's Republic of China in 1949, China adopted the Soviet Union's model of development. In 1958, after China's first five-year plan, Mao adopted the plan of grassroots socialism to turn the country into an industrialized country. The government was the principal source of S&T funding, and the allocations of funds were done through administrative orders. In the 1950s, most of China's technology imports had come from the USSR, and in 1960s, selective acquisition of most advanced technology was made (Nolan, 2004). China began its development strategy based on the policies of import substitution, centralised planning and the dominance of the public sector. In 1978, China adopted the 'open door' policy and followed the 'dual-track' approach with the co-existence of a market economy and planned economy (Sachs and Woo, 1997). The policy emphasised basic research in advanced technologies to generate future growth (Conroy, 1984). In 1981, five-point guideline research policies were announced wherein the emphasis was laid on development of science and technology (S&T) consistent with economic growth and social needs, including the focus on agriculture, light consumer goods and industries. In 1982, the policy document entitled 'Outline report on policy concerning the development of our national science and technology' was adopted, which emphasised the co-ordination between higher authorities and research institutes (Baark, 1987).

  In India, the first five-year plan was also earmarked to build up national laboratories and research institutes under the aegis of the Council for

Scientific and Industrial Research (CSIR)[4]. In the following five-year plans, research was made broader and research facilities in universities and research institutes were strengthened. In the direction of strengthening the industrial base, the Industrial Policy Resolution was enacted in 1958, followed by the Invention Promotion Board. In 1971, the Department of Science and Technology (DST) was set up as the nodal institute for implementation of overall science and technology policies, for promotion of new areas of science and technology, to coordinate multi-agency programmes, for the promotion and utilisation of indigenous technology and international cooperation in transferring technology and for providing grants to research institutes, scientific associations and societies and academics.

During the period, both countries tried to lay the foundation of science and technology through the establishment of various research institutes and universities through government efforts and control.

c *Post-Reform Period (1980s onward):* Since the 1980s, both India and China adopted significant reforms, although the pattern, structure and quantum of reforms varied. In 1985, China followed the policy of 'building the nation with science and education' and the inter-link between research institutes, universities and industry was significantly strengthened. In March 1985, the Central Committee of the Communist Party of China (CCP) earmarked to improve the S&T structure of the country and in this direction, a White Paper on S&T policy was issued by the State Science and Technology Commission (SSTC) in 1986 (Baark, 1987). As of early 1986, China had 1900 research institutes involved in independent technology development. To give impetus to high-technology industries, China drew up two national plans: the High-Tech Research and Development Programme (863 programme) in 1987 and the Torch Programme in 1988. Under these programs, the policy of selective arrangement with major foreign corporations for transferring technology was adopted (Shijun, 1992). By the end of the 1980s, China started developing high-technology industries. In the 1990s, universities and research institutes were encouraged to establish their own enterprises, especially in high-technology sectors (Xiwei and Xiangdon, 2007). China launched the Torch Programme to encourage high-technology zones in 1988, and by the end of 1992, 52 national high-technology zones were established. The state-owned enterprises (SOEs) were liberalised by gradually devolving the decision-making powers related to production, marketing and investment, followed by granting liberalised policies to community-owned enterprises (COEs) (Conroy, 1984). Since 1999, China began to transform government-owned research institutes into enterprises to strengthen the technological capabilities of the enterprises. Thus, it could be concluded that China's approach to economic reforms was experimental and evolutionary under the 'authoritarian political system' (Nolan, 2004). However, despite considerable economic reforms in the late 1980s, China's leadership struck a new balance between plan and market, relying heavily on indirect methods, mainly macroeconomic levers, to guide the economy[5]. India also followed the path of building its technology capabilities through policy implementation. A significant expansion and consolidation of the scientific infrastructure was seen at the time of implementation of the Sixth Five-Year Plan (1980–85). In 1982, the National Council for Science and Technology Communication (NCSTC) was set up to create a new organisational structure to initiate, promote, develop and strengthen S&T activities in the country. But the greatest hallmark of this Plan period was the announcement of the Technology Policy Statement (TPS) in January 1983. But despite these accomplishments, it was recognised that there exist large gaps in terms of capabilities that India possesses and those of the other advanced countries. So the Seventh Five-Year Plan (1985–90) laid emphasis on the development of new areas of S&T such as informatics, biotechnology, material technologies, new frontiers in chemistry, etc. In January 1985, the Department of Scientific and Industrial Research (DSIR) was created as a part of the Ministry of Science and Technology. Further, for indigenous R&D efforts, the Eighth Plan (1992–97) envisaged four thrust programmes for developing S&T in the country – to give priority to basic research in frontier areas, for securing a position of leadership and self-reliance, provision for the diffusion of appropriate technology and to integrate S&T in economic planning.

(i) *FDI and Technology Transfer:* In China, control over FDI was lifted slowly and more strategically compared to India. China adopted the 'quid pro quo' policy that makes technology transfers a pre-condition of foreign firms selling in China (Holmes et al., 2013). It is evident that the 'quid pro quo' policy was explicit[6] prior to China's accession to WTO in 2002 (Ahmad, 1978). But thereafter this policy became implicit. This policy generated mixed results – for example, Ford Motors transferred its technology to get access to the huge Chinese market, whereas Nissan found the policy too onerous. But by the beginning of 2000, China became the largest recipient of FDI in the world. Relatively, India adopted a liberalised policy for FDI after 1991 and adopted two routes for FDI – one FDI up to 100 percent through the automatic approval route, requiring only notification to the Reserve Bank of India; under the second route, approval is required by the government through the Foreign Investment Promotion Board in the Ministry of Finance.

(ii) *Trade and Technology Transfer:* China's attitude towards international trade in the 1980s was to encourage exports[7] and to organise

imports[8] according to needs. Control over foreign trade was relaxed slowly, and China joined the WTO as late as the end of 2001. However, India was the founding member of WTO and joined it in 1995. With joining the institution, India slashed tariffs and other non-tariff barriers to trade very significantly and progressed on the path of liberating the economy from the State's control.

(iii) *Higher Education:* To facilitate researchers, as early as the 1980s, China formulated a liberal policy to encourage researchers by giving rewards, bonuses and patenting rights (Baark, 1987). India adopted the mass education system that has resulted in large inclusion of cheap, low-ended jobs for the Indians in the global value chain in the manufacturing sector and in the services sector.

5. Growth and Structure of National Innovation System in India and China: A Comparative Analysis

Literature (Smith, 2005) argues that although innovation is the most coherent source of growth, it is very difficult to quantify. There are, however, some macro-level input and output indicators of innovation that can lead to international comparability of 'systems'. The 'inputs' of innovation could include variables that could directly or indirectly lead to accumulation of knowledge leading to innovation, like investment in R&D, human capital, conducive infrastructure, organizations and institutions for innovation. On the other hand, there are numerous indicators that could reflect the innovation capability and capacity of the economy, like GDP and sectoral composition, quantum of patents, high-tech trade and standard of living, etc. In this section, a comparison of various input and output indicators of innovation is compared for both China and India.

5.1. Innovation Inputs

Research and Development as a percentage of GDP and *Researchers in R&D per million people* are amongst the important indicators of innovation input. These are directly quantifiable and depict the nature of innovation acumen in different countries. Figure 5.4 shows the *R&D as a percentage of GDP* for India and China. It is seen that the during the mid-1990s, the share of R&D as a percentage of GDP for both India and China was somewhat similar, but thereafter, China increased its R&D expenditure as a percentage of GDP exorbitantly as it reaches about two percent after 2014, whereas in India, R&D as a percentage of GDP remained less than one percent and only 0.6 percent of GDP in 2018. Further, Figure 5.5 shows the quantum of *Researchers in R&D per million people* in India and China and again shows the gap between these two Asian countries are widening with each passing

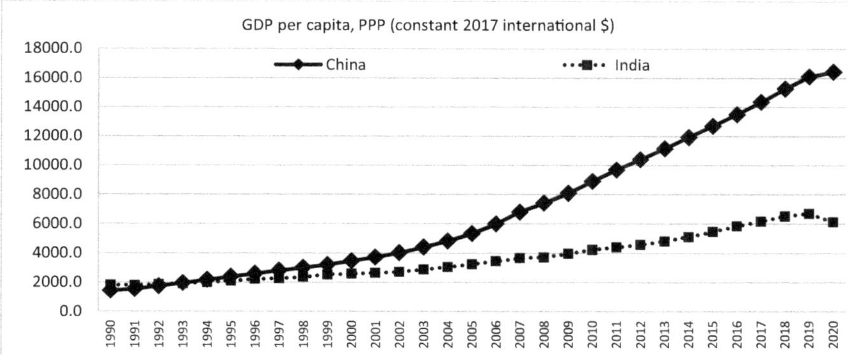

Figure 5.4 R&D Expenditure as a Percentage of GDP: India and China

Source: World Development Indicators

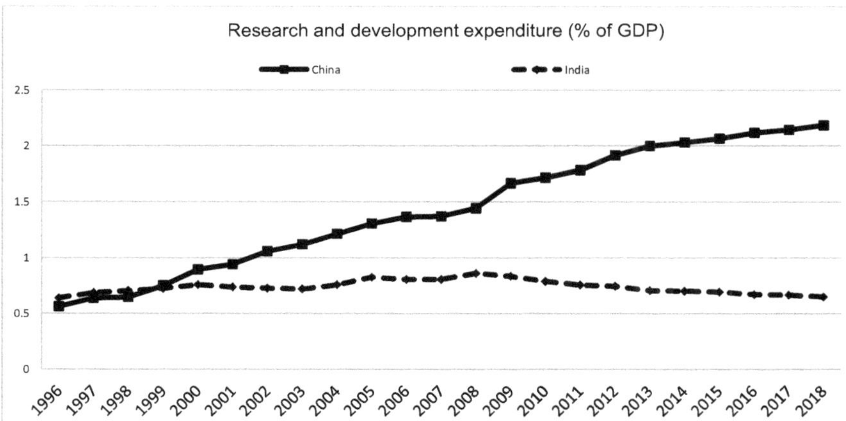

Figure 5.5 Researchers in R&D per Million People: India and China

Source: World Development Indicators

year. In 2018, Researchers in R&D per million people in China were five times higher India.

The sectoral decomposition of value added as a percentage of GDP for three broad sectors of the economy. It was found that the share of agriculture in China was 30 percent in 1980, and subsequently fell to eight percent in 2020. The share of value-added by agriculture of India for 1980 was 36 percent, which fell to 20 percent in 2020. In the case of industries, it was found that the share of value-added as a percentage of GDP for China for

1980 was 48 percent, that fell to 38 percent in 2020; whereas for India, the share of industry remained around 26 percent. Further, it was found that for China, the share of service sector was 22 percent for value-added as a percentage of GDP in 1980, and the share increased to 54 percent in 2020. The subsequent share for India was 37 percent in 1980 and 54 percent in 2020. This shows that 'structural transformation' has happened in both these countries over the years from agriculture to services.

To compare the System of Innovation in India and China, we resort to the data extracted from the 2021 Global Innovation Index. The choice of the

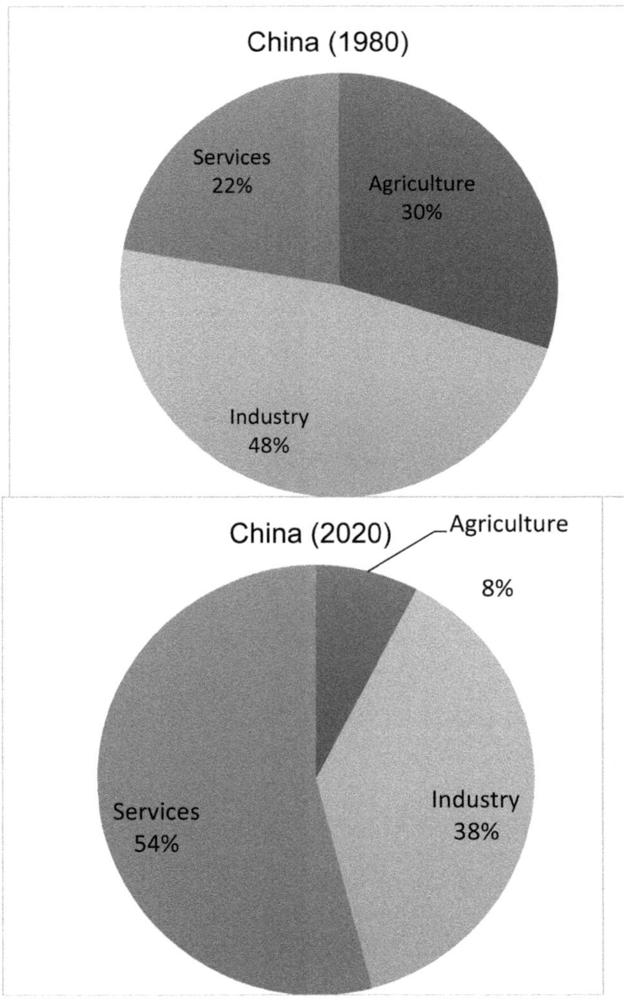

Figure 5.6a Continued

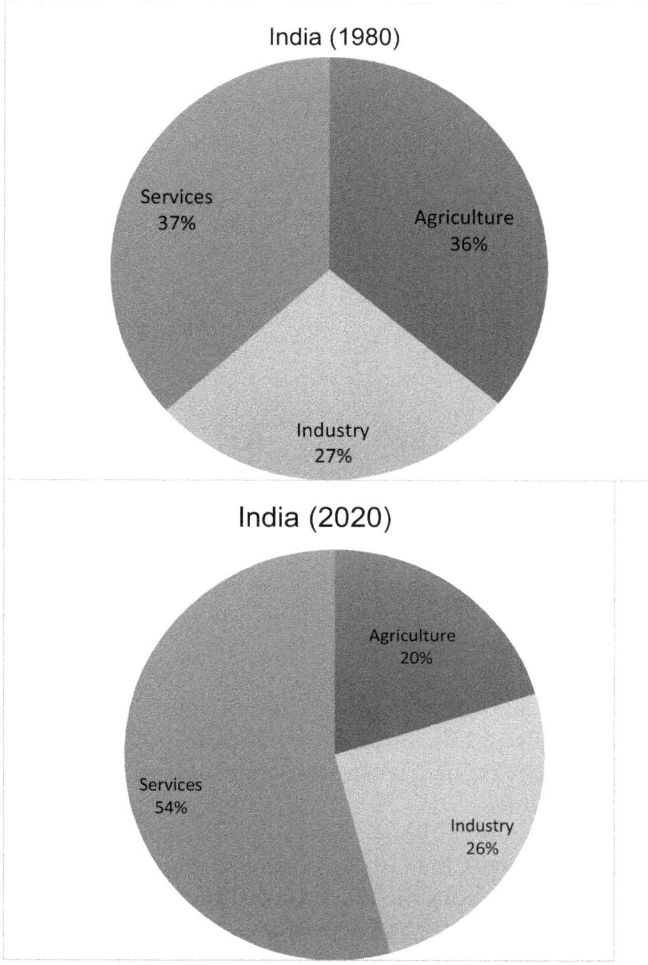

Figure 5.6b Structure of Chinese and Indian Economies: A Comparison
Data Source: World Development Indicators

data is made as it provides the information and comparative data for many indicators of two major components like Organisations and Institutions in the Systems of Innovation approach.

Figure 5.7 gives the comparison of the important components of innovation system of India and China. It is evident that apart from Institutions (Figure 5.8a) with score 64.4, for all the other components namely Human

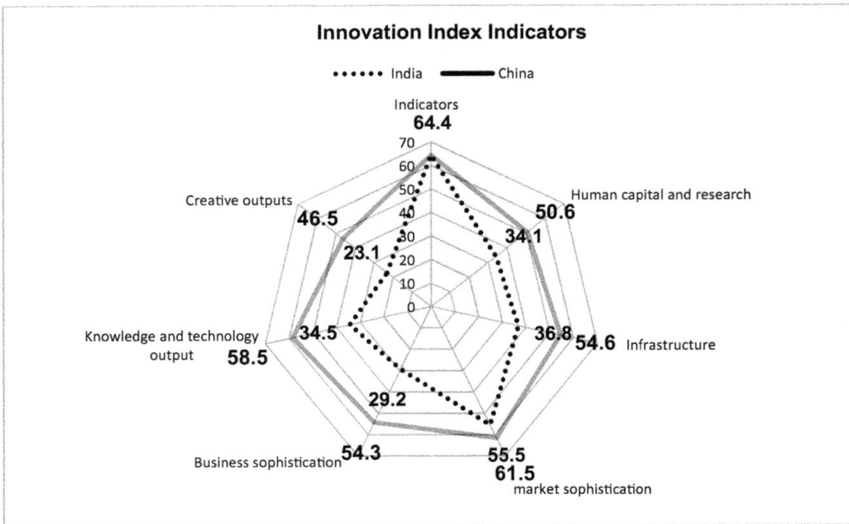

Figure 5.7 Innovation Index Indicators: India and China

Source: Global Innovation Index 2021

and capital research (Figure 5.8b), Infrastructure (Figure 5.8c), Market sophistication (Figure 5.8d), Business sophistication (Figure 5.8e), Knowledge and technology output (Figure 5.8f) and Creative output (Figure 5.8g), China is ahead of India.

Figure 5.8a shows that although the composite score of Institutions is the same for both India and China, there is some divergence for its Institutional sub-components. Data from the 2021 Global Innovation Index shows that China has greater *Political and Operational sustainability* compared to India. The *Government Effectiveness* score for China (62.2) is higher compared to India (54.5). But India's score was high compared to China's in *Regulatory Quality* and *Rule of Law*. Importantly, in *Ease of Starting a Business*, China's score is 94.1 compared to India's 81.6. This indicates that India needs to take initiatives to increase the *Ease of Starting a Business* in the country.

Human Capital and Research are important innovation input component. The component score for India is 34.1, while China's is 50.6 (Figure 5.7). Its important sub-components are *Research and Development expenditure as a percentage of GDP* (Figure 5.4) and *Researchers in R&D per million population* (Figure 5.5), apart from the ones depicted in Figure 5.8b. It was found that in China the *school life expectancy* is 12.4 years, about one year higher than India (11.5 years). Interestingly, Figure 5.8b shows that the

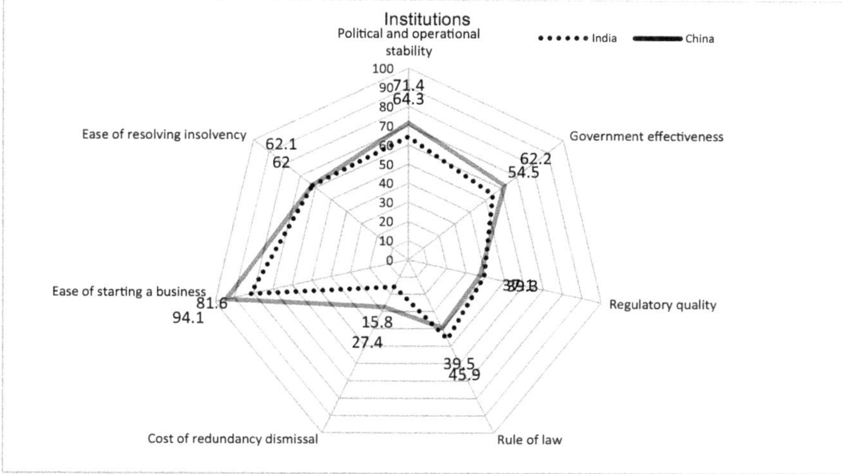

Figure 5.8a Institutions: India and China

Source: Global Innovation Index 2021

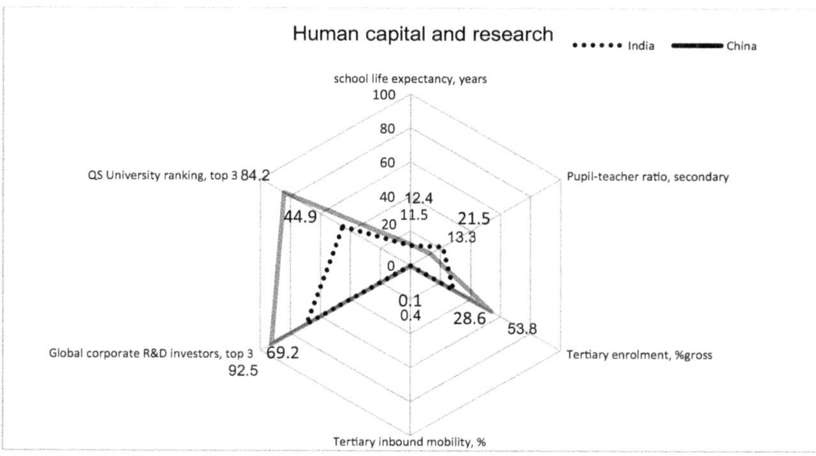

Figure 5.8b Human Capital and Research: India and China

Source: Global Innovation Index 2021

Pupil-teacher ratio in secondary education in India is 21.5, while the ratio for China is only 13.3.

The *gross enrolment in tertiary education* is very high in China (53.8 percent) compared to India (28.6 percent). Another important indicator of

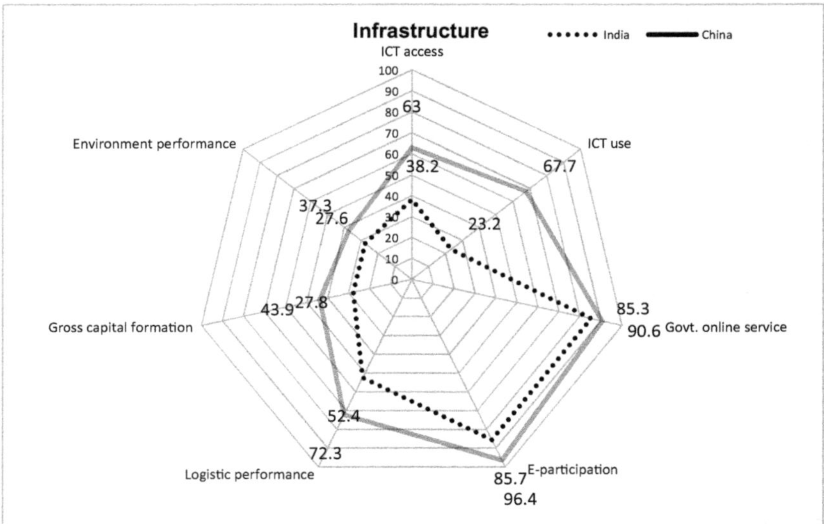

Figure 5.8c Infrastructure: India and China

Source: Global Innovation Index 2021

the education system in a country is captured by *QS University Rankings*, wherein the score of the top three universities in China is 84.2, and India's 44.9. This indicates that India needs to divert resources towards investment in R&D, increasing the researchers per million population and strengthen the overall education and research system in their country to be comparable with China.

Infrastructure is an important component of the system of innovation approach, the sub-components of which were presented in Figure 5.8c. The overall score of *Infrastructure* for India is 36.8 and for China is 54.6 (Figure 5.7). Concerning Information and Communication Technologies (ICTs), it was found that the score of *ICT access* in India is only 38.2 while that for China is 63.0, indicating that there is a need to increase the ICT access in India. But in context of the *Government's online service* and *E-participation*, rates are high for both India and China.

In terms of General Infrastructure, the *Logistic performance score* in India was 52.4 and in China, it was 72.3. Another important infrastructure input, the *Gross capital formation as a percent of GDP*, is found to be 27.8 percent in India and 43.9 percent in China. On account of *Ecological sustainability for GDP per unit energy use*, the score for India was found to be 10.8 while that for China is about 7.5, indicating that there is a need to increase the efficiency that would optimise the use of energy inputs.

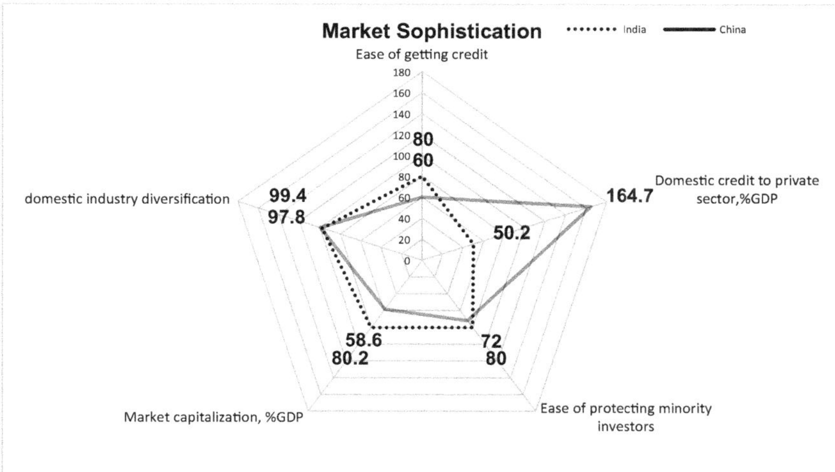

Figure 5.8d Market Sophistication in India and China

Source: Global Innovation Index 2021

Market sophistication is another important sub-component of the systems of innovation approach. A comparison of market sophistication in India and China is presented in Figure 5.8d. It is found that India and China have similar scores for *Domestic Industry diversification* and *Ease of protecting minority investors*. But wide divergences are found for sub-components like *Domestic credit to private sector*; the value of the score for India is about three times less than China. Importantly, India is ahead in *Ease of getting Credit* compared to China. This indicates that market sophistication is comparable for both India and China.

'Learning' is a continuous process that happens with the close interaction between various organisations and institutions. The university-industry linkage is also very important in the process of technology accumulation. Figure 5.8e shows that the *University-Industry R&D collaboration* score is 70.5 for China and 42.7 for India. Therefore, it shows that it is very important for India to increase interrelationships between university-industry linkages for building technological capabilities. Another important sub-component of *Business sophistication* includes the *State of Cluster development*, the score of which is 73.1 for China and 45.6 for India, also shows the need for consistent efforts from the latter. Subsequently, data from the Global Innovation Index of 2021 also shows that the *Research talent as a percent of business* is very high in China compared to India. Further, it was also found that in China around 80 percent of the firms offer *formal training* to the employees to absorb the production process of the firms, while in India,

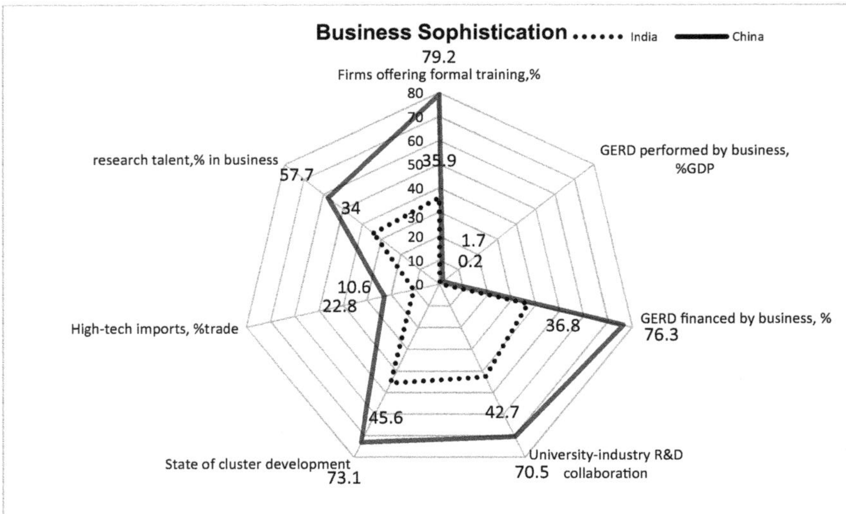

Figure 5.8e Business Sophistication in India and China

Source: Global Innovation Index 2021

only 35.9 percent of the firms offer formal training. This indicates that there is a wide gap between China and India with respect to the investment and efforts in innovation activities that are reflected in the innovation outcomes indicators like GDP per capita, etc, that are presented in Figure 5.8f.

The stronger Innovation system is important to bring forth stronger innovation outputs. In terms of *labour productivity growth*, China is ahead of India. China also scored higher in *Knowledge creation* compared to India. In China, the *Citable documents H-index* score is 58.6 compared to India's 40.8. Another important sub-component of Knowledge outcome is *Knowledge Impact*, on which China scores 52.2 while India scored 23.3. In terms of *knowledge diffusion*, too, the score of China was higher compared to India. China has around 48.5 percent of the *high-tech manufacutring* industrial sector, while India has around 34.1 percent. Further, the proportion of *high-tech exports* is also higher for China compared to India. But in terms of *ICT services exports*, India exports 11.7 percent of the total trade while China exports around two percent of its total trade.

Creative outputs are composed of three important sub-components: *Intangible assets*, *Creative goods and services* and *Online creativity*. Figure 5.8g shows that India scored higher than China in *online creativity*. It was found from the data given in the 2021 Global Innovation Index Report that in terms of *Trademarks by Origin per billion PPP$GDP*, China's score is

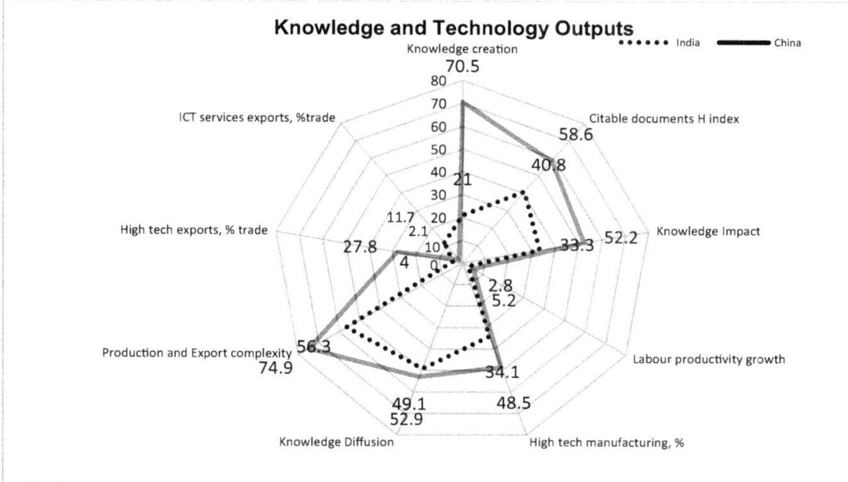

Figure 5.8f Knowledge and Technology Outputs: Comparison of India and China

Source: Global Innovation Index 2021

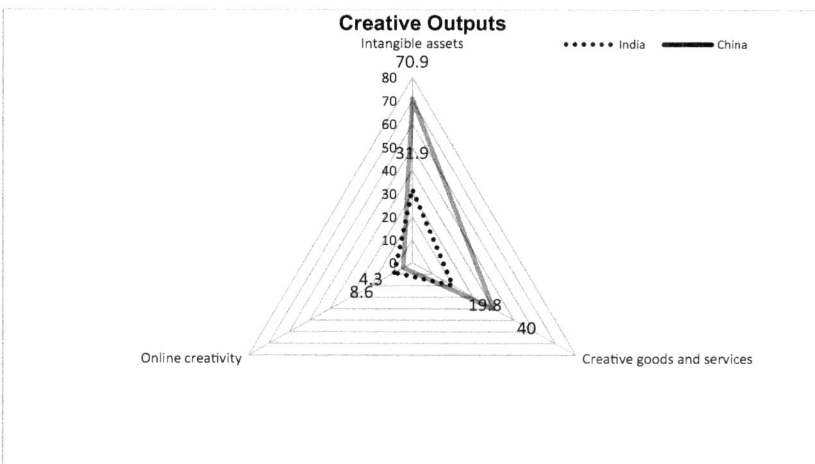

Figure 5.8g Creative Outputs in India and China

Source: Global Innovation Index 2021

about nine times that of the score for India. Also, in terms of *Global Brand Value of top 5000, as a percentage of GDP*, China is 1.6 times that of India. Similarly, in terms of *Industrial Designs by Origin per billion PPP$ GDP*, China is about 29 times that of India. This indicates that in all the variables composing the *Intangible assets*, China is ahead of India. This is an important revelation where the Indian entrepreneurs, researchers and government bodies should concentrate.

On the other hand, in *Creative goods and services*, India is 2.75 times higher than China in terms of *National feature films per million populations in the age group 15 to 69*. Similarly, in *Online creativity*, India scored 23.4 in terms of *Wikipedia edits per million population* and about 13.3 in *Mobile app creation per billion PPP$ GDP*. These results again depict that India's system of innovation needs a boost with investing in innovative inputs that produces innovative outcomes on a comparable basis with China.

To reiterate, the 'system of innovation' approach includes not only the 'technological innovation', but also emphasises the contribution of 'organisational innovations', 'institutional innovations' and the inter-relationship between them (Edquist, 2005). In the edited book by Edquist (2005), a chapter by Edquist and Johnson discusses these factors and their inter-relationship in depth. According to North (1990), organisational innovation includes innovation in the structure of political bodies including city councils, regulatory bodies, political parties, economic bodies like firms, cooperatives, trade unions, social bodies and educational bodies. Institutional innovations include innovations in the working of markets, improvement done in the routines, methodology and habits of working, including innovation in formal and informal laws. The scope of these innovation indicators is very wide and it is equally difficult to capture them properly, but there are some variables discussed that help in doing inter-temporal and inter-country comparison. This analysis depicts that India needs to concentrate more on increasing its efforts for innovation that could boost growth, productivity and inclusive development in the country.

6. Conclusion and Policy Recommendations

Knowledge is widely acclaimed as an inevitable source of growth and development. Accumulation of frontier technology and development of capabilities are the prerequisites of survival and sustainability for any nation. Competitive strength and prospectus of development is determined by the capacity of a knowledge created, accumulated and assimilated by a nation. The theoretical literature for years has been emphasising the importance of technology and innovations in stimulating growth. From exogenous growth theories, the shift towards endogenous growth theories in the late 1980s was an important phase in the development of growth theories. Also, the scholars delved deep in understanding the process of technology generation, along with its accumulation and assimilation. Investment in indigenous R&D is one of the important sources for technology accumulation, along with the investment in human capital. But it is equally important that the whole mechanism in a nation works unanimously and holistically towards the process of technology accumulation. This line of thinking is presented in the literature concerning national innovation systems. Considering innovation as a ubiquitous phenomenon, this approach (Lundvall, 1992; Freeman, 1995) regards the accumulation of knowledge and generation of innovation to be extremely complex. The process of innovation is systematic in nature and is characterised by a holistic approach encompassing the inclusion of not only economic factors but also institutional, organisational, social and political factors (Edquist, 1997). However, given the complexity involved, the literature equally emphasises the role of technology policies of the government.

The state has been central to the rise of most of the world's giant corporations. Far from simply emerging from the free market, the normal path through which the leading corporations developed was through extensive government support (Nolan, 2004; Cimoli et al., 2009).

Public policies were also framed in India and China during the late 1970s to the late 1990s to support the growth of a 'national team' of large firms that could compete with the large corporations. These policies were radically different from the free market orthodoxy (Nolan, 2004). Industrial policy in China has drawn its inspiration from non-mainstream economic theory, and from empirical evidence about the policies pursued in late-industrialising countries. The Chinese political system initially followed the Stalinist political system. The Communist Party remained in power, whereas the political system of India is democratic.

But the empirical evidence shows that although both countries are fast-growing economies in the world, the rate and structure of growth of both countries differs. The structure of the Chinese economy is comparatively more technologically sound compared to India. But both these countries also have some problems on the path of building a strong innovation system. The problem of duplication and scattering of research activities (Conroy, 1984) has hampered the development of the national innovation system of China over the years. Again, Conroy (1984) highlighted that the policy-makers choose low-risk projects that are incremental in nature rather than radical. Most research institutes are not linked to enterprises that result in lack of coordination between research, design and production (Baark, 1987).

Bosworth and Collins (2008) found that there exist serious deficiencies in the education systems of these countries. However, the literature shows that compared to India, China appears to have largely eliminated illiteracy.

It is pertinent to highlight the the importance of building a strong innovation system is the prerequisite for these countries. For both countries, there is a need to focus on need-based, high-quality, high-technology production.

Second, greater emphasis should be laid on building a strong human capital through imparting skill-based education and training to the people. Third, a greater allocation of funds should be earmarked for technology upgradation in these countries, especially in India. Fourth, to avoid duplicity and to encourage radical innovation, inter-linkages between industry, universities and research institutes should be strengthened with an emphasis on building a stronger human capital, especially in India.

Notes

1 By the mid of 2000, China became the fourth largest economy in the world after the United States, Japan and Germany, measured by the official exchange rate. Using purchasing power parity (PPP), it surpassed Germany in 1987, Japan in 1994 and is now second only to United States (Zhang and Liu, 2009).
2 China adopted economic reforms in 1978 while India started with liberalization in 1980s with the major adoption of reforms during 1991.
3 China, to start with adopted the Marxist-Leninist approach under Mao era, known as Maoism and subsequently slipped to 'Decentralized Economic Governance'
4 CSIR was set up in 1940 to provide advice on the nature of research effort necessary for industrial development (Nayar, 1983)
5 Nolan (2004) also made the comparison of Indian and Chine system of working. He asserted that 'unlike the Indian state, the Chinese state does not have to placate the interests of landlords or powerful oligopolistic groups in private industry, or to make deal with any socioeconomic group to seek electoral support'.
6 For example, in 1994, for opening the domestic market for automobile firms, China's State Planning Commission introduced a policy initiative concerning specific technology transfer requirements for these firms (Holmes et al., 2013).
7 A wide array of measures were adopted to promote exports, including foreign exchange retention rights for priority exports sectors, tax rebates and direct rewards to exporters (Nolan, 2004).
8 China maintains a battery of imports control, including state allocation of much foreign exchange and wide array of quantitative allocation. Priority was given to those imports that could enhance the productivity.

References

Ahmad, A. (1978): 'Science and Technology in Development: Policy Options for India and China', *Economic and Political Weekly*, Vol. 13, No. 51/52, 2079+2081+2083+2085+2087+2089–2090.

Amsden, A.H. (2001): *The Rise of "The Rest" Challenges to the West from Late-Industrializing Economies*, Oxford University Press, New York.

Andersen, E.S. (1992): 'Approaching National Systems of Innovation', in Lundvall (ed) *National Systems of Innovation: Towards a Theory of Innovation and Interactive Learning*, Pinter, London and New York.

Baark, E. (1987): 'Commercialized Technology Transfer in China 1981–86: The Impact of Science and Technology Policy Reforms', *The China Quarterly*, No. 111, 390–406.

Beule, F.D. (2010): 'The Role of FDI in Technology Innovation in India and China', in N.S. Siddharthan and K. Narayanan (eds) *Indian and Chinese Enterprises Global Trade, Technology and Investment Regimes*, Routledge, London, 102–116.

Bosworth, B. and Collins, S.M. (2008): 'Accounting for Growth: Comparing China and India', *Journal of Economic Perspectives*, Vol. 22, No. 1, 45–66.

Cimoli, M., Dosi, G. and Stiglitz, J.E. (2009): 'The Political Economy of Capabilities Accumulation, the Past and Future of Policies for Industrial Development', in M. Cimoli, G. Dosi and J.E. Stiglitz (eds) *Industrial Policy and Development the Political Economy of Capabilities Accumulation*, Oxford University Press, New York.

Cimoli, M., Dosi, G. and Stiglitz, J.E. (2009): *Industrial Policy and Development the Political Economy of Capabilities Accumulation*, Oxford University Press, New York.

Coe, D.T. and Helpman, E. (1995): 'International R&D Spillovers', *European Economic Review*, Vol. 39, No. 5, 859–887.

Conroy, R. (1984): 'Technological Innovation in China's Recent Industrialization', *The China Quarterly*, No. 97, 1–23.

Dahlman, C. (2009): 'Growth and Development in China and India', in M. Cimoli, G. Dosi and J. Stiglitz (eds) *Industrial Policy and Development the Political Economy of Capabilities Accumulation*, Oxford University Press, New York, 303–335.

Edquist, C. (1997): 'Systems of Innovation Approaches – Their Emergence and Characteristics', in C. Edquist (ed.) *Systems of Innovation Technologies, Institutions and Organizations*, Pinter, London.

Edquist, C. (2005): 'Systems of Innovation: Perspective and Challenges', in J. Fagerberg, D.C. Mowery and R.R. Nelson (eds) *The Oxford Handbook of Innovation*, Oxford University Press, Oxford, 181–208.

Edquist, C. and Johnson, B. (1997): 'Institutions and Organizations in Systems of Innovation', in C. Edquist (ed) *Systems of Innovation Technologies, Institutions and Organizations*, Pinter, London.

Fagerberg, J. and Godinaho, M.M. (2005): 'Innovation and Catching-Up', in J. Fagerberg, D.C. Mowery and R.R. Nelson (eds) *The Oxford Handbook of Innovation*, Oxford University Press, Oxford, 514–542.

Fleck. J. (1992): 'Configurations: Crystallising Contingency', *The International Journal of Human factors in Manufacturing*, autumn, Vol. 3, No. 1, 15–36.

Freeman, C. (1987): *Technology Policy and Economic Performance: Lessons from Japan*, Pinter, London.

Freeman, C. (1995): 'The National System of Innovation in Historical Perspective', *Cambridge Journal of Economics*, Vol. 19, 5–24.

Grossman, G.M. and Helpman, E. (1991): *Innovation and Growth in the Global Economy*, MIT Press, Cambridge, MA.

Holmes, T., McGrattan, E. and Prescott, E. (2013): 'Quid Pro Quo: Technology Capital Transfers from Market Access in China', Working Paper No. 19249, National Bureau of Economic Research (NBER), Cambridge, MA.

Keller, W. (1998): 'Are International R&D Spillovers Trade Related? Analyzing Spillovers among Randomly Matched Trade Partners', *European Economic Review*, Vol. 42, No. 8, 1469–1481.

Lichtenberg, F. and Potterie, B.P. (1998): 'International R&D Spillovers: A Comment', *European Economic Review*, Vol. 42, No. 8, 1483–1491.

Lucas, R. E. (1988): 'On the Mechanics of Economic Development', *Journal of Monetary Economics*, Vol. 22, No. 1, 3–42.

Lundvall, B.A. (1992): 'Introduction', in *National Systems of Innovation Towards a Theory of Innovation and Interactive Learning*, Pinter, London.

Maio, M.D. (2009): 'Industrial Policies in Developing Countries, History and Perspectives' in M. Cimoli, G. Dosi and J. Stiglitz (eds) *Industrial Policy and Development the Political Economy of Capabilities Accumulation*, Oxford University Press, New York, 107–143.

Mehta, S. (2013): 'Technology Spillovers and Productivity: Analysis of the Indian Manufacturing Sector', *Innovation and Development*, Vol. 3, No. 1, 55–69.

Nayar, B.R. (1983): *India's Quest for Technological Independence Policy Foundation and Policy Change*, Lancers Publishers, New Delhi.

Nelson, R.R. and Winter, S. (1982): *An Evolutionary Theory of Economic Change*, Harvard University Press, Cambridge, MA.

Nolan, P. (2004): *Transforming China Globalization, Transition and Development*, Anthem Press, London.

Romer, P.M. (1986): 'Increasing Returns and Long-Run Growth', *Journal of Political Economy*, Vol. 94, No. 5, 1002–1037.

Sachs, J.D. and Woo, W.T. (1997): 'Understanding China's Economic Performance', NBER Working Paper No. 5935, www.nber.org/papers/w5935.pdf (accessed 5 August 2014).

Saviotti, P.P. (1997): 'Innovation Systems and Evolutionary Theories', in C. Edquist (ed) *Systems of Innovation Technologies, Institutions and Organizations*, Pinter, London.

Schaaper, M. (2009): "Measuring China's Innovation System: National Specificities and International Comparisons", OECD Science, Technology and Industry Working Papers, 2009/01, OECD Publishing. http://dx.doi.org/10.1787/227277262447.

Shijun, Q. (1992): 'High-Tech Industrialization in China: An Analysis of the Current Status', *Asian Survey*, Vol. 32, No. 12, 1124–1136.

Siddharthan, N.S. and Narayanan, K. (2010): *Indian and Chinese Enterprises Global Trade, Technology and Investment Regimes*, Routledge, London, 1–34.

Siddharthan, N.S. and Nollen, S. (2010): 'The Performance of Indian ad Chinese Software Firms', in N.S. Siddharthan and K. Narayanan (eds) *Indian and Chinese Enterprises Global Trade, Technology and Investment Regimes*, Routledge, London, 74–101.

Smith, K. (2005): 'Measuring Innovation', in J. Fagerberg, D.C. Mowery and R.R. Nelson (eds) *The Oxford Handbook of Innovation*, Oxford University Press, New York.

Solow, R. (1956): 'A Contribution to the Theory of Economic Growth', *Quarterly Journal of Economics*, Vol. 70, No. 1, 65–94.

Trivedi, T. (2010): 'Growth and Productivity in the Manufacturing Sector: A Comparative View India and China', in N.S. Siddharthan and K. Narayanan (eds) *Indian and Chinese Enterprises Global Trade, Technology and Investment Regimes*, Routledge, London, 58–73.

Verspagen, B. (2005): 'Innovation and Economic Growth', in J. Fagerberg, D.C. Mowery and R.R. Nelson (eds) *The Oxford Handbook of Innovation*, Oxford University Press, Oxford, 487–513.

Xiwei, Z. and Xiangdong, Y. (2007): 'Science and Technology Policy Reform and Its Impact on China's National Innovation System', *Technology in Society*, Vol. 29, 317–325.

Zhang, W. and Liu, X. (2009): 'Introduction: Success and Challenges: An Overview of China's Economic Growth and Reform Since 1978', *Journal of Chinese Economic and Business Studies*, Vol. 7, No. 2, 127–138.

II

Innovation Systems and Developing Economies

Chapter 6

National Innovation Systems and Technological Innovation Systems for Sustained Growth

A Way Forward to Sri Lanka

Sanika Sulochani Ramanayake

1. Introduction

Traditionally, economists saw economic development as a result of an increase in factors of production such as capital, labour and natural resources that a country possesses (Lundvall et al. 2018). Hence today it is different, because economic development depends on the level of knowledge and technology it possesses (Fagerberg et al. 2010; Lee 2019). This knowledge can be defined as both local and foreign knowledge; hence, most of the developing countries failed to get the foreign knowledge for their development process. Lundvall et al. (2018) mentioned that the ability to tap into these foreign knowledge bases is of utmost importance for the economic development of a nation. Therefore, this chapter focuses on knowledge-based economic development through a national innovation system (NIS) and technological innovation system (TIS). Further, it shows the importance of NIS for sustained growth in developing countries.

In the well-known definitions, the NIS is known as the flow of technology and information among people, enterprises and institutions which is key to the innovative process at the national level; innovation and technology development are the result of a complex set of relationships among actors in the system, which includes enterprises, universities and government research institutes (OECD 1997). It further indicates that for policy-makers, an understanding of the national innovation system can help identify leverage points for enhancing innovative performance and overall competitiveness. It can assist in pinpointing mismatches within the system, both among institutions and in relation to government policies, which can impede technology development and innovation. Freeman, Lundval and Nelson defined more on NIS, and they could be the pioneers for this[1].

According to the existing literature, we can identify several indicators and mechanisms that are related to NIS and TIS. Wagner and Leydesdorff (2005) required a high-quality national education system and public and private R&D system to help link with an advanced global research network. Lee and Kim (2009) indicate that a number of patents and patent

DOI: 10.4324/9781003353904-8

applications is important for growth. Lyasnikov et al. (2014) indicates the social-economic transformations through NIS. They further identified the development of the NIS involves the sustainable development concept, a consistent change of priorities in terms of searching for, developing, testing and adopting all kinds of innovation. Using the case of Thailand, Intarakumnerd et al. (2002) explained that in contrast to developed countries, NIS in developing countries are less successful in technological catching-up. Furthermore, the European Innovation Scoreboard showed that the latecomers in the European Union increased innovation performance with low investment in R&D and more generally in knowledge industries (Galiegue 2014).

When it comes to the newly industrialized countries, mainly East Asian countries, Hikino and Amsden (1994) mentioned that Newly Industrialized Economies (NIEs) in Asia shared common characteristics with many other developing countries. Hence, most of the other developing countries are still in poor stages of technology, and too far from the process of sustained growth. Moreover, Wong (1999) indicates that among the small, late-industrializing economies in the developing world, three (Korea, Taiwan and Singapore) have achieved remarkably rapid industrial and technological catch-up. Furthermore, he mentioned that they have done so by evolving distinctly different models of NIS. Lee (2013) explained the economic catch-up process, particularly in South Korea, through developing manufacturing capacities through new technological innovations. These countries succeeded by implementing industrial policies that allow them to upgrade their competitiveness from low- to middle-, then upper-middle and even high-income countries in a relatively short period.

However, Intarakumnerd (2002) indicates developing countries which are less successful in technological catching-up.[2] Singh (2004) shows the importance of investment expenditure on innovation through R&D in developing countries. Jones and Yokoyama (2006) indicate that increasing productivity growth through innovation is a key to raising living standards.[3] Lee (2013, 2019) indicates that most of the developing countries are unable to take risks and afraid of new technological ladders with poor technological capabilities and investment capital. At the same time in many developing countries, the research capacity of universities is backwards, and they often devote their resources to undergraduate education that mostly utilizes knowledge that is imported from advanced countries (Lee et al. 2009). Therefore, knowledge has increasingly become a key source of economic growth, and with this trend, the university-industry relationship (or UIR or University-Industry Linkage hereafter) has become an important issue (Mazzoleni and Nelson 2005; Sutz 2005; Lee et al. 2009; Ramanayake 2019). Moreover, Wong (1999) says that indigenous firms from the developing countries face two common problems in terms of developing high-tech industrial capabilities: firstly, they were typically distant from the lead user markets in North America, Europe and Japan; secondly, they were also far away from and disconnected from the leading sources of technological innovation in advanced countries.

This chapter is organized as follows. The following section will discusses the mainstream literature on NIS and TIS with some definitions and some other important literature on the topic. Section 3 discusses the NIS and TIS in East Asia, particularly in South Korea and Taiwan, and identifies key factors for NIS and for the sustained growth. Section 4 discusses the NIS in Sri Lanka with progress, weakness and best practice for sustained growth. Section 5 summarises the chapter with some policy suggestions for sustained growth through NIS in Sri Lanka and for other developing countries.

2. Literature Review

2.1. Definitions and Existing Literature on NIS

The term 'national system of innovation' originated when Christopher Freeman and Bengt-Åke Lundvall worked together in the late 1980s. Freeman's research drew heavily on the political economy of Friedrich List and his historical account of the rise of Japan as an economic superpower. Lundvall's work explored the important social interactions between suppliers and customers and their role in encouraging innovation in Denmark. Hence, Lundvall (2008) revealed that the basic ideas behind the concept of NIS go back to Friedrich List (List 1841).

There are some definitions about NIS. The following describe some of them using OECD (1997) and some other sources:

> " *the network of institutions in the public and private sectors whose activities and interactions initiate, import, modify and diffuse new technologies." (Freeman 1987)*
>
> " *the elements and relationships which interact in the production, diffusion and use of new, and economically useful, knowledge . . . and are either located within or rooted inside the borders of a nation state." (Lundvall 1992)*
>
> *"a set of institutions whose interactions determine the innovative performance . . . of national firms." (Nelson 1993)*
>
> *"the national institutions, their incentive structures and their competencies, that determine the rate and direction of technological learning (or the volume and composition of change generating activities) in a country." (Patel and Pavitt 1994)*
>
> *"that set of distinct institutions which jointly and individually contribute to the development and diffusion of new technologies and which provides the framework within which governments form and implement policies to influence the innovation process. As such it is a system of*

interconnected institutions to create, store and transfer the knowledge, skills and artefacts which define new technologies." (Metcalfe 1995)

"National Innovation System (NIS) can be defined as a network of elements which include public, private and academic sector whose interactions and collaborations will induce the creation and use of knowledge for national economic benefit." (Govindaraj 2016)

The OECD report from 1997 explained some measurement and assessment of national innovation systems as follows: 1) interactions among enterprises, primarily joint research activities and other technical collaborations; 2) interactions among enterprises, universities and public research institutes, including joint research, co-patenting, co-publications and more informal linkages; 3) diffusion of knowledge and technology to enterprises, including industry adoption rates for new technologies and diffusion through machinery and equipment; and 4) personnel mobility, focusing on the movement of technical personnel within and between the public and private sectors. Attempts to link these flows to firm performance show that high levels of technical collaboration, technology diffusion and personnel mobility contribute to the improved innovative capacity of enterprises in terms of products, patents and productivity (OECD 1997, p. 7).

2.2. University-Industry Linkage (UIL)

For sustained growth through NIS, knowledge plays an important role. When we talk about knowledge, university-industry linkage comes together as a key phenomenon. However, existing literature and some scholars explained the connection between education, knowledge and UIL. Esham (2008) shows that the significance of university-industry interactions has become very important to the agenda of higher education policy-making at both the national and institutional levels. Lee and Kang (2010) suggest that there is a role for universities for firms in latecomer countries, because the firms have fewer capabilities for R&D. Mazzoleni and Nelson (2005) and Sutz (2005) point to knowledge as a key foundation of economic growth; therefore, university-industry linkages are important. Ramanayake (2019) explains the importance of UILs for sustained growth in developing countries. Seppo and Lilles (2012) measure different types of collaboration activities between universities and industry, and they indicate that a popular indicator for measuring university-industry linkages is the number and amount of patents or licenses. Moreover, with regard to the positive impacts of UILs, Valentín (2000) explains the benefits that arise from university-industry interactions. Franco and Haase (2015) examine the interface between researchers' motivations and interaction channels concerning university-industry cooperation. Furthermore, there are a group of studies that discuss university-industry relationships, such as Branscomb et al. (1999); Etzkowitz et al. (2000); Rosenberg and Nelson (1994) and OECD (2002).

2.3. *Triple Helix Model of Innovation*

There is a robust connection between NIS, UIL and the Triple Helix Model of innovation. The Triple Helix Model refers to a set of interactions between academia, industry and government, to foster economic and social development, as described in concepts such as the knowledge economy and knowledge society. Lundvall (2008) mentioned that knowledge production (Gibbons et al. 1994) and the Triple Helix approach focus on science and the role of universities in innovation. However, Eun et al. (2006) observe that there are diverse modes of the UIR[4], and the UIR in each country tends to take a certain mode depending upon several country- or sector-specific factors. Figure 6.1 indicates the beginning of the Triple Helix Strategic Interaction in a middle-income country. The Triple Helix identified university, industry and government. Figure 6.1 indicates the connectivity between these three helixes.

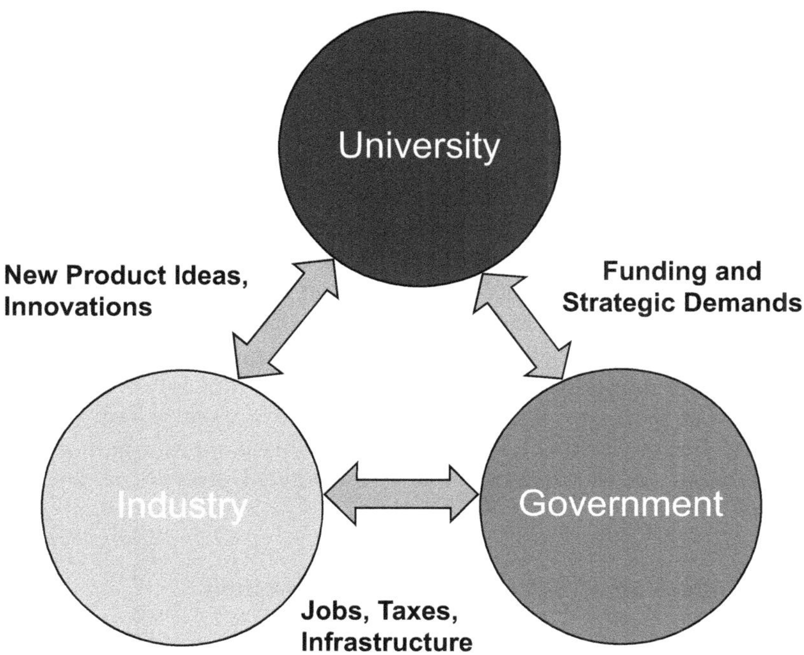

Figure 6.1 Beginning of Triple Helix Strategic Interactions in a Middle-Income Country (Push-Pull)

Sources: Based on Kimatu (2016)

Furthermore, Leydesdorff and Etzkowitz (1998); Etzkowitz and Zhou (2006) and others have been discussed the Triple Helix Model for growth.

3. Some Lessons from East Asia

Taiwan, Korea and Singapore have managed to achieve significantly faster high-tech industrial growth over the last three decades than all other developing countries (Wong 1999). Hence, this growth led the knowledge-based national innovation system. Haggard (2004) indicates that institutions have played a central role in the political economy explanations of East Asia's growth. At the same time, Mok (2012) indicates that national innovation systems of the four Little Tigers in East Asia are in Hong Kong, Singapore, Taiwan and South Korea. Further, he has identified that a national innovation system is characterized by the interactions between the state, industries and universities in promoting innovation. His study has paid particular attention to the role of higher education, specifically, in university-industry collaboration in these four countries.

OECD (1997) and Lee (2019) specify that countries tend to develop along certain technological paths or "trajectories" determined by past and present patterns of knowledge accumulation. Which path a country takes is determined largely by institutional factors, often specific to a country, including the broad range of interactions that characterize the national innovation system.

Wong (1999) indicates some key indicators for sustained growth via TIS in Korea, Singapore and Taiwan. They are: resource-based view of the firm, the network interaction perspective on the technological learning process, and institutional economics perspective on the contexts of late industrialization. At the same time, Amsden (1995) argued that market-friendly state interventions and getting prices right has been rightly criticized as ignoring the substantial state intervention role in these countries. Hence, Lee (2013, 2019) stated that in the case of Korea, the importance of and following of different technological trajectories, taking detours (not following the same technological path of the frontrunners) and advantage of risk-taking (in industrial sectors such as leapfrogging, path following and path creating) are significant for economic growth and sustained growth for developing countries.

3.1. Comparison of NIS Interrelated Dimensions

This section compares interrelated dimensions to NIS in some selected East Asian countries, with a special focus on South Korea and Taiwan. Existing exploration identified some variables as vital for measuring innovative performance of a country. According to Carvalho (2015), number of patents, private & public R&D and percentage of innovative firms are significant measures for innovation performances in a country. Moreover, Kim et al. (2012) indicate that the numbers of patent applications are important for NIS. Therefore, this sector focused on these key indicators as a comparison.

3.1.1. R&D Spending in GDP

Figure 6.2 shows the R&D expenditure in selected East Asian countries. According to the data, South Korea spent 4.8% for R&D in 2018. Combined with the Ministry of Science and ICT, the South Korean government and the private sector's spending of 89.05 trillion won for R&D in 2019. South Korea remains the fifth-largest R&D spender among the OECD countries. Expressively, South Korea's private sector spent 68.5 trillion won in R&D in 2020 and (76.9%), while public sector R&D spend 19.1 trillion won (21.4 % of the total).[5] This condition is significant and unique compared with many other countries.

Tim Mazzarol from the University of Western Australia in Perth, who specializes in innovation and entrepreneurship, said that the high R&D intensity helped South Korea become a global leader in information and communication technologies. At the same time, Korea emerged from a historically top-down innovation system that promotes "close collaboration between government, industry, and the academic community in the process of nation building" (Ref_154_FILE150404190006).[6]

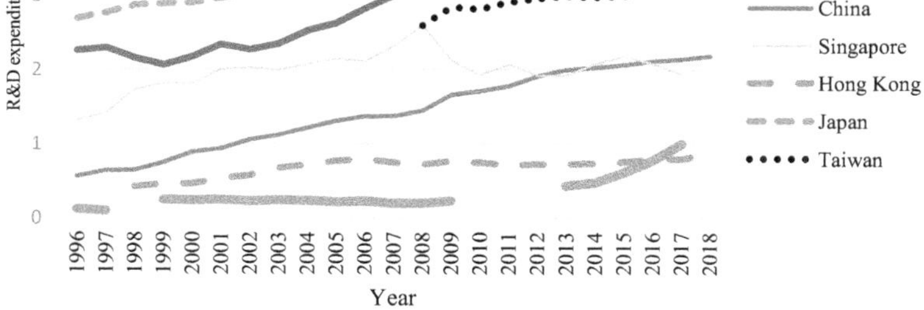

Figure 6.2 R&D Expenditure (% of GDP) – 1996–2018

Source: Using World Bank WDI data created by the Author (*Taiwan data is from Statistica.com)

Taiwan remains the second largest investor on R&D in this figure. Taiwan's R&D spending accounted for 3.36 percent of the national GDP.

China also increased its R&D intensity, particularly after 2000. China's spending on R&D climbed 10.3 percent to 2.44 trillion Chinese yuan ($378 billion) and accounted for 2.4 percent of GDP in 2020. However, China is going to focus on developing a number of technology areas including semiconductors, health care, quantum computing and cloud computing, according to a draft of its five-year plan.[7] At the same time, after 2008, newly emerging Thailand also shows a significant growth on R&D expenditure. It is total 182.357 billion THB in 2019, or 1.11 percent of GDP, and a 17.5 percent increase from the 2018.[8]

3.1.2. Number of Patent Applications

WIPO (2019) indicates that patent applications worldwide grew by 5.2 percent in 2018. In 2018, there were 3.3 million filled patent applications. The report indicates that such strong growth was an exceptional number of filings in China, which received about 160,400 more filings in 2018 than it had in 2017. However, WIPO indicates that five patent offices account for 75 percent of all patents filed and 75 percent of patents granted worldwide. These are the US, Japan, the European Patent Office, South Korea and China.

Table 6.1 presents the top 20 countries in the world for patent applications in 2018. According to the data, South Korea ranked in 4th place, Taiwan ranked 16th and Singapore ranked 18th, while newly emerging China remained first in the world ranking list in 2018.

Table 6.1 Patent applications for the top 20 countries in 2018 in the world

Rank	*Country*	*Patent Applications*	*Rank*	*Country*	*Patent Applications*
1	China	1,542,002	11	Australia	29,957
2	US	597,141	12	Brazil	24,857
3	Japan	313,567	13	UK	20,941
4	South Korea	209,992	14	Mexico	16,424
5	European patent office	174,397	15	France	16,222
6	Taiwan	73,431	16	China Hong Kong SAR	15,986
7	Germany	67,898	17	Iran	12,823
8	India	50,055	18	Singapore	11,845
9	Russian Federation	37,957	19	Italy	9,821
10	Canada	36,161	20	Indonesia	9,754

Sources: WIPO 2019 (www.wipo.int/edocs/pubdocs/en/wipo_pub_941_2019.pdf)

Year	Korea	China	Japan
2010	178,654	308,326	468,441
2011	187,752	436,168	475,070
2012	203,835	561,405	490,271
2013	223,527	734,093	473,139
2014	230,553	837,813	465,971
2015	238,185	1,010,524	457,948
2016	233,801	1,257,425	456,549
2017	226,614	1,306,080	460,771
2018	232,021	1,460,246	460,376
2019	248,427	NA	452,130

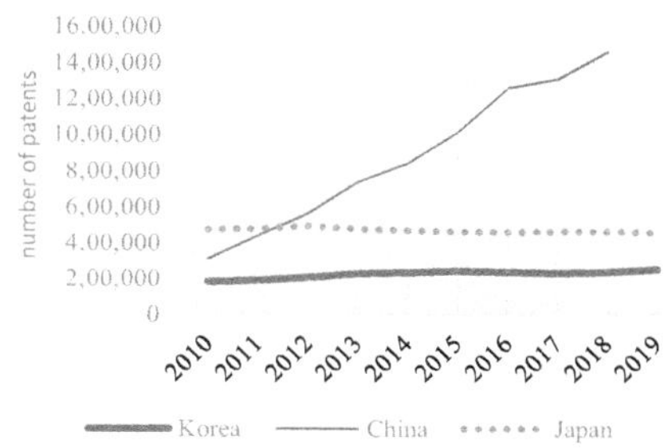

Figure 6.3 Number of Patents in Selected Countries

Source: Using WIPO online data created by the author (NA: Not available)

Furthermore, South Korea continues to file the highest number of patents per unit of GDP, with 8,561 resident patent applications per unit of USD 100 billion GDP (WIPO 2019, p. 16)

According to the TIPO Statistics Report: Patent and Trademark Applications in 2018, Taiwan (ROC) is not a member of the United Nations, and the number of patents filed in Taiwan is not reported separately from China in the indicators. Therefore, the number of patent applications filed with the Taiwan Intellectual Property Office (TIPO) in 2018 was 73,431[9], which would place it in 6th place worldwide for that year, or 2nd place per capita.

The following diagram (Figure 6.3) indicates the number of patents owned by some countries in East Asia. It is clear that Korea and China are increasing their patents, while China's growth is significant since 2010. Also, Japan has declined.

Figure 6.3 indicates the number of patent applications in Korea and China from 2010 to 2019. In the case of Korea, the largest number of patent applications was represented by residents. At the same time, there are some patent applications by nonresidents and abroad applicants. In the case of China, the largest number of patent applications was by by residents and lowest number of applications by nonresidents and abroad applicants. Somehow, there is a significant growth in patent applications by China since 2010.

3.1.3. University-Industry Linkage (UIL) in East Asia

When considering UILs as a new vehicle for catch-up, Lee and Kang (2010) have found that those that have certain R&D capabilities and thus conduct some R&D are the most frequent users of services from universities or public research institutes (PRIs). This implies that the relationship between R&D by firms and that by universities is more complementary than

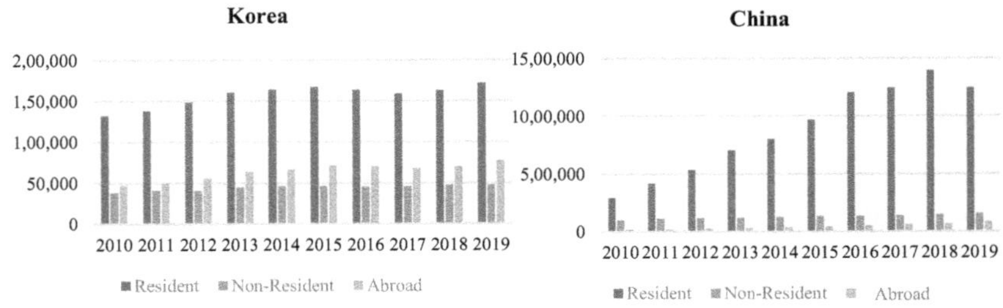

Figure 6.4 Patent Applications in Korea and China

Source: Using WIPO online data created by the author

substituting. It indicates that South Korea's contract-based research and China and Malaysia's joint projects, contract research and licensing have significant contributions to economic growth. Moreover, Lee (2014) found that universities are an important research partner of private firms, although industrialists often do not trust the research capabilities of universities. Further, it suggests that the government policies to promote university-industry R&D cooperation have been strengthening. Also, Sohn et al. (2009) examine the role of the Korean government in creating UILs and in promoting the role of universities as knowledge providers in regional innovation systems. They additionally argued that government policy is the main determinant that drives Korean universities to play the role of knowledge provider for industrial innovation.

In the case of China, Wu (2007) mentions that a key component of China's recent reforms in the national innovation system is driven by the university-based research and technology transfer. Xue (2004) explains that China's innovation system has experienced a dramatic change over the last 15 years. Therefore, the evolution of the university-market linkages in China has been greatly influenced and conditioned by such changes. They further said that the academia-market linkage provides the impact and connection to the global innovation system.

4. The Dynamics of NIS, Innovation and Technological Behaviors in Sri Lanka

According to the OECD (1997), the NIS approach reflects the increasing attention given to the economic role of knowledge; the intent is to evaluate and compare the main channels for knowledge flows at the national level, to identify bottlenecks and to suggest policies and approaches to improve their fluidity. This involves tracing the links and relationships among industry, government and academia in the development of science and technology.

Such analysis may ultimately lead to the ability to measure the "knowledge distribution power" of a national innovation system, which is considered one determinant of growth and competitiveness. Therefore, it is clear that there are some important measurements to develop NIS in a country. This section will discuss some of the key measurements which are principal to the NIS in Sri Lanka.

4.1. Research & Development Intensity (R&D)

Kuen Lee (2013) leads to a more negative conclusion in terms of R&D in developing countries. He argued that middle-income countries generally present low ratios of R&D. This statement is true in the context of Sri Lanka as well.

Figure 6.5 indicates the R&D expenditure in Sri Lanka for the period from 1966 to 2017. In 2010, Sri Lanka's spending on R&D equalled 0.16 percent of GDP. This is comparatively lower than other South Asian neighbours. India is at 0.81 percent, Pakistan at 0.33 percent, and Nepal is at 0.30 percent respectively.[10] At the same time, since 2013 R&D expenditure as a percentage of GDP was 0.11 percent in Sri Lanka, which is still lower than many lower-income countries like Sudan and Ethiopia. Significantly, statistics show that Ethiopia spent 0.6 percent for R&D as a percentage of GDP in 2013.

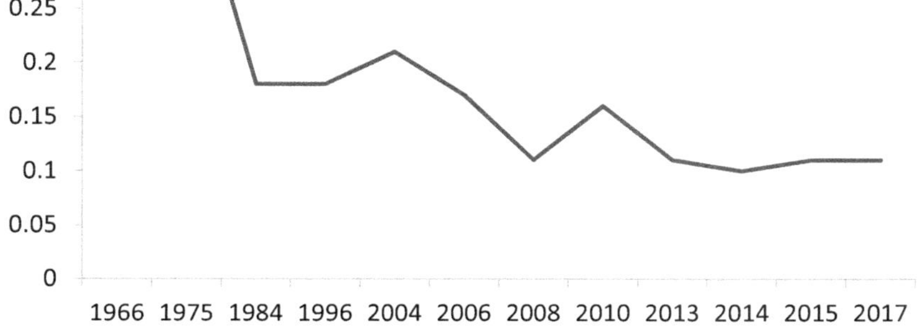

Figure 6.5 Gross Expenditure on R&D in Sri Lanka 1966–2017 (as a % of GDP)

Source: Using data form National R&D Surveys Sri Lanka, 1996 (NARESA), 2000, 2004, 2006, 2008, 2013, 2014 & 2015 (NSF), 2017 (WDI) created by the author

However, Larsen et al. (2016) indicate that Sri Lankan universities have had a low level of R&D activity. In 2010, only 11 percent of R&D expenditure was carried out by universities, compared with 45 percent by government research institutes and 44 percent by business enterprises respectively. According to the statistics from the National Science Foundation (NSF) and the national R&D survey (2015), national gross expenditure on R&D by the government sector uses 34.1 percent, higher education sector uses 32 percent, business enterprise uses 34 percent, and private non-profit sector uses 0.4 percent respectively (see Table 6.2 for more details).

When we compare national R&D expenditure by different disciplines, the highest expenditure is for agricultural science (31.5 percent), and the lowest is for social science and humanities (5.4 percent). Furthermore, natural science was 26.6 percent, engineering and technology 25.1 percent, medical science 8.6 percent, and other was 2.8 percent respectively (see Table 6.3 for the statistics).

However, in Sri Lanka, more of the R&D expenditure was spent for applied research, which is recorded at 55.85 percent. The second-largest is

Table 6.2 National gross expenditure on R&D by sector of performance (year 2015)

Sector	*Recurrent*	*Capital*	*Total*	*%*
Government	3,008.1	1,054.4	4,062.5	34.1
Higher Education	3,749.1	46.2	3,795.3	31.9
Business Enterprise	3,656.3	347.9	4,004.2	33.6
Private Non-Profit	40.1	2.0	42.1	0.4
Total	10,453.6	1,450.5	11,904.1	100.0

Source: National R&D Survey Sri Lanka, 2015 (NSF)

Table 6.3 National R&D expenditure of different sectors by discipline in 2015

Discipline	*Higher Education*	*State Sector*	*Business Enterprise*	*PNP*	*Total*	*%*
Natural Sciences	1,182.8	888.1	1,060.8	38.6	3,170.3	26.6
Engineering & Technology	679.5	683.1	1,629.0	0.2	2,991.8	25.1
Medical Sciences	974.5	42.8	1.8	0.0	1,019.1	8.6
Agricultural Sciences	419.3	2,035.1	1,291.7	0.0	3,746.1	31.5
Social Sciences & Humanities	253.9	390.6	0.0	3.3	647.8	5.4
Other	285.3	22.8	20.9	0.0	329.0	2.8
Total	3,795.3	4,062.5	4,004.2	42.1	11,904.1	100

Source: National R&D Survey Sri Lanka, 2015 (NSF)

for experimental development research, recorded at 30.13 percent. And the lowest R&D spent is for basic research, at 14.02 percent.

4.2. Number of Patent Applications

The World Intellectual Property Organization (WIPO) says that patents are the engine of economic growth. Further, it elaborates that the number of patent applications filed worldwide almost doubled between 1985 and 2004. It rose from 884,400 to 1,599,000 with an average annual rate of increase of 4.75 percent since 1995. A patent is important because it can help safeguard your invention.[11] Therefore, this is focused on patents in Sri Lanka.

Table 6.4 indicates the number of IP fillings and patent applications in Sri Lanka from 2010 to 2019. The data shows some growth of patent applications in all three categories (Resident, Non-resident, and Abroad). In 2010, there were 225 resident patents, which increased to 356 in 2019. At the same time, there were 235 non-resident patents, which increased to 255 in 2019. Likewise, in 2010 it was 18 abroad patents, which increased to 56 in 2019. IP filings in Sri Lanka show some growth from 2010 to 2019. However, this growth is not significant and is unable to boost the Sri Lankan economy. Compared to other countries, particularly in some countries in East Asia, this is significantly low (discussed in section 3).

Figure 6.5 indicates the total number of patent applications and registered patents in Sri Lanka for the period from 1995 to 2018. It signals that the total number of patent applications increased from 114 to 603 during this period. However, the registered number of patents shows stagnation during

Table 6.4 Number of patents & patent applications in Sri Lanka (2010–2019)

Sri Lanka		*IP Filings (Resident + Abroad, Including Regional) and Economy*			*Patent applications*		
Year	*Patent*	*Trademark (class count)*	*Industrial Design (design count)*	*GDP (Constant 2017 US$)*	*Resident*	*Non-Resident*	*Abroad*
2010	243	5,225	381	184.93	225	235	18
2011	214	5,156	686	200.47	194	235	20
2012	n.a.	7,211	678	218.8	n.a.	n.a.	33
2013	445	6,899	295	226.23	328	188	117
2014	n.a.	n.a.	n.a.	237.45	n.a.	n.a.	17
2015	264	7,440	405	249.34	218	263	46
2016	316	9,351	309	260.53	280	293	36
2017	331	n.a.	485	269.85	277	266	54
2018	382	9,161	486	278.78	343	260	39
2019	412	7,987	606	285.14	356	255	56

Source: Using WIPO statistics database (last updated 01–2021) (n.a: Not available)

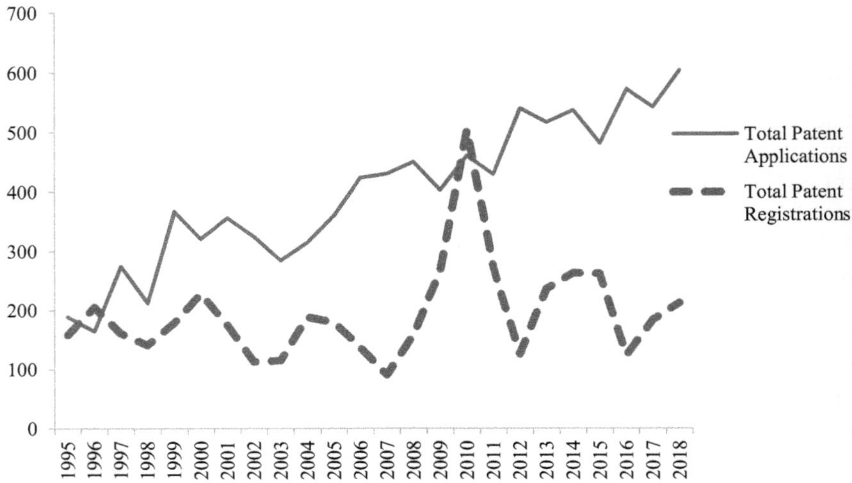

Figure 6.6 Total Patent Applications and Total Patent Registrations – 1995–2018

Source: Using statistics from National Intellectual Property Office, Ministry of Science, Technology and Research created by the Author

this period. Thus, during the period from 2007 to 2012, this shows some increase; however, after that it has declined again. In 2018, there remained only 212 registered patents in Sri Lanka.

Figure 6.6 indicates foreign patents versus domestic patents in terms of registration applications. It shows an increasing trend of domestic patent applications. However, data illustrates that after 2016, domestic patent applications are higher than foreign applications. Nevertheless, in terms of registered patents, immobile foreign patents are higher than the domestic patents.

As indicated earlier, this growth is not significant when we compare it to some emerging countries. The Government of Sri Lanka needs to promote the significance and necessity of patents and patent applications for Sri Lankan universities and business firms. Moreover, IP protection (Institutional Property) in Sri Lanka is still at a very basic level.

4.3. Innovation Process and Growth

As we have seen, evaluating the performance of national innovation systems is not an easy thing to do. Galiegue (2014) indicates that with a low investment in knowledge activities in a country, it is not easy to get a higher return and higher input level in knowledge. Figure 6.6 shows the ranking of Global Innovation Index in 2019, where Sri Lanka ranked 89th in the World.

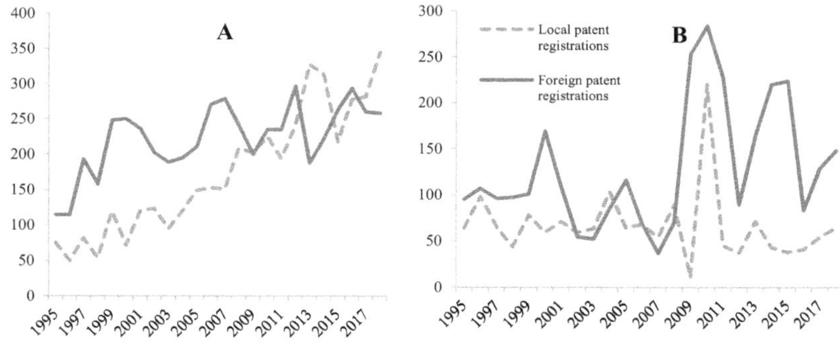

Figure 6.7 Foreign Patents Vs. Domestic (Local) Patents

Source: Using statistics from National Intellectual Property Office, Ministry of Science, Technology and Research created by the Author

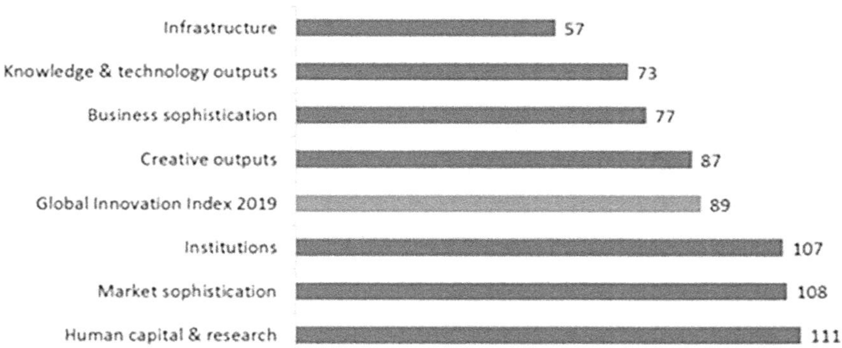

Figure 6.8 Overview of Sri Lanka's Rankings in the 7 GII Areas

Source: Using statistics from National Intellectual Property Office, Ministry of Science, Technology and Research created by the Author

Figure 6.8 indicates the bubble chart between income levels (GDP per capita) and innovation performance (GII score). The trend line gives an indication of the expected innovation performance according to income level. According to this indicator, economies appearing above the trend line are performing better than expected, and those below are considered innovation underperformers relative to GDP (Global Innovation Index 2019). Sri Lanka is below the line.

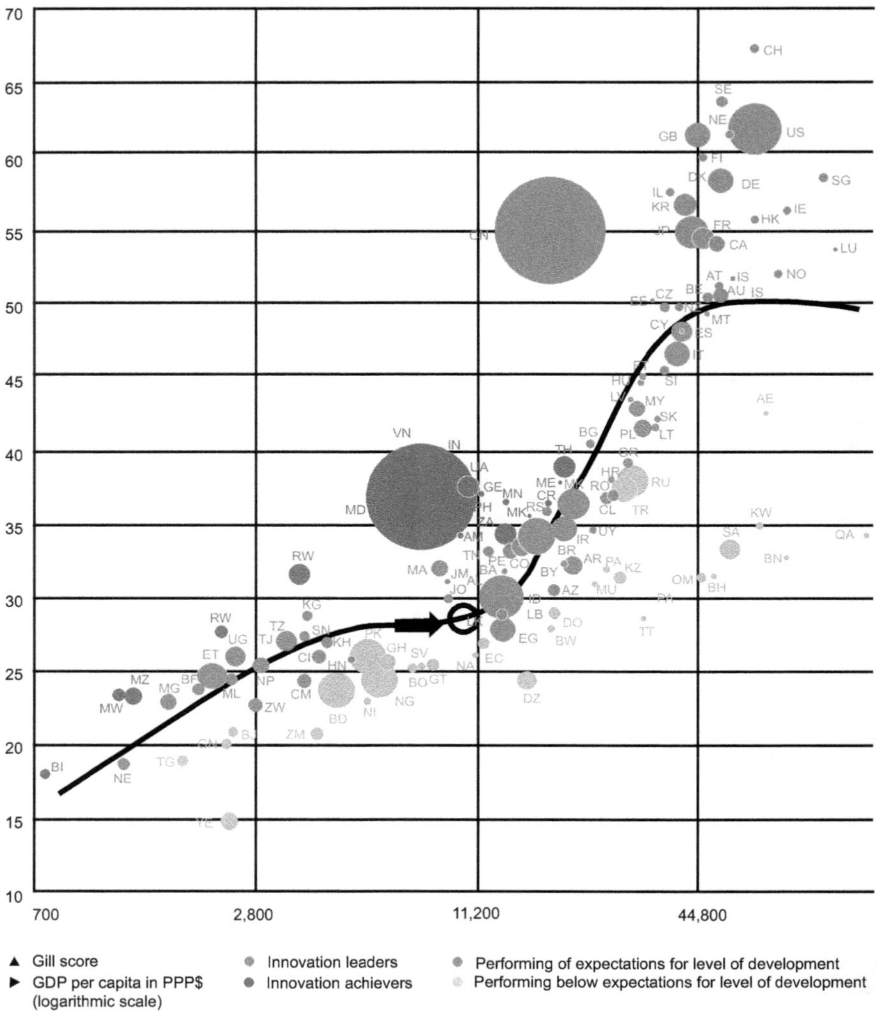

Figure 6.9 GII Scores and GDP Per Capita in PPP US$ (bubbles sized by population)

Source: The Global Innovation Index 2017

4.4. Weakness Found in Sri Lanka to Look Forward

As a section summary, I would like to discuss some of the important elements which connect with NIS and economic growth. Table 6.5 indicates 2019 ranks in GII Sri Lanka. While all of the indicators are important in this list, I highlighted four most important indicators for NIS (highlighted

Table 6.5 Weaknesses and its ranks – Sri Lanka

Source: WIPO, Global Innovation Index 2019 (www.wipo.int/edocs/pubdocs/en/wipo_pub_gii_2019/lk.pdf)

Weaknesses

Code	Indicator name	Rank
1.2	Regulatory environment	127
1.2.3	Cost of redundancy dismissal, salary weeks	126
2	Human capital & research	111
2.1.1	Expenditure on education, % GDP	107
2.1.2	Government funding/pupil, secondary, % GDP/cap	96
2.2	Tertiary education	113
2.2.3	Tertiary inbound mobility, %	96
2.3.2	Gross expenditure on R&D, % GDP	105
2.3.3	Global R&D companies, top 3, in mn US$	43
4.1	Credit	113
4.1.1	Ease of getting credit*	104
5.1.2	Firms offering formal training, % firms	78
5.2.3	GERD financed by abroad, %	87
6.1.4	Scientific & technical articles/bn PPP$ GDP	111

in green). According to that, expenditure on education as a share of GDP in Sri Lanka ranked 107, Tertiary education ranked 113, Gross expenditure on R&D as a share of GDP raked 105 and scientific and technical articles (bn PPP$ GDP) ranked 111.

All of these mentioned indicators have significant impacts on NIS and growth (as you can see from the discussed case studies, and even in China); thus, most of the developing countries, including Sri Lanka, perform very poorly.

4.5. Best Practices to Follow-up

By tradition, universities have been considered the place of invention, education and research (Wallmark 1997; Mian 1994; Esham 2008). Thus, industry is the home of innovation, which thereby creates a kind of distinction. However, the connectivity between these two is a lacuna in Sri Lanka

Table 6.6 High-technology exports in selected countries 2010–2017 (Current US$ Million)

Category	*Country Name*	*2010*	*2013*	*2014*	*2015*	*2016*	*2017*
	Australia	4590	5367	5488	5124	5407	4942
	Canada	27248	32769	29531	28847	26797	27593
Developed countries	France	106441	119315	121376	110206	109317	109359
	Germany	180523	210021	216163	199797	204385	196321
	Israel	10585	11744	12409	13754	12200	12058
	Korea, Rep.	132079	143485	149060	147119	135914	166675
	Japan	130195	111571	107607	98537	99291	106416
East Asia	China	474522	655996	653870	652237	594552	654188
	Singapore	131971	143759	145602	139342	135616	147179
	Malaysia	65679	67099	70965	64475	63220	74136
South East Asia	Philippines	n.a	n.a	n.a	n.a	n.a	33502
	Thailand	37211	37091	38523	38294	38799	n.a
	Vietnam	6069	32759	36377	47524	55215	74114
	India	10779	17965	18345	14616	14301	15161
	Nepal	4	2	4	3	4	6
South Asia	Pakistan	268	354	264	268	311	362
	Sri Lanka	**62**	**72**	**71**	**63**	**67**	**79**
	Bangladesh	38	69		94		
	Ethiopia	9	9	26	17	10	
Africa	Mauritius	6	6	0	1	1	28

Source: World Bank – WDI data

and in many other developing countries. If this connection works well in Sri Lanka (like other advanced or emerging countries like South Korea, China and Taiwan), Sri Lanka could also be a country rich with innovative exports and sustained growth.

4.5.1. High-Tech Exports

When we compare high-technology exports in Sri Lanka, it is declining and limited for labour-intensive primary exports such as textiles and garments, and some agricultural products. According to World Bank data, high-technology exports in Sri Lanka in 2015 was 63 million; in 2017 it was 79 million. The data shows that Sri Lankan high-tech exports are very low compared to most other developing countries. Furthermore, high-technology exports (as a share of manufactured exports) are very low in Sri Lanka, and it is 1 percent from 2010 to 2017 (see Figure 6.8). High-technology exports are products of high R&D intensity, such as aerospace, computers, pharmaceuticals, scientific instruments and electrical machinery. However, Sri Lanka is incapable of fighting with the global market and market competition. Therefore, this can cause growth decline or inability to sustain economic growth.

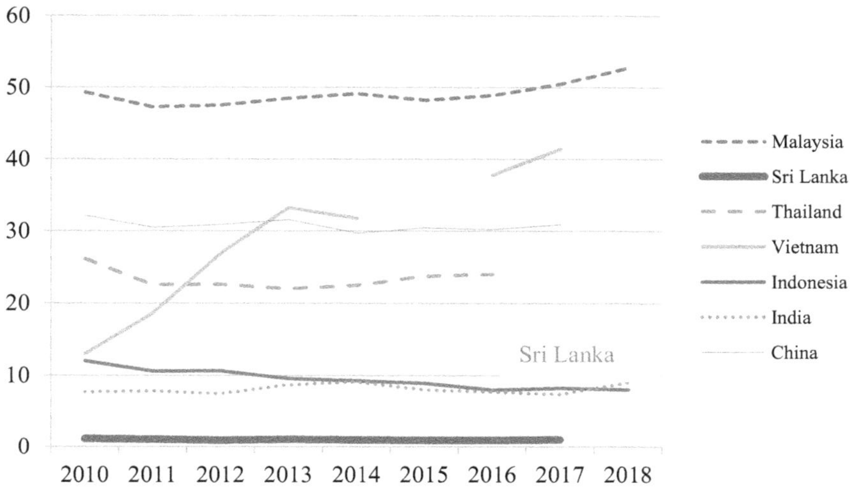

Figure 6.10 High-Technology Exports (% of Manufactured Exports) in Selected Countries

As you can see in the figure, Malaysia is performing so well with high-technological exports. At the same time, literature evidenced that the UILs are strong in Malaysia.[12] Therefore, Malaysia can be a good example for an emerging country with good performance in the global export market.

4.5.2. Research & Development for New Innovations

As explained before, R&D plays a significant role for NIS and sustained growth. Therefore, the government should aim to raise R&D expenditure to at least 1.5 percent of GDP and distribute public funds on innovation in a few high-impact areas. Sri Lankan universities and research labs are not well linked with industry, unlike many other developed and emerging economies. Government interventions to connect universities and industries are necessary to NIS. As an example, in Taiwan over 70 percent of the R&D resources are held by universities (Wang et al. 2013); most of South Korea's universities have their own industrial sectors to produce new inventions by the university systems (ex: Seoul National University hospital, Seoul National University Milk industry etc.).

4.5.3. Business Incubators

Business incubators help entrepreneurs translate their ideas into workable and sustainable businesses by guiding them from inception to becoming a growing and thriving business. Business incubation provides entrepreneurs with expertise, networks and tools that they need to make their ventures successful (National Business Incubation Association). As an example, Taiwan has one of the highest densities of higher-education institutions in the world in 2011 and boasts 163 colleges and universities.[13] There are currently 98 college-level institutions with innovation incubators in Taiwan, and 11 corporate-funded innovation incubators in the area. These business incubators play a role as knowledge and technology sharing hubs for the countries, which in turn helps the NIS and economic growth. Additionally, Mian's (1996) study indicates the importance of business incubators as providing and nurturing environment for new business start-ups.

5. Conclusions and Policy Suggestions

Mainly South Korea and Taiwan achieved sustained growth through the adoption and adaptation of technologies through the NIS. Now, China is escaping the middle-income trap by following the same path through NIS. The technological innovation process has been documented in existing literature for sustained growth (Lee 2013, 2019). At the same time, most of the middle-income countries and developing countries failed to sustain growth because of their specialization in low-technological industries and inability to upgrade their specialization in more advanced technologies. Sri Lanka is one example. Growth-driven NIS-associated indicators are not performing very well in Sri Lanka. Therefore, the Sri Lankan government should take action by introducing and developing new policies to uplift the NIS.

5.1. Suggestions and Policy Development for Sri Lanka

- Link to the development of user innovation, or innovation by users (Gault and Von Hippel, 2009); that is a major source of the innovation product and process. This kind of innovation has been encouraged by the development of the information and communication technologies. Promote adapted technologies and leapfrogging innovation strategies.
- Promote university-industry R&D cooperation; it can be a good strengthening to the NIS. Therefore, the government needs to make some policies to connect the university and industrial sectors for R&D through some newly designed policy programmes.
- Development of good research infrastructure in the universities and maintaining high-quality research with the foreign and local expertise while focusing on industrial linkages. At the same time, improve the indicators used to map interactions in NISs as well as the linkages to the innovative performance of firms.
- Most of the developing countries begin to set up basic industries using low-skilled labor; even in Sri Lanka, Textiles and Clothing (T&C) are

the main export industry. Therefore, Sri Lanka needs to upgrade this specialization to get the comparative advantage from these industries in international trade. Economic activities in Sri Lanka need to be more knowledge-intensive, especially in the export market.

- In terms of productions and export industries, not only upgrade the same industries, but also introduce new innovative industries to grab the market for higher profit gain industries (similar to South Korea: first they were exporting hair wigs, then moved into the garment industry, shipbuilding, semiconductors, Digital TV (LED), mobile, and now into pharmaceuticals which is a long cycle sector with a highly R&D-intensive industry). Relevant policies need to be taken from the government side to encourage the private sector for global market competition with higher profits.

5.2. Policy Suggestions for Development of Sri Lanka

Innovation is the main determinant of long-term economic development. Therefore, strengthening NIS could lead to sustained growth in developing countries.

Introduction of more innovative product cycles are essential in Sri Lanka. Changing the labour-intensive product cycle into a technology-based, more innovative product cycle could be a better policy implication. At the same time, Sri Lanka needs to upgrade this specialization to get a comparative advantage in international trade and global markets. Through this process, the country is able to achieve higher export earnings. As Ramanayake and Lee (2015) suggested, sustained export growth is a key determinant of economic growth for developing countries in the long run since they can invest those export incomes into capital investment. However, today Sri Lanka is facing a huge economic crisis during the post-pandemic era (especially late 2021 and early 2022), due to lack of dollar reserves and high debt rate. Obviously, this caused by many miscontrolled and wrong policies conducted by the previous governments, as well as the current government since independence in 1948. This is a different story that is unable to be addressed in this chapter.

However, to overcome the crisis in the long run, a country like Sri Lanka can promote university-industry R&D cooperation. This can be a backbone of the NIS. Therefore, the government needs to make some policies to connect the university and industrial sectors for R&D. Development of good research infrastructure in the universities and maintaining high-quality research with foreign and local expertise is essential with a focus on industrial linkages. This can lead to an increased number of patents and patent applications.

In terms of productions and export industries, not only upgrading the same industries, but also introducing new innovative industries can grab the market for higher profit-gain industries. Relevant policies need to be taken from the government side to encourage the private sector for global market competition with higher R&D capability.

Policies that promote user innovation could be encouraged by the development of information and communication technologies in other countries. This helps to promote adapted technologies and leapfrogging innovation strategies. Therefore, the government needs private firms on user innovations by providing benefits and encouraging both public and private firms to collaborate with foreign firms with higher technological capabilities, mostly through joint venture companies investing in local firms with government support.

Notes

1 The first edition of Lundvall (1992) and of Nelson (1993), introduced the concept of NIS, was known only by a handful of scholars and policy makers.
2 In case of Thailand.
3 In case of Japan
4 UIR: University Industry Relations
5 S. Korea's R&D spending 5th largest among OECD members in 2019, https://en.yna.co.kr/view/AEN20201209003800320#:~:text=Korea's%20. Accessed on 2020–03–05
6 How South Korea made itself a global innovation leader, www.natureindex.com/news-blog/how-south-korea-made-itself-a-global-innovation-leader-research-science. Accessed on 2021–03–02
7 China spending on research and development to rise 7% per year in push for major tech breakthroughs, www.cnbc.com/2021/03/05/china-to-boost-research-and-development-spend-in-push-for-tech-breakthroughs.html. Accessed on 2021–03–02
8 NXPO announces survey results of 2018 R&D expenditure and R&D personnel, www.nxpo.or.th/th/en/5008/#:~:text=Kitipong%20Promwong%20recently%20announced%20Thailand's,increase%20from%20the%20previous%20year. Accessed on 2021–03–02
9 TIPO Statistics Report: Patent and Trademark Applications in (2018), www.tipo.gov.tw/en/cp-282-699109-b7d57-2.html. Accessed on 2021–02–20
10 For India and Pakistan 2011 data, and for Nepal 2010 data.
11 Patents are engine of economic growth, says WIPO, https://sciencebusiness.net/news/73133/Patents-are-engine-of-economic-growth%2C-says-WIPO#:~:text=The%20number%20of%20patent%20applications,of%20some%205.6%20per%20cent. Accessed on 2021–03–03
12 Chandran at el. (2014)
13 Higher Education in Taiwan, https://ws.moe.edu.tw/Download.ashx?u.pdf

References

Amsden, A. H. (1995). Inductive theory in economic development: A tribute to Wassily Leontief on his 90th birthday. *Structural Change and Economic Dynamics*, 6(3), 279–293.

Branscomb, L. M., Kodama, F., & Florida, R. (Eds.). (1999). *Industrializing knowledge: University-industry linkages in Japan and the United States*. Cambridge, MA: The MIT Press.

Carvalho, N., Carvalho, L., & Nunes, S. (2015). A methodology to measure innovation in European Union through the national innovation system. *International Journal of Innovation and Regional Development*, 6(2), 159–180.

Dayton, L. (2020). *How South Korea made itself a global innovation leader*. www.natureindex.com/news-blog/how-south-korea-made-itself-a-global-innovation-leader-research-science (accessed 2 March 2021).

Esham, M. (2008). Strategies to develop university-industry linkages in Sri Lanka. *National Education Commission Sri Lanka Study Series*, (4), 2007–2008.

Etzkowitz, H., Webster, A., Gebhardt, C., & Terra, B. R. C. (2000). The future of the university and the university of the future: Evolution of ivory tower to entrepreneurial paradigm. *Research Policy*, *29*(2), 313–330.

Etzkowitz, H., & Zhou, C. (2006). Triple Helix twins: Innovation and sustainability. *Science and Public Policy*, *33*(1), 77–83.

Eun, J. H., Lee, K., & Wu, G. (2006). Explaining the "University-run enterprises" in China: A theoretical framework for university – industry relationship in developing countries and its application to China. *Research Policy*, *35*(9), 1329–1346.

Fagerberg, J., Srholec, M., & Verspagen, B. (2010). Innovation and economic development. In *Handbook of the economics of innovation* (Vol. 2, pp. 833–872). North-Holland. Amsterdam, The Netherlands. https://www.sciencedirect.com/handbook/handbook-of-the-economics-of-innovation/vol/2/suppl/C

Franco, M., & Haase, H. (2015). University – industry cooperation: Researchers' motivations and interaction channels. *Journal of Engineering and Technology Management*, *36*, 41–51.

Freeman, C. (1987). Technical innovation, diffusion, and long cycles of economic development. In *The long-wave debate* (pp. 295–309). Berlin; Heidelberg: Springer.

Galiegue, X. (2014, May). National innovation systems and economic catch up: Lessons from recent experiences. In *10th international conference of ASECU*, Cluj-Napoca (pp. 16–17).

Gault, F., & Von Hippel, E. (2009, October). *The prevalence of user innovation and free innovation transfers: Implications for statistical indicators and innovation policy*. Georgia Institute of Technology. https://smartech.gatech.edu/bitstream/handle/1853/35350/1237573208_FG.pdf?sequence=1&isAllowed=y

Gibbons, M., Limoges, C., Nowotny, H., Schwartzman, S., Scott, P., & Trow, M. (1994). *The new production of knowledge: The dynamics of science and research in contemporary societies*. SAGE.

Global Innovation Index. (2019). www.wipo.int/publications/en/details.jsp? (accessed 2 March 2021).

Govindaraj, S. (2016). *A study of the national innovation system of Sri Lanka*. Doctoral dissertation. http://dl.lib.uom.lk/handle/123/11657

Haggard, S. (2004). Institutions and growth in East Asia. *Studies in Comparative International Development*, *38*(4), 53–81.

Hikino, T., & Amsden, A. H. (1994). Staying behind, stumbling back, sneaking up, soaring ahead: Late industrialization in historical perspective. In *Convergence of productivity: Cross-national studies and historical evidence* (pp. 285–315). UK: Oxford University Press.

Intarakumnerd, P., Chairatana, P. A., & Tangchitpiboon, T. (2002). National innovation system in less successful developing countries: The case of Thailand. *Research Policy*, *31*(8–9), 1445–1457.

Jones, R. S., & Yokoyama, T. (2006). *Upgrading Japan's innovation system to sustain economic growth*. OECD Library. https://www.oecd-ilibrary.org/economics/upgrading-japan-s-innovation-system-to-sustain-economic-growth_365562216004
Kim, Y. K., Lee, K., Park, W. G., & Choo, K. (2012). Appropriate intellectual property protection and economic growth in countries at different levels of development. *Research Policy*, *41*(2), 358–375.
Kimatu, J. N. (2016). Evolution of strategic interactions from the triple to quad helix innovation models for sustainable development in the era of globalization. *Journal of Innovation and Entrepreneurship*, *5*(1), 1–7.
Larsen, K., Bandara, D. C., Esham, M., & Unantenne, R. (2016). *Overview of university-industry collaboration in Sri Lanka*. E-library World Bank. https://elibrary.worldbank.org/doi/abs/10.1596/978-1-4648-0922-4_ch1
Lee, K., Joseph, K. J., Abraham, V., Eun, J. H., Wu, G., Wang, Y., . . . & Kang, R. (2009). Promoting effective modes of university-industry interactions and their evolution for economic catch up in Asia. *IDRC Final Report*.
Lee, K., & Kang, R. (2010). University-industry linkages and economic catch-up in Asia. *Millennial Asia*, *1*(2), 151–169.
Lee, K., & Kim, B. Y. (2009). Both institutions and policies matter but differently for different income groups of countries: Determinants of long-run economic growth revisited. *World Development*, *37*(3), 533–549.
Lee, K. R. (2013). *Schumpeterian analysis of economic catch-up: Knowledge, path-creation, and the middle-income trap*. Cambridge: Cambridge University Press.
Lee, K. R. (2014). University – industry R&D collaboration in Korea's national innovation system. *Science, Technology and Society*, *19*(1), 1–25.
Lee, K. R. (2019). *The art of economic catch-up: Barriers, detours and leapfrogging in innovation systems*. Cambridge: Cambridge University Press.
Leydesdorff, L., & Etzkowitz, H. (1998). The triple helix as a model for innovation studies. *Science and Public Policy*, *25*(3), 195–203.
List, F. (1841). *Das nationale der politischen oekonomie*. Cotta. https://books.google.lk/books?hl=en&lr=&id=pnM5AAAAcAAJ&oi=fnd&pg=PA1&dq=List,+F.+(1841).+Das+nationale+der+politischen+oekonomie.+Cotta&ots=F3PCoCaj93&sig=VpgqwS8gOJuKYJiav1oNECoHdLQ&redir_esc=y#v=onepage&q&f=false
Lundvall, B. A. (1992). *National systems of innovation: An analytical framework*. London: Pinter.
Lundvall, B. Å. (2008). *Innovation system research: Where it came from and where it might go*. Georgia Institute of Technology. https://smartech.gatech.edu/handle/1853/43444
Lundvall, B. Å., Fagerberg, J., & Srholec, M. (2018). *National innovation systems, openness and global value chains: Towards a taxonomy*. http://liee.ntua.gr/wp-content/uploads/2018/02/246-National-Innovation-Systems-Openness-and-Global-Value-Chains-.pdf
Lyasnikov, N., Dudin, M., Sekerin, V., Veselovsky, M., & Aleksakhina, V. (2014). The national innovation system: The conditions of its making and factors in its development. *Life Science Journal*, *11*(6), 535–538.
Mazzoleni, R., & Nelson, R. R. (2005). *The roles of research at universities and public labs in economic catch-up* (No. 2006/01). LEM Working Paper Series. https://www.econstor.eu/handle/10419/89427

Metcalfe, J. S. (1995). Technology systems and technology policy in an evolutionary framework. *Cambridge Journal of Economics*, *19*(1), 25–46.
Mian, S. A. (1994). US university-sponsored technology incubators: An overview of management, policies and performance. *Technovation*, *14*(8), 515–528.
Mian, S. A. (1996). The university business incubator: A strategy for developing new research/technology-based firms. *The Journal of High Technology Management Research*, *7*(2), 191–208.
Mok, K. H. (2012). The quest for innovation and entrepreneurship: The changing role of university in East Asia. *Globalisation, Societies and Education*, *10*(3), 317–335.
Nelson, R. R. (Ed.). (1993). *National innovation systems: A comparative analysis*. Oxford: Oxford University Press on Demand.
OECD. (1997). www.oecd.org/science/inno/2101733.pdf
OECD. (2002). *Benchmarking industry-science relationship*. Paris: OECD.
Patel, P., & Pavitt, K. (1994). National innovation systems: Why they are important, and how they might be measured and compared. *Economics of Innovation and New Technology*, *3*(1), 77–95.
Ramanayake, S. S. (2019). *University industry linkage to sustain education & growth in Sri Lanka*. https://www.researchgate.net/profile/Sanika-Ramanayake/publication/345501730_University_Industry_Linkage_to_Sustain_Education_Growth_in_Sri_Lanka/links/5fa7ef12299bf10f732fee8e/University-Industry-Linkage-to-Sustain-Education-Growth-in-Sri-Lanka.pdf
Ramanayake, S. S., & Lee, K. (2015). Does openness lead to sustained economic growth? Export growth versus other variables as determinants of economic growth. *Journal of the Asia Pacific Economy*, *20*(3), 345–368.
Rosenberg, N., & Nelson, R. R. (1994). American universities and technical advance in industry. *Research Policy*, *23*(3), 323–348.
Seppo, M., & Lilles, A. (2012). Indicators measuring university-industry cooperation. *Discussions on Estonian Economic Policy*, *20*(1), 204.
Singh, L. (2004). Globalization, national innovation systems and response of public policy. *International Journal of Technology Management & Sustainable Development*, *3*(3), 215–232.
Sohn, D. W., Kim, H., & Lee, J. H. (2009). Policy-driven university – industry linkages and regional innovation networks in Korea. *Environment and Planning C: Government and Policy*, *27*(4), 647–664.
Sutz, J. (2005). The role of universities in knowledge production. *Himalayan Journal of Sciences*, *3*(5), 53–56.
Valentín, E. M. M. (2000). University – industry cooperation: A framework of benefits and obstacles. *Industry and Higher Education*, *14*(3), 165–172.
Wagner, C. S., & Leydesdorff, L. (2005). Network structure, self-organization, and the growth of international collaboration in science. *Research Policy*, *34*(10), 1608–1618.
Wallmark, J. T. (1997). Inventions and patents at universities: The case of Chalmers University of Technology. *Technovation*, *17*(3), 127–139.
Wang, W. B., Hung, Y. C., & Wang, C. C. (2013). University-industry business incubators in Taiwan. *Open Journal of Business and Management*, *1*(1), 1.
WIPO. (2019). *World intellectual property indicators 2019*. www.wipo.int/edocs/pubdocs/en/wipo_pub_941_2019.pdf (accessed 5 March 2021).

Wong, P. K. (1999, June). National innovation systems for rapid technological catch-up: An analytical framework and a comparative analysis of Korea, Taiwan and Singapore. In *DRUID Summer Conference* (pp. 9–12). https://www.academia.edu/5996386/National_innovation_system_for_rapid_technological_catch_up_An_analytical_framework_and_a_comparative_analysis_of_Korea_Taiwan_and_Singapore

Wu, W. (2007). Cultivating research universities and industrial linkages in China: The case of Shanghai. *World Development*, *35*(6), 1075–1093.

Xue, L. (2004). University – market linkages in China: The case of university-affiliated enterprises. In *Symposium on University, Research Institute and Industry Relations in the US, Taiwan and Mainland China, Stanford Project on Regions of Innovation and Entrepreneurship*, Palo Alto, CA.

Chapter 7

An Innovation Systems Perspective on Agricultural Technology Diffusion

The Case of India's Sericulture

Rajesh GK and Mammo Muchie

A few years ago, one of the authors of this chapter presented a paper on farmer-level adoption of a hybrid silkworm in India in an international conference held at Tampere University. A discussant found the econometric model employed a 'black box' and narrated the following story in substantiating his critique.

> A country in Sub-Saharan Africa developed a high-yielding *dwarf* variety hybrid-corn through an ambitious publicly-funded project. The hybrid was certainly superior to the ruling *tall* variety. However, farmers rejected the hybrid in spite of attractive promotional schemes. Where economists failed, an anthropologist succeeded in bringing to light the rather uncanny reason behind the fiasco. *Tall* corn-fields were serving safe haven to village couples, deprived of privacy in their single-roomed *rondavels* where large families lived. In all likelihood the village folk were horrified at the prospect of the *dwarf* variety replacing their clandestine retreats, potentially exposing the entire community to the threat of imminent depopulation.

The story had no evidence whatsoever. Nevertheless, it was reminiscent of the Rosenbergian expression of the black box: 'necessity to break open and to examine the contents of the black box into which technological change has been consigned by economists' (Rosenberg, 1982).

Technological innovations and their diffusion are major concerns in developing-country agriculture. Agricultural processes and technologies differ from industrial ones on account of being biological processes conditioned by natural environments (Hayami, 1974), marked by location specificity (Evenson, 1974), leading to several adoption and diffusion processes and technological options (Feder et al., 1985). Moreover, the tendency to see agriculture as a science is disputed as it cannot be studied scientifically in all its aspects[1] (Spedding, 1979).

DOI: 10.4324/9781003353904-9

Rosenberg (1970) observed that transfer of technologies in agriculture is difficult as it is an 'open system', subject to interactions between human beings and the natural environment. He identified three hurdles in application of technologies in developing country-agriculture: 1) Solutions to agricultural problems hinge upon knowledge 'which [is] not ordinarily possessed by the cultivato'; 2) Major breakthroughs come through application of scientific breakthroughs in rich countries; and 3) Uncertainty concerning application of new technologies due to high sensitivity to even minor variations in weather conditions, pests and diseases. Thus, abilities of research, ability to produce new knowledge and the element of uncertainty are crucial factors to be taken into consideration during policy formulation in agricultural environments.

The neoclassical economic perspective as applied in agricultural innovations brought to light several factors as 'variables' determining production, innovation and diffusion of agricultural technologies. Nevertheless, such modelling attempts, employing econometric tools, have not been successful in bringing out the entire truth behind the phenomena. The linear, top-down system of agricultural innovations and transfer itself is now considered a major hurdle to the progress of the sector in developing countries (Biggs, 1990, Hall et al., 2003, World Bank, 2009). Historical evolution of theoretical perspectives in agricultural innovation exhibits a paradigm shift from top-down to systemic approaches (Hall, 2007; Hall et al., 2001 and Klerkx et al., 2012). Agricultural Innovation System (AIS) is a relatively recent theoretical perspective in this evolutionary trajectory. AIS is still in its infancy and yet to be fully developed into a dependable 'analytical focusing device' for policy development in developing country agriculture.

This chapter attempts to contextualise agricultural technology diffusion in an 'Innovation Systems' perspective through the case study of a subsystem of Indian agriculture, namely sericulture. The central focus of this chapter is not the empirical investigation of the problem per se. This chapter rather focusses on the theoretical and conceptual issues concerning analysis of diffusion of agricultural innovations in the systemic angle. In this process, the authors demonstrate selection of an analytical framework through a theoretically informed, problem focused and empirically sound method. The rest of the chapter is divided as follows: A review of the Innovation Systems thinking in general and Agricultural Innovation Systems in particular is undertaken in Part I. The problem addressed as a case study is introduced in Part II. In Part III, the application of the theory is demonstrated, and the results of the empirical investigation presented.

1. A Brief Overview of Innovation Systems Thinking

Modern innovation theory has its roots in the works of Joseph Schumpeter. Schumpeter criticised the neoclassical economic theory as being 'ahistorical': hanging in a historical vacuum, 'static: not evolutionary', 'inefficient over time' (though efficient at any point of time), the market being 'not competitive' and compared the neoclassical approach with a 'planned economy' (Schumpeter, 1928, 1934, 1942). Schumpeter proposed two patterns in evolution of the firm-level innovative activity, later known as Schumpeter Mark-I & II. Mark-I presents the case of late-nineteenth-century European industry where small innovative firms found easy entry by replacing the older, less innovative ones and in the process, eliminated the quasi-rents associated with the outdated innovations (Nelson and Winter, 1982; Kamien and Schwartz, 1982). Mark-II was inspired by early-twentieth-century American industry, where large innovative firms with dedicated R&D departments created barriers to entry for new firms (Malerba and Orsenigo, 1995). One important criticism of Schumpeter's later works has been the disproportionate weight he attached to the supply side on matters of innovation. He thought the demand side would passively adjust to the supply side. It is in this setting that the concept of National Innovation Systems took shape, as a criticism of the Schumpeterian inattention of the demand side (Lundvall, 2016), as Schumpeter Mark-III (Lundvall, 2007).

A few early foundational works that nurtured systems thinking dealt with the role of 'interaction and feedback' on firm-level innovations (Rothwell, 1977), evolutionary economics (Nelson and Winter, 1982), sectoral pattern of interactions (Pavitt, 1984), technical change and economic performance (Dosi, 1984), technical change and employment (Freeman and Soete, 1987), the chain-linked model (Kline and Rosenberg, 1986), an empirical study of the Japanese National Innovation System (Freeman, 1988) and studies in relation to foreign trade (Dosi et al., 1990). Now, there are several concepts representing the systemic perspective on innovation: Regional Systems of Innovation (Cooke, 1996), Technological Systems (Carlsson and Stankiewicz, 1991) and Sectoral Systems of Innovation (Breschi and Malerba, 1997), to name a few. The multiplicity of approaches differentiated by narrow margins could be rather startling to someone new to the field.

1.1. National Systems of Innovation

The first, most original, comprehensive and popular concept in this genre is undoubtedly National Systems of Innovation (NSI). The expression was coined by Christopher Freeman and Bengt Ake Lundvall, each 'accusing' the other of its paternity. While Freeman (1995) asserted it was Lundvall in Dosi et al. (1988), Lundvall credited it to Freeman in his book on technology policy and economic performance in Japan (Freeman, 1987). However, one thing both scholars agree upon is their indebtedness to Friedrich List's conception of 'The National System of Political Economy' (1841).

Freeman (1994), in the introduction to his Critical Survey of the Economics of Technical Change, states that it is a paradox that mainstream economics fails to acknowledge the role of 'technical innovation', while Karl Marx and Schumpeter had recognised it as the most important source of dynamism in capitalist economies. Some of the 'reasons' associated with this neglect have been: i) considering technical change as outside the economist's specialisation, hence treated as exogenous (Blaug, 1964); ii) data constraints on quantitative measurement of technology (Jewkes et al., 1958); and iii) predisposition of economists with the 'Keynesian Problem' (Freeman, 1994). The 1980s and 90s saw a renewed interest in innovations. NSI draws considerably from evolutionary economics and recognises NIS as an 'evolutionary concept' stressing knowledge and learning. The evolutionary core of NSI has been built on the following assumptions (Lundvall, 2007):

1) 'Location specificity' of knowledge: Elements of knowledge are localised. They can't be easily transported;
2) 'Tacitness' of knowledge: Elements of knowledge are embodied in the minds and body of people and their interrelations;
3) Learning as 'interactionist' process: Learning and innovation is an outcome of interaction;
4) Learning as a 'socially embedded' process: Being a socially embedded process, a purely economic analysis and interpretation wouldn't suffice;
5) 'Interconnectedness' of learning and innovation: Learning and innovation are connected but not identical processes;
6) 'Production, trade and knowledge base are determinants' of national systems; and
7) 'Systemic' characteristics of national systems: The elements of NSI are interdependent and interrelations are important for the innovation process.

Lundvall (2016) explicitly states that the IS framework is engaged in straight competition with standard economics, as the latter 'disregards diversity of agents' and the processes of 'learning and competence building'. The theoretical foundation of NSI rests on the following principles:

1) Science is important for innovation: NIS upholds the idea that science is a productive force (Lundvall and Lorenz, 2012).
2) Interaction and feedback as roots of innovation: Innovation is characterised by interactive learning (Lundvall, 1985, 1992) between various agents involved in the process. The process from science to innovation is not a linear process, but an interactive process (Freeman, 1994; Lundvall, 1996).
3) Learning by Doing and Learning by Interactions: The basic approach to innovation in NSI is learning by doing, learning by using and learning by interacting (Freeman, 1994; Freeman & Soete 2005). NSI sees knowledge as a mixture of explicit codified elements called 'information', which can

be easily transferred, and passive elements 'embodied' in people called 'tacit knowledge', which is not in the brain, but in the body of people (Freeman, 1991, 1994, 1995; Lundvall, 1999).

4) Experience-based learning versus scientific learning: NIS identifies two types of learning activity as determined by the tacit and codified attributes of knowledge. The STI Mode (Science Technology Innovation) is characterised by science approach, formalisation, 'explicitation' and codification. The DUI mode is characterised by learning by doing, using and interacting. That is experience-based, implicit, embedded and embodied (Freeman, 1991, 1994, 1995; Ernst and Lundvall, 1997; Johnson Lorenz and Lundvall, 2002).
5) The Learning Economy: Lundvall and Johnson, 1994 constructed the idea of 'learning economy' as a concept wherein the capability of individuals to learn becomes essential for success. According to Lundvall and Johnson, 1994 learning is not just acquiring information. It refers to building new competencies and acquiring new skills.

Dosi (2007) in his preface to Christopher Freeman's *Selected Essays*, identifies that Freeman had developed an analytical style combining micro events (say, specific innovations), "meso" dynamics (e.g. the competitiveness and the patterns of evolution of particular industries) and macro patterns concerning income growth, employment and relative success/decline of particular countries. Much in keeping with this style, which Dosi referred to as a 'rare virtue', Lundvall (2016) prescribed a methodology to study the National Innovation System. The steps involved in this methodology moves from 'micro to macro and back again to micro':

- Analyse what takes place inside firms (innovation in the light of organisational setup and human resources while taking into account sector specialisation).
- Analyse interactions among firms and with knowledge infrastructure, including both domestic and international linkages.
- Explain national specificities in these respects with reference to national education, labour markets, financial markets, welfare regimes and intellectual property regimes.
- Use firm organisation and network positioning as factors that explain the specialisation and performance of the innovation system.

The Directorate for Science Technology and Industry at OECD in its report on National Innovation Systems (OECD, 1997) assimilated most of the foundational work and accorded credibility to NIS among policy-makers in OECD countries. The World Bank (2006) recommended use of the Innovation Systems concept in agriculture[2]. The NIS concept is now well-established and used extensively in many countries across all continents.

1.2. Evolution of 'Innovation Systems Thinking' in Agriculture

Originally, agriculture had a linear adoption-diffusion model. Rogers' model (Rogers, 2003) was very strong and was very useful to explain some dynamics but wasn't useful to explain all dynamics, and also had to capture the diversity of producer, the diversity of farming strategies, etc. Criticism about the top-down model popped up in the 1980s. Since then, the concept of 'supply of technologies through pipeline' and 'supply-push from research as the driver of innovation' shifted to learning farmers' constraints through surveys (1980s), transfer of technology approach (Jarrett, 1985), Induced Innovation (Ruttan and Hayami, 1984), Training and Visit System (Hulme, 1992), Participatory Research and Participatory Technology Development (Farrington and Martin, 1988; Neef and Neubert, 2011), Farmer First (Chambers et al., 1989) and Agricultural Knowledge and Information Systems (AKIS) (Röling, 2009). The idea of Agricultural Innovation Systems (AIS) is the latest in this line.

The notion of an 'institutional system' is not new in agriculture. Rosenberg (1970), who studied Japanese agriculture, attributed its success to progression through low-cost fertiliser, new farm implements, high-quality education and extension work towards mechanisation – all operating within a healthy and supportive institutional system. Hence, policy-makers of other countries attempting to catch up with the Japanese success story were intrigued as to how to incorporate these functions in 'an institutional system' that would perform successfully in those countries. Thus, the 'institutional system' was identified as a crucial factor in systems thinking in agriculture. However, the Rosenbergian notion remained underdeveloped until the emergence of AKIS and RAAKS.

Two versions of 'systems thinking' emerged during the 2000s. Neil Roling and Paul Engel proposed these early versions through their ideas of an Agriculture Knowledge Information System[3] (AKIS) and Rapid Appraisal of Agricultural Knowledge Systems[4] (RAAKS) respectively, yet these concepts were never used on the scale they deserved (Röling,1990). Hall (2007) observed that

> the originally well-conceived idea was distorted, overemphasising the strengthening of agricultural education processes. It did recognise that many different sources of information exist, but was still fixated on methods of passing this information to farmers.

Roling's original thinking on AKIS acknowledged the importance of Interactive Learning feedback loops between all kinds of players in the agricultural system, and was based on the idea of knowledge production and use as a systemic process involving a wide range of different actors and interaction (Roling, 1990; Hall, 2007). However, the AKIS model did not become a well-structured policy framework or 'a conceptual focussing device', but was relegated to the ranks of an extension method. AKIS, as originated from the 'extension perspective' and not 'research perspective', focussed more on 'actors and processes in the rural environment'. The AKIS framework ignored the role of physical markets, the private sector, the policy environment and other disciplines and sectors. In spite of its recognition of transfer of information from farmer to research system, it continued to foster a top-down approach when it came to technology transfer (Hall et al., 2006).

Klerkx (2012) acknowledges that AIS emerged parallel to AKIS. It was pioneered by Andy Hall, a Science Policy Research Unit (SPRU) alumnus, and was influenced by National Systems of Innovation (Lundvall, 1992; Hall et al., 2001, 2006). However, AIS did not directly engage with the mainstream Innovation Systems thinking of SPRU; perhaps this was a lost opportunity to impart more theoretical and conceptual strength to the framework!

AIS are defined as:

> a network of organisations, enterprises, and individuals focused on bringing new products, new processes, and new forms of organisation into economic use, together with the institutions and policies that affect the way different agents interact, share, access, exchange and use knowledge.
> (Hall et al., 2006)

Thus, AIS has been a result of deepening of understanding of the nature of innovation as a 'process' and consequent realisation that neoclassical economics alone cannot explain the dynamics of economic systems (Hall et al., 2003). One could perceive in AIS an influence of the empirical works of Freeman et al. (1987) on the 'institutional arrangements associated with innovation performance', the 'evolutionary economics perspective' exemplified by works of Nelson and Winter (1982), the 'complex systems ideas that explain human behaviour' (Clark et al., 1995), the two modes of knowledge production (Gibbons et al., 1995) and the analytical ocussing device of the National Innovation System (NIS) (Lundvall, 1992), which encompassed most of the other ideas. Klerkx et al. (2012) attested to this cross fertilisation. AIS has internalised the fundamental tenets of NSI in the sectoral context; that is, innovations are seen as embedded information that agents can use in different ways, depending on their ability to learn, gather information and use it creatively in response to market opportunities or other social needs, depending on the organisational cultures and ability of agents to interact and exchange knowledge through networks, linkages and interventions ().

There are many concerns regarding the applicability of AIS in developing countries. Spielman (2008) found that 'AIS in the developing country context is nascent and the empirical evidence of its overall effect on generation and diffusion of agricultural innovations is limited'. AIS still is in the process of its evolution into a freestanding, all-encompassing and self-organising theoretical construct that allows its uninhibited and efficient use as a theoretical framework to address important real-life issues in developing country-agriculture. Hall (2007) advised readers to take all 'how-to manuals' on applying innovation systems perspective to the design and implementation of agricultural research projects with a huge pinch of salt.

An important step towards developing a methodology for AIS was taken by Hall, Mytelka and Oyeyinka (2006) and subsequently by the World Bank (2006), by drafting a set of 'operational concepts'. In the process, an 'analytical framework', 'operational framework' and an 'intervention

Table 7.1 Procedure for systemic assessment of AIS

Components of assessment	*Key questions to be answered*
Sector timeline and evolution	i) Triggers of emergence (technical/policy/market/other) ii) Main players and their characteristics (public, private, elite groups of farmers, local or foreign companies, international development agencies) iii) History and evolution (market, technology or policy changes, turning points) iv) Other dynamics in the sector and the manner in which the system copes with it (exit, decline or taking alternative paths).
Sector mapping: (research domain, enterprise domain, demand domain)	i) Main actors and organisations in the sector; what role do they play ii) Which actors and competencies are missing iii) Is policy required to change the role of the public sector, or to encourage others to play different roles/ play existing roles more effectively
Habits and practices of organisations	i) Whether interacting, knowledge flows and learning ii) Whether investing ii) Whether inclusiveness of poor stakeholders and the demand side
Wider policy and support structures	i) Policies encouraging innovation ii) Policies having a positive/negative/neutral impact on the behaviour of actors iii) Contradictory policies that are counteracting each other iv) Polices that do not work being affected by habit, practices and institutions of actors and organisations v) Additional measures/incentives needed to account for non-working policies vi) Are support structures effective and if not, how do they need to be adopted?

Source: Prepared from Hall et al. (2006)

framework' for assessing AIS were developed. The methodology depends on 'understanding of historical patterns of development in order to provide context to an assessment of the current situation' (Hall et al., 2006) and gives a practical procedure to make a systemic assessment of AIS under four broad components of assessment, as detailed in Table 7.1.

Having considered the methodologies outlined for Innovation Systems in general and AIS in particular, the following section undertakes a diagnostic assessment of the 'Sericulture Innovation System (SIS)' as a case study, employing a combination of these methodologies.

2. 'Sericulture Innovation System (SIS)' as a Case Study

Sericulture is the agro industry of silk production. India's sericulture sector evolved through continuous and conscious efforts in technological upgradation. A major preoccupation of these technological up-gradations has been genetic improvement of the indigenous silkworm. This quest to breed a high-yielding and disease-resistant hybrid has contributed to the evolution of a system and vice-versa.

Silk is important to India primarily because of its potential to generate rural employment and environmentally sustainable livelihood options (Jayaram et al., 1998, Benchamin and Giridhar, 2005). The farm component of the industry, namely sericulture, is constrained in India by low productivity, low quality of produce – namely raw silk[5], price instability and import competition[6], consequently threatening the domestic industry[7] (Rajesh and Ramaswamy, 2015). The root cause of these constraints is the poor quantitative and qualitative performance of the prevalent, traditional, low-yielding silkworm varieties. To ameliorate them, a superior hybrid and technology package, the 'Bivoltine-Hybrid Technology (BVHT) package[8]' was evolved as early as the 1970s, and systematic popularisation efforts began during the 1990s. However, BVHT did not diffuse well. The current percentage of BVHT adoption is around only 20.0 per cent (Ramakrishnan, 2001; Kumaresan, 2002 and Rajesh and Ramaswamy, 2015).

Per cent contribution of BVHT in India from the 8th Five-Year Plan to 2017–18 is furnished in Table 7.2; which is indicative of BVHT diffusion over the 25 years. Over this period, the diffusion rate has increased from just three per cent to 26 per cent. While considering the efforts that has gone into the R&D and promotional efforts, the 26 per cent diffusion over a quarter century is a poor diffusion rate.

The diffusion curve illustrated in Figure 7.1 gives a distorted sigmoid curve, unlike the standard 'S' shaped diffusion curves. This is due to absence of rapid growth in diffusion during the decade from 2002 to 2011.

During this period, the total cocoon and silk production in the country was growing at a slower average growth rate of around three per cent per annum.

Table 7.2 Indian silk production over plan periods

Plan	*Year*	*Silk production ton*			*% contribution of BVHT silk*
		BV	*CB*	*Total*	
VIII	1992–97	387	12567	12954	3.0
IX	1997–02	840	15002	15842	5.3
X	2002–07	1089	15436	16525	6.6
XI	2007–08	1175	15070	16245	7.2
	2008–09	1250	14360	15610	8.0
	2009–10	1200	15122	16322	7.4
	2010–11	1400	14960	16360	8.6
	2011–12	1685	16587	18272	9.2
XII	2012–13	1984	16731	18715	10.6
	2013–14	2559	16917	19476	13.1
	2014–15	3870	17520	21390	18.1
	2015–16	4613	15865	20478	22.5
	2016–17	5266	16007	21273	24.8
2017–18	2017–18	5874	16192	22066	26.6

Source: CSB, 2019

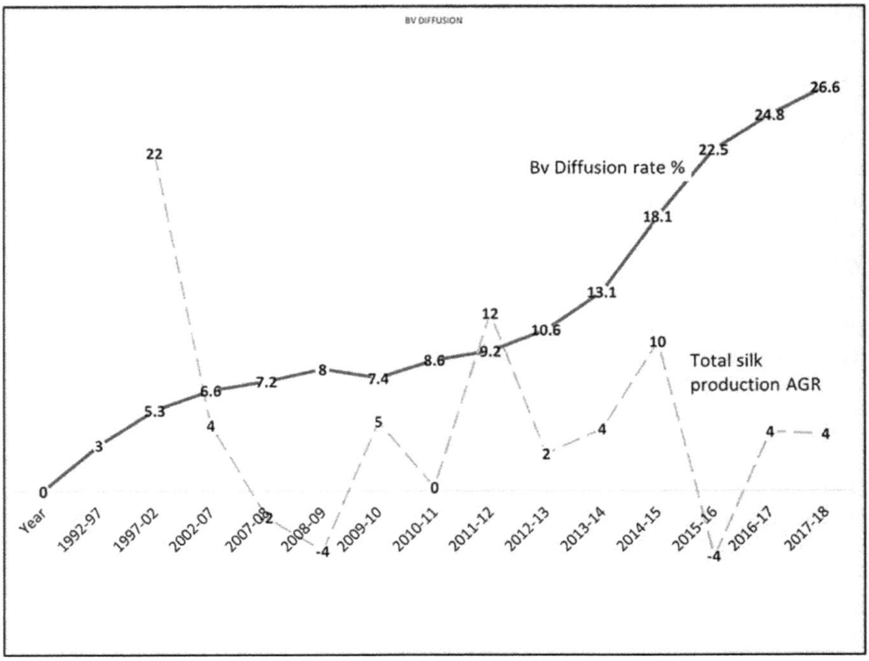

Figure 7.1 Per Cent Diffusion of BVHT in India Since 1992

This phase was also marked by a drastic lowering of import duty on raw silk, by an aggregate 35.0 per cent, until it was hiked in 2013 by 10.0 per cent.

This situation demands a diagnostic assessment of the Sericulture Innovation System, which is a sub-system of the broader AIS. The diagnostic assessment is undertaken using the protocol discussed in the previous section.

2.1. Sector Timeline and Evolution

Indian sericulture has at least 300 years of recorded history. The technological evolution in the sector is summed up in Table 7.3. Since the 1800s, a pattern of intermittent waves of technological transformation interspersed with phases of system-building and consolidation is discernible. The characteristic features of this technological evolution appear to be: i) a constant preoccupation with importation and improvement of the silkworm; ii) continued foreign-expert supervision; iii) active state support; and iv) strategic system-building. Howes (1974) rated the efforts made during the early 70s as a 'successful transfer to application of relatively sophisticated technical knowledge' and attributed the success to the strength of 'initial decisions' pertaining to the technology transfer exercise, which is a 'strong determinant of the subsequent course of events'. There were significant steps towards 'system-building' and 'technology transfer'. The already acquired 'absorptive capacity' was further consolidated through careful planning and choice of men and means, with the objective of gaining 'local control' of the transferred technology.

The sector witnessed two major breakthroughs in technological upgradation during the 1970s and 1990s, the former being locally driven and the latter through foreign collaboration with the Japan International Cooperation Agency (JICA). The JICA model was characterised by seven key features. JICA brought to India only a few silkworm breeds that took 'hybrids' as breeding stock. They were not ready to spare their major pure lines. What in fact made a difference here was the JICA approach of bringing in a 'system'. From the review undertaken, seven key elements of this approach are identified as creating the impact: Building a dedicated team, fine-tuning locally available technology, *In situ* innovations, Addressing system gaps, Mid-term course correction, Field demonstration and a stress on Private participation, as detailed in Table 7.4.

The successful strategies of transfer of foreign technology under the Japan International Cooperation Agency (JICA) project that helped the modernisation of Indian sericulture is summarised in Table 7.4.

The strategies were basically directed at transferring the Japanese knowledge, with special reference to its 'tacit' component, to Indian scientists and technical personnel. This transfer had been by informal means: interaction, observation, motivation etc. The Japanese team leader exercised 'absolute power'. He could call the minister to fix things up (interview, GB Singh, 2018). JICA was rather 'prepared' to tackle the problems associated with

Table 7.3 Technological evolution of S. Indian sericulture

Sericultural evolutionary phases: Timeline	*Key events in Indian sericulture*	*Innovation principles in 'techno economic paradigms' in the contemporary industrial world (Kattel et al., 2009)*
I. Beginnings (1770–1800)	• Pioneering efforts by Tipu Sultan, the local ruler of Mysore, James Anderson in Madras and the British East India Company • Importation of Chinese and European silkworms • Efforts to improve silk reeling by importing Italian machines.	**1771–1829** (Industrial Revolution): Factory production – Mechanisation – Productivity, time keeping and time saving – Fluidity of movement – Local networks
II. First wave of technological transformation (1850–1930)	• Technological transformation under foreign expert guidance. • F1 hybrids of imported silkworm strains commercially exploited. • Systematic race maintenance and multiplication started.	**1829–1875** (Age of steam and railway) Economies of agglomeration – Power centres with national networks – Scale as progress – Standard parts/ machine made machines – Energy where needed (steam) – Inter dependent movement (of machines, transport)
III. Building the 'system' and organisational support (1930 – Late 1960)	• Strengthening of organisational setup by formation of commodity board (Central Silk Board). • National and sub-national systems and five-year plan-wise financial support. • Legal backing to the industry through Acts. • Tariff protection to domestic industry against cheap imports. • Founding of International research station in India. • Overseas training to create a '*pool of expertise*' at the top.	**1875–1908** (Age of steel, electricity and heavy engineering) Giant structures-steel – Economies of scale – Electricity for industry – Science as a productive force – Worldwide networks and empires – Universal standardisation – Cost accounting- Great scale for world market power – Small is successful, if local **1908–1971** (Age of oil, automobile and mass production) Mass production – mass markets – horizontal integration – product standardisation – energy intensity (oil) – synthetic materials – functional specialisation – metropolitan centres & suburbanisation – National powers, world agreements, confrontations

Sericultural evolutionary phases: Timeline	*Key events in Indian sericulture*	*Innovation principles in 'techno economic paradigms' in the contemporary industrial world (Kattel et al., 2009)*
IV. Second wave of technological transformation (1970s–1980)	• Rectification and fine-tuning of agronomy packages. • 'Triple revolution'- research focus shifts to development of 'enabling technologies – hybrid silkworm, HYV food plant and standard agronomy practices, resulting in improvement of food-plant and agronomical practices also. • A period of significant technological advancement established the possibility of tropical BVHT sericulture	
V. External funding, Infrastructure and System building (1980–1990)	• Massive infrastructure-creation under externally funded/supported projects. • Expansion in Research infrastructure, departmental base and manpower strengthens the organisational structure. • Overseas training programs provide exposure.	**Since 1971** (Age of information and telecommunications): Information intensity – decentralised integration – knowledge as capital – heterogeneity, diversity, adaptability, market segmentation–- economics of scope and specialisation – globalisation -clusters, instant global communication and action
VI. Third wave of technological transformation: Japan International Cooperation Agency – JICA (Since 1990)	• Under the Japan International Cooperation Agency (JICA) project, BVHT matured. • Hybrids and meticulous packages of practice evolved for tropics prepare the country for diffusion of BVHT in 1997. • Well-designed and flexible development schemes incentivise BVHT at farmer level, eliciting encouraging response. • Central Silk Board Act, 2010: Massive deregulation and financial incentives attract private participation. • Private BVHT hatcheries mushroom – competitive market gives rise to private extension. • Technology adoption and improvement in BVHT diffusion.	

Source: Survey of literature by author

Table 7.4 Strategies of transfer of foreign technology in Indian sericulture

Strategies	*Outcomes realised*
Generating capabilities to discriminate between extant alternatives before committing to any foreign technology (Howes, 1974)	a) Any new decision would only require short-term foreign expert assistance b) Acquiring foreign 'tacit knowledge' c) Eliminating 'technocratic bias'. d) Rapid assumption of full 'local control' of transferred technology
Modifying available technology and utilising existing viable 'exogenous' technologies (Howes, 1974)	a) Development subject to 'local control' b) Exploit 'absorptive capacity' c) Permitting 'shortcuts' where possible
Team building & overseas training	The team acted as a single-block
Course correction in participatory mode	Local adaptation of foreign technology Removing barriers to learning
Identification and rectification of system gaps	Ensuring longevity of technological gains
Private participation	System building
Demonstration-farmer's movement	Diffusion through social networks
Local innovations: using 'shortcuts' wherever possible	a) Economy: money and time b) Utilisation of local 'tacit knowledge'
Demonstrable models and exploiting farmer's network for its diffusion	The models diffused well and survived

Source: Review of literature

implementation of a sophisticated scheme in the developing country context, with all its inefficiencies. Localised knowledge was taken seriously and modified wherever possible. Thus, most of the technology was 'innovation', based on both local as well as Japanese available technology. Economy of time, money and effort was a priority. Potential 'technocratic biases' were foreseen and eliminated. The Indian counterparts quickly acquired local control over the foreign technology and ensured 'longevity of technical gains' by ensuring a permanent Indian supply of bivoltine parent race. JICA's success was also due to the 'absorptive capacity' already possessed by the Sericulture Innovation System in India and gained through the historical process of technological transformation.

2.2. *Sector Mapping*

Schrempf et al. (2013) identify three important building blocks of Innovation Systems viz. knowledge and technological domain, the actors and networks and the institutions.

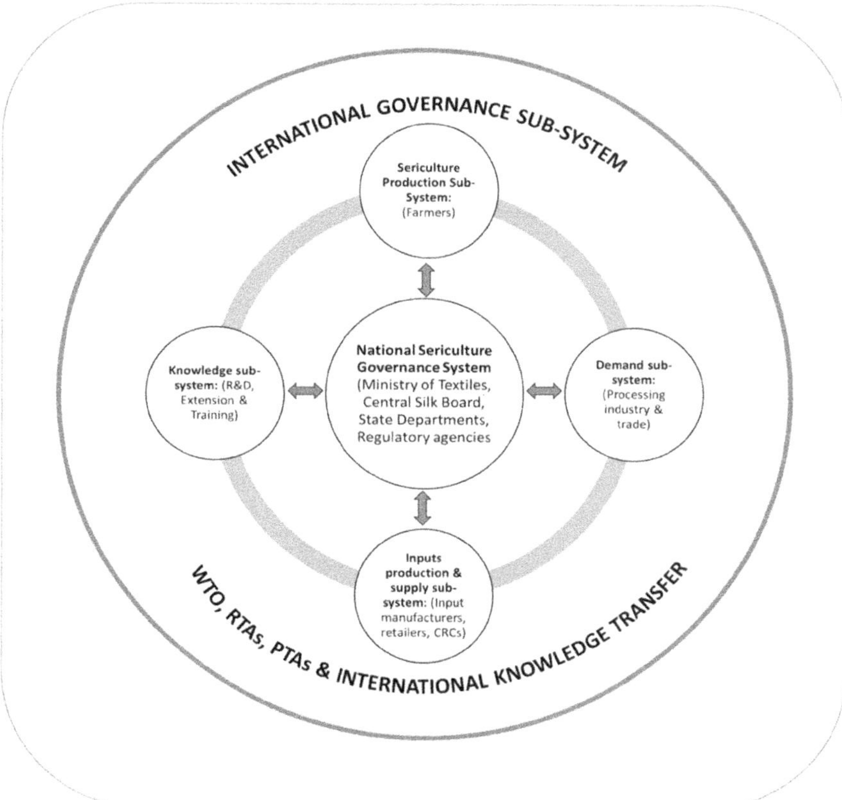

Figure 7.2 India's Sericulture Innovation System

Source: Modified after Joseph et al., 2014

In **Figure 7.2**, a Sericulture Innovation System is conceived with six broad component sub-systems. The National Governance Sub-System is based on the Ministry of Textiles, Government of India and the Commodity Board, namely the Central Silk Board. At the sub-national level, it has integral sub-systems of various state departments of sericulture, as illustrated in **Figure 7.3**. The Production Sub-System is centred around the farmer-producers and their networks. The Supply Sub-System is representative of the private players in the system including the input manufacturers, retailers and seed and Chawky producers (RSPs and CRCs). Demand Sub-System is the entry point to the industrial processing sector and still larger silk industry (which at the moment is considered outside the scope of this analysis, for analytical ease and clarity). The Knowledge Sub-System comprises the research stations, universities and independent researchers, extension

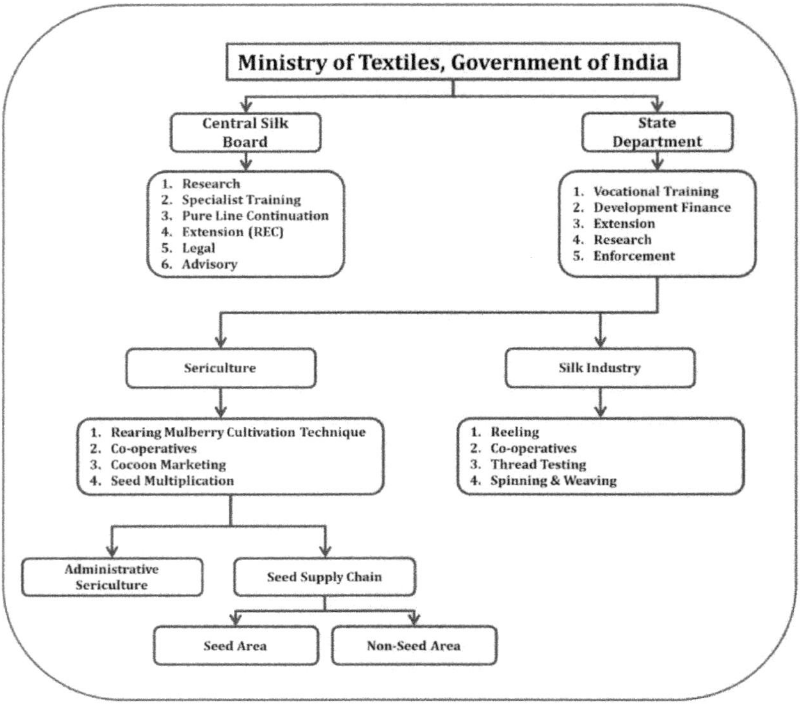

Figure 7.3 The National Governance Sub-System of the SIS

network and training organisations. All these systems, as discussed in this chapter, are involved in constant networking and exchange of knowledge and material among themselves and with the Global Sub-System, represented by the World Trade Organisation (WTO), Regional Trade Agreements (RTAs), Preferential Trade Agreements (PTAs) and knowledge transfer (foreign technology transfer from other sericulture practicing countries).

Malerba defines a Sectoral Innovation System as:

> a Sectoral Innovation System includes a set of established and new products for specific uses and a set of agents supporting and carrying out technological, market, and non-market interactions for the creation, production, and sale of those products.
>
> Malerba (2002)

The Indian sericulture sector qualifies the criteria specified in this definition. It has a well-documented knowledge system with at least 300 years of recorded history. The sericulture knowledge base has been enriched periodically by the import and export of technologies. It has an array of technologies ranging from land preparation, mulberry plantation and agronomy, silkworm raising, silkworm seed production, crop protection, reeling technology and yarn processing technology, with divisions and sub-divisions of activities. The sericulture sector has been highly technology-intensive, with a perpetual focus on product quality improvement through crop improvement and breed improvement. The production inputs of sericulture range from agricultural inputs for mulberry production and silkworm rearing, chemical inputs for crop protection of both the plant and animal, silkworm seed, special equipment for silkworm rearing and silk reeling machinery. The demand for silk is well-defined, existing (and perpetually growing), emergent, and potential. The system comprises both organisational and individual agents. There are firms (sericulture farmers, reelers, silkworm seed producers, chawky suppliers, inputs suppliers, etc.) and non-firm organisations (central and state government research stations, universities, banks and other financial agencies, central and state government departments and extension services, powerful farmer's and reeler's organisations and technical associations). There are institutions characteristic of the sericulture sector (specific laws and acts laid down for controlled extraction of resources like precious genetic material, regulated markets, social conventions governing extraction of natural resources, work division and crop rotation), contracts, traditions, etc. Above all, the system is highly dynamic and sensitive to import and export of material from outside the system boundaries, and finally is characterised by an extremely complex network of players. All these match well with the definition provided by Malerba (2002). Hence, it may be argued that a well-defined Sericulture Innovation System is in place.

Key Agents: The key agents of the Sericulture Innovation System are: Sericulture farmers (commercial sericulturists and seed cocoon rearers), Input suppliers such as: Licenced Seed preparers (graineures), Chawky (young age worm) Rearers, Fertilisers and chemicals suppliers, Suppliers of implements, silkworm rearing equipments etc., State Government Departments and their sericulture extension system, Central Silk Board and its R&D and extension centres, State- and central Government-owned Research and Training stations, Private manufacturers of inputs and their R&D wings, Universities offering sericulture courses and conducting sericulture research, Sericulture farmers' associations, Government silk markets, Silk reelers, manufacturers of reeling machinery, Suppliers of inputs to reeling industry, Government Silk yarn markets, Silk testing and conditioning centres, Researchers, Extension officers, Administrative setup and bureaucracy, Political leaders, agricultural labourers, the banking sector, private money lenders, etc. An exhaustive listing of all the players and defining their roles is outside the scope of this chapter. Therefore, a few important and most visible ones are discussed briefly.

- **Commercial Sericulturists:** The sericulture farmers who are the backbone of the sector. The farmers, although belonging to various socio-economic classes, together form a strong pressure group. The collective bargaining power of sericulture farmers has historically led to many policy initiatives protecting their interests. A recent example is Farmers' organisations campaign and several state- and national-level struggles seeking the restoration of an import duty on silk at 30 per cent.
- **Seed Cocoon Rearers:** These are farmers who are selected and registered as rearers of parental races for the purpose of hybridisation. These are privileged farmers, as they receive close technical guidance aimed at production of cocoons with specific quality standards and they receive high prices for the seed cocoons they produce.
- **Licensed Seed Preparers:** Private producers of commercial silkworm eggs need to obtain licenses as a regulatory measure for the government to ensure quality and 'disease freeness' of silkworm eggs.
- **Chawky Rearers:** Chawky rearing is the centralised rearing of young silkworms up to 10 days, so that farmers could buy them instead of directly buying silkworm eggs. The technology standardised as early as the 1980s but took a long time to diffuse. Now the technology is well diffused.
- **Central Silk Board:** CSB is a Statutory body established in 1948 by an Act of Parliament. It is working under the administrative control of Ministry of Textiles, Government of India. CSB possesses an extensive research system. Three Central Sericultural Research and Training Institutes (CSR&tIs), Central Tasar Research and Training Institute, Central Sericultural Germplasm Resources Centre, Seri-biotech Research Laboratory, Central Muga Eri Research and Training Institute and 11 Regional Research Stations. The National Silkworm Seed Organisation (NSSO) is the organisation responsible for multiplication of basic seed evolved by the research centres and universities.
- **State Departments of Sericulture:** All the major silk-producing states have their own sericulture departments looking after sericulture extension activities and R&D through State Government Research and Training Institutes.
- **Government-Regulated Markets:** There is a well-established Cocoon Marketing System in India. By law, cocoon transaction is facilitated by Government-owned markets where transaction through auction is facilitated. The Karnataka State has 34 Regulated Cocoon Markets in different cocoon production areas. Cocoon markets in Karnataka are mostly located in the major reeling centres.
- **Government Silk Markets:** To support raw silk marketing, silk testing centres are operated by CSB. Recently the state governments have come

up with a proposal to widen the silk testing centre network by establishing silk testing centers in collaboration with the CSB in all the major reeling clusters. The State has organised silk exchanges in major reeling centres to facilitate raw silk sales. It was mandatory for the reelers to transact the silk only in the silk exchanges under the provisions of the Karnataka Silkworm Seed, Cocoon and Silk Yarn (Regulation of production, Supply Distribution and Sale) Act, 1959. This was backed by Silk enforcement.

- **Reeler Cooperatives:** Efforts to organise the reeler cooperatives to support reeling and address raw silk marketing issues have met with limited success. Almost 95 per cent of the reeler cooperative societies have become defunct, and so is the Karnataka Silk Marketing Federation.
- **The Legal Sub-System:** The Karnataka Silkworm Seed Act of 1960 brought each and every sericultural activity under government control. This powerful act, in keeping with the economic policies of the 1960s was 'regulatory' in style and characterised by licensing, invigilation and penalisation. The thorough revision of the act with drastic de-regulation to form the National Silkworm Seed Act of 2010 has brought visible vibrancy to the industry, which is reflected in the enhanced rates of diffusion of technologies.
- **Integration with the International Sub-System:** The Indian Sericulture System is well integrated with the global system, as India is the second-largest producer of silks and the largest importer and consumer of silk yarn (raw silk). The impact of imports on domestic sericulture is illustrative of the strong integration of the national sericulture system with the international governance sub-system of WTO, PTAs and RTAs.

Apart from these components, many more players, such as Manufacturers of reeling machinery, Suppliers of inputs to reeling industry, Government Silk yarn markets, Silk testing and conditioning centres, Researchers, Extension officers, Administrative setup and bureaucracy, Political leaders, Agricultural labourers, sharecroppers, the banking sector and private money lenders play important roles in the sector.

2.3. Habits and Practices of Organisations

It appears that the system has all elements necessary for a functional and sustainable Sectoral Innovation System. However, the system is not without weaknesses. An important weakness of the sector is poor participation of the private sector in Research and Development activities. **Figure 7.4** illustrates the per cent contribution of various research organisations in completed sericulture scientific projects. While the central government institutes dominate with a nearly 75.0 per cent share of projects, the representation of private firms (categorised as other institutes) is just 0.1 per cent. Even

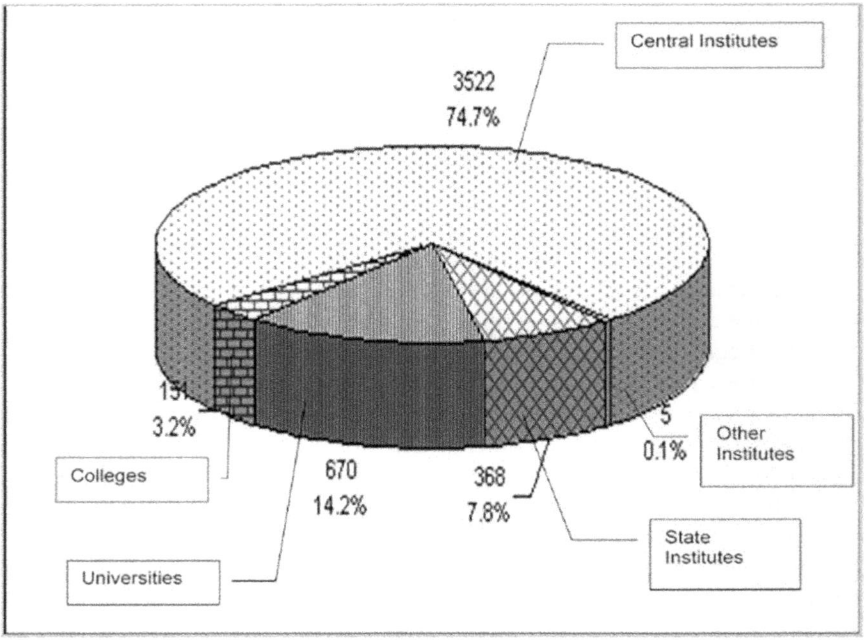

Figure 7.4 Organisational Share of Completed Sericulture Projects

the role of Universities (14 per cent) and State Institutes (7.8 per cent) are limited. **Figure** 7.5 illustrates the share of release of various sericultural technologies by research institutes. While Central government-owned institutes account for 67.0 per cent, private participation is only 3.0 per cent. State R&D institutes contribute to 24.0 per cent, and Universities 6.0 per cent. It is important that the Government devise strategies to vitalise the private sector and encourage their entry into R&D.

Yet another weakness is with respect to the overemphasis placed upon the agricultural aspect and neglect of the industrial aspect of silk reeling and silk technology. In Indian sericulture, the farming community forms a major pressure group capable of influencing policy decisions for their advantage. While this is reasonable, the processing industry receives scanty attention with respect to creation of knowledge, technological innovations and diffusion. The silk reeling sector is marked by low levels of diffusion of technologies, which badly reflect upon the poor quality of silk being produced.

Figures 7.6 and 7.7 give the number of technical experts and number of publications in sericulture. While the lion's share of experts and publications were in the agricultural sector, the silk technological sector received scanty attention. This discussion points to important shortcomings of the

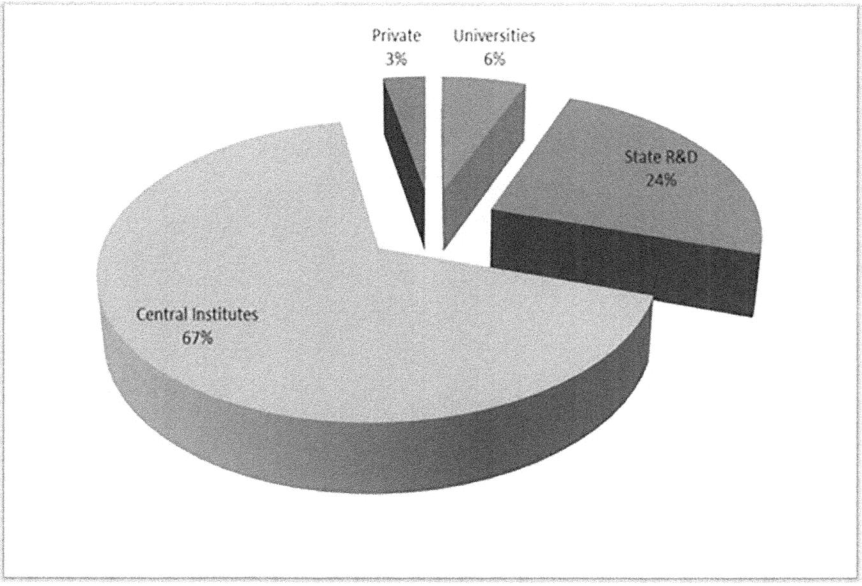

Figure 7.5 Share of Institutes in Release of Technologies

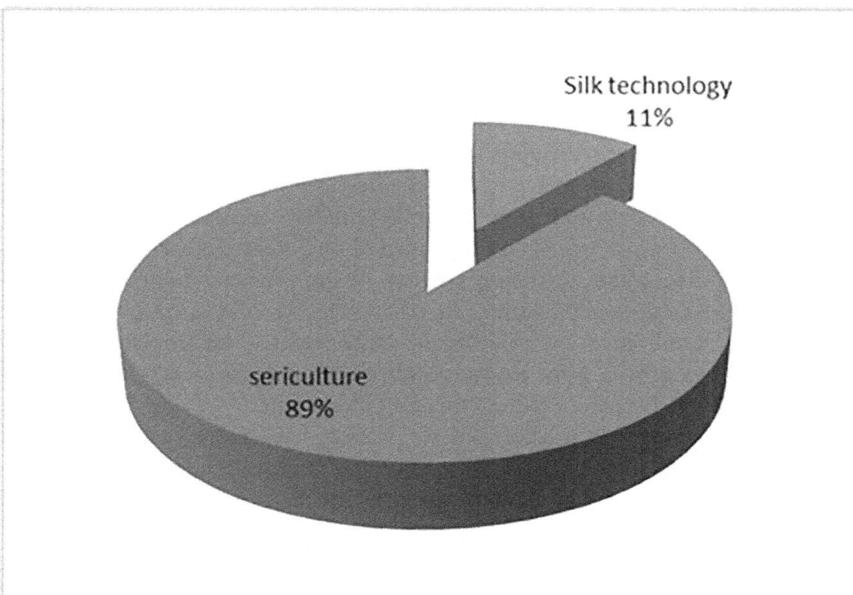

Figure 7.6 Discipline-Wise Number of Scientists

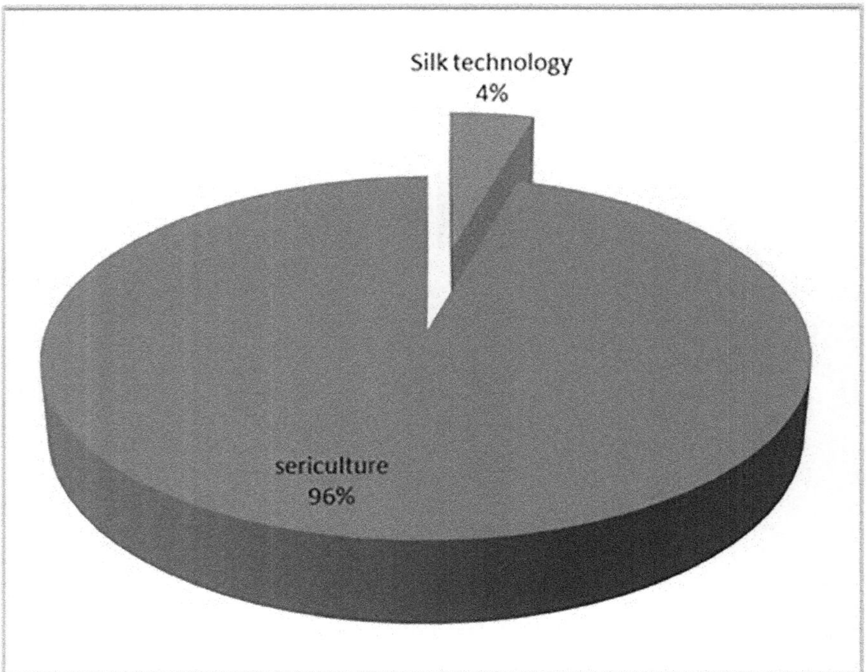

Figure 7.7 Publications in Sericulture by Discipline

Sectoral Innovation System of sericulture in India. There is an urgent need to adopt strategies for rectifying these.

The Indian sericulture sector has all the necessary components of an Innovation System. It is characterised by complex networks and linkages, by way of economic, social, political, organisational and institutional factors influencing the development, diffusion and use of innovations; hence it qualifies as a Sectoral Innovation System in its own right. However, its progress and development are limited by its inherent weaknesses. Two important weaknesses of the system are poor participation of the private sector in R&D and overemphasis of the agricultural aspect of sericulture.

The bulk of innovation efforts in the Indian sericulture sector over past three decades have been focused on evolving highly productive silkworm hybrids capable of producing high-quality silk. In this process, traditional local varieties of the mulberry plant and silkworms were replaced by imported varieties. Matching modernisation efforts were not made in the silk reeling sector. This, coupled with the sub-optimal levels of technology and absorptive capacity of the reeling sector, rendered the whole attempt ineffective. India imported and directly applied policies and best practices in sericulture from industrialised nations as a technological catch-up strategy. However, there are particularities in developing countries which cannot be neglected when studying innovation dynamics in a systemic approach. At times when this fact is neglected, the innovative attempt could lead to systems disruption. The Indian Sericulture Innovation System needs to replace the strategy of direct technology transfer from abroad and undertake an introspective innovation attempt. It is recommended that by bringing in more private participation, by increasing technology absorptive capacity of the silk reeling industry and by incentivising technology adoption in the silk reeling sector, the Indian Sericulture Innovation Sector can benefit.

3. Summary and Conclusion

The technological transformation of Indian sericulture is an interesting case study in transfer of foreign agricultural technology. Technology transfer has been a characteristic feature of the sector from the very beginning. However, a more mature and realistic approach was discernible during the three phases of JICA, which placed both India and Japan in a win-win situation. While Indian sericulture realised quantitative and qualitative improvements in silk production coupled with significant intangible gains in 'system building', Japan benefitted: by equipping India to be a dependable source of quality silk, by engaging an aging generation of sericulture experts in remunerative assignments and above all by being able to exercise 'soft power' in exchange of part of their rich knowledge base, accumulated since the Meiji restoration. JICA spent comparatively less than any other project in financial terms. JICA didn't create any material infrastructure. In that respect, the results created were rather 'intangible' but the impact had been longstanding. JICA exercised a soft power in correcting the system and creating certain useful models.

This chapter has elucidated India's National Sericulture Innovation System (SIS) in the light of the innovation history of the country. It is understood that India has a well-developed and functional SIS, but not without shortcomings and further scope for improvement. The SIS is marked by domination of government participation and highly protective regulatory policies aimed at a) safekeeping the interests of the farming community, b) maintenance of hybrid vigour of the evolved hybrids and c) prevention of incidence of disease. The overemphasis on the farming sector and the regulatory policies had caused poor participation of the private sector. There is no R&D activity in the private sector. The technology transfer is still in the top-down manner, disregarding innovation at industry level. There has been gross neglect on R&D in the industrial aspect of silk reeling and silk technology. The silk reeling sub-system of the SIS is marked by low levels of diffusion of technologies, which badly reflect upon the poor quality of silk being produced. The reeling sector is marked by sub-optimal levels of absorptive capacity.

The SIS of India imported and directly applied policies and best practices from industrialised countries as a technological catch-up strategy. The analysis indicates that India needs to replace the strategy of direct technology transfer from abroad and undertake an introspective innovation attempt. It is recommended that by bringing in more private participation, by increasing technology absorptive capacity of the silk reeling industry and by incentivising technology adoption in the silk reeling sector, the Indian Sericulture Innovation Sector can benefit.

It may be concluded that the transformation achieved through intermittent periods of technological advancements, interspersed with spells of organisation building and consolidation, has led to the evolution of a 'Sericulture Innovation System' in India, on due recognition of which and incorporation of the corrective measures that have emerged from the discussion would improve the performance of the system.

The brief systemic analysis undertaken in this chapter has important policy implications. The SIS of India imported and directly applied policies and best practices from industrialised countries as a technological catch-up strategy. The analysis indicates that India needs to replace the strategy of direct technology transfer from abroad and undertake a more introspective policy. By bringing in more private participation, by increasing technology absorptive capacity of the silk reeling industry and by incentivising technology adoption in the silk reeling sector, the Indian Sericulture Innovation Sector can benefit. Above all, policy-makers need to recognise the Innovation System and consider its various elements/players and their linkages as important functional units of the system. Future policies need to be based on a sound understanding of the existing system, its components and their relative roles. Protectionist regulatory policies favoring any particular component in the systems would be detrimental to the system and subsequently the industry.

Notes

1 Spedding (1979) said, 'The term "agricultural science" is sometimes used to describe the scientific study of agriculture, but this can be rather misleading because agriculture embraces more than the contributing sciences and cannot, therefore, necessarily be studied scientifically in all its aspects. (A similar difficulty applies, for example, to "social science"). "Agricultural science", on the other hand, can be used to group those sciences (or parts of them) that are most relevant to agriculture or underpin its processes and operations.'

2 'The innovation systems concept is derived from direct observations of countries and sectors with strong records of innovation. The concept has been used predominantly to explain patterns of past economic performance in developed countries and has received far less attention as an operational tool. It has been applied

to agriculture in developing countries only recently, but it appears to offer exciting opportunities for understanding how a country's agricultural sector can make better use of new knowledge and for designing alternative interventions that go beyond research system investments' (WB, 2006).

3 An AKIS is a set of agricultural organizations and/or persons, and the links and interactions between them, engaged in such processes as the generation, transformation, transmission, storage, retrieval, integration, diffusion and utilisation of knowledge and information, with the purpose of working synergically to support decision making, problem solving and innovation in a given country's agriculture or a domain thereof (Roling, 2009).

4 RAAKS: Participatory action-research, allowing stakeholders to design improvements in the way they strategise for innovation at the community or sector level. By gathering and analysing information about the way they're organised now, comparing actual impacts with desired results, local and/or institutional stakeholders design ways to strengthen their capacity to achieve change. Outcomes are communication, information and organisational strategies and measures to enhance networking and learning (Engel and Salomon, 1997).

5 Silk is produced by silkworm (*Bombyx mori. L*), an insect belonging to the family of moths and butterflies. Raw silk is the raw yarn reeled out of cocoons, before subjecting it to further processing such as twisting, doubling, bleaching or dyeing.

6 The import price of raw silk has been lower than the domestic silk, as the cost of production of Indian silk is high (Kumaresan, 2002). Moreover, as shown by Naik and Babu (1993), the price of imported Chinese silk is dependent on the prevailing prices of Indian silk, though the causative nature of indigenous silk price has not been clearly elucidated. This has affected the indigenous silk prices and in turn the domestic cocoon prices (Tikku, 1999).

7 With the demand pull created by sophisticated power looms and consequent to relaxation in exim policies, a large quantity of high-quality silk is being imported at prices lower than local silk. This has apparently lowered the demand for domestic silk and adversely affected prices of cocoon and silk (Rajesh, 2011)

8 The Bivoltine Hybrid Technology (BVHT) is a package of numerous technologies that may be broadly classified into three categories viz. Mulberry cultivation, Silkworm rearing technology and Silk reeling technologies. Each of these in turn contain a large number of individual component technologies.

References

Ahmed, K. M. (1997). *Economics of silk reeling with reference to production and marketing in Karnataka*. PhD Thesis Submitted to University of Mysore India.

Benchamin, K. V. (1990). Issues involved in the development of bivoltine sericulture in Karnataka. Indian Silk. Central Silk Board. 32–36.

Benchamin, K. V., & Kshama, G. (2005). Sericulture industry in India. *Conference papers, III, the 20th congress of the international sericultural commission*. Central Silk Board, Bangalore, pp. 158–161.

Bengt-Åke Lundvall, B. A. (1996). The social dimension of the learning economy. Druid working paper no. 96-1, April.

Blaug, M. (1964). *Economic theory and economic history in Great Britain, 1650–1776*.

Breschi, S., & Malerba, F. (1997). Sectoral innovation systems: Technological regimes, Schumpeterian dynamics, and spatial boundaries. *Systems of Innovation: Technologies, Institutions and Organizations*, 1, 130–156.

Carlsson, B., & Stankiewicz, R. (1991). On the nature, function and composition of technological systems. *Journal of Evolutionary Economics*, 1(2), 93–118.

Central Silk Board. (2019). Annual reports of Central Silk Board. *Member Secretary Central Silk Board*. http://www.csb.gov.in/publications/annual-report/

Chambers, R. (1989). The state and rural development: Ideologies and an agenda for the 1990s. *Institute of Development Studies Discussion Papers No. 269*.

Clark, N., Perez-Trejo, F., & Allen, P. (1995). *Evolutionary dynamics and sustainable development: A systems approach*. Edward Elgar Publishing Ltd.

Cooke, P. (1996). The new wave of regional innovation networks: Analysis, characteristics and strategy. *Small Business Economics*, 8(2), 159–171.

CSB. (2019). Annual Report, Central Silk Board, Government of India. https://csb.gov.in/publications/annual-report/

Dandin, S. B., Basavaraja, H. K., & Suresh Kumar, N. (2005). *Silkworm breeds and hybrids at Galore*. Mysore: Central Sericultural Research and Training Institute.

Dosi, G. (1984). *Technical change and industrial transformation: The theory and an application to the semiconductor industry*. Springer.

Dosi, G. (2007). Technological innovation, institutions and human purposefulness in socioeconomic evolution: A preface to Christopher Freeman "*System of innovation*. Selected essays in evolutionary economics" (No. 2007/18). LEM Working Paper Series.

Dosi, G., Freeman, C., Nelson, R., Silverberg, G., & Soete, L. (eds) (1988). *Technical change and economic theory*. London and New York: Pinter.

Dosi, G. et al. (1990). *Technical change end economic theory*. London: Pinter Publishers.

Engel, P. G., & Salomon, M. L. (1997). Facilitating innovation for development: a RAAKS resource box. *Facilitating innovation for development: A RAAKS resource box*.

Ernst, D., & Lundvall, B. Å. (1997). Information technology in the learning economy-challenges for developing countries. *Globalization, Economic Development and Inequality*, 258.

Evenson, R. (1974). International diffusion of agrarian technology. *The Journal of Economic History*, 34(1), 51–73.

Farrington, J., & Martin, A. M. (1988). Farmer participatory research: A review of concepts and recent fieldwork. *Agricultural Administration and Extension*, 29(4), 247–264.

Freeman, C. (1987). *Technology policy and economic performance: Lesson from Japan*. New York: Pinter Publisher.

Freeman, C. (1988). Structural crises of adjustment: Business cycles. In *Technical change and economic theory*. London: Pinter.

Freeman, C. (1991). Networks of innovators: A synthesis of research issues. *Research Policy*, 20(5), 499–514.

Freeman, C. (1994). The economics of technical change. *Cambridge Journal of Economics*, 18(5), 463–514.

Freeman, C. (1995). The 'National System of Innovation' in historical perspective. *Cambridge Journal of Economics*, 19(1), 5–24.

Freeman, C., & Soete, L. (1987). *Technical Change and Full Employment*. Oxford: Blackwell.

Freeman, C., & Soete, L. (2005). 14. A digital society for us all: "old" and "new" policy reflections. *The Economics of the Digital Society*, 330.

Gibbons, M., Limoges, C., Nowotny, H., Schwartzman, S., Scott, P., & Trow, M. (1995). *The new production of knowledge: The dynamics of science and research in contemporary societies*. London: SAGE.

Hall, A. (2007). Challenges to strengthening agricultural innovation systems: Where do we go from here?. UNU-MERIT Working Paper #2007-038. United Nations University - Maastrciht Economic and Social Research and Training Centre on Innovation and Technology.

Hall, A., Bockett, G., Taylor, S., Sivamohan, M. V. K., & Clark, N. (2001). Why research partnerships really matter: Innovation theory, institutional arrangements and implications for developing new technology for the poor. *World Development*, 29(5), 783–797. https://doi.org/10.1016/S0305-750X(01)00004-3

Hall, A. J., Mytelka, L. K., & Oyelaran-Oyeyinka, B. (2006). Concepts and guidelines for diagnostic assessments of agricultural innovation capacity. UNU-MERIT Working Paper 2006-017. *Maastricht: United Nations University – Maastrciht Economic and Social Research and Training Centre on Innovation and Technology*.

Hall, A., Sulaiman, V. R., Clark, N., & Yoganand, B. (2003). From measuring impact to learning institutional lessons: An innovation systems perspective on improving the management of international agricultural research. *Agricultural Systems*, 78(2), 213–241.

Hayami, Y. (1974). Conditions for the diffusion of agricultural technology: An Asian perspective. *The Journal of Economic History*, 34(1).

Howes, M. (1974). The transfer of technology in the Indian Silk Industry, a report based on Visit to the Department of Sericulture, Karnataka, and the Central Silk Board, Bombay, 7–16 October. Science Policy Research Unit, University of Sussex.

Hulme, D. (1992). Enhancing organizational effectiveness in developing countries: The training and visit system revisited. *Public Administration and Development*, 12(5), 433–445.

Jarrett, F. G. (1985). Sources and models of agricultural innovation in developed and developing countries. *Agricultural Administration*, 18(4), 217–234.

Jayaram, H., Mallikarjuna, V., Lakshmanan, S., Ganapathi, Rao, R., & Geetha Devi, R. G. (1998). Labour employment under different Mulberry Farm holdings-a comparative study. *Indian Journal of Sericulture*, 37(1), 52–56.

Jewkes, J. (1958). British Monopoly Policy 1944–56. *The Journal of Law and Economics*, 1, 1–19.

Johnson, B., Lorenz, E., & Lundvall, B. Å. (2002). Why all this fuss about codified and tacit knowledge? *Industrial and Corporate Change*, 11(2), 245–262.
Joseph, K J. (2014). Exploring exclusion in innovation systems: Case of plantation agriculture in India. *Innovation and Development*, 4, 73–90. https://doi.org/10.1080/2157930X.2014.890352.
Kamien, M. I., & Schwartz, N. L. (1982). *Market structure and innovation*. Cambridge University Press.
Kattel, R., Drechsler, W., & Reinert, E. S. (2009). Introduction: Carlota Perez and Evolutionary Economics. In *Techno-economic paradigms: Essays in honour of Carlota Perez*. Eds. W. Drechsler, R. Kattel and E. S. Reinert. London: Anthem Press, pp. 1–18
Kirkpatrick, W. (1811). *An account of the Kingdom of Nepal, being the substance of observations made during a mission to that country, in the year 1793: Illustrated with a map and other engravings* (Vol. 3). Miller.
Kline, S., & Rosenber, G. (1986). An overview of innovation. In *The positive sum strategy: Harnessing technology for economic growth*. Eds. R. Landau and N. Rosenberg. Washington, DC: National Academy Press, pp. 275–305.
Kumaresan, P. (2002). Quality silk production: Some economic issues. *Economic and Political Weekly*, September 28, pp. 4019–4022.
Lefroy, M. H., & Ansorge, E. C. (1915). Report on an inquiry into the Silk Industry in India (1915), Vol. I, Calcutta.
Lundvall, B. Å. (1985). Product innovation and user-producer interaction. *The Learning Economy and the Economics of Hope*, 19, 19–60.
Lundvall, B. Å. (1992). *National systems of innovation: towards a theory of innovation and interactive learning*. In Towards a theory of innovation and interactive learning. London: Pinter.
Lundvall, B. Å. (1999). National business systems and national systems of innovation. *International Studies of Management & Organization*, 29(2), 60–77.
Lundvall, B. Å. (2007). National innovation systems—analytical concept and development tool. *Industry and Innovation*, 14(1), 95–119.
Lundvall, B. Å. (2016). *The learning economy and the economics of hope*. London; New York: Anthem Press.
Lundvall, B. A., & Lorenz, E. (2012). Innovation and competence building in the learning economy: implications for Innovation policy. In *Interactive learning for innovation*. London: Palgrave Macmillan, pp. 33–71.
Lundvall, B. Å., & Johnson, B. (1994). The learning economy. *Journal of Industry Studies*, 1(2), 23–42.
Malerba, F. (2002). Sectoral systems of innovation and production. *Research Policy*, 31(2002), 247–264.
Malerba, F., & Orsenigo, L. (1995). Schumpeterian patterns of innovation. *Cambridge Journal of Economics*, 19(1), 47–65.
Naik, G., & Babu, K. H. (1993). *Demand and supply prospects for high quality silk*. Oxford; New Delhi: IBH Publishing Co. Pvt. Ltd.
Neef, A., & Neubert, D. (2011). Stakeholder participation in agricultural research projects: a conceptual framework for reflection and decision-making. *Agriculture and Human Values*, 28(2), 179–194.
Nelson, R. R., & Winter, S. G. (1982). *An evolutionary theory of economic change*. Cambridge, MA: Harvard University Press.

OECD. (1997). National innovation systems. https://www.oecd.org/science/inno/2101733.pdf (accessed January 2022).
Pavitt, K. (1984). Sectoral patterns of technical change: Towards a taxonomy and a theory. *Research Policy*, 13, 343–373.
Rajesh, G. K. (2011). *Diffusion of Bivoltine hybrid silkworm in India: An economic analysis*. LAP LAMBERT Academic Publishing GmbH & Co.
Rajesh, G. K., & Ramaswamy, S. (2015). Towards building a national sericulture (Mulberry) innovation system in India-Possibilities and prospects. *Sericologia*, 57(3), 169–184.
Ramakrishnan, S. R. (2001). Bivoltine sericulture- a complementary activity. Global Silk Scenario. In *Proceedings of the international conference on sericulture*. Calcutta; Oxford: IBH Publishing Co, pp. 472–477.
Röling, N. (1990). Extension science: Haven't we come of age. *Journal of Extension Systems*, 6(1), 12–15.
Röling, N. (2009). Pathways for impact: Scientists' different perspectives on agricultural innovation. *International Journal of Agricultural Sustainability*, 7(2), 83–94.
Rogers, E. M. (2003). *Diffusion of innovations* (5th ed.). New York: Free Press, p. 221.
Rosenberg, N. (1970). Economic development and the transfer of technology: Some historical perspectives. *Technology and Culture*, 11(4), 550–575. https://doi.org/10.2307/3102691
Rosenberg, N. (1982). *Inside the black box: Technology and economics*. Cambridge: Cambridge University Press.
Rothwell, R. (1977). The characteristics of successful innovators and technically progressive firms (with some comments on innovation research). *R&D Management*, 7(3), 191–206.
Ruttan, V. W., & Hayami, Y. (1984). Toward a theory of induced institutional innovation. *The Journal of Development Studies,* 20(4), 203–223.
Schrempf, B., Kaplan, D., & Schroeder, D. (2013). National, Regional, and Sectoral Systems of Innovation – An overview, Report for FP7 Project "Progress", progressproject.eu
Schumpeter, J. A. (1928). The entrepreneur. In *The entrepreneur: Classic texts by J. Schumpeter*. Eds. M. Becker, T. Knudsen, and R. Swedberg. Stanford, CA: Stanford University Press, pp. 227–260.
Schumpeter, J. A. (1934). *The theory of economic development: An inquiry into profits, capital, credit, interest, and the business cycle*. Harvard University Press.
Schumpeter, J. A. (1942). *Capitalism, socialism and democracy* (Vol. 36). New York: Harper & Row, pp. 132–145.
Shaw, M. (2016). Post-World War I tales: A silk surplus, armistice fashion, and a philanthropic innovator. *National Museum of American History*, October 11. https://americanhistory.si.edu/blog/WWI-silk-fashion (accessed 21 June 2019).
Spedding, C. R. W. (1979). *An Introduction to agricultural systems*. Applied Science Publishers.
Spielman, D. J., Ekboir, J., Davis, K., & Ochieng, C. M. O. (2008). An innovation systems perspective on strengthening agricultural education and training in sub-Saharan Africa. *Agricultural Systems*, 98, 1–9.

Tikku, M. K. (1999). Tangled threads silk growers and imports. *Economic and Political Weekly*, March 6–13, p. 578.

World Bank. (1980). *Staff Appraisal report of Karnataka Sericulture Project*. Washington, DC: World Bank.

World Bank. (2006). Enhancing agricultural innovation: How to go beyond the strengthening of research systems. *The World Bank*. Washington, DC: Agriculture and Rural Development Division.

Chapter 8

Measurement and Determinants of Productivity of the Indian Electronics Industry

2004–05 to 2016–17

Manish Kumar and Pushpa Trivedi

1. Introduction

Irrespective of the objective of firms, which could be to maximize profits, market share or sales, the pursuit of productivity is the driving force for the successful performance of a firm. Solow's (1957) study proved to be a catalyst for the burgeoning literature on measurement of productivity. Productivity is also at the heart of endogenous growth models. Both at the micro and macro levels, innovation is said to result in higher productivity, which ultimately leads to firm growth and economic growth (Romer 1990, 1994; Grossman and Helpman 1991). Productivity increase also involves *creative destruction* through free entry or exit of firms driven by innovation (Aghion and Howitt 1992, Aghion et al. 2015). Evolutionary models too emphasize the centrality of productivity in explaining industrial evolution through differing technology regimes emanating from diverse sources, modes and patterns of innovation, leading to heterogenous distribution and evolution of firm and industry (Dosi and Nelson 2013; Nelson and Winter 1982).

Firm productivity explains the firm performance. The heterogenous distribution leads to different trajectory of firm evolution, survival and growth (Jovanovic 1982; Hopenhayn 1992; Syverson 2011). There are multiple sources of heterogeneous firm productivity. In general, firms in developing countries have lower productivity than those in developed countries (Bloom *et al* 2010). The misallocation of resources and adjustment friction lead to the heterogenous firm productivity in developing countries (Hsieh and Klenow 2009; Bartelsman et al. 2013; Asker et al. 2014). A set of constraints in developing countries, such as infrastructure, informality, regulations, trade policies, human capital, management practices and decision making together reduce the firm-level productivity (Tybout 2000; Bloom et al. 2010; Syverson 2011). At times, even productive firms do not grow as quickly as expected due to financial or organizational constraints. However, once developing countries start reform measures along with work on

DOI: 10.4324/9781003353904-10

infrastructure, institutions and regulatory bodies for better incentives, we observe the productivity level improving at an economy-wide level (Bollard et al. 2013; Goldar et al. 2017).

Some major early work on productivity in India focused on the measurement of productivity and methodological aspects associated with it (Ahluwalia 1991; Balakrishnan and Pushpangadan 1994; Trivedi et al. 2000). Post-liberalization, productivity literature on India has increased in number and quality, while debate over measurement method remains. The improved productivity performance in the 1980s continued after the 1991 reforms with interindustry and interstate differences (Trivedi 2004; Trivedi et al 2011; Kathuria et al. 2013b). In the most recent study following KLEMS framework[1], Goldar et al. (2017) show accelerated productivity growth at 1.8 per cent per annum during 2003–14, with higher labour and capital productivity. This marks a significant increase in productivity growth and manufacturing performance post-liberalization. There is the increasing role of high-tech industry, including electronics, in driving aggregate productivity and growth through continuous innovation (Carlaw and Lipsey 2003; Aghion and Jaravel 2015). However, studies pertaining to the electronics industry in India are too few and are often classed with electrical or grouped as high-tech industries (Ghosh 2009; Majumdar 2010a, 2010b; Sharma 2014; Raju and Saradhi 2021).

The Indian electronics industry has a 2.3 per cent share in India's GDP, while the overall manufacturing share is below 20 per cent[2]. Given the importance of the electronics industry as an independent contributor to the growth of the economy and the input contribution to other sectors, the growth and productivity performance of this industry are crucial from the point of the overall growth of the economy. COVID-19 has reinforced the importance of this industry in the years to come. The electronics industry holds strategic importance at firm- (or country-) level with extensive usage in military, space and security systems, and partly explains the inter-firm (or country) competition to innovate, acquire and maintain the technology gap. The future of automation and artificial intelligence-led revolution rests on the innovation and growth of the electronics industry. Electronics indirectly contribute to the production and growth of intangibles and thus lead to an improved productivity performance of the manufacturing and services sector. However, moving from an old technology regime to new works with a time lag gives rise to a 'productivity paradox', where adoption takes place in waves[3]. Adoption also becomes difficult due to technology skill gaps and organizational barriers (Acemoglu and Zilibotti 2001; Atkin et al. 2017).

Following Bartelsman and Doms (2000) and Syverson (2011) surveys, we endeavour to incorporate the three dimensions of extant productivity literature in our study of the electronics industry. The *first* dimension explores major methodological studies for measurement of productivity undergoing continuous evolution and sophistication, e.g., growth accounting, semi-parametric (Olley and Pakes 1996; Levinsohn and Petrin 2003; Ackerberg et al. 2006; Wooldridge 2009) or parametric methods. The *second* dimension of the literature deals with measuring productivity at different levels of aggregation, like plant, firm, industry, sector or country. The *third* dimension delves into sources or determinants of productivity and explains the level or growth of productivity.

The objective of this study is to estimate and compare productivity estimates using a semi-parametric approach: the Levinsohn and Petrin (2003) and Wooldridge (2009) methods for the electronics industry at a 4-digit level of industrial classification. Thereafter, we identify and examine the determinants of productivity and subsequently their impacts on productivity performance of the Indian electronics industry. For the determinants, one-way and two-way fixed effects models are employed (Rijesh 2015). We inquire further into linkages of policy and reforms with firm performance and its determinants. Our study also owes to the availability of micro data at the firm level, advancement in productivity estimation methods and improvement in computational power (Syverson 2011).

The rest of the chapter is organized as follows: in Section 2, the Indian electronics industry is briefly discussed, followed by a discussion on the literature on determinants of productivity in Section 3. In Section 4, data and variables are outlined along with estimation methods. We discuss empirical results in Section 5, followed by our conclusion in Section 6.

2. Indian Electronics Industry

In this section, we highlight three key features of the Indian electronics industry. First, the production and technological base of the industry is low, especially compared to Asian giants (Joseph 2005; Mani 2016; Raju and Saradhi 2021). For this reason, domestic demand is mostly met through imports while the magnitude of exports is small and of low technology (see Figure 8.1). Second, rising per capita purchasing power, expansion of technological infrastructure and government spending on flagship programs make India a major electronics market[4]. This explains the current size of the electronics market and future growth potential. Third, the trajectory of policy and reforms before and after liberalization tells the tale of evolution and the performance of industry. Reforms to attract foreign competition and investment, leading to efficient allocation of resources that improve productivity with overall higher output, have shaped the electronics industry in the last three decades. We observe an increasing import dependence despite policy intervention.

India was rather late in realizing the importance of this industry. Other countries by then had acquired substantial prior experience, production capacity and supply chain network in the electronics and semiconductors industry and were benefitting from the same. The liberalization process,

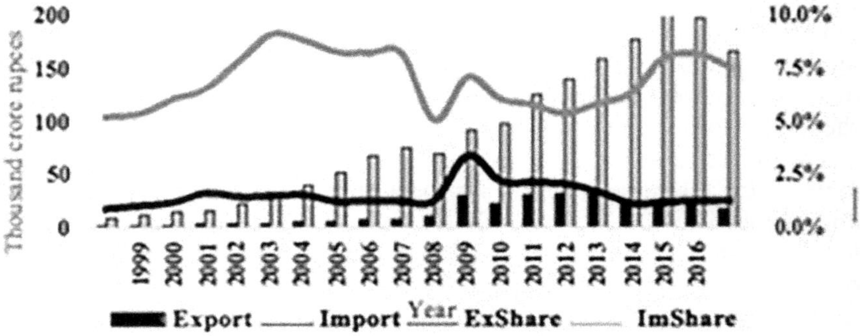

Figure 8.1 Indian Electronics Industry – Trade and Its Share in Total Trade

Source: Authors' compilation based on UN comtrade data

initiated in 1991, led to a reduction in the tariffs on imports of electronic goods. The signing of the Information Technology Agreement (ITA) of the World Trade Organization (WTO) in 1997 and bilateral treaties with Japan, Singapore and ASEAN, etc., have also resulted in a reduction of import duties by India on a wide range of electronics products to zero (Francis 2016). Though a late entrant to the WTO, China has been a big beneficiary of ITA and increased its global market share[5]. Apart from China, India's electronics import is dependent on OECD and Asian-Pacific countries, whereas India's exports go to low-income African countries. This conveys technological differences in imports and exports of electronic goods. Though India imports high-technology products, her exports are mainly in the form of low-technology products (Francis 2016; Raju and Saradhi 2021).

Chinese economic growth is explained by productivity-led growth more than capital investment, with creative restructuring of domestic firms accumulating knowledge and organizational capabilities along with efficient use of inputs and an active role of state (Yu 2015). In comparison, India's slower growth is attributed to services-led growth coupled with late and gradual reforms despite productivity performance converging with Chinese performance after its WTO entry (Wu et al. 2017). The tepid growth of Indian manufacturing is also reflected in slower plant size growth, which indicates lower investment, employment and aggregate productivity growth. The average 40-year-old plant size is 40 per cent larger than the average 5-year-old plant, while the difference is 7 times greater in the USA (Hsieh and Klenow 2014). Higher sunk or entry costs, along with regulatory and institutional hurdles to firm exits, lead to the survival of unprofitable or unproductive firms (Foster et al. 2008). This also distorts the (re)allocation of government subsidies. At the same time, if consumers find enough products to substitute technologically inferior goods, import dependency grows with lowering of trade barriers. In this context, India has consistently lagged behind China in manufacturing in general, and electronics in particular.

The electronics industry is highly capital-, skill- and scale-intensive. It requires specialized materials and components leading to emergence of GVCs, such that manufacturing and knowledge production are spread across geography. The distributed networks operate together as an assembly system with increasing complexity of technology and continuous innovation. Intermediate inputs constitute a major share of electronics production. Therefore, there exists inter-firm (or country) competition to move up the value chain and secure key components and technology, which leads to increased productivity (Melitz 2003; Antras and Helpman 2004; Antras and Chor 2021).

The increased electronics imports into India accompanied by the reduced tariff have given rise to higher trade in intermediate inputs that significantly explain the firms' performance (Amiti and Konings 2007; Goldberg et al. 2010; Topalova and Khandelwal 2011; Halpern et al. 2015; Shu and Steinwender 2019). Higher input imports of electronic goods into India are due to the cheaper, technologically superior and complementary nature of inputs and unavailability in domestic markets, like semiconductor components and devices. Domestic firms lack and lag in innovation to compete with imports and the rapidly changing nature of the industry. However, COVID-19 demonstrates the limitations of global value chains (GVCs) and provides an opportunity for electronics manufacturing in India[6]. Experiences of successful countries, such as China, South Korea and Taiwan suggest a nexus of government-university-industry to accelerate innovation (Cohen et al. 2002; Ernst 2009).

3. Literature Review

In this section, we discuss contemporary literature on measurement and determinants of productivity.

3.1. Measurement of Productivity

The majority of productivity-related studies in India have focused on manufacturing or the industrial sector. These studies are grouped into 3 generations: pre-1980, pre-reform and post-reform studies. Based on the coverage of the study, the extant productivity literature is divided into *macro* (economy level), *meso* (sector or industry level) and *micro* (firm level). With increasingly available data, studies are not limited to a single category alone. To estimate productivity, there are 3 broad approaches: parametric, semi-parametric and non-parametric. These approaches can further be categorized into frontier and non-frontier groups (Kathuria et al. 2013b). In extant literature, early Indian studies are primarily based on growth accounting with a gradual shift towards production function. It is observable that parametric or semi-parametric approaches are used for studies at a disaggregated level, such as industry or manufacturing, while non-parametric is used at the aggregated level. It is noteworthy that productivity measurement, being sensitive to both measurement of output, input and the methodology used, remains a minefield of contesting results and ensuing debates.

Despite the wide variation in productivity estimates obtained using different methods, there is emergent consensus on improvement of manufacturing productivity beginning in the 1980s. There is an interesting caveat. With the majority of Indian manufacturing under unorganized sectors, there is evidence for a widening productivity gap between organized and unorganized, where the former shows growth amid interstate and inter-industry differences. Using growth accounting, Bollard et al. (2013) terms it as miracle of productivity performance led by existing large plants which benefitted from reforms and better access to resources and networks. Trivedi et al. (2011) estimates the productivity growth for both organized and unorganized manufacturing at the country level and also for 15 major states for the period 1980-81 to 2007-08. Using growth accounting, growth for manufacturing during the entire period is reported at 0.99 per cent; however, it shows deceleration in the post-reform period. Metals and chemicals are the best performing industries, with the TFPG at 1.47 and 1.35 per cent respectively during 1980-81 to 2007-2008. Metal continues to shine in the post-reform period but chemicals' gains fizzle out in the same period. On the other hand, textiles and food, beverages and tobacco are the worst-performing industries across the period. The TFP estimates based on production function differs from estimations using growth accounting.

The recent literature increasingly delves into both measurement and determinants of productivity to identify and examine the sources of a 'measure of ignorance'. In Table 8.1, recent studies on productivity of the Indian electronics industry are reported. We observe a prevalence of the Cobb-Douglas production function with application of semi-parametric methods. Majumdar (2010a, 2010b) assesses performance of the electronics industry post-liberalization using parametric method (stochastic frontier) for the period 1993-2004. The findings suggest productivity gains initially and dissipates later; however, labour productivity improves in later periods. In the most recent study on the Indian electronics industry, Raju and Saradhi (2021) employ fixed and random effects estimates of production function for the period from 2000-2018. They highlight key characteristics of the industry with significant contributions of imported technology, R&D and, above all, imported materials in firm-level productivity.

Table 8.1 Recent Indian literature on productivity of electronics industry

Studies	Theme	Data and Method(s)	Results
Ghosh (2009)	Financial Structure and Productivity of Electronics & IT	Prowess, 1996-2007, LP	Firms with lower leverage has high productivity, leverage decided exegenously
Majumdar (2010a, 2010b)	Impact of Liberalization on Indian Electronics Industry	Prowess, 1993-2004, Stochastic production frontier	Effects of reforms minimal, low and slow TFPG compared to Chinese firms in Electronics
Sharma (2010)	Ownership and Firm Productivity	Prowess, 1994-2006, LP	Electronics Industry TFP falling, domestic firms better in TFP than foreign firms
Sharma (2014)	Imported, Inputs, R&D and Firm Productivity	Prowess, 2000-09, System-GMM, LP	Imported inputs and R&D determines productivity of electronics firms, weak relation
Rijesh (2015)	Technology Import and Manufacturing Productivity	Prowess, 1995-2010, LP	Embodied and Disembodied Technology Import positively related to firm productivity
*Francis (2016)**	Impact of Trade Liberalization on Indian Electronics Industry	UN Comtrade, Intra-Industry Trade	Electronics industry more import dependent, low value addition, lack of production base and scale
Satpatky et al (2017)	Determinants of Firm Productivity in Select Industries	Prowess, 1999-2013, LP	Embodied and disembodied technology, imported materials intensity determines TFP
Kumar and Paul (2019)	Productivity Grown under Market Imperfections	ASI, 2009-16, LP	High TFP Growth and markings in Instruments and Components measured at 3-digit level
Raju and Saradhi (2021)	Determinants of Productivity of Indian Electronic Manufacturing	Prowess, 2000-2018, FE, RE	Positive impact of R&D, Export, Import of Materials and Capital Goods on Productivity

*Studies cover trade aspect of electronics industry, relevant to understand export, import and domestic value added.

3.2. *Determinants of Productivity*

At the country level, the lack of inadequate infrastructure including quality power, domestic supply chain and logistics, component manufacturing base and limited design capabilities are major bottlenecks in the growth of the electronics industry (Sharma and Sehgal 2010; Joseph 2005; Ernst 2014; Mani 2016). In addition to external factors operating at the country level, there are firm-level determinants of productivity, like quality labour and capital input, firm age and size, R&D and information technology, management practices and firm structure (Bloom et al. 2010; Kathuria et al. 2013a; Bartz-Zuccala et al. 2018). India is a net import-dependent country in electronics for both inputs and outputs. Firms import capital (embodied and disembodied) and intermediate goods, which significantly explain their performance (Basant and Fikkert 1996; Hasan 2002; Parameswaran 2009; Rijesh 2015; Raju and Saradhi 2021). Intermediate inputs sourced from abroad have inputs complementarity, lower cost and technology transfer through inputs (Goldberg et al. 2010). Trade liberalization facilitates availability, lower cost and higher quality of inputs, which improves both revenue and productivity (Zhang 2017).

The firm age reflects vintage capital effect and '*learning by doing*,' translating into productivity. However, impact of firm age on firm performance is inconclusive (Majumdar 1997; Fort et al. 2013; Haltiwanger et al. 2016; Coad 2016; Esteve-Perez et al. 2018). In general, young firms grow faster but are susceptible to business cycle and early exit, while old firms survive longer with better access to input–output market, finance, etc. For high-tech industries like electronics, young and innovative firms are sources of growth and employment. In Schumpeterian and endogenous growth models, firm size acts a source of resourcefulness to further sales growth, innovation and productivity (Harris and Moffat 2015; Ding et al. 2016). Large firms have advantages of economies of scale and market power, along with investment for R&D and tangible and intangibles capital. Such firms also have better access to government incentives and business that result from deep political connections, especially in developing countries (De and Nagaraj 2014). Amid size heterogeneity, policy and regulations distort growth of firm size in such countries and thus reduce the expected gains in productivity (Tybout 2000).

Firm competition in an industry drives productivity in two ways. First, firms compete to gain market share by reducing cost and in effect become more productive, leading to Darwinian selection as only the productive survive and others are forced to margin or exit. Second, firms take strict measures to increase productivity at firm or plant level to stay in business. Through both channels 'within" and 'between', aggregate productivity increases (Foster et al. 2008, Syverson 2011). Schumpeterian and endogenous growth models vouch for higher market concentration to spur innovation through adequate capital allocation. The competition through trade channels leads to reallocation of resources, both domestic and foreign, and increased rate of innovation and adoption of technology, raising overall productivity (Pavcnik 2002; Melitz 2003; Bloom et al. 2016). The firm also gains on profitability by driving up productivity, leading to more investments (Foster et al. 2008). Profitability and productivity as firm performance variables have a bi-directional relationship where productivity, in general, leads to higher profitability (Bottazzi et al. 2008).

Integrating MNCs with domestic firms through GVCs creates networks for the flow of goods and capital in the electronics industry, contributing to productivity. MNCs drive aggregate productivity in their foreign locations through subsidiary and acquisitions of local plants, apart from being the source of FDI. Innovation, export and management practices help to improve technical efficiency when MNCs drive revenue productivity, whereas different prices across plants lead to increased productivity explained by market structure (Bircan 2019). Prior to that, gradual lowering of trade and investment barriers supported by improvement in transportation and communication technology has paved the way for increased world trade and MNCs-led GVCs. There is widespread consensus on productivity gains from trade reforms accompanied by rising shares of input trade (Pavcnik 2002; Fernandes 2008; Topalova and Khandelwal 2011; Yu 2015; Ahn et al. 2019). Through learning by importing, firms source inputs, accumulate necessary capital and gain in competitiveness. The reduction in tariffs on both inputs and outputs lead to increased trade and aggregate productivity (Amiti and Konings 2007; Defever and Toubal 2013; Garetto 2013; Halpern et al. 2015). At the same time, firms benefit from productivity spillovers via agglomeration, knowledge transfers, thick-input market effects, workers mobility, foreign ownership or joint ventures, R&D cooperation and geographically bounded flow of knowledge (Syverson 2011).

Firms undertake R&D measures to reduce cost of production, create new products and remain competitive while also benefitting from spillover

(Griliches 1979; Bernstein and Nadiri 1988). Government expenditures over R&D, especially for defence and space research, actually crowds *in* the investment by private players, additionally facilitatinf investment being the near-monopsony buyer of their output (Moretti et al. 2019). Public expenditure advances the creation of a skilled workforce by funding education and sponsoring research through public-funded facilities. The growth and globalization of the electronics industry, led by new patents and innovations, depends upon the active role of government, institutions, MNCs and GVCs (Acemoglu and Cao 2015; Branstetter et al. 2019). Literature discussing returns on R&D and productivity of R&D investment has generally shown a varying degree of benefits of R&D investment (Hall et al. 2010; Doraszelski and Jaumandreu 2013; Atkeson and Burstein 2019). In the Indian context, the impact of R&D on productivity has mixed results (Sharma 2014; Khanna and Sharma 2018). In determining the sources of productivity, sector-specific industrial policy, regulations and institutions governing labour laws, intellectual property, etc. have consequential impact by driving the competition, innovation, productivity and growth (Bloom et al. 2013; Garicano et al. 2016; Khanna and Sharma 2018; Liu 2019; Bolatto et al. 2020).

The dominant role of old and/or large firms characterize the Indian manufacturing industry (Alfaro and Chari 2014). Some of these firms also have diverse business investments that help them survive and pool resources within the firm or business group. Such firms also choose to move from high to low technology, determining their product output necessitated by a decline in innovation or productivity. When it comes to availing of subsidies and government benefits, these firms excel due to their size and entrenched networks (Criscuolo et al. 2012). Old and large firms benefitting from subsidies may increase productivity and investment while saving employment (Aghion et al. 2015). At the same time, they may obstruct the reallocation required for other incumbents and new entrants, in the process slowing down overall growth (Acemoglu et al. 2018). Securing high-quality human capital and capital for R&D and IT are big constraints for firms, especially small and young firms (Coad et al. 2016). In this context, an innovative industry like electronics demand relooks into the flow of subsidies along with innovation-driven entrepreneurship. This phenomenon also explains the import-centric approach of domestic firms with a smaller base of technology and capital while facing cheap and technologically superior imports.

4. Productivity Measurement and Determinants Estimates

In this section, we outline data and variables, followed by the productivity estimation method and determinants model.

4.1. Data and Variables

The firm-level data of the electronics industry is drawn from the Centre for Monitoring Indian Economy (CMIE) managed PROWESS database for the period 2004–05 to 2016–17 at a 4-digit level of industry classification, following National Industry Classification (NIC) 2008. Due to missing observations, we construct an unbalanced panel of 148 firms after due cleaning of data. In the sample, firms survive throughout the study period. For this reason, firms joining the industry after 2005 are excluded, while firms exiting during the study period are also left out to minimize selection bias since entry and exit both exert their influence on overall productivity. Peculiar examples also emerge as we look at the firm level. Firms involved in advertising are listed under manufacturing activities and can be identified with zero value of materials input for all years. Similarly, firms providing services with electronic equipment are also part of the original data set obtained from database. After arduous manual checks, we also find a few firms listed as electronics actually turned out to be electricals. For obvious reasons, such firms are excluded from the sample as part of data cleaning. Therefore, the sample selection more or less requires careful examination of all firms within the aforementioned NIC group.

There exists a persistent problem of overlapping manufacturing activities as most firms produce multiple products. For industrial classification they report their main product group. Firms change their main product group over years as their business changes or they are incentivized by government policies and tax regulations. In this regard, electronics and electricals have maximum overlapping compared to other industrial activities. As mentioned earlier, we manually checked firm-level activities to ascertain their industrial group. Based on these, we removed firms from the sample that were primarily electrical firms involved in manufacturing switches, etc. After due cleaning of data, we have an unbalanced sample of 148 firms and 1425 observations over 13 years from 2004–05 to 2016–17 (hereafter, 2005–17 for practical reasons). On an average, datapoints per firm is 9.63 each year against the balanced average of 13. There are 46 firms (31.08%) with datapoints for each year out of 148 firms. The description of industry and subsector is depicted in Table A1.

The variable construction is described in Table A2. This comprises various variables constructed for production function estimation and subsequently to examine for determinants of the productivity. The production function estimation is based on gross revenue or sales output. Capital stock is constructed following Srivastava (1996) using the perpetual inventory method (PIM)[7]. Labour is proxied using compensation to workers and employees (Rijesh 2015). Materials as intermediate input is used as proxy for productivity shock, implying separability of intermediate inputs (Trivedi 2004). Firm age is based on firm incorporation year, and firm size is measured in total assets. Profitability is firm-level profit deflated using total assets. The appropriate and variable specific deflators are mentioned in Table A2. Market concentration is measured using the Herfindahl Hirschman index (HHI), and energy intensity is ratio of power and fuel expenses to sales revenue. The summary of the variables is presented in Table A3. It can be observed that there exists a large firm effect in the sample of the electronics industry. This is evident by large differences between mean and median and high standard deviation. Large firms, in general, belong to business groups, government-run public sector units and foreign firms and their subsidiaries. The large firm effect is visible from the firm size distribution. It can be deduced that on average, firms' sales revenue is increasing and therefore more firms are moving to a higher size class.

In our sample of 148 firms, 119 firms or 80 per cent are exporting, while only 67 firms or 45 per cent undertake R&D investment[8]. The import of inputs is a major characteristic of the electronics industry, as discussed previously. We find 131 firms or 89 per cent importing intermediate inputs; 114 firms or 77 per cent import capital goods (embodied technology), while only 56 firms or 38 per cent import licenced or royalty paid inputs (disembodied technology). This suggests that the majority of firms rely on the import of intermediate inputs and capital goods apart from exporting their output.

4.2. Methodology Used

4.2.1. Methodology for Estimation of Productivity

To begin with, consider a general Cobb-Douglas production function:

$$Y_{it} = A_{it} K_{it}^{\beta_k} \ L_{it}^{\beta_l} M_{it}^{\beta_m} \tag{1}$$

where *Yit* is output of firm *i* in period *t*; *Lit* and *Mit* refer to capital, labour and materials inputs respectively; *Ait* is Hicksian neutral efficiency level of firm *i* in period *t.g*

Taking the natural log on both sides of (1), we have linear production function:

$$y_{it} = \beta_0 + \beta_k k_{it} + \beta_l l_{it} + \beta_m m_{it} + \omega_{it} + u_{it} \tag{2}$$

Such that $(A_{it}) = \beta_0 + w_{it} + u_{it}$; and lower-case letters refer to natural logarithms. The constant term (β_0) measures the mean efficiency level for all firms. Other two terms, w_{it} and u_{it} measure firm-specific unobservable (to econometrician) deviation from the mean. Out of these two, w_{it} refers to observable or predictable parts, at least to the firm, and therefore affects the firm's input decisions and output. This is also called *productivity shock*. The latter part that is *uit* is unobservable to both firms and econometrician and therefore has no impact on input choices. This is assumed to be distributed identically and independently (iid). For example, *wit* stands for managerial ability that is observable to firms and affects input choices and output both while *uit* can be unexpected machine breakdown or weather shocks, etc (Beveren 2012).

The productivity level is estimated as follows:

$$\ln\left(\widehat{A}_{it}\right) = \widehat{\omega}_{it} + \widehat{\beta}_0 + \widehat{u}_{it} = y_{it} - \widehat{\beta}_k k_{it} - \widehat{\beta}_l l_{it} - \widehat{\beta}_m m_{it} \tag{3}$$

Assuming classical measurement error with zero mean, this can be written as:

$$\ln\left(\widehat{A}_{it}\right) = \widehat{\omega}_{it} + \widehat{\beta}_0 = \exp\left(y_{it} - \widehat{\beta}_k k_{it} - \widehat{\beta}_l l_{it} - \widehat{\beta}_m m_{it}\right)$$

This can be estimated using ordinary least squares (OLS). But this requires input decisions to be exogenous. In estimating production function, Marschak and Andrews (1945) pointed out the issues of simultaneity or transmission bias. A profit-maximizing firm decides inputs such that input choices are endogenous to unobserved (to econometrician) productivity. The issue arises with managers (owners) or firms having more information than the econometrician about the productivity. The flexible input(s) transmits the bias since the profit maximizing firm has prior information of productivity-adjust input decisions. Therefore, input choices are no longer exogenous and are correlated with error terms.

Among a multitude of available methods to deal with simultaneity bias, we follow control function approach of semi-parametric methods. These methods, such as Olley and Pakes (1996) [OP], Levinsohn and Petrin (2003) [LP], Ackerberg, Caves and Frazer (2006) [ACF] and Wooldridge (2009), differ in assumptions, proxy variables, timing of input decisions and moment conditions[9]. At the same time, all these methods are based on a monotonicity condition of proxy variable; that is, proxy variables increase monotonically in unobserved productivity terms. Wooldridge (2009) solves issues with OP and LP having two-step estimation procedures with a one-step procedure of generalized method of moments (GMM). He writes two equations with the same dependent variables but uses a different set of instruments. This helps in overcoming the potential identification problem as suggested by ACF in the first stage. Another major benefit emerges by easily obtaining robust standard errors for both serial autocorrelation and heteroskedasticity or both. The bootstrapping technique used to obtain standard errors in two-step methods are inefficient for two reasons: first, contemporaneous correlation in error terms across two equations; second, serial correlation or heteroskedasticity is not addressed properly. Wooldridge (2009) also allows for the Sargan-Hansen test for over-identifying restrictions.

4.2.2. Methodology for Determinants of Productivity

We estimate a determinants model using the fixed effects method. We regress the impact of age, size, profitability and competitiveness on productivity, along with dummy variables for assessing the impact of firm characteristics such as export, import and R&D on productivity. There are 3 broad group of imports: import of embodied technology (capital goods), import of disembodied technology (license, royalty payments, etc.) and import of intermediate input (materials). The Indian electronics industry primarily being dependent on imports for both inputs and final goods makes a strong case for examining their impact on productivity. Both one-way and two-way fixed effects estimation is performed to disentangle the time or year effect given the unbalanced panel.

$$
\begin{aligned}
tfpwd_{it} &= \beta_0 + \beta_1 age_{it} + \beta_2 size_{it} + \beta_3 PFT_{it} + \beta_4 HHI_{it} + \beta_5 ENI_{it} \\
&\quad + \beta_6 EXD_{it} + \beta_7 RDD_{it} + \beta_8 IED_{it} + \beta_9 IDD_{it} + \beta_{10} IMD_{it} + \varepsilon_{it}
\end{aligned} \tag{4}
$$

where tfpwd is TFP in natural logs measured using Wooldridge method, age indicates natural log of firm's age, size is natural log of firm size measured in total assets, PFT is firm profitability, HHI is market concentration and ENI is energy intensity. EXD is dummy for exporting activity, 1 for observation and 0 for no observation, RDD is for R&D, IED is import of embodied technology, IDD is import of disembodied technology and IMD is import of materials.

5. Empirical Results and Discussion

In this section, we report and discuss productivity estimates obtained using LP and Wooldridge methods and determinants of productivity using fixed effects models subsequently.

5.1. Estimates of Productivity

Table 8.2 presents the coefficients estimated for the Cobb-Douglas production function. Before estimating production function, we compute the correlation among variables (see Table A4). The high correlation among capital, labour and materials is on expected lines due to the endogenous nature of inputs in the production process. Input(s) decisions and usage are endogenous due to unobservable discretion of managers or firms and technology. For this, we check for variance inflation factor (VIF) which is 3.45, well below the acceptable limits of 10 (see Table A4). Then, we proceed to estimate production function using OLS, LSDV, FE one-way and two-way, LP and Wooldridge methods. Multiple methods are employed for comparison and the intuitive robustness of estimated parametres[10]. The coefficients of materials are consistently more than 0.5 across all estimates, while the coefficients of labour input are above 0.2, and both are significant at 1 per cent. The coefficient of capital is more than 0.5 across OLS, LP and Wooldridge estimates. In comparison, capital coefficients are downward biased, while labour and material coefficients are upward biased in OLS. All 3 coefficients are smaller in Wooldridge than in LP estimates.

These comparisons suggest that labour and materials play a pivotal role in electronics production. We also estimate production function for the full sample of 148 firms without outliers[11] and find no difference in coefficients with respect to full sample estimates across methods (see Table A5). A similar exercise is run after dropping the year 2017 yielded close results with minor changes in capital and materials coefficients, especially using the Wooldridge method (see Table A5). Considering these two estimations together with Table 8.2, it can be said that estimates of production function are robust. We find that elasticity of output with respect to capital, labour and materials is significant under OLS, LP and Wooldridge methods. The coefficient range of capital, labour and materials is 0.061–0.087, 0.236–0.283 and 0.531–0.663 respectively. LP estimates suggest near-constant returns to scale, whereas Wooldridge points towards decreasing returns to scale, which is evident from the Wald test. The Hansen test for identification in the Wooldridge method is significant at 1 per cent, suggesting validity of variables used.

Table 8.2 Production function estimation – electronics industry

	(1)	*(2)*	*(3)*	*(4)*	*(5)*	*(6)*
Sales (y)	*OLS*	*LSDV*	*FE1*	*FE2*	*LP*	*WD*
Capital (k)	0.0612***	0.0809***	0.0225	0.0597**	0.0874**	0.0817***
	(0.0125)	(0.0120)	(0.0309)	(0.0269)	(0.0433)	(0.0197)
Labour (l)	0.2830***	0.2750***	0.4918***	0.3977***	0.2618***	0.2355***
	(0.0201)	(0.0197)	(0.0713)	(0.0639)	(0.0344)	(0.0177)
Materials (m)	0.6631***	0.6449***	0.5738***	0.5326***	0.5979***	0.5316***
	(0.0189)	(0.0192)	(0.0574)	(0.0581)	(0.0502)	(0.0483)
Constant	1.4868***	1.2316***	1.2293***	1.5115***		
	(0.0644)	(0.0772)	(0.2895)	(0.3104)		
Wald Test					0.89	12.37
P-value					0.35	0.00
Observations	1,425	1,425	1,425	1,425	1,425	1,233
R-squared	0.9529	0.9572	0.7979	0.8295		
Hausman Test			^{2}:35.19*** 3	^{2}:35.68*** 15		
Year FE	NO	YES	NO	YES	NO	NO
No. of Firms	148	148	148	148	148	148

Note: Hansen's J statistic for overidentification in Wooldridge estimation is 26.66***.

Robust standard errors in parentheses; *** $p < 0.01$, ** $p < 0.05$, * $p < 0.1$

5.2. Determinants of Productivity

The FE effects model is well suited for a determinants of productivity study as it is designed to understand the causes of change within a firm. Employing FE saves on potential loss of information compared to using GMM or sys-GMM. Having an unbalanced panel, the increasing number of lags faces the challenge of a limited number of observations. Before presenting our empirical results, we verify for the absence of heteroskedasticity, multicollinearity, and any potential serial correlation. In doing so, we use clustered standard errors that are robust to the correlation between error terms and heteroskedasticity over time in all of our estimations. We further highlight the Pearson correlation coefficient for the main variables used in our empirical analysis (see Table A6). It can be observed that the signs of the correlation coefficients between the explanatory variable and dependent variables are mostly consistent with predicted signs as discussed in Section 4, except for age. We also perform collinearity diagnostic tests using the variance inflation factor (VIF) on the independent variables, which is found to be 1.07, indicating none of these correlations among explanatory variables causes concern regarding multicollinearity.

The cross tabulation of productivity with explanatory variables using quartile distribution reveals their relationship (see Table 8.3). As productivity increases, age and size both increase in each corresponding quartile; however, the increase in mean age is meagre, while the median age rises more than mean age and becomes constant in the third and fourth quartiles. Therefore, firm age may not have a direct linear or positive relationship, but size has strong linear and positive relation. Profitability rises with productivity continuously for first three quartiles but declines thereafter in fourth quartile, creating a local maximum in third quartile. It appears

Table 8.3 Productivity and explanatory variables

tfpwd	*Q1*	*Q2*	*Q3*	*Q4*
	−1.393–2.358	2.358–2.640	2.640–2.915	2.915–4.849
age	3.024	3.066	3.113	3.153
	2.996	*3.045*	*3.178*	*3.178*
size	7.285	8.219	8.906	10.349
	7.013	*8.149*	*8.897*	*10.151*
PFT	0.082	0.122	0.148	0.144
	0.081	*0.118*	*0.137*	*0.130*
HHI	0.154	0.157	0.167	0.183
	0.151	*0.151*	*0.164*	*0.175*
ENI	0.049	0.027	0.017	0.012
	0.022	*0.013*	*0.008*	*0.004*

Source: tfpwd, age and size are in natural logs; first row is mean value; second row (in italics) indicates median value; Q_i represents quartiles.

that profitability has a strong positive and weak non-linear relationship with productivity. Market concentration continuously increases with increasing productivity in all quartiles, suggesting a strong positive and linear relationship. On the other hand, energy intensity follows a direct and negative relationship with productivity. Corresponding to increasing productivity, firm-level energy intensity declines.

5.2.1. Determinants of Productivity Estimates

Moving on to the determinants model, we report both one-way and two-way FE results in Table 8.4. Firm age is positive and significant at a 1 per cent level in all one-way results but negative and not significant in two-way results, except when profitability is excluded from the model. The coefficient of firm size is positive and significant at a 1 per cent level in all models, indicating a strong positive relationship with productivity. Profitability positively explains the productivity level with its coefficient significant at 1 per cent in all model specifications. Market concentration has strong and significant bearings on productivity. Although HHI is not significant in one-way models, it is positive and significant at a 1 per cent level in all two-way models. Energy intensity negatively affects firm-level productivity where its coefficient is negative and significant at 1 per cent in all one-way and two-way models.

Declining energy intensity leading to higher productivity also reiterates continuously innovative industry characteristics, including energy consumption. The relationship between productivity and explanatory variables more or less follows the information available from their cross tabulation (see Table 8.3). Among dummy variables, the coefficient of the import of materials is positive in all specifications and significant in two-way FE models. The R&D and import of embodied technology is not significant; however, the sign of their coefficients is positive in all specifications of the two-way FE model. The coefficient of export and import of disembodied technology is negative and not significant in all model specifications, indicating their limited role in explaining productivity of the Indian electronics industry.

With the inclusion of profitability in the determinants model, there is a possibility of simultaneity bias given the bi-directional relationship between productivity and profitability (Bottazzi et al. 2008). Estimating the model without profitability, we find that signs of previously significant variables remain the same, while the values of their coefficients also more or less remain unchanged. Regressing the determinants model with one period lag of profitability, we find signs of coefficients remain unchanged and significant[12]. This absolves the model of potential simultaneity bias or endogeneity[13]. The inclusion of profitability also takes into account correlation among determinants variables (Campello 2006). Prior to that, we also report the Fisher type panel unit root test with Phillips-Peron equation and trend in Table A7. We reject the null hypothesis of all panels having unit

Table 8.4 Determinants of productivity – fixed effects model

	(1)	*(2)*	*(3)*	*(4)*	*(5)*	*(6)*
Var(s)	*tfpwd*	*tfpwd*	*tfpwd*	*tfpwd*	*tfpwd*	*tfpwd*
Age	0.6207***	–0.0496	0.5915***	–0.0496	0.5554***	0.0294
	(0.1003)	(0.1963)	(0.1101)	(0.1963)	(0.1146)	(0.2194)
Size	0.1926***	0.1801***	0.1926***	0.1801***	0.2006***	0.1888***
	(0.0262)	(0.0271)	(0.0263)	(0.0271)	(0.0282)	(0.0290)
PFT	0.5816***	0.6502***	0.5836***	0.6502***		
	(0.1894)	(0.2235)	(0.1919)	(0.2235)		
HHI			0.2113	4.9031***	0.1326	4.4762***
			(0.2921)	(1.2399)	(0.2986)	(1.4176)
ENI	–0.7109***	–0.7372***	–0.7137***	–0.7372***	-0.7251***	–0.7510***
	(0.2093)	(0.2107)	(0.2086)	(0.2107)	(0.2268)	(0.2311)
EXD	–0.0345	–0.0356	–0.0327	–0.0356	–0.0483	–0.0493
	(0.0484)	(0.0500)	(0.0491)	(0.0500)	(0.0495)	(0.0502)
RDD	–0.0029	0.0107	–0.0011	0.0107	–0.0027	0.0076
	(0.0434)	(0.0367)	(0.0432)	(0.0367)	(0.0438)	(0.0383)
IED	0.0068	0.0013	0.0069	0.0013	0.0091	0.0057
	(0.0198)	(0.0183)	(0.0198)	(0.0183)	(0.0214)	(0.0200)
IDD	–0.0971	–0.0531	–0.0965	–0.0531	–0.1100*	–0.0756
	(0.0642)	(0.0690)	(0.0641)	(0.0690)	(0.0653)	(0.0699)
IMD	0.0439	0.0667*	0.0460	0.0667*	0.0762**	0.0984***
	(0.0382)	(0.0344)	(0.0373)	(0.0344)	(0.0377)	(0.0361)
Constant	–0.9809***	0.8500	–0.9295***	0.1091	–0.8115**	–0.0420
	(0.3129)	(0.5533)	(0.3170)	(0.4127)	(0.3263)	(0.4717)
R^2	0.4056	0.4381	0.4060	0.4381	0.3694	0.3947
Obs	1,425	1,425	1,425	1,425	1,425	1,425
Firms	148	148	148	148	148	148
Hausman Test	^{2}:148.15***	^{2}:19.73	^{2}:154.28***	^{2}:19.73	^{2}:133.08***	^{2}:27.12
	9	20	10	21	9	20
Year FE Test		4.40***	-	4.68***		4.25***
Firm FE Test		22.85***		22.85***		22.93***
Year & Firm Test		28.09***		25.68***		24.51***
Year FE	NO	YES	NO	YES	NO	YES

*Robust standard errors in parentheses; *** p<0.01, ** p<0.05, * p<0.1*

roots; therefore, variables are stationary. Based on our results and diagnostics, we accept the two-way FE model as a better fit and discuss it further.

In Table 8.5, we present the mean difference in TFP based on dummies. When firms report their export, R&D or import of inputs, their corresponding mean TFP is higher and significant at 1 per cent, except for the import

Table 8.5 Mean difference in TFP based on dummy

Dummy	*Obs(1)*	*Mean TFP*	*Obs(0)*	*Mean TFP*	*Mean Diff*
Export (EXD)	961	2.693	464	2.570	0.123***
R&D (RDD)	507	2.735	918	2.607	0.128***
Import of Embodied Technology (IED)	686	2.761	739	2.552	0.209***
Import of Disembodied Technology (IDD)	327	2.803	1098	2.608	0.194***
Import of Materials (IMD)	1076	2.650	349	2.661	–0.011

Notes: (1) indicates presence of corresponding observations, (0) indicates otherwise, *** p<0.01, ** p<0.05, * p<0.1

of materials. It can be said that average productivity of firms increases with export, R&D and import of inputs; however, only the import of materials is significant in the determinants model (see Table 8.4). This signifies that firm characteristics such as decision to export, R&D or import of inputs have bearings on firm productivity.

5.2.2. Determinants of Productivity Estimates – Mean Divide

In this section, we divide samples into two groups based on mean values of age, size, profitability and energy intensity. For firm age, there are 51% observations above the mean termed *old* and the rest as *young*. At the firm-size level, there are 47 per cent observations above the mean considered *large*, and the remaining are *small*. The profitability has 46 per cent observations above the mean labeled as *high*, and the others *low*. Based on the mean of energy intensity, there are 26 per cent observations above mean called *more*, and the rest are *less* energy-intensive. The mean divide explains the distribution across the mean and resulting industry characteristics. On average, firms are old while less energy-intensive, whereas size and profitability are driven by a few large or high-profit firms.

In Table 8.6, we present the mean-based differences in determinants of a productivity model specification using two-way fixed effects[14]. Firm age is not significant in all specifications except for *low* profitable firms, where its coefficient is negative and significant at 10 per cent. Firm size is positive and significant in all cases except for *more* energy-intensive firms. Profitability has a curious case with a sizeable variation in value and significance level of its coefficient. It is observable that profitability positively and significantly boosts productivity for *low* profitable, *large* size, *old* age and *less* energy-intensive firms. Market concentration is positive and significant for all groups, except for young firms with significant variation in the value of the coefficients. Energy intensity has negative and significant relation to productivity in all cases, except for *high* profitable firms with a broad range for

Table 8.6 Determinants of productivity – mean divide

	(1)	*(2)*	*(3)*	*(4)*	*(5)*	*(6)*	*(7)*	*(8)*
	Young	*Old*	*Small*	*Large*	*Low*	*High*	*Less*	*More*
tfpwd	*AGE*	*AGE*	*SIZE*	*SIZE*	*PFT*	*PFT*	*ENI*	*ENI*
age	0.1187	–0.2738	–0.0410	–0.0705	–0.3885*	–0.1962	–0.0485	–0.1829
	(0.3093)	(–0.6552)	(–0.1508)	(–0.3351)	(–1.7673)	(–0.7461)	(–0.2894)	(–0.5337)
size	0.1705***	0.1865***	0.1631***	0.1126***	0.1657***	0.1658***	0.1562***	0.0845
	(5.4360)	(3.7129)	(3.9007)	(2.9992)	(4.3709)	(4.9525)	(6.0322)	(1.3135)
PFT	0.6022	0.6305***	0.3460*	1.0069***	1.7268***	0.2287	0.4724***	0.2321
	(1.5534)	(4.0673)	(1.9524)	(5.1240)	(6.1407)	(1.4868)	(3.4948)	(0.8347)
HHI	3.5453	6.1693***	4.1044**	6.3955***	8.7366***	3.7378*	4.3536***	6.2374**
	(1.0464)	(3.0916)	(2.1640)	(4.8415)	(6.1124)	(1.9366)	(3.6794)	(2.5488)
ENI	–5.7600**	–0.7032***	–3.6397***	–6.5697***	–0.7394***	–0.8618	–28.7166***	–0.6982***
	(–2.0107)	(–3.8121)	(–12.1343)	(–3.4979)	(–4.0878)	(–0.6090)	(–6.3116)	(–4.3724)
EXD	–0.0517	0.0047	–0.0390	0.0109	–0.0234	–0.0378	–0.0267	–0.0037
	(–0.6972)	(0.1297)	(–0.6384)	(0.1979)	(–0.4474)	(–0.3948)	(–0.4609)	(–0.0793)
RDD	–0.0471	0.0532	–0.0581	0.0354	0.0297	–0.0390	–0.0438	–0.0126
	(–0.6731)	(1.3604)	(–0.8331)	(0.9275)	(0.5852)	(–0.9826)	(–1.1966)	(–0.1397)
IED	0.0130	–0.0132	–0.0138	–0.0051	–0.0130	0.0379	–0.0154	0.0147
	(0.4480)	(–0.6086)	(–0.5347)	(–0.1724)	(–0.4345)	(1.3908)	(–0.6902)	(0.5435)
IDD	–0.1470	0.0202	–0.0693	0.0085	0.0402	–0.1749	–0.1119	–0.0398
	(–1.2283)	(0.5106)	(–0.7201)	(0.1764)	(0.8988)	(–1.4181)	(–1.3351)	(–0.4159)
IMD	0.0199	0.1022**	0.0214	0.0519	0.0858*	–0.0015	0.0165	0.1293
	(0.5153)	(2.2350)	(0.5688)	(1.0489)	(1.8855)	(–0.0312)	(0.5224)	(1.4403)
Constant	0.2241	0.4263	0.5424	0.5166	0.3616	1.1140**	0.7917*	0.9069
	(0.4836)	(0.3791)	(1.1842)	(0.9140)	(0.7258)	(1.9803)	(1.9644)	(1.0345)
R^2	0.4200	0.4916	0.4898	0.5512	0.4795	0.4334	0.4974	0.4517
Obs	700	725	757	668	767	658	1,054	371
Firms	86	74	107	77	134	134	128	62

Note: Robust standard errors in parentheses; *** $p < 0.01$, ** $p < 0.05$, * $p < 0.1$

the value of its coefficients. It is no surprise that largest value of coefficient is for less energy-intensive firms.

Among dummies, only the import of materials has significant and positive relation to productivity, but only for *old* and *low* profitable firms. In all other cases, the sign of the coefficient is positive except for *high* profitable firms. The sign of the coefficient of the R&D dummy is positive but not significant for *old*, *large* or *low* profitable firms. For export, it's *old* and *large* firms; for imports of embodied technology, it's *young* and *high* profitable firms; for import of disembodied technology, it's *old*, *large* and *low* profitable firms. Following the mean divide regression, as in Table 8.6, without profitability also yields similar results (see Table A8). The import of materials is positive in all scenarios and significant for *old* and *low* profitable firms.

We find differences of productivity based on mean values of age, size, profitability and energy intensity to be significant at a 1 per cent level, except for age (see Table 8.7). As firm size, profitability and energy intensity cross the industry average, their average productivity is higher than that of below-average values. It points towards the average productivity being biased towards above-mean values. Our study incorporates firm- and industry-level determinant variables, which may result in omitted variable bias. The limitations to our study also emerge from sample selection bias due to data availability and the cleaning process, along with the definition of industry adopted. There is a possibility of results being sensitive to the period of study considered.

The electronics industry requires higher capital investment and continuous innovation. In this regard, vintage capital outweighs learning by doing given the high sunk cost for vintage capital, which confirms our results (Harris and Moffat 2015). At the same time, increasing firm size leads to economies of scale, higher investment and exploitation of business and political connections, translating into higher productivity as evident in our results (De and Nagaraj 2014). Moving from perfect competition to an oligopolistic market structure, productivity increases in the Indian electronics industry. Our results point out that the import of materials input is vital for productivity performance in line with the findings of Sharma (2014, 2016).

Table 8.7 Mean difference in TFP based on mean divide

Variables	*Obs(1)*	*Mean TFP*	*Obs(0)*	*Mean TFP*	*Mean Diff*
age	725	2.671	700	2.635	0.036
size	668	2.882	757	2.451	0.432***
PFT	658	2.775	767	2.548	0.227***
ENI	371	2.363	1054	2.755	-0.392***

Note: (1) indicates values greater than or equal to mean, (0) indicates the rest; *** $p < 0.01$, ** $p < 0.05$, * $p < 0.1$

We observe the difference across the average values of firm age, size, profitability and energy intensity as expected. *Old*, *large* and *low* profitable firms are more productive, while they also productively choose to import inputs, especially materials. Learning by doing and access to input networks and the global value chain play a pivotal role in explaining the productivity performance of the electronics industry. Profitability has a limiting point beyond which productivity declines, suggesting exhaustion of resources and diminishing marginal rate of returns to input(s) set. The oligopolistic market structure benefits firm-level productivity while indicating the presence of a few large firms, similar to the global electronics industry. Schumpeterian growth theory fits the emerging characteristics of the electronics industry with the central role of old and large firms. The declining energy intensity across firms driving up productivity concurs with the innovation-driven industry.

With nearly half of firms involved in R&D, domestic-level innovation is limited but still relevant. Firms prefer one-time lump sum payments for embodied technology instead of disembodied technology, which is in continuation of the pre-liberalization pattern (Joseph 2005). Given the lack of a domestic capital goods market, liberal trade regime or innovative nature of the industry, there is continuous competition to innovate or import inputs. Materials become the cornerstone of input imports through interlinkages of GVCs, partly explained by technology gaps and product life-cycle hypotheses. Exports have a limited role due to low technological content of output, while the major focus lies on domestic demand with limited production capacity. Overall, firm productivity distribution is heterogenous and determined by its size, profitability, market concentration, R&D and import of inputs, especially materials. The electronics industry, characterized by import dependency and rapid innovation, policy and regulation, should be industry-specific to augment innovation and entrepreneurship. Industrial experience from Asian countries suggests the central role of government in (re)allocation of subsidies, licences and contracts, along with building the nexus of government-university-industry.

6. Conclusion

The Indian electronics industry is one of the fastest-growing industries with a 2.3 per cent GDP share. Driven by continuous innovation and demand, electronics are increasingly used on a standalone basis or as intermediate input for other industries, and thus contribute to overall productivity and growth. However, India is a net importer of electronics for both input(s) and output. In this context, it is imperative to assess firm performance measured through productivity and examine sources of its determinants. In doing so, this study aims to empirically explore the measurement of productivity and determinants of productivity of the Indian electronics industry for the period of 2004–05 to 2016–17. We estimate firm-level productivity of an unbalanced panel of 148 firms at a 4-digit level of industrial classification, using the Cobb-Douglas production function. The results show consistent positive signs and near-convergent values of elasticity of capital, labour and materials inputs using semi-parametric LP and Wooldridge methods. We choose Wooldridge estimates over LP, owing to the efficient single-step bootstrapping method for examining the determinants of productivity using two-way FE models. The estimated results show that firm size and profitability positively explain firm-level productivity, while firm age has no significant impact. Increasing market concentration and decreasing energy intensity lead to higher productivity.

Using dummies for firm characteristics, the import of materials input is found to positively and significantly explain productivity. Firms benefit from undertaking R&D and import of embodied technology; however, coefficients are not significant. Exports and imports of disembodied technology are neither positive nor significant suggesting their limited role. We also estimate determinants by dividing the sample based on average values of age, size, profitability and energy intensity. The results of the study do not change qualitatively for *old*, *large* and *low* profitable firms. The results are ascertained with robustness checks showing efficacy of the model. There exist the large firm effects with higher-mean TFP based on firm characteristics. These findings fit well with Schumpeterian and endogenous growth models while conforming with broader characteristics of Indian manufacturing. We propose an active government role in resource (re)allocation and industry-specific policies to foster innovation and entrepreneurship to reduce import dependency in the long run.

Acknowledgement: This book chapter is part of a doctoral dissertation submitted at IIT Bombay. We are thankful to IIT Bombay for the research grant and support. Any or all errors are our own only.

Notes

1 KLEMS framework includes capital (K), labour (L), energy (E), materials (M) and services (S) as inputs. India, China and OECD countries are adopting this for comparable data series and productivity estimates.
2 National Policy on Electronics 2019, Ministry of Electronics and IT, Government of India (NPE 2019).
3 David (1990) points out this productivity paradox attached to innovation through examples of dynamo and computer as technological adoption, diffusion and spillovers take time. Solow (1987) captures it succinctly, 'We see computers everywhere but in productivity statistics'.
4 Government programs like Digital India and BharatNet. are aimed at improving electronics-based infrastructure, while Make In India and Production Linked Incentives (PLI) schemes target increasing electronics manufacturing.
5 India imports 40 per cent of total electronics imports from China, which is 32 per cent of total imports from China. ***https://tinyurl.com/yrxruryb*** Last accessed on March 03, 2021.

6 TIFAC: Focused intervention for 'Make In India' post-COVID-19 https://tinyurl.com/ffxe6hhc Last accessed on March 03, 2021.
7 The PIM assumes that the flow of capital services is proportional to the stock of capital. Although widely used in Indian productivity literature, PIM does not account for capacity utilization, and depreciation rates may vary in reality.
8 Firms reporting R&D, export or import during the study period (one or more observations) are counted as undertaking that activity.
9 There are two major limitations of assumptions associated with semi-parametric methods. First, the underlying assumptions for invertibility of function breeds practical problems. This requires monotonicity of proxy variables for the inverse of the function to be possible. Second, the assumptions of firms facing competitive factor markets or same input prices are not realistic. The condition of scalar observables is violated in the presence of differing input prices for firms (Ackerberg *et al*, 2006).
10 We consider sales, net sales and sales with change in stocks as a measure of output. However, only sales provide consistent and significant results for all methods. Estimations including energy yield very small and not significant coefficients for energy across all methods, so we dropped it.
11 Outliers identified following ($\bar{\cdot} \pm 3$) for output variable and 24 observations were removed out of 1425.
12 One period lag of profitability can determine productivity, but the same is not true the other way around. At the same time, profitability and its lag have a significant correlation among them. Therefore, this rules out the possible endogeneity in our model. We have not produced the regression here for the want of space; this can be produced by the author if and when demanded.
13 The sign and significance of coefficients of fixed-effect determinants models do not change with one period lag of profitability, indicating robustness of estimated parametres.
14 As specified earlier, we discuss two-way FE results since they account for firm-level heterogeneity with both firm and year effect.

References

Acemoglu, D., & Cao, D. (2015). Innovation by entrants and incumbents, *Journal of Economic Theory*, 157, 255–294.

Acemoglu, D., & Zilibotti, F. (2001). Productivity differences, *The Quarterly Journal of Economics*, 116(2), 563–606.

Acemoglu, D., Akcigit, U., Alp, H., Bloom, N., & Kerr, W. (2018). Innovation, reallocation, and growth, *American Economic Review*, 108(11), 3450–3491.

Ackerberg, D., Caves, K., & Frazer, G. (2006). Structural identification of production functions, University of California Los Angeles. Last accessed on 16th May 2021: www.econ.ucla.edu/ackerber/ACF20withtables.pdf

Aghion, P., Akcigit, U., & Howitt, P. (2015). Lessons from Schumpeterian growth theory, *American Economic Review*, 105(5), 94–99.

Aghion, P., & Howitt, P. (1992). A model of growth through creative destruction, *Econometrica*, 60(2), 323–361.

Aghion, P., & Jaravel, X. (2015). Knowledge spillovers, innovation and growth, *The Economic Journal*, 125(583), 533–573.

Ahluwalia, I. J. (1991). *Productivity and Growth in Indian Manufacturing*, Oxford University Press, New Delhi.

Ahn, J., Dabla-Norris, E., Duval, R., Hu, B., & Njie, L. (2019). Reassessing the productivity gains from trade liberalization. *Review of International Economics*, 27(1), 130–154.
Alfaro, L., & Chari, A. (2014). Deregulation, misallocation, and size: Evidence from India, *The Journal of Law and Economics*, 57(4), 897–936.
Amiti, M., & Konings, J. (2007). Trade liberalization, intermediate inputs, and productivity: Evidence from Indonesia, *American Economic Review*, 97(5), 1611–1638.
Antras, P., & Chor, D. (2021). Global value chains, Working Paper 2854, National Bureau of Economic Research.
Antras, P., & Helpman, E. (2004). Global sourcing, *Journal of Political Economy*, 112(3), 552–580.
Asker, J., Collard-Wexler, A., & De Loecker, J. (2014). Dynamic inputs and resource (mis)allocation, *Journal of Political Economy*, 122(5), 1013–1063.
Atkeson, A., & Burstein, A. (2019). Aggregate implications of innovation policy, *Journal of Political Economy*, 127(6), 2625–2683.
Atkin, D., Khandelwal, A. K., & Osman, A. (2017). Exporting and firm performance: Evidence from a randomized experiment, *The Quarterly Journal of Economics*, 132(2), 551–615.
Autor, D., Dorn, D., Katz, L. F., Patterson, C., & Van Reenen, J. (2020). The fall of the labor share and the rise of superstar firms, *The Quarterly Journal of Economics*, 135(2), 645–709.
Balakrishnan, P., & Pushpangadan, K. (1994). Total factor productivity growth in manufacturing industry: A fresh look, *Economic and Political Weekly*, 29(31), 2028–2035.
Bartelsman, E. J., & Doms, M. (2000). Understanding productivity: Lessons from longitudinal microdata. *Journal of Economic Literature*, 38(3), 569–594.
Bartelsman, E., Haltiwanger, J., & Scarpetta, S. (2013). Cross-country differences in productivity: The role of allocation and selection, *American Economic Review*, 103(1), 305–334.
Bartz-Zuccala, W., Mohnen, P., & Schweiger, H. (2018). The role of innovation and management practices in determining firm productivity, *Comparative Economic Studies*, 60(4), 502–530.
Basant, R., & Fikkert, B. (1996). The effects of R&D, foreign technology purchase, and domestic and international spillovers on productivity in Indian firms, *The Review of Economics and Statistics*, 78(2), 187.
Bernstein, J., & Nadiri, M. I. (1988). Interindustry R&D spillovers, rates of return, and production in high-tech industries, Working Paper 2554, National Bureau of Economic Research.
Beveren, I. V. (2012). Total factor productivity estimation: A practical review, *Journal of Economic Surveys*, 26(1), 98–128.
Bircan, Ç. (2019). Ownership structure and productivity of multinationals, *Journal of International Economics*, 116, 125–143.
Bloom, N., Draca, M., & Van Reenen, J. (2016). Trade induced technical change? The impact of Chinese imports on innovation, IT and productivity, *The Review of Economic Studies*, 83(1), 87–117.
Bloom, N., Eifert, B., Mahajan, A., McKenzie, D., & Roberts, J. (2013). Does management matter? Evidence from India, *The Quarterly Journal of Economics*, 128(1), 1–51.

Bloom, N., Mahajan, A., McKenzie, D., & Roberts, J. (2010). Why do firms in developing countries have low productivity? *American Economic Review*, 100(2), 619–623.

Bolatto, S., Naghavi, A., Ottaviano, G., & Kejzar, K. Z. (2020). Intellectual property and the organization of the global value chain, Discussion Paper 1673, Center for Economic Performance, London School of Economics.

Bollard, A., Klenow, P. J., & Sharma, G. (2013). India's mysterious manufacturing miracle, *Review of Economic Dynamics*, 16(1), 59–85.

Bottazzi, G., Secchi, A., & Tamagni, F. (2008). Productivity, profitability and financial performance, *Industrial and Corporate Change*, 17(4), 711–751.

Branstetter, L. G., Glennon, B., & Jensen, J. B. (2019). The IT revolution and the globalization of R&D, *Innovation Policy and the Economy*, 19, 1–37.

Campello, M. (2006). Debt financing: Does it boost or hurt firm performance in product markets? *Journal of Financial Economics*, 82(1), 135–172.

Carlaw, K. I., & Lipsey, R. G. (2003). Productivity, technology and economic growth: What is the relationship? *Journal of Economic Surveys*, 17(3), 457–495.

Coad, A. (2016). Firm age: A survey. *Journal of Evolutionary Economics*, 28(1), 13–43.

Cohen, W. M., Nelson, R. R., & Walsh, J. P. (2002). Links and impacts: The influence of public research on industrial R&D, *Management Science*, 48(1), 1–23.

Criscuolo, C., Martin, R., Overman, H., & Reenen, J. V. (2012). The causal effects of an industrial policy, Working Paper 17842, National Bureau of Economic Research.

De, P. K., & Nagaraj, P. (2014). Productivity and firm size in India, *Small Business Economics*, 42(4), 891–907.

Defever, F., & Toubal, F. (2013). Productivity, relationship-specific inputs and the sourcing modes of multinationals, *Journal of Economic Behaviour & Organization*, 94(10), 345–357.

Ding, S., Sun, P., & Jiang, W. (2016). The effect of import competition on firm productivity and innovation: Does the distance to technology Frontier matter? *Oxford Bulletin of Economics and Statistics*, 78(2), 197–227.

Doraszelski, U., & Jaumandreu, J. (2013). R&D and productivity: Estimating endogenous productivity, *Review of Economic Studies*, 80(4), 1338–1383.

Dosi, G., & Nelson, R. R. (2013). The evolution of technologies: An assessment of the state-of-of-the-art, *Eurasian Business Review*, 3, 3–46.

Ernst, D. (2009). *A New Geography of Knowledge in the Electronics Industry? Asia's Role in Global Innovation Networks*, East-West Centre, Honolulu, HI.

Ernst, D. (2014). *Upgrading India's Electronics Manufacturing Industry: Regulatory Reform and Industrial Policy, A Special Study*, East-West Centre, Honolulu, HI.

Esteve-Perez, S., Pieri, F., & Rodriguez, D. (2018). Age and productivity as determinants of firm survival over the industry life cycle, *Industry and Innovation*, 25(2), 167–198.

Fernandes, A. M. (2008). Firm Productivity in Bangladesh Manufacturing Industries. *World Development*, 36(10), 1725–1744.

Fort, T. C., Haltiwanger, J., Jarmin, R. S., & Miranda, J. (2013). How firms respond to business cycles: The role of firm age and firm size, *IMF Economic Review*, 61(3), 520–559.

Foster, L., Haltiwanger, J., & Syverson, C. (2008). Reallocation, firm turnover, and efficiency: Selection on productivity or profitability? *American Economic Review*, 98(1), 394–425.

Francis, S. (2016). *Impact of Trade Liberalization on Indian Electronics Industry*, Working Paper 192, Institute for Studies in Industrial Development, New Delhi.

Garetto, S. (2013). Input sourcing and multinational production, *American Economic Journal: Macroeconomics*, 5(2), 118–151.

Garicano, L., Lelarge, C., & Van Reenen, J. (2016). Firm size distortions and the productivity distribution: Evidence from France, *American Economic Review*, 106(11), 3439–3479.

Ghosh, S. (2009). Do productivity and ownership really matter for growth? Firm-level evidence, *Economic Modelling*, 26(6), 1403–1413.

Goldar, B., Krishna, K. L., Aggarwal, S. C., Das, D. K., Erumban, A. A., & Das, P. C. (2017). Productivity growth in India since the 1980s: The KLEMS approach, *Indian Economic Review*, 52(1–2), 37–71.

Goldberg, P. K., Khandelwal, A. K., Pavcnik, N., & Topalova, P. (2010). Imported intermediate inputs and domestic product growth: Evidence from India, *The Quarterly Journal of Economics*, 125(4), 1727–1767.

Griliches, Z. (1979). Issues in assessing the contribution of research and development to productivity growth, *The Bell Journal of Economics*, 10(1), 92–116.

Grossman, G. M., & Helpman, E. (1991). *Innovation and Growth in the Global Economy*, MIT Press, Cambridge, MA.

Hall, B. H., Mairesse, J., & Mohnen, P. (2010). Measuring the returns to R&D. In B. H. Hall & N. Rosenberg (Eds.) *Handbook of the Economics of Innovation* (Vol. 2, pp. 1033–1082), Elsevier.

Halpern, L., Koren, M., & Szeidl, A. (2015). Imported inputs and productivity, *American Economic Review*, 105(12), 3660–3703.

Haltiwanger, J., Jarmin, R. S., Kulick, R., & Miranda, J. (2016). High growth young firms: Contribution to job, output, and productivity growth. In *Measuring Entrepreneurial Businesses: Current Knowledge and Challenges* (pp. 11–62), University of Chicago Press, Chicago.

Harris, R., & Moffat, J. (2015). Plant-level determinants of total factor productivity in Great Britain, 1997–2008, *Journal of Productivity Analysis*, 44(1), 1–20.

Hasan, R. (2002). The impact of imported and domestic technologies on the productivity of firms: Panel data evidence from Indian manufacturing firms, *Journal of Development Economics*, 69(1), 23–49.

Hopenhayn, H. A. (1992). Entry, exit, and firm dynamics in long run equilibrium, *Econometrica*, 60(5), 1127–1150.

Hsieh, C.-T., & Klenow, P. J. (2009). Misallocation and manufacturing TFP in China and India, *The Quarterly Journal of Economics*, 124(4), 1403–1448.

Hsieh, C.-T., & Klenow, P. J. (2014). The life cycle of plants in India and Mexico, *The Quarterly Journal of Economics*, 129(3), 1035–1084.

Joseph, K. J. (2005). Strategic approach to strengthening the international competitiveness in knowledge based industries: Electronics industry (No. 22102). East Asian Bureau of Economic Research.

Jovanovic, B. (1982). Selection and the evolution of industry, *Econometrica*, 50(3), 649–670.

Kathuria, V., Raj, S. N. R., & Sen, K. (2013a). Impact of human capital on manufacturing productivity growth in India. In V. Kathuria, S. N. R. Raj, & K. Sen (Eds.) *Human Capital and Development* (pp. 23–37), Springer, India.

Kathuria, V., Raj, S. N. R., & Sen, K. (2013b). Productivity measurement in Indian manufacturing: A comparison of alternative methods, *Journal of Quantitative Economics*, 11(1–2), 148–179.

Khanna, R., & Sharma, C. (2018). Testing the effects of investment in IT and R&D on labour productivity: New method and evidence for Indian firms, *Economics Letters*, 17(3), 30–34.

Kumar, A. R., & Paul, M. (2019). Industry level analysis of productivity growth under market imperfections, *Indian Growth and Development Review*, 13(1), 155–174.

Levinsohn, J., & Petrin, A. (2003). Estimating production functions using inputs to control for unobservables, *Review of Economic Studies*, 70(2), 317–341.

Liu, E. (2019). Industrial policies in production networks, *The Quarterly Journal of Economics*, 134(4), 1883–1948.

Majumdar, R. (2010a). Did liberalization impact productivity of the Indian electronics hardware industry? *International Journal of the Economics of Business*, 17(2), 253–273.

Majumdar, R. (2010b). Indian electronics hardware industry: Growth and productivity (1993–2004), *Economic and Political Weekly*, 45(14), 72–77.

Majumdar, S. K. (1997). The impact of size and age on firm-level performance: Some evidence from India, *Review of Industrial Organization*, 12(2), 231–241.

Mani, S. (2016). *One Size Does Not Fit All: An Analysis of the Importance of the Industry Specific Vertical Policies for Growing High Technology Industries in India* (Discussion paper 16–08), National Graduate Institute for Policy Studies, Tokyo.

Marschak, J., & Andrews, W. H. (1945). Random simultaneous equations and the theory of production, *Econometrica*, 12(3/4), 143–205.

Melitz, M. J. (2003). The impact of trade on intra-industry reallocations and aggregate industry productivity, *Econometrica*, 71(6), 1695–1725.

Ministry of Eletcronics and Information Technology. (2019). *National Policy on Electronics*, https://www.meity.gov.in/writereaddata/files/eGazette_Notification_NPE%202019_dated%2025022019.pdf

Moretti, E., Steinwender, C., & Van Reenen, J. (2019). The intellectual spoils of war? Defense R&D, productivity and international spillovers, Working Paper 26483, National Bureau of Economic Research.

Nelson, R. R., & Winter, S. G. (1982). *An Evolutionary Theory of Economic Change*, Harvard University Press, Cambridge, MA.

Olley, G. S., & Pakes, A. (1996). The dynamics of productivity in the telecommunications equipment industry, *Econometrica*, 64(6), 1263.

Parameswaran, M. (2009). International Trade, R&D Spillovers and Productivity: Evidence from Indian Manufacturing Industry, *Journal of Development Studies*, 45(8), 1249–1266.

Pavcnik, N. (2002). Trade liberalization, exit, and productivity improvements: Evidence from Chilean plants, *The Review of Economic Studies*, 69(1), 245–276.

Raju, S., & Saradhi, V. R. (2021). What ails India's electronic manufacturing industry: An assessment, *The Indian Economic Journal*, 69(1), 1–23.

Rijesh, R. (2015). Technology import and manufacturing productivity in India: Firm level analysis, *Journal of Industry, Competition and Trade*, 15(4), 411–434.
Romer, P. M. (1990). Endogenous technological change, *Journal of Political Economy*, 98(5–2), 71–102.
Romer, P. M. (1994). The origins of endogenous growth, *Journal of Economic Perspectives*, 8(1), 3–22.
Sharma, C. (2010). Does productivity differ in domestic and foreign firms? Evidence from Indian machinery industry, *Indian Economic Review*, 45(1), 87–110.
Sharma, C. (2014). Imported intermediate inputs, R&D, and productivity at firm level: Evidence from Indian manufacturing industries, *The International Trade Journal*, 28(3), 246–263.
Sharma, C. (2016). Does importing more inputs raise productivity and exports? Some evidence from Indian manufacturing. *Economic Issues*, 21(1), 8–21.
Sharma, C., & Sehgal, S. (2010). Impact of infrastructure on output, productivity and efficiency, *Indian Growth and Development Review*, 3(2), 100–121.
Shu, P., & Steinwender, C. (2019). The impact of trade liberalization on firm productivity and innovation, *Innovation Policy and the Economy*, 19, 39–68.
Solow, R. M. (1957). Technical change and the aggregate production function, *The Review of Economics and Statistics*, 39(3), 312–320.
Srivastava, V. (1996). *Liberalization, Productivity and Competition: A Panel Study of Indian Manufacturing*, Oxford University Press, New Delhi.
Syverson, C. (2011). What determines productivity? *Journal of Economic Literature*, 49(2), 326–365.
Topalova, P., & Khandelwal, A. (2011). Trade liberalization and firm productivity: The case of India, *Review of Economics and Statistics*, 93(3), 995–1009.
Trivedi, P. (2004). An inter-state perspective on manufacturing productivity in India: 1980–81 to 2000–01, *Indian Economic Review*, 39(1), 203–237.
Trivedi, P., Lakshmanan, L., Jain, R., & Gupta, Y. K. (2011). Productivity, efficiency and competitiveness of the Indian manufacturing sector, Study No. 37, Development Research Group, Reserve Bank of India, Mumbai.
Trivedi, P., Prakash, A., & Sinate, D. (2000). Productivity in major manufacturing industries in India: 1973–74 to 1997–98, Study No. 20, Development Research Group, Reserve Bank of India, Mumbai.
Tybout, J. R. (2000). Manufacturing firms in developing countries: How well do they do, and why? *Journal of Economic Literature*, 38(1), 11–44.
Wooldridge, J. M. (2009). On estimating firm-level production functions using proxy variables to control for unobservables, *Economics Letters*, 104(3), 112–114.
Wu, H. X., Krishna, K. L., Das, D. K., & Das, P. C. (2017). How Does the Productivity and Economic Growth Performance of China and India Compare in the Post-Reform Era, 1981–2011? *International Productivity Monitor*, 33, 91–113.
Yu, M. (2015). Processing trade, tariff reductions and firm productivity: Evidence from Chinese firms, *The Economic Journal*, 125(585), 943–988.
Zhang, H. (2017). Static and dynamic gains from costly importing of intermediate inputs: Evidence from Colombia, *European Economic Review*, 91(1), 118–145.

Chapter 9

MNC's Affiliation and Their Exports Performance

A Case of the Indian Motor Vehicle Industry

Anurag Anand

1. Introduction

The motor vehicle industry (MVI) is one of the key industries of the Indian economy. The industry has a strong recognition and reputation in the world export market, as the annual production of motor vehicles[1] has increased from 8,18,193 units in 1999 (about 2 per cent of world production) to 51,74,645 units in 2018 (about 8 per cent of world production). The share of passenger cars (15.08 per cent) and commercial vehicles (4.45 per cent) comprises more than 20 per cent of the automobile sector in India (SIAM, 2013). In the category of passenger cars, the market share of Maruti Udyog was 52 per cent, Hyundai Motor's market share was 19 per cent, and Tata Motor's share was 16 per cent in 2012–13. These are the three major companies, having almost 87 per cent of the market share in the passenger car segment in India. Over the last decade, several studies have appeared, linking the export performance of firms with the size of firms and the affiliation with multinational companies (MNCs) (Aggarwal, 2002; Kumar & Siddharthan, 1994). However, the results of these studies are not unambiguous (Siddharthan & Nollen, 2004). Most of the empirical results are either inconsistent or contradictory, especially in the case of developing economies where exports play a crucial role.

The study discusses that the export performance of MNC affiliations is determined differently from domestic firms in case of the Indian motor vehicle industry. The objective of this study is to investigate the role of firm-specific factors in determining inter-firm differences in the export behaviour of firms in India. Some empirical studies analyzed the export behaviour of firms using some form of limited dependent variable estimation techniques. These studies can be broadly classified as those following either a censored regression model, Tobit model, some form of the two-part model as suggested by Cragg (1971), or a sample selection model. In the case of India, empirical studies on the determinants of firm exports have invariably used the Tobit model (Bhat & Narayanan, 2009). For our analysis, we have

DOI: 10.4324/9781003353904-11

extracted data for the period 2001–2016 on the motor vehicle industry in India from the Prowess database.

The MVI chosen for the study is one of the oldest industries in the world as well as in India. The Indian MVI has attracted substantial foreign capital in the last decade or more, especially after 2000. On average, the FDI inflows per annum received by passenger cars only were USD 82.63 million from 2000 to 2002, which further increased to USD 515.92 million from 2007 to 2011, and then stood at USD 794.68 million from 2012 to 2016 (RBI, 2012, p. 201, 2017). This sharp increase in FDI inflows reflected the fact that almost all the leading foreign manufacturing companies have started the production of cars in India (Singh, 2019). The foreign share in sales has increased significantly in the manufacturing of Indian MVI since Indian economic reforms. According to a study by Kumar (1994), the foreign share in total sales was only 19.45 per cent in 1980–81.

According to the study by Singh (2019), until the late 1970s, the full market was controlled by only three indigenous manufacturers (Hindustan Motors, Premier Automobile and Standard Motors). After the changes in policy regime and liberalization of the early 80s were the introduction of several new models of motor vehicles in the Indian market. The share of MNCs increased to 64.19 per cent in 2000 and further to 69.92 per cent in 2016 in Indian MVI. The share of MNCs in total exports is also quite high and increasing over time. It increased from 40.59 per cent in 2000 to 75.69 per cent in 2016. Foreign firms highly dominate the industry. The top five exporting companies from India are MNC affiliates. These are Ford India, Hyundai Motors, Maruti Suzuki, General Motors and Nissan Motors (SIAM, 2018).

We have divided this chapter into three broad sections. Section One sets the background by discussing the phase evolution of MVI and MNC affiliations in India and reviews the market conforming policies over the past three decades. It also discusses the trends and patterns of production, as well as exports of motor vehicles in India. Further, this section sheds some light on the export intensity of the Indian motor vehicles industry. Section Two reviews the literature on MNCs' affiliation and their exporting behaviour. It also provides detailed information on the determinants of exports. In the third section, we discuss the data sources, description of variables and methodology. Further, we explain the research methodology along

with describing models and descriptive statistics, followed by some significant findings and conclusions.

2. Evolution of MNCs' Affiliation in the Indian Motor Vehicles Industry

Several amendments in policies along with liberalization in the early 80s and 90s made possible the launching of several new models of motor vehicles in India. The collaboration started with Japanese and Western manufacturers, leading to a transformation of the prevailing structure of the MVI in India. According to the study by Narayana (1989), the demand for passenger cars in the late 70s and early 80s in India was 38,000 units. Demand for commercial vehicles was 40,000 units, while the demand for two-wheelers was about 30,0000 units for 1978–79 (Narayana, 1989). This demand and production have been increasing over some time. The policy initiative since the economic reforms of 1991 was and remains to develop India as a manufacturing hub by attracting foreign investors from around the world. The government has opened several sectors for foreign investors to make India an international hub for manufacturing products, designs and innovations. The government is pitching India as an investment-friendly destination for manufacturing and exporting goods.

While examining the MNCs' Collaboration with Indian Motor Vehicle Companies in Table 9.1, we have divided the period into three phases. The first phase, from 1947 to 1982, was indicated by progressive regulation, protection and indigenization (Athukorala & Veeramani, 2019). The second phase, from 1983 to 1993, saw some easing of restrictive policies with an emphasis on technological capability through foreign technology collaborations. The final phase, starting in 1993, allowed joint ventures with foreign MNCs and allowed 100 per cent FDI.

a In the first phase, parts and accessories of MVI were mainly controlled by the government subject to state control through industrial licensing. It was a closed-market economy with several restrictive measures due to controlled industry. From 1953 onwards, only firms with completely built-up units were permitted to operate. The government had given priority to commercial vehicle production. The domestic companies were not allowed to make any new collaborations (either financial or technical) with MNCs, and the frequency of model changes was restricted. General Motors and Ford Motors came to India and started assembling trucks and cars in the late 1920s. Both companies left India in 1954 due to regulation and indigenization policies in this period. The full market of MVI was controlled by only three indigenous manufacturers: Hindustan Motors, Premier Automobile and Standard Motors, for well over 40 years. Hindustan Motors made the Ambassador and Premier Automobile Ltd, the Padmini (a Fiat 1100 of the 1950s). Growth of this market was limited to domestic supply (Athukorala & Veeramani, 2019; Narayana, 1989; Singh, 2019).
b The second phase was from 1983 to 1993. In this period, the Government of India allowed foreign technology collaboration with or without equity participation with domestic companies. India was the first to sign in a joint venture with the leading foreign producer, Suzuki, in

Table 9.1 Major MNCs' collaboration with Indian motor vehicle companies

Year of Entry	*Name of MNC (Country)*	*Indian Company*	*Collaboration Type*
Early 1980s	Government of India allowed foreign technology collaboration with or without equity participation with domestic companies.		
1982	Suzuki (Japan)	Maruti Udyog	Technical
1984	Vauxhall Motors (UK)	Hindustan Motors	Technical
1985	Austin Rover (UK)	Standard Motors	Technical
1986	Isuzu (Japan)	Hindustan Motors	Technical
1986	Nissan Motors (Japan)	Premier Automobile Ltd	Technical
1986	Techno license ltd (U.K.)	Premier Automobile Ltd	Technical
1994	DCM-Toyota	Daewoo Corporation	Joint Venture 51:49
1994	General Motors (USA)	Hindustan Motors	Joint Venture 50:50
1994	Peugeot (France)		
1994	Daimler Benz (Germany)	Mercedes-Benz (India)	Joint Venture
1995	Ford (USA)	Mahindra & Mahindra	Joint Venture 50:50
1995	Honda (Japan)	Shriram Group	Joint Venture
1997	Fiat (Italy)	Premier Automobile Ltd	Joint Venture 51:49
1997	Toyota Motors (Japan)	Kirloskar Group	Joint Venture 89:11
1997	Hyundai Motors (S.K.)		
1998	Mitsubishi Motors (Japan)	Hindustan Motors Ltd	Technical
2001	Skoda Auto (Czech Republic)		First 100 per cent subsidiary
2001	Daewoo Motors (South Korea) was acquired by Tata Motors.		
2004	Audi (Germany)	Audi India	100 per cent Subsidiary
2005	Nissan Motors (Japan)	Nissan Motors India	100 per cent Subsidiary
2006	BMW Group started its 100 per cent subsidiary named BMW India		
2012	Isuzu Motors Group started its 100 per cent subsidiary as Isuzu India Motors		

Source: Compiled from companies' official websites and updated from Athukorala & Veeramani, 2019; Singh, 2019

1981. China followed suit in 1984 and formed a joint venture with Volkswagen. Further, Maruti Udyog Ltd came up as a government initiative in collaboration with Japanese Suzuki Motors. Suzuki specialized in small and fuel-efficient cars (D'Costa, 2004). Suzuki's entry

Table 9.2 Some reforms introduced in 1991 onwards in Indian MVI

Year	*Remark*
1991	Licensing requirements were abolished in commercial vehicles
1991	Licensing requirements were abolished in automobile components production
1993	Licensing requirements were abolished in passenger vehicles
1991	Automatic approval of foreign holding of up to 51 per cent of equity announced
1997	Importation of capital goods and automobile components were allowed

Source: Athukorala & Veeramani, 2019

into India was one of the essential landmarks in the history of Indian MVI. As a result, many MNCs came to India and started their business as a technical collaboration with domestic companies (Vauxhall Motors, Techno License Ltd and Austin Rover from the UK, Isuzu and Nissan Motors from Japan) and perceptibly changed the stature of Indian MVI.

c The third phase started in 1993. It was observed that until 1992, only technical collaboration with foreign MNCs was allowed[2]. The economic reforms of early 1991 led to the entry of many foreign MNCs in the forms of joint ventures and wholly-owned subsidiaries. The nature and share of foreign MNCs in the motor vehicles industry changed from technology suppliers to joint venture and equity participation (Singh, 2019). In 1994, the German car company Daimler Benz started a joint venture with TELCO called Mercedes-Benz (India) Ltd. Other joint ventures during this phase include General Motors and Hindustan Motors, Peugeot (France) and Premier Automobile Ltd, Fiat and Premier Automobile Ltd. Ford Motors (USA) started a 50:50 joint venture with Mahindra & Mahindra; Toyota Motors (Japan) started a joint venture with Kirloskar Group of India as 89:11 share. In 2000, the Government of India allowed 100 per cent FDI through automatic routes in the automobile sector. After 2000, many foreign MNCs established their subsidiaries in India, including the Czech Republic company Skoda Auto in 2001. German company Audi established its wholly-owned subsidiary in 2004 as Audi India. Nissan Motors (Japan) in 2005 and BMW (Germany) in 2006 entered India and set up their wholly-owned subsidiaries. As a result of these establishments, foreign MNCs may dominate the domestic market and hence determine the structure of the domestic MVI. Until 1999–2000, only 20 foreign MNCs were working in the Indian motor vehicles and transport equipment industry. It increased to 68 in 2013–14 and further to 88 in 2015–16 (see Figure 9.1).

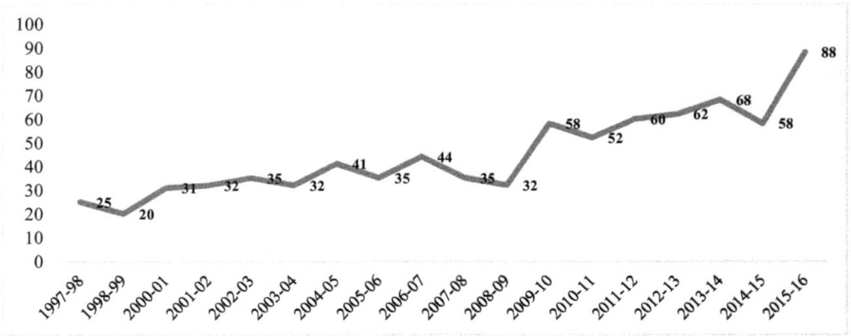

Figure 9.1 MNCs Working in Motor Vehicles Industry in India (in Numbers)

Source: (Finances of FDI Companies, 2016)- RBI, various reports)

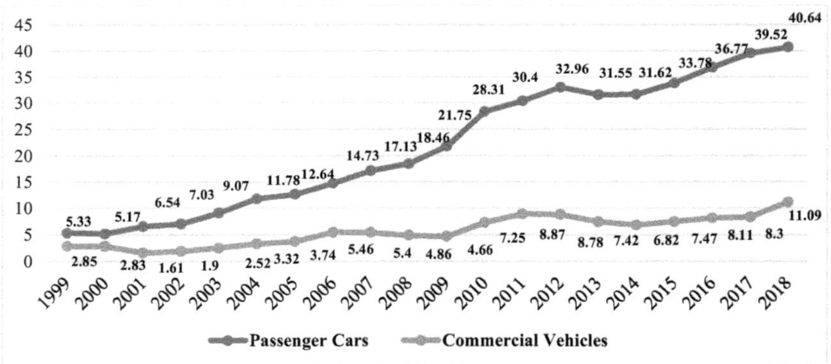

Figure 9.2 Production of Motor Vehicles in India (Qty. in Lakhs)

Source: Data extracted from International Organization of Motor Vehicle Manufacturers (OICA, 2018)

2.1. Production of Motor Vehicles in India

India emerged as the fourth largest car producer with a growth rate of 8.87 per cent in 2016 against the German car market, which grew only 2.8 per cent with 3.8 million of its vehicles sold in the country last year. The Indian MVI grew at 8 per cent, with over 5.17 million units sold in 2018 (see Appendix 9-A). India is now following the USA, China and Japan in terms of car production. The production of passenger cars and commercial vehicles increased from 8,18,193 units in 1999 to over 51,74,645 units in 2018 (see Appendix 9-A). India's share of motor vehicles in total world production has increased from 1.94 per cent in 2000 to 7.34 per cent in 2018 (see Appendix 9-A). The share of passenger cars (15.08 per cent) and commercial vehicles (4.45 per cent) comprises more than 20 per cent of the automobile sector in India (SIAM, 2012, 2013). In the category of passenger cars, the market share of Maruti Udyog was 52 per cent, Hyundai Motor's market share was 19 per cent, and Tata Motor's share was 16 per cent in 2012–13. These are three major companies capturing about 87 per cent of the market share in the passenger car industry in India.

2.2. Exports of Motor Vehicles from India

According to SIAM (2018) statistics, India exported 6,76,193 passenger cars and 99,931 commercial vehicles between January-December 2018. The export of passenger cars was 9.67 per cent less in 2018 compared to 2018. However, during the same period, exports of commercial vehicles from India increased by 3.17 per cent (see Figure 9.3). According to SIAM's (2018) statistical profile of the automobile industry in India, the top five passenger car exporters from India are MNC affiliations. These MNC affiliates were Ford India (23.94 per cent), Hyundai Motors (22.82 per cent), Maruti Suzuki (16 per cent), General Motors (11.33 per cent) and Nissan Motors (9.2 per cent) in 2018. In contrast, the top five exporters of commercial vehicles from India are Tata Motors (52.55 per cent), Mahindra & Mahindra (21.38 per cent), Ashok Leyland (12.16 per cent), Volvo Eicher commercial vehicles (9.84 per cent) and Maruti Suzuki India (2.27 per cent) in 2018.

In 2002, the Government of India allowed 100 per cent FDI in the automobile industry through the automatic route. As a result, many foreign automotive MNCs entered India and established their subsidiaries to sell

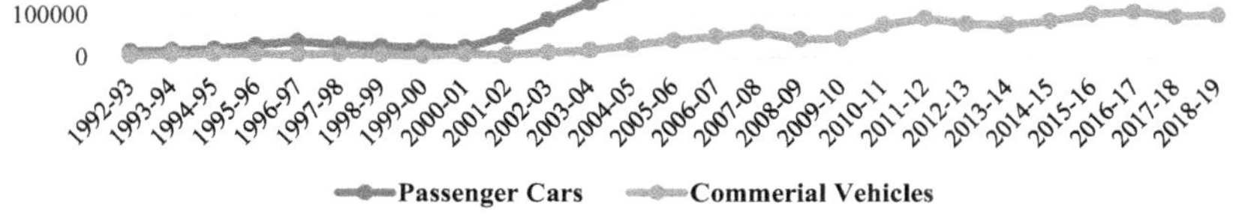

Figure 9.3 Exports of Motor Vehicles from India (Qty. in Numbers)

Source: Appendix 9-B

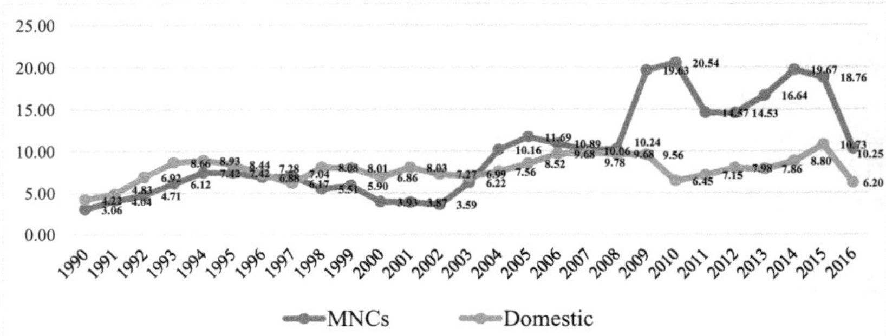

Figure 9.4 Export Intensity of Indian Motor Vehicles Industry (per cent)

Source: Data extracted from (CMIE Prowess IQ, 2016)

and export from India to other countries. Foreign MNCs not only started selling their latest technology but also started designing cars in India. These include Skoda, Audi, Nissan and BMW. Because of this, sales as well as exports of the MNCs started increasing. From 2003 onwards, it is clear that the exports of the MNCs outperformed the exports of domestic companies (See Figure 9.3).

2.3. *Literature Review and Determinants of Exports*

2.3.1. Literature Review

The literature review has been divided into two broad categories: first, the literature on MNC affiliation and their export performance; second, the literature related to MNCs as a source of technology transfer and exports orientation.

A. MNC AFFILIATES AND THEIR EXPORT PERFORMANCE

The presence of MNCs in the domestic market itself may increase the export performance of domestic firms due to technology spillover effects. Therefore, it is essential to study the export and technology performance of MNCs and domestic firms. MNCs account for more than one- fifth of the world's total exports and one-third of the developing country's exports (Aggarwal, 2002). The study by Chacar et al. (2010) argues that MNC affiliates are better performers than domestic firms and the benefits of affiliates increase with age. Another study by Lall & Mohammad (1983) on foreign ownership and export performance taking the case of the large corporate sector in India found that foreign ownership has a positive impact on export performance of the largest corporate firms in India. But on the other side, the study by Pant (1993) found that there was no influence by transnational corporations (MNCs) on the export propensity of the Indian manufacturing industry. MNCs have more globally integrated production and marketing strategies with better trading prospects than other local firms. Aggarwal (1997, 2002) and Kumar & Siddharthan (1997) found that there is a positive relationship between FDI and manufactured exports in developing countries. MNCs with modern technology and the latest machinery can play an important role in promoting India's exports.

The decision to export solely depends on firms' own capability and choice, not on foreign affiliates. Some firms don't export directly, but they provide inputs to other exporting firms. Studies such as Prasanna (2010) discuss the impact of FDI on export performance in India by describing the role of government. The study argues that several liberal policies of the mid-1990s resulted in increasing the FDI inflow into India. The study found that this increasing FDI into India has positively impacted the export performance of the country. A similar study conducted in China by Zheng et al. (2004) on the impact of FDI on the export performance of Chinese indigenous firms found that FDI has less influence on the export performance of indigenous firms. Studies of MNCs and their exports over the years mainly focused on the causality of MNCs on exports and firm efficiency, but not on how MNCs impact the firms' export decisions. The study by Aggarwal (2002) examines the inter-firm determinants of export performance in the Indian manufacturing sector in the late 1990s and concludes that firms with higher foreign equity stakes have not performed distinctly better than firms with lower foreign equity ownerships. Further, high-tech industries do not attract efficiency-seeking FDI, whereas medium-tech industries do. The study by Sharma (2003) also found that there is no significant impact of FDI on India's export performance.

B. MNC AS A SOURCE OF TECHNOLOGY TRANSFER

The theory of heterogeneous firms suggests that MNCs belong in the top productivity layer of firms, as only they can afford the costs of international production. The study by Lall (1999) suggests that to increase the manufacturing exports, countries need to upgrade their technology base by providing better training to domestic firms. For attracting foreign capital, firms need sophisticated technology to "dynamize" their export structures. Another set of studies argues that MNCs are the primary source of technology transfer across borders, too. MNCs can transfer technology to their affiliates based in other countries. They offer the world increased technical efficiency by eliminating the duplication of the joint-input that would occur with independent national firms. They spend a vast majority of the world's R&D activities. In 2002, 700 firms, 98 per cent of which are MNCs, accounted for 46 per cent of the world's total R&D expenditure and 69 per cent of the world's business R&D (UNCTAD, 2005).

Further studies suggest that MNCs increasingly conduct their R&D abroad. UNCTAD (2005) estimated that 28 per cent of the R&D of MNCs in 2003 were based in foreign (not home) countries. The R&D expenditure is generally the primary measurement tool utilized for technology development. It generally indicates a firm's in-house technology content and its effort to be on the edge of technology. R&D investments by MNCs have gotten extra attention due to their role in growth, productivity, employment and competitiveness. While some studies found strong support for the view that in-house R&D is favorable for exports (Basile, 2001; Bhaduri & Ray, 2004), others found that R&D has a positive effect on exports in the medium- to high-technology industries (which include the motor vehicles industry).

The existing studies implicitly undertake that the exports by MNCs and other domestic firms of the host economy are explained in the same way. In this chapter, we argue that MNC affiliates perform differently from other domestic firms and that the magnitude and sign of the coefficients of some determinants of exports will differ between the MNCs and other domestic firms. As the share of MNCs in total exports of goods in the motor vehicle industry is more than 75 per cent, we examine such firms in the manufacturing of MVI in India, which is an essential industry in terms of an increasingly open economy and increasing foreign share.

2.3.2. Determinants of Exports

In this section, we review studies of technological and other firm-specific factors that determine exports. We consider firms' efforts to acquire technologies through both in-house and external means – other firm-specific factors, such as the size of the firm and age of the firm. Advertisement and marketing intensity, import of raw material, indigenous raw material consumed and choice of production technology are also considered as control variables.

The export intensity and R&D intensity: Exporting is one of the most straightforward foreign market entry modes that does not require highly skilled human and financial resources. This strengthens production capability, enhances trade balance, increases the foreign exchange reserves and adds to the industrial productivity (Moghaddam et al., 2012). A firm's export activity boosts the scale as well as the productivity of the firm (Malik, 2014). Export intensity is the most widely used measure to assess firms' export performance (Sousa, 2004). Another variable we use is the R&D intensity. Guner et al. (2010) find that R&D intensity positively influences the firm's export performance.

Investment in R&D enables the firm to be more competitive in areas such as product development, operational efficiency and cost reduction. Export-oriented firms are spending more on R&D because they need to be highly competitive in terms of price, quality of service and product innovation. We have defined export intensity as the ratio of a firm's export of goods to its sales value.

MNC affiliation: MNC affiliates have the edge over their local counterparts in international markets and are likely to enjoy higher export intensity (Aggarwal, 2002). However, many authors postulate a positive relationship between MNCs and exports. They argue that MNCs prefer to control their export-oriented affiliates strictly through high ownership stakes, treating their marketing network as their proprietary asset. We define MNC affiliation as a firm whose foreign share is ten per cent or more and owned by a foreign private group.

Technology import intensity (import of capital goods intensity and royalty and technical fee intensity): Imports of technology are one of the most vital sources of knowledge acquisition by enterprises in developing economies (Aggarwal, 2002). Imported technology consists of both embodied as well as disembodied technology[3]. In the case of R&D, the results of empirical studies examining the effects of imported disembodied technology on exports are diverse. In the case of high-technology intensive industries, a positive relationship between imports of disembodied technology and exports was observed (Kumar & Siddharthan, 1994). In our case, we have defined import of embodied technology (capital goods) intensity as the ratio of a firm's expenditure on import of capital goods to its sales value and import of disembodied technology intensity as the ratio of a firm's expenditure on royalty, and technical fee payments in foreign currency to its sales turnover.

Indigenous raw material intensity: Firms generally acquire embodied technology through the import of capital goods and import of raw materials. The imported machines, equipment and raw materials are based on modern designs and the latest technologies. Hence, not only the import of capital goods but also the import of raw materials are considered as embedded sources of the latest technology. Using these modern and well-designed equipment and raw materials in the production process, most of the firms in the Indian motor vehicles industry can supply products that are equal to global standards. In the case of manufacturing firms in Italy, both Basile (2001 and Sterlacchini (1999) found investment in capital equipment to have a favourable effect on export performance. Aggarwal (2002) argued that after the economic reforms, there had been a positive relationship between imports of embodied technology and exports in the medium- to high-technology industries. Indigenous raw material intensity is defined as expenditure on indigenous (from local market) raw material consumed by the firm as their sales ratio.

Selling cost intensity: Foreign firms enter into the domestic market with abundant capital and high technology. They, however, do not spend much on new research. As their main objective is to capture the market and sell their products, they prefer to spend on marketing, selling and distribution of their products. Extensive market promotion of the product may help a firm in creating a niche market for that product. Furthermore, in the process of creating brand names, firms are compelled to maintain minimum quality standards, which help firms in the overseas market. Kumar & Siddharthan (1994) found advertisement intensity to have a positive effect on exports in five of the Indian industries. We define selling cost intensity as the ratio of a firm's amount spent on selling and distribution to its sales turnover.

Outsourcing intensity: Often, manufacturing and services firms outsource part of their manufacturing processes to other firms. It is not only cost-efficient (as the outsourced firms are generally specialized producers of the given products and services), but it also helps the firm to concentrate on their strengths. The firms may thus produce quality products at competitive prices for the export markets. In the empirical studies, the degree of vertical integration of the firm was considered as a potential determinant of exports. The firm that is relatively less vertically integrated is more likely to outsource part of its manufacturing process. Willmore (1992), in a large sample of Brazilian manufacturing firms, found that higher vertical integration worsened export performance. In the context of India, for the post-reform period, Narayanan (2006) found vertical integration to be unimportant in determining exports. We use outsourcing intensity as the ratio of a firm's amount spent on outsourced manufacturing jobs to its sales turnover.

Choice of technology: The choice of production technology (labour-intensive technology or capital-intensive technology) is also essential in determining a firm's exports. In a labour-abundant and relatively capital-scarce country such as India, adoption of a more labour-intensive technique of production can give a competitive edge to a firm over its rivals in the export market (Kumar & Siddharthan, 1994). However, the effects of the choice of technology on export behaviour are mixed. Athukorala et al. (1995 and Siddharthan & Nollen (2004) found capital intensity to have a positive effect on exports. Others, such as Kumar & Siddharthan (1994) (for six low- and medium-technology industries, including industrial and other chemicals) and Zhao & Zou (2002) (for Chinese manufacturing firms), found a negative relationship between capital intensity and exports. We define the choice of technology intensity as the expenditure on wages and salaries as a proportion of gross fixed assets of the firm.

Size of the firm: The size of the firm is the most commonly used non-technology variable in analyzing export competitiveness (Bhat & Narayanan, 2009). Larger firms are better qualified and able to appropriate returns from their innovative activity for a few reasons. First, they can evade uncertainty and risk of failure by undertaking a large amount of R&D expenditure. Second, larger firms have more systematic and efficient production patterns (Ray & Bhaduri, 2001) due to their low unit cost and higher productivity. Larger firms, with their vast resources and influential positions, have the edge over smaller firms in catering to the needs of domestic as well as international markets (Bhat & Narayanan, 2009). Some studies have found that there is a positive relationship between firm size and export competitiveness, including Aggarwal (2002) for Indian medium- and low-technology industries, Basile (2001) for Italian manufacturing firms, Zhao & Zou (2002) for Chinese manufacturing firms and Narayanan (2006) for the Indian automobile industry. It is argued that the size of the firm is one of the most critical determinants of technological activities. New trade theory postulates a positive impact of the market size given economies of scale. The effect of size has measured by the log value of annual sales turnover of firms.

Age of the firm: This is one of the non-technology factors considered in empirical studies on exports. The age of the firm can determine the accumulated capabilities of the firm over the years of its operation. Thus, a firm's age may positively influence its export behaviour. At the same time, in developing countries such as India in the post-reform period, new firms find it relatively easy to get into foreign markets, rather than competing with the established firms in the domestic market (Bhaduri & Ray, 2004). Joseph & Kakarlapudi (2018) found that the age of the firm has a positive effect in the case of medium- and high-tech industries.

2.4. Data Source, Description of Variables and Methodology

2.4.1. Data Description and Source

This section presents the data, description of variables and the methodology used in the analysis. In this study, we use panel data consisting of 125 firms for 16 years (periods)[4] from 2001 to 2016 for the Motor Vehicle Industry. The study was based on the firm-level data provided by CMIE Prowess IQ (2016). It covers both listed and unlisted firms from a wide cross-section

Table 9.3 Three groups of firms used in this study

NIC Code	*Name of the Industry*	*Domestic*	*MNCs*	*Total*
291	Manufacture of Motor vehicles	07	08	15
292	Manufacture of Bodies (coach work) for motor vehicles	32	04	36
293	Manufacture of Parts and accessories for motor vehicles	64	10	74
	All	103	22	125

Source: (CMIE Prowess IQ, 2016)

of manufacturing, services, utilities and financial industries. Prowess covers information primarily from the income statements and balance sheets of publicly listed companies. This database provides information about companies from 1989 onwards. These companies in the database account for more than 70 per cent of the economic activity in the organized industrial sector of India. It also provides firm-level information where firms have classified into various industries according to the national industrial classification 2008 (NIC). Since our analysis is restricted to the manufacturing of motor vehicles sector only, we drop firms with NIC codes that do not fall under the manufacturing of motor vehicles sector. For example, we exclude the following industries from analysis: NIC 32 (Miscellaneous manufactured articles), NIC 34 (Diversified), NIC 42 (Civil engineering), NIC 47 (Retail trading), NIC 61 (Other miscellaneous services), NIC 68 (Real estate), NIC 77 (Business services and consultancy), NIC 222 (Other chemical products), NIC 281 (General-purpose machinery) and NIC 98 (Undifferentiated goods).

Further, we exclude all those firms that have not reported sales value for more than three years. Three filters are used to define MNCs. First, a firm whose foreign[5] equity share is 10 per cent or more[6]. Second, the company should come under the private (foreign) ownership group. Third, we have included another important indicator to define foreign subsidiaries whose foreign association is denoted in the Prowess with ownership group '(F)'. After filtering, we have a total of 22 foreign companies (MNCs) and 103 domestic firms. Finally, we had 125 firms in our study.

Further, these 125 firms have been categorized in various sub-industries, according to their three-digit NIC code. According to NIC codes 291, 292 and 293, 15 firms have identified as manufacturing of motor vehicles, 36 firms have identified as the manufacture of bodies (coachwork) for motor vehicles, and 74 firms belong to manufacture of parts and accessories for motor vehicles. Table 9.4 presents the definition of variables and symbols used in this study.

2.4.2. Description of Variables

Table 9.4 The variables and their definitions

Sr. No.	*Variables*	*Symbol*	*Definition used in the study*
Dependent Variable			
1	Export intensity	EXPIn	Total export as a proportion of firm's sales
2	Decision to export	DEXPIn	DEXPIn = 0 if firm does not export DEXPIn = 1 if firm export
Independent Variables			
2	MNC affiliation	MNC	MNC = 1 if the firm is MNC MNC = 0 domestic
3	R&D intensity	RDIn	The ratio of a firm's expenditure on R&D to its sales value
4	Import of embodied technology intensity	ICGIn	The ratio of a firm's expenditure on import of capital goods to its sales value
5	Indigenous raw material Consumed	IndeRMI	The ratio of a firm's import of indigenous raw material (in local currency) to sales value
6	Selling cost intensity	SellingIn	Expenditure on Selling & Distribution as percentage of sales turnover of the firm
7	Outsourcing intensity	OutIn	Amount spent on outsourced manufacturing jobs as proportion of sales turnover of the firm
8	Choice of technology	CHOI	Expenditure on wages and salaries as proportion of gross fixed assets of the firm
9	Size of the firm	SIZE	Logarithm of the total assets of the company
10	Age of the firm	Age	Difference between year of incorporation and year in the study
11	Motor vehicles industry (291)	Dmvi	Dmot = 1 if the firm belongs to manufacturing of motor vehicles industry Dmot = 0 otherwise
12	Bodies (coach work) for motor vehicles industry (292)	Dbmv	Dbmv = 1 if the firm belongs to manufacturing of Bodies (coach work) for motor vehicles industry Dbmv = 0 otherwise
13	Parts and accessories for motor vehicles industry (293)	Damv	Damv = 1 if the firm belongs to manufacturing of Parts and accessories for motor vehicles industry Damv = 0 0therwise

2.4.3. *Methodology*

This section consists of four broadheads. First, it starts by describing the models used in this study. The next part discusses the descriptive statistics and correlation metrix. The third part will advance the chapter's major findings, and the final part concludes the chapter.

2.4.3.1. DESCRIPTION OF MODELS

The export behaviour of any firm can be considered to involve two decisions (Athukorala et al., 1995; Vyas et al., 2013): first, either to choose export or not to export; second, to fix the proportion amount of output to be exported. Our data set included both exporting and non- exporting firms. Thus, the export behaviour of firms can be better explained by using both exporters as well as non-exporters. The problem, however, is the presence of observations with zero value. In our sample, the dependent variable (Export Intensity) faces such a problem, having many zero values. Thus, we consider limited dependent model specifications to be appropriate (Vyas et al., 2013). For such a censored sample where information on the dependent variable in a regression is not available for some observations, OLS regression may not be a suitable estimation procedure, as coefficients may be biased towards censored points (zero in this case).

Censoring and Truncation: Censoring is when the limit observations in the sample (only the value of the dependent variable has censored), and truncation is when the observations are not in the sample. The censored sample includes firms who export zero quantities of the product. The truncated sample only includes firms who export positive quantities of products. The censored sample is representative of the population (only the mean for the dependent variable is not) because all observations are included. The truncated sample is not representative of the population because some observations are not included. Truncation is a more significant loss of information than censoring (missing observations rather than values for the dependent variable).

However, the censored regression models do not suffer from this bias (Bhat & Narayanan, 2009). A general approach to deal with the censored sample is the Tobit model (Bhat & Narayanan, 2009; Gujarati, 2009). However, it constrains the participation equation and the intensity equation to have a similar set of explanatory variables and parametrs (Vyas et al., 2013). The Tobit model may be mis-specified in this case, leading to undesirable consequences for the estimates. This limitation can be mixed by involving two separate equations. Cragg (1971) proposed a Double Specification model. Tobit and the two-part Cragg Specification models are exceptional cases of a general sample selection model. The main feature of the Double Specification model is that the probability of exporting and quantity of exports are assumed to stem from two separate choices of firms, and determinants of two decisions are allowed to behave differently.

According to Bhat & Narayanan (2009), the Cragg Specification model relaxes the limit to assume that the decision to export is taken first, and then a decision is made on the amount to be exported by the firms. Then, the decision to export can be specified by a Probit model and the export intensity by a truncated standard model with zero as the point of truncation. Furthermore, in Cragg's model, the factors affecting the decision to export and export intensity need not be the same. However, if the set of factors that affect the decision to export and export intensity are assumed to be the same, then one can construct a likelihood ratio statistic (Greene, 2002, p. 915) to test which of the two models, namely, Tobit or two-part (Probit + Truncation), is more appropriate.

Both Sterlacchini (1999) and Wakelin (1998) have used this approach to choose between the Tobit and the two-part (Probit + Truncation) models for explaining the export behaviour of firms. Therefore, the first part of the Double Specification model using the whole set of data considers the probability to export. Studies including Vyas et al. (2013) used the Probit model to analyze the pharmaceutical sector. For the second part of the model, only the subset of sample exporting abroad has to be considered. Therefore, truncated regression is an appropriate model where the dependent variable is observed only if it is greater than zero. In the same set of variables to check those affecting both the probability of exporting and quantity to export, a likelihood ratio test (LR test) may be used to test which of the two models is better. Therefore, this study compares exports performance of motor vehicle firms in India by using the Tobit model and Cragg's Double Specification model.

The Tobit model for export performance is specified as:

$$\begin{aligned} EXPIn^{*} &= a_0 + a_1 RDIn + a_2 ICGIn + a_3 IndeRawMIn \\ &+ a_4 SellingIn + a_5 OutIn + a_6 CHOI + a_7 SIZE + a_8 Age \\ &+ a_9 Dmvi + a_{10} Dbmv + a_{11} Damv + ui \end{aligned} \tag{1}$$

$$\begin{aligned} EXPIn &= EXPIn^{*} \text{ if } EXPIn^{*} > 0 \\ &= 0 \text{ if } EXPIn^{*} \leq 0 \end{aligned}$$

This model tests the Tobit model as a special case.
The Tobit model is a combination of two models (decisions).
Two-part (Probit + Truncated regression)

The Probit model for probability of exporting can be expressed as follows:

$$\begin{aligned} DEXPIn &= \beta + \beta_1 RDIn + \beta_2 ICGIn + \beta_3 IndeRawM \\ &+ \beta_4 SellingIn + \beta_5 OutIn + \beta_6 CHOI + \beta_7 SIZE + \beta_8 Age \\ &+ \beta_9 Dmvi + \beta_{10} Dbmv + \beta_{11} Damv + ui \end{aligned} \tag{2}$$

DEXPIn = 0 if firm does not export
DEXPIn = 1 if firm export

The second stage of Double Specification model, i.e. Truncation model can be written as:

$$\begin{aligned} EXPIn = {} & \gamma_0 + \gamma_1 RDIn + \gamma_2 ICGIn + \gamma_3 IndeRawM \\ & + \gamma_4 SellingIn + \gamma_5 OutIn + \gamma_6 CHOI + \gamma_7 SIZE + \gamma_8 Age \\ & + \gamma_9 Dmvi + \gamma_{10} Dbmv + \gamma_{11} Damv + ui \end{aligned} \tag{3}$$

Equation (3) is estimated when DEXPIn = 1

2.4.3.2. DESCRIPTIVE STATISTICS AND CORRELATION MATRIX

The differences in the mean of the full sample, MNCs, domestic firms, exporting and non- exporting firms are highlighted in Appendix 9-D of descriptive analysis. The mean export intensity and R&D intensity of domestic firms are higher than MNCs. The mean export intensity of the full sample is 12.63 per cent, but those of domestic firms (13.09 per cent) are higher than that of the full sample as well as MNCs (10.46 per cent). The mean export intensity of exporting firms (14.77 per cent) is higher than the full sample, domestic and MNCs. The mean value of MNCs for import of embodied technology intensity, and selling cost intensity and size of the firm is higher than that of the domestic and full sample. The mean intensity of MNCs for the MVI is the highest and lowest for bodies (coachwork) for the motor vehicle industry. MNCs are new in the market compared to domestic firms because the mean age of MNCs (21.54 years) is lower than that of domestic firms. Domestic firms are more experienced than MNCs. The foreign MNCs are spending more on selling and distribution expenses compared to domestic companies. Therefore, the mean intensity of selling and distribution for MNCs is more than domestic firms.

The differences in the means of firm characteristics have also been highlighted for both exporting and non-exporting firms. Out of total 1609 observations of the full sample, 1376 are exporters, and 232 are non-exporters. The exporter firms are spending more on R&D and import of capital goods than non-exporting firms. Exporting firms are using more indigenous raw material than non-exporting firms. The selling and distribution intensity of exporting firms is more than two times higher than non-exporting firms. The mean intensity of import of capital goods for exporting firms is also higher than non-exporting firms. Comparing the difference between the exporting and non-exporting firm ages, we can infer that exporting firms (24.30 years) are more experienced than non-exporting firms (17.63 years). The R&D

intensity of both exporting and non-exporting firms is almost the same. It is because some firms don't export directly, but they supply inputs to other exporting firms. This shows that exporting firms spend more on selling, distribution and marketing to showcase their products in global markets.

The correlation matrix for the full samples of domestic firms and MNCs have been presented respectively in Appendix 9-E. The variables, like research and development intensity (RDIn), import of capital goods intensity (ICGIn), selling and distribution intensity (SellingIn), outsourced intensity (OutIn), choice of technology (CHOI) and age of firms, have positively correlated with export intensity in the full sample. Other variables like indigenous raw material intensity (IndeRawMIn) and size of the firm (SIZE) have a statistically significant negative correlation with export intensity in the full sample. However, the magnitude of the correlation coefficient is low in all cases. The magnitudes of correlation coefficients between all other variables are also low in all three tables (see Appendix 9-E). The correlation matrix of MNCs explains low levels of pair-wise correlation values among the study variables. All the technology and non-technology variables in the study have a significant positive correlation with export intensity. Only the choice of technology intensity (CHOI) has negatively correlated with export intensity. Hence, there are fewer chances of multicollinearity problems in this study. Nonetheless, we have also estimated Variance Inflating Factor (VIF-test) to check the presence of multicollinearity. The results of the VIF-test show that there is no multicollinearity presence in all the models.

2.4.4. *Major Findings*

Tables 9.5, 9.6 and 9.7 show the final results for the three models discussed in the earlier part of this chapter. The LR test[7] (Bhat & Narayanan, 2009; Vyas et al., 2013) run for the selection of the model suggests that the Double Specification Model (Probit + Truncation) is more suitable than the Tobit model in this study. The results for the truncated regression model that we found are similar to the estimates of the random-effects model, as the objective of this study is to separate between exporting and non-exporting firms and also to find out how the export performances of MNC affiliations are determined differently from domestic firms in the Indian motor vehicle industry. So for the analysis, we have categorized all firms into groups rather than creating firm heterogeneity. Therefore, the random effect model of Tobit, Probit and Truncated regression has taken the empirical analysis.

In the current study, the exports by the firm have two stages: first, to decide whether to export or not (Decision of exporting); second, how much to export (Intensity of exporting). The second stage is applicable only for those firms who have decided to export. The econometric results also support the idea that the effect of independent variables differs on the probability of exporting (Decision of exporting) and on export intensity (Intensity of exporting).

Table 9.5 Panel data estimation of Tobit, Probit and truncated models (full sample)

Expln	*Double Specification Model*		
	Tobit	*Probit*	*Truncation*
RDIn	0.416*	−0.0431	−68.75
	(0.0182)	(0.0317)	(56.76)
ICGIn	0.0756	0.0181	6.987
	(0.0952)	(0.0167)	(7.29)
IndeRawMIn	0.0739***	0.0291***	−4.725
	(0.0229)	(0.0039)	(3.398)
SellingIn	0.363***	0.139***	9.052*
	(0.129)	(0.0396)	(4.959)
OutIn	0.417***	0.0284	31.22
	(0.134)	(0.0237)	(20.89)
CHOI	−0.00959	0.0150*	1.253
	(0.0413)	(0.00776)	(2.094)
SIZE	3.539***	0.898***	−180.1
	(1.274)	(0.184)	(131.8)
Age	0.139*	0.0194**	6.392
	(0.0783)	(0.00931)	(4.753)
Dmvi	−5.505	−1.266**	−79.32
	(5.522)	(0.561)	(128.1)
Damv	3.87	0.202	−24.77
	(3.375)	(0.306)	(52.93)
Constant	−10.40**	−3.397***	−286.7
	(4.23)	(0.608)	(282.4)
No. of firms	125	125	
Observations	1,609	1,609	1,377
Wald chi2	75.17	109.27	31.76
Prob > chi2	0.0000	0.0000	0.0002
Log likelihood	−5487.1417	−407.55084	−4991.683
Likelihood-ratio test of rho=0: chibar2(01)		201.30	(LR Test = 175.81568)
Prob >= chibar2		0.000	

Source: Calculated by author based on the sample extracted from CMIE Prowess IQ, 2016

Note: Standard errors in parentheses
*** Significant level at 1 per cent, ** Significant level at 5 per cent, *Significant level at 10 per cent

The econometric results of tables 9.5, 9.6 and 9.7 found that the Double Specification model is more appropriate than the Tobit model. Therefore, we would discuss the results obtained using the Double Specification model.

2.4.4.1. DETERMINANTS OF PROBABILITY OF EXPORTING

Results show that in-house research & development (RDIn) does not affect the probability of exporting in all three models, i.e., full sample, domestic companies as well as MNCs in the Indian motor vehicle industry. Import

Table 9.6 Data estimation of Tobit, Probit and truncated models (domestic companies)

Expln		*Double Specification Model*	
	Tobit	*Probit*	*Truncation*
RDIn	0.434*	−0.0284	−23.09
	(0.001)	(0.0353)	(18.42)
ICGIn	0.0404	0.0196	1.454
	(0.112)	(0.0181)	(3.587)
IndeRawMIn	0.0519**	0.0244***	−2.993**
	(0.0259)	(0.0041)	(1.442)
SellingIn	0.383**	0.190***	4.680**
	(0.152)	(0.0465)	(2.112)
OutIn	0.395***	0.0301	14.16**
	(0.144)	(0.0246)	(6.212)
CHOI	−0.042	0.0117	1.325
	(0.0461)	(0.00822)	(1.163)
SIZE	2.612*	1.045***	−163.3**
	(1.451)	(0.209)	(75.55)
Age	0.145	0.0165	1.992
	(0.0896)	(0.0103)	(1.239)
Dmvi	−6.388	−1.807**	−110.3
	(7.526)	(0.722)	(110.4)
Damv	4.953	0.316	16.33
	(3.833)	(0.346)	(29.19)
Constant	−7.061	−3.728***	102.3
	(4.797)	(0.679)	(79.6)
No. of firms	103	103	
Observations	1331	1331	1125
Wald chi2	45.42	91.2	27.42
Prob > chi2	0.0000	0.0000	0.0068
Log likelihood	−4557.2872	−344.55386	−4101.5087
Likelihood-ratio test of rho=0: chibar2(01)		201.31	(LR Test =
Prob >= chibar2		0.000	222.44928)

Source: Calculated by author based on the sample extracted from (CMIE Prowess IQ, 2016)

Note: Standard errors in parentheses
*** Significant level at 1 per cent, ** Significant level at 5 per cent, *Significant level at 10 per cent

of capital goods (ICGIn) plays a decisive role in the decision of exporting for the full sample, domestic companies and foreign MNCs, although it is not significantly affecting the probability of export. Import of indigenous raw material (IndeRawMIn) has a positive and significant effect on the firm's probability of exporting for both domestic companies as well as foreign MNCs. Both MNCs and domestic companies buy raw material from the local market, as the Indian domestic parts and accessories industry is well developed. Some small companies do not export directly, but they provide raw materials to other big companies. Expenditure on Selling and

Table 9.7 Panel data estimation of Tobit, Probit and truncated models (MNCs)

Expln	*Double Specification Model*		
	Tobit	*Probit*	*Truncation*
RDIn	0.273	−0.0457	−5.993
	(0.672)	(0.126)	(5.891)
ICGIn	0.0577	0.0197	−0.073
	(0.142)	(0.0573)	(0.794)
IndeRawMIn	0.242***	0.0742***	0.650**
	(0.0409)	(0.0182)	(0.307)
SellingIn	0.306	0.0157	5.006***
	(0.196)	(0.08)	(1.073)
OutIn	0.799	0.15	8.104***
	(0.549)	(0.149)	(2.322)
CHOI	0.330***	0.0552*	−0.872**
	(0.0872)	(0.0286)	(0.426)
SIZE	9.877***	1.331**	71.11***
	(2.287)	(0.668)	(13.96)
Age	−0.0972	−0.00836	0.642**
	(0.137)	(0.0264)	(0.0263)
Dmvi	−11.02	−0.977	−93.77***
	(6.893)	(1.155)	(18.12)
Damv	0.772	−0.392	7.928
	(6.028)	(0.901)	(8.39)
Constant	−37.59***	−5.370**	−299.9***
	(8.015)	(2.513)	(65.64)
No. of firms	22	22	
Observations	278	278	252
Wald chi2	126.12	28.23	34.92
Prob > chi2	0.0000	0.0017	0.0001
Log likelihood	−864.84459	−44.035152	−786.77703
Likelihood-ratio test of rho=0: chibar2(01)		0.51	(LR test =
Prob >= chibar2		0.237	68.064811)

Source: Calculated by author based on the sample extracted from (CMIE Prowess IQ, 2016)

Note: Standard errors in parentheses
***Significant level at 1 per cent, **Significant level at 5 per cent, *Significant level at 10 per cent

Distribution (SellingIn) has a positive and significant sign to the decision of a firm's export behaviour for both domestic companies and foreign MNCs. Usually, to sell the products in the international market, firms need to brand and advertise. Domestic companies need more advertising to enter into the global export market as it helps in creating brand value. Studies found that SellingIn helps companies with showcasing their products globally. The amount spent on outsourced manufacturing jobs (OutIn) is positively determining the decision of exporting of all the three models. Expenditure on wages and salaries (CHOI or choice of technology) has the expected positive effect on the probability of exporting in case of the full sample and foreign MNCs.

On the other hand, the corresponding coefficient in the case of domestic companies is not statistically significant. The size of the firm (SIZE) influences the probability of exporting positively in the case of the full sample, for domestic companies as well as foreign MNCs. The age of the firm (AGE) is positive and significant only for the full sample. It positively determines the probability of exporting of domestic companies only. Age of the firm is not affecting the decision of MNC's export behaviour. One notable exception is Dmvi (Dmvi), which has adverse and significant effects on the decision of exporting in case of the full sample and domestic companies. It does not have any effect on the decision of MNC's export behaviour. Damv has positive effects on the probability to decide to export for the full sample and domestic companies. It has no effects on MNC's exporting decision.

2.4.4.2. DETERMINANTS OF INTENSITY OF EXPORTING

We can see some similarities in the effects of explanatory variables for determining both the probability of export and intensity of export. The Expenditure on Selling and Distribution (SellingIn) have positive and significant effects on both the probability of export and intensity of export. The amount spent on outsourced manufacturing jobs (OutIn) is also positively determining both probabilities of export and intensity of export in the motor vehicle industry. At the same time, Expenditure on Selling and Distribution (SellingIn) turns out to be a more important factor for companies that have already entered the export market. It supports the view that companies need to continuously spend more on sales promotions to maintain and improve their export performance.

Research & Development (RDIn) seems to be less favourable in determining the export intensity of the Indian motor vehicle industry. It shows that the Indian motor vehicle industry is importing technology and raw material from abroad instead of spending their R&D activity. We can see here that the import of capital goods (ICGIn) seems to be positively affecting the export intensity of domestic companies, but it does not favourably affect the MNCs' export intensity. The import of indigenous raw material (IndeRawMIn) does not affect the export intensity of the full sample, although it does negatively affect the domestic company's export intensity. But it appears to be an essential factor in determining the export intensity of foreign MNCs working in the Indian motor vehicle industry. Many foreign MNCs import indigenous raw materials for their production instead of importing raw material from abroad. Nowadays, many small companies, including parts and accessories firms, are supplying raw material to other big MNCs. Small companies do not export directly to the global market, but they provide indigenous raw material to foreign MNCs, which positively determines their export intensity.

The Expenditure on Selling and Distribution (SellingIn) seems to have a positive and significant factor in determining the export intensity of the full sample of domestic companies and MNCs. It is one of the essential factors for companies to showcase their products in the global market. Selling is also a proxy indicator for product differentiation. The motor vehicle industry seems to have more scope for product differentiation. The amount spent on outsourced manufacturing jobs (OutIn) also positively and significantly determines the intensity of exports in both domestic companies as well as foreign MNCs working in the Indian motor vehicle industry. Expenditure on wages and salaries (CHOI) has positive coefficients for determining the export intensity of full and domestic companies, but it turns out to be negatively impacting the export performance of foreign MNCs. The size of the firm (SIZE) does not have any effect on the performance of export intensity in case of the full sample and it is negatively affecting the intensity of domestic company's export performance. But size turns out to be positively and significantly affecting the export performance of foreign MNCs. The mean size of foreign MNCs is also higher than domestic companies (see Appendix 9-D of Descriptive Statistics).

The age of the firm (Age) has positive coefficients for determining the export intensity for full sample and domestic companies. It significantly affects the export intensity of foreign MNCs. The Double Specific model suggests that younger companies are more export-intensive as compared to older companies. The mean age of MNCs is also lower than domestic companies (see Appendix 9-D). After the liberalization, many foreign MNCs entered India through joint ventures and full subsidiaries. They are relatively new compared to domestic companies in the Indian motor vehicle industry. Therefore, newer companies (foreign MNCs in this case) enter the industry with the latest technology and better production skills.

3. Summary and Conclusion

This chapter attempts to analyze the role of MNC affiliations in determining the export intensity and their performance, and how they are determined differently from domestic companies in the case of the Indian motor vehicle industry. The export performance of companies has considered two main aspects: first, to decide regarding whether to export or not; second, if they are exporting, then how much to export. To conduct this study, we used a panel of data consisting of 125 firms for 16 years from 2001 to 2016 for the Indian Motor Vehicle Industry based on the firm-level data provided by CMIE Prowess IQ (2016). Also, for presenting the econometric results of the analysis, we have carried out using two different models: namely, the Tobit model and a Double Specification (Probit + Truncation) model. When comparing the results of these two models, we found some evidence to contend that there are differences in the determinants to decide the probability to exports and intensity to export. Therefore, to analyze the export performance of the companies, a Double Specification (Probit + Truncation) model is more suitable than the widely used Tobit model.

MNC affiliations appeared to affect the export performance of companies of the Indian motor vehicle industry significantly. Considering the MNCs (Table 9.7), it is evident that import of indigenous raw material, selling cost intensity, outsourced intensity and size of the firm influence positively the probability of exporting as well as the intensity of exporting. The age of MNCs' affiliations is not influencing the probability of export. However, it does affect positively the intensity of exports of the MNCs affiliated to the Indian motor vehicle industry. The study found that the size of MNCs' affiliation positively influences both decision and intensity of exports. There is clear evidence that younger companies are more successful in the export market.

Further, the plants and machinery of newer firms are expected to be more modern technologies. The results suggest that domestic companies are more experienced than foreign MNCs in the Indian motor vehicle industry. However, experienced companies may be better able to cope with risks and uncertainties associated with exporting. The results of the regressions are mixed. Affiliations of foreign MNCs are looking forward to the international market to remain in the industry. In the case of domestic companies, age has a positive sign for both the decision and the intensity to export.

Regarding the domestic companies (Table 9.6), research & development intensity do not affect the export performance of the Indian motor vehicle industry. Domestic companies have been importing the latest technology and capital from other countries. So, instead of spending on R&D, domestic companies spend on advertisement and promotion of sales to boost exports. The selling cost intensity for domestic companies indicates a positive and significant effect on both the export decision as well as the intensity of exports.

As a concluding remark, to promote exports in the Indian motor vehicle industry, firm-level and industry-level factors are very important. The role of government is also essential to improve the international competitiveness of domestic companies. Indigenous raw material by domestic companies has a positive effect on the probability of exporting, but it is negatively affecting the quantity of exports. So, efforts should be made to improve the quality and technology of indigenous raw materials. It can be developed by supporting indigenous capital equipment and accelerating training of workers with the latest machinery.

The study provides evidence of the impact that FDI still has on export performance. It also helps to understand the importance of FDI in a particular industry for the global integration of the economy. From a policy perspective, the study suggests that the indigenous raw material by domestic companies has a positive effect on the probability of exporting, but it is negatively affecting the quantity of exports. So, the government's efforts should be on improving the quality and technology of indigenous raw materials. The government can provide subsidies and other incentives to support indigenous capital equipment and accelerate the training of workers with the latest machinery. It is also important to have greater resource efficiency in the motor vehicle industry in India, and this can be achieved by investing in and introducing the latest and most technologically advanced electric vehicles. Including the petrol and diesel segment in PLI (production linked incentive) schemes can facilitate India's commitment towards reducing oil imports, and then it can easily move towards the environmentally sustainable and more efficient electric vehicle-based industry. Also, more in-house R&D expenditure is needed with more technical collaborations for the growth and higher export rates of the Indian motor vehicle industry.

Notes

1 Motor vehicles include production of passenger cars and commercial vehicles www.oica.net/category/production-statistics/2018-statistics/
2 In the automotive sector, the joint venture with Japanese company Suzuki Motors was an exception. Suzuki entered India through a joint venture with Maruti Udyog.
3 Embodied technology is acquired through a firm's expenditure on the import of capital goods. Disembodied technology import is calculated by royalty payments and technical fee payment in foreign currency.
4 The study period shows significance from various portions. First, India pursued liberal policies and moved from FERA to FEMA regime in 1999, particularly concerning foreign capital flows. Second, the Government of India allowed 100 per cent FDI through automatic routes in the automobile sector in 2001. 2001 marked a year of inflexion with a significant increase in foreign capital inflows. During the period from 2001–2014, the automobile sector in India remained one of the major sectors attracting on an average about 5.5 per cent of annual FDI inflows.
5 Foreign promotors (per cent) include foreign individual promotors, foreign corporate bodies (per cent) and foreign promotor institutions (per cent).
6 This threshold is suggested and used by IMF and was adopted by RBI (as per the Balance of Payment manual, 5th edition, 1995)
7 2(Ln Probit + Ln Truncation – Ln Tobit), where Ln is the log-likelihood ratio. If LR test is greater than the critical value of the chi-square distribution for the relevant degree of freedom, the unrestricted model specification based on the combination of Probit and Truncated regression is more suitable than restricted Tobit model.

References

Aggarwal, A. (1997). Liberalization, internationalization advantages and foreign direct investment: The Indian experience in the 1980s. *Transnational Corporations*, *6*, 33–56.

Aggarwal, A. (2002). Liberalisation, multinational enterprises and export performance: Evidence from Indian manufacturing. *Journal of Development Studies*, *38*(3), 119–137.

Athukorala, P., Jayasuriya, S., & Oczkowski, E. (1995). Multinational firms and export performance in developing countries: Some analytical issues and new empirical evidence. *Journal of Development Economics*, *46*(1), 109–122.

Athukorala, P., & Veeramani, C. (2019). From import substitution to integration into global production networks: The case of the Indian automobile industry. *Asian Development Review*, *36*(2), 72–99.

Basile, R. (2001). Export behaviour of Italian manufacturing firms over the nineties: The role of innovation. *Research Policy*, *30*(8), 1185–1201.

Bhaduri, S., & Ray, A. S. (2004). Exporting through technological capability: Econometric evidence from India's pharmaceutical and electrical/electronics firms. *Oxford Development Studies*, *32*(1), 87–100.

Bhat, S., & Narayanan, K. (2009). Technological efforts, firm size and exports in the basic chemical industry in India. *Oxford Development Studies*, *37*(2), 145–169.

Chacar, A. S., Celo, S., & Thams, Y. (2010). The performance of multinational affiliates versus domestic firms. *Journal of Management Policy and Practice*, *11*(4), 47–59.

CMIE Prowess IQ. (2016). *Centre for monitoring Indian economy*. https://prowessiq.cmie.com/

Cragg, J. G. (1971). Some statistical models for limited dependent variables with application to the demand for durable goods. *Econometrica (Pre-1986)*, *39*(5), 829.

D'Costa, A. P. (2004). Flexible practices for mass production goals: Economic governance in the Indian automobile industry. *Industrial and Corporate Change*, *13*(2), 335–367.

Finances of FDI Companies. (2016). *Reserve Bank of India Bulletin- various reports*. https://m.rbi.org.in/Scripts/Pr_DataRelease.aspx?SectionID=363&DateFilter=Year

Greene, W. H. (2002). *Econometric analysis*. Pearson Education India.

Gujarati, D. N. (2009). *Basic econometrics* (Fifth ed.). Tata McGraw-Hill Education.

Guner, B., Lee, J., & Lucius, H. W. (2010). The impact of industry characteristics on export performance: A three country study. *International Journal of Business and Economics Perspectives*, *5*(2), 126–142.

Joseph, K. J., & Kakarlapudi, K. K. (2018). Technology-productivity conundrum in India's manufacturing under globalization: A preliminary exploration using innovation system perspective. *FGKS*, 24.

Kumar, N. (1994). *Multinational enterprises and industrial organization: The case of India*. SAGE.

Kumar, N., & Siddharthan, N. S. (1994). Technology, firm size and export behaviour in developing countries: The case of Indian enterprises. *The Journal of Development Studies*, *31*(2), 289–309.

Kumar, N., & Siddharthan, N. S. (1997). *Technology, market structure and internationalization: Issues and policies for developing countries*. Routledge.

Lall, S. (1999). India's manufactured exports: Comparative Structure and prospects. *World Development*, *27*(10), 1769–1786. https://doi.org/10.1016/S0305-750X(99)00084-4

Lall, S., & Mohammad, S. (1983). Foreign ownership and export performance in the large corporate sector of India. *The Journal of Development Studies*, *20*(1), 56–67. https://doi.org/10.1080/00220388308421888

Malik, S. K. (2014). Conditional technology spillovers from foreign direct investment: Evidence from Indian manufacturing industries. *Journal of Productivity Analysis*, *43*(2), 183–198. https://doi.org/10.1007/s11123-014-0425-8

Moghaddam, F. M., Hamid, A. B. B. A., & Aliakbar, E. (2012). Management influence on the export performance of firms: A review of the empirical literature 1989–2009. *African Journal of Business Management*, *6*(15), 5150–5158.

Narayana, D. (1989). *The motor vehicle industry in industry: Growth within a regulatory policy environment*. Centre for Development Studies Occasional Paper Series.

Narayanan, K. (2006). Technology acquisition and export competitiveness: Evidence from Indian automobile industry. In *India: Industrialization in a reforming economy* (pp. 439–470). Academic Foundation.

OICA. (2018). *2018 Statistics | OICA*. www.oica.net/category/production- statistics/2018-statistics/

Pant, M. (1993). Export performance, transnational corporations and the manufacturing sector: A Case study of India. *Indian Economic Review*, *28*(1), 41–54.

Prasanna, N. (2010). Impact of foreign direct investment on export performance in India. *Journal of Social Sciences*, *24*(1), 65–71. https://doi.org/10.1080/09718923.2010.11892838

Ray, A. S., & Bhaduri, S. (2001). R&D and technological learning in Indian industry: Econometric estimation of the research production function. *Oxford Development Studies*, *29*(2), 155–171.

RBI. (2012). *Reserve Bank of India*. www.rbi.org.in/home.aspx

RBI. (2017). *Reserve Bank of India – publications*. www.rbi.org.in/Scripts/PublicationsView.aspx?id=17931

Sharma, K. (2003). Factors determining India's export performance. *Journal of Asian Economics*, *14*(3), 435–446. https://doi.org/10.1016/S1049-0078(03)00036-8

SIAM. (2012). *Society of Indian automobile manufactures*. www.siamindia.com/statistics.aspx?mpgid=8&pgidtrail=13

SIAM. (2013). *Society of Indian automobile manufacturers, statistical profile 2012–13*. https://www.siam.in/statistics.aspx?mpgid=8&pgidtrail=15

SIAM. (2018). *Society of Indian automobile manufacturers, statistical profile 2017–18*. www.siamindia.com/statistics.aspx?mpgid=8&pgidtrail=15

Siddharthan, N. S., & Nollen, S. (2004). MNE affiliation, firm size and exports revisited: A study of information technology firms in India. *Journal of Development Studies*, *40*(6), 146–168.

Singh, J. (2019). *Global players and the Indian car industry: Trade, technology and structural change*. Routledge India.

Sousa, C. M. (2004). Export performance measurement: An evaluation of the empirical research in the literature. *Academy of Marketing Science Review*, *2004*, 1.

Sterlacchini, A. (1999). Do innovative activities matter to small firms in non-R&D-intensive industries? An application to export performance. *Research Policy*, *28*(8), 819–832.

UNCTAD. (2005). *Transnational corporations and the Internationalization of R&D*. United Nations. https://unctad.org/en/docs/wir2005_en.pdf

Vyas, V., Narayanan, K., & Ramanathan, A. (2013). Mergers and acquisitions, technological efforts and exports: A study of pharmaceutical sector in India. *Innovation and Development*, *3*(2), 169–186.

Wakelin, K. (1998). Innovation and export behaviour at the firm level. *Research Policy*, *26*(7–8), 829–841.

Willmore, L. (1992). Tansnationals and foreign trade: Evidence from Brazil. *The Journal of Development Studies*, *28*(2), 314–335.
Zhao, H., & Zou, S. (2002). The impact of industry concentration and firm location on export propensity and intensity: An empirical analysis of Chinese manufacturing firms. *Journal of International Marketing*, *10*(1), 52–71.
Zheng, P., Siler, P., & Giorgioni, G. (2004). FDI and the export performance of Chinese indigenous firms: A regional approach. *Journal of Chinese Economic and Business Studies*, *2*(1), 55–71. https://doi.org/10.1080/14765280310001631381

III

Institutions, Organizations and Inter-Linkages in Sub-National Innovation Systems

Chapter 10

Digital India as an Innovation System

Nirvikar Singh

1. Introduction

"Digital India" is the name of an initiative of the Government of India, announced in 2014 and formulated over the following year, which has "a vision to transform India into a digitally empowered society and knowledge economy."[1] "Digital India" is also the title of a report from McKinsey Global Institute (Kaka et al., 2019), which has a sweeping vision in its subtitle: "Technology to transform a connected nation." The emphasis of the two visions is somewhat different, with the MGI report giving more attention to specific applications and sectors of the economy, whereas the government initiative is mostly focused on aspects of e-governance. In this chapter, we outline a conceptualization of Digital India as an innovation system. Doing so, we would argue, provides the basis for a more realistic assessment of how and to what extent India can indeed use digital technology in various ways to enable empowerment of citizens, economic growth and societal transformation.

What is an "innovation system"? Friedrich List used the term "national system" in 1841,[2] but he connects this to "political economy." In essence, he argues for an alignment of commercial and political union at the level of the nation, and is skeptical of free trade as a universally beneficial policy. While he does not focus on innovation per se, the idea of industrial development by acquisition and refinement of manufacturing capabilities is clearly related. Indeed, Freeman (1995) argues forcefully that List's focus in economic development is on "learning about new technology and applying it" (p. 5). A century later, Schumpeter (1942) emphasized the importance of innovation in coining the term "creative destruction," but it is with Lundvall (1985 [2016]) that a systemic aspect of innovation begins to emerge (p. 21): "We shall regard innovations as the result of collisions between technical opportunity and user needs." The full-fledged concept and terminology seem to first explicitly appear in Freeman (1987): a national innovation system is "the network of institutions in the public and private sectors whose activities and interactions initiate, import, modify and diffuse new technologies."[3]

DOI: 10.4324/9781003353904-13

There are many other similar articulations of the concept of an innovation system, and an enormous global literature output applying the concept to numerous economies. Freeman's early discussion of Japan still remains paradigmatic in this large set of studies. Studies of India are characteristic of how most analyses are done. Fan (2008) compares India and China, using indicators such as export of high-technology and other "knowledge" products, patents, expenditure on R&D, number of scientific and technical personnel, government policies and firms' innovation capabilities in biotech and pharmaceuticals. Datta and Saad (2011) focus on the contribution of India's universities to its innovation system, and suggest that the record is mixed, but not insignificant. Bokachev (2019) focuses on India's spending on R&D and how it is distributed across various types of institutions. He also describes the pattern of FDI across sectors, and the evolution of government policies for import substitution and development of technological capabilities. Herstatt et al. (2008) provide a comprehensive discussion, including all the aggregate indicators used in other studies, along with more detailed analysis of government policies, as well as the state of India's educational system, physical infrastructure measures and demand factors. In addition, they surveyed a set of firms to understand their innovation capabilities and perspectives on their external environment as it shaped those capabilities.

A significant exception to the typical qualitative studies, such as those described, is the work of Mehta (2018). She uses quantitative measures for the inputs and outputs of innovation, including GDP per capita, R&D expenditure, patents, science and technology personnel, physical infrastructure and trade openness. She estimates a simultaneous equation model for inputs and for innovation performance, separately for the periods before and after the 1991 economic reforms that are typically viewed as marking a break in the functioning of the Indian economy, making it less state-controlled and more market-oriented. Among her results are evidence of a positive impact of government R&D, openness and the stock of science and technology personnel on India's innovation performance. Mehta also suggests that India lags behind other countries in the levels of these variables that matter for a successful innovation system.

Rather than the national innovation system, Joseph (2009) focuses on India's information and communications technology (ICT) sector. In other respects, this is the typical qualitative analysis of the innovation system, though it is based on various kinds of data. He documents the growth of software- and IT-enabled services as well as hardware. He discusses the overall policy regime, the availability and growth of engineering education, the role played by domestic and multinational firms, and the impact of R&D and of institutional networks, including universities and other types of R&D institutions. The outcome of this system is detailed: namely, the movement of Indian IT firms into higher value-added niches and their increasing global presence, including offshoring in addition to taking on outsourced work in

India. Joseph notes the dominance of Southern India in this sector, as well as the failure of the ICT sector's innovation system to have much impact on the other parts of India's economy, especially manufacturing. Hence, Joseph raises, without answering a central issue, the concept of Digital India as an innovation system.

In this chapter, we use the conceptual framework of an innovation system to discuss the manner in which digital technology can have an impact on the entire economy. Hence, our focus is not on the entire national innovation system, nor is it on the IT sector alone (we will use this acronym in preference to ICT). Our focus on digital technology is because of its status as a transformative factor for the economy.[4] The rest of the chapter is organized as follows. In the next section, we discuss the visions of Digital India as conceptualized by the Indian government and in the McKinsey report, and briefly outline what is missing in terms of how one might evaluate an innovation system based on digital technology. In the following three sections, we consider infrastructure, skills, and education and research, as inputs into the innovation system. We then discuss the importance and characteristics of a start-up ecosystem, before turning to various applications of digital technology, in sectors such as retailing, manufacturing, education, and health. The final section is a summary conclusion.

2. Visions of Digital India

The national government's vision of Digital India is centered on three areas: digital infrastructure as a utility for all citizens, governance and services on demand and digital empowerment of citizens. This is a plausible and appealing categorization, although it seems to omit the role of digital technology in business by focusing on government and consumers. Further description does highlight provision of digital government services for making it easier to do business, but this only addresses the government-business interface, not the internal workings of business.

The next level of detail in the conceptualization of Digital India lists nine "pillars." The first three pillars come under the first vision area: broadband highways, universal access to (mobile) phones and a public Internet access programme address different aspects of infrastructure, with the third pillar referring specifically to an ongoing effort to create rural "Common Service Centres" as well as extending the services of post offices in this direction.

The next two pillars are e-Governance and electronic delivery of services (e-Kranti). These both fit within the second vision area, with e-Governance referring to the use of digital technology to re-engineer internal government processes and functioning. Therefore, these two pillars are complementary, although the first is in some ways more important than the second since citizen services can only achieve cosmetic improvement without a fundamental internal reorganization of government. The range of services listed is impressive but daunting, including health, education and finance, but conceptual coherence starts to break down when target groups are also listed (especially farmers), and there are references to e-prisons, e-courts and e-police. The latter group seems to refer to portals for those law-and-order functions, but their presence and presentation is incongruous. Cyber-security, which is a fundamental and vital aspect of digital infrastructure, is clearly misplaced in the e-Kranti category.

The sixth pillar has the sweeping designation of "information for all." This would potentially come under the third vision area, digital empowerment, though empowerment implies much more than information access. There are three components of this pillar. One is clearly laudable and important – making government data open and accessible to citizens. But this is really a corollary of the fourth and fifth pillars. A second component is a platform for citizen engagement, MyGov.in, supposedly "engaging with over 9 lakh citizens for enabling and empowering them to participate directly in policy formulation and program implementation." This seems to be mostly cosmetic, unless it is part of a major overhaul of government functioning. The third component simply consists of a plan to digitally push government-generated messages at citizens. The sixth pillar is, therefore, conceptually weak and unclear.

The last three pillars do not even fit into the three vision areas, although they still matter. The seventh pillar, Electronics Manufacturing, has an explicit target of zero net imports. Developing domestic capabilities in the design and manufacture of digital devices, including writing the software that they use, is clearly an important objective. But "zero net imports" is an unrealistic and unnecessary target. This so-called pillar ought to have been conceived of more broadly, and at the higher level of a vision area. This would also bring business more squarely into the vision.

The eighth pillar is "IT for Jobs," covering a broad range of skills and types of jobs. Aside from the failure to acknowledge the enormous challenge and ongoing failure to provide all kinds of skills (not just for IT) to India's population, this pillar does not connect well to the existing vision areas, although it could fit with a broadened "digital capabilities" area that includes manufacturing, software development, IT maintenance and IT-enabled services.

The last pillar, of "Early Harvest Programmes" is a grab-bag of completely miscellaneous programmes that are already under development. But there are so many aspects of the other eight pillars that are ongoing or specific that separating a long list of random programmes in this manner is unhelpful.

The McKinsey vision of Digital India (Kaka et al., 2019) has a very different focus than that of the government. It begins with the premise that the rapid growth in Internet subscribers will drive a "digital surge" on the consumer side. On the other hand, their survey of over 600 firms leads them to conclude that "digital adoption among businesses has been uneven across all sectors." Nevertheless, small firms are described as closing the digital gap with large firms, especially in areas such as digital payments. One important fact emphasized in this analysis is that data costs dropped by 95 percent from 2013 to 2019, spurring increased Internet usage. On the government side, the expansion of the Aadhaar digital identification programme and the introduction of the Goods and Services Tax Network are also viewed as important drivers of digitization. In sum, the McKinsey vision of Digital India is more specific than that of the government, in terms of quantifying trends in access and usage, though of course it has the advantage of recency, and therefore the ability to describe trends more concretely.

The McKinsey conceptual framework is somewhat more coherent than the "pillars" of the government's vision. A key organizing principle in this approach is that of the types of sectors, three are identified. First are core digital sectors: these include IT and IT-enabled services (ITES),[5] telecoms and other digital communications and electronics manufacturing. Second are sectors where digitization is already being introduced in ways that add value: these include agriculture, education, energy, financial services, healthcare, logistics and retailing. Applications can be as diverse as digital tracking of vehicles in logistics to collecting and analyzing data on soil conditions in farming. The third set of areas in which digitization can play a significant role are not really sectors as such, but cross-cutting areas such as government services and labor markets. So, the typology is not perfect, but it is more systematic than the government's "pillars." Indeed, several of those pillars are in the third McKinsey group, whereas the government framework does not systematically address different sectors in the second group.

With respect to jobs and skills, the McKinsey report is also conceptually clearer. An important point that it makes up front is that "the need for functional digital literacy will increase across the board." At the same time, in other work situations, there will be an increased demand for creativity and problem-solving. All of these developments will put new demands on India's systems of education and training, which are already deficient in some respects. Of course, there will be increased demand for those with all levels of skills related to software development and programming, manufacturing of hardware and all kinds of maintenance and repair activities, whether for software, access devices or network equipment. The last of these, in particular, tends to be taken for granted in these kinds of discussions, but it is not a trivial aspect of the new kinds of skills that will be needed in a "Digital India." This is true in non-obvious places – while maintaining network cables and routers is an obvious aspect of digitization, the fact that something like repairing increasingly digitized automobiles requires very different skills can be easy to ignore.

While the McKinsey vision is broader, more concrete and more coherent than that of the national government, neither really offers a systemic perspective. The McKinsey report does use "ecosystem" many times, often to refer to data ecosystems, and at other times to sectoral ecosystems, in cases such as agriculture and logistics. But this does not really constitute a systemic perspective in the sense of a "system of innovation." In some cases, as for skilling or cybersecurity, there is little beyond brief mentions or exhortations that these are important issues. In particular, there is no assessment of India's system of higher education or its capabilities in research and development (R&D).[6]

In an important component of what is required for a digital system of innovation – namely, the use of digital tools by firms – while this issue is mostly absent from the government's vision, the McKinsey report provides a lengthy analysis of disparities in digital adoption. However, it seems that it fails to put the analysis in the context of a configuration of industry that has an unusual size distribution, with relatively few large firms and many small firms, the latter often in the informal sector – the "missing middle" in Indian industry. Furthermore, there is the decades-long failure for manufacturing to grow fast enough to create an adequate number of jobs, indicating structural problems that are deeper than the absence of a digital adoption strategy. Even reliability and cost of electric power are major issues for many smaller Indian firms, potentially making digital infrastructure an unattractive investment for firms.[7]

Finally, other illustrations of what is missing from these conceptualizations of Digital India are an absence of consideration of trade and trade policies, foreign direct investment (FDI) and technology transfer, the intellectual property rights (IPR) regime and the start-up ecosystem. The research on India's national innovation system indicates these are important in general, and they are likely to be more so for any digital transformation.

3. Infrastructure

Digital infrastructure is obviously a critical foundation for any progress with a digital economy. The hardware of this infrastructure is costly and complex, including towers, cables, routers, servers, access devices and so on. There is just as much, if not more, complexity in the software that is equally necessary for a robust digital infrastructure, ranging in functions from the basic functioning of the hardware through storage, processing, data traffic management, communications, cybersecurity and any number of applications.

The government's own listing of initiatives within Digital India under the category of infrastructure (www.digitalindia.gov.in/infrastructure) is again somewhat miscellaneous. Two key elements of physical infrastructure highlighted in this list are BharatNet, a mission to provide fiber-optic cable to village governments throughout the country, and Common Service Centres (CSCs), which are meant to provide rural residents with access points for government and non-government services by digital means.[8] As usual with national government initiatives, it is difficult to assess actual performance and impacts, but the evidence suggests that what has been achieved so far is well short of the vision (e.g., Mudliar, 2016, 2020).

More broadly and concretely, the McKinsey report offers a Digital Adoption Index (DAI), which has three components (each with sub-components): foundation (which is one aspect of infrastructure), reach (which is another aspect) and value (which is partly about infrastructure, and partly other factors). Specifically, the first component measures the cost, speed and reliability of Internet connections; reach measures access levels, data usage and app downloads; and value measures engagement by chatting, shopping, streaming and so on. Compared to 16 other developed and developing economies, India has the lowest DAI, below Indonesia, South Africa, Brazil and China, although the report stresses a rapid increase in the past few years. A combination of government initiatives and private sector investment are credited for this pace of change.

Other digital infrastructure indices provide similar information, as well as additional insights. In particular, the World Bank (2016) DAI ranks India at 92 out of 180 countries. But it also provides rankings of three components: people, business and government. In the first category, India's rank is 132, in the second it is 114, and in the third it is a remarkably high 22. One does not have to accept the last case as necessarily a true ranking of how well India's citizens are able to digitally access government services. Indeed, the low rankings for people and business suggest that there may be an imbalance in India's digital infrastructure. Sophisticated governmental digital infrastructure will still not help those without the capabilities to access it. The World Bank index may be considered to be obsolete, given rapid recent progress in India, but another ranking from 2019, Cisco's Global Digital Readiness Index, puts India at 101 out of 141 countries (Cisco, 2020).[9]

Since each index is based on different factors and each is broader than just a pure measure of digital infrastructure, it is difficult to draw conclusions that are very sharp, but it seems reasonable to assert that India, despite its considerable progress in the last few years, is not yet at a level that would support a robust digital innovation system. Arguably, bandwidth and reliability are still short of where they could be, and while there is widespread use of smartphones, access to more sophisticated devices such as laptops and tablets is much more limited.[10] Of course, low incomes are a major factor in this, but there does not seem to be much analysis of how to promote shared access in locations such as schools or universities, or how to provide cutting-edge infrastructure for these institutions, and for small and medium firms. Two other areas where anecdotal evidence suggests there are limitations or constraints are cybersecurity and local language content.

4. Skills

The boundary between skilling and training on one hand and education on the other is unavoidably fuzzy. The need for much broader functional digital literacy as digital technology becomes more pervasive will be addressed in the next section, under education, although the acquisition of specific skills, such as word processing or web design, could be considered as vocational training. In any case, India's system of skilling is notoriously deficient, even aside from the new demands created by the spread of digital technology. The government's vision does not seem to address the issue of what skills will be needed for this situation: the pillar of "IT for Jobs" envisages mostly BPM-type jobs, and the actual implementation seems to only consist of trying to create such jobs in the Northeast region of India. The McKinsey report's discussion of skills is generic and non-specific, and the processes by which these skills will be acquired is not addressed. Other discussions of skilling (e.g., Seth et al., 2020) are at the level of advanced skills which are acquired in addition to higher education: in the context of IT, examples are expertise in artificial intelligence, data analytics, human-computer interfaces and so on. Here we focus on basic skills such as maintenance and repair of the various components of the complex digital infrastructure.

India has a significant number of Industrial Training Institutes and Industrial Training Centres, run by government and the private sector respectively, regulated by the National Council for Vocational Education and Training (NCVET). This was created in 2018, subsuming two separate regulators. The range of trades or skills that are addressed is naturally quite diverse, but it does include several that are relevant to various aspects of a digital economy, such as data entry, mechanics who deal with electronics in different industries, network technicians, and many more. This is not surprising. In 2009, a National Skill Development Policy was put in place, and it led to a National Vocational Education Qualification Framework (NVEQF), which created a listing and inventory of skills and occupations.

In practice, there have been problems in translating the bureaucratic and regulatory superstructure into effective training in the classroom, lab or factory floor. The NVEQF attempts to define learning standards, but it is short on detail, does not have the right structure and lacks any specification of learning outcomes. Ultimately, the problems are with inadequate capacity, lack of qualified trainers and an imbalance of the skills being imparted relative to market needs (Herstatt et al., 2008; Sharma and Nagendra, 2016; Kumar et al., 2019). The last of these, in particular, is related to the government-dominated approach to this kind of skilling. Furthermore, India has little in the way of internships and apprenticeships beyond what happens through the elite business schools. Despite discussions or proposals to upgrade training institutes or even make them into universities, there does not seem to have been much focused effort to learn from Germany on the apprenticeship front, or the US and its tradition of agricultural universities.

There are, however, some successful examples of adaptation to needs when there is a focused requirement. The National Skill Development Corporation (NSDC), a public-private partnership set up in 2008, collaborated with the Institute of Company Secretaries of India in 2017 to train about 100,000 people as GST Account Assistants, for helping companies transition to the GST. This training was subsidized by a government programme, but it was a very specific two-week course, designed for those with existing baseline skills. This is very different from, say, training an electrician or computer repair person from scratch. Nevertheless, the NSDC represents the beginning of a different approach to skills training in India, emphasizing greater use of the private sector for imparting this training. Another example is TeamLease Skills University, established with the support of the Gujarat state government, which provides more advanced vocational education, including areas such as IT and "mechatronics," and perhaps falls more in the category of education.

Perhaps a better example of new possibilities for training are purely private institutes, such as the Prizm Institute established in 2015 in Mumbai, which offers training in repairing mobile phones and various types of computers. It offers online courses as well, although is difficult to assess how effective that can be for this kind of training. Furthermore, it offers relatively clear guidance on entry qualifications and career prospects. There are several variants on the basic model, including franchising and combining technical training with entrepreneurship training. Some even offer guidance on finding jobs in Indian migrant destinations such as the Gulf states. Examples include Britco & Bridco, headquartered in Kerala, and the Expert Institute, headquartered in Delhi.

There are, of course, many others, and there is tremendous variation in the range and level of courses offered, the kinds of certification provided, and the extent of government oversight. From the information provided by government agencies, it is difficult to assess the size, quality and other features of these kinds of offerings. This reflects the common problem of government initiatives in India: that they often do not translate effectively from overarching visions to detailed assessment of implementation and outcomes. What is clear, however, is that innovations of the kind illustrated by these private institutes will need to be much faster, and scaled up in a manner that has escaped the government so far. Arguably, there may be a need for importing trainers from developed countries, in order to achieve the requisite speed of expansion of vocational training. This may seem paradoxical, since these are not traditionally viewed as high-skilled, knowledge-intensive occupations. But the central point to be made is that in a digital economy, even basic tasks such as repair and maintenance require much greater specialized training than in the past.

5. Education and Research

Education is a much broader topic than skilling, but it has also received much more attention. At the primary level, it is now well established that increases in school enrollment rates have not been well reflected in learning outcomes.[11] The reasons for this are numerous, but the main proximate cause is lack of incentives for teachers to teach.[12] It is also the case that teachers are not well trained themselves. The underlying causes of these two phenomena are inadequate expenditure and poor regulation. A well-known response to these problems has been for parents to place their children in fee-charging private schools, rather than "free" government schools. Unfortunately, one government counter-response has been to increase the regulation of private schools, making it more difficult for them to provide low-cost educational services.

In this context, the issue of digital literacy seems to be of second-order importance. Nevertheless, it cannot be neglected as efforts to reform primary and secondary education are undertaken. The 2020 National Education Policy (NEP) envisages some major structural reforms in education, de-emphasizing intensive and extensive rote learning and make-or-break examinations, in favor of fostering creativity and problem-solving. It is not clear how positive changes will come about without extensive changes in teacher incentives and training, but it is a step in the right direction. There is also a move to create more vocational tracking in secondary school, although this has the danger of prematurely excluding some students from high-paying or satisfying occupations and careers. Indeed, this kind of tracking should probably be done after high school, and opportunities for practical learning should be enhanced for everyone. The NEP does have a couple of brief mentions of digital literacy, but there is not any substantive discussion of what this entails or how to achieve it, especially if teachers themselves are lacking in this competence.

The NEP gives much more attention to digital access, and makes repeated promises to reduce the digital divide. This can be considered to be an aspect of infrastructure (networks and devices), which we discussed previously, or of digital services (educational content), which we treat in a later section. The promise of widespread online education has been held out for years before the NEP, and the coronavirus pandemic has illustrated how far India has to go in providing anything like adequate options. Furthermore, electricity, water and toilets are also priorities for making Indian schools more effective, perhaps before digital tools can make a difference.[13]

This area is another where the articulation with the government's Digital India mission is weak. That initiative refers to a National Digital Literacy Mission (NDLM) under infrastructure, but the focus is on employees or agents of the government, such as Anganwadi, ASHA workers and authorized ration dealers, rather than a universal educational goal. Furthermore, the NDLM website seems to consist only of guidance on how to prepare for and apply for various government jobs, rather than any programmes for digital literacy.

Turning to higher education in India, that topic has also received considerable attention.[14] Attendance and quality of college and university teachers are less severe problems at this level, but there is clearly a severe shortage of faculty, given the level of demand in India. Of course, there are a few dozen elite institutions, especially in fields such as engineering and management, but there is arguably a considerable drop-off in quality as one goes outside the top tier. Here, too, private universities have stepped into the gap created by an insufficient supply of public education, but their quality is still somewhat variable and difficult for prospective students to judge ex ante. Here also the NEP offers some reform possibilities, with proposals for streamlining and rationalizing regulation, but one of the most severe constraints may simply be lack of funding, especially for some of the science and engineering fields.

In the context of the development of IT and ITES in India beginning in the 1990s, the story of the rapid expansion of regional engineering colleges, especially in several states in South India, is well-known. It is also acknowledged that the average quality of graduates is often low, so that only a small fraction of them are employable by the major software firms in India, and even then will require considerable training. To some extent, the need for job-specific training is common, even in advanced countries with better educational systems, so the difference is a matter of degree, rather than of kind. In addition to resource constraints such as lack of up-to-date equipment, laboratories and software, perhaps the most severe constraint is once again insufficient numbers of high-quality faculty. In this case, teaching skills are not the only desideratum, since research-active faculty are important for education in fields such as IT, where there are rapid developments in what is considered state-of-the-art.

At the apex of the education system is research and development (R&D), technically not a necessary component of education, but inextricably linked to it in the modern university system. In this respect, however, India is quite weak. Public universities in India have been underfunded, and countries like the US and UK have siphoned off many of the best students for graduate work. Premier engineering institutions such as the IITs do not, with some exceptions, have robust research efforts. Changing this situation with respect to digital technologies will require considerable investments in facilities, as well as incentives to attract leading faculty from around the world: China, Hong Kong and Singapore are examples of successful efforts to upgrade university research capabilities in this manner. Meanwhile, government research institutions do continue to provide some oases of excellence, echoing their role as sources of human capital for India's initial progress in IT, but their aggregate impact is far short of what an economy the size of India requires.

In the case of digital technologies, the bright spot in R&D is the capabilities of the IT firms themselves. Some of these capabilities are found in the start-up ecosystem, discussed in the next section. What is particularly significant is that numerous large US corporations have set up R&D centers in India, especially in places like Bengaluru, which is emerging as a global hub in this respect. Indeed, India-based R&D is generating US patents at a significant rate. Frontier research possibilities in areas such as Artificial Intelligence (AI) are also an exception to the government's somewhat fuzzy plans for Digital India, with NITI Aayog (2018, 2020) producing excellent roadmaps.[15] As another example, NASSCOM is mapping out what it calls Global Capability Centres (GCCs) in areas such as cybersecurity (KPMG, 2020).

Overall, then, at least in the case of IT, India appears to be developing strong research capabilities that leverage the success of its IT firms and the emergence of places like Bengaluru as knowledge hubs. What is noteworthy is that this has been accomplished without proportionate development of the foundational layers of the nation's education system. This lack of balance will be a severe constraint in the future unless it is addressed in a strong manner.[16]

6. Start-up Ecosystem

Overall, India's rate of new business creation is below what its per capita income levels would predict. However, in parallel with the emergence of IT-centred R&D hubs in India, the same locations are becoming start-up hubs as well. A report on the country's tech start-up ecosystem (NASSCOM-Zinnov, 2020) is very positive in its assessment. It counts more than 10,000 such firms created since 2015, the cumulative number growing at 8-10% a year. Of these, 38 have valuations over USD 1B (so-called "unicorns"), with a dozen of those entering that category in 2020 alone. This start-up landscape has breadth and a presence on the frontier of technology.[17] The range of sectors where start-ups are emerging includes retailing, finance, education, health and media, as well as back-end technologies for internal businesses operations or supply chains. The report details "deep-tech" start-ups, in frontier areas such as artificial intelligence, blockchain and big data. This is a far cry from the early days of doing routine and back-end services for global firms, to the extent that the country's software workers were dismissed as "techno-coolies."

However, while there are over 500 incubators and accelerators spread across more than 100 cities, the success rate among these is characterized as "abysmal." One positive example given is the Bharat Inclusion Initiative at IIM-Ahmedabad, but there is no indication of what sets it apart. A review of other evidence suggests that these incubators often lack sufficient funding of their own, and even more, lack both their own management expertise and the expertise needed to provide quality mentorship. Physical infrastructure and routine services are necessary, and governments and universities can provide those, but are not overcoming the scarcity of financial and human capital. The creation of a start-up ecosystem may require effective clusters rather than incubators, so the government may do better by making sure that high-quality digital infrastructure is available for everyone (not just within incubators), along with general promotion of ease of doing business.[18]

Clusters also have the potential advantage of critical mass – this may also be a problem for Indian incubators. For example, China's start-up incubators are larger and go further in achieving the requisite critical mass (Tang et al., 2013). Of course, China has a longer track record in this dimension, and that supports both size and effectiveness through learning by doing. India has to catch up in this respect. Other areas where China illustrates a possible pathway for India are in the importance of universities and of intellectual property and patents. China has made great strides in the quality of its universities, and as discussed earlier, India needs to do better in this dimension.

On the patent front, it does appear that the government's Start-Up India Mission is promoting easier protection of intellectual property, along with reductions of bureaucratic hurdles and improvements in tax treatment of start-ups. More can probably be done on the tax front to make risk-taking attractive, but overall, there are hints that India is moving in a direction that could finally change its below-average record in new business creation.

7. Applications

The applications of digital technologies across different sectors of the economy are the essence of the special nature of IT as a "general purpose technology" (GPT)[19]. It is impossible to provide a comprehensive account of all such applications; instead, we provide an overview. In the abstract, the three basic dimensions of digital technology, namely, storage, processing and communication of information, drive every application. As emphasized earlier, a complex infrastructure of hardware, including network equipment and access devices, has to be created and maintained to support the more ethereal information economy. And the variety of possibilities for "amplifying brain power"[20] make IT even more transformative than previous GPTs such as electric power.[21]

As already discussed, the government's Digital India initiative focuses on government operations and citizen services, and on some aspects of infrastructure. It includes electronics manufacturing as one of its pillars, but does not dig into applications of IT that fall outside the delivery of citizen services. On the other hand, the McKinsey report focuses much more on the business side of IT adoption, although it does not analyze the reasons for uneven adoption of digital technologies by Indian firms.[22]

Financial services are an obvious candidate for applying IT, since financial records and transfers are all potentially reduced to digital form. Payments and transfers, credit, loans, insurance and savings represent a wide range of possible financial services that can be digitized. The main obstacles to achieving this are higher needs for data security and consumer knowledge, as well as greater dangers of fraud and systemic instability. After some delays in adoption because of India's size and regulatory caution, it does seem that digital financial services are beginning to become part of the Indian economy. In some cases, this is being driven by the government, as welfare transfers and tax systems are digitized. In other cases, the growth of other digital applications, such as retailing, is driving adoption for simpler services such as payments.

The McKinsey report treats financial services in a scattered manner, but has separate sections on agriculture, healthcare, retailing and logistics as specific sectors. Energy, education, governance and job markets also receive brief discussions. The precise nature of applications can vary across different sectors, and there is enormous potential variety, but there are some fundamental tasks that can be performed efficiently using digital technologies. These include remote sensing (e.g., in agriculture, energy or healthcare), remote tracking across locations (e.g., in logistics or retailing), one-way information gathering and processing (e.g., education, retailing, job markets or healthcare), two-way human interactions (e.g., healthcare, education, job markets or agriculture) and so on. The key principle is that the costs of certain kinds of interactions are brought down dramatically, making them economically feasible, where they were not before, or information can be gathered and processed usefully in ways that would have been prohibitively costly without information technology, so that new types of services are enabled (Singh, 2008).

A key idea here is that, while adoption of digital technology is itself an innovation, doing so enables further innovation. However, there are a couple of potential obstacles. One may be fixed costs and the need to achieve sufficient scale to benefit from the change. Another is that a large network may be needed for individual members of the network to benefit enough to want to participate. This can be true for networks where everyone can interact, or where there are two sides, as in a digital marketplace. A third obstacle is that several complementary innovations are required for any one of them to work (e.g., retailing and payments, although cash on delivery was an initial workaround in India).[23] Some of these obstacles were apparent in failed early attempts to bring Internet-enabled services to rural India (Singh, 2016). However, as the costs of storage, processing and communications have continued to fall dramatically, especially in the last half-decade, there does seem to be potential for significant adoption and innovation in many sectors of the Indian economy. In some cases, there may still be a need for overcoming switching costs, through one-time subsidies or other incentives. The growth of a diverse and competitive start-up ecosystem (NASSCOM-Zinnov, 2020) is also a signal of the potential for digital adoption for many sectors to take off in India.

8. Conclusion

The falling cost of information technology, along with the accumulation of capabilities in India's IT and ITES sector and the increased size of that sector, together represent a major opportunity for digital technology to emerge as the foundation for a national system of innovation. Digital information technology has some aspects that give it unique potential to be transformative in this manner. The government's Digital India programme, while it has significant gaps and uneven implementation, does represent a relatively supportive stance by the government for achieving this transformation, as does its Startup India initiative. Government attempts to increase digitization in systems of welfare transfers and taxation, as well as gradual updating of regulations in areas such as financial services, also represent positive developments.

The weaknesses for achieving a robust system of innovation include an infrastructure that needs significant broadening and deepening, despite fast progress in the past few years. Preserving competitiveness and equity while accelerating the development of digital infrastructure will be a major challenge, given India's political economy. Also, more basic types of infrastructure, such as the distribution of reliable and low-cost electric power, are an important precondition for a digital economy. The greatest weakness of the Indian economy, not just in the realm of creating a national system of innovation based on digital technology, is in building human capital, both in specific skills and broader educational outcomes. For digital innovation, this includes a range of new skills that will be required to maintain a high-performing digital infrastructure, and to use digital technologies effectively in a range of applications, as well as high-level skills such as programming, software design, cybersecurity, data analytics and various "deep-tech" applications. In the education sector as a whole, the effective use of digital technology falls far short of what is possible, but improvements in organization and regulation, and increased entry and competition may be even more important for a robust innovation system than the increased deployment of technology. Expanding capabilities in this manner will also be important if existing economic inequalities are not to be exacerbated.

Notes

1 See www.digitalindia.gov.in/, where the effort is described as a "flagship programme."
2 This is a translation of the original German, but the words are almost identical in the two languages. The standard English translation is List (1909).
3 See also Dosi et al. (1988), especially the contributions by Nelson and Freeman, which specifically add institutions such as governments and universities to producers and users, in thinking about "national innovation systems."
4 The special features of digital technology from an economic perspective are discussed in detail in Singh (2016), which also reviews many features of India's economy and its use of digital technology.

5 The report uses the term Business Process Management (BPM), which is somewhat narrower, but perhaps more apt, since ITES may be in non-core sectors.
6 There is a reference to a previous McKinsey report (McKinsey Center for Government, 2013), which documented the shortcoming of India's training and skilling programs, but the data is from the 1990s.
7 See Sharma and Singh (2013) for a detailed empirical analysis of these issues.
8 The CSC plan was actually introduced in 2006, well before the national Digital India initiative. Given that length of time, its progress seems to be disappointing.
9 These are not the only such measures. The IMD World Digital Competitiveness Ranking (IMD, 2019) places India at 44 out of 63 economies. An even broader Digital Evolution Scorecard (Chakravorti et al., 2020) ranks India at 61 out of 90 economies.
10 There have been notable failures in this respect, including the One Laptop Per Child project (Shah, 2011), and the Aakash Tablet (Phalkey and Chattapadhyay, 2015).
11 Annual reports on surveys conducted by the NGO Pratham document this problem in great detail. For example, see Pratham (2019), as well as previous reports.
12 Many studies document the problems of teacher absence and poor incentives. For an overview of the policy issues with respect to schooling in India, see Muralidharan (2013).
13 A useful controlled experiment that isolates and measure the impacts of digital tools for learning at the school level is described in Muralidharan et al. (2019).
14 For example, see Kapur and Mehta (2017). One issue that often gets neglected in discussions of education is the low availability of education services and content in regional Indian languages: digital technology may help in relaxing this constraint, if focused attention is paid to this problem.
15 On AI, see also Kathuria et al. (2020) and NASSCOM (2020).
16 For a general analysis of the challenges of broad-based development in India via IT, see Singh (2004).
17 See also Government of India (2018), for additional perspectives on start-ups in India, including detailed state-level comparisons.
18 For quantitative analysis of these issues, see Joshi and Satyanarayana (2014) and Joshi (2018).
19 Again, see Singh (2016) for a detailed discussion of the origins of this term and the characteristics of IT that lead to this classification.
20 This description is due to economist Bradford DeLong, as quoted in Woodall (2000).
21 For a specific discussion of the special characteristics of IT with respect to the process of innovation, see Singh (2008).
22 Again, see Sharma and Singh (2013) for an empirical analysis of manufacturing firms.
23 This is captured in McKinsey's use of the term "ecosystem" to describe digital developments in various sectors. The term is somewhat elastic in its various usages. Ecosystems are not necessarily sector-specific, with payments being an important cross-cutting example. A start-up ecosystem represents a different formulation from sectoral ecosystems.

References

Bokachev, IN (2019). National innovation system of India: genesis and key performance indicators. *RUDN Journal of Economics*, 27 (4), 774–785.

Chakravorti, B, Chaturvedi, RS, Filipovic, C, and Brewer, G (2020). *Digital in the Time of Covid: Trust in the Digital Economy and Its Evolution across 90 Economies as the Planet Paused for a Pandemic*. Boston: The Fletcher School at Tufts University.

Cisco (2020). *Cisco Global Digital Readiness Index 2019*. White paper. San Jose, CA: Cisco Public. Available at https://www.cisco.com/c/dam/en_us/about/csr/reports/global-digital-readiness-index.pdf. Accessed 25 September 2022.

Datta, S, and Saad, M (2011). University and innovation systems: the case of India. *Science and Public Policy*, 38 (1), 7–17.

Dosi, G, Freeman, C, Nelson, R, Silverberg, G, and Soete, L (1988). *Technical Change and Economic Theory*. Pisa: Laboratory of Economics and Management, Sant'Anna School of Advanced Studies.

Fan, P (2008). Innovation capacity and economic development: China and India, WIDER Research Paper, No. 2008/31, The United Nations University World Institute for Development Economics Research (UNU-WIDER), Helsinki.

Freeman, C (1987). *Technology Policy and Economic Performance: Lessons from Japan*. London: Francis Pinter.

Freeman, C (1995). The 'national system of innovation' in historical perspective. *Cambridge Journal of Economics*, 19, 5–24.

Government of India (2018). *States' Startup Ranking 2018*. New Delhi: Ministry of Commerce & Industry, Department of Industrial Policy & Promotion.

Herstatt, C, Tiwari, R, Ernst, D, and Buse, S (2008). India's National Innovation System: Key Elements and Corporate Perspectives. TIM/TUHH Working Paper 51, Hamburg University of Technology.

IMD (2019). *IMD World Digital Competitiveness Ranking 2019*. Lausanne, Switzerland: IMD World Competitiveness Center. Available at https://www.imd.org/globalassets/wcc/docs/release-2019/digital/imd-world-digital-competitiveness-rankings-2019.pdf. Accessed 25 September 2022.

Joseph, KJ (2009). Sectoral innovation systems in developing countries: The case of ICT in India. In Lundvall, B-A, Joseph, KJ, Chaminade, C, and Jan Vang, J (eds) *Handbook of Innovation Systems and Developing Countries: Building Domestic Capabilities in a Global Setting*. London: Edward Elgar, 291–346.

Joshi, K (2018). Emergence and persistence of high-tech start-up clusters: An empirical study of six Indian clusters. *International Journal of Global Business and Competitiveness*, 13 (1), 15–34.

Joshi, K, and Satyanaraya, K (2014). What ecosystem factors impact the growth of high-tech start-ups in India? *Asian Journal of Innovation and Policy*, 3 (2), 216–244.

Kaka, N, Madgavkar, A, Kshirsagar, A, Gupta, R, Manyika, J, Bahl, K, and Gupta, S (2019). *Digital India: Technology to Transform a Connected Nation*. San Francisco: McKinsey Global Institute.

Kapur, D, and Mehta PB (2017). *Navigating the Labyrinth: Perspectives on India's Higher Education*. New Delhi: Orient Blackswan.

Kathuria, R, Kedia, M, and Kapilavai, S (2020). *Implications of AI on the Indian Economy*. New Delhi: ICRIER and NASSCOM.

KPMG (2020). *Secure in India 2020: GCC at the Forefront of Managing Global Digital Risks*. New Delhi: KPMG and NASSCOM.

Kumar, R, Mandava, S, and Gopanapalli, VS (2019). Vocational training in India: Determinants of participation and effect on wages. *Empirical Research in Vocational Education and Training*, 11, 3.

List, F (1909). *The National System of Political Economy*, trans. Lloyd, SS. London: Longmans, Green and Co.

Lundvall, B-A (1985 [2016]). Product innovation and user-producer interaction, Industrial Development Research Series, vol. 31, Aalborg, Aalborg University Press. In Lundvall, B-A (ed.), *The Learning Economy and the Economics of Hope*. London: Anthem Press.

McKinsey Center for Government (2013). *Education to Employment: Designing a System That Works*. Boston: McKinsey Center for Government. Available at https://www.mckinsey.com/industries/education/our-insights/education-to-employment-designing-a-system-that-works. Accessed 25 September 2022.

Mehta, S (2018). National innovation system of India: An empirical analysis. *Millennial Asia*, 9(2), 203–224.

Mudliar, P (2016). *Rural India on the National Optic Fibre Network: What Happens Next?* (Policy Report No. 19). Chennai, India: The Hindu Centre for Politics & Public Policy.

Mudliar, P (2020). A reality check on India's search for digital Utopia. *The Hindu Centre for Politics & Public Policy*, August 28. www.thehinducentre.com/the-arena/current-issues/article32444675.ece.

Muralidharan, K (2013). Priorities for primary education policy in India's 12th five-year plan. *India Policy Forum*, 9 (1), 1–61.

Muralidharan, K, Singh, A, and Ganimian, AJ (2019). Disrupting education? Experimental evidence on technology-aided instruction in India. *American Economic Review*, 109 (4), 1426–1460.

NASSCOM (2020). *Unlocking Value from Data and AI: The India Opportunity*. New Delhi: NASSCOM.

NASSCOM-Zinnov (2020). *Indian Tech Start-up Ecosystem*. New Delhi: NASSCOM.

NITI Aayog (2018). *National Strategy for Artificial Intelligence*. New Delhi: NITI Aayog.

NITI Aayog (2020). *AIRAWAT: Establishing AI Specific Cloud Computing Infrastructure for India*. New Delhi: NITI Aayog.

Phalkey, J, and Chattapadhyay, S (2015). The Aakash tablet and technological imaginaries of mass education in contemporary India. *History and Technology*, 31 (4), 452–481.

Pratham (2019). *Annual Survey of Education Report: Early Years*. New Delhi: ASER Centre.

Schumpeter, J (1942 [1994]). *Capitalism, Socialism and Democracy*. London: Routledge.

Seth, K, Aswani, R, and Arora, K (2020). *Future Skilling for the Digital Economy*. Noida: NASSCOM and Deloitte.

Shah, N (2011). A blurry vision: Reconsidering the failure of the one laptop per child initiative. *WR: Journal of the Arts & Sciences Writing Program*, 3, 89–98.

Sharma, L, and Nagendra, A (2016). Skill development in India: Challenges and opportunities. *Indian Journal of Science and Technology*, 9 (48), 1–8.

Sharma, S, and Singh, N (2013). Information technology and productivity in Indian manufacturing. *India Policy Forum*, 9, 187–229.

Singh, N (2004). Information technology and India's economic development. In Basu, K (ed.) *India's Emerging Economy: Performance and Prospects in the 1990's and Beyond*. Cambridge, MA: MIT Press, 223–261.

Singh, N (2008). Transaction costs, information technology and development. *Indian Growth and Development Review*, 1 (2), 212–236.

Singh, N (2016). Information technology and its role in India's economic development: A review. In Dev, SM, and Babu, PG (eds), *Development in India: Micro and Macro Perspectives*. Singapore: Springer, 283–312.

Tang, M, Baskaran, A, Pancholi, J, and Lu, Y (2013). Technology business incubators in China and India: A comparative analysis. *Journal of Global Information Technology Management*, 16 (2), 33–58.

Woodall, P (2000). The new economy. *The Economist*, September 21, 6.

World Bank (2016). *World Development Report: Digital Dividends*. Washington, DC: World Bank.

Chapter 11

Innovation and Institutions: A Study of the Economy of the North Eastern Region of India in the Context of the Act East Policy

Bhagirathi Panda

Ever since the central government renamed the Look East Policy (LEP) of the Government of India as the Act East Policy (AEP) in 2014, the interest of development practitioners and academicians in this policy has significantly increased. This is precisely because the rechristening has the implication of being associated with a major tectonic shift in the philosophy and strategy of development for the country as a whole, and the North Eastern Region (NER) in particular. The story of the journey of development of the NER post-independence, albeit its contribution to creation of some socio-economic overheads, is a classic case of 'development prisoned to heightened security' and 'development outsourced to contractors'. The Act East Policy in its North Eastern edition is a reimagination of development for the region based on the philosophy of 'Retreat, Reimagine and Reclaim (RRR)' through promotion of 'Commerce, Culture and Connectivity (CCC)'. The retreat is about jettisoning the earlier distorted inward-looking dependent model of development fostered through pumping of money from Delhi. Reimagination is all about creatively thinking of promotion of economic development through the strategy of regional economic integration. Reclaiming is all about getting back the pre-partition primacy of wealth and employment status of the NER amongst the states of the country through promotion of entrepreneurship and sustainable use of all available resources. In fact, NEP is now dubbed as the macro development strategy for development of the NER by promoting commerce (trade and investment) with the neighbouring countries of South East Asia, East Asia including Bangladesh, cultural exchange (people to people contact) and improvement of physical and digital connectivity.

In the meantime, 19 years have gone by since the LEP was initiated by the central government way back in 1991, and 7 years have elapsed since it was rechristened as the AEP in 2014. Assessment of scholars (Sarma, 2017; Panda, 2020) shows that except some limited progress in the front of the connectivity and cultural exchange, nothing much has happened with

DOI: 10.4324/9781003353904-14

respect to trade and investment. It has been continuously argued by this author (Panda, 2017a, 2020) that the eventual success of AEP depends on the achievements in the front of trade (merchandise and services) and realisation of investment. To happen, this requires the region to provide for a critical scale of manufacturing and services activities, which is not visible at this juncture. The primary reason for the absence of the critical scale of manufacturing and services and investment activities is attributed to the presence of high transactions costs, the distorted nature of its structural transformation and the absence of an adequate innovation environment. The presence of high transaction costs and absence of enabling innovation ecosystems can be attributed to the deficiency and malfunctioning of the required institutions, both formal and informal. One of the important requirements for growth of industry and enterprise is the innovation ecosystem in the region. When this author wrote his earlier articles on this very subject, there was no credible data available with respect to the innovation ecosystem. Recently, NITI Aayog, a premier think-tank of the central government, has come up with its maiden report on innovation, 'Indian Innovation Index 2019'. This now gives an opportunity to analyse the innovation ecosystem in the region and contextualise the industrial and investment environment in relation to it.

This chapter is presented in five sections. Section II gives an account of the region, highlighting the nature of its structural transformation in the space of income and employment. Section III analyses the innovation and institution ecosystem for the region and Section IV concludes with some critical policy recommendations.

1. The Region and Its Structural Transformation

The North-Eastern Region (NER) of India comprises the eight states of Arunachal Pradesh, Assam, Manipur, Meghalaya, Mizoram, Nagaland, Sikkim and Tripura. Its geographical area is 8 percent of the total geographical area of the country, and its share of population approximately 3.77 percent of the country's total population. The region has an international border of 5,182 km with the neighbouring countries. In the North, it shares a distance of 1,395 km with Tibet Autonomous Region; in the east, a distance of 1,643 km with Myanmar; in the south-west, a distance of 1,596 km with Bangladesh; in the west a distance of 97 km with Nepal; and in the north-west a distance of 455 km with Bhutan (Chauhan, 2021). The economy of the region showed no appreciable growth in the income and employment space during the decades of the 80s and 90s. Post-2000 and particularly 2010, some signs of improvement are visible in the income space, as evidenced from Figure 11.1. However, as the figure shows there are four states–Meghalaya, Nagaland, Manipur and Arunachal Pradesh–in the region experiencing average annual growth rate (AAGR) of GSDP of less than the national average (6.95%) during the period 2012–19. In fact,

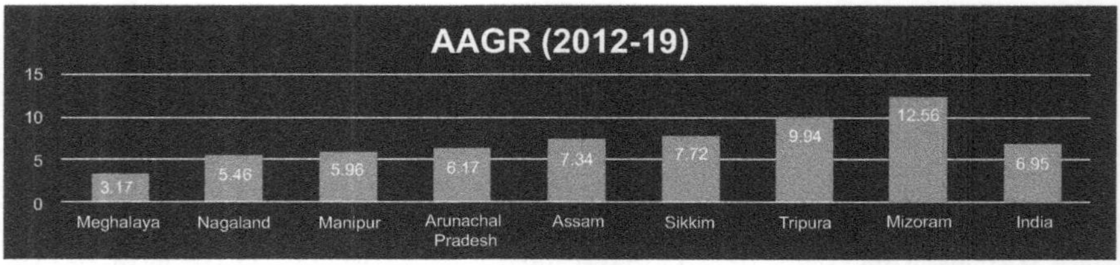

Figure 11.1 Average Annual Growth of GSDP of the NER, 2012–19

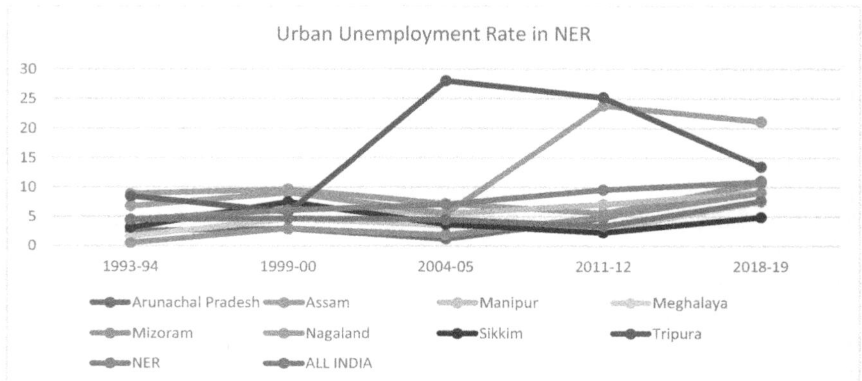

Figure 11.2 Urban Unemployment Rate in NER

amongst 33 states and union territories of the country, these states rank 32, 29, 24 and 22 respectively. The other four states of Assam, Sikkim, Tripura and Mizoram have AAGR above the national average. It is heartening to see here that the largest economy of the region (Assam) is experiencing above national AAGR of GSDP, and the state of Mizoram has realised the highest AAGR of 12.56 in the country during the period from 2012–19.

Similarly, the urban and rural unemployment rates in the region over different periods of time from 1999–20 to 2018–19 (Figures 11.2 and 11.3) have been much above the national averages. Two of the states in the region (Tripura and Nagaland) are experiencing very high unemployment rates both in their rural and urban sectors.

In the literature of development economics, one of the central theoretical explanations of the process of economic growth and development in an economy or society is the theory of structural transformation. (Lewis, 1954; Myrdal, 1957; Kuznets,1966). Structural transformation primarily implies a continuous reallocation of factors of production from low-productivity

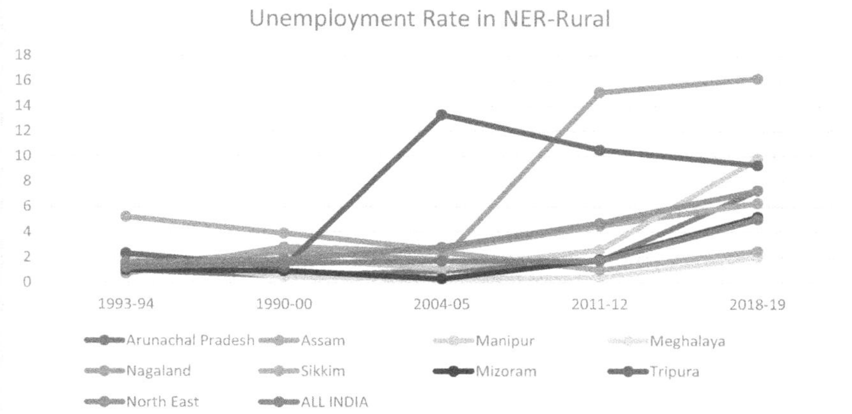

Figure 11.3 Rural Unemployment Rate in NER

sectors to high-productivity sectors, thereby increasing the productivity of the economy. Its actual realisation, based on the experience of most of the developed and fast developing transitional economies, suggests a secular movement of workforce from the agricultural sector to the industrial sector and then to the high-end services sector. The rural economy of the North-East at the macro level, based on analysis of data with respect to the nature of growth of GSDP and changing profile of the workforce in employment, shows no appreciable signs of confirmation to the structural transformation theory. Alternatively, its rural labour market remains inefficient and heterogeneous and signals the presence of distress diversification and casualisation of employment (Panda, 2017b, 2018).

2. The Innovation and Institution Ecosystem in the Region

It was Schumpeter who very rightly mentioned that economic development happens through 'creative destruction', meaning that an existing arrangement of producing and marketing of goods and services needs to be creatively destroyed to bring in new goods and services and new ways of marketing. The basis to realise creative destruction was suggested to be through continuous innovation. Never in the history of the economies of the world had a moment come when Schumpeter was so relevant and so immediate as it stands today. Historically, the world production hub has revolved around the countries/regions that did have the advantage in labour cost, along with the provision of a critical innovation and skilling environment.

However, today's economies like China and the USA, which are losing/have lost their core advantage in labour cost of production, are seriously trying to offset it through 5th generation innovations. Colonial powers did not promote any meaningful innovation in Indian industry for their own vested interests. Post-colonial India is also not known for its state-of-the-art innovation in industrial production. However, contemporary India boasts one of the best innovation environments in the IT services sector in the world. As mentioned in the introductory section of this chapter, the success of AEP, particularly in its NER edition, requires substantial reduction in transaction costs, improvement in its institutional arrangement and promotion of an innovation environment. We begin this section then with an analysis of the innovation ecosystem in the region based on the data provided in the maiden report of the NITI Aayog, 'Indian Innovation Index 2019'. This subsequently is followed by an analysis of the institutional environment in the region (based on the works of other authors and the 'North-eastern Region District SDG Index Report & Dashboard 2021–22' of NITI), to be concluded finally with an exploration of the relationship between innovations and institutions. Descriptive statistics, tables, charts and a linear bivariate regression analysis have been used as tools to decipher the situation in this context. Since the details of the variables taken, their sources and the methodology adopted to construct the various indices are already contained in both the reports ('Indian Innovation Index 2019' and 'North-eastern Region District SDG Index Report & Dashboard 2021–22' of NITI), we consider it unnecessary to repeat the same.

(a) The State of Innovation in the Region

As evidenced from Table 11.1, the Innovation score of all the NER states is below the national average. The lowest rank in the Index for the country is 36, and there are three states in the NER, i.e. Meghalaya, Mizoram and Nagaland, that are in the bottom 5 ranks of the country (Rank 35, 34, 33 respectively). Out of the 8 NER states, 6 of them are in the bottom 10 ranks of the country. As explained in the methodology section of the report, this index is prepared on two dimensions: enabler and performance. The enabler dimension consists of 5 indicators: (i) human capital, (ii) investment, (iii) knowledge workers, (iv) business environment and (v) safety and legal environment; the performance dimension consists of 2 indicators: (i) knowledge output and (ii) knowledge diffusion. An examination of the details of the enabler dimension scores in Table 11.2 reveals that Assam is at the bottom of the list among the NER states, and Sikkim is at the top of the list. However, Assam tops the list in the performance dimension, and Sikkim is at the bottom. This indicates the fact that Assam has been able to efficiently use its enabler factors to convert them into performance, whereas Sikkim has not been able to do that. However, Sikkim has all the potential to convert it to better performance in days

Table 11.1 NER states and their Innovation Index score

States	*Innovation Index Score*	*Rank in NER*	*Rank in India*
SIKKIM	13.12	1	13
MANIPUR	11.69	2	23
TRIPURA	8.54	3	27
ARUNACHAL PRADESH	8.50	4	28
ASSAM	7.74	5	25
NAGALAND	7.49	6	33
MIZORAM	6.88	7	34
MEGHALAYA	6.38	8	35
INDIA	15.6	-	-

Source: Computed by the author based on India Innovation index 2019, NITI, Govt of India

Table 11.2 Innovation Index (dimension score): The case of the North-eastern states in India

States	*Innovation Index Score*	*Dimension Score*	
		Enabler	*Performance*
SIKKIM	13.12(1)	29.98(1)	1.01(8)
MANIPUR	11.69(2)	18.50(2)	4.87(2)
TRIPURA	8.54(3)	15.51(3)	1.56(5)
ARUNACHAL PRADESH	8.50(4)	13.00(4)	4.00(3)
ASSAM	7.74(5)	7.99(8)	7,48(1)
NAGALAND	7.49(6)	11.76(6)	3.21(4)
MIZORAM	6.88(7)	12.31(5)	1.46(7)
MEGHALAYA	6.38(8)	11.09(7)	1.66(6)

Source: Computed by the author based on India Innovation index 2019, NITI, Govt of India

Note: *Figures in the parentheses show the relative rank of the state in NER

to come. The reading of the details of the IIS (Innovation Index Score), its dimensions scores, etc. are like the capability vector score of Amartya Sen's capability approach, where capabilities are basically the basket of potential functionings. Hence, the IIS here needs to be understood in the realm of possibilities and potentials. One can also find a lot of spread in the IIS, dimension and performance scores among all the states of the region.

Table 11.3 deconstructs the enabler dimension score in terms of its different indicator values. With respect to the human capital indicator, Sikkim tops the list with a score of 39.34, followed closely by Mizoram and Tripura. On this indicator, all the NER states do well vis a vis the country. In terms of the investment indicator, Meghalaya and Assam score very poorly. The most striking observation from this table is the extremely poor situation

Table 11.3 Innovation Index ('enabler' dimension scores): The case of the NER

States	*Enabler Score*	*Enabler Dimension Indicator Scores*				
		Human Capital	*Investment*	*Knowledge Workers*	*Business Environment*	*Safety and Legal Environment*
Sikkim	29.98(1)	39.34	4.29	33.62	3.41	68.74
Manipur	18.50(2)	24.36	14.54	24.82	4.38	24.42
Tripura	15.51(3)	30.02	7.90	5.14	5.42	29.05
Arunachal Pradesh	13.00(4)	24.86	11.38	4.64	4.36	19.76
Assam	7.99(8)	19.91	0.80	4.74	4.81	9.70
Nagaland	11.76(6)	24.20	3.63	5.81	4.55	20.54
Mizoram	12.31(5)	33.36	5.25	1.11	4.80	17.01
Meghalaya	11.09(7)	27.79	0.21	9.76	5.23	12.46

Source: Computed by the author based on India Innovation index 2019, NITI, Govt of India

Note: *Figures in the parentheses show the relative rank of the state in NER.

of all the NER states with respect to the Business Environment. All the NER states are way below the national average. For the knowledge worker indicator, the state of Sikkim ranks 2nd from the top in the whole country. The situation of Manipur and Meghalaya is comparatively better. In terms of safety and legal environment Sikkim tops the country.

The range of variation on this score is very high in the North-east. Assam, the biggest economy in NER, ranks lowest with a score of only 9.70 (which is the 3rd lowest in the country). It is a surprise that two of the states with better connectivity to the rest of India rank lowest in the investment and safety and legal environment indicators. This is a matter for introspection. It somewhat negates the common perception that poor infrastructure is the biggest obstacle in the way of investment and industrialisation. This also indicates the fact that institutional arrangements, including governance, are comparatively in a poor state in these two states.

Table 11.4 delves into the performance dimension indicator scores. Here, the NER does extremely poorly. In the front of knowledge diffusion, all the NER states except for Assam perform very badly. In fact, the bottom 7 ranked states of the country are from the North-east. Similarly, with respect to the knowledge output indicator, the ^{2n}d-^{5t}h lowest-ranked states are from the NER.

(b) Is there a relationship between innovation ecosystem and institutions in the NER?

As indicated earlier, the presence of high transaction costs and absence of enabling innovation ecosystems has been attributed to the deficiency and

Table 11.4 Innovation Index ('performance' dimension scores): The case of the NER

States	*Performance Score*	*Performance Dimension Indicator score*	
		Knowledge Output	*Knowledge Diffusion*
SIKKIM	1.01(8)	0.94(8)	1.07(5)
MANIPUR	4.87(2)	7.33(2)	2.42(2)
TRIPURA	1.56(5)	3.13(5)	0.00(8)
ARUNACHAL PRADESH	4.00(3)	7.39(1)	0.62(6)
ASSAM	7,48(8)	5.90(3)	9.07(1)
NAGALAND	3.21(4)	4.61(4)	1.82(3)
MIZORAM	1.46(7)	2.31(6)	0.61(7)
MEGHALAYA	1.66(6)	1.73(7)	1.60(4)

Source: Computed by the author based on India Innovation index 2019, NITI, Govt of India

Note: *Figures in the parentheses show the relative rank of the state in NER.

malfunctioning of the required institutions, both formal and informal in the NER (Panda, 2020; Basumatary and Panda, 2020). Deficiency and malfunctioning of institutions are reflected in the form of presence of corruption, rent-seeking, lack of property rights, presence of information asymmetry, poor law and order, insurgency, ethnic conflicts and lack of robust modern legal system. Quoting ***Transparency NE***, a body set up very recently by some social and anti-corruption activists as well as retired bureaucrats, Basumatary and Panda (2020) write, 'About 50 to 60 per cent of the funds meant for infrastructure and other development and welfare schemes in the region are siphoned. In states like Manipur and Nagaland, the amount goes up to even 70 per cent'. Mizoram anti-corruption watchdog PRISM (People's Right to Information & Development Implementing Society of Mizoram) claims that corruption is the major obstacle for development of the North-east and the main cause for the socio-economic ills, including militancy, troubling the region. Datta (2000) makes insurgency and violence responsible for perpetuation of underdevelopment in the NER. Kikhi (2009) gives a very interesting example to measure the increase in transaction costs because of deficiency in law and order. He says moving a truckload of goods from Moreh to Dimapur, a distance of 316 km, costs Rs 50,000 because the trucker has to pay huge extortion demands on the route.

A lack of appropriate and reliable data does not permit researchers to study at the macro level the relationship between institutions and innovation, thus industrialisation and economic development. Publications of two recent important reports of the NITI Aayog, ' Indian Innovation Index 2019' and 'North Eastern Region District SDG Index Report & Dashboard 2021–22' have given us an opportunity to analyse this kind of relationship, albeit with some limitations. In the absence of appropriate time series data for both the variables at the macro level, we have chosen a cross-section of data provided in both the reports to examine the relationship by invoking a bivariate linear regression model of the form:

$$\mathbf{Y = a + bX + e},$$

Where Y is the dependent variable,
b is the regression coefficient,
a is the intercept and
e is the residual.

Now putting the actual variables in the study, the model can be written as:

$$\text{INIFIND} = a + b\ \text{INSIND} + e$$

Where Y is the Innovation and Infrastructure Index score (INIFIND),
X is the Institution Index Score (INSIND)

The results after running the regression gives us the following equation for the best fitting line:

$$\text{INIFIND} = -9.329 + 1.13\ \text{INSIND} + e$$

The scatterplot model is as follows in Figure 11.4:

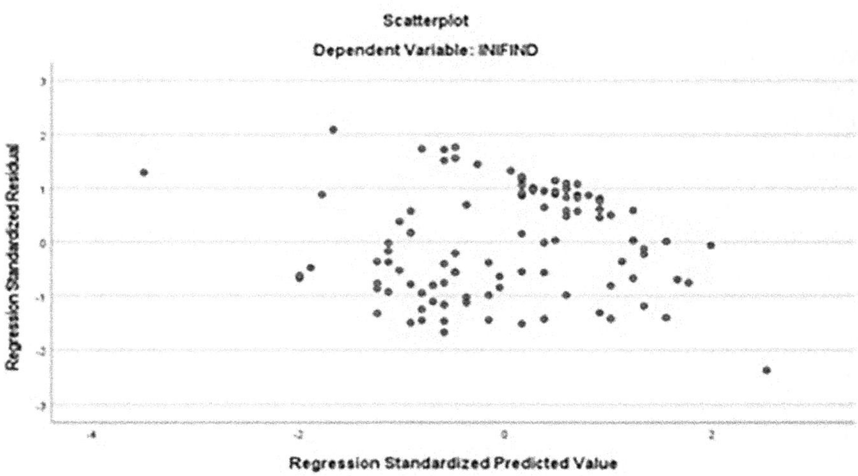

Figure 11.4 Scatterplot

The regression result shows that the model is a good fit, and the independent variable coefficient is statistically significant at 1% level. The data were tested for normality before the run of the regression. The scatterplot here shows good concentration. Although the R Square value is .22, considering the robustness of all other tests, we can safely assume that the institution variable is a reasonably good predictor of the innovation variable. The implication of this result for the economy of the NER is that a reasonably good amount of improvement in the innovation ecosystem can be made by providing for and improving upon the institutional arrangements.

3. Conclusion

The AEP as a reimagination of development for the NER is based on the philosophy of 'Retreat, Reimagine and Reclaim (RRR)' through promotion of 'Commerce, Culture and Connectivity (CCC)'. Success of the AEP as a macro development strategy for the region depends upon the degree of economic integration with its neighbours in Southeast and East Asia, including Bangladesh. To realise such effective regional economic integration, the region needs to be engaged in a critical volume of trade and investment, which at this juncture is not happening. Trade in merchandise to reach the critical size requires the region to produce goods and services in the framework of the global system of fragmented networked value-chain based production arrangement. This cannot happen without a conducive structural transformation happening in the income and employment space. For such a structural transformation to happen requires an increase in the productivity of its factors of production through Schumpeterian suggested practice of creative destruction. Increased industrialisation and services sector growth through creative destruction in the contemporary world requires seamless innovation. The NER economy, as our analysis shows, is a laggard in the field of innovation. Based on our analysis, it is convincing that the innovation system in the region significantly responds to improvements in institutions. The region at this time is still held hostage to institutions such as corruption, rent-seeking, ethnic violence, extortions, lack of property rights, lack of conducive and responsive governance including law and order. A concerted effort should therefore be made from the side of the government, market (private players) and community to come together on a regular basis in a formalised arrangement to improve upon the institutional ecosystem in the region. The success of the AEP fundamentally therefore depends upon the improvement of the institutional and innovation ecosystem in the region.

References

Basumatary, N. and B. Panda (2020). A review of institutional and developmental issues in North-East India, *Indian Journal of Public Administration*, 66(2), 206–218.

Chauhan, S. (2021). Insurgencies of the North East. *Financial Express*, November 18.
Datta, S. (2000). Northeast turmoil: Vital determinants. *Strategic Analysis*, 23(12), 2123–2133. https://www.financialexpress.com/defence/insurgencies-of-the-north-east-part-ii/2371632/
Kikhi, K. (2009). What ails the North-East? Challenges and responses. *Sociological Bulletin*, 58(3), 346–366.
Kuznets, S. (1966). *Modern economic growth: Rate, structure and spread*. New Haven, CT: Yale University Press.
Lewis, W. A. (1954). Economic development with unlimited supplies of labour. *The Manchester School*, 22(2): 139–191.
Myrdal, G. (1957). *Economic theory and underdeveloped regions*. London: University Paperbacks, Methuen.
Panda, B. (2017a). Act East policy and Northeast India: The role of transactions costs. In A. Sarma and S. Choudhury (Eds.), *Mainstreaming the Northeast in India's look and act East policy*. Singapore: Palgrave Macmillan.
Panda, B. (2017b). Rural employment diversification in Northeast India: An analysis. *Journal of Rural Development,* 36(2), 166–179.
Panda, B. (2018). Rural non-farm employment in North-East India: A temporal and spatial analysis. In V. Xaxa, D. Saha and R. Singha (Eds.), *Employment and labour market in North-East India: Interrogating structural changes*. New York: Routledge.
Panda, B. (2020). Act East policy, India's northeastern region and ASEAN: An essay in regional economic integration, *Man and Society: A Journal of North East Studies*, 17(1), 86–98.
Sarma, A. (2017). Integrating Northeast with South East Asia: Great Expectations and Ground Realities. In A. Sarma and S. Choudhury (Eds.), *Mainstreaming the Northeast in India's Look and Act East Policy*. Singapore: Palgrave Macmillan.

Chapter 12

Local Firms and Global Standards on the Ground

Informality and Labour in Indian Clusters

Keshab Das

1. Introduction

The phenomenal pace and spread of market globalization during the last three decades or so have prompted enquiries into understanding the functional dynamics and implications of growing interface between local firms, global buyers and consumers. For global out-tasking to be an (if not *the*) efficient strategy of production organization one needs to look closer into the context and terms under which such contracts are carried out. The nature of the governance structures assumes particular importance as one deals with in-contracting firms belonging to developing and poor economies – often chosen for 'rent-poor' activities by the lead firms. As global production networks (GPNs) essentially are directed by lead-firm strategies to access a larger share of the global market through raw material sourcing, product differentiation, cost-cutting, prompt delivery and product innovations, a particularly noticeable tendency of lead-firms across sectors has been the compromising of labour, environmental, health, social and ethical issues, while remaining focused on maintaining product standards (Damodaran, 2010; Suresh, 2010; Rahman and Langford, 2012; Jha and Chakraborty, 2014; Das, 2016; Roy, 2017). This eventuality has been possible to a large extent due to the preponderance of informality in both the labour and production processes and the presence of weak institutions – both formal and informal – that fail to be vigilant.

It is important to explore if, how and to what extent local micro, small and medium enterprises (MSMEs) in clusters in the global South have been responding to and shaping the labour and environmental standards as these firms participate in GPNs. In understanding these processes, at the MSME cluster level, of aligning with and/or reconfiguring voluntary private sustainability standards as well as public (domestic state and global intergovernmental) standards, it is important to recognise that local values and approaches to producing for the layered markets (domestic and beyond) do matter. That informality in both the production and labour processes in Indian industrial clusters persists as a dominant characteristic needs to be

DOI: 10.4324/9781003353904-15

recognized for a nuanced and realistic understanding of how global standards are navigated by the local enterprises (Das, 2017).

One of the central foci of the larger collaborative research project ('Rising Powers, Labour Standards and Governance of Global Production Networks' supported by the Economic and Social Research Council, UK) of which this study forms a part has been to explore if, how and to what extent MSMEs in clusters, especially from the Rising Powers (emerging economies, but with a focus on India, China and Brazil), have been responding to and shaping the labour and social standards as these firms participate in GPNs (Nadvi, 2014). The chapter puts together observations and insights from field studies in three clusters from southern and western India.

Following much deliberation with the co-researchers and other scholars, it was decided to select two sub-sectors with excellent records in export performance or long experience in dealing with global markets; the sub-sectors chosen were: i. knitwear; and ii. diamond polishing as linked to the gems and jewellery sector. With additional rounds of consultations with scholars and local resource persons, the Tiruppur Knitwear Cluster in Tiruppur in Tamil Nadu was chosen. The units surveyed were all integrated large and medium enterprises with complete focus on exports (exports turnover > Rs. 35 crore). They reported that no work was outsourced to any smaller units. Secondly, a field survey was conducted at the diamond polishing cluster in Surat (Gujarat), and some interactions were made with owners of the gems and jewellery cluster of Mumbai. The surveys were conducted around the last quarter of 2015 to the first quarter of 2016.

2. Standards at Tiruppur Knitwear Cluster (TKC): Nature and Compliance

The rise of TKC in the global market may be traced to the soaring of exports observed since the early 1980s, led mainly by cotton t-shirts. Table 12.1 provides an idea about the growth in exports from the TKC. Table 12.2 gives an impression about the distribution of units by operation. Despite being a prominent export cluster, unfortunately, reliable and comprehensive statistics on basic variables such as number of units, employment, value of production, etc. are unavailable.

While product standards are stipulated by the (foreign) buyers, they often provide guidelines on process standards concerning labour, social, environment and sustainability issues. The standards followed by firms at TKC include Confidence in Textiles, Global Organic Textile Standard (GOTS), Organic-100, Worldwide Responsible Accredited Production (WRAP), Social Accreditation SA8000, ISO 9001 2008 and Business Social Compliance Initiative (BSCI). Some orders received are for products that meet certified standards not just at the manufacturing unit, but down the supply chain also: for example, certified Fair-Trade Organic with Traceability.

Table 12.1 Exports of knitwear from TKC, 1984–2016

Year	*Value of Exports (Rs. Crore)*
1984–85	15
1989–90	300
1994–95	1500
1999–2000	3500
2004–05	6500
2009–10	11500
2014–15	20500
2015–16	23000*

Source: an informal discussion with the CA of Sripuram Trust

Note: Estimate.

Table 12.2 Number of units in TKC by operation, 2010

Operations	*Number of Units*
Knitting Units	1500
Dyeing and Bleaching	700
Fabric Printing	500
Garment Making	2500
Embroidery	250
Other Ancillary Units	500
Compacting and Calendaring	300
Total	6250

Source: www.tiruppur.tn.nic.in/textile.html

However, there exists scope for minor flexibilities as manufacturers can negotiate small modifications for effective execution and to suit local realities. The buyers understand constraints, especially with reference to environment standards where the state does not provide better cost-effective solutions at the level of the collective. The buyers often conduct surprise audits to ensure that the firms adhere to the standards agreed upon. These visits also help learning, as the visiting team of experts suggests improvements that benefit the firm. It is claimed that during the last decade and a half, Tiruppur has earned the trust of its buyers with regard to standards compliance.

Besides these, there are standards that local governments stipulate relating to labour, social and environment aspects. But often the government guidelines lack clarity, leaving much to be desired so far as the implementation is concerned. There could be instances of harassment by 'inspectors' who engage in approaches not constructive to the business or the cluster.

Expectations on standards of buyers from advanced countries are often at substantial variance with or 'exceed' those stipulated by local governments. While it is not difficult to meet most of the expectations on standards –

especially concerning product standards – the standards compliance certification process is time-consuming and expensive, as there are only a few foreign accreditation/certifying agencies with few alternatives. Further, national standards in certain instances are in an evolving stage. For instance, the initiative by the Apparel Export Promotion Council (AEPC), namely Driving Industry towards Sustainable Human Capital Advancement (DISHA), is a qualitative assessment of Indian garment manufacturer exporters to achieve international standards in productivity and social standards. But this is yet to take off in a big way.

While the cluster or the TEA does not seem directly to drive the standards agenda for individual firms, it does hold learning events on standards and demonstrates their benefits to the cluster as well as individual firms. There are fora or groups of firms (for example, TTPK and Sripuram Trust)[1] and a few thought leaders who are now striving for Tiruppur's own standard setting and the promotion of Tiruppur as a brand.

Most of the evolved firms in Tiruppur have, since almost the mid-1990s, realized that compliance with standards brings in business benefits in terms of efficiency, ability to attract new and more profit-making buyers, finding buyers from high-end segments or more vibrant markets and earning respect and referrals among buyers. Hence, many proactive factory owners are seeing compliance not as a cost or burden but as an investment for future business growth. However, this is true for medium and large firms who can afford it. For many smaller firms (say, those with annual turnover less than Rs. 15 crore), the standards certifications are a significant cost both in terms of money and effort.

For example, if a buyer wants Fair-Trade certified products, then applying for, obtaining and retaining Flocert certification entails a minimum of about Rs. 4–5 lakh annually. Other than this, the unit has to have capital and human resources to manage the planned and surprise audits. This is for obtaining just one standard and one certification. There could be six to eight such certifications demanded by different buyers.[2] Other challenges to small suppliers relate to the fact that their order sizes are often small – sometimes as small as 3000 pieces per order. There is no guarantee that the same buyer will place another order (with the same certification requirements) in the same year. Hence, even though these certifications become necessary to get the order, the returns do not always justify the costs – at least in the short or medium term. It does take effort on the part of the firm and consume some resources when new standards are proposed or expected by buyers; for example, reducing energy footprint or water offset. The returns may accrue in the longer term and are hard to measure or attribute directly, whereas the effort and cost/investment are immediate.

Some standards requirements – especially with respect to labour standards; for instance, limits on working hours per day and 'cap' on overtime (OT) to 50 hours/quarter – need to be understood in a context where the local practice among workers is to work OT to earn 200 per cent additional pay to maximize total earnings. A typical worker wishes to work a 32–40-hour regular week plus 12 to 15 hours OT in a week because there is a cent per cent premium in India for OT, whereas in many countries the same is only 50 per cent.

It was understood from reliable sources that the practice of 'fudging' documents did exist, especially in labour records, to mask the fact that 20 to 30 per cent of workers within the firm premises had been engaged on a temporary basis through contractors. The labour records (including PF and ESI records) are manipulated to show that a set of employees are on the rolls of the firm, while they are not. These 'contract' workers earn a wage as they agree with their contractor. The contract workers are paid on a piece rate. Rampant fudging could be one of the reasons why 90 per cent firms here do not deploy standard ERP software by SAP, Tally, Siebel, etc. Local software developers and even in-house programmers have designed independent, tailor-made and company-specific solutions which are not deliberately integrated or standardized to the modules. For example, the production planning department has one software and the human resources another. Similarly, employee compensation would be a separate module. Even though it is possible to integrate these modules of production planning, human resource allocation and compensation-reward-incentives, to optimize or analyze costs better, or achieve efficiency or delineate traceability – these are not integrated purposefully, as discrete modules are easier to manipulate. Auditors also cannot easily find out anomalies.

Even the large knitwear units who make value-added fashion garments like t-shirts face a challenge. The designs in the order are unique and also keep changing – this calls for different skill sets from workers, but order sizes are modest – sometimes as low as 3000 pieces. So every order is like a 'project' and nothing is 'run-of-the-mill'. This also sometimes forces the unit managers to hire skill sets on a temporary basis per the needs/specifications of a particular order, rather than hire workers on a more permanent basis and then struggle when they do not possess the skill sets required for the next product variant. Some skills are project-specific. Those skills are required in a short-term engagement only.

Some standards expectations, for example concerning living conditions, are a function of the government's actions in providing or enabling services such as affordable housing, public healthcare, public schools, public transport, water and sanitation, sports and recreation, etc. For example, as explained by an SME owner, if a buyer expects certain living conditions for labour, the supplier firm has little say in how or where its workers live. Some very large firms have good hostels or living quarters, whereas most SMEs cannot create hostels or townships. In Tiruppur, house rentals are exorbitantly high in the relatively better endowed areas. Eventually, some workers prefer to live in groups in low-rent areas, often sharing the house or living space. This is despite the fact that even a low-skilled worker earns about Rs. 9000 per month and may be willing to pay about Rs. 1000 as rent. Unless the government creates affordable housing, this situation of sub-standard living conditions will continue. Under the scheme of Central Assistance to States for Developing Export Infrastructure and Allied Activities (ASIDE), TEA has built hostels in two places – one for 1000 workers and another for 750 workers. One hostel has also been constructed inside the Apparel Park to accommodate 1000 women workers. But this is not sufficient, nor is it the best solution. The government has to create townships with affordable services and amenities – health, education, transportation, water, sanitation, waste disposal, sports and recreation, etc. Only then the quality of life will be good for everyone.

Social practices and norms outside of the workplace also influence the quality of life of workers. The firms have little or no direct control over these. This was an indirect reference to the caste systems and practices among Tamil-speaking local workers made by our key contact. It appears that there had been a few caste-based disputes during the time preceding the field survey, among groups of workers, perhaps triggered by an inter-caste marriage. Firm owners made no specific comments on the possibility of workplace discrimination based on local traditional practices, caste or religion.

Most of the medium and large units are perceived as good or responsible businesses – both by insiders and outsiders.[3] They were of the opinion that 70 to 75 per cent of the firms (mostly large and medium) in TKC were good employers. Those firms also undertook social work or CSR activities like health camps, education scholarship and tree plantation. The remaining 20 to 30 per cent of firms (almost all small units like 'banian' or vest quality checking units) were where employees suffered. The large and medium enterprises (mainly exporters) had one or the other buyer-visit/audit going on throughout the year. They would not risk tarnishing their image.

Many large and medium-size firms have active CSR activities with reasonable budgets that are not necessarily linked to profits or earnings. They usually connect with local charitable organizations or NGOs to implement their CSR activities. These include developing nearby village infrastructure (Kanimpundi village), supporting rural primary education, aanganwadi, drinking water and sanitation in village schools, mobilizing help during local/village emergencies (like complicated childbirth) and calamities like tsunamis. Others reported working with NGOs, especially for cancer patients or old people[4], vermi-composting, recycling, reducing/preventing use of plastic, using paper prudently and planting more trees. A few factory owners mentioned supporting animal welfare or bestowing compassion towards old animals through a relatively recent NGO named GoDhan.

The firms claim that CSR – usually around charity, health, education, tree plantation, etc. – is voluntary in nature and not due to any government stipulation. However, many buyers and foreign brands do press the CSR agenda – especially on the environment, water use, energy use, people-friendly policies and welfare of employees. Most buyers/brands insist on these activities by including them in their business discussions linked to buying/sourcing. Their planned and surprise audit teams also discuss CSR with the firm owners – this drives home the point that the buyer expects the supplier to engage in CSR activities. As an example, 24 Swedish brands have come together to push the Sweden Textile Water Initiative under the Stockholm International Water Institute. With this, they will help the suppliers and sub-suppliers to become part of the global resource efficient factory network. They will get consulting services to adopt best practices and business intelligence. The factories have to pay a one-time participation fee of 10,000 Swedish Krona (appx Rs. 85000). The services come almost free of cost to the participating suppliers.

3. Labour Dynamics at TKC

At least since 2012, there has been a marked change in labour dynamics at TKC. The labour shortage has emerged as a perennial issue of concern at TKC. Families of labour of Tamil Nadu origin seem to have benefited from the Mahatma Gandhi National Rural Employment Guarantee Act (MGNREGA) and a slew of generous schemes of the state government.[5] Other growing industries, particularly poultry, metal fabrication and agro-processing and similar activities in the rural non-farm sector, have generated employment closer to the native villages of many workers. Workers have demanded and received higher wages. Tiruppur is no longer the *only* option for Tamil workers.

The local labour shortage has led to a piquant situation whereby almost 25 per cent of the low-skill workforce, especially in the smaller units, are now from eastern India, and workers from the north eastern states have also started coming in. It was learnt through the field survey that a few small firms owned by north Indians and Gujaratis had appointed agents to get labour from states like Odisha and Bihar. Workers from eastern India seem to have taken up jobs with higher uncertainties and lower rewards and incentives. Firm owners and labour contractors are now used to the new reality and challenge where workers change jobs frequently – sometimes within a week or two of joining a factory. There seems to be a competition among units to acquire workers by paying more or offering other incentives like free or subsidized lunch, tea, etc. Many workers are now said to prefer to work only 4 days a week! A tailor with very modest skills, who clocks 32 regular hours plus 12 OT hours in a week, is able to earn a total of about Rs. 3200 at the end of the 4-day work week. There are tailors who earn Rs. 700 a day for 10 days and then take a break of 5 days to go to their native villages (usually in Tamil Nadu, Kerala and Karnataka) and work on their small (usually 2 acre) farms, return to take up another 10 days of work in the units in TKC, then go back to villages for 5 days. That works out to be for a local or rather south Indian worker at TKC 10 days at Tiruppur and 5 days are spent in the native village farm for every fortnight.

In order to understand the dynamics of labour at TKC, it may be useful to relate to an instance of labour unrest as observed during the field survey. A faction of labour was said to have been demanding higher pay and bonuses since mid-2015. Tiruppur turned uneasy in October 2015, when the Centre of Indian Trade Unions (CITU) and regional political parties apparently got involved. Simmering issues like local (Tamil) versus outside labour also boiled over. According to some respondents and our key contact, until about 2000, roughly 30 per cent of labour was local (from Tiruppur), and 60 per cent came from rural Tamil Nadu and Palakkad in the bordering Kerala state. Hence, about 90 per cent of the labour was Tamil-speaking. The remaining roughly 10 per cent of workers were mostly migrants from eastern India (Odisha and Bihar) and Nepal. Since about 2007 or so, migrant labourers (roughly 80 per cent of them are men) have come in big numbers from eastern India (mainly Bihar, Jharkhand, Odisha and eastern Uttar Pradesh) and north-eastern regions (Assam and Meghalaya, especially). These migrants form roughly 20–25 per cent of the total labour during the survey period (a rough estimate puts the total labour engaged in the TKC at about 5–7 lakh, and according to the President of TEA, there were 1000 exporting firms in the cluster, with 4 lakh workers). The number of migrant labourers has been increasing every year. Mostly, as reported, they were taking jobs from those 60 per cent rural Tamil Nadu workers who were seasonal intra-state migrants. Usually, these jobs involved lower skill levels. Very much like the Tamil rural workers, the migrants (typically from northern and eastern India) also return to their native villages for about 5 months during the farming seasons every year.

About 40–50 per cent of migrants could be working in units with turnover less than Rs. 20 crore per annum. These are small units, mostly focusing on low-end products, largely for the domestic and certain Asian markets. Larger numbers of migrants work for factory owners of north Indian or Gujarati origin. These migrant workers are willing to work at lower wages compared to what their Tamil counterparts receive, as even these lower wages are unavailable in their native states. The migrant workers socialize in their groups and do not join local labour unions (of the six such unions, CITU remains the most visible, vocal and influential). Some factions of Tamil labour are unhappy about the influx of migrants, although there have been no violent incidents. Local politicians often stoke the Tamil vs non-Tamil (or, 'local' vs 'outsider') issue, leading to anxiety and conflicts among workers as well as some unit owners. As learnt from respondents, these issues have always been temporary in nature and would subside once the local politicians vacate the scene.

The three large and medium enterprises covered under this study seemed to be well-designed modern structures with worker-friendly workstations along with functioning, accessible and decent amenities – drinking water, ventilation, separate toilet and bathroom blocks for men and women, creche or baby care facilities on the ground floor (in a safe and visible place) with a play area for toddlers, canteen or a catering booth and locker room. This suggests that the business response to labour standards in particular and decent working conditions in general has been influenced by the nature and extent of the interface of local producers with buyers as well as the changing dynamics of labour market resilience.

4. Sumangali: Note on a Despicable Labour Engagement Practice in TKC

Until about 2010, the Sumangali system of recruitment of young female labour was commonly practised, especially among labour under contractors at spinning and fabric mills in Coimbatore and Erode and some small-scale apparel makers in Tiruppur. Almost 90 per cent of these workers were Tamil girls, and others spoke Malayalam, Telugu or Kannada. The Sumangali Scheme (also known as 'camp coolie system', or 'thirumangalam thiruman thittam') may have originated in spinning mills around Coimbatore around the late 1990s. Although more commonly (some estimates put this at about 80 per cent) found in the textile mills, this practice was also present in TKC. In short, this was a practice of labour contract whereby factories started hiring young women workers, particularly from poor households, on a long-term (3-year) contract basis, promising a lump sum payment at the end of the contract that could supplement huge expenses during the woman's marriage, especially as a dowry. For poor families with few income opportunities, the:

> Sumangali scheme seemed to be a win-win situation for all: parents received a sizeable sum at the end of 3 years that could be used towards the marriage of their daughter and the mills got workers willing to work in the mills continuously as 'apprentices,' mostly for no/little statutory benefits and for wages lower than their male counterparts (p. 7).[6]

This despicable practice (which was closely linked to the legally prohibited system of dowry) was a subject of much contention (especially as buyers found this unacceptable). The International Labour Organization, along with several local and global labour agencies, played a crucial role in finally putting an end to this.

As understood from the field survey, since 2011 the practice had come down drastically especially in Tiruppur due to various factors – activism by NGOs, awareness among families of girls in far-off rural areas, schemes of the Government of Tamil Nadu that reduced family expenses and pressure by buyers and international brands – especially European and US brands, active participation of TEA, formation of a task force (called *Tiruppur Stakeholders Forum* formed with the keen involvement of TEA), ethical work groups formed with the support of some international brands and some local political parties leveraging the issue to appease the predominantly dalit vote banks.

Large and medium enterprises that make garments for leading global brands and firm owners who have a reputation to protect – for their own business interests – have been cautious and avoid contractors and labour who are likely to be in such arrangements. There are many labour contractors who follow fairer practices than others. If a firm wants to avoid any contractor who engages in Sumangali arrangements, they can, as they have better choices.

It is possible that some small firms (manufacturing for domestic markets) in TKC are still engaging contractors who practice Sumangali arrangements. But no such evidence could be gathered during the field survey, except that a Sumangali Helpline number (1800 425 1092) promoted by the Centre for Social Education and Development was found functional by the end of 2014. This perhaps indicated that the practice was not fully gone.

5. Emerging Issues in TKC

As may be surmised from a contemporary press report (*Economic Times*, March 16, 2016), Indian suppliers to global buyers, including established global brands such as Gap, H&M and Marks & Spencer, were to be subjected to monitoring for unfair trade practices. This follows from an agreement reached by a consortium of global agencies including UNICEF, Stop Child Labour and Solidaridad. This agreement on sustainable garments and textiles, the drafting of which was overseen by the Social and Economic Council of the Netherlands, had been signed by a broad coalition of industry organizations, trade unions, civil society organizations and the Dutch government. Even as this has exerted some pressure to comply, *inter alia* to labour standards, TEA president A. Sakthivel insisted on the firms being "clean and compliant". With consumers getting conscious (about the clean supply chain) and forcing brands to source ethically, this agreement would serve a significant role in cleansing the Indian supply chain. Companies such as Gap and H&M have in the past forced their Indian suppliers to comply before they 'resumed' business, he said. Apparel exporters from the knitwear cluster in Tiruppur, which caters to companies including Tommy Hilfiger, Nike and Gap, have been accused of practising bonded labour under the guise of the Sumungali social security scheme.

At one level, as Vijayabaskar (2021) points out, the absence of institutional support for innovation, neglect of social and cluster-specific infrastructure coupled with an obsession with cost reduction undermine incentives to upgrade socially and economically. At another level, the emerging concern in TKC has been the growing shift in preference from cotton hosiery to manmade fibre (MMF) clothing, which is not TKC's strength; Asian countries like Vietnam, Taiwan, China and South Korea are better positioned to cater to the new demand.

6. Business at Surat Diamond Polishing Cluster (SDPC)

By mid-2014, the global market demand for diamonds had started slowing down and by the end of2014 the decline was rapid. By mid-2015, several diamond manufacturer-exporters (SMEs, mostly) in India, who were on a debt-fuelled aggressive growth strategy since 2013, faltered. There were massive business losses and job losses in the diamond and diamond jewellery manufacturing clusters. Many units were running at 50 per cent capacity, underemployment, half-pay, etc. The SDPC, however, appeared to be on a slow road to recovery by early 2016.

In 2015, the SDPC had an estimated annual turnover of Rs 900,000 to Rs. 10,00,000 million and employed about 0.7 million artisans (diamond workers). The exact number of manufacturers in Surat is not known, although the Surat Diamond Association (SDA) suggested that the figure of member-manufacturers could be well above 500. In the SDPC, tentatively, large manufacturers account for 30 per cent of enterprises and process 70 per cent of the diamonds by value. The remaining 30 per cent of processing (in value terms) is shared among 70 per cent of the units that are SMEs. The 'Big League' (or large enterprises) in the SDPC is understood as any firm with an annual turnover above Rs. 3000 million (at 2015 prices). Many Big League *diamantaires* also focus only on high-value diamonds (every stone of a minimum value of USD 300). For the large and medium firms, 80–85 per cent of their market is b2b exports and only 15–20 per cent is domestic b2b.

A specific issue related to the privileges enjoyed by select large enterprises: banks prefer to lend to a few large accounts; hence, they favour the Big League diamantaires. The SMEs find it difficult to access mainstream bank financing, even as the diamond SMEs' inventory is, in fact, a real recoverable asset, unlike, say, perishables in the food processing business where the inventory is a risk and liability. Banks demand 125 per cent collateral from SMEs (field example: bank guarantee of Rs. 100 million). Banks follow a points system or ranking system that currently favours the large or Big League firms and puts the SMEs at a disadvantage[7]. Eventually, SMEs end up borrowing from various sources of private finance and compromise with competitiveness; at times this dependence on private financing pushes them to pursue financial/accounting practices that are neither salubrious nor fair.

It was reported during the surveys that until about 2010, the foreign buyers (including a small proportion of persons of Indian origin) seemed to be better aware of the products and more concerned about global issues such as treatment of labour, blood diamonds and ethical diamonds. However, in 2015–16, all domestic (Indian) buyers engaging in b2b were equally well informed about the product and were concerned about issues in sustainability. Domestic buyers like Tanishq (of Tata Group) have always been as good as any global buyer, perhaps a notch above, when it came to their information about and concerns over ethical diamonds, labour issues, etc.

In appreciating the functioning of the SDPC, the role of the Surat Diamond Association (SDA), registered as a Society, needs to be recognized. It has been representing the local G&J industry while catering to the interests of the community of diamond processing firms since 1988. With a membership comprising manufacturers (more than 500), brokers, Diamond Trading Company (DTC) sight holders, traders, importers, exporters and institutions, the SDA represents almost all of the major companies who have their operations in Surat. To promote the growth of the local diamond industry, the SDA has undertaken a number of initiatives, such as the Empower ID program to address labour-related issues in the SME sector, conducting seminars and fairs to increase awareness about the rapidly changing technology and business trends of the sector and educational programmes for the local community.

The SDA, in association with the Gems and Jewellery Export Promotion Council of India (GJEPCI), has initiated the 'Empower ID' Programme as the first step towards organizing the highly unorganized SME sector of the local diamond industry. The programme aims at developing an inclusive database of the 700,000 artisans associated with the Surat diamond industry. Upon completion of the database, the SDA plans to approach the state and central governments about programmes that would improve the welfare of the artisans in areas such as health, education and more. The first milestone set was to create a database of 100,000 artisans by March 2016; as of February 2016, 94,000 ID cards had been issued.

7. Standards in Practice

The respondents did not answer specific queries about standards, except they said that in this business the emphasis was on the product (each stone) – its specifications, qualities, standards, etc. They emphasized that they never faced any problems meeting the standards expectations of buyers across continents. The large firms appeared to value all standards – product and process including labour, social and environmental aspects. Their workplaces/facilities were ultra-modern, their processes and management, as explained, seemed fair and transparent and they possessed all the popular certifications, such as the Kimberley Process Certification. They confirmed that they were carrying out importing of rough diamonds and exporting polished diamonds in strict compliance with the Kimberley Process Certification Scheme (to avoid blood diamonds) and the System of Warranties, refraining from any transactions with individuals, entities or organizations that have been blocked or banned by national or international sanctions.

The diamantaires of the Big League source their diamonds directly from prominent suppliers (mining and distribution companies) like DTC and Rio Tinto. However, in contrast, the small firms are willing to take the risk of procuring 'stolen' rough stones from a few African countries. As revealed by a young entrepreneur, working with his relative in a small unit in Surat, his uncle (also a small diamond unit owner with 8 *ghantis*) had been robbed of Rs. 2.5 million and shot dead in 2010 in a shady diamond town in South Africa, where he had gone to buy stolen rough diamonds, as he had done on several earlier occasions. Many small unit owners apparently still do the same, despite being aware of the risks. It was an 'open secret' amongst local firms in the SDPC that in the African diamond mining countries, several such towns dominated by gangsters exist, where stolen rough diamonds are sold.

An example of improvement in business process standards at the SDPC was cited with reference to the gradual discarding of the 6-decade-old *chitthi* system of payment, which was based on an informal trade instrument drawing upon mutual trust. Basically, it is a handwritten note on a slip of paper, given by a buyer to a seller, describing the product specifications (size, carat, colour and purity of diamonds) purchased (taken physical possession of) and promising payment of a large amount (in millions of rupees) on a said future date. Following an increase in defaults and cheating cases, the small and medium diamond unit owners were readying to embrace a more reliable system of *jhangad*, a kind of promissory note to arm fraud victims with stronger evidence for legal action. Since September 2014, defaults at least to the tune of Rs. 500 crore have been reported in Surat (by the time the field survey was conducted). The SDA launched a campaign in 2015 to persuade traders and manufacturers to adopt this more reliable system of *jhangad*. Some have switched over, but many were expected to do so in the coming months. In fact, as a newspaper report (*Times of India*, January 5, 2016, Surat Edition) suggested, the *chitthi* system had now been banished.

> Diamantaires in the multi-billion-dollar world's biggest diamond cutting and polishing centre in Surat have abolished the age-old 'chitti' system for a foolproof promissory note mode . . . Surat Diamond Association (SDA) has made it mandatory for diamond merchants and manufacturers to buy and sell diamonds by exchanging promissory note, which is a valid sales document. 'Around 85 per cent of merchants and manufacturers have banished paper chits for promissory note system. The campaign was started last year. We have now decided to make promissory note mandatory for diamond trade', SDA president Dinesh Navadiya said.

Underscoring the importance of responsible supply chains, the respondents confirmed that in every process, big or small, care was taken to ensure that all health and safety measures, labour regulations and environmental protection measures were strictly adhered to, both in letter and spirit. The diamond processing steps were so designed, it was held, as to be least harmful and in many cases, these were even better than global best practices. Since 1996, the firms in the SDPC have been taking recourse on the internet to organize distribution of diamonds. This has not only been one of the most inexpensive ways but also the most environment-friendly manner to distribute the product; both travel time and costs of customers have been reduced due to this. It was emphasized that the SDPC continues to hold a pioneering position as one of the most trusted and ethical loose diamond suppliers in the e-commerce arena. Besides complying with prescribed policies and procedures, the local firms regularly imparted training and took various sessions on Venus Jewel values, anti-discrimination, anti-sexual harassment, wages, benefits, health and safety and a host of other topics.

An interesting practice in the SDPC was related to actively monitoring and developing a culture of reduced paper use. To illustrate, received envelopes are reused for unimportant local communications, duplex printing is encouraged and internal communication is primarily done through the use of the internet. Further, these firms have been making efforts to ensure responsible disposal of waste and have a focused approach towards waste management. Even as diamond processors do not release any significant effluents, gases, vapours and smoke, waste is segregated, stored and disposed of with authorized recyclers in adherence to applicable legislations. Hazardous waste (notably, a very small quantity of concentrated acids used for deep cleansing some diamonds before processing) and e-waste are disposed to recyclers who possess the required clearances from the Pollution Control Boards.

Further, the single piece packaging and certification system (first introduced in the mid-1980s) – a price book for each diamond – developed by a few leading visionary large diamantaires lent much credibility to the cluster. As observed during the field survey, such innovations in manufacturing technologies are very important as they provide quantum leaps in value creation or loss reduction (as much as 35 per cent of a raw stone is lost to wastage/process losses – any small reduction is valuable).

8. Labour at SDPC

According to the president of the SDA, there is no labour union in SDPC. A diamond artisan/worker – typically male – usually belongs to the Patidar community from the Saurashtra region of Gujarat. There are a few migrant workers in some units, but they are inconspicuous. There have been recent attempts by some firms to set up all-women units (one unit in Jasdan, Gujarat and another proposed near Dangs). With very low levels of formal education, workers find employment as they are willing to build up their skill and ability to learn various activities of the business. It was learnt during the surveys that there exists a caste/religious bias favouring Hindu Patidar workers to acquire higher skills for executing tasks that allow an employee to learn and grow; this is particularly the case when an employee prepares to learn aspects of business. The stronghold of higher castes such as Patidars, Jains, Marwaris and Banias in the business represents the social discrimination prevalent mostly among the MSME units.

As the labour process is dominated by informal practices, a mere roughly 10 per cent of the employees of an SME would be on fixed salaries; typically, these would be the administrative or office staff. The diamond artisans/workers are paid on a piece rate basis, which is closely linked to the worker's performance. It was reported that the logic for reward and the IT systems (as in the Big League) that manage the rewards and the compensation processes are transparent. This actually drives a culture of excellence and competition among the workforce. Many diamond workers, especially in the large and medium enterprises, have average monthly compensation consistently above Rs. 80,000, while educated employees in administration or sales sections might be earning about Rs. 25,000 fixed pay per month. Even if a worker's performance is extremely poor, he can still earn Rs. 15,000 minimum (just by attending work every day) + Rs. 10,000 production linked pay = Rs. 25,000 per month. So a worker almost always earns at least as much as an office employee does.

9. Concluding Observations

In the Tiruppur cluster, while low wages and disregard for decent working conditions have often been reported, the agency of labour (especially trade unions) has been quite active during recent years. While adhering to standards (both product and process) has been recognized as important to improve business prospects globally, the small enterprises have been reluctant to practice the same. An influx of workers from other states – who have taken up jobs with higher uncertainties, lower rewards and incentives – has not only imbalanced wage structures but has angered local workers. In contrast, the labour process in the Surat cluster is dominated by informal practices, where workers are paid on a piece rate system which is closely linked to their performance. This is despite the unmatched skills and acumen of the workers here. No trade union activity is noticed here. A passive state has contributed to compromising labour standards. Further, while an increasing awareness of the business benefits of following global standards has been recognized by the local firms, there is little to suggest that these firms are even at the threshold of coming up with alternative standards that could threaten the prevailing ones. While much detailed research is called for in unravelling the dynamics of global standards as they play out in local informal cluster settings, even from this limited analysis here, it seems obvious that product standards have remained the priority area for buyers and not process standards. This is worrisome.

Notes

1 Since 2011, the Tirupur Thozhil Pathukappu Kulu (TTPK) has been one of the active associations in TKC, largely working towards the interest of the textile and apparel segment and exporters. The association came into being in response to the crisis in pollution due to dyeing surfacing in the cluster, and has coordinated with all stakeholders in establishing common effluent treatment plants (CETP) in TKC. This association has been involved in regularly organizing programmes like seminars and workshops and interventions related to technology upgrading, credit linkages and productivity enhancement. http://perfectsourcingmag.blogspot.in/2016/05/tirupur-thozhil-pathukappu-kulu-ttpk.html (accessed November 2, 2016). The Sripuram Trust, founded by entrepreneurs and philanthropists of Tiruppur, works towards developing local infrastructure to keep the city green and clean, improving labour resources and conducting skill development programs for workers. http://sripuram.co.in/aboutus.html (accessed November 2, 2016).
2 http://ecosalon.com/textile-certification-guide-green-clothing-tag-labels/
3 Based on informal chats with two software programmers, an employee of a firm that supplies lubricants in the cluster, a software solutions provider from Sri Lanka, two watchmen, four middle-aged taxi drivers who had earlier worked in the factories, two truck drivers, three young hotel employees (one from Assam) who were earlier employed in knitwear factories and a middle-level executive of a garment firm in Palakkad who has risen from the ranks.
4 These respondents did not wish to name the NGO.
5 These schemes include the Free Rice Scheme (20 kg of free rice to every 1.85 crore card-holder beneficiaries under the Public Distribution System (PDS), and 35 kg of free rice to every 19 lakh 'Antyodaya Anna Yojana' beneficiaries. This is apart from the 'One Rupee per kg Rice Scheme' for certain categories of beneficiaries: the allotted quota of 4 kg per adult and 2 kg per child is supplied subject to a minimum of 12 kg and a maximum of 20 kg per month per card, except in the Nilgiris where the minimum is fixed at 16 kg and the maximum 24 kg.) including the supply of ultra-affordable grocery items through PDS.
6 www.solidaridadnetwork.org/sites/solidaridadnetwork.org/files/publications/Understanding_Sumangali_Scheme_in_Tamil_Nadu.pdf
7 The respondent refused to elaborate on this as he did not want his comments about the banking sector's bias to be documented as they would need them.

Acknowledgements

This study is a component of a larger collaborative research project, "Rising Powers, Labour Standards and Governance of Global Production Networks", based at the University of Manchester, UK and supported by the Economic and Social Research Council (ESRC), UK (Grant Number ES/J013234/1). It was a great experience in learning and unlearning as on numerous occasions I closely interacted with my co-researchers Khalid Nadvi, Peter Knorringa, Rudolf Sinkovics, Mansueto Almeida, Chris Chan King, Natalie Langford, Corinna Braun-Munzinger and Bimal Arora. For crucial logistic and other support, I greatly appreciate help received from Kirubakara Sudhan, Vittaleswar Alapati, Madhav M. Shanbhag, Satyakam Joshi, Kiran Desai, Kamlesh Yagnik, Mihir Shah and Swati Mehta. For helpful comments on the draft of this paper, sincere thanks are due to

M. Vijayabaskar. For excellent professional support including conducting field surveys and preparing detailed notes, Hareesh Belawadi's contribution is truly praiseworthy. Special thanks to him as he undertook these exercises despite facing some health challenges both on the personal and family front.

References

Damodaran, S., 'Upgradation of Flexible Casualization? Exploring the Dynamics of Global Value Chain Incorporation in the Indian Leather Industry', in A. Posthuma and D. Nathan (Eds.), *Labour in Global Production Networks in India*, Oxford University Press, New Delhi, 2010, pp. 231–250.

Das, K., 'Situating Labour in the Global Production Network Debate: As If the "South" Mattered', *The Indian Journal of Labour Economics*, 59 (3), 2016, pp. 343–362.

Das, K., 'Industrial Clustering in India: Local Dynamics and the Global Debate', in K. Das (Ed.), *Indian Industrial Clusters*, Routledge, London, 2017, pp. 1–19.

Jha, P. and A. Chakraborty, 'Post-Fordism, Global Production Networks and Implications for Labour: Some Case Studies from National Capital Region, India', Working Paper No. 172, Institute for Studies in Industrial Development, 2014, New Delhi.

Nadvi, K., '"Rising Powers" and Labour and Environmental Standards', *Oxford Development Studies*, 42 (2), 2014, pp. 137–150.

Rahman, Z. and T. Langford, 'Why Labour Unions Have Failed Bangladesh's Garment Workers', in S. Mosoetsa and M. Williams (Eds.), *Labour in the Global South: Challenges and Alternatives for Workers*, International Labour Organization, Geneva, 2012, pp. 87–106.

Roy, S., 'Rent and Surplus in the Global Production Network: Identifying "Value Capture" from the South', *Agrarian South: Journal of Political Economy*, 6 (1), 2017, pp. 32–52.

Suresh, T. G., 'Cost Cutting Pressures and Labour Relations in Tamil Nadu's Automobile Components Supply Chain', in A. Posthuma and D. Nathan (Eds.), *Labour in Global Production Networks in India*, Oxford University Press, New Delhi, 2010, pp. 251–271.

Vijayabaskar, M., 'Constraints to Upgrading and Employment Expansion in the Tiruppur Knitwear Cluster', in R. Nagaraj (Ed.), *Industrialisation for Employment and Growth in India: Lessons from Small Firm Clusters and Beyond*, Cambridge University Press, New Delhi, 2021, pp. 49–71.

Chapter 13

Indigenous and Exogenous Reverse Innovations

Application to Microfinance Products

Surender Mor and Arvind Ashta

1. Introduction

Global spending on Research & Development has seen a record upsurge to almost US$ 1.7 trillion, 80 per cent of which is spent by 10 countries (UIS, 2019). The high-income economies like Switzerland, Sweden, USA, UK, Netherlands, Denmark, Finland, Singapore, Germany and Republic of Korea (South) continue to be the top-performing economies in the Global Innovation Index (2020). However, India, China, the Philippines, and Viet Nam have made significant progress in their Global Innovation Index ranking over time, and all are now in the top 50 (WIPO, 2020). New products and services require a huge investment, carried out in mostly capital-intensive countries, that the developing countries cannot afford. The trends and patterns of innovations across the globe show that development and innovations usually go hand in hand; however, some economies break from this pattern. Except for China, all innovation leaders are high-income economies (WIPO, 2020). That's why most products/services originate in developed countries and move towards developing countries for consumption by adapting them according to the market (Prahalad, 2006). This process is also known as 'Glocalisation', implying the diffusion of innovations to developing countries from developed countries, but in the case of reverse innovation, the products/services flow in the reverse direction.

The term 'Reverse Innovation' refers to those innovations which are made to a product in a poor or emerging country. Thereafter, the improved product is introduced in the markets of advanced countries (Govindarajan, 2012). It incorporates any innovation that is realised first in developing markets and then adapted and adopted in developed markets (Immelt et al., 2009). Brown and Hagel (2005) were the first to propagate the concept of 'blowback innovation', which underlines the multinational companies' approach to rethinking their way of doing business in emerging markets instead of only adapting products for them. However, Immelt et al. (2009) used the new idea of reverse innovation contrary to the concept of 'glocalisation'. This new paradigm of innovation, which serves as the basis

DOI: 10.4324/9781003353904-16

for the next phase of globalisation, has posed some interesting puzzles for mainstream theories of innovation management (Govindarajan & Trimble, 2012). These theoretical challenges can be classified into three dimensions. Firstly, we need to understand that the fundamental driver of reverse innovation is the income gap between the emerging and developed markets. The developing countries have huge markets with micro consumers, which require products with improved price-performance features, portability and usability, suggesting MNCs rethink their business models for emerging markets (Prahalad, 2006; Ramamurti & Singh, 2009; Ramamurti, 2009).

Second Corsi et al. (2014) regarded reverse innovation as a continuum of disruptive innovation, resulting in worse product performance in the mainstream market. It may be a cheaper, smaller, simpler version of the exiting product and convenient to use (Christensen & Bower, 1995). Reserve innovation results from the income gap, infrastructure gap and sustainability gap in rich and poor economies (Govindarajan & Trimble, 2009). Disruptive innovation may lead to new markets that are more inclusive if the new technology permits the lowering of prices. Therefore, reverse innovation and disruptive innovation could be connected well via the income gap between the North and South. Third, reverse innovation could be disruptive because Asian firms succeeded in creating disruptive innovations in developed countries (Hart & Christensen, 2002). Nevertheless, technology is a powerful force even within developed countries, and fintech operators are eating the banking system by nibbling at small niche markets (Ashta & Biot-Paquerot, 2018). Each target of disruptive innovation is too small for incumbent banks to safeguard. If banks do not innovate, the fintech operators will eat their lunch. Of course, banks have many options: do nothing, experiment directly or adopt a wait-and-see policy and take over a fintech operator that seems to be winning. The problem is that incumbents are cautious: they do not want to experiment in their markets for fear of cannibalisation into their main bread-and-butter markets. Therefore, they want to experiment far from their market. One possibility is to experiment in a poor and isolated country.

Microfinance has spread worldwide but unevenly, as South Asia possesses more than over 80 per cent of clientele, while Africa has relatively few. The success of the 'Gramin Model' of Bangladesh and the Self-Help Group (SHG) model of NABARD in India gave the microfinance revolution a great momentum. There are cases of reverse innovation in financial services, especially in the microfinance sector. Research (Buchanan, 2012; Sinha, 2013) established that the developed countries tried the group lending innovation originating in the developing world; mobile payments that are now widely used in Europe and the USA have origins from the Philippines, Kenya and Tanzania (Hossain et al., 2016). If these developments in the microfinance arena are triggering the growth of microfinance service in 'The North', then it will be a case of reverse innovations, i.e. the transfer of learning from developing to developed countries. The reverse innovation in microfinance is not country-specific, i.e. the innovative social practices adopted in developed countries do not require any litmus test.

In this chapter, we examine whether the microfinance innovations that occurred in South Asia represent reverse innovation (trickle-up), or if it is just a diffusion of knowledge by examining some well-known models of microfinance, like the business correspondent model, electronic money issuers (EMI), payments banks and mobile payments, etc., across the world.

Section 2 deals with the review of the extant literature on reverse innovations besides the conceptual framework. Section 3 deals with business correspondent models and mobile payments models that excelled in developing countries. Section 4 concludes the cases of reverse innovation.

2. Review of Extant Literature

Reverse innovation, initially launched in an emerging economy and later adopted in an advanced country, is classified as weak or strong based on the number of phases involved in developing nations to trickle up to the developed market (von Zedtwitz et al., 2014). Corsi and von Zedtwitz (2016) use the term 'Reverse Innovations', which are explicitly designed and invented in developing markets and later on introduced into the markets of advanced countries. Govindarajan and Ramamurti (2016) talk about reverse innovation cases practised in developing economies before being adopted in rich countries. Ashta and Mor (2020) used three concepts of reverse innovation, i.e. narrow, intermediate and broad. The broad concept refers to the adoption of innovation in an emerging economy in the developing economy, which is the reverse innovation in the real sense. In contrast, the innovation under the intermediate and narrow sense is undertaken by MNCs either in the home or host countries and then exported to developed countries for adoption. Whatever the case may be, reverse innovation has been adopted by both rich and poor economies to reap its benefits for opening new vistas for growth and catering to consumer demand in the globe, besides the prolonged survival and sustaining the culture of competition (Vadera, 2019).

Classic innovation mostly took place in developed nations and then trickled down to emerging economies, but this innovation pattern in the world economy appears to be changing due to an upsurge of innovations in China and India (Govindarajan & Ramamurti, 2016). The multinational organisations are increasingly applying reverse innovation to facilitate better market access y efficiently deploying their resources (Miranda et al., 2013). Hussler and Burger-Helmchen (2020) examined the drivers and challenges of reverse innovation that lead to adjustments in the market phenomena using disruptive innovation lenses. Banerjee (2013) considers that these micro-level drivers and challenges of this phenomenon remain understudied, despite the promises of reverse innovation. Borini et al. (2016) analyse the cases for reverse innovation in 167 companies in Brazil and highlight that organisational structure is necessary for reverse innovation which stems from headquarters' support, autonomy and integration. India, Korea, Mexico, Brazil and China have made huge contributions in exploring reverse innovation opportunities in global markets (Vadera, 2019). The poor emerging markets contribute in innovations to the rest of the world from time to time and are no longer just borrowers of innovations from developed countries (Govindarajan & Ramamurti, 2016; Hussler & Burger-Helmchen, 2020).

Therefore, the MNC's strategy for reverse innovation cannot be termed as deliberate or planned; instead, the MNC during its effort to penetrate and expand its outreach in the emerging country's market launched many low-cost products which at the same time found a sizable market in the host country (Corsi et al., 2014). But this diffusion of innovation is full of challenges; as has been observed in four case studies in India and China, its success depends on the vast knowledge of market conditions of emerging countries, evolving and matching local capabilities and sustained R&D efforts (Chang-Chieh et al., 2010). If innovation management succeeds in developing countries, we then need to bring it back, which requires addressing other issues. Major problems in bringing back reverse innovations are related to organisational structure, culture and resource-base (von Janda et al., 2018). The organisational structural problems include how strongly developing country units are embedded in the headquarters, whether there is a central market intelligence unit and whether the different geographical units allow information to pass through. The cultural problems are linked to the fear of cannibalisation of the existing high-margin developed market product by the low-priced, low-margin developing country product; lack of management diversity; and lack of an open mindset to innovations originating elsewhere. Parallel to this, there are many inventions and innovations in emerging countries competing with products manufactured in developed countries. There are also many associated concepts, such as 'Jugaad Innovation' (Radjou et al., 2012), frugal innovation (Zeschky et al., 2011) and bottom of the pyramid innovation (Prahalad, 2009) that capture the competitiveness of innovations made in emerging and developing economies. There have been some attempts in the literature to link or differentiate between the different concepts. For example, Zeschky et al. (2014) find that low-cost innovation and frugal innovations are all linked to products and markets to different degrees. However, reverse innovation is linked to adapting the former innovations to different geographical markets elsewhere. Hossain et al. (2016) also indicate that reverse innovations are a subset of frugal innovations and that not all frugal innovation will reach developed countries. Here it is pertinent to mention that in case of these product-based innovations, it is not necessary that the same firm which innovates a product in a developing country will introduce it in the developed markets. It may be a different firm exporting the products to a developed country. Radojević (2015) opined that reverse innovation should include all innovations taking place in the secondary market and moving towards a company's primary market, instead of limited to the innovations trickle up to rich countries from emerging economies. According to Corsi and Di Minin (2014), reverse innovation is only a specific disruptive innovation (Christensen et al., 2000, 2002, 2015), and it adds a geographical dimension. Disruptive innovation in the developed country can be done by new start-ups or by the incumbent firm's by-products. Similarly, innovations to appeal to the long tail small consumers' in emerging countries can be done by local firms or multinational enterprises. This long tail of consumers are those that comprise a large number with very low purchasing power.

From the various perspectives mentioned here, reverse innovation can be understood in the indigenous sense and exogenous sense. The indigenous sense of reverse innovation forms the diffusion of original/basic ideas from emerging economies and then trickled up to the advanced countries naturally, i.e. without using the ideas of developed countries or MNCs' efforts. However, in the exogenous sense, the innovations occurred in developed countries, tested/readapted in developing countries, and trickled back to developed economies. The latter may itself have preceded on two paths: one in which the MNCs belonging to the advanced country do innovate, invent

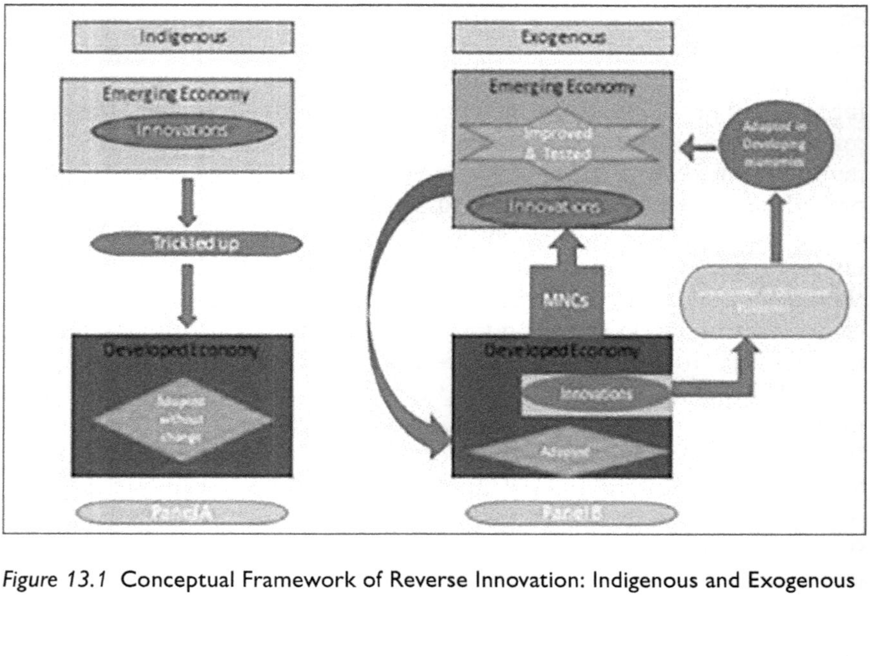

Figure 13.1 Conceptual Framework of Reverse Innovation: Indigenous and Exogenous

and test in developing economies and then bring back the innovation to the home country owing to cost and competitive advantages (Winter & Govindarajan, 2015). In contrast, in the second path, the innovation that fails in developed economies is adopted and tested in emerging markets and altered to bring back to developed countries. This is represented in Figure 13.1.

In the next section, we apply this perspective to innovations from the microfinance sector that spread from the South to the North.

3. Microfinance Product and Reverse Innovation

Microfinance refers to a construct of many types of financial services like small loans, insurance and savings encompassing many concepts like microcredit, microloans, savings and checking accounts, microinsurance and payment systems and other services (Sammi, 2018).

Microfinance has been regarded as one of the most powerful tools to fight poverty and generate ample employment opportunities, because the small loans given to microbusiness are utilised to grow their businesses and support their families, paving the way for strong and prosperous economies (Yunus, 2003). It is a way to reduce inequalities and increase income, consumption and welfare (Mahjabeen, 2008). However, the microfinance sector in India fails to promote the well-being of masses owing to the existence of substantial technical inefficiencies Singh, Goyal & Sharma (2013), unable to promote gender equality despite the participation of more than 97 per cent of women clientele (Singh, 2017) due to high transaction cost of microfinancing operations (Mor, 2015). Third-world countries, especially India, require more social organisation innovations beyond traditional microfinance instruments (Ashta & Mor, 2017). Promoting the culture of innovations proves to be very handy in enhancing well-being across the globe (Mor & Ashta, 2018). A review of many impact studies indicates that impact in microfinance is far from being established (Duvendack et al., 2011).

This discussion has not documented the adoption of emerging countries' ideas to rich countries by companies different from the original company, whether MNC or emerging country firms. These ideas are concepts, which are often not patentable. When the reverse innovation comes to the developed country, it requires changing institutions in the developed country, as is often the case of radical innovation from below (Govindarajan, 2012). Similarly, when an idea is appropriated from a developing country background, it needs to be aligned with the developed country's institutions or institutions that need to be changed. To illustrate, we describe three such ideas or concepts: self-help groups, the business correspondent model and the payments bank model. We do not use microcredit, because a recent study has shown that it does not constitute a reverse innovation. After all, microcredit's essential features in the South are not retained by those offering microcredit in the North (Ashta & Mor, 2020).

3.1. Business Correspondent Model

The business correspondent model or agent-based banking model uses non-bank businesses as agents of the bank to collect money and make payments, allowing customers to be served where no bank is present. This model is often attributed to Brazil, which started this form of branchless banking in 1973 (Riolino & Dias, 2009). In 1990, this was formalised to include financial institutions that other financial institutions could correspond with. By 1999, the kind of services that could be performed by agents included: receiving and forwarding account (savings and demand) opening applications; payments and deposits in savings, investments, and demand accounts; third-party payments (bill payments); payments and deposits for the bank itself; receiving and forwarding loan applications; analysis of credit and background information; collection services; and control and data processing related to the transactions conducted through the agent. However, the bank itself retained responsibility for regulatory compliance. Based on this regulation, Caixa Econômica Federal partnered with over 9,000 lottery outlets. All banks together had about 64,000 agents in 2000 (CGAP, 2010). By 2003, the Brazilian government decided that all types of financial institutions could hire correspondents, including credit cooperatives and microcredit institutions, and any commercial establishment or financial institution could be a correspondent (Riolino & Dias, 2009). The number of agents had increased to 150,000 by 2010, with Caixa leading with almost 14,000 (CGAP, 2010).

Besides lottery establishments, there have been many other kinds of partnerships to distribute financial services. The Banco Bradesco in Brazil used post offices as agents (Ivatury & Mas, 2008). In the Philippines, several banks partnered with the SMART mobile operator, and Standard Bank in South Africa partnered with MTN, also a mobile operator. In Kenya, Equity Bank partnered with the Nakumatt chain of retail stores. In South Africa, WIZZIT partnered with Dunn's chain of about 400 clothing stores (Ivatury & Mas, 2008). In Mexico, banks have partnered with telegram offices, retail chains such as 7–11 and mobile airtime top-up agents. The major insight was that banks were able to reduce their costs of distributing financial services significantly using retail agents.

We have recently seen that debit cards are being sold in France through tobacco shops (Le Bret, 2013). Although the idea is the same as in the developing countries, a recent interview with the CEO indicates that Nickel's founder took the idea from observing the behaviour of the family and friends of poor immigrants (Ashta and Courtois, 2020). This means that ideas travel in strange ways and not necessarily as a deliberative policy. Nickel was established in 2012, while banking correspondents existed in Brazil many decades before. Therefore, this can be considered as an indigenous innovation.

3.2. Mobile Payments, E-money Issuers and Payments Banks

Barely three decades ago, one could not think of using the cellular phone to perform financial transactions, buy movie tickets, arrange travel and even order pizza. Since then, a lot has changed, and mobile-based wallets like Smart and M-Pesa have been associated with catering to the needs of millions of previously unbanked populations, especially in third-world countries (Scott-Briggs, 2016). Global banking and payment services have been revolutionised by enhancing outreach to unbanked populations in emerging economies and offering new opportunities with added conveniences in developed countries (Gupta, 2013).

The Philippines introduced its first instrument (Smart) for transferring person-to-person remittances in 2000 (Runde, 2015). A year later, the first mobile-based 'Smart Money' was launched by Banco de Oro in collaboration with Smart Communications for enhancing the financial outreach to unbanked populations through the use of their mobile program for facilitating personal finance and strengthening the banking infrastructure in the country (Hasnain et al., 2016). Many banks and non-banks are now in the fray to offer e-financial services through mobile and e-applications (Llanto et al., 2018).

M-Pesa was launched in 2007 in Kenya by Vodafone and Safaricom. It refers to a mobile phone facility permitting transfer of payments as well as microfinance service which allow users to transfer, withdraw money, deposit money, make the payment from a network of agents, shopping and access to credit and saving accounts, all with the help of a mobile device (Saylor, 2012). By 2010, M-Pesa had become the most powerful mobile-based platform for financial services in emerging markets (Jack & Suri, 2010). The services enable millions of unbanked people to get access to the financial system, additionally reducing crime. The Communications Commission of Kenya reported the opening of more than 17 million accounts by the end of 2012[1]. Initially, M-Pesa was created to provide a microfinance platform just for the convenience of the microfinance borrowers in receiving and paying the small loans using Safaricom services; subsequently it was equipped with the facility of sending of remittance across the country and for making payments (Hughes & Lonie, 2007).

Wizzit was launched in South Africa in 2004 and had 250,000 accounts by 2008. Later, visualising this growth and potential, M-Pesa spread to this country by Vodacom in partnership with Nedbank to serve the more than 13 million unbanked people (Writer, 2010) by working on a target to add 10 million customers in the first three years of its launching. However, the growth of M-Pesa in South Africa is lower than that of Kenya, as there were only 76,000 active users till 2016. This may be attributed to the strict banking regulations existing in South Africa (Mbele, 2016).

The transformative success of mobile-based money transfer platform M-Pesa in making a turnaround in the Kenyan economy since its launching in 2004 received explosive growth, with over 237 million person-to-person transactions in 2013 (Runde, 2015). M-Shwari is a new service of M-Pesa with the facility of opening bank accounts via mobile phone and is operational in many other neighbouring nations; it partners with MTN in Uganda, Vodacom in Tanzania, FNB in South Africa, and GCash as well as SmartMoney in the Philippines (Cobert et al., 2012).

The first payments bank in Mexico was established in December 2009. Mexican regulation provides for the creation of niche banks under a license that allows deposit-taking for processing payments (CGAP, 2011, p. 4). However, there was only one bank that took it up (Dias & Staschen, 2019).

In India, mobile banking guidelines came out in 2008 and were modified in 2009 (Ashta, 2017). Two years later, on April 18, 2013, M-Pesa was launched in India in partnership with ICICI Bank (Russell, 2013). This was formalised by India, where the regulator allowed such 'payments banks' in 2014. The first payments bank started in 2017, and there are four operational now. Only banks that have received one-time approval from RBI are permitted to provide this facility to customers.

Each of these payments banks is piggybacking on a distribution network. The India Post Payment Bank uses the post office distribution network; Paytm uses its customer network; Airtel uses mobile phone customers and Fino uses its network of business correspondents. It is interesting to note that in a period of a little more than three years since its emergence, FINO (a financial services technology provider) has reached 10 million poor clients with various financial services on behalf of banks. However, their long-term sustainability is in doubt (Ashta & Pillarisetti, 2020; Dias & Staschen, 2019), since they have a host of banking regulations to comply with. For example, Vodaphone's facility was shut down on July 15, 2019, due to regulatory curbs and stress in this sector (Kurup, 2019).

We can see that the governments in developing economies are keen to launch and promote mobile banking for payment of social security (Pickens, Porteous, & Rotman, 2009) and at the same time to enhance outreach with minimum cost (Ashta, 2011; Morawczynski, 2011). In developing countries with minimal payment infrastructure, entirely new payment platforms have emerged to make the most of the ubiquity of basic mobile devices that can use text-based payments. In China and India, mobile wallets like Alipay, Tenpay and Paytm are mainly used to shop online or in marketplaces. Vodafone's M-Pesa mobile money transfer and payment service is the world's leading mobile money product. It has more than 20 million active users across Africa, the Middle East, Asia and (Eastern) Europe. With services like M-Pesa, financial services have reached 2.5 billion people with limited access to financial services (Wallets, 2016). Recent research shows that mobile payments have positively impacted the welfare of rural populations in Bangladesh (Lee et al., 2021) and in India (Siddiqui & Siddiqui, 2020). Therefore, it is generally believed that non-bank E-money issuers (EMI) would be easier to operate. The only difference from payments banks is that they would not be allowed to give interest on the deposits they collect (Dias & Staschen, 2019).

Initial experiments with mobile payments started earlier in developed countries. The first innovative instance of the use of the mobile wallet was by Coca Cola with the introduction of vending machines allowing consumers to purchase drinks through text message in Helsinki in 1997 (Scott-Briggs, 2016); in the same year, ExxonMobile began offering their customers the option of contactless payment (Fung, 2014). Although the European Payment Services Directive (PSD1) of 2007 predates many of the initiatives in developing countries, there was no serious mobile payment activity in Europe since European governments wanted to play safe (Ashta, 2017).

The initial idea of mobile payments in the developed world, therefore, started in developing countries. After seeing the high growth rate of mobile and online commerce, the ever-increasing access to smartphones and the scope of digital wallets in developing countries, it became explicitly evident that the mobile space could be used profitably in every corner of the globe (Wallets, 2016), and it came back to developed countries.

We can see that most of the mobile payment services started later in the developed world. For example, Nickel started its payment services in France in 2012 (Ashta, 2021). Similarly, in Denmark, MobilePay was launched only in May 2013, initially as a P2P mobile payment service. Japan is the only exception, where NTT Docomo has provided a mobile wallet in the market since 2004. Also, Osaifu-Keitai was one of the first initiatives to offer a digital wallet as a substitute to the physical wallet.

Not all transpositions of the innovation succeeded. M-Pesa entered Eastern Europe through Romania in March 2014, intending to expand its

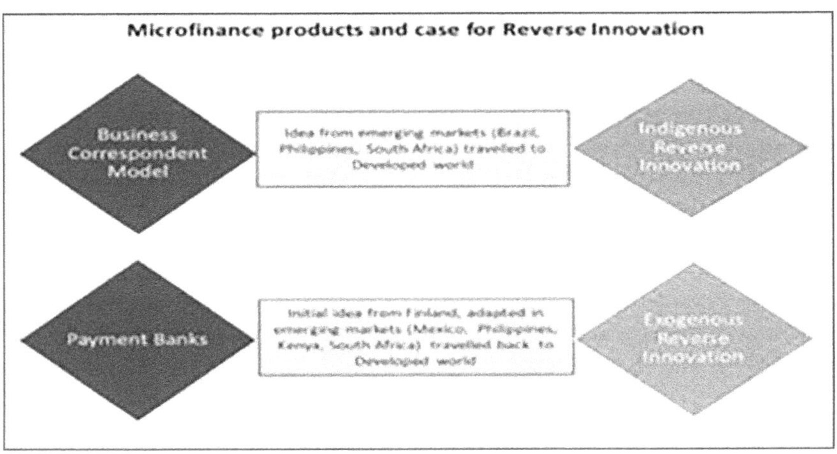

Figure 13.2 Diagrammatic Representation: Indigenous and Exogenous Reverse Innovations

outreach to many people having mobile but no bank accounts, but the facility was closed in December 2017 (Seceleanu, 2017). Similarly, the M-Pesa services were introduced in Albania in May 2015 but unable to sustain beyond July 2017 (Macharia, 2017).

4. Conclusion

We have proposed bifurcating reverse innovations into two models: the exogenous and indigenous models, based on the origin of the innovative idea. If the idea came from developing countries, we call it indigenous, and if it came from developed countries, we call it exogenous. We have illustrated the theory with two applications: the business correspondents model and payments banks. First, we have examined the business correspondents model and established that those ideas came from Brazil many decades before their use in developed markets in the 2010s. Business correspondents are operating in many other countries like Kenya, Mexico and the Philippines and are successful, and therefore, it is termed as a case of indigenous reverse innovation. Second, the case for Mobile Payments, E-money Issuers and Payments Banks as reverse innovations has been investigated, and our review shows that the first mobile payment experiments were in a developed country (Finland). However, these were then tested and spread in many developing countries such as the Philippines, Kenya, South Africa, Tanzania, Mexico and India, and then travelled to Europe. This therefore represents a case for exogenous reverse innovation. It is possible that the reason for the developed countries to proceed with caution is that they already had a good financial system and they were averse to damaging the system: they preferred to see how it would work in developing countries before adopting it (Ashta, 2017).

The implication of this division of reverse innovation into indigenous and exogenous is that that both the developed and developing countries can learn from the innovation and experience of each other and pass on the benefits of reverse innovation to the consumers, often needy people. The various microfinance tools like mobile banking and correspondents banks are successfully serving the unbanked segment of the population in many parts of the world, and need to be promoted to the rest of the world where financial inclusion has not taken place. Financial exclusion may be increasing in the developed world, especially in rural areas, as banks retreat from providing expensive outlets. Yet, the ageing population of people in rural areas may make them unable to use automated services in machines or on the internet. Therefore, banking correspondents, such as tobacco shops, may need to offer basic services. However, such sharing of knowledge and innovations needs to take into account fears of leaders of developed countries who may be blocking access to reverse innovations by erecting trade and capital barriers to technology that is not made in the developed world.

Future research needs to dwell upon how developed countries' leaders can be educated and their fears allayed to allow the development of reverse innovation. At a more specific level, other researchers can examine the case of microinsurance, micro saving and other financial products and non-financial products. The research can also examine the case for reverse innovation that trickled up in various phases to developed markers in the microfinance sector.

Note

1 https://en.wikipedia.org/wiki/M-Pesa

References

Ashta, A. (Ed). (2011). *Advanced Technologies for Microfinance: Solutions and challenges*. Hershey, PA: IGI Global.

Ashta, A. (2017). Evolution of mobile banking regulations: A case study on legislator's behavior. *Strategic Change: Briefings in Entrepreneurial Finance*, *26*(1), 3–20. https://doi.org/10.1002/jsc.2105

Ashta, A., & Biot-Paquerot, G. (2018). Fintech evolution: Strategic value management issues in a fast-changing industry. *Strategic Change: Briefings in Entrepreneurial Finance*, *27*(4), 301–312.

Ashta, A., & Courtois, T. (2020). Lessons from an incumbent taking over a challenger. *Journal Entreprendre & Innover*, (3), 56–65.

Ashta, A., & Mor, S. (2017). Fostering well-being through cultural change: Lessons from microfinance for social entrepreneurs. In A. K. Sinha, A. K. Mohapatra & T. Banerjee (EdS.), *Good governance and growth in global economy* (pp. 21–30). New Delhi: Bloomsbury India.

Ashta, A., & Mor, S. (2020). Is microcredit a reverse innovation? *FIIB Business Review, 11*(2), 225–234. https://doi/10.1177/2319714520962924

Ashta, A., & Pillarisetti, S. (2020). Can microsavings work without microcredit? A case study of India Post Payments Bank (IPPB). *Strategic Change*, *29*(3), 331–340. https://doi.org/10.1002/jsc.2332

Banerjee, P. M. (2013). The "frugal" in frugal innovation. In *Evolution of innovation management* (pp. 290–310). London: Palgrave Macmillan. https://doi/10.1057/9781137299994_13

Borini, F., Costa, S., & Oliveira Junior, M. (2016). Reverse innovation antecedents. *International Journal of Emerging Markets*, *11*, 175–189. https://doi.org/10.1108/IJoEM-11-2013-0194

Brown, J., & Hagel, J. (2005). Innovation blowback: Disruptive management practices from Asia. *The McKinsey Quarterly*, *1*(1), 35–45.

Buchanan, L. (2012). The world as R+D Lab: An interview with Vijay Govindarajan. Inc., 34(May), 98–100. Retrieved from http://search.ebscohost.com/login.aspx?direct=true&db=bth&AN=74731457&site=ehost-live

CGAP. (2010). *Update on regulation of branchless banking in Brazil*. Available at https://www.cgap.org/sites/default/files/CGAP-Regulation-of-Branchless-Banking-in-Brazil-Jan-2010.pdf

CGAP. (2011). *Technology program country note MEXICO*. Available at https://www.cgap.org/sites/default/files/CGAP-Technology-Program-Country-Note-Mexico-Mar-2011.pdf

Chang-Chieh, H., Jin, C., & Subramian, A. M. (2010). Developing disruptive products for emerging economies: Lessons from Asian cases. *Research-Technology Management*, *53*(4), 21–26. https://doi.org/10.1080/08956308.2010.11657637

Christensen, C. M., Bohmer, R., & Kenagy, J. (2000). Will disruptive innovations cure health care? *Harvard Business Review*, *78*(5), 102–112. http://search.ebscohost.com/login.aspx?direct=true&db=bth&AN=3521277&site=ehost-live

Christensen, C. M., & Bower, J. L. (1995). Disruptive technologies: Catching the wave. *Harvard Business Review*, *73*(1), 43–53.

Christensen, C. M., Johnson, M. W., & Rigby, D. K. (2002). Foundations for growth. *MIT Sloan Management Review*, *43*(3), 22–31. http://search.ebscohost.com/login.aspx?direct=true&db=bth&AN=6553416&site=ehost-live

Christensen, C. M., Raynor, M., & McDonald, R. (2015). What is disruptive innovation? *Harvard Business Review*, *93*(12), 44–53. http://search.ebscohost.com/login.aspx?direct=true&db=bth&AN=111099338&site=ehost-live

Cobert, B., Helms, B., & Parker, D. (2012). *Mobile money: Getting to scale in emerging markets*. www.mckinsey.com/industries/public-and-social-sector/our-insights/mobile-money-getting-to-scale-in-emerging-markets#

Corsi, S., & Di Minin, A. (2014). Disruptive innovation in reverse: Adding a geographical dimension to disruptive innovation theory. *Creativity & Innovation Management*, *23*(1), 76–90. https://doi.org/10.1111/claim.12043

Corsi, S., & von Zedtwitz, M. (2016). Reverse innovation: A new world order for global innovation? *The European Business Review*, 11/12, 73–77.

Dias, D., & Staschen, S. (2019). *Nonbank e-money issuers vs. payments banks: How do they compare? Technical note*. Washington, DC: CGAP.

Duvendack, M., Palmer-Jones, R., Copestake, J. G., Hooper, L., Loke, Y., & Rao, N. (2011). *What is the evidence of the impact of microfinance on the well-being of poor people? EPPI-Centre, Social Science Research Unit, Institute of Education*. London: University of London.

Fadel Riolino, R. P., & Dias, D. (2009). *Branchless banking and consumer protection in Brazil*. Available at https://www.cgap.org/sites/default/files/CGAP-Branchless-Banking-and-Consumer-Protection-in-Brazil-Dec-2009.pdf

Fung, B. (2014). The history of the mobile phone. *The Washington Post*. www.washingtonpost.com/blogs/the-switch/wp/2014/09/09/the-history-of-the-mobile-phone/

Govindarajan, V. (2012). A reverse-innovation playbook. *Harvard Business Review*, *90*(4), 120–124. http://search.ebscohost.com/login.aspx?direct=true&db=bth&AN=73564900&site=ehost-live

Govindarajan, V., & Ramamurti, R. (2016). Reverse innovation in emerging markets. In J. Haar & R. Ernst (Eds.), *Innovation in emerging markets. International political economy series*. London: Palgrave Macmillan. https://doi.org/10.1057/9781137480293_8

Govindarajan, V., & Trimble, C. (2009). Is reverse Innovation like disruptive Innovation? *Harvard Business Review*. http://blogs.hbr.org/2009/09/is-reverse-innovation-like-dis/ (accessed 30 October 2020).

Govindarajan, V., & Trimble, C. (2012). *Reverse innovation: Create far from home, win everywhere*. Boston, MA: Harvard Business School Press.

Gupta, S. (2013). The mobile banking and payment revolution. *European Financial Review*, February-March, pp. 3–6.

Hart, S. L., & Christensen, C. M. (2002). The great leap: Driving innovation from the base of the global pyramid. *MIT Sloan Management Review*, *44*(1), 51–56.

Hasnain, S., Komu, A., & Blackburn, C. (2016). *GSMA | Mobile money in the Philippines: Market conditions drive innovation with Smart Money and GCash | Mobile for Development*. www.gsma.com/mobilefordevelopment/programme/mobile-money/mobile-money-philippines-market-conditions-drive-innovation-smart-money-gcash-philippines-becoming-mobile-money-innovation-hub/

Hossain, M., Simula, H., & Halme, M. (2016). Can frugal go global? Diffusion patterns of frugal innovations. *Technology in Society*, *46*, 132–139. https://doi.org/10.1016/j.techsoc.2016.04.005

Hughes, N., & Lonie, S. (2007). M-PESA: Mobile Money for the "unbanked" turning cellphones into 24-hour tellers in Kenya. *Innovations: Technology, Governance, Globalization*, *2*(1–2), 63–81. https://doi.org/10.1162/itgg.2007.2.1-2.63

Hussler, C., & Burger-Helmchen, T. (2020). Opening the reverse innovation black box to pinpoint its drivers and challenges in Western MNCs. *European Journal of International Management*, *14*(5), 941–954. https://doi.org/10.1504/EJIM.2020.109820

Immelt, J. R., Govindarajan, V., & Trimble, C. (2009). How GE is disrupting itself. *Harvard Business Review*, *87*(10), 56–65.

Ivatury, G., & Mas, I. (2008). The early experience with branchless banking. Focus Note 46. Washington, D.C.: CGAP, available at https://www.cgap.org/sites/default/files/researches/documents/CGAP-Focus-Note-The-Early-Experience-with-Branchless-Banking-Apr-2008.pdf

Jack, W., & Suri, T. (2010). *The economics of M-PESA*. www.mit.edu/~tavneet/M-PESA.pdf

Kurup, R. (2019). Voda's M-Pesa shuts shop in India. *The Hindu Business Line*. www.thehindubusinessline.com/info-tech/vodas-m-pesa-shuts-shop-in-india/article28659123.ece

Le Bret, H. (2013). *No Bank: L'incroyable histoire d'un entrepreneur de banlieue qui veut révolutionner la banque*. Paris: Les Arenes, Editions Points.

Lee, J. N., Morduch, J., Ravindran, S., Shonchoy, A., & Zaman H. (2021). Poverty and migration in the digital age: Experimental evidence on mobile banking in Bangladesh. *American Economic Journal: Applied Economics*, *13*(1), 38–71.

Llanto, G. M., Ane, M., Rosellon, D., Kristina, M., & Ortiz, P. (2018). *E-finance in the Philippines: Status and prospects for digital financial inclusion*. Discussion paper series. www.pids.gov.ph

Macharia, K. (2017). Vodafone to shut down M-Pesa in Albania – Capital Business. *Capital Business*. www.capitalfm.co.ke/business/2017/07/vodafone-shut-m-pesa-albania/

Mahjabeen, R. (2008). Microfinancing in Bangladesh: Impact on households, consumption and welfare. *Journal of Policy Modeling*, *30*(6), 1083–1092.

Mbele, L. (2016). Why M-Pesa failed in South Africa. *BBC News*. www.bbc.com/news/world-africa-36260348

Miranda, G., Heras, D., & Casado, G. (2013). Application of reverse innovation in SMEs. In C. H. Iglesias & J. M. Pérez Ríos (Eds.), *Book of proceedings of the 7th international conference on industrial engineering and industrial management*

– *XVII Congreso de Ingeniería de Organización* (pp. 180–188). Valladolid: Universidad de Valladolid.

Mor, S. (2015). Transaction cost and technical efficiency: The case of Indian microfinance institutions. *EPRA International Journal of Agriculture and Rural Economic Research*, *3*(1), 152–160.

Mor, S., & Ashta, A. (2018). Fostering the culture of learning and experimentations: An introduction. In S. Mor (Ed.), *Culture of learning and experimentation for well-being* (pp. 1–18). New Delhi: Bloomsbury India.

Morawczynski, O. (2011). Saving through the mobile: A study of M-PESA in Kenya. In A. Ashta (Ed.), *Advanced technologies for microfinance: Solutions and challenges*. Hershey, PA: IGI Global.

Pickens, M., Porteous, D., & Rotman S. (2009). *Banking the Poor through G2P Payments*. Focus Note 58. Consultancy Group to Assist the Poor (CGAP): Washington, D.C.

Prahalad, C. K. (2006). *The fortune at the bottom of the pyramid: Eradicating poverty through profits*. Upper Saddle River, NJ: The Wharton School Publishing.

Prahalad, C. K. (2009). *The fortune at the bottom of the pyramid, revised and updated 5th anniversary edition: Eradicating poverty through profits*. Pearson FT Press. https://www.informit.com/store/fortune-at-the-bottom-of-the-pyramid-revised-and-updated-9780133829136.

Radjou, N., Prabhu, J., & Ahuja, S. (2012). *Jugaad innovation: Think frugal, be flexible, generate breakthrough growth*. John Wiley & Sons, San Francisco, Ca. https://www.wiley.com/en-us/Jugaad+Innovation%3A+Think+Frugal%2C+Be+Flexible%2C+Generate+Breakthrough+Growth-p-9781118249741.

Radojević, N. (2015). Reverse innovation reconceptualised: Much geo-economic ado about primary market shift. *Management International*, *19*(4), 70–82. https://doi.org/10.7202/1043077ar

Ramamurti, R. (2009). What have we learned about emerging-market MNEs? In R. Ramamurti & J. V. Singh (Eds.), *Emerging multinationals in emerging markets* (pp. 399–426). Cambridge: Cambridge University Press.

Ramamurti, R., & Singh, J. V. (2009). Indian multinationals: Generic internationalisation strategies. In R. Ramamurti & J. V. Singh (Eds.), *Emerging multinationals in emerging markets* (pp. 110–166). Cambridge: Cambridge University Press.

Runde, D. (2015). *M-Pesa and the Rise of the Global Mobile Money Market*. www.forbes.com/sites/danielrunde/2015/08/12/m-pesa-and-the-rise-of-the-global-mobile-money-market/?sh=4b3b15845aec

Russell, J. (2013). Vodafone launches M-Pesa mobile banking service in India, targeting 700m "unbanked" people. *The Next Web*. https://thenextweb.com/in/2013/04/17/vodafone-launches-m-pesa-mobile-banking-service-in-india-targets-700m-unbanked-people/

Sammi. (2018, April 23). Microfinance: What it is and why it matters. *Business News Daily*.

Saylor, M. (2012). *The mobile wave: How mobile intelligence will change everything*. Perseus Books/Vanguard Press. https://archive.org/details/mobilewavehowmob0000sayl

Scott-Briggs, A. (2016). What is a mobile wallet, origin and history in financial technology? *TechBullion*. www.techbullion.com/mobile-wallet-origin-history-financial-technology/

Seceleanu, A. (2017). *Grupul Vodafone pune capăt experimentului M-Pesa din România: serviciul de plăți de pe telefonul mobil se închide la 1 decembrie.*

www.zf.ro/business-hi-tech/grupul-vodafone-pune-capat-experimentului-m-pesa-din-romania-serviciul-de-plati-de-pe-telefonul-mobil-se-inchide-la-1-decembrie-16766209
Siddiqui, T. A., & Siddiqui, K. I. (2020). FinTech in India: An analysis on impact of telecommunication on financial inclusion. *Strategic Change*, *29*(3), 321–330.
Singh, S. (2017). Do transaction costs affect technical efficiency? Case of Indian microfinance institutions. *International Journal of Management and Development Studies*, *6*, 16–25.
Singh, S., Goyal, S., & Sharma, S. K. (2013). Technical efficiency and its determinants in microfinance institutions in India: A firm-level analysis. *Journal of Innovation Economics Management*, (1), 15–31.
Sinha, R. (2013). Reverse innovation: A gift from developing economy to developed economy. *Business Perspectives & Research*, *2*(1), 69–78. https://doi.org/10.1177/2278533720130106
UIS (UNESCO Institute for Statistics). (2019). *How does your county invest in R & D*. http://uis.unesco.org/apps/visualisations/research-and-development-spending/
Vadera, S. (2019). Exploring reverse Innovation: Emerging markets saga. *Asia Pacific Journal of Research*, *1*(86), 43–45.
von Janda, S., Schuhmacher, M. C., & Kuester, S. (2018). Reversing gears: Inverting the innovation-flow paradigm with reverse innovation. *Research-Technology Management*, *61*(1), 46–57. https://doi.org/10.1080/08956308.2018.1399023
von Zedtwitz, M., Corsi, S., Søberg, P., & Frega, R. (2014). A typology of reverse innovation. *Journal of Product Innovation Management*, *32*(1), 12–28.
Wallets, M. (2016). *The evolution of digital and mobile wallets (issue August)*. www.ericsson.com/mobility-report.
Winter, A., & Govindarajan, V. (2015). What engineering a reverse innovation looks like. *Harvard Business Review Digital Articles*, 2–5. http://search.ebscohost.com/login.aspx?direct=true&db=bth&AN=118667521&site=ehost-live
WIPO (World Intellectual Property Organisation). (2020). *Global innovation index 2020. Who will finance Innovation?* www.wipo.int/global_innovation_index/en/2020/
Writer, S. (2010). M-PESA launched in South Africa. *How We Made It in Africa*. www.howwemadeitinafrica.com/m-pesa-launched-in-south-africa/3611/s
Yunus, M. (2003). *Banker to the poor: Micro-lending and the battle against world poverty*. New York: Public Affairs.
Zeschky, M. B., Winterhalter, S., & Gassmann, O. (2014). From cost to frugal and reverse innovation: Mapping the field and implications for global competitiveness. *Research-Technology Management*, *57*(4), 20–27. https://doi.org/10.5437/08956308X5704235
Zeschky, M., Widenmayer, B., & Gassmann, O. (2011). Frugal innovation in emerging markets. *Research-Technology Management*, *54*(4), 38–45.

IV

Innovation, Growth and Sustainability

Chapter 14

Governance and Management Innovations in Producer Organizations in India

A Case Study of NDDB's Milk Producers' Companies

Sukhpal Singh

1. Introduction[1]

Institutions and institutional context are important determinants of development. Institutions refer to the "rules of the game" in a society or, more formally, the socially designed constraints and enablers that shape human interactions within action situations (Gatzweiler 2016). They are made up of formal and informal constraints and opportunities such as rules and laws, norms of behaviour or codes of conduct, and their enforcement characteristics, and they altogether define the incentive structure of the society and economy.[2]

> Innovation is the implementation (use) of something new or improved (whether technology or otherwise) in products (goods or services), processes, marketing, or organizational methods. In other words, it means applying ideas, knowledge, or practices that are new to a particular context with the purpose of creating positive change that will provide a way to meet needs, take on challenges, or seize opportunities. Such novelties and useful changes could be substantial (a large change or improvement) or cumulative (small changes that together produce a significant improvement)
>
> (IICA 2014, p. 3)

A novel idea implemented in a particular way can be considered an innovation if it is new in the context, even though it may not be new to the world (IICA 2014, p. 3; Raffaelli and Glynn 2015).

There are many types of innovations such as technological, social, product, process, marketing, and organizational, and institutional innovation is one type (IICA 2014). There could be path dependence in institutions (Ebbinghaus 2005) versus innovations in institutions. Path dependence refers to the recognition in institutional theory that the past shapes the future or that history matters. Thus, path dependence could be about an unplanned "trodden trail" that emerges due to repeated use of the path spontaneously

DOI: 10.4324/9781003353904-18

chosen by an institution; by others, which leads to diffusion of the persistence of the same institution; or about a "road juncture," which is a branching point at which one of the available paths needs to be chosen to continue the journey, which is about institutional change (Ebbinghaus 2005).

In the Indian context, the various amendments in the Cooperative Societies' Act could be more about path dependence, and the Producer Company Act more about institutional change. Institutional innovations could be in land system, labor system, social systems, and the organization of activity-production and marketing, including market and policy reforms, and innovations could take place in a top-down or bottom-up manner. Institutional innovations entail a change of policies, standards, regulations, processes, agreements, models, ways of organizing, institutional practices, or relationships with other organizations, to create a more dynamic environment that encourages improvements in the performance of an institution or system to make it more interactive and competitive (IICA 2014, p. 4). It can be a continuous process of incremental change, or a response to a crisis or a failure and, therefore, a more radical change (Shiller 2006; Mendoza and Thelen 2008), or a process of creative destruction (Gatzweiler 2016). Therefore, institutional innovation can be the creation of new institutions or a change in existing institutions (Raffaelli and Glynn 2015). The emergence of second-hand tractor markets in the Indian Punjab can be seen as an institutional innovation in response to a crisis of over-tractorization and nonviable use of the machine in the post-Green Revolution period (Singh 1999). There have also been many other innovations in the production and marketing of various crops, including paddy rice in India (Singh 2017). Contract farming has been studied as an institutional innovation in agribusiness (Maertens and Velde 2017; Bhanot et al. 2020).

It is important to realize that, for farmer incomes to improve, they need to have a presence not in primary production, but in value-added products that have higher margins. For this to happen, farmers need to own or control some of the downstream links in the value chain, which requires capital and capability. It is here that the role of PCs comes in, as they are more like business entities with no interference from the state or any other external entity (Mahajan 2015). This is where PCs, which are newer, more market-oriented cooperative companies that can help farmers buy and sell more effectively, come in. They have gained currency across India during the last decade when the amendment to the Companies Act made this possible in 2003 and India now has thousands of such PCs, many of them supported by state agencies (Neti et al. 2020).

The PCs suffer from a lack of finance in the formative years as the kind of support provided by the MP government has not come from any other state government or the union government until recently. But their own mobilization from members remains low in most cases (Singh and Singh 2014). In fact, the idea of a co-operative (read PC) is not only for pooling of produce, but also for pooling members' capital (Shah 2016). Singh and Singh

(2014) find that most of the Madhya Pradesh District Poverty Initiative Project (MPDPIP) PCs were in a seed production business, which is not a very good business as it involves a small number of members and has a high cost. Therefore, it does not create member centrality or the large patronage needed for the PC to scale up. The viability of the PCs was dependent on different factors in different contexts ranging from scale, nature of farmers, and crops/produce handled to professional management of the value chain and women members' involvement. Thus, scale and governance emerge as the major concerns of PCs which give rise to many other problems, like capital constraint, lack of member loyalty, or external trust in the business for market linkages.

Governance, which can be defined as non-market co-ordination of economic activities and can include defining the products, processes, and standards for suppliers (Singh 2013), is also amenable to plenty of innovations especially in a co-operative structure; it is a severally owned body with very unique objectives in mostly difficult situations, where other enterprises (public or private) have generally failed to make a difference. This chapter examines the innovations in NDS promoted milk PCs in terms of their governance and management, which have led to them being relatively successful compared with many other PCs in India, despite higher competition from other multinational, national, and local milk buyers. The next section profiles 4 of the 6 milk PCs directly promoted by NDS and studies their farmer impact, followed by governance and management factors behind such success in terms of innovations in Section 3. The last section concludes the chapter.

2. Milk PCs of NDS: Profiles and Impact

2.1. *Baani Milk PC, Punjab*

Baani Milk Producer Company (BMPC) was incorporated on 11 August 2014, with its head office in Patiala, Punjab. The main objective of the BMPCL was to increase the milk production of its member producers, decreasing the cost of milk production and providing them better services and competitive prices of milk. It came into operation w.e.f. 6 November 2014 as an independent organization for improving the livelihoods of marginal farmers and empowering women milk producers in Punjab. Currently, it is procuring milk from 8 districts of Punjab: Bathinda, Mansa, Barnala, Faridkot, Ferozepur, Moga, Sri Muktsar Sahib, and Sangrur. At the time of establishment, the PC had 5000 member producers, and in early 2018, they numbered 20000 with a coverage area of about 1181 villages. There are 13 milk chilling centres of the PC. BMPCL also provides 2 types of cattle feed and 1 type of mineral mixture to the farmers.

Baani involved a third party, Kansal Feed Industries Pvt. Ltd., Khanna, for the manufacturing of all types of feeds. However, it is not compulsory for the member producers to purchase these inputs from the PC. They can purchase any other kind from the market also. The payment for these inputs is not paid in cash by the farmers; rather, it is deducted when they receive payment for the milk. The PC also launched three types of training and extension programmes to educate the member producers regarding better milk production (BMP) approaches through the involvement of Non-Governmental Organisations (NGOs). Each programme is organized once in a year in each village. These three types of programmes are the Clean Milk Production Programme (CMPP), Women Awareness Programme (WAP), and Producer Awareness Programme (PAP). The PC did not provide any kind of veterinary or credit facilities (Kaur 2019).

The physical and financial performance of Baani shows that it has been able to triple its turnover within four years and has doubled its membership and paid-up capital and even profit, but it has not grown much in its milk procurement or inclusion of women members. Financially, it has doubled its profits and increased its reserves and surpluses substantially (Table 14.1). However, the paid-up capital performance remains modest.

Table 14.1 Profile and performance of Baani milk PC

Year> *Parameters*	*2014–15*	*2015–16*	*2016–17*	*2017–18*	*2018–19*
Revenue from operations (Rs. in crore) and total revenue in ()	87 (87.14)	201 (201.69)	258 (260.05)	356 (357.63)	363 (365.15)
Total member shareholders and % of women in total in ()	22972 (11.7)	33218 (11.7)	43023 (21.1)	43073 (24)	50603 (25)
Number of Board of Directors and % of women in total in ()	14 (21)	15(20)	15(20)	15(13)	14(14)
Authorized capital (Rs. crore)	20	20	20	20	20
Paid up Capital (Rs. crore) and %age of authorised capital	1.38 (7)	4.32 (21)	7.61 (38)	8.69 (43)	9.78 (49)
Net Profit after tax (Rs. crore)	2.16	1.05	1.67	5.15	5.35
Total Dividend and (EPS)	0.17 (416.97)	–0.05 (58.14)	–0.4 (33.54)	–0.66 (66.5)	–0.93 (57.2)
Total milk pooling points (MPPs)	484	917	1386	764	1321
Milk procurement (Lakh Litres/day)	1.7	1.59	1.8	2.53	2.75
Reserves and surpluses (Rs. crore)	1.99	2.52	4.19	8.60	13.11

Source: Annual reports of Baani

A survey of 100 members of Baani Milk PC and 100 non-member informal channel supplying farmers found that member-operated land was higher (10 acres) than that of non-members (9 acres) though owned land was not that different across two categories (9 acres and 8.6 acres) and Baani members leased somewhat higher land on average than non-members. There were also more landless among the non-members compared to members. Baani members also had more acreage under cotton than that by the non-members, but the cropping intensity of members was lower than that of the non-members. The level of education among member was somewhat higher on an average (10 years) compared with that of non-members (8.4 years), and both members and non-members had similar assets: more than 70% of both owned tractors, and all medium and large farmers in both categories also had milking machines. Even the marketed surplus was the same (83%) in both categories. Farmers sold milk to Baani due to good relations, proximity from home, timely payment, and higher prices. On the other hand, non-members did not sell to Baani due to their good relations with other buyers, distance from residence, and fixed higher price irrespective of fat and SNF (Kaur 2019).

2.2. *Saahaj Milk PC*

Headquartered at Agra, Saahaj was registered on 17 October 2014 and sells 5 types of milk, ghee, and buttermilk, as well as supplying cattle feed to its members. Mother Dairy already had its presence in the districts since 2007, and all milk producers supplying milk to Mother Dairy became members of Saahaj. It is present in 8 districts, wherein it overlaps with Amul in 3 districts. Out of the 369 villages, 41 had BMCs established by Saahaj and run and managed by the consigners. The Dairy *sahayak* (chosen by members) received Rs. 1.2/litre at the Milk Pooling Point (MPP) and a consigner Rs. 1.05/litre at Bulk Milk Chiller (BMC) level. It sells cattle feed, mineral mixture, and has a facility for Artificial Insemination.

Producers from only those villages become members where there is MPP (milk pooling point: 2661) or a BMC (bulk milk chillers: 366). In 2015-16, it had 80871 supplying members, of whom 606062 had been admitted (24% of them being women members and 72% being small producers) as members; the rest were still provisional members.

The dealing with non-members was negligible at 1% and exclusive members that dealt only with PC were about 55% of the total. The Board of Directors (BoD) is selected, not elected, and they must fulfil the primary criteria of members. The BoD also includes 1–3 expert directors for a total of 12–15 over different years.

In 2016–17 A grade members supplied 57% of total procurement, B grade 18% and C grade 25%; accordingly, there were 3 types of BoD chosen from 3 categories of members in proportion to the milk supplied by each category of member. The PC claims that most of the farmers have 1–3 milk animals, though there are those with more than 6 animals who are called large producers (Singh 2021).

Saahaj had scale in terms of membership, equity base, and level of business turnover. It had profits of the order of Rs. 13 core and had mobilized most of its authorized capital, which was of the order of Rs. 30 crore and earlier Rs. 20 crore. 50% members supplied milk exclusively to Saahaj, but it had a modest spread of operations and membership and share of women members in total (Table 14.2).

The average owned land was 4.82 acres for members and 1.92 for non-members. Thus, the PC milk producer members were larger landholders, and their operating average land area was even higher at 10.11 acres, wherein the case of non-members, it was same as owned land average. The reason for the very high operational holding was the fact that a member had 60 acres, mostly leased in. By owned land, 60% of the members were marginal owners but they owned only 17% of total area; 30% were semi-medium

Table 14.2 Profile and performance of Saahaj MPC

Year> Parameters	*2014–15*	*2015–16*	*2016–17*	*2017–18*	*2018–19*
Revenue from operations (Rs. crore)	158.24	489.44	497.99	773.19	841.85
Authorized capital (Rs. crore)	20	20	20	20	30
Paid up Capital (Rs. crore)	2.21 (11%)	8.97(45)	15.33 (76%)	18.56 (93%)	23.03(77%)
Total member shareholders and women as % of all	44999 (21)	60606(24)	80952 (27)	60901 (31)	76540(32)
Number of BoD and %age of Women in BoD	12 (17)	15(17)	15(17)	13(15)	14(0)
Net Profit after tax (Rs. crore)	4.63	9.96	1.79	12.15)	13.49
Dividend in Rs. Lakh (EPS)	22.20 (375/-)	108 (Rs. 10 per share) 329/-	148 Rs. 8/share 17.5	179 76.3	222 Rs. 8/ share/71.5
Total MPPs	1855	2661	3455	3455	3455
Milk procurement (LLPD)	-	3.68	3.45	5.04	5.94
Reserves and surpluses (Rs. Crore)	4.36	13.24	15.03	25.71	37.41

Source: Annual reports

and 10% medium by ownership, accounting for 58% and 26% of all owned land respectively. By operated land, among members, 50% were marginal and had 8% of all operated land; 10% small with 3% of land; 20% semi-medium with 18% land; and 10% each medium and large with 12% and 59% land. The non-members were much smaller operators, with 60% being marginal and operating 27% land, with 30% small and 10% semi-medium and medium, each operating 47% and 26% of operated land (Singh 2021).

More importantly, the livestock ownership among members was predominantly made up of buffalo (90% farmers having them) and cows, with an average of 3 such livestock making up 46% of all animals. Cows were owned by 80% and averaged 3 each, and were 39% of the total livestock owned by members. The average of 3 goats per household led to their share of 16% in total livestock, though only 30% of farmers owned them. The livestock ownership of non-members was more towards goats, with 20% owning 21 goats, accounting for 43% of all livestock owned by non-members; buffaloes were another 41% and cows only 12%, with only 50% farmers owning cows and all farmers owning buffaloes. However, the average size of livestock per household was lower here, with 2 buffaloes, 1 cow, and 11 goats per household. The cropping intensity of members (1.2) was lower than that of non-members (2).

Only 60% of members knew that PC was owned by member famers; 20% and 10% though it was owned by PC employees or a promoting agency (NDS/NDDB). 10% had no idea about its ownership. Among non-members, awareness was even poorer, as only 20% thought it belonged to farmers, 40% reporting it to be PC employee-owned, and 4% not knowing about it at all (Singh 2021).

Seven farmers out of 10 reported selling milk to PC in the case of buffalo milk and 4 farmers were selling cow milk, where the quantity of milk supplied had increased over the last 3 years. Four members sold buffalo milk and 3 members sold cow milk to the other POs earlier and were still selling in those channels currently. And other channels, like local dairies, had declined completely as there were other co-operatives in the area in the case of members. The members reported a price increase of 16-20% over the previous channel price. Against this, in case of non-members, only 4 out of 8 buffalo milk farmers reported selling to other milk POs, and the other 3 out of 4 cow milk producers continued with local dairies. There was a significant increase (29%) in the number of buffaloes owned by farmer member, and an increase in milk yield by 25–50%; therefore, marketed surplus increased by 50–60% in the cases of cow and buffalo milk respectively (Singh 2021).

2.3. Paayas Milk PC

The Paayas Milk PC has its origins in the Mother Dairy (NDDB) project, which began in 2009 in Rajasthan. However, Mother Dairy didn't have a formal structure of cooperative membership of milk producers. The Paayas was set up in 2012. By 2016, it covered 2400 villages in 8 districts with a membership of 74533, of whom 39% were small holders and 41% were women. It was procuring 4.91 lakh litres of milk per day. It had by then 2571 MPPs, employed 1228 LRPs, and covered 1.44 lakh animals and had covered 2985 villages with Artificial Insemination (AI). For example, one of the villages, which was 32 kms from a milk collection centre (MCC) (Figures 14.1a and 14.1b), had 65 registered members and 60 were delivering milk. totalling 570 litres per day. It was run by a local farmer as a sahayak (assistant) and one facilitator from the PC.

The PC had presence in 3300 villages, which covered 38% of milk animal-owning households in these villages. 40% of the milk for Paayas came from non-members. Its sales were 85% institutional and 15% retail. The institutional sales were mainly to Mother Dairy, and a small quantity also went to the Rajasthan Co-operative Dairy Federation (RDDF).

There are informal groups of the local community: a village contact group (VCG) and a member relation group, which act as a bridge between the members and the PC as the procurement at the village level is now undertaken by private individuals. The VCG has 3-5 members at the MPP level, while

Figure 14.1a A Milk Collection Centre of Paayas

Figure 14.1b A Details of Membership and milk Procurement at MCC of Paayas

the Member Relations Group (MRG) has 10-12 members at the milk route level. While the VCG encourages farmers to become members and make the members adhere to the rules of the PC, the MRG is more about supporting the PC in organizing various campaigns, meetings, and workshops.

The elected board of directors had 10 farmer shareholders based on their category of membership, which itself is based on patronage; 3 expert directors, who were subject matter specialists; and a Chief Executive Office (CEO). Of the 10 elected farmer members, there was a ratio of 7:3 of male:female, and 3, 2 and 5 each were elected from A, B and C categories.

It had outsourced facilities for processing and packing up to 1.5 lakh litres a day, cold storage capacity of 1 lakh litres, and ghee making capacity of 4.5 metric tonnes per day. The PC had 125 distributors and 4000 retailers. Over the years, it was gaining market share while RCDF was losing its market share.

The PC supplied cattle feed and various other inputs and services like mineral mixture, fodder seeds, group medical insurance, and an AI facility, which were used by 90% of the members. It also supplied milking machines for large dairy animal holders. It supplied rations like Urea Molasses Blocks (UMBs) and other specific types of feed and nutrients for animals. Many of its services were provided to both members and non-members, because non-members are potential members who could help expand procurement and turnover of the PC. The PC also provided bunkers for biomass and fodder storage at the household level, which were provided for free or at 50% cost to women dairy farmers. It claimed that the ration balancing intervention led to 0.22 kg. increase in average milk yield, 0.08 percent increase in milk fat and Rs. 2.25 reduction in cost of feeding, leading to reduction of Rs. 19 per animal per day. This led to Rs. 28 per animal increase in daily income of farmers and 10 percent reduction in feed cost per kg of milk. The PC also set up 14 model dairy farms in 3 districts, and more than 800 farmers were trained in model dairy farming.

Major problems the PC experienced per the promoter's opinion were that the mindset of the Board of Directors was still of the traditional cooperative type, which it was trying to change with training and orientation. Furthermore, it was working on an asset-light high-turnover business model which would have to change as the scale increased, which would require more reliable systems of handling raw materials as well as finished products. More importantly, the state did not provide a level playing field for the PC as it only subsidized cooperatives (Singh 2021).

Rajasthan is the second-largest milk-producing state in the country despite being in the dryland region. The major competitors of Paayas include RCDF – a state milk cooperative procuring 28 lakhs litre annually, with 40% coming from non-members and the largest player in buying and selling milk in this state; Gujarat Co-operative Milk Marketing Federation (GCMMF) (Amul) – 11 lakh litres procurement, mainly sourcing from neighbouring milk unions in Gujarat; private players, which include Modi Dairy with Lotus Brand, procuring five lakh litres annually through a mix of direct procurement and through intermediaries; Dharmapala Satyapal with Ksheer Brand, handling one lakh litres mainly procured through intermediaries; and Patanjali Foods, procuring 1.5 lakh litres through a mix of direct buying and through intermediaries. The latter two players are of recent origin, whereas Lotus has been there for more than 25 years, and Amul entered this market before that. Reliance and Kwality dairies had shut down their operations, while Heritage, Rufil, and Dev Milk Foods were new entrants to the state milk market (Singh 2021).

However, due to the state government's patronage, RCDF offers a subsidy of Rs. 2/- per litre which has been increased to Rs. 5/- now, which leads to unfair competition for the PC. Payaas milk PC had turnover of more than Rs, 1000 crore per year and profits of the order of more than Rs. 10 crore per year, and surplus of Rs. 29–61 crore per year. It had also mobilized most of its authorized equity from members (Table 14.3).

Average land owned by a member milk producer was 1.3 acres, with all of them being marginal or landless farmers. In terms of operated land, which

Table 14.3 Profile and performance of Payaas PC

Year > *Parameter*	*2015–16*	*2016–17*	*2017–18*	*2018–19*
Turnover (Rs. crore)	845	1062	1282	1429.5
Authorized capital (Rs. crore)	30	35	35	50
Share capital (Rs. crore) and %age in total in ()	22.8(76)	30.72(88)	33.89(97)	37.4(75)
Number of shareholders (in lakh) and (% of women in total)	–	1.12	97816 (39)	1.04 (38)
Profit (Rs. crore)	12.89	11.15	16.84	13.03
Reserves and Surplus (Rs. lakh)	1.80	2923	4754.1	6119.0
Assets (Rs. Lakh)	44.26	4511.6	3479.2	2587.5
Milk Procurement (Lakh litres per day)	4.91	6.5	645	8.6

Source: Singh 2021

was on average 1.4 acres, the distribution of farmers remained the same. However, due to some leasing in and leasing out, all the farmers became operating landowners but remained marginal in size.

The average owned land among non-members was 2 acres, with 83% marginal and 17% semi-medium. Due to some leasing in and leasing out, average operated land was around 2.3 acres, with 67% operators being marginal scale, 23% small and 8% semi-medium. The latter 8% of farmers accounted for 21% of the operated area. Interestingly, there was no farmers in the category of medium or large farmers in ownership and operation of land. The cropping intensity of member farmers was 1.89, and of non-members was 2. This information shows that the milk PC members were really marginal or landless land operators and livestock rearers.

80% of members knew that the PCs belonged to the farmers. In 40% of cases, it was PC employees who made them join the PC. Another 10% were influenced by promoters and PC employees and others, and 30% by friends and other farmers. The PC made a good impact on their livelihoods, with various interventions like input supply and milk procurement, along with supplying fodder seed and other services (Singh 2021).

Before the PC intervention, all farmers sold milk either to other Producer Organisations (POs) or did not sell at all. There was a 60% increase in buffalo milk sales because of the PC intervention, though the price came down recently compared to the alternative channels of sale. While only 60% sold to the PC a few years ago, 100% started selling to it after a few years of its entry. In terms of channels, earlier they dealt with traditional cooperative and the PC, and have since moved over to the PC completely. The member farmers reported a price increase of 13% over previous channel prices. 25% of non-member farmers reported membership in another PO, which was the local milk cooperative society (of RCDF), and they had been members of the same for many years. In fact, 83% of them were aware of the milk PC, and 42% reported that it was owned by farmers.

2.4. Maahi PC

Maahi Milk Producer Company Limited was incorporated on 7 June 2012 and commenced its commercial operations on 18 March 2013. It is the oldest PC among all milk PCs promoted by NDS. Initially, milk procurement of the PC came from the districts of Saurashtra and Kutch region of Gujarat, covering 1,912 villages and 2,142 MPPs. At that time, 85,194 milk producers were members. In 2016–17, the memberships of 7865 members were cancelled due to nonfulfillment of membership criteria, and 262 members fully surrendered their shares while four members partially surrendered. As of 31 March 2017, only 50,199 members are entitled to voting rights, and 49,714 members who did not pour milk for at least 200 days totalling 500 litres in a previous financial year (2016–17) lost their voting rights and were not entitled to vote at the ensuing Annual General Meeting. There was enrolment of 13,730 new members in 2017–18.

Maahi has taken over the cattle feed factory situated at Khandheri from NDDB on a long lease w.e.f. 1 April 2018, and renamed the Unit as the Animal Feed & Nutrition Unit (AFNU). The unit has the capacity to produce 200 MT of cattle feed per day. It has a mineral mixture plant with 10 MT production capacity per day. The unit is equipped with a Bypass "Protein Feed" plant, and Maahi is manufacturing all its cattle feed variants at the AFNU, which also manufactures Mineral Mixture for other PCs like Saahaj, Sreeja Mahila, Balinee, Bapudham, and Indujaa Mahila Milk PC. PC's sales and distribution network was spread out from Saurashtra and Kutch region, in the cities of Ahmedabad, Vadodara, Surat, and Vapi. Maahi was manufacturing all its cattle feed variants, i.e. Maahi Dan Power (Bureau of Indian Standards (BIS) Type II), Maahi Dan Sampoorna (BIS Type I-22% protein and 7% FAT), Maahi Dan Junior (23% protein and 4% FAT), using formaldehyde-treated protein sources, and Mineral Mixture under the Brand name of "Maahi Min".

Though Maahi PC was located in a milk-rich state, its physical performance has been more modest and its financial performance more mixed (Table 14.4). This could be due to the fact that it has strong competition from Amul in Gujarat, along with many private dairy brands based in Ahmedabad (Singh 2017).

Table 14.4 Profile and performance of Maahi PC

Year> Parameter	*2014–15*	*2015–16*	*2016–17*	*2017–18*	*2018–19*
Revenue from operations (in crore) and Total revenue in ()	979.25 (985.8)	1007.73 (1014.59)	1178.26 (1190.17)	1436.87 (1444.73)	1449.26 (1459.76)
Authorized capital (Rs. crore)	35	35	35	35	50
Paid up Capital (Rs. crore) and % of authorized mobilized ()	26.22 (75)	26.91(77)	30.61(87)	32.46(93)	34.72(69)
Total member shareholders and % of women in total ()	86938 (NA)	88253 (NA)	99913 (NA)	116511 (NA)	109608 (25)
Number of Board of Directors and % of women in BoD	15 (13)	14 (14)	15 (13)	14 (14)	15(20)
Net Profit after tax (Rs. crore)	12.78	14.76	17.75	18.25	19.55
Total Dividend and EPS	–2.86 (52.98)	–2.96 (52.21)	–3.2 (66.67)	–3.3 (60.52)	–3.51 (62.86)
Total milk pooling points (MPPs)	2144	2296	2792	2881	–
Milk procurement (Lakh Litres/day)	5.35	5.72	6.36	7.69	8.12
Reserves and surpluses (Rs. crore)	10.32	21.85	41.13	59.73	79.7

Source: Maahi website

3. Innovations in PC Governance and Management

As this analysis of cases of milk PCs shows, they have been able to perform better on many parametres, despite being new entities. All of the PCs were set up under the National Dairy Support Project and financed by the World Bank for 5 years. The relatively better physical and financial performance of the four PCs, though varying on various parametres, is also corroborated by a recent assessment of their performance. They had achieved the targets of farmer membership, including women members and small-holder producers, but fell short on the number of villages covered at the end of the project period. The membership ranged from a low of 51,590 in Baani to as high as 104,603 in Paayas, with the other two having 95,000 (Maahi) and 91,000 (Saahaj) members each. The women membership out of the total stood at between 25% and 26% (Baani and Maahi respectively) and 35% and 38% (Saahaj and Paayas respectively). Likewise, small-holder percentage of total membership was the lowest at 34% and 35% for Paayas and Baani respectively, and the highest for Saahaj at 64%, with Maahi at 52%. Over time, the share of smallholders in Paayas and Saahaj was declining due to the existing members expanding their herd size on average. However, Paayas and Maahi stood apart from others in milk procurement at more than eight lakh litres per day, while Baani and Saahaj were less than three lakh and six lakh litres each respectively. This was reflected in turnover figures as well. Finally, the share capital mobilization by Baani was the poorest, and that of Paayas and Maahi was the best; Saahaj fell between these two extremes (WB 2020).

The financial ratio analysis (liquidity, solvency, efficiency, and profitability) also showed average or modest performance, especially in profitability, but that was more due to the fact that like co-operatives, PCs have also been passing on the surplus to members as patronage-based price incentive as well as dividends on share capital benefits. Further, they face competition in terms of meeting producer expectations and also exploring new markets in the presence of large co-operative and private dairy entities. The earnings per share analysis showed better performance, but still there was a need for better capital management. Only Maahi and Paayas had good solvency positions (WB 2020).

Given this evidence, it is important to examine what made these entities relatively successful way when many other PCs are still struggling to sustain in India. One of the reasons for milk PCs' relatively good performance was its governance and business models, which were very tight and foolproof. It relied on a low-asset/high-turnover model and strictly enforced member discipline, along with the professional input it had from the NDDB team, which is known for their expertise in promoting milk producer co-operatives. Further, the NDDB-promoted PCs have no dairy cooperative society at the village level, but have a *sahayak* to manage procurement.

NDDB's model of promoting milk PCs was based on certain rules of governance to enhance patron cohesiveness, governance, and operating effectiveness; these include: they will do business with only members, new members can join only during specific windows in each year, only those with minimum supplies of milk can vote, and the BoD are chosen from 3 categories of members (Table 14.5) in proportion to the milk supplied by each category of members. Compare this with a traditional milk co-operative, like Milkfed Punjab, which categorizes farmers in only 2 types: commercial dairy farmers (selling 50 kg re more milk/day) and small milk producers (selling <50 kg milk/day) (Kaur 2019).

The members have to maintain a ratio of 3:1 flush to lean milk supply and must increase their shareholding after a year; also, there are classes of

Table 14.5 Categories of membership in NDS promoted milk PCs

Parameter>	*No. of days of milk supply needed in a year*				*Quantity of milk supplied needed in a year (litres)*				*Min. No. of shares needed and value of shares held in Rs. (one share of Rs. 100)*			
PC> Member Category	*Baani*	*Maahi*	*Saahaj*	*Paayas*	*Baani*	*Maahi*	*Saahaj*	*Paayas*	*Baani*	*Maahi*	*Saahaj*	*Paayas*
A	>=300	>=330	>=330	>=330	>=7000	>=10000	>=12000	>=10000	100	70	120	100
B	269–299	>=270	>=300	>=270	2500 – 6999	>=4000	>=6000	>=4000	40	25	60	40
C	200–268	>=200	>=200	>=200	500–2499	>=500	500–6000	>=500	5	5	5	5

* Note 1: All members have to maintain a lean-flush ratio of 1:3.
Note 2: For Maahi:

a) The actual share contribution or the actual milk quantity supplied, whichever is lower, will be considered for the purpose of arriving at the categorization of class.

b) For the purpose of patronage calculation, the following shall be considered:

(i) Members who were admitted during the previous financial year and have not yet completed 365 days of their membership but have subscribed the minimum required share capital for the class chosen by them shall be considered to belong to that class.

(ii) Any member who will not meet the criteria under Class A or Class B may slide to an appropriate lower class for which the member meets the criteria. However, they will not be eligible to contest for the Board of Directors position for that year.

(iii) Those members who are not fulfilling the required criteria to retain at least 'Class C' will be issued notice for cancellation of membership as per the provisions of Article 4.3 read with Article 8 of the Articles of Association of the Company.

Source: Kaur 2019; Singh 2021; Maahi website.

membership; the face value of the share is revalued periodically and existing members can leave the PC and retire their equity capital at present valuation, besides 20% of the directors being co-opted experts. The elected board members are forbidden from holding any political office and have staggered terms where one-third retired every year/2 years (Singh 2021). This has led to a sense of seriousness among the members who can't think of free riding without serious consequences for their participation and benefits from the PC. This enhances the understanding of the business orientation of the PC among membership and helps appreciate their role in 'organizing' to create an agency for their empowerment.

Furthermore, there are very serious conditions for membership. For example, in case of Maahi, other conditions for membership included:

A.1 An individual Producer, who is engaged in production of milk from milch animals owned by him/her and responsible for the care and management of cow(s) and buffalo(es).

2 A person cannot become a member of the Company, a) if he has any business interest which is in conflict with business of the Company. and b) He/she was in employment of PC directly on its rolls or through a contractor or employed on a contractual basis with the PC for not less than consecutive six months in any of the two financial years, immediately preceding the financial year or during the current financial year in which he/she is proposed to be enrolled.

3 Membership is limited to only one milk producer from each household who is of the age exceeding 18 years.

4 A milk producer desirous of becoming a Member of the PC shall have to apply in prescribed application form to the PC (when the membership drive is open) and undertake in writing to abide by the provisions of the Memorandum and the Articles of Association of the PC. Further, a non-refundable admission fee of Rs. 100/- for male members and Rs. 50/-admission fee for a woman is required to be paid. He/she has to subscribe for at least five equity shares of Rs. 150/- each (including Rs. 50 per share towards premium).
The Producer shall agree to in writing to subscribe for minimum of Five Equity Shares of Rs. 150/- each. (Rs. 100/- towards Share Capital and Rs. 50/- towards Share Premium).

5 To undertake to supply good quality milk according to the quality standards laid down by the PC from time to time.

6 To undertake not to engage in trading of milk other than own produce.

7 The effective date of membership shall be from the date on which membership is approved by the Board.

8 Such other conditions as may be prescribed by the Board from time to time.

In addition, the conditions for continuation of membership were:

1 Membership shall continue as long as a Member does not fail to meet the following criteria:

  a) The member is engaged in production of milk from milch animals owned by him and responsible for the care and management of cow(s) and buffalo(es). Member is not indulging in an act which is detrimental to the functioning of the PC and also which is against the interest of the PC; b) member has supplied milk for at least 200 days during the previous financial year and poured a minimum of 500 litres of milk annually; c) member has subscribed for shares matching the annual quantity of milk supplied; d) total milk supplied to the PC during the winter months namely November to February shall not exceed three times the milk supplied during the summer months namely April to July during the previous financial year; e) the milk supplied by the member has met all the quality standards as stipulated by the PC from time to time and f) such other conditions as may be prescribed by the Board from time to time (Source: Maahi website).

The large member base and involvement is crucial for achieving business viability as well as better governance, as suggested by NDDB experience across states to achieve economies of scale and scope and obtain member centrality and patronage, which create agency and empowerment.

4. Conclusions

As this analysis of the three PCs of NDS shows, they have been able to scale up and become viable despite entering the market when it was highly competitive across states where the PCs are located. A significant part of their performance can be explained with the help of an analysis of innovations undertaken by NDS while designing and setting up the PCs, which range from innovations in membership profile and role, business model, and operational management of the PCs.

What also emerges from this analysis is the bringing in of elements of contract farming among PC members to ensure commitment of some supply of milk, so that business plans could be executed successfully for trustworthy presence in the market, and free riding and horizon problems typical in a traditional co-operative could be avoided to a large extent. This was achieved by linking milk delivery rights to equity and the other ways besides patronage leading to eligibility for participation in the governance of the PCs through board membership.

Although PCs generally focus on small producers to achieve inclusiveness, there is some merit in mixed-member PCs in terms of farmer base, as that helps achieve scale and mobilize more equity. It is also argued that, if they are composed of only small and marginal producers, they find it difficult to break even sooner; and later, because of the small scale of their operations, bringing in larger farmers at a later stage creates problems of governance as PCs were originally designed with patronage cohesiveness. But scale is only one factor, and others such as differentiation and meeting buyer preferences or serving niches are also important as part of the strategy (Penrose-Buckley 2007). That a large member base and involvement are crucial is also suggested by these milk PCs' experience across states to achieve economies of scale and scope and obtain member centrality and patronage (Shah 2016).

The PCs also need to choose their activity portfolio carefully, keeping in mind the member centrality. They should also do adequate value-chain mapping of the relevant commodity/sector/service before undertaking any intervention. It is possible to identify new activities in local areas that are valuable for small farmers (e.g. custom hiring of farm machinery and equipment that they can't afford to buy, but can rent).

Further, like the New generation Co-operatives (NGCs), PCs can also discourage, if not restrict, large membership via by-laws to remain viable and not become unwieldy in size, as has been done to some extent by PCs promoted by NDDB. The PCs need to identify other businesses that can bring in a larger number of members to reach scale and cater to the diverse interests of members.

Notes

1 This section borrows heavily from author's own paper Singh (2017) given in reference list.

2 Institutions are different from organizations – the former being the rules of the game and the latter the players in the game. But both of them influence each other: which organizations come up and how they evolve is determined by the institutional framework (rules of the game), and they in turn influence how the institutional framework itself evolves.

References

Bhanot D, Kathuria V and Das D (2021): Can institutional innovations in agri – marketing channels alleviate distress selling? Evidence from India, *World Development*, 137, https://doi.org/10/1016/j.worlddev.2020.1'05202

Ebbinghaus B. (2005): Can path dependence explain institutional change? Two approaches applied to welfare state reform. MPIfG Discussion paper no. 05/2. Max Plank Institute for the Study of Societies, Cologne.

Gatzweiler FW (2016): Institutional and technological innovations in polycentric systems: pathways for escaping marginality. In: Gatzweiler FW, von Braun J, editors. *Technological and institutional innovations for marginalised smallholders in agricultural development*. London: Springer Open, pp. 25–40.

IICA (2014): *Innovation in agriculture: a key process for sustainable development. Institutional position paper*. San José, Costa Rica: Inter-American Institute for Cooperation in Agriculture (IICA).

Kaur M (2019): An economic analysis of production and marketing of milk under formal and informal milk markets in Punjab, PhD thesis, Dept of Economic Studies, School of Social Sciences, Central University of Punjab, January.

Maertens M and Velde KV (2017): Contract farming in staple food chains: the case of rice in Benin, *World Development*, 95, 73–87.

Mahajan V (2015): Farmers' producer companies: need for capital and capability to capture the value added. In: Access Development Services, editor. *State of India's Livelihoods Report 2014*. New Delhi: OUP.

Mendoza RU and Thelen N (2008): Innovations to make markets more inclusive for the poor. *Development Policy Review*, 26(4), 427–458.

Neti A, Govil, R and Rao MR (2020): *Farmer producer companies: Past, present and future*. Bangalore: Azim Premji University.

Penrose-Buckley C (2007): *Producer organisations: a guide to developing collective rural enterprises*. Oxford: Oxfam GB.

Raffaelli R and Glynn MA (2015): Institutional innovation: novel, useful and legitimate. In: Shalley CE, Hitt MA, Zhou J, editors. *The Oxford handbook of creativity, innovation and entrepreneurship*. Oxford: Oxford University Press.

Shah T (2016): Farmer producer companies: fermenting new wine for new bottles. *Economic and Political Weekly*, 51(8), 15–20.

Shiller RJ (2006): Behavioral economics and institutional innovation. *Southern Economic Journal*, 72(2), 269–283.

Singh S (1999): Institutional innovations in Indian agriculture: a case of input markets. *Institutional Development*, 6(2), 3–9.

Singh S (2013): *Governance and upgrading in export grape global production networks in India* (Capturing the Gains Working Paper 33). Manchester: The University of Manchester.

Singh S (2017): Institutional innovations in paddy rice production and marketing in India: Experience and strategies. In: Mohanty S, Chengappa PG, Mruthyunjaya, Ladha JK, Baruah S, Kannan K, Manjunatha AV, editors. *The future rice strategy for India*. London: Academic Press (Elsevier), Chapter 12, pp. 335–357.

Singh S (2021): Understanding performance and impact of producer companies: Cases studies across States and Promoters in India (Final report). IIM Ahmedabad: CMA.

Singh S and Singh T (2014): *Producer companies in India: Organisation and performance*. New Delhi: Allied.

WB (2020): Implementation completion and results report IDA-50740, national dairy support project, Report No. ICR00005044, South Asian Region. Washington, DC: World Bank.

Chapter 15

Molecular Diagnostics (MDs) Innovation Systems in India

Analysis of System Failures and Challenges

Nidhi Singh

1. Introduction

Molecular diagnostics, or MDs, is a broad term describing the class of diagnostic tests that assess a person's health at a molecular level, detecting and measuring specific genetic sequences in deoxyribonucleic acid (DNA) or ribonucleic acid (RNA) or the proteins they express (Constance, 2010). MDs identifies gene, RNA and protein variations that shed light on whether a specific person is predisposed to have a disease, whether the person actually has a disease or whether a certain treatment option is likely to be effective for a specific disease (AdvaMedDx and DxInsights, 2013). MDs is one of the most dynamic and transformative areas of diagnostics, leading to advances in research and treatment that are revolutionizing healthcare across a wide range of diseases and health conditions (Poste, 2001).

The Innovation System for MDs in India is being built on the expectations that it will perform more accurate and sensitive diagnoses to reduce the delays and initiation of treatments for highly dangerous infectious diseases like TB, Malaria and HIV and non-infectious diseases like cancer and diabetes, where conditions of these diseases are also specific to India. These potential expectations need to be fulfilled through the development of a robust innovation ecosystem and the relevant actors contributing to innovation making. Only by embedding the emerging technology system of MDs into the local needs and addressing the constraints involving capacity and capability development, as well as accessibility and affordability for the new healthcare technologies within the medical community, can India realize the full potential of MDs innovation system development.

MDs are at present emerging technology in India[1]; the Indian innovation system for healthcare lacks capabilities for modern biomedical technological developments (Chaturvedi, 2007). Medical pluralism, low government spending, high out-of-pocket spending and a large unregulated private sector characterize MDs ecosystems (Engel et al., 2015). Healthcare providers range from highly qualified specialists to unqualified practitioners and local healers, and large state-of-the-art laboratory chains, medium-sized facilities

DOI: 10.4324/9781003353904-19

and small neighborhood labs offer associated laboratory services. They are largely commercial players driven by profit motives (market-based calculation) and lack formal/official quality assurance or accreditation (Engle etal., 2015).

In this context, the current need is for India to develop the innovative capability to meet the domestic needs of the country. Development of the innovation process for an emerging technology such as MD requires a framework that can capture the dynamic interplay of the innovation actors and the institutional structure that governs and directs knowledge creation, accumulation and diffusion. The evaluation of system-building activities in MD innovation requires a more holistic understanding of innovation systems, which considers context-specific challenges embedded in the country, like innovation-making for resource-poor healthcare settings as well as adoption and absorption of imported MD. Being an emerging biomedical scientific field, the creation and diffusion of MDs knowledge to meet the country-specific health challenges depend upon building an effective interactive explorative learning and competence building under a resource-poor economic context. As a technology-follower country, the technological capability building for successful catch-up in MDs innovation in India requires a detailed assessment of the System building issues across actors and the identification of component failures.

Public sector R&D organizations, foreign firms, large domestic firms or young start-ups can be made to respond favourably and contribute to the development of an innovation system for MDs to address the local needs. However, the challenge of building structural systems and components for MDs innovation requires a comprehensive goal-oriented policy strategy that addresses market and non-market based social calculations. For an emerging technology with significant complexity and scientific knowledge sphere, MDs innovation is expected to transform the current practice of diagnostic needs and requirements of society. Therefore, there is a need to address the perceived weakness and system failures that go beyond the weaknesses in the market and structural component failures. This requires a multi-level perspective that addresses the challenge of strategic transformation of broader systems of production and consumption.

In this regard, the present chapter attempts to ascertain the number of system failure issues of the innovative actors of MDs in India. As such, the objective of this study is to evaluate the issues and challenges experienced in the performance of system building activities by the three major innovation actors: *Science Base actors, Translational Base actors and Industrial Base actors* for the development of an emerging MDs innovation system in India. By examining these challenges, we will be able to identify the underlying System weakness and underperforming component of the MDs innovation structure. The analysis of issues and challenges is done in terms of 'System Failure' analysis that would help in developing an understanding about the sectoral specific lacunae persisting in the system, which need to be addressed to achieve a socially responsible innovation system for MDs in the country. For this purpose, the technology innovation system in MDs is examined through three important *properties* of innovation systems: market, structure and transformation change.

The chapter is divided into the following Sections. Section 2 describes the methodology and data; Section 3 highlights the innovation system merits, technology function shortcomings, challenges and failures of the Science base in MDs innovation systems. Section 4 evaluates the system-based merits, functional patterns, challenges and failures of the Translational base actors of MDs. Section 5 examines the industry base actors' performance, technology functioning, system issues and failures. Section 6 evaluates the challenges of MDs system building in the context of catch-up, institutional change and policy issues. Section 7 concludes.

2. Methodology and Data Sources

In order to address the *challenge of* building MDs innovation system according to the needs and requirements of the country-specific needs, we follow the *System Failure Framework*, initially developed by Woolthuis et al. (2005), van Mierlo et al. (2010) and later provided institutional legitimization by Weber and Rohracher (2012).

Innovation system failures are defined as system weaknesses that are blocking innovation mechanisms, which are collectively called systemic failures (Chaminade and Edquist, 2010; Jacobsson and Johnson, 2000; Smith and Stirling, 2010; OECD, 2016). Table 15.1 provides the matrix of innovation system failures covering the three broad areas of the innovation system framework, i.e., Market Based System, Structural System and Transformational System. The development of innovation systems for MDs requires identification of all possible innovating agents in these systems and designs policies to address the issue of system failure that hinder and block generation and diffusion of innovation process in the economy.

Analysis of the innovation system failure is done using secondary data sources. The research data is collected from various databases, including: (a)Publications in MDs are mapped by using an indexed database *Web of Science*, which is a collection of online journals and academic citations provided by Thomson Reuters; (b) Information on Extramural Research Projects (EMR) is collected from the database of the Department of National Science and Technology Management Information System (NSTMIS), available at the Department of Science and Technology (DST) website; (c) The datasets on patents are obtained by using the search engine *www.ipindia.nic.in/*, supported by the Department of Industrial Policy and Promotion (DIPP), Ministry of Commerce and Industry and Government of India. Further, the website's search and study of annual reports of industries, research institutes, universities and departments of government has been done; (d)

Table 15.1 Innovation system failures in diagnostic innovation system

Categories of Failures	*Types of Failure*
Market failures	Information asymmetries (Uncertainty about the outcomes lead to undersupply of funding for R&D) Knowledge spillover (Public good character of knowledge and leakage lead to socially sub-optimal investment in R&D) Externalization of costs
Structural system failures	Infrastructural failure (Lack of physical and knowledge infrastructure) Institutional failures (Absence, excess or shortcomings of formal institutions such as law, regulations and standards) Interaction or network failure (network failure between the different actors) Capability failure (Lack of appropriate competencies and resources at actor and firm level)
Transformational system Failures	Directionality failure (Lack of shared vision, coordination, insufficient regulation and lack of funding) Demand articulation failure (lack of anticipation about users' need to enable the uptake of innovations by users) Policy coordination failure (Lack of policy coordination across different systemic levels) Reflexivity failure (Inadequacy to monitor, anticipate and involve actors in process of self-governance)

Source: Adapted from Weber and Rohracher (2012)

Databases of Government promotional schemes set up for supporting innovation actors in the area of medical diagnostics, like Biotechnology Industry Research Assistance Programme (BIRAP), Biotechnology Industry Partnership Programme (BIPP), The Small Business Innovation Research Initiative (SBIRI), Biotechnology Industry Research Assistance Council (BIRAC) and The New Millennium Indian Technology Leadership Initiative (NMITLI). Innovation actors receiving funds from international donor and funding organizations in India to strengthen their system building activities have been checked;(e) The industry- and trade-level data were collected from Prowess (CMIE), Bloomberg Professional Terminal, UN Comtrade, DGCI&S and WPI from Office of Economic Advisor, Government of India.

3. Critical Evaluation of MDs Innovation Development: Analysis of System Failures in Science Base

The analytical exercise, based on a number of technological parametres, reveals that the System building activities are facing a number of issues and challenges. The persistence of these innovation weaknesses reveals the presence of sub-optimal functioning of technological innovation processes, and these System component Failures hinder the progress of successful scientific knowledge catch-up in MDs.

3.1. Persisting Innovation Issues in the Science Base Sector

(a) Inadequate Resource Mobilization and Fund Direction for Competence Building

We find that even though during the past 10 years the Department of Biotechnology (DBT) has increased MDs research funding, compared to other biomedical area, there is lack of funding for exploratory learning. The distribution of Extramural Research (EMR) funding is heavily concentrated towards selected organizations, like the Institutes of National Importance (INIs), at the expense of universities and national research laboratories to strengthen the science base (Figure 15.1). There is also evidence of a lack of infrastructure for the development of advanced MDs like microfludic MDs and biosensor-based options in the country (Figure 15.2).

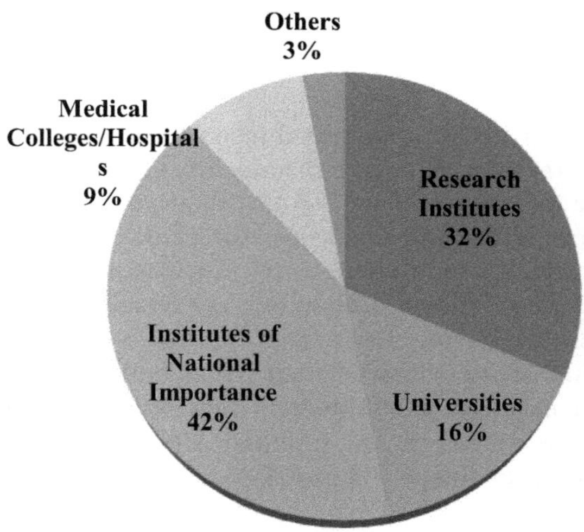

Figure 15.1 Distribution of EMR Funding to Types of Institutes (2000–2016)

Note: We select the type of Institutions where science base for MDs is located

Source: Authors' calculation based on the data collected from National Science and Technology Management Information System (NSTMIS) Database

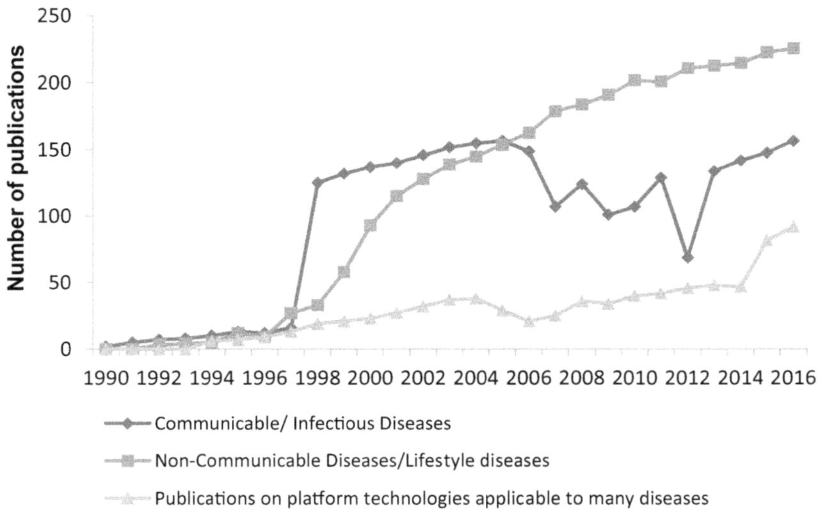

Figure 15.2 Number of Publications Activities: By Diseases (1990–2016)

Source: Author's calculation based on the data collected from Web of Science Database

(b) Lack of Specialized Human Resources

In spite of a continuous effort of DBT for the development of human resources over time, the proportion of specialized manpower dedicated for MDs research is very small. In terms of intra-discipline catch-up, the proportion of active researchers[2] and star researchers[3] in this area has been significantly small (Figure 15.3). This is largely because of the scant involvement from medical colleges and hospitals, where the proportion of Doctoral students in the specialized area of MDs in the last five years has also been very low: only 1.3 of the total PhDs enrolled in biomedical disciplines (Figure 15.4).

(c) Lack of Scientific Capabilities to Meet Country-Specific Health Challenges

The funding pattern of EMR has shifted from communicable diseases to non-communicable diseases, which reflects a lack in the priority setting for targeted research (Figure 15.5). Since the development of MDs requires convergence and co-dependencies of various disciplines like molecular biology, biotechnology, clinical biology and biochemistry, the lack of coordination and interaction between the different scientific actors hinders socially responsible scientific knowledge creation and diffusion. Most of

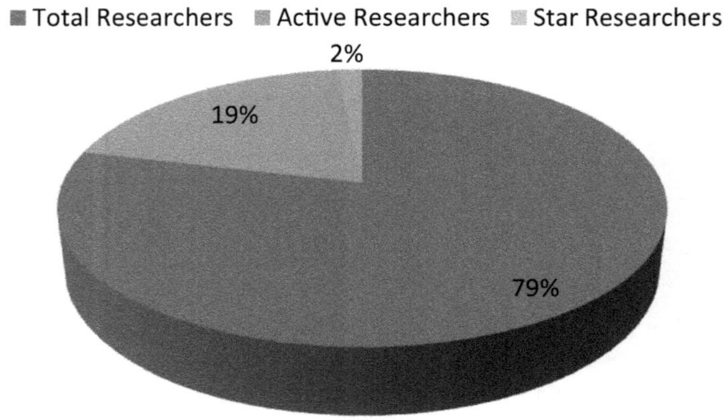

Figure 15.3 Distribution of Type of Researchers (2007–2016)

Source: Author's calculation based on the data collected from Web of Science database

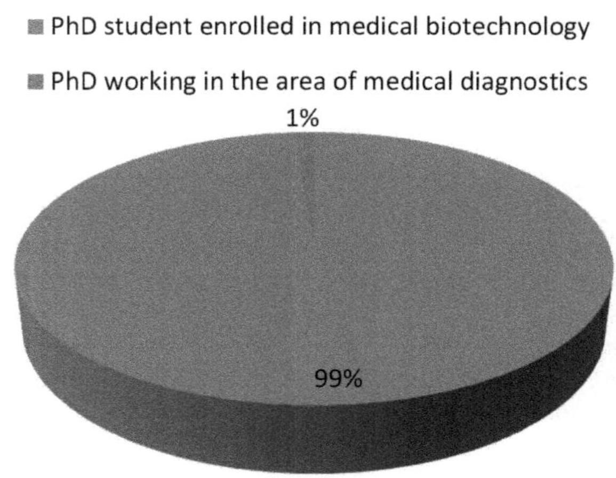

Figure 15.4 Distribution of PhD Researchers Working in the Area of Medical Diagnostics (2012–2016)

Source: Author's calculation based on the data collected from annual institutional reports

the knowledge produced for exploratory learning is at present restricted to basic research, and the knowledge production for applied research is extremely weak (Figure 15.6). We know that the exploratory nature of learning is required to solve the resource constraint setting-specific problems, like patients near testing and point-of-care diagnostics. This requires

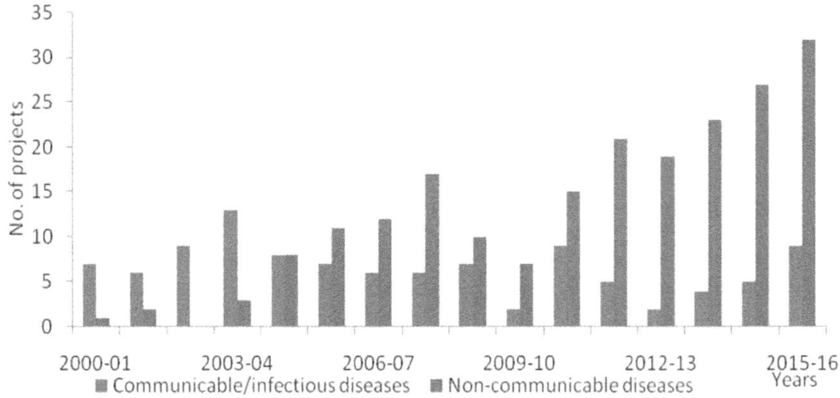

Figure 15.5 Distribution of EMR Funding for Communicable and Non-communicable Diseases (2000–2016)

Source: Author's calculation based on the data collected from NSTMIS database

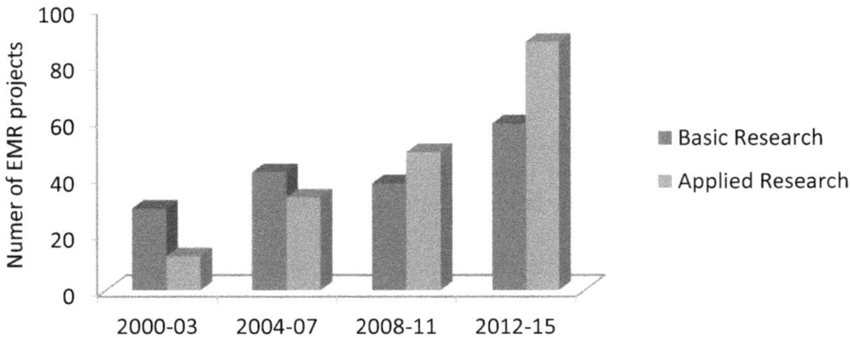

Figure 15.6 Pattern of Distribution of EMR Projects (2000–2016)

Source: Author's calculation based on the data collected from NSTMIS database

promotions of disciplines like biosensors, molecular markers and sequencers are very much limited in the science base at present.

Overall, the presence of these *System Challenges* reveals that the science base for MDs innovation systems lack problem-solving goal-oriented research outlooks. System building for translating research into product development is still missing in the Indian science base. System building is not very directed towards meeting the diagnostic-specific needs, and as a result, there are still various gaps in research for priority diseases in the country. The challenges observed in the technology innovation process of system building activities for the science base in MDs system in the country indicate the persistence of number of *System Failures* that hamper the effective creation and transfer of knowledge required for a socially responsible innovation system in India. Sub-section 3.2 discusses the analysis of System Failures in the MDs Science Base.

3.2. MDs Innovation System Failures: Science Base

The presence of some of the innovation system building formation problems in the scientific organization structure of Indian MDs segment points out that several structural parts are underperforming or that adequate knowledge development is lacking. The complexity of the scientific content of MDs requires a detailed assessment of the nature of system challenges so that proper policy prescriptions can be prepared to address these issues. The identification of system failures is done based on a number of challenges that we noticed from our empirical analysis. For analytical purpose, the list of system failures is categorized across three heads: Market-Based Failures, System Component Failures and Transformational System Failures. The detailed categories and the sources of failure mechanism based on system challenges are given in Table 15.2.

We can observe that the system building activities for exploratory learning are majorly guided by economic market calculations. The knowledge accumulation through the interaction of market forces in the Science Base organization face the problem of information asymmetry, negative spillover knowledge externality and failure to meet society's vital health problems. Some of the major factors behind these important market lacunas are due to the presence of large uncertainty, rewards and recognition for scientists, poor conversion rate from basic research to applied research and misdirection of research efforts towards diseases that are not very specific to a majority of Indian population. The move towards a market-oriented research focus is found to drive the incentives and rewards away from undertaking scientific MDs innovative research towards the local needs of the country.

In the existing innovation system component, there is a clear absence of exploratory learning efforts by the scientific community because of infrastructure failures, capability failures and interaction or network failures. The absence of well-developed scientific research facilities and labs prevents scientific development of Micro fluidics development, Bio Safety Levels (BSL3&4), etc. The knowledge failure is further aggravated by a lack of indigenous product capability development of reagents, enzymes and vectors, which are currently sourced from abroad. Since technology interaction among various organizational heads are critical, the institutional-level failure indicates the absence of interactive learning, coordination between

Table 15.2 Overview of system failures in MDs: Science-based actors

Categories of Failures	*Types of Failure (Failure Mechanism)*
Market Failures	**Problem of Information Asymmetry and Market Distortions** (Lack of incentive for research laboratories to undertake MDs research due to inadequate utilization of research) **Issue of Knowledge Externality** (Severe sub-optimal/underinvestment in knowledge as the rewards and recognitions for scientists to undertake diagnostic research are very low in India, concentration of basic research) **Failure to Meet Social-based Calculations** (Inclination of research towards the diseases which are not very specific to Indian population, lack of applied research)
Structural System Failures	**Infrastructure Failure** (Lack of Infrastructure facilities for highly sophisticated research like fabrication facilities for Micro fluidics development, Bio Safety Levels [BSL3 & 4 etc]) **Capability Failure** (Lack of indigenous innovation for the development of reagents, enzymes and vectors for which the country is heavily dependent on imports, poor conversion rate from basic research to applied research) **Interaction/Network Failure** (Lack of convergence and co-ordinations between different minds and ideas, absence of proper validation process (rules) for MDs technologies)
Transformational System Failures	**Directionality Failure** (Lack of targeted goal-oriented research to prioritize the needs of the country) **Demand Articulation Failure** (Absence of monitoring system to help the improvement of the quality of public expenditures and R&D for improved implementation of technology) **Policy Co-ordination Failure** (Inability of the science base institutes to integrate the country-specific diagnostic problems into their healthcare research system) **Reflexivity Failure** (Problem in swift adaptation to scientific knowledge changes, Lack of research and investment for Communicable Diseases and Non-Communicable Diseases (CDs/NCDs) which constitutes the highly burden and for advanced technologies like biosensors, biomarkers etc shows the failure of demand articulation)

Source: Author's compilation

different agents' ideas, absence of validation process and insufficient regulatory policies to provide emerging demands of the health sector in the country.

Apart from the structural weaknesses that prevent optimal creation and diffusion of scientific knowledge and innovative efforts, the science base actors face additional challenges that are multi-level in nature. This brings us to the issue of dealing with Transformational system failures in terms of lack of vision and directions to prioritize scientific research, absence of reflexivity for development of monitoring system to evaluate the performances of the innovation actors, lack of policy co-ordination and demand articulation due to insufficient conducts of system building activities to meet the social demand. In overall terms, the system-building activities of the Indian science base is currently immature in developing socially responsible innovation systems for MDs. As an emerging technology, the future development requires coherent policy vision and directions to induce exploratory learning towards social-based calculations.

4. Critical Evaluation of MDs Innovation Development: Analysis of System Failures in Translational Base

We find that the System building activities for Translational research for MDs development were incorporated into biomedical innovation systems of India through the efforts of DBT in the mid-2000s. The realization of the importance of the Translational scientific base led to the formation of the National Biotechnology Development Strategy (NBDS), which provided support for the development of skilled workforces and dedicated research facilities. We observe a number of efforts towards the development of global consortia to enhance interdisciplinary learning, interaction between the various stakeholders (research institutes, hospitals, companies, etc.), facilitation of international collaborations, public-private partnerships and regulatory guidelines in the past few years. We find the establishment of dedicated System building organizations such as Translational Health Sciences and Technology Institute (THSTI) and various public sectors research laboratories by mobilizing financial resources from EMR funding by the DBT. In terms of research outcomes, there is evidence of increased knowledge production (i.e., research publication) in the frontier technology areas of MDs such as biomarkers, next-generation sequencing, point-of-care technologies, rapid molecular test and DNA microarrays, increased research effort towards diseases like tuberculosis, cancer, glaucoma, HIV and malaria and emerging competence building through research collaborations and interactive learning. However, despite these significant research advancements, a number of *challenging issues* are faced by the innovating actors/organizations.

4.1. Persisting Innovation Issues in the Translational Base Sector

(a) Availability of Research Funding and Capability Issues

A major challenge in Translational research is the relatively lower incidence of healthcare research funding compared to other medical devices projects. Since the Translational field contains basic science and clinical research, the presence of considerable uncertainties in bringing new research projects diminishes the core scientific knowledge output. At present, the knowledge output from Translational research is comparatively lower than basic research, and very few basic ideas are followed to clinical applications (Figure 15.7). We observe that only a handful of research institutes have the knowledge capability to conduct research, and the level of granted patents is very low (Figures15.8 and 15.9).

(b) Lack of Interactive Learning and Regulatory Issues

We find the level of interaction between industry-academia and clinicians-researchers for building the ecosystem for Translational research is very limited (Figures: 15.10 and 15.11). There are several unexplored research areas because the present system building lacks significant interactive learning and exchange. In cases where interactive learning was fostered – for example, the development of affordable diagnostics such as the Tuberculosis (TB) 'Truenat' test from Biotechnology Industry Research Assistance Council (BIRAC) initiatives – there is evidence of meeting the priority of

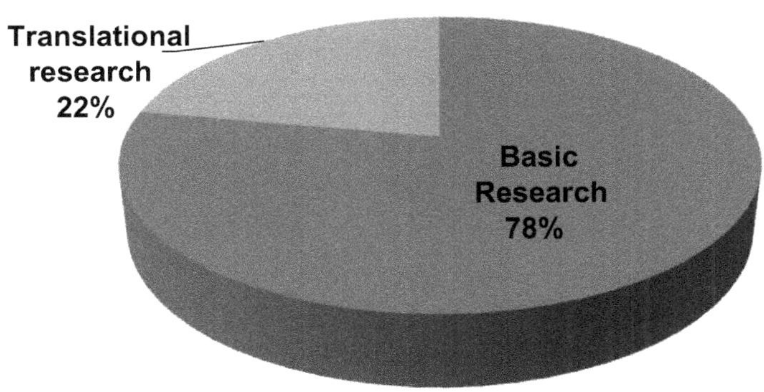

Figure 15.7 Comparative Analysis of Basic Research and Translational Research in MDs (2006–2016)

Source: Author's calculation based on the data collected from Web of Science database

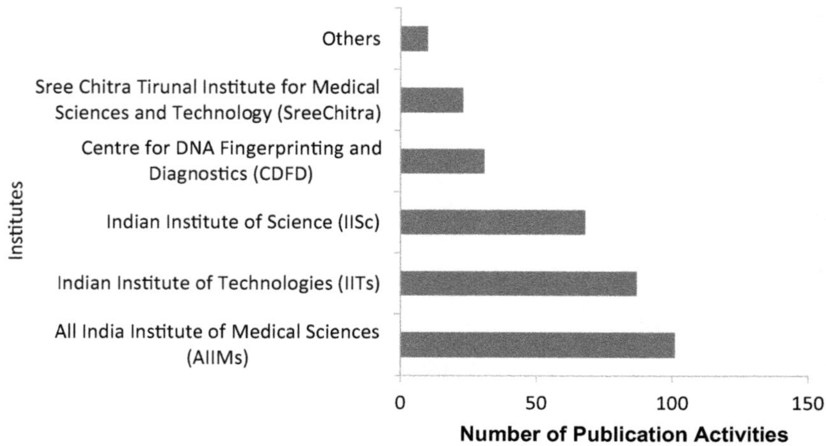

Figure 15.8 Location of Translational Research: Major Institutes in India (2006–2016)

Source: Author's calculation based on the data collected from Web of Science database

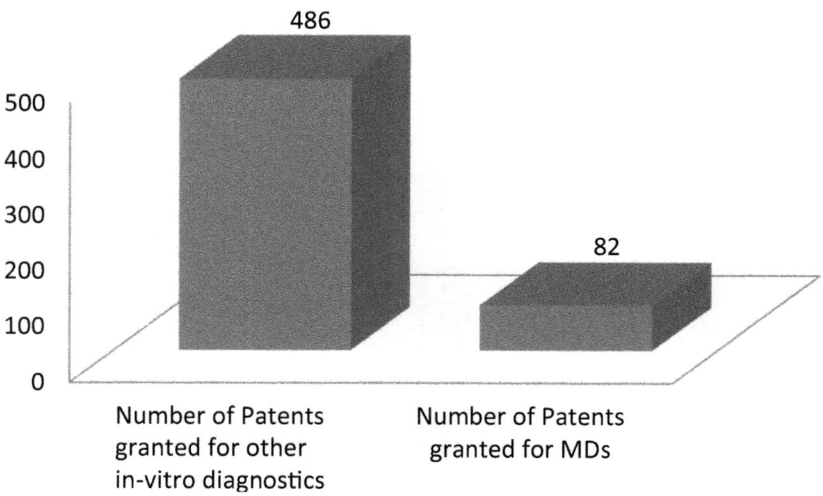

Figure 15.9 Comparative Analysis of Total Patents Granted for In-Vitro Diagnostics and MDs: 2006–2016

Source: Author's calculation based on the data collected from Indian Patent Office database

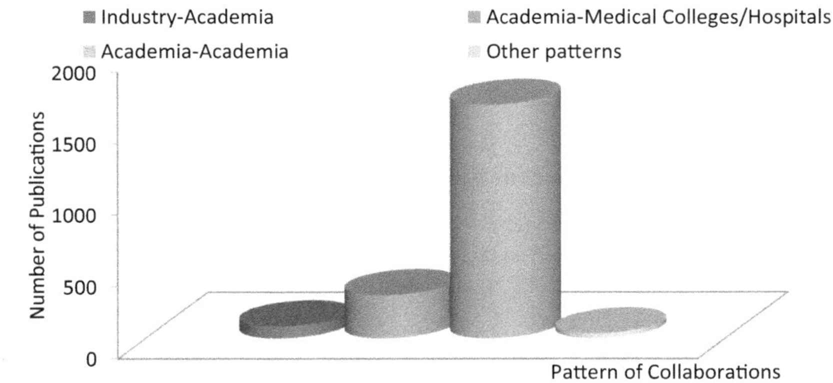

Figure 15.10 Ratio of Intra and Inter-Institutional Collaborations: 1991–2016 (%)

Source: Author's calculation based on the data collected from Web of Science database

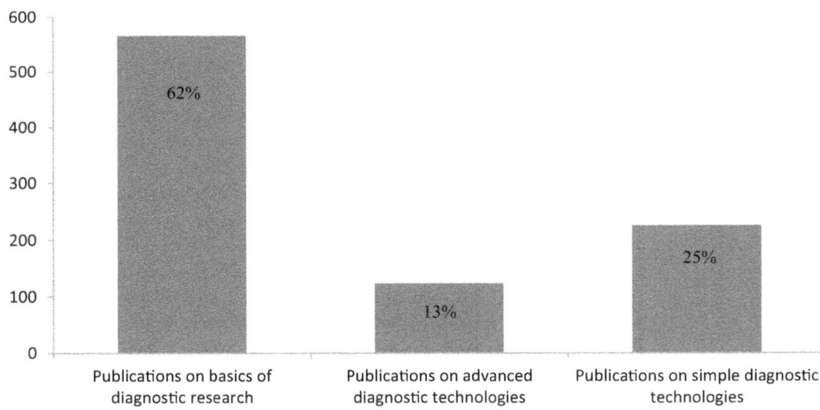

Figure 15.11 Pattern of Technological Focus of Collaborative Activities (1991–2016)

Source: Author's calculation based on the data collected from Web of Science Database

country-specific diagnostic needs. Moreover, the current environment lacks country-specific regulatory rules and guidelines for quality assessment.

To sum up, the Technological functional failures that are most common among the Translation research actors are relatively lower levels of knowledge output, lack of adequate fund mobilization, knowledge diffusion across discipline and proper regulatory institutional Legitimation. The prevalence of these innovation challenges implies that the innovation system components for the Translation base of MDs have several weaknesses and deficiencies. The comprehensive account of system underperformance factors can be delineated through the identification of *System Failures*. This is attempted in Sub-section 4.2.

4.2. MDs Innovation System Failures: Translational Base

As before, we classified the entire System failures into three groups: namely, market-based failures, structural system component failure and transformational failures (see Table 15.3). In the case of market-based failures, the

Table 15.3 Overview of system failures in MDs: Translation base actors

Categories of Failures	*Types of Failure (Failure Mechanism)*
Market Failures	**Issue of knowledge externality** (Lack of incentives to convert basic ideas into applications for research laboratories)
	Information asymmetry (Lack of interest of researchers in undertaking projects that have considerable knowledge uncertainty in the short period, continued mindset of risk-averse research)
Structural System Failures	**Institutional Failure** (Absence of proper formal regulatory bodies for transparent rules and guidelines)
	Network/Interaction Failure (Lack of interaction between industry-academia and clinicians-researchers, absence of mechanisms of strategic collaboration and coordination between different actors hindering the information to flow between the global private sector, the research community and the government, insufficient involvements in the interactive learning that prevent translation of MDs from bench to bedside, i.e., from laboratory to poor clinical settings)
	CapabilityFailure (Lack of trained manpower (HRD) in the area like genetic testing, absence of quality ideas towards meeting unmet needs and requirements)
Transformational System Failures	**Directionality Failure** (Lack of policy direction towards achieving socially relevant Health demand)
	Reflexivity Failure (Insufficient monitoring of recent developments in research platform, insufficient space for interactive learning and experimentation)
	Policy Co-Ordination Failure (Absence of mentoring support towards entrepreneurship development to help in the transition from science-based research to market-driven commercialization)
	Demand Articulation Failure (Insufficient deployment of capabilities and resources focused on cutting-edge frontier research and commercialization to meet the local needs)

Source: Author's compilation

challenge of conversion of basic scientific research into clinical application indicates the presence of considerable gap in knowledge accumulation and positive spillovers. This further implies the absence of complete information between various stakeholders which has led to sub-optimal investment in Translational-based research. The risk aversion and clinical and basis scientific knowledge uncertainty further induce the market to perform inefficiently. Unless efforts towards meeting socially desirable health issues of wider sections of populations are not addressed, the market-based calculations will be directed towards serving commercial-profit making incentives of the various stakeholders.

The structural system components analysis reveals the presence of failures in developing sufficient *knowledge capabilities, sound network or interaction among various disciplines* and *inadequate institutional apparatus*. Considering the acute healthcare issues of the population, India needs to supply considerable scientific knowledge personals dedicated towards core scientific area such as genetic testing. The knowledge creation and diffusion often fail to materialize because of a lack of productive interaction between academia and industry, foreign private entities and the government bodies, especially those related to research collaborations in Translating MDs from bench to bedside. This further requires a sound legitimized legal apparatus that is specific to the needs and requirement of this field.

Most of the structural failures result from lack of a clear policy vision and goal-oriented program by the State. This brings the need to study additional system failure components in terms of Transformational system change. Based on this framework, we find that there is lack of directionality, reflexivity, demand articulation and policy coordination among various stakeholders. The current environment of liberal policy regime that favours market-based calculations sabotages the need to direct research towards some critical social needs and requirements. As the technology becomes more complex, the system should have the capability to monitor and adapt to their research focus and design. This requires consistent policy coordination between different government heads and departments. Assuch, we can conclude from the analysis that the existing policy regime for innovation is not sufficient for building an ecosystem for translational research for the development of socially responsible requirements of the healthcare system of India.

5. Critical Evaluation of MDs Innovation Development: Analysis of System Failures in Industry Base

The system building activities of the Industrial base in India is constituted by the formation of entrepreneurial activities by the foreign firms, large domestic firms, and young-start-up firms. Most of the foreign manufacturing firms supply the domestic market using imported products. System building activities of the domestic firms are concentrated in the development of low-priced, high-volume segments. However, the high import of finished MDs equipment is found to be the dominant feature of the industry. Most the indigenous product development were largely carried out by the young start-up firms that are specific for local diagnostic needs such as TB, Malaria and HIV. We find that the government has been an important institutional player for industrial development by initiating policy initiatives such as Make-in-India, development of medical technology clusters/parks, initiatives to foster PPPs/PDPs and promotional schemes to strengthen firms' R&D. In recent periods, the government has introduced several changes in the medical diagnostic regulatory policies to promote proper validations and accreditation of the tests that are introduced in the market.

5.1. Persisting Innovation Issues in the Industry Base Sector

We find that the System building activities of the industrial base is largely emerging in India. However, the sector is experiencing a number of innovation issues to meet the buoyant diagnostic demand. The most prominent issues are the following.

(a) Lack of Domestic Innovation Capability

The empirical analysis reveals that the present structure of the organized industrial base in India lacks the capability to manufacture indigenous products that serve the demand of healthcare system under resource-poor settings. Since the domestic industry is largely import-dependent and highly concentrated in the presence of large MNCs, there is very limited positive knowledge externality for domestic manufacturing firms (Figures 15.12 and 15.13). Imported products from other countries, both as original equipment manufacturer and in finished form, are still prevalent. Needless to say, the innovative activities through formal R&D by manufacturing firms lags far behind that of leading MNCs in the market.

(b) Lack of Investments Capability

We find that the investment in system building activities for competence building is lacking among the industrial actors (Table 15.4). Although the government has made some efforts towards assisting young-start-up firms, these are largely small, especially when considering the requirements of needs and competence building. Emphasis on indigenous research has been notably lacking amongst the local players owing to the deficiency of required skills, technical expertise and the infrastructure to support the elevated costs for conducting research and development for products, and the share of domestic players has been considerably lowered. There is evidence of lack of

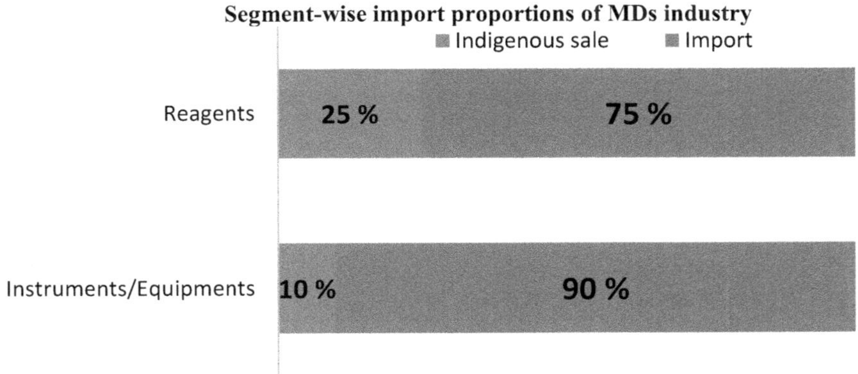

Figure 15.12 Segment-wise Import Proportions of MDs Industry

Source: Adapted from the Association of Indian Medical Device Industry (AIMED)

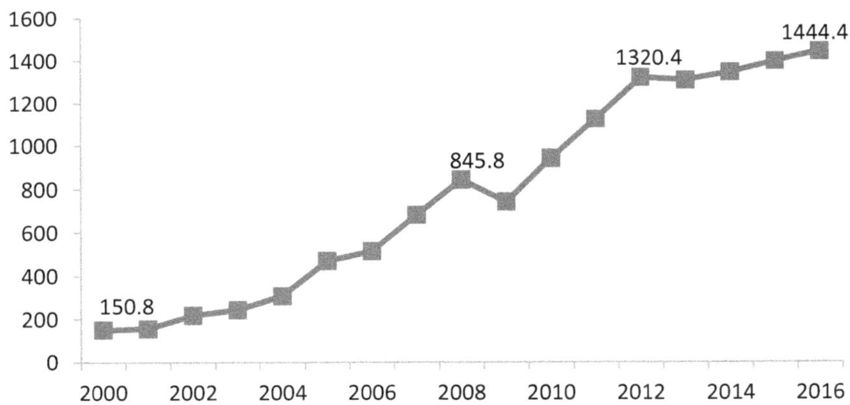

Figure 15.13 Trend in Import of MDs in India (2000–2016) Million US$

Source: Author's calculations based on UN Comtrade data, accessed from WITS online portal

sufficient public investment in the process of learning, competence building and innovation making (see Singh and Abrol, 2017)

(c) Absence of Social Calculation-based System Building Activities by Large Foreign Firms and Domestic Firms

We observe that in the context of the ongoing trade liberalizations policy regime, the production choices of large domestic and foreign firms' system

Table 15.4 Production, investment and technological capability of MDs manufacturing industry: Select indicators

Type of Firms	*Indicators*	*Share Analysis (%)*				*CAGR (%)*
		2000	*2005*	*2010*	*2016*	*2000–2016*
Domestic Firms	Sales Composition	4.3	7.2	7.5	3.9	8.5
	Export Composition	6.0	31.4	47.4	48.2	26.5
	Import Composition	3.8	7.9	12.2	3.6	14.6
	GFA/Sales	62.7	42.1	40.7	12.5	–0.5
	LP Index (2005 = 100)		100.0	189.9	204.3	6.1
	R&D Intensity	0.3	0.5	2.8	1.3	23.3
	Finished Goods Import Intensity	0.0	0.0	35.4	0.0	0.0
	Royalty, Technical Fees Intensity	0.0	0.3	0.1	0.9	0.0
Foreign Firms	Sales Composition	95.7	92.8	92.5	96.1	9.3
	Export Composition	94.0	68.6	52.6	51.8	7.0
	Import Composition	96.2	92.1	87.8	96.4	14.9
	GFA/Sales	20.2	15.4	24.2	9.7	5.8
	LP Index (2005 = 100)		100.0	130.7	178.3	4.9
	R&D Intensity	0.6	0.3	0.1	0.0	–5.9
	Finished Goods Import Intensity	33.1	58.4	79.9	33.1	14.9
	Royalty, Technical Fees Intensity	0.8	0.0	0.0	0.0	–100.0
Total MDs (Rs. Millions)	Sales Composition	100.0 (4438.1)	100.0 (5623.9)	100.0 (8560.0)	100.0 (18278.8)	9.3
	Export Composition	100.0 (57.9)	100.0 (58.9)	100.0 (115.3)	100.0 (312.2)	11.1
	Import Composition	100.0 (375.5)	100.0 (584.9)	100.0 (1546.6)	100.0 (2405.9)	14.9
	GFA/Sales	22.0 (859.1)	17.3 (1004.3)	25.4 (2720.1)	9.8 (2682.6)	5.3
	LP Index (2005 = 100)		100.0	96.6	147.3	3.3
	R&D Intensity	0.5 (21.1)	0.3 (16.7)	0.3 (34.9)	0.1 (22.0)	0.3
	Finished Goods Import Intensity	31.9 (119.6)	53.8 (314.4)	74.4 (1151.2)	31.9 (1099.4)	14.9
	Royalty, Technical Fees Intensity	0.7 (28.8)	0.0 (1.1)	0.0 (1.2)	0.0 (9.9)	–6.5

Note: (a) The total Rs. Million for Sales and GFA is at 2004–05 = 100 prices. The rest of the series are in current prices, (b) The share figures for Sales, Exports, Imports and Finished Goods import are based on aggregate total MDs of respective categories in %, (c) GFA denotes Gross Fixed Capital Asset (i.e., Investment), (d) LP denotes Labour Productivity Index, base 2005 = 100, (e) CAGR corresponds to compound annual growth rates in percent, (f) Total MDs represents the aggregate values of domestic and foreign firms in the database.

Source: Author's calculations based on PROWESS IQ, CMIE database

building activities have largely ignored social calculations. Since the commercial markets are motivated by profit-seeking incentives and incomes are skewed towards high-wealth accumulators, there is a tendency to neglect the supply of cost-effective and larger welfare-oriented MDs products in the market. Even though the entrepreneurs of start-up firms are helped through mobilization of financial resources like EMR and promotional schemes promoting Public Private Partnerships (PPPs), the market formation of these firms is often weakened because of competitive imported products. The indigenous products of start-ups face comparative disadvantages in a market dominated largely by foreign firms.

One of the distinguishing features of the MDs industry is the emergence of young start-up firms, which are changing the landscape of product development. Compared to foreign firms and large domestic firms, the young start-ups are playing a significant role in developing system-building activities for development of MDs (*knowledge creation, development learning and diffusion)* that are relevant for country's specific diagnostic needs (Singh and Abrol, 2017). Most of the founding members are scientists who later converted to entrepreneurs (*formation of entrepreneurship in the market*). In Table 15.5, we provide details of major *young start-up firms*active in MDs with their key focus areas for innovation specific to local needs (*social calculations and valorization process)*.

The young firms are supported by various critical drivers, such as emergence of seed funding, medtech product development expertise nurtured by product development centres of various MNCs and translational capability in public research system. Innovation funding platforms such as the SBIRI and BIPP/BIRAC created by DBT and TDB by DST, Grand Challenges Canada, etc., have received several applications for development of affordable devices and diagnostics that are relevant for the country (see Table 15.6). Over the last decade, various Private Equity (PE) and Venture Capital (VC) fundingshave emergedto promote business development and incubation services in the medical biotechnological sector (see Table 15.7).

The public-private involvement (PPP) plays a critical role in the development of system building activities like Human Resource Development (HRD), research and infrastructure development. At present, BIRAC is the main government agency that supports the*PPPs* model through devolution of funds for the development of medical technologies. Some examples of *PPPs*in the area of MDs development are given in Table 15.8.

(d) Lack of Regulation

The current deregulation policy regime of the government has resulted in large imports of finished MDs products that are found to be maladapted to resource-poor settings of India. India lacksan effective analytical and clinical validation process that involves accreditation from a clinical laboratory

Table 15.5 Young start-up firms with their founders and key focus area for MDs innovation

Start-Up Firms	*Founder(S)*	*Key focus area*
XCyton	Dr. Ravi Kumar, PhD in neurochemistry from the Indian Institute of Science (IISc), Bangalore. Later he was a project coordinator and research leader in Astra Research Centre (now AstraZeneca), Bangalore.	• Mapping of unmet clinical needs in the Indian market • Infectious diseases specific to India and other developing countries
Bigtec	Chandrasekhar Nair is achemical engineer. He worked in the field of bioprocess modelling in India and Canada.	• Infectious diseases specific to India and developing countries
ReaMetrix	Dr. Bala S. Manian is a Silicon Valley serial entrepreneur of Indian origin with a PhD in electronic engineering. He founded several successful companies and has extensive industry expertise in the biological applications of optometrics.	• Extensive mapping of market niches for future products in the Indian market • Diseases specific to India and developing countries
Achira	Dr. Dhananjaya Dendukuri is a returning Indian with a PhD in microfluidics from MIT in the US; Dr. Suri Venkatachalam did PhD in condensed matter physics from IISc and post-doctoral work in computational neuroscience from UC, San Diego. After returning to India, he briefly worked in the local biotech industry. Subsequently, he founded Achira's mother company Connexios Life Sciences. He also co-founded Group Lifespring which invested in Achira.	• The microfluidic chips with a dedicated low-throughput fluorescence reader will target the fragmented private healthcare market • The silk fabric chips which do not require a fluorescence reader will be cheaper and for the government health market

Source: Compiled by the authors on the basis of information available on industries' websites and annual reports

performing diagnostic tests in order to get certification from a regulatory body (National Accreditation Board for Testing and Calibration Laboratories (NABL)), Clinical Laboratory Improvement Amendments (CLIA) and College of American Pathologists (CAP) in India. We find that the regulatory measures for diagnostics are poorly developed, as less than 10 percent of clinical laboratories are currently accredited. The burden of cost for implementation of quality control programmes and a general lack of awareness are leading to a lack of pressure for appropriate innovation[4]. Although

Table 15.6 Examples of small ventures supported by various funding schemes

Funding Scheme Supports	*Small ventures receiving funds*
Biotechnology Industry Partnership Program (BIPP) in 2010 under the management of Biotechnology Industry Research. BIRAC has been set up with a vision to stimulate, foster and enhance the strategic research and innovation capabilities of the Indian biotech industry, particularly SMEs	• Supporting Big-Tech lab for the Point-of-Care detection of infectious disease using handheld micro-PCR. • Supporting Revelations Biotech for the development of low-cost rapid quantitative PCR technology. • Supporting Chromous Biotech Multiplex FastPCR-based diagnosis and prognosis of tuberculosis. • Supporting Genomix Molecular Diagnostics (P) for developing diagnostics for malaria.
Small Business Innovation Research Initiative (SBIRI) in 2005. SBIRI is managed by the Biotechnology Industry Research Assistance Council (BIRAC). SBIRI is set up to promote PPP	
CSIR launched the programme of New Millennium Indian Technology Leadership Initiative (NMITLI) in 2001. NMITLI is set up to promote PPP	• Supporting Big-Tech labs for the development of novel diseases and low-vision enhancement devices. • Supporting Big-Tech labs for the development of Point-of-Care rapid diagnostic kits for TB.
Department of Health Research (DHR)	• Supporting Achira Labs for the development of Point-of-Care glucose sensor devices for diabetes.

Source: Compiled on the basis of information available on Websites of DBT, CSIR, DHR

Table 15.7 List of PE/VC supporting the development of MDs firms in India

Private equity (P/E) and venture capital (VC)	*Affiliations*	*Features*
Biotech Consortium India Ltd. (BCIL)	Department of Biotechnology	• Involved in technology transfer, project consultancy, fund syndication, information dissemination, manpower training and placement related to biotechnology. • **Services provided by BCIL are**: Technology transfer, Project consultancy, Certification services, Information services, Bio safety, Biotech Industrial Training Programme and Project management

(*Continued*)

Table 15.7 (Continued)

Private equity (P/E) and venture capital (VC)	*Affiliations*	*Features*
Centre for Innovation Incubation and Entrepreneurship	Government-funded Incubator centre at Indian Institute of Management Ahmadabad	• Fosters innovation driven entrepreneurship in India through incubation, investment and training.
Centre for Cellular and Molecular Platforms (C-CAMP)	Department of Biotechnology	• C-CAMP is engaged in development of novel diagnostic technologies and tools and development of novel modalities for the existing tools and technologies
Foundation for Innovative New Diagnostics	Bill and Melinda Gates Foundation	• FIND is a non-profit foundation for developing and implementing new, affordable, easy-to-use and cutting-edge diagnostics for poverty-relateddiseases. • Current disease programmes include tuberculosis, malaria and human African trypanosomiasis (HAT), also known as sleeping sickness.
European Business and Technology Centre, EBTC	Co-funded by the European Union and implemented by EUROCHAMBRES	• Activities of EBTC are geared towards generating new business opportunities and technology transfer, with a focus on energy, environment, transport and biotechnology.
Institute of Bioinformatics and Applied Biotechnology (IBAB)	Supported by the Government of Karnataka, DST, DBT, DIT	• Promote entrepreneurships, conduct training programs, provide contract research services and undertake research and development.
Indian Angel Network (IAN)	Supported by DST	• Helps connect entrepreneurs with relevant and experienced Mentors from IAN's members. • Working closely with the incubates, the assigned. IAN mentors and incubation managers help strategies, identify and plug the gaps.

Source: Adapted from Diagnostic Guide India, FINPRO India, 2015

Table 15.8 Public private partnerships for the development of MDs: Selected cases

Public Private Partnerships (PPPs)	*Title of the Project Supported*	*Supported by*
Bhat Bio-Tech India (P) Limited, Bangalore **in collaboration with** National Institute of Malaria Research, New Delhi	HRP-II/p-LDH-baseddiagnostic kits for the differential detection of malarial parasites	BIRAC
Genomix Molecular Diagnostics (P) Limited, Hyderabad **in collaboration with** BITS, Pilani, NIMR, New Delhi, NIMR, Jabalpur, Osmania University, Hyderabad	Sensitive, inexpensive and handheld diagnostic Point-of-Care (POC) instrumentation to detect Malaria and other pathogens	BIRAC
BigTech labs in collaboration with Indian Institute of Science, Bangalore	Molecular diagnostics for infectious disease and TB.	BIRAC
BigTech labs in collaboration with Indian Institute of Science, Bangalore	TruelabM system (low-cost near-patient platform) for detection of infectious disease.	NMITLI

Source: Compiled on the basis of information available on Websites of DBT and CSIR as of July 2015

the government has introduced several steps to develop a properly defined regulatory framework for the medical devices industry, the institutionalization and legitimation system building functions involving regulatory apparatus is currently lacking in MDs.

5.2. MDs Innovation System Failures: Industrial Base

The challenges observed in the performances of system building activities for building up an industrial base for MDs innovation systems in the country are due to the presence of several *System Failures* that are listed in Table 15.9.

The MDs market structure is characterized by market imperfections and knowledge asymmetry because of the concentration of production technology in the hands of few large foreign firms. The presence of high-level technical complexity and uncertainty has resulted in considerable information asymmetry and underinvestment in knowledge accumulation by private Indian firms. Since knowledge has public good characteristics, the private market calculations will often undermine the external social cost to the environment in which the firms operate. This further discourages additional investments in in-house R&D of domestic firms and indigenous supply of products that meet the healthcare demand of the larger sections of society. The presence of marketfailures suggests that there is a need to increase public investments to become the catalyst of knowledge diffusion in the domestic market.

Table 15.9 Overview of system failures in MDs: Industry base actors

Categories of Failures	*Types of Failure (Failure Mechanism)*
Market Failures	**Issue of Information Asymmetry** (Technology complexity and uncertainty leads to undersupply of financial resources towards discovery of new equipments, lack of R&D investments, Heavy market competition from MNCs including Chinese companies, high technology uncertainty, financial support for domestic Start-up firms) **Issue of Knowledge Externality** (Public good nature of knowledge prevents complete recovery of research costs, under investments in knowledge creation, poor domestic R&D investments) **Failure to meet Social-based Calculations** (Lack of economic incentive of domestic firms to undertake indigenous product innovations, Heavy import-dependency serving profit-calculations)
Structural System Failures	**Network Failure** (Clear absence of industry-academia partnership, lack of collaborative research effort by start-up firms) **Infrastructure Failure** (Low level of private investment in knowledge creation, Lack of adequate finance for R&D investment, low entry barriers in the service provider market creates heavy domestic competition from foreign service providers) **Capability Failure** (Market monopoly and entry barriers impede domestic firms knowledge creation and diffusion, lack of innovation capability – R&D) by large and small domestic firms, problem of local adaptability and high manufacturing cost incurred by Foreign Firms, severe market competition hampers product development for start-up firms **Institutional Failure** (Absence of proper regulatory accreditation bodies, uncertainty in rules and procedures for quality checking, Lack of supply chain regulations, costly regulatory procedures towards initiating manufacturing activities for start-up firms, non-complacent regulatory regime and uncertainty related to existing clinical practices faced by service providers and high-level service quality competition increases cost of operations for service providers)
Transformational System Failures	**Directionality Failure** (Lack of policy direction towards developing indigenous domestic substitute for costly imported diagnostic products from abroad, lack of shared vision and goal towards serving severe health challenges of the society)

Table 15.9 (Continued)

Categories of Failures	*Types of Failure (Failure Mechanism)*
	Demand Articulation Failure (Insufficient thrust towards providing public investments for manufacturing products that correctly anticipate and learn from society's demand for economically efficient health diagnostic tools, heavy reliance on imported diagnostic machines that fail to serve needs and requirement of health care under resource-poor condition of the economy)
	Policy Coordination Failure (Absence of proper synchronization between different departmental policies, including IPR Policy, Trade and Investment Policy, Innovation Policy and Manufacturing Policy, Conflicting policy objectives evident from "Make-in-India" and liberal import of parts and components of diagnostic equipment that hinder domestic manufacturing capability)

Source: Author's compilation

The existence of a considerably small manufacturing base of the MDs industry reflects the lack of fully developed ecosystem conducive for domestic production and indigenous product development. This relates to the failure to create well-functioning system components including sufficient infrastructure facilities, network interdependencies, supply-side capabilities and formal institutional regulatory mechanisms. As evident from the scientific and translation base actors, the lack of collaborative and interactive functioning has led to major knowledge network failure in the industrial sector.

Since the industry has low levels of private investment in knowledge creation and inadequate finances for undertaking R&D investments, the infrastructure failure creates further problems at the supplyside. This in turn affects the domestic players' manufacturing capability, as there are considerable entry barriers in terms of MNCs' monopoly in knowledge asset and R&D investments. The maladapted imported products from abroad further erode the competitive position of emerging domestic players in the market. Such capability failures are directly related to the failure of the government to create a proper regulatory apparatus. These institutional inadequacies are reflected in terms of insufficient regulatory accreditation bodies, inadequate rules and procedures for quality checking, supply chain mismanagement, costly procedures in setting up manufacturing activities for start-up firms and non-complacent regulatory practices and uncertainty involved in clinical practices faced by service providers.

The failure to enhance the competitive landscape of developing domestic manufacturing with cost-effective indigenous industrial products is further reflected in the analysis of system building activities under a multi-dimension of functions. In terms of Transformative change, there are failures in directionality, demand articulation and policy coordination. Since the resource-poor context of India demands the development of inexpensive and effective products that are directed towards social health goals, the increased reliance on imported innovative products from abroad reflects directionality failure. This indicates the absence of a goal-oriented policy orientation that is shared equally across government departments. Given that the majority of the population has limited economic means and suffers from a number of health hazards, the failure to anticipate correctly the effective demand of reagents and equipments suggests the problem of demand articulation by the manufacturing firms. Since the innovation landscape is influenced by diverse policy goals, including industrial policy, trade policy, innovation policy, IPR and standards, there should be coherence between different policy choices. This is clearly lacking as is evident from the increased thrust for making industrial goods domestically under the 'Make-in-India' initiatives (industrial policy) while simultaneously witnessing considerable importing of finished MDs products because of the steep reduction in tariffs and NTBs (trade policy) on MDs products.

6. MDs Innovation System Building Challenges and Policy Issues

The analysis of innovation system failures experienced by the various actors of MDs in India indicates that there are considerable policy challenges in building an effective ecosystem of innovation in the resource-poor context of the country. In the context of increased inflow of foreign products that are often ill-adapted and ill-directed to serve the social needs, there is a need to direct innovative activities towards improving productive efficiency and capability for indigenization. At present, the level of indigenously manufactured products that are cost-effective and specific to diagnostic needs of the country is very low and is carried mostly by the youngstart-up companies. There is a significant challenge in creating a socially calculative incentive structure under which the majority of large domestic and foreign firms invest their resources and technological capabilities. The building of capacity to catch-up and develop competitive products depends on the increased industry-scientific academia collaboration and interactions.

At present, the scientific knowledge base of MDs devotes considerably less effort towards socially desirable health needs of the country. As explained before, the neglect of exploratory research, inadequate reward system, infrastructure bottlenecks and institutional rigidity deter proper valorization of scientific knowledge in research labs. The effort to building a socially responsible innovation system requires that the policy instruments have to address these context-specific failures and challenges. The structural rigidities in terms of lack of adequate resource personnel, scientific uncertainties and financial constraints further restrict applied research and Translational effort from laboratory results to clinical practices.

In this context, there is ample scope for ***Public Policy***to intervene effectively to correct the underperforming system component and facilitate knowledge creation and diffusion at a socially optimum scale. Since the innovative actors operate under the policy rules and regulations, the institutional characteristics will have a major impact on knowledge creation and distribution across organizations. At present, the thrust towards economic integration and liberal policy regime tend to favour the market competition and resource efficiency of private sector firms. There is a lack of deliberate effort to nurture and expand various public sector organizations that can facilitate socially desirable investment in critical health needs of the country. As an emerging technology field with considerable market uncertainty, knowledge complexity and inter-dependency, what is required is a proactive involvement of the State in various stages of product development and diffusion. The challenge of policy is to plan and design the right mix of policy coordination and actions.

7. Conclusion

The purpose of this study is to bring out clearly the System building failures and challenges in the MDs innovation system in India. Using the innovation system framework, we were able to identify the technological knowledge processes across various actors of MDs. Although considerable progress has been made, there are a number of issues that prevent the innovation system from developingin a socially desirable manner to serving the health requirement of the country. We tried to analytically categorize these issues and identify system failures across Science base, Translational base and Industry base actors of MDs. The analysis of failures was classed in terms of market-failure, structural system component failure and transformational change failure. Under each innovation system failure, the underperforming TIS functions were used as a guide to derive the failure mechanism across actors.

We find that the current pattern of innovation development in MDs suffers from a number of system weakness and challenges. The innovative actor's effort towards knowledge creation and development is hampered through the presence of several system failures. There is a lack of thrust towards creating exploratory learning, valorization and applied scientific research. The thrust towards Translational research from research lab to clinical laboratories involving multidisciplinary fields is found to have emergedvery late in India. Some of the major barriers for inadequate socially responsible scientific research are the failure to engage and collaborate with industry and other academic research organizations. The absence of targeted research and inadequate fund mobilization creates an unfavourable environment for knowledge creation at both scientific and industry segments. The industry landscape suffers from an inadequate institutional policy regime, which favours bulk imports at the expense of indigenous production that serves local needs and requirements of the health sector in the country. The market concentration, lack of investment in capability building through formal R&D, collaborations and interactive failures further dampen the entry and emergence of incumbent firms in the market. The small size of the market players is further constrained by increased market competition, inadequate regulations, and policy directions and coordination. Under these circumstances, there is a need for a well-articulated goal-oriented targeted policy strategy from the State to assist and develop the innovation pathway for serving socially desirable objectives.

Notes

1 MDs is based on a modern biomedical approach.
2 Active Researchers are those who have published for each year from 1997–2016
3 Star researchers having 10 or more paper publications in the last 10 years (2006–2016)
4 Among all the laboratories participating in quality control programme, 75% exist in only five states, accounting for 30% of the population. Since most of these laboratories are private, the population residing in rural areas not only lacks access to private labs, but also is more likely to undergo maladapted and substandard testing which is subject to inadequate safety protection.

References

AdvaMedDx and DxInsights. (2013). Introduction to molecular diagnostics: The essentials of diagnostics series, Copyright ©2013 DxInsights / AdvaMedDx, www.dxinsights.org advameddx.org.

Chaminade, C., & Edquist, C. (2010). Rationales for public policy intervention in the innovation process: A systems of innovation approach. In S. Kuhlman, P. Shapira, & R. Smits (Eds.), *The theory and practice of innovation policy. An international research handbook*. London: Edward Elgar Publishers.

Chaturvedi, S. (2007). Exploring interlinkages between national and sectoral innovation systems for rapid technological catch-up: Case of Indian biopharmaceutical industry. *Technology Analysis & Strategic Management*, *19*(5), 643–657.

Constance, A. (2010). *The future of molecular diagnostics; innovative technologies driving market opportunities in personalized medicine*. Copyright © 2010 Business Insights Ltd.

Engel N, Ganesh G, Patil M, Yellappa V, Pant Pai N, Vadnais C, et al. (2015) Barriers to point-of-care testing in India: Results from qualitative research across different settings, users and major diseases. *PLoS ONE*, *10*(8), e0135112. https://doi.org/10.1371/journal.pone.0135112.

Jacobsson, S., & Johnson, A. (2000). The diffusion of renewable energy technology: an analytical framework and key issues for research. *Energy Policy*, *28*(9), 625–40.

Nora Engel, Gayatri Ganesh, Mamata Patil, Vijayashree Yellappa, Nitika Pant Pai, Caroline Vadnais, Madhukar Pai. (2015). Barriers to point-of-care testing in India: Results from qualitative research across different settings, users and major diseases. *PLoS ONE, 10*(8), e0135112. https://doi.org/10.1371/journal.pone.0135112.

OECD. (2010). *Biomedicine and health innovation: Synthesis report*. OECD Publications. https://www.oecd.org/sti/emerging-tech/biomedicineandhealthinnovation-synthesisreport.htm

Poste, G. (2001). Molecular diagnostics: A powerful new component of the health-care value chain. *Expert Review of Molecular Diagnostics*, *1*(1).

Singh, N., & Abrol, D. (2017). In-Vitro Diagnostics (IVDs) Innovations for resource-poor settings: The Indian experience. *African Journal of Science, Technology, Innovation and Development*, *9*(5), 617–636.

Smith, A., & Stirling, A. (2010). The politics of social-ecological resilience and sustainable socio-technical transitions. *Ecology and Society*, *15*(1).

Van Mierlo, B., Arkesteijn, M., & Leeuwis, C. (2010). Enhancing the reflexivity of system innovation projects with system analyses. *American Journal of Evaluation*, *31*(2), 143–161.

Weber, K. M., & Rohracher, H. (2012). Legitimizing research, technology and innovation policies for transformative change: Combining insights from innovation systems and multi-level perspective in a comprehensive 'failures' framework. *Research Policy*, *41*(6), 1037–1047.

Woolthuis, R. K., Lankhuizen, M., & Gilsing, V. (2005). A system failure framework for innovation policy design. *Technovation*, *25*(6), 609–619.

Chapter 16

Building the Solar Energy Market in Malaysia

Role of Public Policy and Institutions

VGR Chandran, Angathevar Baskaran, & Sonia Kumari Selvarajan

Acknowledgement: We would like to acknowledge the financial support provided by The RU Geran – Fakulti Program, University of Malaya under the Research grant no: GPF002P-2018. This is also part of a larger project supported by the European Commission Marie Skłodowska-Curie Actions Research and Innovation Staff Exchange (H2020 MGA MSCA-RISE – Multi) grant no: 778398.

1. Introduction

Countries' commitment to climate change and attempts to reduce carbon footprints have forced governments around the world to take deliberate policy action. This effort also aligns with the larger context of sustainable development goals. One such move is to promote renewable energy (RE) uptake domestically – particularly to build the renewable energy market and production as well as supply. However, managing renewable energy uptake and production requires governments to establish proper institutions and policies that would work to promote renewable energy as an important source of the energy mix. Specifically, building a more competitive industrial structure would allow cost reduction efforts and effective applications that promote domestic market uptake. Indeed, globally, state intervention is required due to market failures to support the development of renewable energy. Market failures exist in investing in these new industries as well as in financing those industries, given the risk-averse behaviour of firms and financial institutions. Indeed, given the asymmetric information and huge transition cost, the government acts to mitigate and intervene in the market to help kick-start the industry.

Scholars suggest that the renewable energy sector is expected to grow rapidly in the coming decades. The estimate by the International Energy Agency (2019) is that by 2026, for the total energy supply contribution globally, 15–20% is expected to come from renewable sources that include

DOI: 10.4324/9781003353904-20

solar energy. Investment in renewable energy sources for electricity, heating, and in biofuels has increased considerably. The global solar energy industry is expected to reach $422 billion by 2022 from $86 billion in 2015, growing at a CAGR of 24.2% from 2016 to 2022 (Allied Market Research, 2014). Solar energy is harnessed by using various technologies such as solar heating, photovoltaic cells, and others. The growth of the solar energy market is driven by increase in environmental pollution and provision of government and tax incentives to install solar panels. The demand for solar cells has gained major traction owing to a surge in rooftop installations. The demand for parabolic troughs and solar power towers in electricity generation is expected to boost the demand for concentrated solar power systems. Based on technology, the global solar energy industry is bifurcated into photovoltaic cells and concentrated solar power systems (CSP). Photovoltaic cells are further segmented into inorganic and organic cells, whereas CSP systems are sub-segmented into parabolic troughs, solar power towers, and others. Accordingly, the solar module market is categorized into monocrystalline silicon cells, polycrystalline silicon cells, cadmium telluride silicon cells, amorphous silicon cells, and others. In the global solar value chain, North America and Europe have largely focused on research to maximize solar potential; Asian countries such as China and Japan have significantly increased the production of solar technologies owing to governmental tariffs and mergers and acquisitions of local manufacturers; and the Middle East and Africa have also gained owing to increases in applications of solar energy for power generation, agriculture, and architecture (McGrath, 2012). The race towards tapping the renewable energy market has been explored via various industrial policy instruments, with the state playing a critical role. It is also important for countries using industrialization strategies to structurally change their industrial composition to consider the new development so that the countries can move forward from being trapped in the so-called "middle-income trap". Given that these countries engage in bringing new industries with new growth potential, and building this requires significant efforts on the part of the government, particularly building the entire ecosystem of a particular industry, various policies and instruments were utilized to promote the renewable energy industry. Nevertheless, less is known about how specific countries undertake their efforts to pursue their goals in committing to climate change and carbon footprint efforts by building renewable energy markets: in our case, the solar energy market in Malaysia.

In this context, this chapter aims to explore the solar industry ecosystem in Malaysia, which has seen significant growth over the last decade. In doing so, we assess Malaysia's dual development goals: to promote its solar industry as an export-orientated industry as well as the development of downstream activities near to user that helped the development of its solar energy uptake in the energy sector, particularly in the electricity market. We examine both the investment and production and the efforts of building the domestic demand in terms of solar energy uptake, particularly in the electricity market. This chapter aims to investigate the following research questions: (1) What policies and institutional settings help to build the solar industry market in Malaysia, both in solar energy uptake and production and supply? (2) What lesson can we learn from Malaysia? and (3) What are the limitations and further actions needed as a way forward in greening the future?

2. Malaysia's Commitment to Climate Change and Carbon Footprint

Malaysia, relative to the emission intensity of GDP in 2005, has committed to reduce its greenhouse gas emissions intensity of GDP by 45% by 2030, which consist of a 35% unconditional commitment and a 10% conditional commitment with financial, technology transfer, and capacity development assistance from the developed world. This commitment requires Malaysia to build its renewable energy uptake and green industrial policy to encourage investment, trade, and production of renewable energy. Examining the sources of CO_2 emissions indicates the electricity and heating sector to be the largest sector contributing to greenhouse gas emissions in Malaysia, representing 130.3 million tonnes of CO_2 equivalents (see Figure 16.1). It is critical that the energy mix in these sectors move towards renewable energy to limit the undesirable externalities to

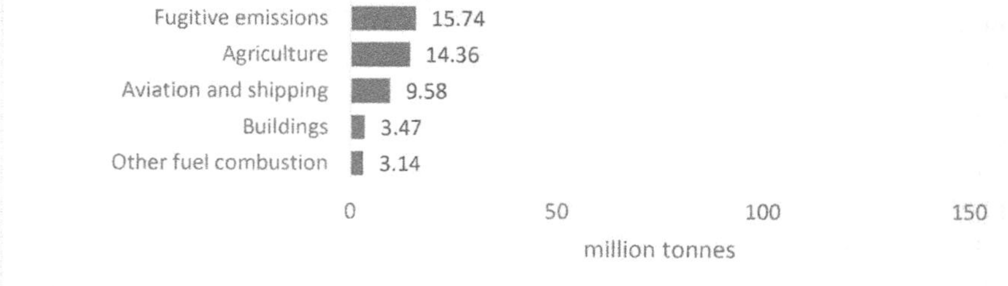

Figure 16.1 Greenhouse Gas Emissions by Sector, Malaysia, 2019

Source: CAIT Climate Data Explorer and Our World in Data

Note: Greenhouse gas emission are measured in tonnes of carbon dioxide-equivalents.

Table 16.1 Primary energy supply (Ktoe), Malaysia, 2010–2018

Years	*Crude Oil*	*Petroleum Products*	*Natural Gas*	*Coal and Coke*	*Hydro power*	*Bio diesel*	*Solar*	*Biomass*	*Biogas*	*Renewable Mix*
2010	22487	2521	35447	14777	1577					
2011	24679	2224	35740	14772	1850	24				2.36
2012	28053	1449	38648	15882	2150	115	11	183	4	2.85
2013	27154	5320	39973	15067	2688	188	38	297	6	3.55
2014	26765	6657	40113	15357	3038	300	63	181	12	3.89
2015	24971	4195	41853	17406	3582	389	75	189	18	4.59
2016	27757	3570	41257	18744	4501	389	90	198	21	5.39
2017	27471	1908	41201	20771	6240	379	93	194	41	7.07
2018	25735	3694	40939	22280	6230	436	172	241	147	7.24

Source: Compiled by authors based on Energy Commission reports.

the environment. Other key sectors include transportation and manufacturing and construction sectors.

The primary energy supply indicates that Malaysia is still relatively low in targeting the renewable energy mix (hydro, biodiesel, solar, biomass, and biogas), with only 7.2% of renewable mix in the total primary energy supply in 2018. Hydro accounts for the highest among the renewable energy supply (Table 16.1). Deliberate policy action by the government indicates the improving solar energy capacity in Malaysia. Given that Malaysia has placed greater potential for solar energy as an important renewable energy source, the government has implemented various policies and institutional frameworks to promote the solar energy market. This includes attempts to build the domestic market for solar energy as well as promoting investment, trade, and production (see Table 16.1).

3. Policies and Institutional Settings

Building the solar industry and promoting the uptake of renewable energy requires adequate institutional and policy framework. Given the risk-averse nature and high uncertainty of any new venture of industries, the government, in most cases, steps forward in driving the initiatives. In doing so, proper policy and institutions are required to drive the supply side of the industries by promoting investments, trade, and production, as well as the building of domestic demand for renewable energy. In the next section, we discuss the policy and institutional setting of Malaysia in promoting the solar market. Our focus is on the energy sectors, specifically the electricity market. In doing so, we assessed the public policy and institutional setting that was aligned to manage the supply and demand of promoting solar energy as an important source of energy mix.

3.1. Building the Solar Industry Ecosystem through Policy and Institutional Setting: Supply and Demand Side

The government in Malaysia has initiated a number of measures to develop the solar industry in Malaysia, including providing various incentives. Understanding the Malaysian solar industry ecosystem is critical to assess the importance of policy and institutional instruments in promoting solar energy uptake in the electricity market. Malaysia was successful in building the needed industrial ecosystem by ensuring the important segments and value chain of the solar industry were promoted via investment and trade. To complement that, the government has also developed downstream activities that are nearer to the user market where the deployment can be further encouraged. It is clear that Malaysia has taken a dual development policy approach, in that the target was to promote the solar industry via the export promotion strategy, while simultaneously trying to build a domestic market for solar energy uptake in the electricity market. In doing so, various policy and institutional settings were formulated.

In promoting the solar industry, the government has taken a value chain approach where the missing gaps are filled up by attracting investments and financing through targeted fiscal incentives and programs (see Table 16.2). Indeed, the first movers within the segments of the value chain were targeted, and time-based incentives were designed and used to promote and complement the industry ecosystem. Common fiscal incentives are tax incentives and allowances. The solar industry can enjoy a 15-year tax holiday, including tax exemptions and investment tax allowance for the purchase of green technology assets[1]. Foreign multinational corporations were allowed 100% ownership to operate in Malaysia. Trade has been liberalized and tariffs for solar panels were virtually eliminated. Likewise, import duty exemptions are given for those operating within the export processing zones.

Tax incentives, particularly for green technologies and assets, feature an important move to encourage the uptake of green technologies. A total of 301 projects (226 solar projects) were approved from 2016–2019 under the Green Investment Tax Allowance (GITA), and 28 services under Green Income Tax Exemption (GITE)[2] (MGTC, 2019). Other facilitations such as customs and trade facilitation including trade promotion were critical. Institutional settings include the role of Malaysian Investment Development Authority (MIDA) and Malaysia External Trade Development Corporation (MATRADE) in ensuring the right investment and promotional activities are fostered with the sectors.

In addition, the Green Technology Financing Scheme (GTFS) was established to support green technology. The financing policy and program was instrumental in supporting the development of green technologies, including solar. Indeed, most of this financing goes to supporting solar technologies[3]. The scheme was announced in 2010 with financing amounting to RM 1.5 billion with an additional allocation of 2 billion in 2013 to 2017. The financing was not only instrumental in supporting the industry; it was critical in bringing additional investment in the industry as well as creating green jobs. A total of RM 3.6 billion was financed under the scheme, with 319 projects (85 projects in the energy sector) and 28 participating financial institutions between 2010 to 2017 (MGTC, 2019). The project has also brought in RM 7.053 billion in green investment values. Additionally, in April 2018, a financing amount of 5 billion was announced under the so-called GTFS 2.0. The scheme was discontinued due to the change of government in May 2018; however, beginning in March 2019 it was continued until the end of 2020. GTFS 2.0 have nearly approved RM 900 million of funding with 28 participating financial institutions[4].

Likewise, in the capital market, development of the sukuk and green bonds was kickstarted in 2014. The Sustainable and Responsible Investment Sukuk Framework was established by the Securities Commission Malaysia in 2014. Green bonds and green sukuk markets started to expand in 2017 with the emergence of the renewable energy sector in Malaysia (Chandran, 2021). By January 2021, Malaysia was one of the leading economies in the issuance of sukuk with 16 sukuk. Facilitating financing access largely depends on the critical role played by Malaysian Green Technology Corporation, Security Commissions, Central Bank, and financial institutions.

Apart from incentives and programs to promote investment, it is critical that policy coordination is also established to promote renewable energy in the domestic markets. Without targeted policy framework, the incentives for firms and consumers to adopt and deploy renewable energy, more specifically solar energy, is critical. Table 16.3 summarizes the critical policy framework adopted in moving forward the energy sectors onto a greener path. In 2000, Malaysia engaged in establishing renewable energy as the fifth energy source, targeting 5% of its energy mix. Progressively, the government initiated various other policies and programs in achieving its renewable energy targets. The deployment strategies are mainly to levelize the cost of renewable energy so that the demand can be promoted. Programs such as Feed-in-Tariff (FiT) (2011), Net Energy Metering (NEM), and Large-Scale Solar (LSS) (2016) allow the government to build the renewable energy market. Innovative approaches, such as peer-to-peer energy trading (P2P), were launched in 2019. The trial phase of P2P is ongoing, where data is collected to assess the viability. P2P allows households to sell renewable energy directly to others, and power companies will not be part of the process. Likewise, the Supply Agreement for Renewable Energy (SARE) program allows consumers to lease solar panels without having to pay for the upfront cost of installation, but instead pay a monthly leasing fee with the capacity to generate solar energy. Critically, these programs aided the development of the solar industry, especially the downstream activities.

These policies and programs helped Malaysia build its solar ecosystem. Three distinct broad segments of the solar industry can be identified (see Table 16.4). First are the module segments: the product (solar panels) that involves the manufacturing sectors and processes that range from

Table 16.2 Fiscal incentives and programs

Incentives/Programs	*Description*
Investment and Tax Incentives	(1) Pioneer status with tax exemption of 100% of statutory income, and an extension of the pioneer status from 5 years to 10 years; (2) Investment tax allowance of 100% on qualifying capital expenditures incurred within a 5-year period, with the allowance offset against 100% of statutory income for each year of assessment; and (3) 100% Foreign Ownership Structure (4) Green Technology Tax Incentive – Green Investment Tax Allowance and Green Income Tax Exemption
Trade Policy	(1) Export Processing Zone (2) Trade liberalization – 0% Tariff Rates for Solar Panels (3) Import Duty exemptions
Financing	(1) Green Technology Financing Scheme- Total loan amount of RM 3.5 billion for producers (max RM 50 million) and users of green technology (max RM 10 million) with 2% interest subsidy by the government & 60% government guarantee.
Capital Market Financing	Green Sukuk and Bond Market – Establishment of Sustainable Responsible Investment Sukuk Framework to complement the other incentives and financing schemes.

Source: Chandran (2017) (updated)

the development of polysilicon, wafers, cells, and modules based on the upstream activities (**Segment 1** of the value chain – upstream activities). On the other hand, the system integrators and the BOS (**Segment 2** – downstream activities) play a critical role in the deployment of solar energy in the domestic market. Apart from that, other services industries (**Segment 3** – downstream activities) involved in supplying components such as cables, mounting, tracking systems, and other electrical components are also critical. Services such as project development, wholesale distribution, design, engineering, construction, and maintenance also play a critical role in supporting the deployment of solar energy in the local market via large-scale projects.

In building Segment 1 of the solar value chain, the government has utilized its trade and investment policy successfully. Malaysia largely depends on foreign direct investment in driving the capital-intensive industries in the upstream segments. Using the incentives system, Malaysia managed to attract key global players within the segment. Companies such as First Solar, Panasonic, SunPower, Nanopac, JA Solar, LONGi, Jinko Solar, and Hanwha Q-CELLS to name a few, have their manufacturing base in Malaysia producing cells and modules. OCI Specialty of the Republic of Korea is involved in the polycrystalline silicon manufacturing by acquiring it from Tokuyama.

Table 16.3 RE policies and institutions

2000	Fifth Fuel Policy – Targeting Renewable Energy as the fifth energy source – Target of 5% in energy mix by 2005.
2001	Small Renewable Energy Program (SREP) – Program to develop and intensify utilization of RE as the fifth energy source.
2005	Malaysia Building Integrated Photovoltaic (MBIPV) Program – Jointly funded by Global Environment Facility and the Government of Malaysia to accelerate policy, technology, and market development of PV as a RE source.
2006	Malaysia Development Plan (9th Malaysia Plan) – Target of 350MW RE installation by 2010.
2009	Establishment of Ministry of Energy, Green Technology, and Water – The ministry will be in charge of driving the development of RE and green technology through planning and formulating policies for the green technology sector.
	National Green Technology Policy – Green technology identified as a driver to promote economy and sustainable development.
2010	National Renewable Energy Policy and Action Plan – Positions RE as an important component of national energy mix, and propose strategies for widespread application of RE.
2011	Renewable Energy Act – Introduction of Renewable Energy Fund and feed-in-tariff for four types of RE including PV, biomass, biogas, and small hydro.
	Sustainable Energy Development Authority Act – Establishment of Sustainable Energy Development Authority (SEDA)
	Feed-in-Tariff program with the establishment of Renewable Energy Fund
2016	Net Energy Metering – Installation of PV system primarily for own use with excess electricity exported to grid. At present, 3 series of NEM have been launched
	Large-Scale Solar Program – Solar power plants in the range of 1–50MW to be awarded through bidding process.
	MySuria – Installation of PV systems on houses of B40 group, with FiT paid to the house for the duration of 10 years.
2017	Malaysia Green Technology Master Plan 2017–2030 (GTMP)
2019	Supply Agreement for Renewable Energy (SARE)
	Peer-to-Peer Solar Energy Trading (P2P)

Source: Chandran (2016 & 2017), updated

Development of these segments helped Malaysia to promote exports of PV solar. Within the module segment, a large number of local manufacturers have invested: namely, Malaysian Solar Resources, Solartif, Promelight, and PV Hi Tech[5]. Some of these companies also participate in large-scale solar farm initiatives, hence promoting the solar energy deployment. For instance, LONGi was awarded to supply modules to 2 of the 5 projects under the Large-Scale Solar for commercial operation in 2021. The project is expected to generate 190MW solar energy to achieve the government target of 20%

of RE by 2025 (LONGi, 2021[6]). In 2016, the MIDA survey of the top solar firms indicates that the industry exports around RM 11.1 billion with local sourcing of RM 1.42 billion (Lee, 2017). According to market research, in 2015, the total global shipment of solar PV amounted to 50.8GW, with China contributing 48%, Taiwan 20%, Malaysia 12%, and Japan 6%. Malaysia aimed to emerge as the world's second-largest PV producer by 2020 by increasing the current output of 12% of global production to 20% (Malaysian Reserve, 2017). With the trade war between China and the US, Malaysia is home to many Chinese solar manufacturers. The relocation was mainly due to the fact that China wants to take advantage of the growing Asia Pacific market for solar energy.

In driving Segments 2 and 3 of the industry, which are near the end-user of the solar value chain, the domestic deployment programs and policies were instrumental. Malaysia sets a tall order in terms of targets of a renewable energy mix at 20% by 2025. For this, various policies were put forth, and we critically assessed the policy initiatives. On analyzing the demand side of how policy and institutions work, we focus on the deployment of the solar energy in Malaysia. Solar has been earmarked as one of the potential sources of renewable energy within the electricity market, given the geographical position of Malaysia where the potential of the sun can be leveraged. Nevertheless, the transition towards solar and decarbonizing the supply side requires close engagement with the deployment at the end user, which is closely linked to the demand side management. As such, due to market failures on the side of deployment, given its cost and other factors, a range of policy instruments is needed to promote deployment strategies. It is also important to note that domestic deployment could further leverage the cost reduction that allows subsequent installation to be cheaper since economies of scale can kick-start. Malaysia has experimented with various policies, and the learning curve on investment provides insights on the demand management. The critical policies and programs include SREP/MBIPV, FiT, NEM, LSS, and MySuria. Table 16.5 shows the targeted capacity of the solar energy. With these targets, the domestic players were able to play a critical role in supplying the needed installation capacity.

Since 2005, the downstream industry of the solar PV has kickstarted with the implementation of the Malaysia Building Integrated PV (MBIPV) program, which is funded by the Malaysian government and the Global Environment Facility and implemented by the United Nations Development Program. The program also developed the capacity for Malaysia in designing policy and awareness as well as technical, market, and technological skills. With the Renewable Energy Act enactment in 2011, the establishment of Feed-in-Tariff (FiT) funded by the Renewable Energy Fund marks the significant development of the downstream industry. The FiT system administrated by Sustainable Energy Development Authority (SEDA) allows the sales of electricity from RE systems at a fixed premium price for 21 years.

Table 16.4 Solar industry value chain

Segment	*Companies*	*Segment*
Polysilicon	OCI	Polysilicon productions
Ingot	LONGi	Ingot production of crystal pulling, machining and polishing
Wafer	LONGi; Panasonic	Wafer fabrication
Cells	Panasonic; Hanwha Q-Cells; LONGi; Jinko Solar; JA Solar; SunPower; TS Solartech	Cells
Module	Panasonic; Hanwha Q-Cells; Jinko Solar; Trina Solar; Yingli Solar; First Solar; Nanopac; Flextronics; Solartif; PV HiTech; Malaysian Solar Resources; Promelight	Solar PV modules
Balance of System	ETI Tech; Tamura Electronics; Huber + Suhner; ABB; Schneider Electric; EM Kabel; KVC Industry Supplies; Ezis; Misa; Superspan; Barysol; Sunrise Prima	BOS equipment such as batteries, inverters, circuit-breakers, cables and mounting structures comprise all the equipment in a PV system
System Integrators[1]	Largest segment with estimated 150 companies	Leveraging the domestic market – installation at residential, commercial and large-scale solar farms

Note: [1]Malaysian Photovoltaic Industry Association represents the segment.
Source: MIGHT (2015) and Chandran and Wong (2019)

And with the grid connectivity, the solar PV market recorded substantial growth. FiT scheme alone allocated 450 MW of renewable energy.

With the discontinued FiT scheme in 2017, new schemes were established. The Net Energy Metering (NEM) and Large-Scale Solar (LSS) allowed the installed capacity to increase further. From 2016 to 2020, 500 MW was allocated for NEM, while the newly launched NEM 3.0 allocated additional 400 MW. Three series of LSS projects allocating 1.3 GW of renewable energy capacity have been launched since 2016. Specifically, the third LSS was announced in 2019 with a RM 2 billion project with a 500 MW capacity. Through competitive bidding, the solar tariff was brought down as low as RM 0.1777, which is lower than the gas-dependent power generation that stands at RM 0.32 per KWh[7]. In March 2021, 30 bidders were announced for the fourth LSS, which allocates 1 Gigawatt that would generate 823 MW energy. In addition, the MySuria program, launched in 2017, aims

Table 16.5 Targeted installation capacity under various programs

Policy	*2001–2011*	*2012–2015*	*2016*	*2017*	*2018*	*2019*	*2020*	*2021–2023*
SREP/MBIPV	2MW							
FiT		450MW						
NEM			100MW	100MW	100MW	100MW	100MW	400MW
LSS				1.3 GW				1 GW
MySuria					4.86MW			

Note: * Achieved as of April 2021.
Source: Sustainable Energy Development Authority (SEDA), Malaysia[8]; and Energy Commission (2021).

to promote 1,620 households from the bottom 40% to generate income through the renewable energy scheme. It is important to note that building the solar industry ecosystem is critical in the downstream, namely the balance of system and system integrators industries within the value chain that have implications for the domestic uptake of renewable energy. In 2017, Malaysia launched the Malaysian Solar PV Roadmap 2030 to drive the country's solar PV industry forward, and it is ranked as the world's third-largest producer of PV cells and modules.

4. Key Lessons, Limitations, and Alternative Policy Options

Critical success factors for the development of the solar market were the ability to coordinate policies that were instrumental at various levels, from investment, trade, finance, and domestic mechanism, to mitigate the risk of the technologies as well as reduce the cost of adoption for the end user. This section discusses the key lessons from the case of Malaysia in building its solar energy market ecosystem. With it, we discuss some limitations and alternative policy options that would complement the current efforts. We discuss the lessons by assessing the major policies that facilitated the energy transition process.

4.1. Investment and Trade Policy

Malaysia was able to design critical investment policies to attract firms to invest in Malaysia. Malaysia's long experience in attracting foreign investment was instrumental in designing an effective investment policy, and the learning experience of MIDA was able to allow Malaysia to design a complete ecosystem for the solar industry. In terms of trade policy, trade liberalization with the reduction in tariff rate for modules has allowed Malaysia to deploy the technologies. Nevertheless, the fact remains that in reducing the domestic cost of solar technology adoptions, trade barriers in other supporting sectors are critical. For instance, cables, batteries, and inverters are important components that go into installation of the solar panels. However, the average ad valorem tariff rates remained high, adding cost to the overall solar panel and installations. The average tariff for batteries (critical for energy storage) is 20%, while for cables it stands at 30%. Likewise, for fuses and breakers and surge protection devices, the tariffs are 15%. The industry indicates that these components are mostly sourced from abroad, namely from Germany, Switzerland, Italy, the US, Spain, the UK, Taiwan, and China. It suggests that policy-makers should be thinking of liberalizing the other sectors related to solar panel production to encourage the progress of the industry, as well as to reap the welfare gains for the end users.

Other limitations include the inability of the other actors in the value chain to buy the cells or solar panels directly from the manufacturers in Malaysia. For instance, system integrators are unable to purchase those items locally due to the requirements that module producers are mainly encouraged to export their products. This limits the emergence of new creative industry that would otherwise be able to assemble their modules in a more cost-effective way.

4.2. Financing Policy and Framework

Malaysia has used various investment and financing instruments in promoting and supporting the solar industry. However, de-risking investment does not only depend on ensuring that adequate financing is available for the industry. It is equally important to understand how fuel subsidies are limiting the investments, as well as how depending entirely on national energy companies would crowd out investment in renewables. Additionally, de-risking involves ensuring that financial institutions are capable of assessing the risk of new technologies in a more adequate way so that they can become less risk-averse. Learning on risk assessment of new technologies allows banking and financial institutions to come forward to offer financial services more willingly, without as much guarantee from the government side. More work is needed in reporting and managing green technology risk, regulatory framework for green technology assets, deployment of incentives for green investment (including via public procurement), as well as integrating green technology risks into financial sectors regulations and the environmental, social, and governance framework. Blended financing in managing risk is becoming a potential solution. All these require proactive updating and innovative solutions on designing financial regulatory framework.

4.3. Deployment Approach and Policies

Malaysia's deployment approach and policies are largely concentrated on the levelized cost of energy by introducing adequate mechanisms such as FiT, NEM, and LSS. While these are the global standards deployment strategies, Malaysia also requires other complementary policies. The first is the need to assess the effectiveness and efficiency of such subsidies so that institutions can internalize the knowledge and design better policies and programs.

The complementary policies should target the barriers faced in the deployment of solar energy. The first is barrier-free connectivity to the grid, where diversification of renewable energy technology adopters and owners can play a critical role. Indeed, encouraging standardization enables sharing and integration of systems, as well as allows systems integrators to share knowledge and information. For instance, rooftop installers could internalize standards with regards to installation steps and system integrations, relying on other parties to involve in the process. Other non-carbon price-based policies include green technology certification[9] as well as consumer standards. Indeed, government may promote the uptake of certain technologies through regulatory amendments. For instance, the green building codes and index established by Malaysia would be critical. Sectoral policies for other industrial sectors are also important for the deployment of solar energy. This should be aligned with the industrial and specific sectorial policies and roadmaps.

In improving the demand for solar energy, Malaysia has designed various programs to increase the uptake of solar technologies. Demand management is critical in that the domestic market adopts technology and engages in renewable energy usage. However, shifting demand for renewable energy requires deliberate actions on the part of the government in the following aspects: (1) reducing the peak demand for electricity, shifting it to non-peak hours through time-of-use tariffs; (2) promoting significant energy-saving technologies to industries; and (3) reducing the transaction cost related to energy transitions – e.g. the managing of stranded assets and others.

4.4. Research and Development and Innovation

While policies and programs were critically well coordinated, the other missing link is the support for Research and Development (R&D) with regards to renewable energy. The ecosystem remained limited with participation of universities in undertaking renewable energy research. Predominantly, R&D activities remained weak among the industrial sectors, and more so by system integrators and balance of systems. Indeed, service providers need to be more innovative in finding solutions to minimize cost of adoption. The idea of capital incentives and technology adoption financing should be complemented by the idea of leveraging the cost of learning by the stakeholders within the value chain to be innovative. For instance, learning and financing innovative solutions among the solar panel manufacturers, BOS, and system integrators could be more instrumental in reducing the solar panel adoption cost. So could the system integrators who could accumulate learning experience in integrating various components and connectivity systems to allow standardization with minimal customization to leverage on the economies of scale for applications like rooftops and other small solar energy generations. Achieving all this requires greater support systems for R&D, and public-private partnership is essential. Indeed, system integrators could also move into other segments of the market, integrating themselves vertically to reduce the cost of the system at large. Vertical integration would also mean that domestic players can expand their businesses. However, it should be noted that vertical integration should be exercised in a path that allows cost reduction and not market dominance. Therefore, government policy facilitation is required so that the vertical integration is solely to encourage innovation and R&D. Another approach is to create a consortium to encourage R&D and innovation activities across and within certain segments of the industry. Policy and program design are crucial in these aspects.

4.5. Managing Market Uncertainty

As government policies and programs drive solar energy, the progress of the solar industry is also largely dependent on the continuity of the policies and programs, globally and domestically. Given the fiscal constraints added by the pandemic with reallocation for health and other measures, it is often seen that the programs are less sustainable under economic uncertainty. While the EU focuses on developing its green industry as the recovery plan, others in Asia, including Malaysia, have not placed solar industry and the green industry as its frontier sectors to move forward. Managing uncertainty requires policy continuality and most importantly, long-term policy commitments to manage uncertainty.

5. Concluding Remarks

Malaysia has been successful in building its solar industry market using various policies and programs with dedicated institutional settings. Its ability to learn and progress in designing new mechanisms does not only help build the upstream industry but also local business at the downstream activities. This includes manufacturers of solar panels as well as system integrators, supporting industries, and other service providers. Some of the initiatives were also instrumental in democratizing technology to benefit poor households. What started as a rural electrification project and industrial development strategies have moved into building a more resilient green industrial policy combining industrial development paths with exportation and building a domestic market to achieve Malaysia's renewable targets. In the upstream activities, the role of investment and trade was critical and with high capital-intensive industries, the role of MNCs have provided the impetus for Malaysia to gain traction. The participation in the global value chain offered Malaysia a way to build its upstream activities. Institutions specifically designed for investment and trade promotion activities were crucial in building the industrial ecosystem. Likewise, the building of the domestic market for solar is dependent entirely on the renewable energy policy and programs. However, the deployment of solar PV in the domestic market is still limited and achieving its renewable energy target requires much effort. On a positive note, Malaysia can serve as a model for other countries that aim to develop their solar potential to contribute towards the renewable target. The lessons and limitations serve as a critical juncture for countries to learn how public policies and programs can be designed to help build new industries. What is critical is the policy learning and coordination among various stakeholders within the industrial ecosystem.

Notes

1 A company approved with a Pioneer Status certificate can enjoy income tax exemption between 70% – 100% of statutory income for 5 to 10 years, whereas for Investment Tax Allowance, a company can get allowances between 60% – 100% on qualifying capital expenditure incurred within a period of 5 to 10 years.
2 GITA is for companies that qualify for green technology (assets) projects for business and own consumption, while GITE is for qualified green technology services providers. Please refer to Malaysia Green Technology Corporation's annual report available at www.mgtc.gov.my/annualreport2019/download/Annual-Report2019.pdf
3 Based on the GTFS as of 2015, 40% of the financing goes to solar technologies.
4 Based on the GreenTech Malaysia website figures, available at www.gtfs.my/
5 MSR and Solartif are also involved in system integration.
6 Press release available at https://en.longi-solar.com/home/events/press_detail/id/320.html
7 Refer to https://aseanenergy.org/asean-solar-sector-2019-highlights/
8 Refer to www.seda.gov.my/ and www.st.gov.my/en/
9 Malaysia has already launched the MyHijau program that certifies products and services that meet local and international environmental standards under one single mark.

References

Allied Market Research. (2014). *Solar energy market-Global opportunity analysis & industry forecast, 2014–2022*. Allied Market Research. Available at: www.alliedmarketresearch.com/solar-energy-market

Chandran V.G.R. (2016). Greening the economy with low carbon energy system: developments, policy initiatives and lessons from Malaysia. In: Anbumozhi V., Kalirajan K., Kimura F., & Yao X. (eds) *Investing on Low-Carbon Energy Systems*. Springer, Singapore. https://doi.org/10.1007/978-981-10-0761-3_5.

Chandran V.G.R. (2017). INDC and low-carbon technology deployment scenarios: Malaysia. In: Kalirajan, K., & Anbu, V. (eds) *Globalization of Low-Carbon Technologies: The Impact of the Paris Agreement* (pp. 115–148). Springer, Singapore.

Chandran V.G.R. (2022). Trade, sustainability and finance: Leveraging on sustainable trade financing instruments and policy framework. In Rajah R., Gopi, K. & Azleen O.R. eds, *Financing Sustainability Critical Issues with East Asian Experiences* (pp. 37–56). University of Malaya Press, Malaysia.

Chandran V.G.R. & Wong, P.W. (2019). Spatial re-localisation in global production networks: a path creation perspective of Solar Panel Industry in Malaysia, presented at UNU-MERIT.

Energy Commission. (2021). *The Energy Commission's statement on natural gas price review for non-electricity sector in Peninsular Malaysia*. Retrieved from www.st.gov.my/en/web/consumer/details/2/10.

International Energy Agency. (2019). *Africa Energy Outlook 2019*. IEA, Paris. Available at: www.iea.org/africa2019

Lee, J. (2017, June 19). A growing solar industry. *The Star Online*. Available at: www.thestar.com.my/metro/smebiz/focus/2017/06/19/a-growing-solar-industry/.

LONGi. (2021, April 9). *LONGi to supply modules for projects in Malaysia's latest LSS3 tender*. Retrieved from https://en.longi-solar.com/home/events/press_detail/id/320.html.

Malaysian Reserve. (2017, April 3). Malaysia to be hub for solar cell manufacturing by 2030. *Malaysian Reserve*. Available at: https://themalaysianreserve.com/2017/04/03/malaysia-to-be-hub-for-solar-cell-manufacturing-by-2030/.

McGrath, M. (2012, January 23). Solar storm as desert plan to power Europe falters. *BBC*. Available at: www.bbc.co.uk/news/science-environment-20357167.

MGTC. (2019). *Greening the future, annual report 2019*. Malaysian Green Technology Corporation. Available at: www.mgtc.gov.my/annualreport2019/download/AnnualReport2019.pdf.

MIGHT. (2015). *Solar industry survey 2015. Unpublished datasets*. Malaysia Industry Group for High Technology, Cyberjaya, Malaysia.

Chapter 17

Mission-Oriented Innovation Systems in the Climate Change Context

The Case of Agriculture and Renewable Energy Sector in India

Manish Anand[1], *Rita Pandey*[2] *and Shailly Kedia*[3]

1. Introduction

Narrow sector-specific approaches to foster basic research and develop specific technologies in accordance with state-defined goals in sectors such as defence, nuclear, space, telecommunications, energy, and agriculture have been pursued in the past and are high on the agenda of many nations. These technology-specific approaches set concrete directions with clearly defined goals, objectives, and challenges; are usually state-sponsored and centrally administered; are generally undertaken by a small group of experts and firms; and have a focus on technical achievements, with little regard for their social acceptance and economic feasibility (Robinson & Mazzucato, 2019; Soete & Arundel, 1993). These approaches had a strong focus on scientific and technological solutions. For instance, the 'Green Revolution' in agriculture was marked by productivity growth and modernization brought about by intensive use of high-yielding seed varieties, irrigation, chemical fertilizers, and pesticides (Wright, 2012). Similarly, in the energy sector, the focus has been on the development and diffusion of renewable energy technologies, with scant attention paid to how the potential of these technologies can be realized in substantially transforming the energy sector (Jacobsson & Bergek, 2004). In other words, earlier approaches were often seen from a science and technology systems perspective rather than an innovation systems perspective, embodying dynamic links between a variety of actors and institutions (Freeman, 1995).

Current grand societal and socio-economic challenges like climate change, loss of biodiversity and degradation of ecosystem integrity, and ageing problems in Western nations have led to the adoption of 'mission'-oriented approaches by policy-makers in terms of setting concrete directions and facilitating a portfolio of innovation projects in the key sectors (Mazzucato, 2018; Fisher et al., 2018; Georghiou et al., 2018). Unlike 'narrow' science and technology system-based mission approaches of the past, in modern times mission-oriented policies to address grand challenges

DOI: 10.4324/9781003353904-21

are socio-economic and not just technical, are characterized by complexity owing to fewer clear technological challenges, and are often not related to well-defined outcomes (Foray, 2005). In these modern 'broad-based' mission-oriented policies, grand societal challenges are defined with a complex mix of goals and objectives, have multiple sources of financing, and there is a decentralized control with a wide range of actors involved across many value chains and innovation ecosystems (Robinson & Mazzucato, 2019). This has inspired innovation scholars to analyze the mission-oriented policies from an innovation systems perspective, introducing the concept of mission-oriented innovation systems (Hekkert et al., 2020).

India, under the National Action Plan on Climate Change (NAPCC), prepared in 2008, had adopted several missions including the National Solar Mission, National Mission for Enhanced Energy Efficiency, National Mission on Sustainable Habitat, National Water Mission, National Mission for Sustaining the Himalayan Ecosystem, National Mission for a Green India, National Mission for Sustainable Agriculture, and National Mission on Strategic Knowledge for Climate Change (GOI, 2008). These missions were intended to serve as a roadmap for how India plans to combat climate change, uniting it with the country's development concerns and the need to sustain economic growth. Further, the Draft Fifth Science, Technology, and Innovation Policy (STIP) 2020 of India aims at bringing profound changes via short-term, medium-term, and long-term mission mode projects in alignment with the United Nations' Sustainable Development Goals (UN-SDGs) (GOI, 2020). This aims to achieve a nurtured ecosystem that promotes research and innovation on the part of individuals and organizations, as well as providing renewed impetus to the mainstreaming of equity and inclusion.

This chapter examines the case of National Missions on sustainable agriculture and renewable energy under NAPCC, using the concept of mission-oriented innovation systems. Analysis of the Missions in the context of their respective innovation ecosystems is undertaken for critically reflecting upon "how mission-oriented policies are nationally and supra-nationally embedded and how this loops back on the process of innovation and system change" (Klerkx & Begemann, 2020). To this end, the chapter adopts a 'structural-functional approach' to examine the evolution of a mission-oriented innovation system in the sectors concerned. The basis of choosing these two missions is their relevance to both basic human development needs and to environmental sustainability. The remainder of this chapter is organized as follows. First, we explain the theoretical perspectives and the analytical framework for undertaking such an analysis. Second, we map and analyze the contours and dynamics of the innovation ecosystems, taking the case of the National Mission on Sustainable Agriculture and National Solar Mission, by delineating the structure (actors, networks and institutions) and the key processes – also labelled as functions of innovation systems –

that are being served or need to be served for system build-up. Third, the evolution of mission-oriented innovation systems in the agriculture and renewable energy sector is discussed and analyzed. Finally, the concluding observations based on the analytical insights derived from the study are presented.

2. Literature Review and Analytical Framework

Several innovation system theories have been developed since the 1980s based on the different boundaries of the system, such as national innovation systems (Freeman, 1988; Lundvall, 1992; Nelson, 1993; Edquist & Johnson, 1996), regional innovation systems (Cooke, 1992), sectoral innovation systems focusing on firm-level or sectoral boundaries (Breschi & Malerba, 1997), international systems of innovation (Fromhold-Eisebith, 2006; Desai, 2009), and technological innovation systems (Carlsson & Stankiewicz, 1991; Bergek et al., 2008; Hekkert et al., 2007; Markard & Truffer, 2008), focusing on technological fields as the level of analysis. Looking at these different models, the notion common to all of them is to explain how an innovation system develops, diffuses, and utilizes innovations (technological, social, institutional innovation) within different contexts, taking into account a broad set of societal factors driving and directing innovation. Innovation studies scholars have proposed analyzing innovation systems both in terms of their structural components (described by the constituent elements: actor, networks, and institutions), as well as their functional components (diagnosis of various functions which provide valuable insights in the dynamics and performance of the innovation system) (Hekkert et al., 2007). Such analysis can help develop targeted innovation policies to fix market and systems failures.

Though innovation systems theory provides a heuristic framework that enables optimization of system performance in terms of nature and quality of the interactions of actors, the framework has limitations in terms of addressing directional failures and in creating, shaping, and directing markets and industries towards transformative change (Weber & Rohracher, 2012). To this end, the concept of a mission-oriented innovation systems approach has been introduced by scholars (Robinson & Mazzucato, 2019; Hekkert et al., 2020). The concept of mission-oriented innovation systems is defined as "the network of agents and set of institutions that contribute to the development and diffusion of innovative solutions with the aim to define, pursue and complete a societal mission" (Hekkert et al., 2020: 77). The mission-oriented policy approach, which serves as an intermediary layer to translate the broad societal and socio-economic challenges into concrete actions (Mazzucato, 2017), makes an interesting case for analysis by innovation scholars. Identification of gaps and opportunities for mainstreaming these missions provide avenues for studying innovation systems as mission-oriented innovation systems. This would create insights for policy-makers and relevant actors on directionality, equity, and inclusivity of innovation systems, and devise policy mixes for enabling sustainability transformations in the sectors concerned.

The literature on mission-oriented innovation systems is emergent and currently focused in the setting of the global North. The concept can be applied to the setting of developing countries like India to critically reflect on the missions undertaken to address environmental and development-related challenges. Figure 17.1 illustrates the structure, dynamics, functions, and trajectories of an innovation system in the context of National Missions towards a mission-oriented innovation system. The structural-functional analysis of innovation systems in the context of national missions permits a more systematic method of mapping determinants of innovation, and has the potential to fix directional failures by delivering a clear set of policy targets as well as instruments to meet these targets. To critically reflect on how the missions, and the sub-missions that underpin them, are embedded nationally in their respective innovation ecosystems, the analytical framework aims at: mapping the diversity of actors and identifying the actors relevant for mainstreaming the missions; mapping the network of actors driving innovation systems and the relevant networks required for mainstreaming mission and systems-building in the desired direction; understanding institutional arrangements and the need to redesign them towards addressing the grand challenges and understanding the characteristics of the innovation system in terms of functions fulfilment and pressures, drivers, and barriers towards sustainability transformations. For types of functions for developing

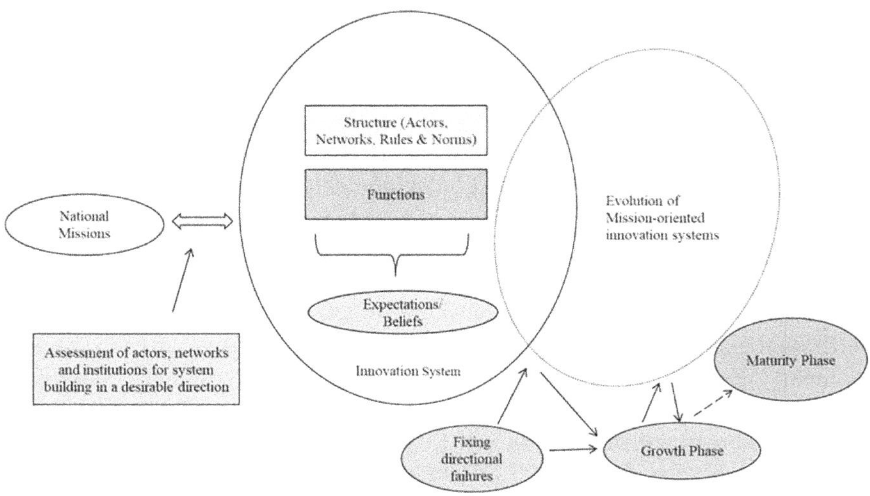

Figure 17.1 Analytical Framework

countries, seven functions will be considered based on Edsand (2016) and Esmailzadeh et al. (2020). These seven functions include: knowledge development[4]; resource mobilization[5]; market formation[6]; guidance of the search[7]; knowledge diffusion[8]; entrepreneurial activities[9]; and institutionalization and legitimation[10]. Within knowledge development, two aspects of absorptive capacity and technological learning will be considered. In addition, to address directionality dilemma, co-benefit, life-cycle, and multi-stakeholder approaches will be considered to better understand aspects related to environmental and social benefits (Urmetzer & Pyka, 2019).

3. Innovation Ecosystems Linked to Societal Challenges

3.1. The Case of National Mission for Sustainable Agriculture

According to the National Action Plan on Climate Change (NAPCC), the National Mission for Sustainable Agriculture (NMSA) would aim to devise strategies to make Indian agriculture more resilient to climate change (GOI, 2008: 7). Thus, NMSA derives its mandate from NAPCC. According to NAPCC, the role of "agricultural research systems" should be oriented to monitor and evaluate climate change and recommend changes in agricultural practices accordingly. NMSA is envisaged to focus on four areas crucial to agriculture in adapting to climate change, namely dryland agriculture, risk management, access to information, and use of biotechnology (GOI, 2008: 36).

The Department of Agriculture and Farmers Welfare (DOAFW) under the Ministry of Agriculture & Farmers Welfare (MOAFW) is the nodal ministry for the implementation of NMSA. The NMSA Mission Document, accorded 'in principle' approval by Prime Minister's Council on Climate Change (PMCCC) in September 2010, aims at promoting sustainable agriculture through adaptation by focusing on ten key dimensions encompassing Indian agriculture namely: "improved crop seeds, livestock, and fish cultures, water use efficiency, pest management, improved farm practices, nutrient management, agricultural insurance, credit support, markets, access to information, and livelihood diversification" (MOAFW, 2019).

At the national level, for NMSA, there is a National Advisory Committee (NAC) under Chairmanship of Secretary (Agriculture and Cooperation) with members from Ministry of Water Resources, Ministry of Rural Development, Ministry of Panchayati Raj, Ministry of Environment, Forest & Climate Change, Ministry of Food Processing Industries, Ministry of Tribal Affairs, Department of Agricultural Research & Education, Department of Animal Husbandry Dairying & Fisheries, Department of Land Resources, National Rainfed Area Authority, and Department of Agriculture & Farmers Welfare. At the state level, the State Level Committee (SLC) will oversee planning and implementation of the Mission. States also have an option to set up an autonomous State Mission for Sustainable Agriculture (SMSA) for implementation of NMSA. At the district level, District Mission Committee (DMC) will be entrusted with project formulation and implementation and monitoring of NMSA. Notably, at the national level, there is an absence of a representative from the Ministry of Science and Technology (MOST), since under NAPCC there is also a focus on climate risks. MOST is the nodal ministry of the National Mission on Strategic Knowledge for Climate Change (NMSKCC), which is also crucial for understanding the climate scenarios and resulting impacts. The linkage with the crop insurance scheme of 'Pradhan Mantri Fasal Bima Yojana' is also unclear.

A Project Sanctioning Committee (PSC) prioritizes and approves projects under NMSA. The Standing Technical Committee (STC) at the national level aims to provide knowledge support and technical feedback to the Project Sanctioning Committee and National Advisory Committee of NMSA to decide the policy content or change in any component if required. The STC is envisaged to be represented by Central Research Institute for Dryland Agriculture, Central Arid Zone Research Institute, Indian Council of Agricultural Research, Indian Institute of Soil Science, Indian Agricultural Research Institute, selected State Agricultural Universities, and professionals of national/international eminence. Climate Change Cell (CCC) of DOAFW, along with Soil & Land Use Survey of India (SLUSI), is expected to serve as a knowledge networking centre. Soil and Land Use Survey of India, National Centre of Organic Farming, and Central Fertilizer Quality Control & Training Institute are expected to serve as subordinate organizations/for the implementation and monitoring of NMSA.

There are five components under NMSA: Rainfed Area Development (RAD); Sub-Mission on Agroforestry (SMAF); National Bamboo Mission (NBM); Soil Health Management (SHM); and Climate Change and Sustainable Agriculture: Monitoring, Modeling and Networking (CCSAMMN).

As per the report 'Performance of the National Action Plan on Climate Change (NAPCC)' of the Committee on Estimates of the Lok Sabha Secretariat, some scientific endeavours were identified under NMSA (LSS, 2018). These include the development of InfoCrop, indigenously developed at the Centre for Environment Science and Climate Resilient Agriculture (CESCRA) of IARI, which is a generic crop model that simulates the effects of weather, soils, agronomic management (planting, nitrogen, residues, and irrigation), and major pests on crop growth, yield, soil carbon, nitrogen, and water, and greenhouse gas emissions. Another aspect mentioned is the National Innovation for Climate Resilient Agriculture (NICRA), which in 2012 identified about 450 climate-resilient varieties of crops.

Beyond some activities of RAD, SMAF, NBM and SHM, outcomes of "improved crop seeds, livestock and fish cultures, water use efficiency, pest management, improved farm practices, nutrient management, agricultural insurance, credit support, markets, access to information, and livelihood diversification" are not presently monitored. A key gap in the present structure of NMSA is the lack of monitoring of the CCSAMMN component through management information systems (MIS).

Furthermore, a holistic and integrated approach to meet the objectives of food and nutrition security, sustainability, and climate change adaptation and mitigation demands would involve major reorientation of R&D practices and institutions based on the status and requirements of each agro-ecological region. This would involve knowledge development by undertaking time-bound research and developing appropriate technologies for each of the country's agro-ecological regions. To this end, adequate resource mobilization in terms of financial and human resources through budgetary provisions need to be ensured. Further, dissemination of this information and knowledge among farming communities by way of piloting climate change adaptation/mitigation research model projects in the domain of climate-smart sustainable management practices would be important. NMSA has been formulated for enhancing agricultural productivity, especially in rainfed areas focusing on integrated farming, water use efficiency, soil health management, and synergizing resource conservation; however, the institutional and regulatory structures and R&D efforts of the sector are still oriented towards irrigated agriculture. In the following, we provide suggestions for how the evolution and mainstreaming of mission-oriented innovation systems in the context of NMSA can be improved based on adjusting the functions of innovation systems.

In terms of *knowledge development* and *diffusion*, it is important that research on climate-smart agriculture production systems and development and commercialization of innovative technologies be done simultaneously in government and private sectors from their specific perspectives. The ecosystem needs to encourage and facilitate the upscaling of technologies that have been developed by the private sector. Further, focus on increasing the knowledge, skills, and learning capacity of farmers, employees in agricultural institutions, and agricultural education students would be important to create adaptive capacity (Anand et al., 2021). Closing the loop between R&D organizations and farmers would ensure necessary feedback from the ground level that needs to be incorporated into research design and technology development processes, which are required in the areas of climate-smart research and technologies in agriculture, given the uncertainties associated with climate change and its impact.

Improving the affordability and access to agricultural insurance schemes for farmers, ensuring responsible contract farming agreements, and providing business management training to farmer organizations and small and medium enterprises so that they can negotiate with agribusiness firms as more equitable partners will further *entrepreneurial activities*. There is a need to check perverse incentive systems that promote unsustainable use of water, energy, and land. A *market-oriented regime* that facilitates more sustainable practices and crop diversification suited to agro-ecological conditions over the long term is required for the agricultural sector.

In terms of *resource mobilization*, private sector investment in climate-smart agriculture, such as resource-efficient technologies related to agricultural value-chain and natural resource management, can help achieve the desired impact at scale. Increased participation of farmer organizations and civil society organizations (CSOs) are vital in the *creation of legitimacy*. To this end, addressing barriers related to limited access to finance and marketing opportunities, information asymmetry, low access to technologies, and limited linkages with research and extension agencies may enable increased participation of CSOs and community institutions, which can play a central role in supporting rural economies and creating sustainable food systems.

In terms of the *guidance of the search* function, the development plans in the agriculture sector aim to improve adaptation outcomes while in most cases also optimizing mitigation co-benefits, primarily focusing on soil management (organic farming, zero tillage, retention of agricultural residues); crop diversification, cropping system optimization, and management (crop rotations, changing cropping pattern and crop mix, short-duration crop varieties, development of seed varieties tolerant to biotic and abiotic stresses); water management (extending the coverage of irrigation and improving water use efficiency through laser land levelling, micro-irrigation systems); sustainable land management (agroforestry, conservation agriculture); risk sharing (co-investment, community engagement), risk transfer (crop/livestock insurance), and improved forecasting and agro-advisory (localized weather forecasting, SMS, and dedicated web portals for farmers). Ensuring development outcomes in the agriculture sector in the context of climate change and for effective evolution of mission-oriented innovation systems would require effective coordination at different levels of governance. In the federal setup in India, agriculture is a State subject under the Indian Constitution, so planning and policy implementation in agriculture falls substantially within the purview of respective States and local institutions, with the Central government providing the broader policy framework and guidelines. However, given the national goals of sustainable development and climate change mitigation, prioritizing adaptation and mitigation options and building synergies at the national, state, and local levels and across different departments has to be viewed holistically.

The conceptualization of NMSA and methods followed to achieve the objectives currently adopt a compartmentalized approach. It is important to highlight that the agricultural system is dynamic, complex, and multi-functional, and that systems thinking is essential when looking at the agri-food system as an integrated complex whole with interdependencies, feedback loops, and trade-offs. A systematic understanding of the wider context and linkages that influence mission-oriented innovation systems

to be considered in the case of NMSA includes establishing collaborative links with similar missions for water and forest. Further, the state-level climate action plans do incorporate the requirements of the national missions, but institutional structures and planning mechanisms have yet to get fully aligned, and additional budget support for adaptation is low. In particular, actions to implement the Sustainable Development Goals (SDGs) and the Missions related to climate change mitigation and adaptation have to be integrated and trade-offs have to be effectively managed for evolution of mission-oriented innovation systems. In this regard, NITI Aayog (National Institution for Transforming India) – a public policy think-tank of the Government of India, identified as a nodal agency for coordination and overseeing implementation of SDGs in India – can provide insights for better horizontal (among Ministries) and vertical (Central and State levels) coordination and management of trade-offs.

3.2. The Case of National Solar Mission

The National Solar Mission (NSM) was launched in January 2011 as one of the eight key National Missions of India's National Action Plan on Climate Change (NAPCC). Long-term energy security and ecological security are its key objectives. The NSM laid down a comprehensive strategy to develop both grid-connected and off-grid applications of solar energy in a phased manner (Table 17.1), with an emphasis on developing domestic manufacturing and indigenous technologies through a comprehensive research and development (R&D) programme.

Table 17.1 NSM: Application segments, targets, and achievements, 2010–22

Application Segment	*Phase – I Target and Achievement (2010–13)*	*Phase – II Target and Achievement (2013–17)*	*Phase – III Target (2017–22)*
Grid-tied solar power (Plants, rooftop and distribution plants)	1100 MW (1686.44 MW)	10000 MW (12288.83 MW)	100000 MW
Standalone solar applications (Home lighting systems, street lighting, and lanterns)	200 MW (252.5 MW)	1000 MW (1000 MW)	2000 MW
Solar Thermal Collectors (Solar heating and cooling systems, industrial heat processes etc.)	7 million square meter area (7.01 million square meter area)	15 million square meter area (15 million square meter area)	20 million square meter area

Source: Adapted from Kumar et al. (2018)

Ministry of New and Renewable Energy (MNRE) is the nodal Ministry of the Government of India for all matters relating to new and RE programmes, including the solar energy programmes. MNRE has specialized technical institutions i.e. Solar Energy Center (SEC), now the autonomous National Institute of Solar Energy (NISE), which acts as the nodal agency for R&D, and supports the Government of India in its solar testing, calibration, and benchmarking initiatives and offers knowledge services and facilitates technology commercialization initiatives. Indian Renewable Energy Development Agency Limited (IREDA), under the administrative control of MNRE, has been established to promote, develop, and extend financial assistance for renewable energy projects. In the solar energy segment, IREDA has also played the role of programme administrator for the generation-based incentives (GBI) under the Rooftop PV and Small Solar Power Generation Programme (RPSSGP) scheme in NSM Phase I, and is responsible for project allotment and disbursement of GBI. Solar Energy Corporation of India (SECI), which is supported by NISE and IREDA in the achievement of NSM, functions as a solar planning, management, and implementation institution. Further, for implementation for solar energy projects at the State level, State Nodal Agencies (SNA) are responsible for grid as well as off-grid solar power project/programme implementation.

Regarding functions of mission-oriented innovation ecosystems in the context of NSM, for *knowledge development* a focus on creating absorptive capacity as well as technological learning is required. SECI Expression of Interest for setting up an integrated manufacturing facility of 20 GW capacity within three years acted as a big driver in achieving targets. Development of off-grid systems that are 'grid-ready' for rural and remote areas and making by-laws for new buildings that are grid-connected as 'rooftop ready' should be the suggested goals for the future. Further, a focus on advanced forecasting of solar power generation, artificial intelligence, and big data to address generation uncertainty is required. Considerable technological learning pertaining to innovations in floating solar PV plant structures, inverter designs, rooftop solar system features, and more flexible and integrated power systems to cope with the variable nature of solar energy are needed.

Resource mobilization initiatives to bring in larger investments for large projects and for small disaggregates applications through RE-Investors Meet & Expo and involvement of important actors including IREDA, service providers, and Regional Rural Banks have been an important driver. However, to achieve the 100 GW target of solar energy by 2022, India needs to invest $65 billion. A major part of it has to be raised within the country, as the performance of the renewable energy sector in attracting foreign direct investment (FDI) so far has been less than encouraging.

In terms of *market formation* function, reverse bidding as the market-oriented procurement mechanism against the practice of feed-in-tariff and capital subsidies resulted in substantial reduction of solar electricity supply prices. The NSM also introduced bundling (selling together) of solar power with coal-based power to reduce the cost of power supplied to the utilities, to lower the average price of bundled electricity, thus creating a huge demand for solar energy projects and equipment. Bulk buying of solar panels through EESL (Energy Efficiency Services Limited) for applications such as solar irrigation pump sets and custom and excise duty concessions and exemptions on specific capital equipment, critical materials, and components have further enabled solar energy technology diffusion. However, more market innovations are required to develop a large market for distributed solar power in a short time in order to strengthen the solar rooftop programme. Energy for alternate business models such as small and micro enterprises warrants attention. Peer trading and community ownership models and pay-as-you-go models make small electricity generators (e.g., solar panel home systems) affordable for the end-user, facilitated by mobile payment technologies that are easily accessible in remote areas.

Regarding *knowledge diffusion*, there are a number of solar energy programmes which are undertaken, and coordination is limited to the specific programmes. SECI, in discharging its role of program implementation, needs support from other MNRE institutions such as NISE and IREDA on critical factors like solar radiation data, site and technology attractiveness, and financing for implementation of solar programmes. There is no established framework for coordination between the SNAs and institutions such as NISE, SECI, and IREDA. In this regard, a framework to facilitate state and center coordination aimed at solar sector development could leverage synergies across different programmes.

A lot needs to be done to improve domestic manufacturing and develop a competitive industry and to further improve *entrepreneurial activities* in the sector. On the domestic manufacturing front, India's performance has been slow, rendering the solar energy in the country import-dependent, both in generation and transmission, despite several efforts by SECI for the development of the Interstate Transmission System (ISTS) connected Solar Photovoltaic (PV) Power Plant. To reduce the risks for solar power producers and to provide support to entrepreneurs, solar radiation monitoring stations were also set up across India, and net metering and interstate power purchase by bulk consumers, such as the Delhi Metro, have been undertaken. In skill development, providing skills for jobs of engineers, manufacturers, suppliers, repairs, maintenance, and testing facilitators are some of the important challenges before the state agencies.

In terms of *creation of legitimacy*, given the level of support and policy thrust in this technology, the solar energy sector has gained immense significance and potential in the overall energy landscape in India. Creation of larger projects to further bring down the capital investments in solar power generation projects, development of dedicated transmission grids for areas with an abundance of sunlight or wind to create solar and wind energy, and addressing the issue of limited land availability have further facilitated the use of this technology and thwarted any resistance to change.

The *guidance of the search* function indicates that expectations set by the government related to this area in terms of policy goals and incentives have guided the system evolution. Regulatory and policy provisions for renewable energy comprise a number of incentives for solar promotion besides the umbrella Electricity Act 2003 and the National Electricity Policy. Under the NSM, a policy and regulatory framework has been created which provides a predictable incentive structure that enables rapid and large-scale capital investment in solar energy applications and encourages technical innovation and lowering of costs. A comprehensive policy on research, design, development, and demonstration (RDD&D) is in place to develop the technologies, processes, materials, components, sub-systems, products & services, standards, and resource assessment in order to indigenously manufacture solar energy systems and devices. However, a lot needs to be done to establish India as a global leader in solar energy, by creating the policy conditions for rapid diffusion across the country.

The Government of India is leading by example through the installation of solar rooftops widely on government buildings, airports, railway networks, educational institutions, residential sectors, and commercial complexes. It is to be noted that unlike thermal power plants, rooftop PV generation (RTPV) is consumer-dominated, and peoples' participation and acceptance are critical issues for its success. At the national level, manufacturing capacity, investment in R&D, an investor-friendly environment, skill development, low-voltage grid connectivity of variable solar resource and regulatory decisions are major challenges to be resolved. As the penetration of RTPV has to increase, a boost to manufacturing capabilities, not only in solar modules but also in inverters and batteries, is must.

An outlook for linking solar energy targets with the current missions on 'Make in India', 'Smart city mission' and 'Digital India' as a promise for developing capabilities and transformation of entire power system in the country is recommended. Development of off-grid systems that are 'grid-ready' for rural and remote areas and making by-laws for new buildings for the grid connected as 'rooftop-ready' should be the suggested goals for the future. Development of solar parks in association with states, providing technical advisory and administrative support for solar parks, and incubating off-grid business models in partnership with SNAs will help ensure the ease of capacity creation and further evolution of the mission.

4. Evolution of Mission-oriented Innovation Systems in the Agriculture and Energy Sector

In terms of innovation system structure, the agricultural innovation system is largely public sector-driven and the organizational and institutional processes have constructed a technological regime and a lock-in situation that hinders the sustainable development of the sector, constraining farmers' capacity in discerning and managing climate risks. Mainstreaming of mission-oriented systems would necessitate adopting a holistic and integrated approach to sustainable food and land use systems, including establishing collaborative links between agriculture, water, and forest missions. Further, focusing on non-state actors such as start-ups, social enterprises, and farmers' producer organizations, and toning down the scale and impact of actors such as agro-chemical companies, would be pivotal.

The innovation system evolution in agriculture was led by Green Revolution-era technology development, diffusion of high-yielding varieties, and provisioning of regulated doses of fertilizers and water, resulting in higher yields. The entire revolution was furthermore realized because of the scientific competence of Indian researchers in the public laboratory system, their links with laboratories in the US, and ease in technology transfer without charging high royalties in the near absence of an intellectual property rights system. The NMSA, which evolved in the backdrop of increasing realization of limitations of the Green Revolution and the negative impacts of climate change, did not get enough traction in the initial years. The need to reconsider the mission strategies in order to build resilience has been emphasized in the context of the predominance of small and marginal agricultural holdings (86% of all holdings), and that 60% of India's cropped area is rainfed. The mission rightly identifies the challenges and the differential needs of the farmers based on their socio-economic status, and its programme of action focuses on the four intervention areas pertaining to research and development; technology, products, and practices; infrastructure; and, capacity building. These constitute an important dimension of the evolution of mission-oriented innovation systems in agriculture. However, there are challenges that limit the formation of mission-oriented innovation systems in the sector.

For NMSA, since climate resilience in considering future scenarios is key, climate modelling and climate risk research is vital for planning activities for the mission. However, NMSA has yet to integrate this crucial aspect in mission planning and monitoring systems. In terms of the structure, considering the overall objectives of NMSA, there is a glaring gap in terms of the exclusion of the Ministry of Science, which is the nodal ministry of the National Mission on Strategic Knowledge for Climate Change. A key gap in the present structure of NMSA is the lack of monitoring of the CCSAMMN component through management information systems (MIS). There is also a need for the innovation systems to integrate knowledge from initiatives such as NICRA and InfoCrop. Models with holistic programmes that address all ten dimensions of NMSA in terms of "improved crop seeds, livestock and fish cultures, water use efficiency, pest management, improved farm practices, nutrient management, agricultural insurance, credit support, markets, access to information, and livelihood diversification" are not presently monitored. For the latter five dimensions, interdisciplinary approaches and a better integration with social science discipline are key.

A paradigm shift is needed, from the top-down model of the Green Revolution of single commodity intensification and productivity enhancement, towards the intensification of location-specific farming systems and systems productivity and enhancing household income. Tremendous effort needs to be made to align it with the goals and objectives of missions on sustainable agricultural systems. This would require ambidexterity and a deft policy hand to manage the trade-offs, including exnovation (disincentivizing non-sustainable agricultural technology or practices; scrutinizing prevalent policy frames, goals, and policy instruments) and build upon the synergies, including developing innovation capabilities, networks, and policies to overcome lock-in and support food systems transformation (Turner et al., 2017). Institutional design focusing on improving the sub-national level management and governance mechanisms for integrating local objectives with national goals and international frameworks and enhancing institutional capacities in local governance and resource management, particularly related to the commons and strengthening Panchayat Raj, co-operatives, and other stakeholder institutions, is absolutely necessary. Such institutional bases are a prerequisite for evolving local and agro-ecological mechanisms for programme design, credit access, filling in infrastructure gaps, marketing, etc. To this end, investments for building decentralized and local institutional capacities need to be made to enable 'iterative planning implementation-learning cycles' by local institutions (FOLU, 2019).

In the renewable energy sector, a mission-oriented approach with a defined target (100 GW in solar energy by 2022; 40 GW rooftop projects; and 60 GW large-scale projects) to be achieved by development and deployment of a technology (solar photovoltaic) offers product-focused innovation opportunities and has set the momentum for evolution of mission-oriented innovation systems in the sector. Such a mission-oriented approach by the Government to promote solar power in the country has resulted in notable growth in the solar capacity in the period from 2010–2020; from 10 MW in 2010 to 34.6 GW in 2020. Economics of low-carbon power such as renewables, driven by a distinctive cost structure characterized by high upfront costs followed by minimal operating costs, entail significant R&D investments in the sector by state and non-state actors, development of appropriate regulatory standards as an important driver for catalyzing investments in the sector, and provisioning of fiscal subsidies in offsetting high upfront capital cost of energy-saving investments for households and companies. The government has enacted strategies for attracting more investment in the sector from both local and foreign sources, through promoting schemes of 'plug and play', focusing on infrastructure development, including clearances in hand required to start the industry. As a result, there has been a significant reduction in solar-tariffs in India from 2010–2020, from 17.91 INR/kWh to 2.44 INR/kWh in 2020. The renewable energy case suggests that infant industry subsidies for emerging technologies are an effective policy tool to derive economies of scale and learning curve effects to drive cost reductions.

Thus, it may be inferred from this that a mix of vertical and horizontal policies targeting different stages of the innovation chain has enabled and facilitated the evolution of mission-oriented innovation system in the renewable energy sector. In the upstream end, mission-oriented vertical policies focused on directing change created landscapes in which different actors can operate, and raised expectations in the private sector for new growth opportunities in the sector. This, supplemented with horizontal policy measures focused on creating background conditions like investments for infrastructure development and supporting and promoting the involvement of the private sector, stimulated the increased participation of different actors and shaped innovation activities at different levels. Thus, clear direction-setting, investment by different types of actors, a portfolio of projects taking into account risks and uncertainties, and a reflexive policy approach to avoid lock-in scenarios have enabled the evolution of mission-oriented innovation systems in the renewable energy sector. To move towards the maturity phase, the innovation system expectations and product performance should align well, and there should be clarity on direction of the technology trajectory, which will be conditional upon the presence of institutions that embody the social, economic, and political infrastructure of the technological innovation.

5. Conclusions

Both in the agriculture sector and in the energy sector, there were/are inherent path dependencies and technology lock-ins. In terms of innovation system functions, the knowledge and innovation agenda for both sectors harbours different missions/sub-missions. Scrutinizing prevalent policy frames, goals, and policy instruments in the sectors provides important insights on the evolution of mission-oriented innovation systems.

The case of the Solar Mission can be considered an alternative innovation system driven internationally with different sets of actor configurations and networks compared to the energy innovation system dominated by coal. Energy systems are highly globalized, and as such systems transformation in the sector is much shaped/influenced by the pace of international developments in the arenas of policy, technology, and capital flow. As a result, the actors in the conventional and alternative innovation systems have a strong international presence. Therefore, for enacting the missions, the drivers of change, constellation of actors, and networks ought to be more international/national-led (top-down). Also, energy being in the concurrent list in the Indian Constitution allows for better policy manoeuvring by the federal governments compared to the agriculture sector, which is under the state list. Furthermore, the main narrative in the energy sector has been the climate change impacts of the sector and the need for transformation thereof in the context of sustainable energy security.

In the case of NMSA, the evolution of the mission ought to be nested within the dominant innovation system. In the agriculture sector, the main narrative has been the impacts of climate change on production systems, food security, and the role of sustainable agricultural systems in building resilience and adaptive capacity at the local level. Therefore, for enacting the missions, the drivers of change, constellation of actors, and networks in the agriculture sector ought to be more national/state-led (bottom-up). This is also exemplified by the different pace of development of missions in agriculture in different states, due to differences in state governance and socioeconomic and regulatory contexts. As such, unlike the renewable energy sector there are no targets defined, which has offered solutions focused on innovation opportunities.

The sustainability and efficacy of developments in the agriculture sector is intrinsically linked to integrating the issues of poverty, inclusivity, and environment, including climate change, in the long-term development strategy at all levels of planning. This would involve altering the role and intonations of actors in the sector to develop new patterns of alliance and governances and to engage in new sectoral business models that are reflective of the regional and local vulnerability contexts, as well as the capacity to undertake interventions. In this regard, strategic planning at the agro-climatic zone level, customized interventions to enhance productivity, creating knowledge and institutional support, linking laboratory to land more effectively, and paying special attention to dryland farming would be crucial. For that to happen in a concerted way, it is imperative that there be a good understanding and cooperation between the national and state-level policies, plans, and vision, and the importance and relevance of sub-national and local actors needs to be brought to the fore. The case of renewables also offers teachings for the agriculture sector in this regard. The mission-oriented policies can prioritize and adopt similar plug-and-play projects in agriculture and agro-processing, focusing on infrastructure development in terms of road connectivity, cold storages, shaping and creating technologies, markets, and developing intersectoral linkages.

Notes

1 Senior Fellow, The Energy and Resources Institute (TERI), New Delhi. Email: manand@teri.res.in
2 Senior Fellow, National Institute of Public Finance and Policy, New Delhi. Email: rita.pandey@nipfp.org.in
3 Senior Fellow, The Energy and Resources Institute (TERI), New Delhi. Email: shailly.kedia@teri.res.in

4 Existence of robust scientific organizations – universities, public and private research institutions – wherein knowledge, having potential for technological innovation is being generated
5 Requirement of financial and human resources (skilled labour) for research and innovation
6 Institutional changes like the development of temporary niche markets, the formation of standards, and the creation of a (temporary) competitive advantage by favourable tax regimes, are often a prerequisite for markets to evolve (Hekkert et al., 2007; Bergek et al., 2008).
7 Involves several activities that positively lead to the formation of priorities for the technology and have effects on the directions of actors and consumers (Bergek et al., 2008).
8 Transfer and diffusion of knowledge and formation of networks for knowledge, policy, market, and competitors' interactions constitute an important dimension and key issues in any innovation system (Hekkert et al., 2007).
9 Refers to entrepreneurs' efforts to develop marketable technological applications. The existence of entrepreneurs and firms active in a technology field is regarded as one of the most important factors for development of innovation systems (Hekkert et al., 2007; Bergek et al., 2008).
10 Activities that provide legitimacy for new technologies and gain approval from key actors and policymakers

References

Anand, M., J. D. Syiemlieh and S. Kedia (2021). *State of Science, Technology and Innovation Skills for Sustainability of India's Food and Land-Use Systems*, New Delhi: The Energy and Resources Institute and Food and Land Use Coalition.

Bergek, A., S. Jacobsson, B. Carlsson, S. Lindmark and A. Rickne (2008). Analyzing the functional dynamics of technological innovation systems: A scheme of analysis, *Research Policy*, 37: 407–429.

Breschi, S. and F. Malerba (1997). Sectoral innovation systems: technological regimes, Schumpeterian dynamics, and spatial boundaries. In C. Edquist (Ed.): *Systems of Innovation: Technologies, Institutions and Organizations*, London: Pinter, 130–154.

Carlsson, B. and R. Stankiewicz (1991). On the nature, function and composition of technological systems, *Journal of Evolutionary Economics*, 1: 93–118.

Cooke, P. (1992). Regional innovation systems: competitive regulation in the new Europe, *Geoforum*, 23(3): 365–382.

Desai, P. N. (2009). Globalization of innovations: changing nature of India's science and technology cooperation policy, *International Journal of Institutions and Economies*, 1(1): 52–77.

Edquist, C. and B. Johnson (1996). Institutions and organizations in systems of innovation, Working Paper 165, Department of Technology and Social Change, 37 pp.

Edsand, H.-E. (2016). Technological Innovation Systems and the Wider Context: A Framework for Developing Countries. UNU-MERIT Working Paper Series, 2016–017.

Esmailzadeh, M., S. Noori, A. Aliahmadi, H. Nouralizadeh, and M. Bogers (2020). A Functional analysis of technological innovation systems in developing countries: An evaluation of Iran's photovoltaic innovation system, *Sustainability*, 12(5): 1–20.

Fisher, R., J. Chicot, A. Domini, W. Polt, A. Türk, M. Unger, H. Kuittinen, E. Arrilucea, F. van der Zee, A. Goetheer, A. Pelkonen, J. Lehenkari, and F.S. Kristensen (2018). Mission-oriented research and innovation: inventory and characterisation of initiatives. Report Prepared for the European Commission by the JIIP.

FOLU (The Food and Land Use Coalition) (2019). Sustainable Food and Land Use Systems in India, National Roundtable Summary Report, May 13, 2019, New Delhi, pp. 21.

Foray, D. (2005). Generation and distribution of technological knowledge: incentives, norms, and institutions. In C. Edquist (Ed.), *Systems of Innovation: Technologies, Institutions and Organizations*, Oxon: Routledge, 64–85.

Freeman, C. (1988). Japan: A new national system of innovation? In G. Dosi, C. Freeman, R. Nelson, G. Silverberg, and L. Soete (Eds.): *Technical Change and Economic Theory*, London and New York: Frances Pinter, 330–348.

Freeman, C. (1995). The 'National System of Innovation' in historical perspective, *Cambridge Journal of Economics*, 19(1): 5–24.

Fromhold-Eisebith, M. (2006). Effectively linking international, national and regional innovation systems: insights from India and Indonesia. In B.-Å. Lundvall, P. Intarakumnerd and J. Vang (Eds.): *Asia's Innovation Systems in Transition*, Cheltenham: Edward Elgar Publishing Limited.

Georghiou, L., D. Tataj, J. Celio, S. Gianni, D. Pavalkis, R. Vegranti and A. Renda (2018). *Mission-oriented research and innovation policy: A RISE perspective*, Brussels: Publications Office, European Commission, Directorate-General for Research and Innovation. https://data.europa.eu/doi/10.2777/426921

GOI (Government of India) (2008). *National Action Plan on Climate Change*, New Delhi: Government of India.

GOI (Government of India) (2020). *Science, Technology, and Innovation Policy, Draft Document, Ministry of Science & Technology, Department of Science & Technology*, New Delhi: Government of India. Available at: https://dst.gov.in/sites/default/files/STIP_Doc_1.4_Dec2020.pdf (accessed 10 February 2021).

Hekkert, M. P., M. J. Janssen, J. H. Wesseling, and S. O. Negro (2020). Mission-oriented innovation systems, *Environmental Innovation and Societal Transitions*, 34: 76–79.

Hekkert, M. P., R. A. A. Suurs, S. O. Negro, S. Kuhlmann, and R. E. H. M. Smits (2007). Functions of innovation systems: A new approach for analysing technological change, *Technological Forecasting and Social Change*, 74(4): 413–432.

Jacobsson, S. and A. Bergek (2004). Transforming the energy sector: the evolution of technological systems in renewable energy technology, *Industrial and Corporate Change*, 13(5): 815–849.

Klerkx, L. and S. Begemann (2020). Supporting food systems transformation: The what, why, who, where and how of mission-oriented agricultural innovation systems, *Agricultural Systems*, 184: 102901.

Kumar, A., Patel, N., Gupta, N., and V. Gupta (2018). Photovoltaic power generation in Indian prospective considering off-grid and grid-connected systems, *International Journal of Renewable Energy Research*, 8(4): 1936–1950.

LSS (Lok Sabha Secretariat) (2018). *Performance of the National Action Plan on Climate Change (NAPCC), Report of Committee on Estimates of the Lok Sabha Secretariat*, New Delhi: Lok Sabha Secretariat.

Lundvall, B.-Å. (1992). *National Systems of Innovation: Towards a Theory of Innovation and Interactive Learning*, London: Frances Pinter Publishers.

Markard, J. and B. Truffer (2008). Technological innovation systems and the multi-level perspective: Towards an integrated framework, *Research Policy*, 37: 596–615.

Mazzucato, M. (2017). *Mission-Oriented Innovation Policy: Challenges and Opportunities*. IIPP Working Paper Series WP 2017–01, London: Institute for Innovation and Public Purpose. www.ucl.ac.uk/bartlett/public-purpose/

Mazzucato, M. (2018). *Mission-Oriented Research & Innovation in the European Union: A Problem-Solving Approach to Fuel Innovation-Led Growth*. Brussels: European Commission. https://doi.org/10.2777/36546.

MOAFW (Ministry of Agriculture & Farmers Welfare) (2019). National Mission for Sustainable Agriculture. https://nmsa.dac.gov.in/Default.aspx (accessed 2 August 2021).

Nelson, R. R. (1993). *National Systems of Innovation: A Comparative Analysis*, Oxford: Oxford University Press.

Robinson, D. K., and M. Mazzucato (2019). The evolution of mission-oriented policies: Exploring changing market creating policies in the US and European space sector, *Research Policy*, 48(4): 936–948.

Soete, L., and Arundel, A. (Eds.) (1993). *An Integrated Approach to European Innovation and Technology Diffusion Policy: A Maastricht Memorandum*, Luxembourg: Commission of the European Communities.

Turner, J. A., L. Klerkx, T. White, T. Nelson, J. Everett-Hincks, A. Mackay, and N. Botha (2017). Unpacking systemic innovation capacity as strategic ambidexterity: How projects dynamically configure capabilities for agricultural innovation, *Land Use Policy*, 68: 503–523.

Urmetzer, S., and A. Pyka (2019). Innovation systems for sustainability. In W. Leal Filho (Ed.), *Decent Work and Economic Growth – The Encyclopedia of the UN Sustainable Development Goals*, Cham: Springer.

Weber, K. M., and H. Rohracher (2012). Legitimizing research, technology and innovation policies for transformative change: Combining insights from innovation systems and multi-level perspective in a comprehensive 'failures' framework, *Research Policy*, 41(6): 1037–1047.

Wright, B. D. (2012). Grand missions of agricultural innovation, *Research Policy*, 41(10): 1716–1728.

Appendix

List of selected Research Publications of Professor Lakhwinder Singh

Books Published:

- **Reimaging Innovation System in the Covid and Post-Covid World,** Routledge, New Delhi (edited with K J Joseph and Susan Cozzens) Forthcoming 2022.
- **Covid-19 Pandemic and Economic Development: Public Policy Lessons from Punjab Experience**, Palgrave Macmillan, Singapore, 2021 (Co-edited with Sukhpal Singh and Kamal Vatta).
- **Agriculture Innovation System in Asia: Towards Inclusive Rural Development,** Routledge, London, New York, New Delhi (jointly edited with Anita Gill), 2020.
- **Agrarian Distress and Farmer Suicides in North India**, Routledge-Taylor and Francis Group, London, New York and New Delhi, Second edition 2020 and first edition 2016 (Jointly with K S Bhangoo and Rakesh Sharma).
- **Economic Transformation of a Developing Economy: The Experience of Punjab, India,** Springer Nature, Singapore, 2016 (Jointly edited with Nirvikar Singh).
- **Technology, Innovations and Economic Development: Essays in Honour of Robert E. Evenson,** (Jointly edited with K J Joseph and Daniel K N Johnson) SAGE Publications, New Delhi, London and Los Angles, 2015.
- **Economic and Environmental Sustainability of the Asian Region** (Jointly edited with Sucha Singh Gill and Reena Marwah) Routledge, London, New York and New Delhi, 2010 and 2016 (Paper Back edition).
- **Economic Cooperation and Infrastructure Linkages between Two Punjabs: Way Ahead** (Jointly with Sucha Singh Gill et.al) CRRID Publications, Chandigarh, 2010.

- **Status of Local Agricultural Labour in Punjab,** The Punjab State Farmers Commission, Government of Punjab, Mohali, 2007 (Jointly with R. S. Ghuman and Inderjeet Singh)

Selected Journal Articles and Book Chapters:

- Human Capital Accumulation and Economic Growth of Ethiopian Economy, **African Journal of Science, Technology, Innovation and Development,** 2022 (with Zemed Degu). https://doi.org/10.1080/2042 1338.2022.2062652.
- Separating Wheat from the Chaff: Farm Acts, Farmers Protest and Outcomes, **Millennial Asia: An International Journal of Asian Studies,** Vol. 12, No.3, 390–410, December 2021 (with Baldev Singh Shergill).
- Punjab's Migration Crisis under lockdown and Beyond: Some Suggestion for Public Policy in Sukhpal Singh, Lakhwinder Singh and Kamal Vatta (eds.) **Covid-19 Pandemic and Economic Development: Emerging Public Policy Lessons from Indian Punjab,** Palgrave Macmillan, Singapore, 2021.
- Fiscal Policy and Private Investment in Developing Economies: Evidence From Ethiopia, **African Journal of Science Technology Innovation and Development**, Routledge, 2021 (with Fekadu Mekonnen Bedhiye) https://doi.org/10.1080/20421338.2021.1982664
- The Deadly Cost of Informal Lending: An Economic Model of Agrarian Suicides in Punjab, (With Daniel Johnson et al). January 2020 *SSRN Electronic Journal* DOI: *10.2139/ssrn.3743099*
- Global Spread and Socio-Economic Determinants of COVID-19 Pandemic, **Seoul Journal of Economics,** Vol. 33, No. 4, 2020 (With Varinder Jain).
- Agriculture Innovation System and Productivity Growth Across North Indian States, in Lakhwinder Singh and Anita Gill (eds.) **Agriculture Innovation System in Asia: Towards Inclusive Rural Development,** Routledge, London, New York and New Delhi, 2020 (with Anita Gill and Rakesh Sharma).
- Asia's Economic Development Experience in the 21st Century, **Millennial Asia: An International Journal of Asian Studies,** Vol. 10, No.3, 2019 (with Sukhpal Singh and Reena Marwah).
- Short run and Long run Technical Efficiency Analysis: Application to the Ethiopian Manufacturing Firms, **Seoul Journal of Economics,** Vol. 32, No. 4, 2019 (Jointly with Yismaw Ayelign).
- Skill Formation, Competitiveness and Industrialization: The South Asian Experience, in Sachin Chaturvedi and Sabayasachi Saha (eds.) **Manufacturing and Jobs in South Asia: Strategy for Sustainable Economic Growth,** Springer Nature, Singapore, 2019.

- Interconnection between R&D and Industrial Production Structure: The Experience of India, **Millennial Asia: An International Journal of Asian Studies**, Vol. 9, No. 3:278294, 2018 SAGE publishers (with Deepika Chawla).
- Structural Change and Economic Growth across Major States of India, **Millennial Asia: An International Journal of Asian Studies**, Vol. 9, No. 2, 2018:162–182, SAGE Publications (with Monica Thind).
- The Determinants of Food Security among the Pastoral Households of Amibara District in AFAR National Regional State, **International Journal of Research and Analytical Reviews**, Vol. 5, No. 3, 2018 (with Abdurhman Kader).
- Quality Standards and Technological Capabilities: Empirical Evidence from Indian Firms, **Journal of Regional Development and Planning**, Vol.7, No. 2, 2018: 29–39, India (With Kriman).
- Knowledge Spillovers Across Developing Economies, **Seoul Journal of Economics**, Vol. 30, No. 3, 2017 (with Manjinder Kaur).
- R&D Expenditure and Economic Growth: An Empirical Analysis, **International Journal of Technology Management and Sustainable Development**, Vol. 15, No. 3, 2016 (with Manjinder Kaur).
- Knowledge in the Economic Growth of Developing Economies, **African Journal of Science, Technology, Innovation and Development**, Vol. 8, No. 2, 2016 (with Manjinder Kaur).
- Emergence of Innovative Manufacturing Firms across Asian Countries, **Seoul Journal of Economics**, Vol. 29, No. 1, 2016 (with Anita Gill).
- Decent Work and Economic Growth, in Pramod Kumar (ed.) **Vision Document 2030 for the State of Punjab**, Chandigarh: Department of Planning, Government of Punjab and Institute of Development and Communication, 2016.
- Towards Alternative Strategy for Economic Development in Punjab, **Journal of Punjab Studies**, Vol. 22, No. 2, 2015.
- Intra Household Allocation of Resources in Rural Punjab: Comparative Analysis of Migrants and Non Migrants Households, **Journal of Agricultural Development and Policy**, Vol. 25, No. 2, 2015 (with Samita Behl).
- Technological Capability, Employment Growth and Industrial Development: A Quantitative Anatomy of the Indian Scenario, in Lakhwinder Singh, K. J. Joseph and Daniel K N Johnson (eds.) **Technology, Innovations and Economic Development: Essays in Honour of Robert E Evenson,** SAGE Publishers, New Delhi 2015 (with Baldev Singh Shergill).
- Economic Governance and Punjab's Economic Growth, in **Punjab's Economic Development in the Era of Globalisation** (eds.) Inderjeet Singh and Sukhwinder Singh and Lakhwinder Singh, 2014.

- Cancer Suffering Households in Punjab: Economic and Financial Consequences, in **Punjab's Economic Development in the Era of Globalisation** (eds.) Inderjeet Singh, Sukhwinder Singh and Lakhwinder Singh), 2014 (with Inderjeet Singh and Parmod Kumar).
- Dealing with the Innovation-Inequality Conundrum: The Indian Experience, in Mario Scerri, Maria Clara Couto Soares and Rasigan Maharajh (eds.) **Inequality and Development Challenges**, Routledge, London, 2014 (with K J Joseph and Vinoj Abraham).
- Understanding India's Economic Growth: Implications for India-Korea Economic Cooperation, **Seoul Journal of Economics**, Vol. 27, No. 1, 2014, South Korea (with Keun Lee).
- The State, Systems of Innovation and Economic Growth: Comparative Perspectives from India and South Korea, **Seoul Journal of Economics**, Vol. 27, No. 1, 2014, South Korea (with K S Bhangoo).
- Internationalization of Firms from China and India: Theory, Evidence and Policy, **Millennial Asia: An International Journal of Asian Studies**, Vol. 3, No. 1, 2012, India (with Anita Gill).
- Post-Reform Economic Development in Punjab: A Comparative Perspective and Alternative Strategy, in H. S. Shergill, Sucha Singh Gill and Gurmail Singh (eds.)
  Understanding North-West Indian Economy, Serials Publications, New Delhi, 2011, India.
- Economic Development, Foreign Direct Investment and Policy in India, in Sucha Singh Gill, Lakhwinder Singh and Reena Marwah (eds.) **Economic and Environmental Sustainability of the Asian Region**, Routledge, London, New York and New Delhi, 2010.
- Changing Contours of Indian Investment Abroad: Evolution, Diagnosis and Public Policy, in Mustafa ZihniTunca (ed.) **Sustainable Economic Development and the**
  Influence of Information Technologies: Dynamics of Knowledge Society Transformation, IGI Global Publishers, 2010. USA, (with Varinder Jain).
- Emerging Pattern of Employment in the Organised Manufacturing Sector of India, in R.S. Ghuman, Surjit Singh and J S Brar (eds.) **Globalisation and the State: Perspectives from Punjab-Essays in Honour of Prof. Sucha Singh Gill**, Rawat Publishers, Jaipur, (with Baldev Singh Shergill) 2010, India.
- Changing Character of Rural Economy and Migrant Labour in Punjab, **Journal of Punjab Studies**, Vol. 16, No. 1, 2009, USA. (with Inderjeet Singh and R. S. Ghuman).
- Capability Building for Innovations, Public Policy and Economic Growth in Asia: Lessons for Science and Technology Policy, **Current Politics and Economics of Asia**, Vol. 17, No. 4, 2008, New York, USA.
- Growth and Dynamics of Unorganised Industries in Punjab, **International Journal of Business and Globalisation**, Vol. 1, No. 1, 2007, UK (with Varinder Jain).

- Innovations, High Tech Trade and Industrial Development: Theory, Evidence and Policy, in George Mavrotas and Anthony Shorrocks (eds.) **Advancing Development: Core Themes in Global Economics, WIDER Development Studies Series,** Hampshire: Palgrave Macmillan, 2007, UK **and -WIDER Research Paper No. 2006/27.**
- Farmers' Suicides and Response of Public Policy: Evidence, Diagnosis and Alternatives from Punjab, **Economic and Political Weekly**, Vol. 41, No. 26, June 30, 2006, Mumbai, India (with Anita Gill).
- Deceleration of Industrial Growth and Rural Industrialization Strategy for Indian Punjab, **Journal of Punjab Studies,** Vol.12, No.2, 2005, USA.
- "Techno-Industrial Cooperation for Development in the Two Punjabs", **Journal of Peace and Democracy in South Asia**, Vol. 1, No.2, 2005, Sweden.
- Globalization, National Innovation Systems and Response of Public Policy, **International Journal of Technology Management and Sustainable Development,** Vol. 3, No. 3, December 2004, UK.
- Technological Progress, Structural Change and Productivity Growth in Manufacturing Sector of South Korea, **World Review of Science, Technology and Sustainable Development,** Vol. 1, No. 1, 2004, UK.
- Domestic and International Knowledge Spillovers in Manufacturing Industries in South Korea, **Economic and Political Weekly**, Vol. 39, No. 5, January 31, 2004, Mumbai, India.
- Post-Reform Employment Growth in Organised Manufacturing Sector of India; A Disaggregative Analysis, **Manpower Journal**, Vol. 38, No. 1, April-June 2002, New Delhi, India (with Anita Gill).
- Deceleration of Economic Growth in Punjab: Evidence, Explanation and A Way Out, **Economic and Political Weekly**, vol. 37, No. 6, February 9–15, 2002, Mumbai, India (with Sukhpal Singh).
- Restructuring Monetary and Fiscal Policies for the Indian Federation, in R.N. Pal (ed.) **Indian Constitution: A Review**, Chandigarh: CRRID Publications, 2002, India.
- Public Policy and Expenditure on R&D in Industry, **Economic and Political Weekly**, Vol. 36, No. 31, August 4–10, 2001, Mumbai, India.
- International R&D Spillovers and Economic Growth in Asia, in Ashok Guha, K.L. Krishna and Ashok Lehari (eds.) **Industry and Trade: Essays by NIPFP – Ford Foundation Fellows**, NIPFP and Vikas Publishers, New Delhi, 2001, India.
- Technological Spillovers and India's Industrial Growth, **The Indian Journal of Economics**, Vol. LXXX, No. 318, January 2000, Allahabad, India.
- Economic Growth, International Technological Spillovers and Public Policy: Theory and Epirical Evidence from Asia, **Indian Management Studies Journal,** Vol. 4, No. 2, October 2000, Patiala, India (with R.E. Evenson).

- Productivity, Competitiveness and Export Growth in a Less Developed Economy: A Study of Indian Punjab, in Pritam Singh and Shinder S. Thandi (eds.) **Punjabi Identity in a Global Context,** Oxford University Press, New Delhi, 1999, India.
- Employment, Wages and Productivity in Public Sector Enterprises in India, **The Indian Jurnal of Labour Economics,** Vol. 41, No. 4, October-December 1998 (with R.S. Guman), New Delhi, India.
- "Globalisation and Economic Growth in Asia" in Gopal Singh (ed.) **South Asia: Democracy, Discontent and Societal Conflicts,** Anamika Publishers Pvt. Ltd., Delhi, India, 1998.
- Industrial Development in Punjab: An Analysis of Growth of Productivity and Structure of Wages, **Finance India** Vol. 7, No. 1, March 1993, New Delhi, India.
- Aspects of Growth and Structural Change in Industrial Sector of Punjab, **Man & Development,** Vol. 14, No.2, June 1992, Chandigarh, India.
- Changes in the Inter-Industry Structure of Wages: The Case of Punjab, **Indian Journal of Industrial Relations,** Vol. 27, No. 2, October 1991, New Delhi, India.
- Foreign Trade of India: A Macro View, **Indian Management Studies Journal,** Vol. I, No. 1, October 1989 (with R.S. Ghuman), Patiala, India.
- Productivity Trends and Factor Substitutability in Punjab Industry, **The Indian Journal of Economics,** Vol. LXVII, Part III, No. 266, January 1987, Allahabad, India.
- Capital-Labour Substitution in Punjab Industry, **Indian Journal of Industrial Relations,** Vol. 21, October 1985 (with K.C. Singhal), New Delhi, India.

Working/Discussion Papers

- "Productivity, Competitiveness, and Export Growth in a Less Developed Economy: A Study of Indian Punjab", **Discussion Paper No. 722,** Economic Growth Centre, Yale University, USA, 1994
- "Economic Growth, International Technological Spillovers and Public Policy: Theory and Empirical Evidence from Asia" **Discussion Paper No. 785,** Economic Growth Centre, Yale University, USA, 1997 (with Robert E. Evenson)
- Technological Progress, Structural Change and Productivity Growth in Manufacturing Sector of South Korea, **Discussion Paper No. 50,** Institute of Economic Research, Seoul National University, Seoul, South Korea, 2002.
- Domestic and International Knowledge Spillovers in the South Korean Manufacturing Industries, **Discussion Paper No. 51,** Institute of Economic Research, Seoul National University, Seoul, South Korea, 2002

- Crisis of Agrarian Capitalism, Farmers' Suicides and Response of Public Policy: Evidence, Diagnosis and Alternatives, **Working Paper No. 5,** Government Policy Spaces (GAPS) Project, Centre for Economic and Social Studies, Hyderabad, 2005 (with Anita Gill)
- The State, Systems of Innovation and Economic Growth: Comparative Perspectives from India and South Korea, **Discussion Paper No. 2,** CDEIS, Punjabi University, October 2013 (with Kesar Singh Bhangoo)
- Services Sector as an Engine of Economic Growth: Implications for India-South Korea Economic Cooperation, **Discussion Paper No. 3,** CDEIS, Punjabi University, October 2013 (with Inderjeet Singh)
- Economic and Financial Consequences of Cancer from Patient's Family Perspective: A Case Study of Punjab, **Discussion Paper No. 5,** CDEIS, Punjabi University, October 2013 (with Inderjeet Singh and Parmod Kumar)
- Emergence of Innovative Manufacturing Firms across Asian Countries, **Discussion Paper No. 11,** CDEIS, Punjabi University, Patiala, December 2015 (with Anita Gill).
- Knowledge in Economic Growth of Developing Economies, **Discussion Paper No. 12,** CDEIS, Punjabi University, December 2015 (with Manjinder Kaur).
- Towards all Alternative Strategy of Economic Development in Punjab, Discussion Paper No. 14, CDEIS, Punjabi University, November, 2016.
- Global Spread and Determinants of Initial Phase of COVID-19 Pandemic, **Discussion Paper No. 18,** CDEIS, Punjabi University, Patiala, June 2020 (with Varinder Jain).

Selected Research Project Reports:

- **Principles and Measures determining Salary Structure of Punjab Government Employees,** Sixth Punjab Pay Commission, Government of Punjab, Chandigarh, 2019–2020.
- **Rural-Urban Migration, Informal Sector Employment and Income/ Earning Differentials: Reflections from Two Indian States-Punjab and Haryana,** Indian Council of Social Science Research, New Delhi 2018 (with Sukhwinder Singh and Deepak Kumar)
- **Farmers' and Agriculture Labourers' Suicides in Seven Districts of Punjab,** October 2017, Department of Revenue, Rehabilitation and Disaster Management, Government of Punjab, Chandigarh.
- **Agrarian Distress in Punjab: Suicides of Farmers and Labourers,** Indian Council of Social Science Research (ICSSR), New Delhi, 2013.
- **Restructuring Economic Governance in Punjab 2011,** Punjab Governance Reform Commission, Government of Punjab, Chandigarh (With B. S. Ghuman).

- **Human Development Report of Sangrur District 2009,** Planning Commission of India and UNDP, New Delhi (with Sucha Singh Gill et.al)
- **Status of Local Agricultural Labour in Punjab,** The Punjab State Farmers Commission, Government of Punjab, December 2007 (with R. S. Ghuman et.al).
- **Infrastructure Linkages in Two Punjabs,** Department of Economics, Punjabi University Patiala, sponsored by Two Punjabs Centre, CRRID, Chandigarh, December, 2005 (with Sucha Singh Gill et.al).
- **Globalisation and Economic Growth in Asia,** Dept. of Economics, Punjabi University, sponsored by UGC, August 1999.
- **Impact of 1994–95 Budget Changes Relating to Central Excise on Small Scale Sector** National Institute of Public Finance and Policy, January 1995 (with A. Bagchi *et al.*).

Appendix

Table A1 Electronics industry – NIC 2008 classification

Class	*Description*	*Contents*	*Firms*
2610	Manufacture of Electronic ***Components***	Semiconductors, Integrated Circuits, Transistors, Capacitors, Microprocessors, Display Components, Cables etc.	**63**
2620	Manufacture of ***Computer*** and Peripherals Equipment	Computers, Laptops, Servers, Storage Devices, Printers, Scanners, Projectors, ATMs etc.	**06**
2630	Manufacture of Communication Equipment ***Telecom***	Radio & TV Studio Equipment, Telephone & Fax Equipment, Mobile & Cellular Equipment, Routers, Bridges, DTHs, etc.	**23**
2640	Manufacture of ***Consumer*** Electronics	TV, Monitors, Displays, Audio Recordings & Duplicating Systems, CD & DVD Players, Radio Receivers, Stereo, Speaker, Karaoke etc.	**12**
2651	Manufacture of Measuring, Testing, Navigating, and Control Equipment ***Instruments***	Emission testing, Physical properties Testing and Inspection Equipment, Consumption and Counting Meters, Radar, GPS, Meteorological Devices etc.	**44**

Author's compilation

Table A2: Variable Construction

Variables	Definition	Deflator	Exp Sign
Production Function Variables			
Output (Y)	Sales	WPI-Electronics	NA
Capital (K)	Gross Fixed Assets	Capital Deflator	+
Labour (L)	Compensation to Employees	CPI-Industrial Workers	+
Materials (M)	Raw Materials Expenses	Input Price I/O Tables	+
Firm Characteristics			
Age (AGE)	Firm's Incorporation Year	NA	+/-
Size (SIZE)	Total Assets	WPI	+/-
Profit (PFT)	Profitability or Profit Before Tax	Total Assets	+
HHI	Herfindahl Hirschman Index	Calculated	+
ENI	Energy Intensity	Energy expanses/ Sales	-
Dummy Variables			

Notes: EXD For firms reporting export in a particular year
IDD For firms reporting royalty etc. in a specific year
IDD For firms reporting Materials Import in each year
IED For firms reporting Import of Capital Goods every year
RDD For firms reporting R&D expenses in a year
1=Export, 0=No Export
1=Import, 0=No Import
1=Import, 0=No Import
1=Import, 0=NO Import
1= R&D, 0=NO R&D

Table A3 Descriptive statistics

Variables	*Obs*	*Mean*	*Median*	*SD*	*Min*	*Max*
Production Function Estimation						
Sales (y)	1,425	8.8633	8.7949	1.8515	1.5063	15.6083
Capital (k)	1,425	7.5145	7.4204	1.6747	1.9191	13.5312
Labour (l)	1,425	5.9945	5.8478	1.6161	0.3214	11.3850
Materials (m)	1,425	7.8720	7.9120	2.0087	0.6243	14.5329
Firm Characteristics						
Age (age)	1,425	3.0888	3.0910	0.4565	0.6931	4.6347
Size (size)	1,425	8.6888	8.4984	1.8025	4.7189	14.7607
Profitability (PFT)	1,425	0.1237	0.1164	0.1281	–0.4850	2.0139
Herfindahl Hirschman Index (HHI)	1,425	0.1650	0.1537	0.0393	0.1205	0.2504
Energy Intensity (ENI)	1,425	0.0262	0.0093	0.1275	0.0002	4.5839

Source: Variables in lower case are in natural logs, in thousand Indian Rupees at constant 2004–05 prices Figure 3 Firm Size Distribution based on Sales

Table A4 Production function estimation – correlation matrix and VIF

Variables	*y*	*k*	*l*	*m*	*Variables*	*VIF*	*1/VIF*
Output (y)	1.00				**Capital (k)**	4.12	0.24
Capital (k)	0.79***	1.00			**Labour (l)**	3.18	0.31
Labour (l)	0.88***	0.81***	1.00		**Materials (m)**	3.04	0.33
Materials (m)	0.96***	0.74***	0.82***	1.00	**Mean VIF**	3.45	.

Notes: *** p<0.01, ** p<0.05, * p<0.1

Table A5 Production function estimation – robustness check

	A. Without Outliers				B. Without Year 2017		
Sales (y)	*OLS*	*LP*	*WD*	*Sales (y)*	*OLS*	*LP*	*WD*
Capital (k)	0.0558***	0.0806**	0.0859***	***Capital (k)***	0.0644***	0.0902*	0.0959***
	(0.0121)	(0.0415)	(0.0202)		(0.0126)	(0.0461)	(0.0249)
Labour (l)	0.2787***	0.2589***	0.2333***	***Labour (l)***	0.2851***	0.2670***	0.2409***
	(0.0201)	(0.0347)	(0.0180)		(0.0196)	(0.0363)	(0.0166)
Materials (m)	0.6581***	0.5901***	0.5534***	***Materials (m)***	0.6555***	0.5922***	0.5109***
	(0.0189)	(0.0514)	(0.0444)		(0.0192)	(0.0523)	(0.0523)
Constant	1.5499***			***Constant***	1.5025***		
	(0.0450)				(0.0664)		
Wald Test		1.78	10.19	***Wald Test***		0.88	13.18
		0.18	0.00			0.35	0.00
Observations	1,401	1,401	1,211	***Observations***	1,351	1,351	1,161
R-squared	0.9469			***R-squared***	0.9520		
No. of Firms		148	148	***No. of Firms***		148	148
*Hansen's J statistic for overidentification estimation is 24.47****				*Hansen's J statistic for overidentification estimation is 23.09****			

*Robust standard errors in parentheses; *** p<0.01, ** p<0.05, * p<0.1*

Table A6 Determinants of productivity – correlation matrix and VIF

Var(s)	*tfpwd*	*age*	*size*	*PFT*	*HHI*	*ENI*
tfpwd	1.00					
Age	0.12***	1.00				
Size	0.63***	0.28***	1.00			
PFT	0.17***	−0.06**	−0.01	1.00		
HHI	0.24***–	0.23	0.17	−0.08***	1.00	
ENI	0.22***	0.04	−0.06**	−0.08***	0.06**	1.00

Var(s)	*VIF*	*1/VIF*
AGE	1.13	0.8854
SIZE	1.10	0.9061
PFT	1.08	0.9296
HHI	1.01	0.9853
ENI	1.01	0.9861
Mean VIF	1.07	

Note: *** p<0.01, ** p<0.05, * p<0.1

Table A7 Fisher Type panel unit root test

Var(s)	P_m *statistic*
k	16.66***
l	23.62***
m	12.12***
	age402.62***
	size21.28***
	PFT30.58***
	HHI22.11***
	ENI14.46***

Note: The test was performed using Phillips-Peron equation with trend, *** p<0.01, ** p<0.05, * p<0.1

Table A8 Determinants of productivity – continuous vs dummy

Tfpwd	*(1)*	*(2)*	*(3)*	*(4)*
age	0.6028***	−0.0531		
	(0.1102)	(0.2019)		
size	0.1871***	0.1785***		
	(0.0266)	(0.0276)		
PFT	0.6114***	0.6812***		
	(0.1909)	(0.2230)		
HHI	0.2223	4.8952***		
	(0.2949)	(1.1702)		
ENI	−0.7138***	−0.7381***		
	(0.2070)	(0.2114)		
EXD			−0.076	−0.043
			(0.059)	(0.054)
RDD			0.129**	0.077*
			(0.056)	(0.043)
IED			0.041	0.020
			(0.032)	(0.023)

Table A8: (Continued)

Tfpwd	*(1)*	*(2)*	*(3)*	*(4)*
IDD			−0.099	−0.031
			(0.065)	(0.071)
IMD			0.050	0.120**
			(0.056)	(0.046)
Constant	−0.9283***	0.1451	2.624***	2.168***
R^2	(0.3204)	(0.4348)	(0.062)	(0.078)
	0.3985	0.4335	0.019	0.257
Obs	1,425	1,425	1,425	1,425
Firms	148	148	148	148
Hausman Test	^{2}:123.17***	^{2}:11.44	^{2}:64.56***	^{2}:60.57***
	5	16	5	17
Year F-Test	–	4.56***	–	15.47***
Year FE	NO	YES	NO	YES

Notes: Robust standard errors in parentheses; *** p<0.01, ** p<0.05, * p<0.1

Table A9 Determinants of productivity – mean divide (without profitability)

	(1)	*(2)*	*(3)*	*(4)*	*(5)*	*(6)*	*(7)*	*(8)*
	Young	*Old*	*Small*	*Large*	*Low*	*High*	*Less*	*More*
tfpwd	*age*	*age*	*size*	*size*	*PFT*	*PFT*	*ENI*	*ENI*
age	0.2742	−0.1282	−0.0213	0.1157	−0.1859	−0.1956	−0.0201	−0.1931
	(0.6882)	(−0.2756)	(−0.0702)	(0.4721)	(−0.6924)	(−0.7578)	(−0.1107)	(−0.5667)
size	0.1809***	0.1930***	0.1679***	0.1114**	0.2126***	0.1544***	0.1561***	0.0964
	(5.5897)	(3.3230)	(3.9870)	(2.5279)	(5.1731)	(4.2982)	(5.8752)	(1.3730)
HHI	2.1409	5.7940**	4.1166**	5.2605***	7.3297***	4.0589**	4.2210***	6.2078**
	(0.6148)	(2.4627)	(2.0050)	(3.3580)	(4.3310)	(2.0884)	(3.4717)	(2.5478)
ENI	−6.3169**	−0.7189***	−3.7817***	−7.8845***	−0.7375***	−1.4577	−31.7335***	−0.6951***
	(−2.3741)	(−3.5227)	(−13.3486)	(−3.8439)	(−3.6316)	(−0.8875)	(−6.6626)	(−4.3125)
EXD	−0.0673	−0.0033	−0.0487	0.0001	−0.0254	−0.0413	−0.0349	−0.0016
	(−0.9213)	(−0.0921)	(−0.7870)	(0.0024)	(−0.4999)	(−0.4392)	(−0.6063)	(−0.0315)
RDD	−0.0401	0.0455	−0.0619	0.0246	0.0516	−0.0405	−0.0490	−0.0139
	(−0.5432)	(1.0589)	(−0.8863)	(0.6156)	(0.9062)	(−1.0346)	(−1.3401)	(−0.1516)
IED	0.0148	−0.0099	−0.0083	−0.0121	−0.0245	0.0417	−0.0120	0.0143
	(0.4555)	(−0.4278)	(−0.3068)	(−0.3380)	(−0.8391)	(1.5567)	(−0.5102)	(0.5162)
IDD	−0.1610	−0.0108	−0.0832	−0.0266	0.0544	−0.1822	−0.1315	−0.0546
	(−1.3553)	(−0.2559)	(−0.8642)	(−0.4949)	(1.0327)	(−1.5121)	(−1.6019)	(−0.5655)
IMD	0.0286	0.1545***	0.0397	0.0853	0.0944*	0.0049	0.0346	0.1413
	(0.7068)	(2.8644)	(1.0844)	(1.3993)	(1.9677)	(0.1045)	(1.0879)	(1.6220)
Constant	0.0896	0.0135	0.4932	0.3291	−0.2886	1.2104**	0.8276*	0.8621
	(0.1767)	(0.0107)	(0.9377)	(0.4862)	(−0.4821)	(2.2352)	(1.9300)	(1.0005)
Observations	700	725	757	668	767	658	1,054	371
R-squared	0.3820	0.4528	0.4711	0.4889	0.4109	0.4260	0.4748	0.4440
Firms	86	74	107	77	134	134	128	62

Notes: Robust standard errors in parentheses, *** p<0.01, ** p<0.05, * p<0.1

Appendix 9-A

Production of Total Motor Vehicles in India and World

Year	*(Qty. in Numbers)*		*Change over previous year (per cent)*		*India's Share in World Production*
	India	*World*	*India*	*World*	*India (in per cent)*
1999	818193	3,97,59,847			2.058
2000	801360	4,12,15,653	–2.06	3.66	1.944
2001	814611	4,01,44,189	1.65	–2.60	2.029
2002	894769	4,13,58,394	9.84	3.02	2.163
2003	1161523	4,20,11,951	29.81	1.58	2.765
2004	1511157	4,45,54,268	30.10	6.05	3.392
2005	1638674	4,60,08,847	8.44	3.26	3.562
2006	2019808	4,99,18,578	23.26	8.50	4.046
2007	2253729	5,30,49,391	11.58	6.27	4.248
2008	2332328	5,28,41,125	3.49	–0.39	4.414
2009	2641550	4,77,72,598	13.26	–9.59	5.529
2010	3557073	5,82,64,852	34.66	21.96	6.105
2011	3927411	5,99,29,016	10.41	2.86	6.553
2012	4174713	6,30,81,024	6.30	5.26	6.618
2013	3898425	6,54,62,496	–6.62	3.78	5.955
2014	3844857	6,77,82,035	–1.37	3.54	5.672
2015	4125744	6,85,39,516	7.31	1.12	6.020
2016	4488965	7,23,88,433	8.80	5.62	6.201
2017	4782896	7,26,63,013	6.55	0.38	6.582
2018	5174645	7,04,66,344	8.19	–3.02	7.343

Source: Data extracted from International Organization of Motor Vehicle Manufacturers (OICA correspondents survey) www.oica.net/category/production-statistics/1999-statistics/

Appendix 9-B

Exports of Motor Vehicles from India (Qty. in Numbers)

Year	*Exports from India*	
	Passenger Cars	*Commercial Vehicles*
1994–95	20406	8069
1995–96	28851	7829
1996–97	37161	7670
1997–98	29722	8204
1998–99	25468	5564
1999–00	23272	4193
2000–01	22990	8260
2001–02	50108	6770

Appendix 9-B: (Continued)

Year	*Exports from India*	
	Passenger Cars	*Commercial Vehicles*
2002–03	88970	12576
2003–04	129291	17432
2004–05	166402	29940
2005–06	175572	40600
2006–07	198452	49537
2007–08	218401	58994
2008–09	335729	42625
2009–10	446146	45009
2010–11	453479	76297
2011–12	508783	92258
2012–13	554686	79,944
2013–14	596142	77,050
2014–15	621341	86939
2015–16	653053	103124
2016–17	758727	108271
2017–18	748366	96865
2018–19	676193	99931

Source: Automatic Component Manufacturers Association of India (ACMA: Facts & Figures, various annual reports) www.acma.in/annual-report.php

Appendix 9-C

Sales and Exports of Motor Vehicles Industry in India

Year	*Sales (Rs. Million)*		*Exports of Goods (Rs. Million)*	
	MNCs	*Domestic*	*MNCs*	*Domestic*
1990	20880.3	22633.6	726.1	1036.7
1991	24804.7	29214.2	1172.7	1313.6
1992	10665.1	34430.2	3262.6	2466.8
1993	9637.2	33533.8	2543	3113
1994	39975.6	41845.3	3778.1	3878.4
1995	56971.6	64930.4	4683.1	5929.3
1996	88913.8	87947.8	6804.9	6627.2
1997	109800.9	107047.7	7516.6	6870
1998	104572.6	78063.4	6389.2	6170.2
1999	113792.8	70169.3	7379.2	5224.5
2000	168596.4	91025.1	7229.1	6228.3
2001	174484.9	83526.1	7512.7	7364.9
2002	180098	91091.4	6765.3	6381.8
2003	187838.4	112852.8	11693.1	5044.2

(*Continued*)

Appendix 9-C: (Continued)

Year	*Sales (Rs. Million)*		*Exports of Goods (Rs. Million)*	
	MNCs	*Domestic*	*MNCs*	*Domestic*
2004	236918.8	161958.6	23294.5	10389.6
2005	305880.8	211102.3	35913.4	14902.2
2006	3,48,312	242663.8	36086.5	22418
2007	4,38,638	317222.4	42563.3	27478.5
2008	510357.1	333250.2	51924.3	28313.1
2009	551016.6	305369.8	106543.7	23659.3
2010	766076.8	445365.5	152039.5	24194.4
2011	874013.8	611234.8	124044.8	37090.3
2012	981031.6	765101	143102.7	41085.5
2013	1135771	783051	187544.9	38071.5
2014	1299237	690078.6	254542.4	47426
2015	1575850.8	596467.1	301493.8	53884.7
2016	1813494.3	899368.8	187677.1	7931.4

Source: Compiled from CMIE Prowess IQ dataset

Appendix 9-D

Descriptive Statistics

Full Sample					
VARIABLES	*Observations*	*Mean*	*S.D.*	*Minimum*	*Maximum*
Expln	1610	12.63	17.39	0	96.13
RDIn	1610	.47	1.94	0	38.72
ICGIn	1610	1.52	3.25	0	39.26
IndeRawMIn	1610	37.23	19.21	0	76.29
Sellingln	1610	3.33	3.21	0	41.68
Outln	1610	1.91	3.2	0	21.74
CHOI	1641	15.67	11.72	0	87.76
SIZE	1644	3.24	.72	1.01	5.79
Age	2000	23.53	15.24	1	73
Dmvi	2000	.12	.32	0	1
Dbmv	2000	.28	.45	0	1
Damv	2000	0.59	0.49	0	1
Domestic Firms					
Expln	1332	13.09	18.07	0	96.13
RDIn	1332	.49	2.07	0	38.72
ICGIn	1332	1.35	3.26	0	39.26
IndeRawMIn	1332	37.05	19.91	0	76.29
Sellingln	1332	3.29	3.23	0	41.68
Outln	1332	2.13	3.40	0	21.74
CHOI	1352	16.76	11.89	0	87.76

Appendix 9-D: (Continued)

Full Sample					
VARIABLES	*Observations*	*Mean*	*S.D.*	*Minimum*	*Maximum*
SIZE	1355	3.12	.64	1.01	5.79
Age	1648	23.95	15.12	1	73
Dmvi	1648	.06	.25	0	1
Dbmv	1648	.31	.46	0	1
Damv	1648	.62	.48	0	1
MNCs					
Expln	278	10.46	13.44	0	57.45
RDIn	278	.38	1.12	0	17.05
ICGIn	278	2.37	3.04	0	18.57
IndeRawMIn	278	38.07	15.38	0	67.29
Sellingln	278	3.57	3.14	0	25.33
Outln	278	.83	1.65	0	8.72
CHOI	289	10.54	9.32	0	57.79
SIZE	289	3.84	.78	1.08	5.63
Age	352	21.54	15.61	1	68
Dmvi	352	.36	.48	0	1
Dbmv	352	.18	.38	0	1
Damv	352	.45	.49	0	1
Exporting Firms					
Expln	1377	14.77	17.94	.001	96.13
RDIn	1377	.47	1.76	0	38.72
ICGIn	1377	1.55	3.15	0	37.16
IndeRawMIn	1377	39.33	17.69	0	75.95
Sellingln	1377	3.58	3.29	0	41.68
Outln	1377	1.92	3.08	0	20.62
CHOI	1409	15.98	11.64	0	87.76
SIZE	1411	3.3	.7	1.01	5.74
Age	1767	24.3	15.4	1	72
Dmvi	1767	.12	.33	0	1
Dbmv	1767	.27	.44	0	1
Damv	1767	.59	.49	0	1
Non-Exporting Firms					
Expln	233	–	–	–	–
RDIn	233	.45	2.79	0	34.01
ICGIn	233	1.34	3.79	0	39.26
IndeRawMIn	233	24.87	22.81	0	76.29
Sellingln	233	1.87	2.22	0	15.23
Outln	233	1.81	3.84	0	21.74
CHOI	233	13.77	12.05	0	73.78
SIZE	233	2.88	.75	1.08	5.79
Age	233	17.63	12.48	0	73
Dmvi	233	.06	.24	0	1
Dbmv	233	.36	.48	0	1
Damv	233	.57	.49	0	1

Appendix 9-E

Correlation Matrix

Total Companies (125)

	Expln	*RDln*	*ICGln*	*IndeRln*	*Sellingln*	*Outln*	*CHOI*	*SIZE*	*Age*	*Dmvi*	*Dbmv*	*MNCs*	*VIF*	*1/VIF*
Expln	1.0000													
RDln	–0.0475	1.0000											1.06	0.941768
ICGln	0.0080	0.0209	1.0000										1.10	0.907931
IndeRawMln	–0.0468	–0.0148	–0.0705*	1.0000									1.13	0.884032
Sellingln	0.2052*	0.1350*	–0.0413	0.0376	1.0000								1.21	0.823792
Outln	0.2219*	–0.0255	–0.0117	–0.0442	0.0551	1.0000							1.14	0.877266
CHOI	0.0394	0.0293	–0.1951*	0.0538	0.0523	–0.0917*	1.0000						1.19	0.840152
SIZE	–0.1159*	0.1186*	0.1278*	0.2491*	0.0034	–0.2370*	–0.2280*	1.0000					2.12	0.472570
Age	0.1036*	0.0418	–0.1567*	0.1468*	0.2241*	–0.0173	0.1605*	0.2065*	1.0000				1.35	0.742830
Dmvi	–0.0797*	0.1385*	0.0884*	0.2063*	0.2336*	–0.1330*	–0.1567*	0.5804*	–0.0376	1.0000			2.10	0.477129
Damv	0.0851*	– 0.0309	– 0.1006*	– 0.1177*	0.0093	0.0480	0.1200*	–0.3028*	0.1693*	–0.4448*	1.0000		1.34	0.747389
MNCs	–0.0571	–0.0213	0.1191*	0.0201	0.0331	–0.1528*	–0.2022*	0.3813*	–0.0602*	0.3465*	–0.1293*	1.0000	1.38	0.722262
Mean VIF														**1.37**

Note: Values with stars show significance level at 1 per cent or more.

Domestic Companies (103)

	Expln	*RDln*	*ICGln*	*IndeRln*	*Sellingln*	*Outln*	*CHOI*	*SIZE*	*Age*	*Dmvi*	*Dbmv*	*VIF*	*1/VIF*
Expln	1.0000												
RDln	– 0.0538	1.0000										1.07	0.935638
ICGln	– 0.0059	0.0226	1.0000									1.09	0.918848
IndeRawMln	– 0.0827*	– 0.0143	– 0.0841*	1.0000								1.12	0.896373
Sellingln	0.2173*	0.1049*	–0.0737*	0.0041	1.0000							1.19	0.841426
Outln	0.2152*	– 0.0287	0.0043	– 0.0343	0.0689	1.0000						1.14	0.880264
CHOI	0.0483	0.0316	– 0.1763*	0.0862*	0.0909*	– 0.1489*	1.0000					1.15	0.868716
SIZE	– 0.1862*	0.1452*	0.0646	0.2352*	– 0.0647	– 0.2021*	– 0.1476*	1.0000				1.56	0.640935
Age	0.0724*	0.0342	–0.1726*	0.1318*	0.2442*	–0.0541	0.1544*	0.2368*	1.0000			1.32	0.756141
Dmvi	– 0.0834*	0.1851*	0.0319	0.2044*	0.2070*	– 0.0359	– 0.0149	0.4066*	– 0.0077	1.0000		1.49	0.670963
Damv	0.1149*	– 0.0191	– 0.0831*	– 0.0806*	0.0660	0.0038	0.0688	– 0.1578*	0.1961*	– 0.3459*	1.0	1.22	0.822382
Mean VIF													**1.23**

Note: Values with stars show significance level at 1 per cent or more.

MNCs (22)

	Expln	*RDln*	*ICGln*	*IndeRawMln*	*Sellingln*	*Outln*	*CHOI*	*SIZE*	*Age*	*Dmvi*	*Dbmv*	*VIF*	*1/VIF*
Expln	1.0000												
RDln	0.0082	1.0000										1.31	0.761944
ICGln	0.1595*	0.0365	1.0000									1.19	0.837718
IndeRawMln	0.2640*	– 0.0159	– 0.0037	1.0000								1.47	0.682267
Sellingln	0.1491	0.4387*	0.1034	0.2480*	1.0000							1.78	0.562386
Outln	0.2463*	– 0.0356	0.0329	–0.1388	– 0.0064	1.0000						1.30	0.769777
CHOI	– 0.1323	– 0.0408	– 0.1792*	– 0.1574*	– 0.1320	0.1506	1.0000					1.26	0.792245
SIZE	0.3324*	0.1241	0.1960*	0.4198*	0.2097*	– 0.2178*	– 0.2743*	1.0000				4.50	0.222272
Age	0.2823*	0.1061	–0.0613	0.2467*	0.1420	0.2467*	0.1755*	0.2439*	1.0000			1.77	0.566190
Dmvi	– 0.0251	0.1690*	0.0962	0.3269*	0.3645*	– 0.3800*	– 0.3456*	0.7573*	– 0.0448	1.0000		4.73	0.211416
Damv	– 0.1432	– 0.1663*	– 0.1046	– 0.3322*	– 0.2345*	0.2751*	0.2648*	– 0.7273*	0.0177	– 0.6901*	1.0000	2.66	0.375786
Mean VIF													**2.08**

Note: Values with stars show significance level at 1 per cent or more.

Index

For Product Safety Concerns and Information please contact our EU
representative GPSR@taylorandfrancis.com
Taylor & Francis Verlag GmbH, Kaufingerstraße 24, 80331 München, Germany

www.ingramcontent.com/pod-product-compliance
Ingram Content Group UK Ltd.
Pitfield, Milton Keynes, MK11 3LW, UK
UKHW022318250926
475702UK00046B/945
* 9 7 8 1 0 3 2 2 6 6 0 5 3 *